SCHOOL OF
ORIENTAL AND AFRICAN STUDIES

Studies in the Economic History of the Middle East

Studies
in the
Economic History
of the
Middle East

from the rise of Islam to the present day

EDITED BY

M. A. COOK

Lecturer in Economic History
with reference to the
Middle East,
School of Oriental
and African Studies

London

OXFORD UNIVERSITY PRESS

New York Toronto

1970

eml

Oxford University Press, Ely House, London, W.1
GLASGOW NEW YORK TORONTO MELBOURNE WELLINGTON
CAPE TOWN SALISBURY IBADAN NAIROBI LUSAKA ADDIS ABABA
BOMBAY CALCUTTA MADRAS KARACHI LAHORE DACCA
KUALA LUMPUR SINGAPORE HONG KONG TOKYO

SBN 19 713561 7

Printed in Great Britain
by Butler & Tanner Limited, Frome, Somerset

Contents

PART THREE

The Nineteenth and Twentieth Centuries

Preface

A CONFERENCE on the economic history of the Middle East since the rise of Islam was held at the School of Oriental and African Studies in the University of London in July 1967. It would be pointless to restate the original aims of the organizers here. What the conference in fact achieved for most of its participants was to give them a clearer and more comprehensive idea of the state and prospects of research in the field than they had had before.

This volume consists of the papers submitted to the conference, with such revisions as their authors chose to make in the course of the following months. Three scholars who were unable to attend the conference sent papers, and these are included here; one paper (my own) has been omitted. The papers are grouped broadly by period, each group being introduced by a short critical essay. I hope that these essays may help to give the volume some perspective, and at the same time preserve some of the more significant features of the discussions which took place at the conference.

The conference was financed by a generous grant from the Joint Committee on the Middle East of the Social Science Research Council (New York) and the American Council of Learned Societies, together with an allocation from the funds of the School. I would like to thank the administrative staff of the School, particularly Mr. Gatehouse, for their help in organizing the conference, and the Publications Committee of the School for accepting this volume for publication at the School's expense.

Two abbreviations have been used throughout:

EI[1] (*EI*[2]) *The Encyclopaedia of Islam*, 1st (2nd) edition
JESHO *Journal of the Economic and Social History of the Orient.*

M. A. COOK

PART ONE

The Middle Ages

Introductory Remarks

ABRAHAM UDOVITCH

'BEHOLD, your child lives,' the prophet Elijah announced to the widow of Zarephath after a period of famine and drought had threatened the life of her offspring (I Kings 17 : 23). A similar message of hope and optimism can be proclaimed concerning the vitality and future of the economic history of the medieval Near East. After decades of comparative neglect, and even despair, the summer of 1967 witnessed a truly impressive upsurge in interest, encouragement and activity in this sector of Near Eastern Studies. The London conference (in early July) on the Economic History of the Middle East, with its special section devoted to the medieval period, was preceded by a colloquium at All Souls College, Oxford, on Islam and the Trade of Asia, which focused almost entirely on the Middle Ages, and was followed in mid-August by a panel devoted to medieval Near Eastern economic history at the 27th International Congress of Orientalists in Ann Arbor, Michigan, the first such session in the long and venerable history of these meetings.

Thus, if after the summer of 1967 it is incontestable that 'the child lives', it is equally certain that the study of medieval Near Eastern economic history is still in its early developmental stages, especially when compared to other branches of historical study such as intellectual and political history. One of the most important contributing factors to this comparative immaturity is the nature of our sources. Dearth of appropriate documentary sources comparable to those preserved in the medieval West has been a recurrent lament of all those seeking to toil in the vineyards of medieval Islamic economic history. While there is justice in this complaint, only new discoveries will rectify it, and in the interim one has to follow the advice of 'Seek and ye shall find' by extracting from the available sources, both documentary and other, all the relevant information that they might yield. From Professor Lewis' survey, it is clear that while the medieval East may be relatively impoverished with regard to archival and other unmediated documentary material, it is amply endowed (far more than the medieval West) with a wide range of literary and archaeological sources. Even the documentary sources are not yet fully exploited. Of an estimated 50,000 Arabic papyri extant, only 5,000 have so far been published, and Geniza research is only at its beginnings. It is to be hoped that the existence of a heightened demand for and interest in this material and its content will, in accordance with the time-honoured economic principle, result in a more steady supply of publications and studies.

In connection with the Geniza material some amplification of Professor Lewis' remarks is, I believe, called for. These documents are important not only as things in themselves, that is, for the particular information they contain, but also for the indirect guidance they provide with respect to institutions and practices from both earlier and later periods. In spite of the limitation imposed by its 'minority' provenance, from a methodological point of view the significance of the data in these documents exceeds both the limits of the ethnic group from which they stem as well as the chronological boundaries of the few centuries in which these documents originated. For example, with regard to the business methods reflected in the Geniza material, there is little in general outline and even in substantial detail that is not anticipated or implied in some of the earliest Islamic legal writings. Scholars, however, have been hesitant to use Islamic legal material for historical purposes, i.e., to project social and economic institutions and practices on the basis of what has been considered as almost entirely theoretical source material. In light of the close correspondence of Geniza data to the legal economic institutions treated in Islamic legal works, we can assert that many of the latter were indeed transformed into actual economic institutions. This permits us to go a step further and postulate the existence of these commercial institutions in an earlier period, as well as to scan legal sources for information on commercial matters that are absent or only partially manifested in the Geniza documents.

This is but one example of the methodological advance made possible by the Geniza material. Many others, which cannot be detailed here, are to be found pertaining to a variety of social and economic practices and institutions, monetary history, urban taxation and governmental relations to commerce. The myriad of details on seafaring, land-travel, packing and transport, mail services, finance and banking throws light not only on the practices of the eleventh through thirteenth centuries, but also provides us with a wedge and opening into hitherto closed areas of earlier and later periods, illuminating and placing in clearer perspective the fragmentary data yielded by non-documentary sources.

As Professor Lewis implies, even such obvious sources of medieval economic information as coins and inscriptions have been far from fully exploited. It is not only concerning the hoards of Islamic coins from Northern and Eastern Europe that many questions loom large. Very few of the numerous hoards found within the Islamic world have been properly studied with the application of the rigorous methods and techniques developed by numismatists and historians who have made comparable finds in the West yield a great deal of valuable information. (A notable and exemplary exception in this regard is G. D. Miles' analysis of the hoard of *dirhams* found at the excavations in Susa, cf. 'Trésor du Dirhems du IXe Siècle', *Mémoires de la Mission Archéologique en Iran*, vol. XXXVII.) With respect to inscriptions, economic historians have apparently been daunted by the rather narrow range of information they contain. Yet their importance goes far beyond their specific formulaic content. Would it not, for example, be of prime interest to economic historians to collate and collect building inscriptions from various localities so that we could, in conjunction with other evidence, at least indulge in some semi-educated speculations on the problem of 'investment in culture', i.e., on the withdrawal of capital from economic activity and its allocation for other purposes? A host of other similarly relevant problems could be devised to be brought to the attention of epigraphers and archaeologists. The latter, especially, all too often allow their understandable preoccupation with purely archaeological and art-historical concerns to obscure the many other historical problems for which their findings might have relevance.

Generally one might comment that the study of all immediate, contemporary materials—coins, inscriptions, archaeological artifacts, etc.—will not only answer questions that we already have, but just as importantly, raise relevant problems and questions that we haven't yet thought of.

Professor Lewis is certainly correct in stating that the entire vast range of medieval Arabic writings is a legitimate source for economic history. It is sufficient to recall that some excellent studies of early Byzantine economic history were written from data garnered largely from saints' lives. Beginning with the inimitable Qur'ān and going through the chronicles, collections of traditions, *dīwāns* of poetry, treatises on theology, etc., a great deal of economically significant data is given in a casual and almost off-hand manner, sometimes not even articulated, but implied, and is, therefore, for the most part probably authentic. The systematic collection, collation and analysis of this material would certainly add considerably to our knowledge in a wide range of subjects pertaining to economic history.

The ample numismatic remains from the Islamic middle ages are, of course, useful for numerous historical purposes (chronology, dynastic personnel, administration, etc.); but our immediate concern is their use for economic history. The plethora of medieval Islamic coins as well as copious supportive literary and documentary evidence indisputably points to a developed monetary economy. This should not, however, blur the fact that a barter economy persisted simultaneously, especially in the area of petty exchange. For example, the monetary units in which many transactions and economic functions were evaluated did not correspond to actual currency, and thus often no actual money was exchanged but payment was made in kind.

Professor Ehrenkreutz correctly emphasizes the importance of differentiating various types of coins according to size, weight and metallic content. It is from this vantage-point that surviving medieval coins could be of greatest significance for some of the key questions of medieval economic life, such as prices and wages. In view of the fact that, except for exceptional and short periods of time, there was no way of enforcing any given exchange rate (even though minting was a function of the central governmental administration), a knowledge of the weights and alloys is particularly important in determining the economic significance of coins. Coins found their level of value on the basis of the gold–silver ratio prevalent at the time. To be sure, other factors may also have influenced exchange-rates and purchasing power of given coins, e.g. supply and demand, but these were definitely secondary; the basic determinants in this regard were their intrinsic value.

The volume of coinage issued in any given year would, of course, be nice to know, but its importance as a meaningful index of economic life is considerably qualified and reduced by a number of factors. (*a*) Barter, i.e., goods or merchandise as a means of exchange can be assumed, throughout the Middle Ages, to have been an important element in the total volume of goods and services exchanged. (*b*) We have no way of knowing the extent of credit operations; but since we do know that the techniques for commercial credit were highly developed, we may assume that they were utilized and accounted for a sizable proportion of the exchange of goods and services. (*c*) Old coins remained in circulation simultaneously with newer ones for long periods. (*d*) Low quality coins such as copper and lead *dirhams* could often be made to do service on a local or regional level in face of the inadequate supply of good-quality coins, with the latter effectively reserved for long-distance trade. (*e*) We do not know the velocity of exchange and circulation. The volume of coins minted annually, therefore, was only one of several determinants of the volume and intensity of economic life, and it was not necessarily the most important.

In any case, it is questionable whether we can estimate the number of coins produced in any given period *within a tolerable margin of error*. There are inherent shortcomings in the coin-die method of calculation. We are totally dependent on extant coins with no knowledge of their relationship to the coin types originally issued. Furthermore, we cannot be sure that each die was used for the maximum number of strikes, or even anything close to it.

Professor Goitein's paper provides a striking example of the kind of information available in the Geniza papers and of the type of studies that this exciting source makes possible. One of the very valuable features of these documents is that they serve as a combined source for both the qualitative and quantitative aspects of economic life. Even without the Geniza, simply on the basis of non-documentary literary sources, we could have postulated the complexity of the economy and the variety of commodities exchanged. Not only does the Geniza data confirm this general notion and add further substantial details to such questions as the co-existence of specialization and diversification of the merchant class, the inter-relationship of sedentary to itinerant traders and the complexities and subtleties of the organization of trade, but it also provides unique quantitative information, thus bringing together, as it were, for the first time the body and soul of medieval Near Eastern economic life.

Professor Goitein's paper, of course, offers us only a slight foretaste of the rich and varied fare of new information which the Geniza contains. The contents of this cornucopia in its fullness are now available in Professor Goitein's recent book *A Mediterranean Society*. Particularly precious are the details about seafaring and maritime organization, such as the change from the Muslim ownership of ships in the eleventh century to the Christian-European dominance in the twelfth century. This of course ties in with the broad historical processes which the Mediterranean area was passing through at this time, viz., the shift in hegemony and in political and economic initiative from its southern and south-eastern shores to the north and north-west. Of even greater historical interest is the remarkable fact emerging from the Geniza that fully a century and a half before the Crusades, Christian-European merchants were active in significant numbers in Egypt and Tunisia. They were not only there, but apparently exerted some impact on the economic life of the Near East, affecting prices and market conditions by their substantial purchases, and influencing popular consumer taste with their imported European commodities. Historical research, after having some forty years ago shattered the unity of the Mediterranean, is apparently, like all the king's men, slowly putting it back together again, and pushing back the date of the 'One Mediterranean' ever earlier. We now see that the lively interaction between East and West on the Mediterranean and the mutual and frequent access to its waters as a pre-Crusade condition. Could it be that further study and new sources will yet reveal that trade and contacts across the Mediterranean was the normal situation, and that interruptions were the exception and of much shorter duration than previously suspected?

Dr. Labib's summary of Egyptian commercial policy in the Middle Ages seems to support this view, and the 10th century shift of the centre of international trade that he points to from Iraq to Egypt, whatever its reasons within the context of the Oriental world, is probably not unconnected with the European resurgence in the Mediterranean area.

One especially noteworthy feature of Professor Labib's discussion is his enumeration of the various customs dues, taxes and tolls imposed upon commercial activity, as well as the exemptions from them. Drawing attention to these extra-canonical taxes offers us the possibility of investigating the fiscal policy of medieval Islamic governments. While realizing that many actions and policies of these regimes were often quite arbitrary and governed by short-term considerations, there may still be, implicit in the whole taxation and fiscal structure, a rationality that will illuminate for us much of the economic dynamics of the medieval Near East. Here again, it is important to see the total picture, and move away from our narrower concerns with the canonical taxation structure (*kharāj*, *jizya*, *ʿushr*, etc.). These too, of course, should be further explored; but while doing so one should always bear in mind that in spite of their theoretical exclusiveness they were, in the real world, only one segment of a much larger and more complex fiscal structure.

In discussing the economic problems of Egypt in the later Middle Ages, the big bogey man has always been 'state intervention'. While there are numerous difficulties that can be attributed to the government's intervention into economic affairs, we should not over-estimate its importance, and by inference, adopt the attitude that *laissez-faire* would have been best. Rather, it is necessary to probe beneath the overt, short-sighted actions of the various regimes and inquire into the underlying processes and motives for them. For government initiative and policy of the proper sort could very well have been beneficial to economic life and development, as was frequently the case in medieval Europe. The reasons for which no such policy was forthcoming should form the proper subject of our investigations in this regard.

Of all the sub-areas within the economic history of the medieval Near East, the terrain which is as yet the most uncharted and unknown is that of agriculture. This gap in our knowledge is particularly distressing because there can be no doubt that most people derived their livelihood from it and that if we could calculate the GNP of the medieval Islamic world, agriculture would certainly constitute the single largest contributing item.

In this regard, we are faced with a very real and obstinate difficulty of source materials; for our medieval authors, if not always urbane, were almost always urban. Certain aspects of land tenure have been successfully and profitably explored, and we have at our disposal some obvious, if limited, sources such as the papyri that should be further mined for relevant information. But the basic direction of research in this field will probably be of the kind represented by Mr. Rabie's paper, viz., careful and patient collation of random gleanings connected with agriculture, land tenure, agricultural income and productivity, crops and land utilization.

Professor Baer's paper straddles the medieval and modern periods. Our attention is drawn to the particular importance of the careful and precise use of terminology for historical descriptions, especially when we are dealing with categories and institutional nomenclature which grew primarily out of the European historical experience. For medieval times, the foremost example is probably the term 'feudalism', which carries with it certain legal, social and economic connotations distinctive to the Western medieval milieu, but which in the Islamic, Near Eastern context should, as Claude Cahen has pointed out, be used sparingly and with the appropriate qualifications. Professor Baer subjects another major institutional term of Western provenance—guild—to a careful scrutiny *vis-à-vis* its applicability to medieval Near Eastern society. This term has been rather carelessly employed with regard to the very general references to professional associations in the medieval Near East, and Professor Baer shows that until the fifteenth and sixteenth centuries there is no evidence of any guild organizations in the Near East. Instead, what we find are loose trade associations of various sorts in which more than one profession may have been involved.

Since, if we use the term with some precision and accuracy, there were no guilds, and since our Western categories do not seem to fit too well or too closely, the question arises of how the professional classes in particular, and medieval Islamic society generally were organized. Or, put another way, what were, from a historical point of view, the effective groups of action, change and continuity that provided the social setting of medieval Islamic economic life?

These are the problems to which Professor Rodinson addresses himself.

The alleged classlessness of Islamic society from a religious point of view is not only highly questionable, it is also quite irrelevant. The absence of social distinctions based on genealogy or wealth on the Day of Judgment does not in any way diminish their importance in the real world on all the days preceding that one. Furthermore, even if we disregard *dhimmīs* and slaves, a number of institutions of Islamic religious Law *do* accept social status as a criterion for certain rights and privileges. Islamic society was subject to stratification and differentiation; the question is, on what basis?

Islamic society does not readily lend itself to classification along economic lines, as some believe that European medieval society does. The task, therefore, is to discover the multiple criteria—economic, political, ethnic and others—for the stratification of classes and groups in Islamic society. The particular blend of these ingredients, or, to use Professor Rodinson's phrase, the 'synthetic gradation' that made various groups historically effective or ineffective remains yet to be elucidated. The tentative suggestions put forward by Professor Rodinson provide a starting point for a search of this kind and for the application and refinement of these concepts with respect to the various periods and locales that constitute medieval Near Eastern history.

In the final analysis, economic history cannot be understood, much less written, independently of social and political history. For example, the passive attitude of the Islamic world in the face of European initiative in the Mediterranean and Indian Ocean in the later middle ages, and even earlier, is inexplicable except in terms of the social and political structure of Islamic society. The disjunction of constructive economic initiative and policy from effective military and political power was apparently a persistent feature of Islamic society in the Near East: its study will perhaps go a long way towards elucidating the broad configurations of the area's economic development in the Middle Ages.

This phenomenon also highlights the thrust of Professor Cahen's observations that it was not one or two dramatic events that led to the economic decline of the Islamic Near East, but rather the persistent underlying weaknesses in its structure which rendered it unable to react to outside challenges and to withstand various reversals in the economic and commercial field. He is, I believe, the first to suggest that the absence of surplus production as an incentive to expanded trade in the Near East was one of its basic long-term economic handicaps. The production of surpluses, however—and we are presumably speaking primarily of agricultural surpluses—may have had a rather tenuous relationship to trade and been governed by an entirely different set of determinants, and their presence or absence, both in the agricultural and industrial sector, was undoubtedly subject to wide variations from time to time and place to place. It is thus now the task of scholarship to subject this potentially germane hypothesis to a careful scrutiny in order to establish whether indeed such surpluses were consistently absent, if so, why, and how precisely this might have affected trade and commerce. Such inquiries will almost certainly lead us beyond the confines of economic history to questions of technological innovation and to problems of social and cultural history.

Guilds in Middle Eastern History

GABRIEL BAER

THE approach of the present writer to this rather large but important and fascinating theme will be in accordance with the aim of the Economic History Conference as formulated in the instructions sent to the participants: this will be a survey rather than a research paper, it will try to review the present state of research and point out the main gaps in our knowledge, and, at the end, it will make some attempt at synthesis. It will deal with the time from the tenth to the twentieth centuries and with the area comprised in the present-day Egypt, Syria and Turkey: Egypt and Syria were most of the time closely connected with each other, and the Ottoman occupation created a link with Turkey which had a decisive influence on the guild history of these countries. Iraq, on the other hand, had much stronger ties with the countries east of it. The history of the guilds in those countries should be studied separately before the links with Egypt, Syria and Turkey can be established and mutual influences evaluated. The same is true for the Maghrib, about whose guilds in modern times we are quite well informed, but not about their earlier history.

In view of what has been written about guilds in the Middle East, it does not seem to be superfluous first to define what a guild is. In doing so, we have taken into account a minimum of criteria in order to be able to include Middle Eastern guilds and those of different countries in Europe at different times within the framework of a common term. We have used the term 'guild' and not one of the Arabic or Turkish terms—*ḥirfa, ṭāʾifa, ṣinf, esnaf*, etc.,—because these terms are extremely ambiguous: they mean both a profession and a professional organization, and some of them mean many other things as well. Their use would have obscured the problem with which we are dealing and not furthered its solution in any way.

The obvious statement that a guild is a *professional* organization cannot, apparently, be reiterated too often. For a long time this characterization of a guild had been ignored and all *futuwwa* organizations had been identified as guilds without further inquiries into their specific character. But even after this error had been dealt with in detail,[1] it has been repeated in a book published in 1965.[2]

[1] Cl. Cahen, *Mouvements populaires et autonomisme urbain dans l'Asie musulmane du moyen âge*, Leiden 1952, pp. 64, 67 n. 6, 69–70.

[2] Subhi Y. Labib, *Handelsgeschichte Ägyptens im Spätmittelalter (1171–1517)*, Wiesbaden 1965, pp. 222–6. It should be pointed out, however, that the relevant passages are somewhat ambiguous.

It seems, however, to be equally important to stress that a guild is a professional *organization*. Quite a number of writers speak about 'the guilds' whenever they mean the urban craftsmen or merchants without taking trouble to verify whether the sources really indicate the existence of an organization.[3] This leads, of course, to the question what the characteristic attributes of such an organization are. It would seem to us that one may be justified in speaking of the existence of guilds if all the people occupied in a branch of the urban economy within a definite area constitute a unit which fulfils at one and the same time various purposes, such as economically restrictive practices, fiscal, administrative or social functions. A further condition is the existence of a framework of officers or functionaries chosen from among the members of such a unit and headed by a headman.

Obviously this is only a general framework for dealing with the particular problems arising as we ask ourselves when and where guilds existed in Middle Eastern history and what their traits were. The following survey has been arranged according to three periods: (*a*) the tenth to fifteenth centuries; (*b*) the Ottoman guilds—the sixteenth to eighteenth centuries; (*c*) the nineteenth and twentieth centuries. In each period the findings will be specified for each of the three areas with which we are dealing: Egypt, Syria, and Turkey.

(*a*) *The tenth to fifteenth centuries*

Three recently published studies in the economic history of Fāṭimid, Ayyūbid and Mamlūk Egypt virtually arrive at the same conclusion: the sources do not justify the prevalent assumption that Egypt's craftsmen and traders were at that time organized in guilds. Summarizing his thorough investigation of the records of the Cairo Geniza, S. D. Goitein states that 'rigidly organized professional corporations' were non-existent during the eleventh and twelfth centuries.[4] To judge by what Prof. Goitein says further on, his statement is correct even without the qualification 'rigidly organized'. If, however, the qualification means that he has found traces of loose professional organizations, this would be interesting for guild history and should then be further investigated.

Similarly, L. A. Semenova has come to the conclusion that in Ayyūbid and Mamlūk Egypt there were no 'important' organizations of craftsmen like those of Western Europe.[5] She assumes, however, that there were

[3] Cf. Subhi Y. Lahib. *Handelsgeschichte Ägyptens im Spätmittelalter (1171–1517)*, Wiesbaden 1965, pp. 180, 229–30; for further examples see below.

[4] S. D. Goitein, 'The working people of the Mediterranean area during the High Middle Ages', *Studies in Islamic History and Institutions*, Leiden 1966, pp. 267–70.

[5] L. A. Semenova, *Salah ad-Din i mamlyuki v Egipte*, Moscow 1966, p. 166. I am grateful to Prof. E. Ashtor for having drawn my attention to this study, and to Mr. A. Wolfson for a translation of the relevant passages.

primitive local organizations of craftsmen headed by the elders of the community. This assumption would be more convincing if a larger number of examples of the existence of such rudiments of a professional organization had been found in the sources, and if we had some details about the character and function of the *ruʾasāʾ ahl ṣanāyiʿihim* on whom the assumption is based.[6]

The most detailed, but unfortunately somewhat inconsistent, treatment of the subject is that of S. Y. Labib. On the one hand, he says the following: 'Doch deuten gewisse Faktoren darauf hin, dass eine dem abendländischen Zunftwesen ähnliche Entwicklung in Ägypten nicht stattgefunden hat; denn die Quellen sprechen sowohl zur Zeit der Faṭimiden als auch nach deren Herrschaft stets von Handwerkern und Gewerbetreibenden und nicht von Zunftgenossen'; and later he says that 'handlungsfähige Gewerbezünfte' were absent.[7] He does not mention any guilds in his chapters on taxation, on bankers, or on the market. On the other hand, he adopts Massignon's theory about the flourishing of 'the guilds' in the eleventh and twelfth centuries under Shīʿite influence and claims that they played a relatively great role in the economic life of medieval Egypt—without substantiating this claim.[8] He takes the existence of guilds for granted and speaks about 'the guilds' whenever he means the craftsmen and traders—although the sources he quotes do not justify this.[9] A case in point is his treatment of the *ʿarīf*, pl. *ʿurafāʾ*, or the *ʿurafāʾ al-aswāq*, who are invariably called *Zunftmeister* by him.[10] The examination of one of Labib's most important sources, the *ḥisba* manual of al-Shayzarī which dates from the time of Ṣalāḥ al-Dīn,[11] shows clearly that at the time in Egypt the *ʿarīf* was no more than an assistant of the *muḥtasib* whose task was to supervise for the *muḥtasib* and together with him certain kinds of craftsmen and traders, about whose organization nothing is said.[12] Similarly, Labib cites Shayzarī for his statement: 'Der Muhtasib registrierte die Namen der Kaufleute, Händler *und Innungen*.'[13] But what Shayzarī says is that the *muḥtasib* should register the names of the bankers and roasters. Nothing is said about any 'Innungen'.[14] On the contrary, had they been organized in guilds, the *muḥtasib* would not

[6] Semenova gives three references to Ibn al-Furāt's history. One seems to us to be irrelevant. In the other two the death of *raʾīs ahl ṣināʿatihi fī'l-madḥ wa'l-ghinā bi'l-kaff* and *raʾīs al-qurrāʾ . . . wa-shaykh al-wiʿāẓ . . . (wa-raʾīs) ahl juwaq al-muqriyyīn* respectively is reported. The first passage mentions, in addition, that in March 1388 five *ruʾasāʾ ṣanāyiʿihim* died in one week. See *Taʾrīkh Ibn al-Furāt*, ed. C. K. Zurayk and N. Izzeddin, vol. IX, pt. 1, Beirut 1936, p. 26, and vol. IX, pt. 2, Beirut 1938, p. 328.

[7] Labib, pp. 222, 258.

[8] *Ibid.*, pp. 219–20.

[9] See, for instance, *ibid.*, pp. 229–30, 408.

[10] *Ibid.*, pp. 180, 220–1, 335.

[11] ʿAbd al-Raḥmān b. Naṣr al-Shayzarī, *Kitāb nihāyat al-rutba fī ṭalab al-ḥisba*, Cairo 1946.

[12] *Ibid.*, pp. 12, 27, 36, 40, 54, 65. For the same conclusion drawn from other *ḥisba* books see Goitein, p. 268 and n. 1.

[13] Labib, p. 183 and n. 113. Our italics.

[14] Shayzarī, pp. 22, 30.

have been compelled to register them one by one; in later centuries it was the guild *shaykh*, not an officer of the government, who registered the guild members. Labib relates various details about 'the guild of weavers',[15] but no documented facts about the existence of this or any other guild are presented by him, although at least fifteen pages are devoted to this subject. In view of the wide range of his sources, this seems to be significant. Perhaps there were beginnings, or scattered instances, of a professional organization, but unless new sources are brought to light we shall not know this for certain.

Attempts to discover traces of guilds in medieval Syria have not yet led to conclusions which are fundamentally different from those arrived at with regard to Egypt. Again we must begin with a warning against those writers who just call the craftsmen and merchants 'the guilds'. Thus we have a whole article on 'the corporations' of Damascus under Nūr al-Dīn[16] in which not a single indication is given that all those artisans and traders enumerated in the list compiled by the author were organized in a corporation, a guild, or any professional organization. For the sake of clarity, this fashion of some economic and social historians should be strongly discouraged.

The most detailed investigation of the guilds in medieval Syria is contained in two studies by E. Ashtor.[17] Ashtor too begins by summarizing Massignon's theories for which he, like others, has not found corroboration in the sources. He then goes on to relate what he found in the Arabic sources of the period and has to admit, with regard to both the earlier and the later of the periods studied by him, that the sources contain very little on the life of the artisans and nothing at all on internal affairs of corporations.[18] In view of this statement it is interesting, though perhaps not convincing to read: 'Mais quoi qu'il en soit, il est certain que les corporations jouissaient a cette époque [of the Crusades] d'une certaine autonomie. On peut supposer qu'elles pouvaient régler beaucoup de leurs affaires sans que les autorités intervenissent'.[19]

Suppositions apart, Ashtor's actual information on Syrian 'guilds' is confined to two functionaries. One is the *ʿarīf*, who, as we have seen, has also figured prominently as a proof for some writers of the existence of guilds in Egypt at that time. Like those writers Ashtor assumes the *ʿarīfs* to have been 'les maîtres des corps de métiers', but he also quotes passages

[15] Labib, pp. 228–9.

[16] N. Elisséeff, 'Corporations de Damas sous Nūr al-Dīn', *Arabica*, 3, 1956, pp. 61–79.

[17] E. Ashtor-Strauss, 'L'administration urbaine en Syrie médiévale', *Rivista degli Studi Orientali*, 31, 1956, pp. 71–128 (Ashtor 1956 in later references); E. Ashtor, 'L'urbanisme syrien à la basse-époque', *ibid.*, 33, 1958, pp. 181–209 (Ashtor 1958 in later references).

[18] Ashtor 1956, p. 86; Ashtor 1958, p. 202.

[19] Ashtor 1956, p. 86 (no sources indicated). In contrast to Ashtor, Cl. Cahen (*op. cit.*, p. 24) is convinced that the Syrian *aḥdāth* were not organized according to professional divisions.

which show that they were some kind of government inspectors of certain localities. The *ḥisba* manuals are cited and according to them the *ʿarīfs* were appointed by the *muḥtasib* as supervisors of certain professions, but on the other hand an incident is related in which the *ʿarīfs* fulfilled representative functions. Since the evidence is not conclusive, Ashtor suggests that there were perhaps two kinds of *ʿarīfs*, those appointed by the authorities and those fulfilling social functions of the guilds.[20] To sum up, we know very little about the *ʿarīf* and even less about 'the guilds' the heads of which the *ʿarīfs* are supposed to have been.

The second functionary is the *raʾīs al-aṭibbāʾ*, the head of the physicians. Throughout the period under survey the government appointed a chief physician, whose task was to supervise the members of the profession and to issue certificates allowing physicians to practise medicine. The appointment of the Syrian chiefs of the physicians had in certain periods to be approved by the Egyptian chief of the profession. The sources also mention different heads of the physicians (*aṭibbāʾ*), oculists (*kaḥḥālīn*) and surgeons (*jarāʾiḥiyya*).[21] There can be no doubt that, like the *ʿarīfs*, they were appointed by the authorities and therefore, even if this indicated the existence of a professional organization (which it does not do conclusively), it certainly does not justify any conclusions about 'a certain autonomy' of these groups. Nevertheless, for at least one reason the information about the chiefs of the physicians is of interest in the context of the history of the guilds: one of our major sources for the study of Egyptian guilds after the Ottoman conquest is a manuscript whose author was closely connected with the guilds of barbers and physicians.[22] It would be interesting and significant if a connection between the later guilds and the earlier heads of the physicians could be established.

These conclusions are confirmed by the latest, most detailed and best documented study of Syrian and Egyptian towns in Mamlūk times so far published, that of Ira M. Lapidus.[23] Speaking of the *raʾīses* of the physicians, surgeons and oculists, Lapidus says that there is no indication that these functionaries, who were appointed by the state, represented guilds. Similarly, the *raʾīs* of the merchants was an official and not the leader of a guild, nor were the *shaykhs* of the Damascus markets chiefs of merchant corporations. The *ʿarīfs* were appointed by the *muḥtasibs* to be their agents and agents of the state authority. Aside from the silk workers of Damascus,

[20] *Ibid.*; and also Ashtor 1958, pp. 186, 201–2.

[21] Ashtor 1956, p. 88; Ashtor 1958, pp. 187, 202. Cf. Qalqashandī, *Ṣubḥ al-Aʿshā*, vol. 4, Cairo 1914, pp. 194, 222; vol. 5, Cairo 1915, p. 467.

[22] *Kitāb al-dhakhāʾir waʾl-tuḥaf fī bīr al-ṣanāʾiʿ waʾl-ḥiraf*, Gotha, Landesbibliothek, Arabische Handschrift No. 903. The guild material contained in this MS. has been studied in great detail in G. Baer, *Egyptian guilds in modern times*, Jerusalem 1964 (see below). For particulars of the MS. and its connection with the physicians, see *ibid.*, pp. 2–3.

[23] Ira M. Lapidus, *Muslim cities in the later Middle Ages*, Cambridge, Mass., 1967 pp. 96. 98, 101.

Lapidus has not found any signs of craft-based religious fraternities. Summing up, the author says: 'Neither the European nor the Byzantine type of guild was to be found in the bazaars of the Muslim city. . . . Considered from the point of view of political organization, economic regulation, or even corporate fraternal life, there were no guilds in Muslim cities in this period in any usual sense of the term.'

Unfortunately, the early history of guilds in Turkey is at least as obscure as that of Egypt and Syria. Fr. Taeschner, the outstanding authority in this field, says that 'in the absence of clear evidence, one cannot state with any certainty what the organization of the guilds was like in the Middle Ages . . . . The few guild documents which we do possess are of a relatively more recent date (at the earliest of the 9th/15th century).'[24] Similarly, Fr. Babinger did not find any traces of guilds in his sources for the time of Mehmet the Conqueror.[25] It seems to be clear that the prevalent kind of association in Anatolia of the thirteenth and fourteenth centuries was the organization of the *akhī* movement of young men who adopted the ideals of the *futuwwa*; although they were recruited mainly among the craftsmen, the association as such was non-professional.[26] However, the changes in the political situation in Anatolia brought about by the rise of Ottoman power were unfavourable to the existence of free associations such as those of the *akhīs*. This, according to Taeschner, was the reason for the fusion of the *akhī* movement with 'anderen zünftlerischen Anfängen' and the creation of a guild system, in which the *akhī* traditions survived.[27] The best known of such guilds was that of the tanners, whose patron saint was the *akhī* saint Akhī Evran of Kırşehir. The head of this order, who was called Akhī Baba, was the head of all tanners' guilds and of those of other leather workers (saddlers and shoemakers) in Turkey, and it was his task to carry out the initiation of apprentices into these guilds by the ceremony of girding. Gradually the Akhī Babas succeeded in extending their ascendancy over other guilds and in bringing under their control almost the whole Turkish guild organization.[28] Like some other guilds, the tanners had their special *fütüvvetname*, a book of rules dealing primarily with the organization and the ritual of the guild.[29] A similar book of rules for guilds, also influenced

[24] Fr. Taeschner, 'Futuwwa', *EI*², vol. 2, p. 967. Cf. *id.*, 'Futuwwa, eine gemeinschaftbildende Idee im mittelalterlichen Orient und ihre verschiedenen Erscheinungsformen', *Schweizerisches Archiv für Volkskunde*, 52, 1956, Heft 2/3, p. 151.

[25] 'Garnichts verlautet bislang über fachgenossenschaftliche Vereinigungen, Zünfte der Handwerker, wie sie im Osmanenreich des 16. und vor allem des 17. Jahrhunderts aus Schilderungen erweisbar sind'. Franz Babinger, *Mehmed der Eroberer und seine Zeit*, München 1953, p. 491.

[26] See Fr. Taeschner, 'Akhī', *EI*², vol. 1, pp. 321–3.

[27] *Id.*, 'Das Zunftwesen in der Türkei', *Leipziger Vierteljahrsschrift für Südosteuropa*, 5, 1941, p. 173.

[28] *Ibid.*, pp. 173–4; *id.*, 'Akhī Baba', *EI*², vol. 1, pp. 323–4.

[29] On the whole group of *fütüvvetnames* see Taeschner's writings as quoted in the previous notes and further works mentioned in the bibliographies of these writings.

by the *futuwwa* literature, is the above mentioned *kitāb al-dhakhā'ir* of the Egyptian physicians and barbers. This literature which flourished in the sixteenth century seems to reflect a period of transition from the old free *futuwwa* associations to a system of professional guilds. Its framework is the conceptual superstructure of the *futuwwa*, while many of its concrete examples and stories are taken from the life of professional guilds. In the words of Taeschner: 'Ich glaube, dass wir berechtigt sind, in dieser gelegentlichen Berücksichtigung des Handwerkertums die Wirklichkeit des damaligen Zunftwesens durch die theoretische Hülle des allgemeinen Futuvvet-Bundeswesens hindurchschimmern zu sehen. Seyyid Mehemmed scheint somit in seinem 'Grossen Futuvvetname' einen Übergangszustand zu schildern, in dem das alte freie Bundeswesen in Begriffe stand, sich in ein spezifisches Zunftwesen umzuwandeln. In der Wirklichkeit wird diese Umwandlung damals bereits vollzogen gewesen sein; doch war die Theorie der Wirklichkeit noch nicht nachgekommen'.[30]

Before dealing in detail with the outcome of this transition, which led in the seventeenth century to the establishment of a comprehensive and ramified guild system, it should be useful to summarize the development up to the fifteenth century. At least until the second half of the fifteenth century, we have no information whatever about any guilds in Egypt, Syria or Turkey, their membership, organization, structure or any of their possible functions. All assumptions about the existence of guilds are pure conjecture, based mainly on scattered items of information about the holders of a certain post, called *ʿarīfs*, or about the headmen of various branches of the medical profession or of unspecified crafts (Ibn al-Furāt's *ruʾasāʾ ahl ṣanāyiʿihim*). It is not difficult to explain the origin of this strong impulse among economic and social historians to assume the existence of guilds in medieval Turkey, Egypt and Syria: the elaborate guild system of the seventeenth century must have had some beginnings in earlier times (hence Taeschner's 'andere zünftlerische Anfänge'). This is all very well and it is to be hoped that such beginnings, and even more their connection with the later development, will be discovered in hitherto unknown sources. However, one should clearly distinguish between text and conjecture.

(*b*) *The Ottoman guilds—the sixteenth to eighteenth centuries*

The contrast between the clear picture of the Ottoman guild system unfolding before our eyes and the darkness in which 'guild history' (if there was any) is wrapped until the fifteenth century is indeed striking. For Turkish guilds (*esnaf*, later *lonca*) of the seventeenth and eighteenth centuries we have the description of Evliya Çelebi, the copious information contained in Osman Nuri's work, and the documents in the Ottoman

[30] *Id.*, 'Das Zunftwesen in der Türkei', p. 178.

archives, only a small part of which has been used up till now.[31] This material has been used in at least three short studies of the Turkish guilds at that time,[32] but a comprehensive work on this important theme has still to be written.

According to Evliya, early in the seventeenth century there were in Istanbul 1,001 guilds divided into 57 groups for reasons of administrative expediency. Though his figures may not be accurate, his detailed account shows that the whole population of Istanbul, with the exception of the military, government officials, and foreigners, was organized in guilds. The guild system comprised Muslims as well as non-Muslims—sometimes in separate and sometimes in mixed guilds.[33] There were guilds of artisans and merchants, as well as of people engaged in transport and in services, including entertainment. It was an all-embracing system; indeed, it was the only system in which the whole town population was organized and which was recognized by the government.[34] The affairs of each guild were managed by two officers, the *kethuda* (*kâhya*) or steward, and the *yiğit başı* or chief fellow, together with a council of elders, *ihtiyariye*, which apparently consisted of the veterans of the guild. Usually the *yiğit başı* was elected by the elders of the guild without government intervention, whereas in the appointment of the *kethuda* the government's say gradually increased; in any case, his choice had to be ratified by the *qāḍī*. This was the result of the fact that it was the *kethuda* who represented the guild in its dealings with the government and that the secular functions of the guild gradually superseded the ritual functions which the guilds had inherited from the *futuwwa* and *akhī* brotherhoods. Functionaries formerly concerned with the ceremonial aspects were in the course of time supplanted by new secular officers of the guild.[35]

The most important function of the guilds in Turkey in the seventeenth and eighteenth centuries was to serve as a framework for effective control by the government. Such a framework could be effective only if each guild had a monopoly of its branch. Therefore nobody was allowed to open a shop or to practise a profession without the permission of the guild; the number of people engaged in a specific branch was restricted, and their control by the guild, and thereby by the government, ensured. Specified

[31] Evliya Çelebi, *Seyahatname*, vol. 1, Istanbul A.H. 1314 (1898), p. 506 ff.; Osman Nuri, *Mecelle-i umur-u belediye*, Istanbul 1922 (especially ch. 6, pp. 478 ff.). Material from Ottoman archives has been used for guild history by Mantran (see following note).

[32] Fr. Taeschner, 'Das Zunftwesen in der Türkei' (see above, note 26); H. A. R. Gibb and H. Bowen, *Islamic Society and the West*, vol. 1, Part I, Oxford 1950, pp. 281–92; R. Mantran, *Istanbul dans la seconde moitié du XVIIe siècle*, Paris 1962, ch. 4, p. 349 ff. (also chs. 5–7). Three detailed studies on Turkish guilds by the present writer are to appear in 1970.

[33] Gibb and Bowen, p. 289; Mantran, pp. 374–5.

[34] Cf. Mantran, pp. 357–60; Taeschner, p. 180 (he includes the military and government officials as well).

[35] Gibb and Bowen, p. 284; Mantran, pp. 373–7.

crimes and offences were punished, with official sanction, by the exclusion of the offender from the guild, i.e., by preventing him from exercising his craft or profession.[36]

In addition, the guilds were required to supply non-combatant manpower for military campaigns. In such cases they were assembled in large processions to be mustered.[37] However, the guilds' processions were held also on the occasion of other public festivals and ceremonies, thus fulfilling an important social function. Another social function of the guilds was arbitration of disputes among the guild's members with which the *kethuda* was officially charged. Also some of the guilds had arrangements for mutual help among their members.[38]

In contrast with research on Turkish guilds in the seventeenth and eighteenth centuries, archive material and original documents on Egyptian guilds at that time have not yet been collected and published. The following remarks are based on two main sources: first, Evliya Çelebi's account of Egyptian guilds at the time of his visit to Egypt in the 1670's,[39] and secondly, the *Kitāb al-dhakhā'ir* mentioned above. Essentially they are a summary of the first chapter and of some scattered remarks in our study of Egyptian guilds in modern times.[40]

When Evliya Çelebi visited Cairo he found there a ramified network of almost 300 guilds comprising the whole gainfully occupied town population except the higher bureaucracy, the army, and the *ʿulamā'*. The guild system embraced owners of shops, of workshops, of large stores, people who worked in their own houses as well as salaried workers and government employees. Both rich and poor had their guilds, natives of Cairo as well as people born in Nubia and Upper Egypt, and there were even guilds of beggars, pickpockets and prostitutes. As in Istanbul, the guilds were divided into groups. There were thirty such groups of affined occupations in Cairo, each of which formed a separate contingent in the various public processions in which the guilds participated, headed by an officer of the government who controlled that group of guilds. These officers gave 'their' guilds protection and collected their taxes. In the eighteenth century there were apparently three large groups of guilds in Cairo, each of them controlled by a special officer of the government.[41] It should be mentioned that the *Kitāb al-dhakhā'ir* contains evidence for the existence of guilds in more than ten other towns of Egypt.[42]

The two most important officers of a guild in Egypt were the *shaykh* (headman) and the *naqīb* (master of ceremonies). It seems that by the

[36] Mantran, pp. 360, 384, 387–8; Taeschner, pp. 183–4.
[37] Taeschner, pp. 180–1 (with examples).
[38] *Ibid.*, p. 183; Mantran, pp. 375; 379–80.
[39] Evliya Çelebi, *Seyahatname: Mısır, Sudan, Habeş (1672–1680)*, vol. 10, Istanbul 1938, pp. 358–86.
[40] See note 22 above. [41] Baer, pp. 40–3. [42] *Ibid.*, p. 20.

seventeenth century it had become the rule that the *shaykhs* of the guilds were appointed by the *qāḍī* from whom they received a document of investiture (*ḥujja*). Like the Turkish *kethuda*, the *shaykh* of the Egyptian guild was the link between the guild and the government. The more he turned into a tool in the hands of the rulers for the execution of their administrative and fiscal policy, the further estranged he became from the guild members and their traditions. This is what seems to have happened in the seventeenth century. The opponents of the *shaykhs* tried to magnify the importance of the *naqībs*, who were the keepers of the traditional lore and ceremonies of the guilds. However, since the secular aspect of the guilds grew stronger while the conceptual traditions (based on *futuwwa* and similar ideologies) continued to decline, the position of the *shaykh* persisted while the *naqīb* was gradually replaced by a sub-*shaykh* with another title.[43] Parallel developments took place at the same time in Turkish guilds, as we have seen above.

There were some differences between the functions of Egyptian guilds in the seventeenth and eighteenth centuries and those of Turkish guilds at that time. The importance of the fiscal function, i.e., the guilds' constituting a unit for taxation, is much more evident in sources on Egyptian guilds than in those on Turkish ones.[44] However, in Egypt as in Turkey it was the permission of the *shaykh* of a guild (*ijāza*) that was required if anybody wanted to practise the craft or trade of that guild.[45] Although it was the *muḥtasib* who fixed the prices of comestibles, water, fuel and wood, this took place in the presence of the *shaykhs* of the guilds concerned.[46] The *shaykh* of the guild was responsible to the police for the conduct of all the members of the guild, and in order to enforce discipline he seems to have had some power of coercion, including, apparently, the right of corporal punishment.[47] Like the Turkish *kethuda*, the Egyptian *shaykh* used to arbitrate disputes among the guild members,[48] but we have not found any indication in our sources that Egyptian guilds at that time had arrangements or funds for mutual help. Finally, in Egypt too it was one of the important social functions of the guilds to participate in public festivities and ceremonies, and there seem also to have been special ceremonies of single guilds.[49]

Sources on Syrian guilds from the sixteenth to the eighteenth centuries are very poor. Evliya Çelebi, a major source for Turkey and Egypt, does not say a word on the guilds of the Syrian towns described in the ninth volume of his *Seyahatname*. This may be one indication that the guilds in Syria were not as important as units of government control and taxation as they were in Turkey and Egypt. Another indication may be found

[43] Cf. Baer, pp. 11–15.
[44] *Ibid.*, pp. 12–13, 84–5.
[45] *Ibid.*, pp. 56, 105.
[46] *Ibid.*, p. 101.
[47] *Ibid.*, pp. 56 n. 41, 80, 82.
[48] *Ibid.*, pp. 56, 113.
[49] *Ibid.*, pp. 117–18.

in the fact that in the local contemporary chronicles too material on the guild organization is very scarce, even in al-Budayrī's work, written by a barber, which is the best from our point of view.[50] Archive material has not yet been studied or collected from the point of view of guild history. There is, finally, Qudsī's work on the guilds of Damascus in the nineteenth century,[51] which has been frequently used as if it were equally valid for earlier times,[52] or, for that matter, as if it were a general treatise on 'Islamic guilds' regardless of time and place. We shall use it in this section only for information specifically related by Qudsī as belonging to earlier times; it will serve us in the next section as our main source for information on Syrian guilds in the nineteenth century.

Notwithstanding this poverty of the sources, there can be no doubt that at that time the population of Syrian towns, like that of Egyptian and Turkish towns, was organized in professional guilds. Qudsī tells us that a few generations before his time there were more than two hundred guilds in Damascus,[53] and Russell says about Aleppo in the middle of the eighteenth century: 'The trades are divided into different companies under their respective Sheikhs.'[54] The Damascus guilds (as well as the Ṣūfī orders) were controlled by a superior *shaykh*, the *shaykh al-mashāyikh*, whose position, according to Qudsī, was hereditary in a certain family,[55] and who judged them and arbitrated their disputes. He was assisted by a *naqīb* or a number of *naqībs*[56] who in turn were headed by a *naqīb al-nuqabāʾ fī Dimashq ʿalā al-ḥiraf waʾl-ṣanāʾiʿ waʾl-ṭuruq*.[57] It would seem that Damascus was unique in having such an autonomous framework uniting all the guilds under an indigenous head-*shaykh*.[58]

Information on the function of the guilds is also very scanty. They apparently served as a unit of taxation, but for this purpose the *ḥāra* (town quarter) seems to have been at least as important as the guilds.[59] Thus we are told that early in the eighteenth century there were certain taxes which were collected from the guilds and the town quarters of Damascus once

[50] Aḥmad Budayrī al-Ḥallāq, *Ḥawādith Dimashq al-yawmiyya 1154–1175 (1741–1762)*, Cairo 1959. For references to this work (as well as for those given in notes 65 and 66 below) I am indebted to Mr. Amos Gilboa, who permitted me to use his unpublished seminar paper on 'Damascus in the eighteenth and nineteenth centuries' (Jerusalem 1966).

[51] Ilyās Qudsī (Elia Qoudsî), 'Nubdha ta'rīkhiyya fī'l-ḥiraf al-dimashqiyya' ('Notice sur les corporations de Damas'), *Actes du sixième Congrès International des Orientalistes*, deuxième partie, Section 1: Semitique, Leiden 1885.

[52] For instance, Gibb and Bowen, pp. 292–4.

[53] Qudsī, p. 10.

[54] Alexander Russell, *The Natural History of Aleppo*, second edition, London 1794, vol. 1, pp. 160–1.

[55] Other sources, however, show that the post was occupied not only by the ʿAjlānī family, as claimed by Qudsī, but also by other families, such as the Murādīs.

[56] Qudsī, pp. 10–12.

[57] Budayrī, p. 39.

[58] For discussion of this point see Baer, pp. 22–3.

[59] On the great importance of the *ḥāra* in Syrian history see Ashtor 1956, pp. 84–5, and Ashtor 1958, pp. 208–9. For its fiscal function in the nineteenth century, in contrast to that of the guilds, see below.

or twice a year (*amwāl tufraḍ ʿalā al-ḥiraf waʾl-ṣanāʾiʿ waʾl-ḥārāt fīʾl-Shām marra ʾaw marratayn fīʾl-sana*).[60] In addition to their fiscal function, the only other task of the Syrian guilds mentioned in the sources was the ceremonial one of participating in public festivities by forming processions in which each guild demonstrated its craft.[61]

(*c*) *The nineteenth and twentieth centuries*

The first detailed work to be published on the guilds of any Middle Eastern country in the nineteenth century was the above mentioned paper on the guilds of Damascus by Ilyās Qudsī, which has been frequently quoted by many scholars. It showed for the first time the persistence in the nineteenth century of a guild system embracing the whole town population, divided into grades of proficiency from apprentice to master. The transition from grade to grade involved elaborate ceremonies of initiation, which were described in detail by Qudsī. These Damascene guilds had a hierarchy of guild officers, the head of which was the *shaykh*, who either inherited his post or was freely chosen by the elders of the guild; the election had to be confirmed by the *shaykh al-mashāyikh* (see above), but not by the government. Thus the guilds of Damascus seem to have been more autonomous than those of other countries of the Middle East.[62] The *shaykh* punished members of the guild who committed an offence against the guild and he arbitrated disputes among the guild's members as well as between a member of the guild and an outsider.[63]

Qudsī's information on the guilds' functions is not as systematic as that on their structure. He mentions the *shaykh's* task of finding work for labourers and punishing those who use false weights or adulterate precious metals (though in general the guilds did not guarantee the quality of the products of their members).[64] The restrictive and monopolistic character of the guilds is implied in his description of the requirements for exercising a craft or a trade. But he has nothing to say about the fiscal function of the guilds. The reason may well be that, in contrast with Egypt, the guild in Syria was not the most important urban unit of taxation. From time to time special taxes were imposed on certain guilds,[65] but apparently the town quarter remained at least as important a unit of taxation as the guild. Thus, when the Egyptians had occupied Syria and decided in 1833 to impose the *firda*, they first tried to have the population registered for this

[60] Budayrī, p. 45.

[61] *Ibid.*, pp. 233–4; Russell, *ibid.*

[62] Qudsī, pp. 11–14; cf. Baer, p. 72 and n. 102. In Ḥamā, however, the *shaykhs* of the important guilds were appointed by the government. See J. Gaulmier, 'Notes sur le mouvement syndicaliste à Hama', *Revue des Etudes Islamiques*, 1932, p. 97.

[63] Qudsī, p. 13; Gaulmier, *ibid.*

[64] Qudsī, pp. 32–3; Gaulmier, pp. 97–8; cf. Baer, pp. 96–7.

[65] See, for instance, Mikhā'īl al-Dimashqī, *Ta'rīkh ḥawādith al-Shām wa-Lubnān min sanat 1197 ilā sanat 1257*, Beirut 1912, p. 21.

purpose by the *shaykhs* of the town quarters. When the results appeared to them to be unsatisfactory they imposed the new tax on the guilds. However, this did not succeed either, and they returned to their original plan and collected the *firda* by using the town quarters as units of taxation.[66]

Various signs of the decline of the Damascus guilds had been discerned already by Qudsī in his paper. First of all, by the second half of the nineteenth century the *shaykh al-mashāyikh* had lost most of his functions, and even his approval of the appointment of the guilds' *shaykhs* had become insufficient (and thus superfluous) since the election had to be approved by the government.[67] The *naqībs*, or masters of ceremonies, had lost their importance, the *shadd* ceremony was neglected because the government licence had become the requirement for opening a shop, craftsmanship had declined and many of the traditional crafts had disappeared.[68] In 1912, the government of the Young Turks abolished the traditional guilds by a law which provided for the establishment of modern professional chambers or syndicates.[69] Nevertheless, they seem to have existed, though very much weakened, as late as the 1920's. At Ḥamā they were 'mourantes sinon mortes' . . . 'Les vestiges des corporations sont si faibles à Hama que la plupart des gens les ignorent tout à fait.'[70] In Damascus, in 1927, only about 10 per cent of the gainfully occupied population was organized in the traditional guilds, and almost none of the traditional ceremonies remained, although the Mandatory government did not interfere with their old customs.[71] By that time new forms of economic organization, both chambers of commerce and labour unions, had superseded the old guild system.

Like Syrian guilds of the last century and a half, Turkish guilds of that period too have not yet been the subject of a thorough investigation—though existing sources are certainly ample enough for a scholarly study. But even without such a study it is clear that throughout most of the nineteenth century the guilds in Turkey comprised the whole urban gainfully-occupied population. Moreover, the guild system became such an important element of government control that newly emerging professions or modern branches of the economy were organized by law as a guild.[72]

[66] Qusṭanṭīn al-Bāshā al-Mukhliṣī (ed.), *Mudhakkirāt ta'rīkhiyya . . . biqalam aḥad kuttāb al-ḥukūma al-dimashqiyyīn*, Ḥarīṣā n.d., pp. 90–2.

[67] Qudsī, pp. 11–12.

[68] *Ibid.*, pp. 12, 16, 18. For the decline of the *shadd* ceremony in Egypt see Baer, pp. 62–3.

[69] Law of 20 Jumādā al-Ūlā 1330/7 May 1912. See *Düstur, tertib-i sani*, vol. 4, Istanbul 1331, pp. 483–8. For an Arabic version see Gaulmier, pp. 121–3 (Annexe I).

[70] Gaulmier, p. 96.

[71] L. Massignon, 'La structure du travail à Damas en 1927', *Cahiers Internationaux de Sociologie*, 15, 1953, pp. 34–52.

[72] Cf. H. Schurtz, 'Türkische Basare und Zünfte', *Zeitschrift für Socialwissenschaft* (Berlin), vi, 1903, pp. 683–706. For some examples see G. Young, *Corps de droit Ottoman*, Oxford 1905–6, vol. 4, p. 32; vol. 5, p. 291; etc. For guilds newly established in nineteenth-century Egypt see Baer, pp. 134–6.

Effective government control certainly was an important reason for the extreme subdivision of the guilds into very many small specialized groups—a phenomenon that has been mentioned by many observers.[73] There were great variations in the internal structure of the different guilds. In addition to the head of the guild, the *kâhya*, many had retained the old post of *yiğit başı*,[74] and some the post of *shaykh* as well.[75] However, the modern 'sub-*shaykh*' was generally called *vekil*.[76] Some guilds also had a sort of informal committee or council.[77]

It was one of the main functions of the Turkish guilds in the nineteenth century to restrict the number of people exercising a certain trade. In many cases a maximum number was fixed. No shop could be opened without the permission of the guild's officers and the sanction of the *qāḍī*.[78] A special way of enforcing this restriction was the *gedik* system, the heritable right of a craftsman to exercise his trade in a specific shop.[79] These monopolistic practices, which originated of course in the economic interest of the guild members to evade competition, were sanctioned by the government because they facilitated administrative and fiscal control of the town population. It should be remarked, however, that the exact character of the fiscal function of the Turkish guilds, as well as its development before and during the nineteenth century, still remains to be established by a detailed study of these guilds.

Various other economic functions of Turkish guilds have been mentioned in the sources. The *shaykh* of the Istanbul booksellers collected the rent of their shops and paid the sum to the Imperial *waqfs*, and the officers of the jewellers' guild acted as trustees for deposited personal property of minors or travellers.[80] Some guilds seem to have acted as purchasers of raw materials which were then equitably distributed among the guilds' members.[81] Here and there the guilds controlled the prices and the quality of goods sold by their members, but apparently this was not the rule.[82] As against this, Turkish guilds apparently fulfilled some important social functions. The arbitration of disputes among members of the guild was an officially sanctioned function of all guild *shaykhs*, *kâhyas* or guild councils.[83] Moreover, many Turkish guilds seem to have maintained a

[73] For interesting examples see Ch. White, *Three Years in Constantinople*, London 1845, vol. 1, pp. 8–9, 193, 290; vol. 3, pp. 51, 84, 113, 120. For an earlier period see Taeschner, 'Das Zunftwesen in der Türkei', p. 180. For Egypt cf. Baer, pp. 25–7.

[74] Young, vol. 5, pp. 288–9.

[75] White, vol. 1, p. 202; vol. 2, p. 287; etc.

[76] *Ibid.*, vol. 1, p. 52; vol. 3, pp. 149, 324–5.

[77] *Ibid.*, vol. 2, pp. 158, 228, 254.

[78] *Ibid.*, vol. 1, pp. 98, 310; vol. 2, pp. 17, 154, 210; vol. 3, pp. 148, 325; etc.

[79] For explanations, examples and references see Baer, pp. 107 (and notes 9–10), 110, 157–8.

[80] White, vol. 2, pp. 158, 228.

[81] Taeschner, *ibid.*, p. 186.

[82] For examples see *ibid.*, and White, vol. 2, p. 254; Schurtz, p. 706. For Egypt cf. Baer, pp. 96–7, 100–5.

[83] Young, vol. 5, pp. 288–9. For Egypt cf. Baer, pp. 113–14.

fund for mutual assistance—which in the Arab countries was the exception rather than the rule.[84] Finally, a common feature of a Turkish guild was an annual festival in honour of its patron saint or other annual celebrations specific to single guilds—in addition, of course, to their participation in general processions of the guilds.[85]

Since Turkish guilds have not yet been the subject of a detailed study, we have no exact information about the different stages of their decline. The general process has been summarized as follows—without documentation: 'In ein kritisches Stadium der Auflösung aber gerieten die türkischen Zünfte im 19. Jahrhundert, als im Gefolge der Europäisierungsbestrebungen der Regierung in der Zeit der Reformen, der sog. Tanzimatzeit, europäische Wirtschaftsformen immer mehr in die Türkei eindrangen. Dadurch wurden die alten Zünfte immer mehr gegenstandslos und begannen zu verfallen.'[86] In 1910 the guilds of Istanbul were abolished by law, and the abolition of those of other towns of the Ottoman Empire followed two years later.[87]

Egyptian guilds in modern times have been the subject of a detailed study by the present writer. In the following we have briefly summarized what seems to us to be relevant to the present survey.[88]

It has been the assumption of most writers who touched on this subject that the creation of large-scale industry by Muḥammad ʿAlī was responsible for the guilds' decline or even for their disappearance. The obvious proof of the fallacy of this theory is the fact that until the 1880's a ramified system of guilds existed in Cairo and in many other towns of Egypt, comprising almost the whole indigenous gainfully-occupied population. Throughout the century the *shaykhs* of the guilds controlled and supervised the guild members' activities and ensured that the instructions of the government were carried out; they were made responsible for the misdemeanours of their guilds' members; they supplied labour and services to the government and private employers; and they arbitrated in disputes among members of the guilds. Until the last quarter of the century the *shaykhs* were responsible for the payment of taxes by the guild members, collected these taxes, and their advice was sought with regard to the assessment of the taxes to be paid by the guilds; until 1880 they fixed maximum wages for guild members; and until the late 1860's they assisted

[84] Gibb and Bowen, pp. 286–7; Baer, pp. 114–16.

[85] Gibb and Bowen, *ibid.*; Taeschner, *ibid.*, pp. 186–7. For details about Egypt see Baer, pp. 116–24.

[86] Taeschner, *ibid.*, p. 188. For the description of a weakened guild system in some Turkish towns early in this century see Schurtz, pp. 704–5.

[87] For the law of 16 Ṣafar 1328/26 February 1910 see *Düstur, tertib-i sani*, vol. 2, Istanbul 1330, pp. 123–7. Cf. Taeschner in *Schweizerisches Archiv für Volkskunde*, pp. 157–8. For the law of 1912 see above, note 69.

[88] No references to our study have been given here: for each statement the reader will find detailed examples and documentation in the relevant parts of that study.

the authorities in fixing prices of comestibles. It was the function of the guilds to restrict the number of people exercising a specific trade, and in many occupations the guilds kept a monopoly of their trades until the last decade of the nineteenth century.

The interest of the government in maintaining the guild system was not the only reason for its long survival. Not less important was the fact that the guild did not disintegrate as a result of class struggle among the various strata of its members. There was no rigid system of apprenticeship, no clear-cut distinction between apprentice and journeyman and it was relatively easy for an apprentice or journeyman to become a master. No associations of journeymen emerged in Egypt, and no sharp economic or social differentiation developed between the guilds' masters and the *shaykhs*, whose economic and social position did not rise much above that of other members of the guilds. With one or two exceptions, *shaykhs* did not become contractors, and no such transformation occurred in artisan guilds. This was mainly due to the fact that, after the failure of Muḥammad ʿAlī's industrial experiment, no serious industrial development took place in Egypt for decades. Therefore, the emergence of new kinds of economic organization capable of superseding the traditional guilds was delayed for a long time. Indigenous merchants did not form chambers of commerce and industry before the second decade of the twentieth century. The first labour trade union was established in 1899, and by 1911 there were no more than eleven unions, some of them with exclusively foreign membership.

The final decline and disappearance of the guilds was mainly the result of the influx of European goods and of Europeans settling in Egypt. This happened during the second half of the nineteenth century. By the end of the century many branches of Egypt's local crafts had succumbed to European competition. Merchant guilds were equally hit by a complete change of Egypt's commercial system. On the one hand, the traditional organization of the *sūq* gradually dissolved, retail trade spreading all over the town and foreigners infiltrating into branches which previously had been monopolized by Egyptian merchants. Thus the control of the guild *shaykhs* was made impossible. On the other hand, foreign trade was completely transformed: in the past it had dealt mainly in Sudanese, Arabian and Oriental goods, Cairo being one of the most important centres of this trade and Egyptian, Syrian and Turkish merchants being engaged in it. During the nineteenth century the export of cotton to Europe, and the import of European industrial goods into Egypt, became the main business of foreign trade, and Greeks and other Europeans became the principal importers and exporters. Moreover, like the artisans, Egyptian merchants suffered from a large variety of oppressive taxes and duties, from which foreign merchants were exempted by the capitulations.

The heaviest blow, however, was dealt to the guilds towards the end of the century, when Europeans began to disregard the *shaykhs* of the guilds as suppliers of labour. This was made possible by the growth of Egyptian towns, especially during the last quarter of the century. The influx of people into towns considerably increased the number of those who were not members of guilds and thus made it difficult for the guilds to maintain their monopolies.

Finally, towards the end of the nineteenth century, Egypt's administration was reorganized and became more efficient. Thus the state could do without the link of the guilds, and step by step their administrative, fiscal and economic functions shrank until they lost most of them. About the middle of the century, changes in the system of taxation deprived the *shaykhs* of the function of allocating among the members of the guilds a fixed tax-quota imposed on the guild as a whole. Saʿīd officially abolished the monopolies of the guilds (1854–6), but did not succeed in carrying out his decrees in this respect. No further changes in the guilds' functions were introduced during the rule of Ismāʿīl (1863–79). But in the 1880's and the 1890's the government published a series of decrees providing for professional permits to be issued by official authority, not by the guild *shaykhs*. Another group of decrees fixed wages for a number of public services, thereby curtailing the *shaykhs*' function in this matter. In 1881 the *shaykhs* were relieved of the task of collecting the taxes, and by 1892 all taxes on the guilds, and thereby the remaining fiscal functions of the *shaykhs*, had been abolished. Monopolistic practices of specific guilds were prohibited during the years 1887–90, and in 1890 the complete freedom of all trades was announced. The last of the more important functions of the guild *shaykhs*, that of supplying labour, disappeared during the first decade of the twentieth century. By that time, however, not many of the guilds had survived, and after the First World War guilds no longer performed any function in the public life of Egypt.

Summary and conclusion

The foregoing survey of the present state of our knowledge of the history of guilds in Egypt, Syria and Turkey from the tenth to the twentieth centuries may be summarized as follows: we have no definite information about the existence of guilds, let alone their structure or functions, before the fifteenth century. Up to that time the sources have nothing but scattered items of information about chiefs of specific crafts or trades. The first guild documents date from the second half of the fifteenth century and relate to Anatolia (the fusion of the *akhī* movement with specific guilds). Similar documents relating to specific guilds in Egypt (the *Kitāb al-dhakhāʾir* of the barbers and physicians) date from the late sixteenth or early seventeenth century. By the end of the seventeenth century the guilds in Turkey as well as in Egypt had become an all-embracing system of organization of the urban population. The situation in the eighteenth century has not yet been sufficiently investigated, but we know that during most of the nineteenth century the guilds still comprised the whole indigenous gainfully-occupied town population and constituted the most important framework of its administrative and fiscal control by the government. During that century, however, the guilds began to decline, and they finally disappeared at the end of the nineteenth or early in the twentieth century as a result of the modernization of Middle Eastern administration and economy.

Before drawing some general conclusions from this summary we must raise the question whether we have not been misled by the fortuitous character of the sources. In other words, is it not possible that later sources are so much better than earlier ones that they reflect the existence of guilds while the earlier ones don't, although guilds existed at that time? May not our historical perspective have been distorted by the accident that late in the seventeenth century Evliya Çelebi wrote his *Seyahatname*? The answer is that these hypotheses seem to us to be highly improbable. The existence of guilds is reflected in chronicles of the later period which were written in the traditional manner and which are by no means superior in quality to medieval Arabic histories or other relevant sources, while no trace of guilds has been found in such important documents of the economic and social history of the medieval Middle East as the Geniza material and the archives of the Italian cities.

How, then, are we to explain the diametrical contrast between the results of our survey and former theories about the history of Islamic guilds, which assumed that the guilds flourished in the eleventh and twelfth centuries, were suppressed by the re-establishment of Sunnī rule after the overthrow of the Fāṭimids, gradually lost their privileges and continued to 'vegetate' 'in very humble forms' under Ottoman rule until 'they became' modern syndicates in the twentieth century?[89] The explanation seems to be simple. Scholars writing about 'the guilds' until quite recently meant any kind of association with popular membership. Thus 'the guilds' were first associations connected with the Qarmaṭī movement, later *futuwwa* and *akhī* associations and still later veritable guilds, and the

[89] See in particular L. Massignon, 'Ṣinf', *EI*[1]; *id.*, 'Guilds, Islamic', *Encyclopedia of Social Sciences*, vol. 7, p. 215; *id.*, 'Les corps de métiers et la cité islamique', *Revue Internationale de Sociologie*, 28, 1920, pp. 473–89. Cf. also B. Lewis, 'The Islamic Guilds', *Economic History Review*, 1937, pp. 20–37. For critical remarks on Massignon's theory see Cl. Cahen, 'La changeante portée sociale de quelques doctrines religieuses', in *L'Elaboration de l'Islam* (Colloque de Strasbourg, 12–14 juin 1959), Paris 1961, pp. 14–15 (I am indebted to Professor William M. Brinner for this reference); and especially a hitherto unpublished paper submitted by Professor Claude Cahen to a conference on the Muslim city held in Oxford in 1965. I am grateful to Professor Cahen for having been so kind as to let me see the manuscript of this paper before publication.

decline of the Qarmaṭī movement or of the *futuwwa* was considered to have meant the decline of the guilds. As a result of this indiscriminate treatment of associations of fundamentally different character a crucial fact of guild history has been overlooked, namely that the rise of the guilds was closely connected with the decline of the free *futuwwa* and *akhī* associations, as Taeschner has clearly shown with regard to Turkey. The *Kitāb al-dhakhā'ir* reflects the same stage of transition in Egypt, showing as it does how the *futuwwa* traditions and rites gradually declined and how they had to cope with a developing and ever growing range of guilds including more and more crafts and professions.[90]

However, there remains the question how it could have been the prevalent view of guild history in the Middle East that the guilds 'vegetated in very humble forms' under Ottoman rule while in fact it was Ottoman rule which developed the guild system into a comprehensive framework of organization of the urban population. This view can be accounted for only by the existence of a presupposition that a guild is an association organized democratically from below, preferably in revolt against the government but at least free from any official influence or interference. The 'real guilds', therefore, were the revolutionary movements in Islamic history, while the 'official' guilds of the Ottomans do not count according to this view. However, no proof whatever has been produced so far to show that the popular, democratic or revolutionary movements in Middle Eastern history were organized on a professional basis, i.e., as guilds. On the other hand, even if we assume that there were beginnings of spontaneous professional organizations established from below before the sixteenth century, there can be no doubt that these organizations never came near to anything like the comprehensiveness and importance of the elaborate and ramified network of the guild system established by the Ottoman government in the seventeenth century. Therefore, whatever our ideas are about what a guild should be or what a guild was in other parts of the world, with regard to Turkey and Egypt, at least, the guild organization achieved its fullest development by sanction of the government, under its auspices and as the result of its administrative and fiscal policy. The guilds of these countries were maintained from above, and the system in which they were integrated was organized from above, not from below.[91]

Many of the characteristic traits of guilds in the Middle East are closely

[90] Cf. Baer, pp. 9–10.

[91] 'Die Osmanen-Sultane haben das Zunftwesen, das die einzige Form war, in der die Gesamtbevölkerung des Reiches . . . organisiert und erfassbar war, geschützt; sie waren an seiner Erhaltung interessiert. . . . Sie beliessen den Zünften eine weitgehende Autonomie und wiesen gelegentlich ihre Beamten an, diese zu achten und das traditionelle Zunftwesen gegen auf seine Zersetzung abzielende Bestrebungen in Schutz zu nehmen'. F. Taeschner, 'Ein Zunft-Fermān Sultan Muṣṭafā's III. von 1773', *Westöstliche Abhandlungen, R. Tschudi,* Wiesbaden 1954, p. 331.

connected with this basic feature of their history. Since the time of the emergence of the guilds, the guild chiefs, both in Egypt and Turkey, were either appointed by the government (usually by the *qāḍī*) or their choice had to be officially approved. The main function of the guilds was the effective control of the urban population by the government for purposes of security, taxation and the supply of manpower. As long as no other system of control was available, the government ordered the establishment of a new guild whenever a number of people were engaged in a new branch of the economy. When modern systems of administration and taxation evolved, the guilds lost their use for the government and the result was that they disappeared. Moreover, this strong connection between the guilds and government is reflected in the fact that we find the strongest and most comprehensive system of guilds in the two principal seats of government in the Middle East—Istanbul and Cairo; in none of the provincial towns did a comparable guild system emerge. It certainly is significant that the guilds of Damascus, which were more autonomous than those of Cairo and Istanbul, were less important as an economic framework and, apparently, also from other points of view.

The misconception of 'Islamic guilds' as popular or even revolutionary organizations has led to various errors; we shall conclude this paper with short comments on two of them. First, writers on the Middle East have stressed again and again the close connection between the guilds and the Ṣūfī orders. Unfortunately, to the best of our knowledge none of these writers has so far substantiated this claim. In any case, our examination of the situation in Egypt has led to the conclusion that, because of their different functions, guilds and *ṭarīqas* were not associated with each other but rather co-existed on different levels. There were many points of contact but no system of connections.[92]

Secondly, in his article 'Ṣinf' in the first edition of the *Encyclopaedia of Islam*, L. Massignon says: 'Since 1917 the ancient Muslim guilds have tended to become *naḳābāt* or syndicates for the new professions, dependent on the Third International (Moscow).' At least in Egypt, which is mentioned by Professor Massignon as one of the countries in which this change was noticed, nothing of the kind happened. The 'ancient guilds' disappeared at the end of the nineteenth and the beginning of the twentieth century, when they were not needed any more by the government. The emergence of the trade union movement in Egypt had no connection whatever with the traditional guilds.

[92] Baer, pp. 125–6. The same seems to have been the case in the Maghrib. See *ibid.*, note 39.

Quelques Mots sur le Déclin Commercial du Monde Musulman à la Fin du Moyen Age*

CLAUDE CAHEN

Quelle qu'ait été la place, variable selon les moments et les lieux, de l'économie marchande dans le monde musulman médiéval,[1] il est certain qu'au haut Moyen Age, si on le compare à l'Europe, elle le caractérise. Au bas Moyen Age au contraire,[2] et plus encore aux temps modernes, c'est l'Europe qui prend les devants, le distançant de plus en plus. On s'est souvent interrogé sur les causes de cette interversion. Sans pouvoir faire plus dans le temps qui m'est imparti, je présenterai à ce sujet quelques réflexions.

Par définition une économie marchande ne peut s'étudier dans un seul domaine clos,[3] sans référence à ce qui l'entoure. En ce qui concerne le domaine musulman, on constate d'une part que les phénomènes qui l'affectent lui sont communs avec d'autres sociétés, d'autre part qu' ils ne sont pas dûs uniquement à une évolution interne, mais aussi au contrecoup des évolutions qui l'entourent. Sans aller jusqu'à l'Extrême Orient, la même décadence a affecté Byzance,[4] avant d'affecter même ceux des

* Le présent exposé a été fait, à quelques phrases près, dans le cadre d'un «panel» au Congrès des Orientalistes à Ann Arbor le 14 août 1967. Il avait été précédé d'un exposé dans lequel un collègue avait en un quart d'heure indiqué les facteurs de l'essor économique musulman aux premiers siècles de l'hégire. Je disposais à mon tour d'un quart d'heure. Je conserve ici mon texte, mais en y ajoutant des notes. Je dois remercier B. Lewis d'avoir eu la gentillesse de me le demander, malgré mon absence, que je regrette vivement, à la Conférence de Londres.

[1] Il faut se garder d'un certain romantisme qui incline à voir des caravanes ou des flottes de marchands musulmans sillonnant sans arrêt le monde. La terre reste probablement presque partout la source essentielle de la richesse, et le commerce ne commande pas tous les domaines de l'économie. Mais l'importance de l'économie marchande reste évidente si on compare la société musulmane à celles qui l'entourent dans le temps ou dans l'espace.

[2] Il est difficile, et sans grand intérêt pour notre objet, de préciser une chronologie qui peut varier non seulement suivant les régions, mais aussi suivant les facteurs considérés· Nous n'avons pas de statistiques, et il serait tentant de se laisser aller à un certain subjectivisme. Il faut cependant ne pas exagérer non plus l'indifférence au temps, et il est en général instructif de souligner les synchronismes, tant entre faits d'ordres divers qu'entre domaines économiques différents.

[3] L'étendue du domaine musulman ne dispense pas de cette règle: il consiste en une bande de territoires relativement similaires, dont le commerce extérieur a toujours été de plus de portée que le commerce intérieur, sinon de plus de volume.

[4] Longtemps avant sa conquête par les Turcs, qu'elle a naturellement favorisée. Les prodromes en remontent en gros au XIe siècle, c'est-à-dire à la même époque que ceux de la décadence musulmane. C'est en 1082 que, pour des raisons il est vrai en partie fortuites,

Méditerranéens d'Occident qui n'auront pas su à temps convertir leur économie: l'économie moderne aura son centre dans l'Europe du nord-ouest, et non plus à Venise ou à Florence.[5] C'est donc tout un système qui décline, dont le monde musulman n'est qu'une partie, même si cette partie y présente quelques traits originaux. Et d'autre part, quelles qu'aient pu être les causes internes de faiblesse de ce monde musulman, elles vont être aggravées par le fait même de la prépondérance européenne nouvelle, qui fera régresser l'économie des pays non modernisés en deçà du niveau où d'elle-même elle se serait maintenue.[6] A cet égard le vrai problème est moins celui du déclin de l'Orient que de l'essor de l'Occident,[7] et, pour l'historien de l'Orient, la question fondamentale est de savoir comment il se fait qu'en une période donnée – fin du Moyen Age, début des temps modernes[8] – il s'est produit le renversement de tendance dû à ce que les premiers progrès de l'Europe n'ont plus pu être suivis par l'Orient.

On dit souvent que l'évènement principal qui a entrainé la décadence de l'économie musulmane consiste dans les Grandes Découvertes. Certes la découverte de l'Amérique, dont les effets économiques n'ont commencé à se faire sentir que vers le milieu du XVIe siècle, était extérieure au domaine de réaction possible du monde musulman. Mais la découverte de la route du Cap de Bonne Espérance, elle, à y regarder de près, apparait bien plus comme un des derniers actes du drame que comme le prélude de celui-ci.[9] Car enfin comment se fait-il que l'Egypte placée comme elle l'était, n'ait pu ni interdire militairement[10] ni neutraliser économiquement

---

est signé l'acte de capitulation de la flotte byzantine devant Venise; il n'aurait pas été sī définitif s'il n'y avait eu que ces raisons.

[5] Le déplacement des axes commerciaux finira par nuire même à Gênes, mais celle-ci gardera un certain temps sa puissance financière, parce qu'elle aura su prendre des intérêts dans les entreprises nouvelles des pays occidentaux, y compris dans les Grandes Découvertes elles-mêmes; de bon ou de mauvais gré selon les moments, son sort était moins que celui de Venise lié exclusivement à celui de l'Orient, et, contre Venise, elle cherchait autre chose.

[6] C'est donc une faute méthodologique de juger des attitudes économiques, pour ne parler que de celles-là, des Proche-Orientaux du Moyen Age d'après ce qu'on peut constater de leurs attitudes dans les secteurs traditionnels de leur économie contemporaine ou récente.

[7] Méthodologiquement aussi il est évidemment plus facile d'étudier le développement occidental qui a eu lieu que l'absence de développement oriental, et les causes de celui-là que de celle-ci.

[8] Il y a décalage en faveur de l'Empire Ottoman, ou du moins de ses provinces centrales, mais peut-être seulement parce que la situation de force là a permis d'y concentrer ce qui restait d'activité économique ailleurs. La Puissance nouvelle n'a pas plus pu que l'Egypte des Mamluks garder à l'Islam la maîtrise de l'Océan Indien.

[9] On ne saurait cependant reprocher aux Musulmans d'Occident, quand ils étaient encore maîtres de la mer, de n'avoir pas réalisé cette découverte. Ils ont exploré la côte nord-occidentale de l'Afrique, mais n'avaient aucune incitation économique à vouloir tourner leurs coréligionnaires d'Orient. Il ne faut pas exagérer la portée économique des conflits politico-religieux.

[10] Excellent exposé de D. Ayalon dans son *Gunpowder and Firearms in the Mamluk Kingdom*, London 1956.

l'expansion portugaise dans l'Océan Indien? A cet égard les entreprises de Vasco de Gama et de ses successeurs, avant de l'aggraver, révèlent une faiblesse qui leur préexistait.[11] C'est cette faiblesse qu'il nous faut tâcher de comprendre.

Le monde de l'Islam est vaste, et à vrai dire, si l'activité marchande à travers l'Egypte peut faire quelqu' illusion jusqu'au XVe siècle, la plupart des pays musulmans sont déjà bien avant cette date économiquement affaiblis.[12] Ni la religion, ni le Droit de l'Islam n'y sont pour rien. [13] Des causes occasionnelles y ont contribué, qu'il ne faut ni sousestimer ni exagérer: la relative pauvreté minière et l'épuisement de certains gisements,[14] a une époque où l'Europe découvrait les siens, mais où néanmoins l'échelle des besoins restait basse; la Peste Noire et autres épidémies, qui cependant n'ont pas moins touché l'Europe;[15] les invasions, intérieures comme celle des Hilāliens en Afrique du Nord, ou venue du dehors comme celle plus vaste des Mongols en Asie, invasions qui ont plus ou moins directement ruiné l'agriculture et certaines villes, mais qui elles aussi néanmoins avaient révélé des faiblesses avant de les aggraver:[16] de

[11] Sur un point particulier, le comportement du pilote yéménite Ibn Mājid aidan Vasco de Gama repose sur une opposition des marins d'Aden aux prétentions monopolisatrices de l'Egypte. Ils pensaient pouvoir devenir, eux, les intermédiaires et bénéficiaires dans la nouvelle voie commerciale.

[12] L'Asie musulmane a été appauvrie entre autres causes par le développement même de la concurrence égyptienne dans le transit Océan Indien–Mediterranée; l'Afrique du Nord l'est, entre autres causes, par la part croissante prise par les Italiens et Ibériques aux acquisitions de l'or soudanais.

[13] Cela a été fortement établi ces derniers temps, pour ce qui concerne la religion, par Maxime Rodinson dans son *Islam et Capitalisme*, Paris 1966. Il faut remarquer que, même si l'on veut voir dans l'Islam un côté fataliste (qui ne s'est développé en ce sens que lorsqu'une certaine «fatalité» s'est apesantie sur l'Islam, aux temps modernes), il n'y a pas plus fataliste que le protestantisme calviniste, dont le rôle dans l'essor du capitalisme est cependant indiscutable. En ce qui concerne le Droit, celui de l'Islam était sur quelques points en avance sur celui de Rome, Byzance et l'Europe du haut Moyen Age; voir par exemple A. Udovitch, «At the origins of the Western Commenda», *Speculum*, 37, 1962. On a dit par contre que la commende italienne du bas Moyen Age était en avance sur l'islamique, en ce qu'elle pouvait être conclue sur des marchandises et non seulement sur des espèces monétaires; mais, outre qu'en fait nous possédons des exemples de commendes musulmanes sur marchandises (voir H. R. Idris dans *JESHO*, iv, 1961) l'opposition est beaucoup plus formelle que réelle. Le contrat musulman stipule l'avance en valeur monétaire, en raison de son souci de la précision de la somme à rendre, mais, même si l'avance a été effectivement faite en espèces, le marchand qui va commercer au loin en réalise tout de suite en général une partie en marchandises. Et dans les actes italiens, si l'avance est souvent faite en marchandises (mais non toujours), la valeur en est toujours précisée; on revient donc pratiquement au cas précédent.

[14] En particulier les gisements d'or de Nubie épuisés pratiquement depuis la fin du XIIe siècle; en Egypte encore, l'alun a dû baisser ou devenir comparativement moins rentable; l'Egypte a toujours dû importer son fer.

[15] Voir les communications ci-jointes de Lopez, Miskimin et Udovitch.

[16] Le rôle des Hilāliens dans la ruine de l'Afrique du nord a été remis en question par J. Poncet dans deux articles des *Cahiers de Tunisie*, 1954, et des *Annales* (*Economies, Sociétés, Civilisations*), 1967; voir aussi mes notes dans *JESHO*, 1968 et 1969. Sur les

toute façon le monde musulman ne forme pas un marché unique, et la ruine de l'Asie Centrale[17] n'a aucune raison d'avoir affecté l'Egypte. Il est difficile de doser l'influence respective des facteurs: ceux-ci doivent leur relative importance au fait qu'ils ont pu momentanément accentuer un décalage de l'Orient par rapport à l'Occident, et par conséquent rendre plus difficile la concurrence et le redressement; mais il ne faut pas oublier que l'Europe du XIVe et du XVe siècle est elle-même en état de crise.

Des causes sociales peuvent être invoquées, en particulier, en Egypte et ailleurs, la domination sur l'Etat d'une aristocratie militaire qui d'un côté participait aux diverses formes de l'économie, mais qui de l'autre au moindre besoin prenait des mesures coercitives incompatibles avec la santé de celle-ci.[18] Mais, outre que de tels régimes politiques révèlent les limites de l'économie marchande, c'est également l'interférence d'Etats que la classe marchande ne dominait pas qui a dès avant la Peste Noire causé les grands krachs de la Banque italienne.[19]

Sans suggérer aucune exclusive, il y a lieu de rechercher les éléments de faiblesse relative qui pouvaient exister dans la structure de l'économie marchande elle-même.[20] Plutôt que de poursuivre une énumération sommaire, je voudrais essayer de parler de deux facteurs qui me paraissent avoir une certaine importance et n'avoir pas été jusqu'ici suffisamment mis en relief.

Pendant le Moyen Age entier les marchands du monde musulman ont été chercher, de l'Europe orientale à la Chine, et tout autour de l'Océan Indien, les produits dont ils avaient besoin pour leur commerce ailleurs ou leur consommation. Les mêmes Proche-Orientaux, et cette fois aussi les Byzantins, ont très tôt, avant d'y être aucunement contraints, laissé les Italiens s'assurer le quasi-monopole des transports méditerranéens. Je ne peux discuter ici les raisons d'un pareil contraste,[21] qui a pu

Mongols comme pour eux, il faut distinguer en tous cas les circonstances de l'invasion elle-même et la place économico-sociale occupée ensuite dans la société résultante.

[17] Difficilement discutable, mais difficile à dater et à préciser, la formation momentanée de l'Empire Timuride y ayant ramené artificiellement certaines formes d'activité.

[18] La situation à cet égard a été récemment analysée de façon très pertinente par I. M. Lapidus, *Muslim Cities in the later Middle Ages*, Cambridge, Mass., 1967.

[19] Entre autres, par exemple, les arrêts de paiement, par suite de leur guerre, des gouvernements français et anglais aux Bardi et Peruzzi de Florence.

[20] Cette question a fait l'objet de discussions au sein de l'Institut d'Etudes Islamiques de l'Université de Paris en 1962; malheureusement les procès-verbaux n'ont pu en être distribués qu'à usage interne.

[21] J'en ai un peu parlé dans ma communication sur «Quelques problèmes concernant l'expansion économique musulmane au Moyen Age», dans *L'Occidente e l'Islam nell'alto Medioevo*, *Settimane di studio del centro italiano sull'alto Medioevo*, xii, Spolète 1965, surtout p. 423 sq. Maurice Lombard, dans *Le Navire, Travaux du Deuxième Colloque International d'Histoire Maritime, 1957* (article «Arsenaux et bois de marine dans la Méditerranée musulmane, VII–XIIe siècles» a insisté sur l'insuffisance croissante du bois de construction navale dans les pays musulmans de la Méditerranée; l'argument, sans être dépourvu d'intérêt, n'a qu'une portée limitée, en raison de l'échelle modique des

momentanément paraître présenter certains avantages fiscaux;[22] il suffit de souligner qu'il aboutissait, face à l'Europe, à une attitude partiellement passive au moment où les difficultés de la concurrence auraient exigé le déploiement de toutes les énergies d'initiative. Et bien entendu, mais plus tard seulement, la découverte de la route du Cap de Bonne Espérance devait ruiner à la fois les deux branches du système.

Il y a cependant, je crois, plus intérieur encore. L'économie marchande du Moyen Age musulman, comme celle de l'Antiquité, était surtout une économie de spéculation et d'acquisition. De spéculation: je veux dire que le but conscient des marchands était d'acheter quelque part à bas prix des produits qu'ils pourraient ensuite revendre ailleurs avec une grosse marge bénéficiaire.[23] Economie d'acquisition: je veux dire que l'objectif des Etats et de l'aristocratie utilisatrice du commerce était de se procurer les éléments de leur puissance ou de l'aisance de vie, pour autant qu'ils ne pouvaient se les procurer dans leur pays même, non pas d'écouler une production. Certes, pour se procurer des marchandises, il faut bien, si l'on n'a pas assez de moyens monétaires, vendre en compensation des produits de l'économie indigène; mais le monde musulman, qui a eu pendant longtemps une grande aisance monétaire, n'a pas eu à apporter à cet aspect des choses une attention particulière. Jamais en tous cas l'écoulement de la production intérieure ne parait avoir été envisagé pour lui-méme, et souvent même il a été découragé,[24] comme privant un Etat des témoignages de son prestige, ou, en raison des bornes techniques du rendement, des disponibilités nécessaires aux besoins de ses sujets. L'idée d'alimenter un commerce grâce à un surplus de production, pour assurer ou augmenter le travail et les ressources des producteurs ou simplement pour équilibrer en valeurs marchandes importation et exportation, cette idée, élémentaire pour tout Etat moderne, n'a probablement jamais effleuré un Etat du Proche Orient médiéval,[25] parce que plus souvent, au niveau de la technique où l'on se

---

besoins, d'approvisionnements possibles en Asie Mineure et en pays chrétiens, et surtout de la constatation d'une part de la décadence simultanée de Byzance, d'autre part de la continuation, au moins en certaines périodes, de la piraterie maritime.

[22] Et de prestige. Les «barbares» doivent venir constater sur place la richesse de la Ville Impériale, disait-on à Byzance. Et en outre il vaut mieux qu'ils viennent, eux, payer des droits de douane et dépenser sur place l'argent qu'ils gagneront plutôt que d'envoyer les nôtres en faire autant chez eux.

[23] Cela est formulé très explicitement aussi bien les *Maḥāsin al-Tijāra* d'Abū'l-Faḍl al Dimashqī (période et territoire fāṭimide) que dans le *Tabaṣṣur fī'l-Tijāra* attribué (à tort) à Jāḥiẓ (Iraq ʿabbāside). Et c'est la raison d'être des lettres que s'écrivent les marchands juifs connus par la Geniza, les marchands italiens, etc. Sinbad le Marin ne fait rien d'autre. . . .

[24] Cela résulte de manière éloquente des règlements étudiés dans le *Minhāj* d'al-Makhzūmī (Egypte, XIIe siècle), voir mes «Douanes et Commerce dans les ports méditerranéens de l'Egypte médiévale», *JESHO*, vii, 1964, en particulier p. 262 sq.

[25] Je ne prétends naturellement pas qu'il n'y ait eu aucune industrie ou production à clientèle étrangère, telle l'industrie textile de Tinnīs, qui vendait normalement à Constantinople, semble-t-il; mais cela reste des cas exceptionnels.

trouvait, les possibilités de la vente intérieure restaient supérieures à celles de la production,[26] mais avec le résultat réciproque que cette production n'était pas encouragée à dépasser son niveau technique ou son rendement.

Or justement on peut se demander, par comparaison, si, cette conversion, l'Europe occidentale, peut-être à peine consciemment, n'était pas en train de la faire. Elle aussi certainement avait d'abord pensé à acheter plus qu'à vendre; mais monétairement elle était défavorisée, si bien que, même si le but restait l'importation, elle avait été pratiquement obligée de mettre l'accent sur l'exportation des marchandises dont elle pouvait disposer, sur leur production, sur leur transport par ses propres forces. Au milieu du Moyen Age le commerce de l'Egypte faisait encore une place saine à la vente de ses produits, mais à la fin du Moyen Age, même elle, réputée jadis pour son industrie textile, était envahie par les étoffes de l'industrie flamande ou florentine,[27] sans parler des importations d'armes, et de bien d'autres. Le commerce alors n'y consiste plus qu'à assister passivement a l'échange, qui se fait sur son territoire, des produits en transit de l'Extrême Orient contre les produits en transit de l'Occident. Tel avait été le cas deux siècles tôt déjà de ce commerce momentané de l'Empire mongol sur lequel la participation des Italiens ne doit pas faire illusion,[28] et qui de toute façon n'avait pas duré: il traversait le pays, il ne lui appartenait pas. Certes des bénéfices fiscaux, des bénéfices privés pour les importateurs de l'Extrême Orient pouvaient encore être réalisés en Egypte à la fin du XVe siècle; mais qu'arrive alors la Découverte Portugaise, et puisque le transit était tout, tout alors en un jour s'écroule. Je sais qu'il se réorganisera aux temps modernes un «commerce du Levant», mais déjà maintenant dans le cadre de la suprématie européenne,[29] et trop tard pour que le Levant en tirât aucun vrai profit. S'il n'y avait pas eu les Grandes Découvertes, le déclin aurait été plus lent, moins absolu peut-être; mais il n'est pas douteux qu'il avait largement commencé avant elles, et que grosso modo le résultat aurait fini par être le même.

[26] En matière alimentaire, il y avait crainte de disette.

[27] Les Occidentaux apportent, il est vrai, encore des espèces monétaires, mais pour financer leurs achats des denrées en transit; et cette monnaie a maintenant cours dans tout l'Orient, dont la frappe indigène est en ruine, ce qui signifie que, à considérer l'ensemble des circuits commerciaux, les Italiens se procurent assez de métaux précieux pour déborder lour propre aire commerciale.

[28] Cette participation, en projetant sur le commerce une documentation dont nous n'avons pas l'équivalent pour la période antérieure, risque de faire illusion: elle ne suffit pas à elle seule à établir que le commerce, en changeant quelque peu de mains, ait augmenté de volume, ni que les populations intermédiaires en aient tiré plus de profit. Il y a même des cas où l'extension du commerce compense le déclin de la production indigène pour les besoins de l'aristocratie, et où réciproquement elle peut nuire à cette production.

[29] Aux mains des Européens du nord-ouest, et essentiellement du type «colonial», pour achat de matières premières.

Monetary Aspects of Medieval Near Eastern Economic History

ANDREW S. EHRENKREUTZ

To achieve meaningful progress in the field of medieval Near Eastern economic history one must take into account its monetary aspects. This postulate is based on the following premises:

(*a*) Money, or rather a highly elaborate monetary system constituted one of the fundamental institutions in the economic life of medieval Near Eastern society.

(*b*) If properly explored and correlated, historical monetary data may be turned into a heuristic tool permitting an attempt to measure medieval Near Eastern economic accomplishments by means of statistical evaluation.

The Islamic Caliphate was born in a milieu exposed to the circulation of metallic money of Byzantine and Sāsānid origin.[1] Following their victorious expansion in the Near East, Muslim authorities found themselves in control of peoples and territories whose economy had for many centuries been characterized by a sophisticated monetary system. The monetary system inherited by the Muslim conquerors consisted of gold coinage which constituted an imperial monopoly of the Byzantine state, and of silver coinage of the defunct Sāsānid Empire.[2] Military, political, social and economic circumstances produced by the triumph of the Arabs generated major changes with regard to the circulation of money. To begin with, military operations, captures or submissions of towns, palaces, churches and monasteries brought about a process of dethesaurization releasing tremendous quantities of precious metals, coins, jewels, etc., for circulation. Secondly, the territorial extension of the Caliphate resulted in the acquisition of, or at least, accessibility to the rich oriferous and argentiferous areas of the Near East. Finally, by inaugurating the system of *ʿaṭāʾ*, i.e., the institution of regular cash stipends to which all fully-fledged members of the Muslim community were entitled, the Caliphate stimulated production and wide distribution of coinage. One must remember that the beneficiaries of this welfare system were local Near Easterners. In Byzantine times, imperial

[1] Although Ḥimyarite coins were also in circulation (al-Balādhurī, *Futūḥ al-buldān*, ed. de Goeje, 1866, p. 467) they did not seem to play any direct part in the foundation of the Islamic monetary system.

[2] Copper coinage (*fulūs*) because of its inferior, limited and localized function, will not come under consideration in the present paper.

authorities exploited Near Eastern taxpayers and resources to promote the well-being of the court in Constantinople or to finance military campaigns in Europe. Byzantine aristocracy or imperial officials, after serving and earning money in Near Eastern provinces, would retire in the metropolitan district of Constantinople. Indeed, the whole economy of the Byzantine empire was geared to meet the needs of the great consumer and production centre such as Constantinople happened to be. Since the mint of Constantinople was the most important institution producing imperial gold coinage, a lot of Near Eastern gold must have been flowing into the Byzantine capital. Manufacturing activities of gold- and silversmiths of Constantinople must have absorbed substantial quantities of gold and silver bullion imported from Near Eastern provinces. The drainage of Near Eastern gold and silver stopped with the victory of the Muslims. Arab military and administrative aristocracy, or even the rank and file supporting the new regime resided in the Near East. From an economic point of view they represented a class of the nouveau riche consumers, spending money, squandering it or investing it locally, to the benefit of Near Eastern caterers, labourers, producers, merchants, etc. The availability of cash in the hands of the Arab invaders or immigrants stimulated agricultural production, manufacturing and commercial activities and urban developments. All these factors contributed to an intensive circulation of coinage.

Such a situation forced the Caliphate to proceed with appropriate measures to secure an adequate supply of coinage. At first the mints of the new regime continued to strike coins in imitation of traditional Byzantine and Sāsānid types of coins. Before long, however, more precisely towards the end of the seventh century of the Christian era, Muslim administration felt strong enough, politically and economically, to do away with the monetary vestiges of Byzantine and Persian domination of the Near East. In the 690's the mints of the Caliphate began to produce new 'Islamic' coinage consisting of two basic metallic types: silver (*dirham*) and gold (*dīnār*). This event, usually referred to as the monetary reform of ʿAbd al-Malik, received considerable attention in modern scholarly literature but so far its treatment has been mainly limited to numismatic and culturological aspects. Numismatists have registered that event as the inception of a new type of Near Eastern coinage characterized by specific Arab-Islamic stylistic, epigraphical, metrological and other external features. Historians interested in the cultural and ideological evolution of the Caliphate rightly defined the reform of ʿAbd al-Malik as a manifestation of his policy to accomplish arabization of his administration. Still others interpreted the appearance of the purely Islamic, 'impersonal' type of coinage as an expression of a propaganda warfare against the internal and external enemies of the Umayyad regime.

On the other hand little attention has been given to the basic historical function of that reform, namely its economic significance. The reform of ʿAbd al-Malik meant that after a period of transition the new regime established by Arab conquerors decided to assume responsibility with regard to the monetary system of the Caliphate. The very adoption of a uniform bi-metallic coinage was of major economic consequence. It is true that the measure involving silver coins was not too revolutionary in view of the total extinction of the Sāsānid Empire whose function in respect of silver coinage supply was taken over by the Caliphate. In contrast the minting of gold by the Caliphate constituted an outstanding event in medieval economic history. After humiliating the Byzantines on Near Eastern battlefields, the Arab leadership contested the traditional imperial monopoly in respect of gold coinage. This challenge to Byzantine monetary supremacy could not have been undertaken without strong economic foundations and confidence in commercial competitive potentials of Near Eastern society under the new political and religious regime. Thus before the rising silhouettes of Muslim minarets began to dominate Mediterranean horizons, Islamic *dīnārs* had proclaimed the end of economic submissiveness of the Near East and the beginning of its drive in quest of 'international' monetary surpremacy.

The monetary system instituted by the Umayyads entailed more than the adoption of bi-metallic coinage as official currency. Judging by the activities of al-Ḥajjāj and of Hishām[3] the administration of the Caliphate assumed responsibility for the organization of the supply of the official currency. The problems of the procurement of raw materials, in this case of precious metals; of the supervision over the operations of the mints; and of the means of distribution of coinage constituted important areas of governmental involvement in the functioning of Islamic monetary systems.

Subsequent history of that important institution abounded in organizational diversifications and economic modulations. A decentralized network of regional mints replaced the highly centralized Umayyad system of coinage production. The responsibility of the sovereign to safeguard the integrity of coinage was delegated to specially appointed officials. The coinage itself underwent manifold mutations. Money changers and bankers became instrumental agents in the promotion of money circulation. All these historical processes notwithstanding one can hardly question the fact that the monetary system founded by the Umayyads remained one of the fundamental features of the dynamic medieval Near Eastern economy.

How dynamic? To expect a meaningful answer to this question is to presuppose that economic developments in the medieval Near East lend themselves to an analysis by means of some comparative approximation. It

[3] Cf. 'Dār al-ḍarb', *EI*[2], vol. ii, p. 117.

is precisely in this area of historical comparative interpretation that a proper utilization of our knowledge of the medieval Near Eastern monetary system may produce relevant analytical data.

To begin with one should stress the role of monetary evaluation in the pattern of social stratification. Whether one refers to the early Arab hierarchy or to the Mamlūk regime in Egypt the ascriptive and accomplished status enjoyed by the beneficiaries of the two respective systems was evaluated in strict monetary figures.[4] Fiscal activities of the Caliphate operated according to annual budgetary evaluation.[5] Taxes or salaries were not necessarily paid in cash but their level was always stated in terms of official monetary units. This practice of monetary evaluation was even more striking in other sectors of economic life. Medieval literary sources do not lack quotations of the value of real estate, of land and of housing, produce and rent, of the costs of free, conscript and slave labour, as well as of prices prevalent on internal and external markets.

To utilize such value data for the purpose of a reconstructive analysis of economic history one basic prerequisite must be achieved: the understanding of the value of Islamic money itself. This is necessitated by the fact that besides its basic metallic and denominational categories Islamic coinage was characterized by a lack of uniformity as far as its standards of weight and fineness were concerned. As a result of the decentralization and proliferation of coinage production in the ʿAbbāsid period different mints at different times produced coinage according to their local standards. Consequently the markets of the medieval Near East witnessed the circulation of different types of Muslim currency, of the same basic denominational and metallic categories but of unequal purchasing value. To expedite bookkeeping operations medieval fiscal administrations adopted the system of fictitious account money such for instance as the *dīnār jayshī* in Mamlūk Egypt. Unfortunately medieval sources as a rule quote monetary data not in terms of a standardized money of account but in those of the contemporary market currency. To fail to differentiate between various types of currency is to run the risk of complete misinterpretation of relevant sources of historical information. As an illustration of the danger of such interpretative fallacy one may furnish the following example:

In the seventh century of the Christian era the highest stipend in the *ʿaṭāʾ* system as set up by ʿUmar ibn al-Khaṭṭāb was that of ʿĀʾisha, amounting to 12,000 *dirhams* a year.[6] In the fifteenth century the monthly pay (*jāmakiyya*) of a Mamlūk soldier amounted to 2,000 *dirhams*, or 24,000

[4] One may add here that the members of the fiscally underprivileged community, i.e., the *ahl al-dhimmah*, were also stratified according to their economic status.

[5] Cf. the recent article by Makoto Shimizu, 'Les finances publiques de l'Etat ʿabbāsside', *Der Islam*, 42, 1965, pp. 1–24.

[6] Cf. Matti I. Moosa, 'The dīwān of ʿUmar ibn al-Khaṭṭāb', *Studies in Islam*, 2, 1965, p. 68.

dirhams on an annual basis.[7] If uncritically accepted these two statements would suggest that the services of an ordinary warrior in the Mamlūk system were considered twice as valuable as those of the Prophet's widow. However, after investigating the exchange value of the seventh and the fifteenth century *dirhams*, one would find that the rate of exchange of the former was about 14 *dirhams* to a *dīnār*, while that of the latter was 370 to 1 in A.D. 1455 (A.H. 859).[8] In the light of this observation one could deduce that in terms of the seventh century exchange rates the *jāmakiyya* in question amounted to about 900 *dirhams* annually. This amount in turn would appear fairly close to the 500 to 600 *dirhams* payable annually to an ordinary warrior on the *ʿaṭāʾ* list of ʿUmar ibn al-Khaṭṭāb.[9]

This example has been presented here to stress the importance of the need for exercise of extreme caution in studying monetary data for the purpose of an analysis of economic phenomena in medieval Near Eastern history. As a relevant remark one should observe that medieval Near Eastern units of measure of weight, capacity, volume, etc., were not uniform either. Thus even if the economic status of a particular currency unit happens to be established, there still remains the question of the actual size, weight or volume referred to in a price quotation.

PROBLEMS OF SOURCES

Until recently source materials pertaining to the economic past of the Caliphate have either been mistreated or completely ignored. This regrettable situation has given rise to the opinion that evidence relating to the medieval period is unsystematic and episodic. It is hoped that the following survey of the nature of sources available for the study of monetary developments alone will inspire more confidence in the viability of heuristic undertakings in the field of medieval economic history of the Near East. Truly, historians specializing in that particular field are not as privileged as their colleagues dealing with later periods, and whose research is facilitated by the existence of archival or modern statistical documentation. It is my contention, however, that evidence for the medieval period if properly, systematically and exhaustively handled permits attempts at statistical sampling and even mass interpretation. For the purpose of the present discussion the evidence in question has been arranged into two basic categories: textual and numismatic.

A. Textual evidence

(*i*) *Medieval historical and geographical literature*

This type of evidence is listed first because it constitutes an indispensable base for any endeavours in the field of medieval Near Eastern history.

[7] Cf. D. Ayalon, 'The system of payment in Mamlūk military society', *JESHO*, 1, 1957, p. 54. [8] *Supra*. [9] Matti I. Moosa, *art. cit.*, p. 68.

Historians like al-Balādhurī (d. 892), al-Ṭabarī (d. 923), Ibn al-Jawzī (d. 1201), Ibn al-Athīr (d. 1233), al-Maqrīzī (d. 1442) or Ibn Khaldūn (d. 1406), and geographers like al-Yaʿqūbī (d. 897?), al-Maqdisī (b. 946) or Yāqūt (d. 1229), do not need any introduction to those involved in the study of general or particular aspects of Near Eastern society in the Middle Ages. In the specific field of monetary history, sources included in that broad category are important because of their occasional references to: (*a*) location of gold and silver mines,[10] (*b*) location of mints,[11] (*c*) decisions concerning the operations of the mints,[12] (*d*) decisions concerning the types and quality of coinage,[13] (*e*) monetary exchange rates,[14] (*f*) prices and wages,[15] (*h*) state budgets.[16]

(ii) *Specialized literature dealing with diverse subjects*

This category involves medieval texts containing entire sections devoted to monetary or related problems. Juridical texts such as the *Kitāb al-kharāj* of Abū Yūsuf (d. 798), administrative handbooks such as the *Kitāb al-manāzil* of al-Būzajānī (d. 998) or the *Kitāb qawānīn al-dawāwīn* of Ibn Mammātī (d. 1209), diplomatic compendia such as the *Ṣubḥ al-Aʿshā* of al-Qalqashandī or even mathematical monographs such as the *Kāfī fī'l-ḥisāb* by al-Karajī (d. 1016) may be listed as typical examples of this type of source which should be considered in the pursuit of monetary data.

(iii) *Specialized literature devoted exclusively to monetary or directly pertinent problems*

As perfect examples of this kind of source one has to list the *Shudhūr al-ʿuqūd* of al-Maqrīzī, the *Kashf al-asrār al-ʿilmiyya bidār al-ḍarb al-miṣriyya* by Ibn Baʿra (13th cent.),[17] the *Kitāb al-taysīr* of al-Asadī (15th cent.),[18]

[10] Cf. D. M. Dunlop, 'Sources of gold and silver in Islam according to al-Hamdānī', *Studia Islamica*, 8, 1957, pp. 29–49.

[11] Cf. A. S. Ehrenkreutz, 'Contributions to the knowledge of the fiscal administration of Egypt in the Middle Ages', *Bulletin of the School of Oriental and African Studies*, 16, 1954, pp. 508–9.

[12] Cf. al-Balādhurī, *op. cit.*, pp. 468–9.

[13] Cf. A. S. Ehrenkreutz, 'Studies in the monetary history of the Near East in the Middle Ages', *JESHO*, 2, 1959, p. 138.

[14] Cf. tabulations compiled by W. Popper, *Egypt and Syria under the Circassian sultans, 1382–1468 A.D., Systematic notes* . . . (University of California publications in Semitic philology, vol. 16), 1957, pp. 74–5.

[15] Cf. the latest of the numerous publications of E. Ashtor, 'I salari nel Medio Oriente durante l'epoca medievale', *Rivista Storica Italiana*, 78, 1966, p. 322 f. Also *idem*, 'La recherche des prix dans l'Orient Médiéval. Sources, méthodes et problèmes', *Studia Islamica*, 21, 1964, pp. 101–44.

[16] Cf. A. von Kremer, 'Über das Einnahmebudget des Abbassiden-Reiches vom Jahre 306 H. (918–19)', *Denkschriften der Akademie der Wissenschaften in Wienna, Phil. Hist. Klasse*, 36, 1888, p. 307.

[17] Cf. A. S. Ehrenkreutz, 'Extracts from the technical manual on the Ayyūbid mint in Cairo', *Bulletin of the School of Oriental and African Studies*, 15, 1953, pp. 423–47.

[18] Cf. Subhi Labib, 'Al-Asadī und sein Bericht über Verwaltungs- und Geldreform im 15. Jahrhundert', *JESHO*, 8, 1965, pp. 312–16.

or *al-Dawḥa al-mushtabika fī ḍawābiṭ dār al-sikka* by Abū'l-Ḥasan ʿAlī ibn Yūsuf al-Ḥakīm.[19]

(iv) *Quasi-archival documents*

Albeit disadvantaged by the lack of regular archival materials historians engaged in the study of medieval Near Eastern monetary developments have at their disposal great quantities of documents of quasi-archival nature. I refer here to the Egyptian papyri as well as to the famous Geniza collection. The joint chronological coverage of these materials extends over the entire period of the Islamic Middle Ages, furnishing copious information pertaining to monetary transactions, exchange rates, prices of various commodities, real estate and similar business details. How much one can learn from these otherwise prosaic and very complex materials has been demonstrated by the brilliant editorial accomplishments of A. Grohmann[20] and S. D. Goitein.[21]

To a certain extent the critical remarks expressed in the introduction to the present survey of sources apply to the manner in which textual materials have been treated by modern monetary historians. Any discussion of the modern studies of Islamic monetary developments should begin with a tribute to the monumental accomplishment of Henri Sauvaire (1831–96) who was so successful in carrying out a project of the publication of an impressive body of published and unpublished data pertaining to Near Eastern monetary institutions. The contribution of Sauvaire, which first appeared in a series of articles in *Journal Asiatique* between 1879 and 1887, under the title *Matériaux pour servir à l'histoire de la numismatique et de la métrologie musulmanes*, was of major consequence in the development of this branch of Islamic history. From a methodological point of view the significance of Sauvaire's pioneering achievement results from the fact that he successfully demonstrated the feasibility of a project consisting of establishing and organizing a scattered, dispersed and fragmented mass of historical evidence into a coherent body of information which constitutes a fundamental prerequisite for the study of monetary developments. The merit of Sauvaire's achievement may be fully appreciated when one realizes that ever since their appearance the *Matériaux* have served as a basic reference tool for any historian confronted with Islamic monetary or metrological phenomena. Paradoxically enough, the very accomplishment of Henri Sauvaire dealt a setback to subsequent heuristic activities in the field under present discussion. I mean here that scholars engaged in the

[19] Cf. ed. by Ḥussain Monés, *Regimen de la casa de la moneda*, Madrid 1960.

[20] Cf. A. Grohmann, 'Einführung und Chrestomathie zur arabischen Papyrusurkunde' (*Monografie Archivu Orientálního*, vol. 13, i), 1955.

[21] Cf. his recent contribution 'The exchange rate of gold and silver money in Fatimid and Ayyubid times. A preliminary study of the relevant Geniza material', *JESHO*, 8, 1965, pp. 1–46. Also, S. Shaked, *A tentative bibliography of Geniza documents*, 1964.

study of medieval Near Eastern economic and monetary history were so generously accommodated with the wealth of the published *economica* that they failed to follow up the inspiring example of the French savant. Several decades had elapsed before new published economic data appeared in academic circulation. The contributions of Grohmann who has been engaged in the arduous task of interpreting the contents of the papyri; of Goitein who has been unveiling the dormant resources from the Geniza collection; of Ashtor who has been tabulating economic evidence from all kinds of medieval texts—may serve as instances of heuristic undertakings marking the beginning of a new phase in the field of Near Eastern monetary history. A phase which is characterized by a systematic effort to expand and deepen our research control over textual source materials.

B. Numismatic evidence

If students of medieval Near Eastern monetary history are handicapped by the unsystematic and episodic character of textual evidence, they are overcompensated by the nature of numismatic source materials. The great significance of medieval Islamic numismatic evidence arises from the fact that, as a rule, gold and silver coinage dating from the classical period of the Caliphate displays multiple material features reflecting the religious, political, aesthetic and above all economic background of the institutions or authorities responsible for its production.

The phenomenon of the existence of tremendous quantities of surviving Islamic coin specimens, available in public and private collections, in the hands of coin or antique dealers, or surfacing in treasure troves which keep being discovered in Africa, Asia and Europe has led to the rise of many outstanding specialists excelling in the field of Muslim numismatics. Valuable information derived from Muslim coins and registered by several generations of professional numismatists[22] has eventually attracted the attention of scholars interested in Medieval Near Eastern history. They did not fail to appreciate the services rendered by the ancillary discipline in supplementing textual or other archaeological evidence. Political historians could verify or even reconstruct chronology of political events, the nature of relation between different political regimes, territorial extension of authority of particular rulers, their religious or, if one prefers ideological affiliations, etc. Historians interested in the study of diplomatics could examine the nature

[22] Cf. L. A. Mayer, *Bibliography of Moslem numismatics* (Oriental Translation Fund, 35) 1954; also, A. Kmietowicz, 'Supplements to L. Mayer's "Bibliography of Moslem numismatics" ', *Folia Orientalia*, 2, 1960, pp. 259–75; also George C. Miles, 'Islamic and Sasanian numismatics: retrospect and prospect', *Rapports*, *Congrès International de Numismatique*, 1953, vol. i, pp. 129–44; also *idem*, 'Islamic numismatics: a progress report', *Relazioni*, *Congresso Internazionale di Numismatica*, 1961, vol. i, pp. 181–92; also T. Lewicki, 'Nouveaux travaux russes concernant les trésors de monnaies musulmanes trouvés en Europe Orientale et en Asie Centrale (1959–1963)', *JESHO*, 8, 1965, pp. 81–90.

of political and religious titles of the people whose names were mentioned in the inscriptions on the coins. Those concerned with the problem of palaeography, heraldry or of art in general, would eagerly observe stylistic aspects of the coins. Students of the history of science could utilize coinage to study technological, chemical and metallurgical problems involved in the refining and coining of metals. In short, historians have realized the importance of Islamic numismatic materials. They have been aware of the manifold character of historical information to be extracted from this type of evidence. They saw and handled many problems related to or raised by Muslim coinage, but—perhaps because of this topical multiplicity and complexity—they have failed to exploit the availability of these paramount source materials for a serious consideration of the most appropriate subject connected with Islamic coinage. For one can hardly dispute the fact that the most important attribute of Islamic coinage from the point of view of historical discipline, is that it constitutes a direct, physical trace or—to use Bernheim's definition—unintentional material relic of a monetary system. After all, these coins, these *dīnārs, dirhams* or *fulūs* were not struck to satisfy the curiosity of historians or vanity of coin collectors of the modern age, but to serve as money, as currency in the monetary system of the medieval Near Eastern world. Consequently, the most logical direct and obvious question which should be asked of surviving medieval Muslim coins is what they can reveal in respect to medieval Near Eastern monetary history.

The situation arising from the underdeveloped state of numismatic evidence in the reconstruction of the monetary history of the Near East is quite absurd. There are millions of Muslim coins available for statistical tabulation and interpretation and yet few steps have been undertaken in this direction. This statement must not be understood as an accusation of carelessness or ineptitude levelled against the established authorities in the field of Islamic numismatics. Our indebtedness to professional numismatists has been registered above. The blame rests with historians studying monetary and economic phenomena of the Islamic Near East, who have failed to utilize or to insist upon the supply of more detailed and analytical information pertaining to numismatic source materials. For a historian differs from a numismatist in his approach to numismatic sources. A numismatist looks for historical information to produce an exhaustive description of a coin specimen. A monetary historian looks for numismatic evidence to help him achieve an exhaustive reconstruction of a historical phenomenon. The difference of approach is also evident in the evaluation of the importance of a numismatic specimen. Some rare specimens, e.g., the 'standing caliph' type of *dīnārs* of the transitional period prior to the great reform of ʿAbd al-Malik, rate as extremely valuable coins on numismatic markets. The monetary historian, on the other hand, may interpret the rarity of these specimens as an indication of their low value or unpopularity as currency units, leading to their withdrawal from circulation and a further drop in their market price. Neither is the numismatist interested in statistical tabulations. And yet the question of the total numbers of preserved Muslim coins is of historical significance. It has been stated above that millions of Muslim coins are available for a study of monetary history. How many millions? What is the total of Muslim coins which have been saved from obliteration? Does not that total represent a certain minimum of precious metal which has been withdrawn from circulation, hurting the economy of the institutions responsible for their production? Should not the number of all specimens of Muslim coins scattered in various collections be tabulated? Should not such tabulations indicate specific totals of specimens according to the year and place of their production?

Any such tabulations must take typological variants into account. Numismatic catalogues normally refer to the precise weight of described specimens but they do not specify the exact nature of their alloy. Traditional segregation into gold and silver category is of a limited pragmatic consequence to the monetary historian for he is interested in knowing how much gold or silver the alloy of a coin contains. After all, if coins struck by the same mint display a deterioration or improvement in their alloy such phenomena must have been produced by some factors or decisions based most frequently—though not always—on economic considerations.

That an inquiry into the nature of the alloy of numismatic specimens lies within the realm of research viability has been demonstrated by a series of recent or even current investigations. The application of the specific gravity measurements for the study of *dīnārs*[23] and *dirhams*,[24] the use of X-ray spectrographic analysis for the study of *dirhams*,[25] and finally the application of the method of radioactivation which reveals the total composition and the percentage of all elements in the alloy structure of examined specimens,[26] these are some of the examples of sustained research efforts aiming at a more exhaustive and analytical exploitation of numismatic evidence.

While the primary function of Islamic numismatic materials is to furnish

[23] Cf. P. Naster, 'Numismatique et méthodes de laboratoire', *Rapports, Congrès International de Numismatique*, 1953, vol. i, pp. 171–92; also E. R. Caley, 'Validity of the specific gravity method for the determination of the fineness of gold objects', *Ohio Journal of Science*, 49, 1949, pp. 73–82; also A. S. Ehrenkreutz, 'Studies in the monetary history of the Near East in the Middle Ages, II.', *JESHO*, 6, 1963, pp. 248–50.

[24] Cf. E. R. Caley, 'Estimation of composition of ancient metal objects', *Analytical Chemistry*, 24, 1952, pp. 676–81.

[25] Cf. J. L. Bacharach, 'History, science and coins', *Michigan Technic*, Jan. 1964, pp. 24–6; also O. I. Smirnova, *Katalog monet gorodishcha Pendzhikent*, 1963; also E. A. Davidovich, 'Iz oblasti denezhnogo obrashcheniya v Sredney Azii', *Numizmatika i Epigrafika*, 2, 1960, p. 102 f.

[26] Cf. J. L. Bacharach and A. A. Gordus, 'Studies on the fineness of silver coins', *JESHO*, 11, 1968, pp. 298–317. Cf. also Alan K. Craig, 'Neutrons and numismatics', *The Numismatist*, 76, 1963, pp. 1085–6.

information concerning the different types of medieval Near Eastern currency, one may also exploit them for the study of the production of coinage. A copious amount of information concerning the identification of geographic, chronological and personal references displayed by Islamic coin specimens, which has been furnished by several generations of outstanding numismatists, has made it possible to trace the evolution of medieval Near Eastern mint production from the vantage point of economic (relation of the mints to the sources of precious metals; to trade routes and markets) and political considerations (relation of the mints to political organization or institutions). The correlating of the external and intrinsic characteristics of the surviving specimens may yield interesting information concerning the quality of production of particular mints.

Another extremely important aspect of the production of coinage is the annual output of individual mints. Without resorting to sophisticated equations defining the relationship between prices and the volume of coins in circulation, one may state that one of the major factors conditioning the price and wage situation in the medieval Near East was the volume of coins available for the needs of its society. One of the salient features of the monetary system of the medieval caliphate was that it depended on its mints for coinage supply. For this reason the problem of Islamic coinage production acquires a significant status in the field of economic history.

In spite of the deplorable lack of textual information,[27] an inquiry into the productivity of Islamic mints can be undertaken by resorting to numismatic evidence, applying the method of the 'coin-die count'. This method involves two basic phases: (i) the estimation of the number of dies employed in the production of a coinage series, and (ii) the estimation of the quantity of coins which the dies were capable of producing. Phase (i) calls for the discernment of traces of coin die variants in a random sample of specimens belonging to a series. The ratio of coin die variants to the number of random samples has been accepted as a basis for calculations aiming at a statistical estimate of the actual number of dies involved in the production of the series.[28] Phase (ii) culminates in the multiplication of the total of estimated dies by the average number of coins which these dies were capable of producing.

Unfortunately, the problem of estimating the capacity or longevity of coin dies can hardly, if at all, be resolved. In spite of this methodological 'cul-de-sac' the application of the coin-die count procedure constitutes a step forward in the attempt at a quantitative assessment of the annual output of

[27] Interpretative limitations arising from the shortage of textual evidence are discussed in a report in *JESHO*, 9, 1966.

[28] For the most recent discussion of the problem of various formulae for establishing die totals see P. Grierson, 'Byzantine coinage as source materials', *Thirteenth International Congress of Byzantine Studies*, Oxford 1966, *Main Papers*, x, pp. 1–17.

individual mints. This point may be illustrated by means of the following hypothetical example. Let us assume that a tabulation of all surviving *dīnār* specimens struck in A.H. 300 would reveal that there are 1,000 specimens from Baghdad and five specimens from Egypt. In the light of such a quantitative contrast one might be inclined to conclude that the output of the Baghdad mint in A.H. 300 was much higher than that of Egypt. And yet upon a closer scrutiny of the Baghdādī specimens one may establish that they were struck by one, only one, set of dies. On the other hand it may be established that each of the five Egyptian specimens was struck by a different set of dies. This revelation would have to force one to postulate that the output of the Egyptian mint in A.H. 300 exceeded five times the total of *dīnārs* struck in Baghdad.

The viability of the coin-die count method and the value of the results yielded by such an inquiry has been successfully tested by a seminar team at the University of Michigan. During the summer of 1966 the members of the seminar undertook a preliminary investigation involving the Umayyad *dīnārs* and *dirhams* and presently they are engaged in a project concerning the annual output of gold coinage by the medieval Egyptian mints.[29]

A final important problem which should be elucidated by means of a proper exploitation of numismatic materials pertains to the geographic extension of the circulation of the medieval Near Eastern currency. This problem is of 'international' interest since it raises the question of monetary relations between Europe and the Near East during the Middle Ages. As far as the West European aspect of this problem is concerned a scholarly debate has for the past few decades revolved around the preliminary but fundamental question as to whether Muslim gold coins were at all in circulation in Christian markets.[30] Following the enunciation of several, sometimes diametrically opposed theories on the subject,[31] a sobering tone was introduced to the debate in question, consisting of an important contribution by J. Duplessy, 'La circulation des monnaies arabes en Europe occidentale du VIIIe au XIIIe siècle'.[32] The main significance of Duplessy's achievement lies in the fact that after having taken stock of earlier contributions on the subject, he boldly challenged the validity of

[29] A full report on the procedures and results of the seminar, entitled 'Early Islamic mint output. A preliminary inquiry into the methodology and application of the "Coin-die count" method' has appeared in *JESHO*, 9, 1966, pp. 212–41.

[30] For a recent succinct summary of the polemics, and pertinent bibliographical references, see Cl. Cahen, 'Quelques problèmes concernant l'expansion économique musulmane au Haut Moyen Age', *L'Occidente e l'Islam nell'alto Medioevo, Settimane di studio del Centro italiano di studi sull' alto medioevo*, 12, 1965, pp. 392–3.

[31] E.g., those postulated by M. Lombard, 'Les bases monétaires d'une suprematie économique. L'or musulman du VII au XI siècle', *Annales* (*Economies, Sociétés, Civilisations*), 2, 1947, pp. 143–60, and by Fr. Himly, 'Y a-t-il emprise musulmane sur l'économie des Etats européens du VIII aux X siècle', *Revue Suisse d'Histoire*, 5, 1955, pp. 31–81.

[32] *Revue Numismatique*, V serie, 18, 1956, pp. 101–63.

numismatic foundations on which the arguments supporting some sweeping theories were made to rest. The modest number of Muslim coins (241 whole and fractionary *dīnārs*, 153 whole and fractionary *dirhams*, 1 copper coin) originating from 36 West European treasure troves, can hardly be regarded as adequate numismatic evidence warranting any generalizations. Furthermore, this meagre numismatic evidence was neither properly analysed nor correlated with pertinent textual evidence. To restore the air of methodological integrity to the important debate Duplessy made an essential preliminary step by presenting a survey of relevant numismatic and textual materials.[33] He emphasized, however, that before any definitive and categorical conclusions are formulated many more studies must be undertaken, such as 'étude critique des textes arabes, dépouillement complet et classement par régions des chartes et documents divers de l'Europe occidentale; recherches sur les raisons de chacun des enfouissements connus, sur le pouvoir d'achat des monnaies d'or, sur les relations commerciales et les produits échangés'.[34]

Unlike the situation in Western Europe, numismatic evidence yielded by Central, North and East European hoards is so voluminous that the fact of the presence of Muslim coinage on early medieval Slavic and Scandinavian markets does not constitute a debatable issue. Indeed, according to an authoritative study published in 1960 by R. Kiersnowski, the totals of Islamic numismatic materials registered in those regions consisted of about 1,400 troves and about 200,000 specimens of Arabic coins.[35] It is obvious that, the lack of textual evidence notwithstanding, the tremendous volume of numismatic sources accumulated in Central, Northern and Eastern Europe, warrants serious investigations and reconstructive hypotheses concerning the circulation of Near Eastern currency, based on a quantitative method of statistical analysis.[36]

'*Ars longa – vita brevis*'

Methodological goals outlined in the quoted statement of Duplessy apply to the entire field of medieval Near Eastern monetary history. Naturally, the idea of amassing and interpreting monetary data for the purpose of economic evaluations presents an enormous task, hardly feasible if undertaken by ordinary means of analytical treatment. In this respect the application of modern electronic computing devices is of utmost importance. The

[33] *Ibid.*, pp. 121–52. [34] *Ibid.*, p. 119.

[35] R. Kiersnowski, *Pieniądz kruszcowy w Polsce Średniowiecznej*, 1960, p. 103.

[36] The contribution of Kiersnowski offers an excellent example of such an undertaking. The main topic of his investigation is the question of the role which 'foreign' coins and weights played in the inception of the 'national' monetary and weight system of the Polish state around the turn of the first Christian millenium. His accomplishment is significant not only because of many interesting conclusions but because of its methodological aspects.

above mentioned seminar group of the University of Michigan resorted to electronic computers in its tedious task of tabulating the copious data pertaining to Umayyad coin dies. The results obtained from such a procedure proved to be extremely rewarding. The total number of index cards containing a great diversity of coin and coin-die specifications amounted to 1,440. It is true that preparatory activities such as the typing of special key punch cards or the formulating and executing of the computer programming, were time-consuming. However, once the computer was fed with 1,440 punch cards it took only 1 minute 20·7 seconds to process and type the data consisting of 2,756 lines presented on 53 pages. These results speak for themselves. The value of computers in historical research, whenever large volumes of data are involved—which happens to be the case of monetary history—can hardly be disputed.

From now on those scholars who commit their lives to the task of collecting prosaic monetary data need not fear that they might leave the amassed materials uninterpreted. Indeed, future progress in the field of medieval Near Eastern monetary history will depend on the degree to which historians utilize modern laboratory techniques to control the source materials salvaged from the past.

Mediterranean Trade in the Eleventh Century: Some Facts and Problems*

S. D. GOITEIN

DID the Crusades pave the way for the lively flow of Mediterranean trade so characteristic of the later Middle Ages? Or were the Crusades themselves made possible by the meteoric rise of international commerce in the eleventh century, which was accompanied by a similar increase in maritime traffic and naval power, subsequently providing the indispensable supply lines for the Christian warriors? If so, what do we know about the objects, scope and organization of that trade?

The European side of the problem has been treated in comprehensive works which have become classics in their field—W. Heyd's *Histoire du commerce du Levant au Moyen-Age*[1] and A. Schaube's *Handelsgeschichte der romanischen Völker des Mittelmeergebiets bis zum Ende der Kreuzzüge.*[2] Subsequent research has elucidated many additional facets.[3] Attention should be drawn to a paper by Robert S. Lopez showing that already the tenth century witnessed a great social and economic upsurge in western and Central Europe, and, in particular, in Italy.[4] Still, as late as 1963 the *Cambridge Economic History of Europe* admitted: 'Of the organization of trade before the twelfth century, not much, if anything, is known.'[5] Thus we see that, despite generations of research, our information even about the European end of the Mediterranean trade in the eleventh century is still rather incomplete. The Islamic side, which then included also most of Spain and Sicily, still awaits elucidation altogether.

The literary sources illustrating the Islamic trade of the tenth century have been carefully collected by Adam Mez in the last six chapters of his *Die Renaissance des Islams.*[6] To be sure, his references are more copious with regard to the eastern part of the Islamic world than to the Mediterranean area. At all events, no similar work has been done for the eleventh century; and it would seem to be rather unpromising because of the incompleteness of our present knowledge of Islamic historical and

* This paper has been published in *Diogenes*, 59, 1967, and appears here by kind permission of the editor.

[1] Leipzig 1885–1886. Reprint Amsterdam 1959, 2 vols.

[2] München and Berlin 1906.

[3] See the biographical survey of A. Sapori, *Le Marchand italien au moyen age,* Paris 1952.

[4] 'Still another Renaissance?', *American Historical Review*, 57, 1959, pp. 1–21.

[5] Ed. M. M. Postan, E. E. Rich and Edward Miller, Cambridge 1963, p. 46. The statement is by R. de Roover of Brooklyn College, New York.

[6] Heidelberg 1922. There exist English, Spanish and Arabic translations, the latter two containing additional material.

geographical literature related to this century. Archibald R. Lewis' *Naval Power and Trade in the Mediterranean A.D. 500–1100* has its merits, but does not contain new source material of the character provided by Adam Mez.[7]

In the following pages, an attempt is made to describe the Mediterranean commerce in the century preceding the Crusades with the use of a vast, hitherto untapped source: the documents of the Cairo Geniza. The term refers to manuscripts mostly in Hebrew characters, but in Arabic language, originally preserved in a synagogue, partly also in a cemetery, of Fusṭāṭ (Old Cairo), the ancient capital of Islamic Egypt. The material originated all over the Mediterranean area (inclusive of the sea route to India) and comprises every conceivable type of writing, such as official, business and private correspondence, detailed court records and other juridical documents, contracts, accounts, checks, receipts and inventories, writs of marriage, divorce and manumission, prescriptions, charms, children's exercises and the like. The Geniza contains also several hundreds of papers in Arabic script, partly emanating from Muslim and Christian hands, but the bulk of the material, naturally, is of Jewish origin, and, consequently, there arises the question as to how far it may be used for the description of Mediterranean trade in general.[8]

To answer this question we have to keep in mind that no ghetto existed in Fusṭāṭ, Alexandria or Qayrawān (then the capital of the country now known as Tunisia), or even in a holy city like Jerusalem, or a provincial capital and industrial centre like al-Maḥalla in Lower Egypt. In contracts or other documents preserved from all these places we find that houses belonging to Jews bordered on Muslim and/or Christian properties. Muslims lived together with Jewish tenants in houses belonging to Jews and vice versa. Neither was there an occupational ghetto. Jews were prominent in certain industries, such as gold smithing and silver smithing, the fabrication and dyeing of textiles, glassblowing, and, in particular, pharmaceutical products, but here, too, there were no watertight compartments. In commerce, as we shall see, the Jews were more active in some fields than in others, but they did not monopolize any. We find partnerships between Muslims and Jews in both industry and commerce and there were many other ways of cooperation. Naturally, the same money and the same means of transportation were used by both. Still, the specific character of the environment in which the Geniza documents originated has to be taken into consideration when they are used for historical research. Examples of caution exercised in this matter will be found, explicitly or implicitly, throughout our discussion.

[7] Princeton 1951. I could not use E. Eickhoff, *Seekrieg und Seepolitik zwischen Islam und Abendland*, Berlin 1966.

[8] See S. D. Goitein, *Studies in Islamic History and Institutions*, Leiden 1966, ch. xiv: 'The Documents of the Cairo Geniza as a Source for Islamic Social History'. Also *EI*[2], s.v. 'Geniza'.

With only a few exceptions, the material used in the following has not yet been edited. The manuscripts are preserved in the University Library, Cambridge, the Bodleian Library, Oxford, the British Museum, the Jewish Theological Seminary of America, New York, the Dropsie College, Philadelphia, and many other libraries. All statements made in this paper are verified by exact references to the relevant manuscripts, provided in my book *A Mediterranean Society: The Jewish Communities of the Arab World, as Portrayed in the Documents of the Cairo Geniza*, vol. I, *Economic Foundations* (published by the University of California Press and the Cambridge University Press). This book deals with the 'classical' Geniza period (approximately 965–1265) in toto. Here, as a rule, only data referring to the century and a half preceding the Crusades will be used.

The European Impact. The documents of the Cairo Geniza are a vivid testimony to the strong influence exercised by Europe on Islamic trade already in the first decades of the eleventh century, if not earlier. A Hebrew document of July 959, i.e., ten years prior to the conquest of Egypt by the Fāṭimids, makes mention of a market of the Greeks in the 'Fortress of the Candles', the pre-Islamic nucleus of the city of Fusṭāṭ. The Hebrew word for 'Greek' renders the Arabic *Rūm*, which was the common denomination for Byzantine and Italian as well as other west European merchants. I was not successful in finding a reference to this market of the Rūm in any Islamic source and assume that it was abolished at the beginning of Fāṭimid rule over Egypt. This surmise seems to be corroborated by the reports about the massacre in May 996 of 160 or 170 Italian merchants who were suspected of having set on fire the warships being made ready in the harbour of Fusṭāṭ for the war against the Byzantines. The foreign merchants were then concentrated with their wares not in a market within the city, but in the Dār Mānak, the toll- and warehouse on the quay of the Nile, later so frequently mentioned in the Geniza papers.[9] I wonder whether Mānak, which has no derivation in Arabic, does not echo a Greek or Italian name, which would indicate that this toll station for export overseas (for such appears to be its role in the Geniza documents) originally goes back to a European foundation.

Commercial terms which must be derived from Italian make their appearance surprisingly early. This is especially true of the word *barqalū* (*barcalo*) which designates a bale for shipment overseas smaller than the standard *ʿidl.* The Italian skippers, in order to increase their mobility, in the case of storms or attacks of pirates (when bales were often jettisoned), introduced these smaller bales, and their practicality soon was recognized

[9] See Claude Cahen, 'Un Texte peu connu relatif au commerce oriental d'Amalfi au Xe siècle', *Archivio Storico per le Province Napoletane*, N.S., 34, 1953–4, pp. 1–8. For Dār Mānak see *idem*, *JESHO*, 7, 1964, p. 237. The reading Mānak is ascertained from many Geniza references.

by their colleagues to the south. The term occurs in a letter from Alexandria, received in the office of the great merchant of Fusṭāṭ, Joseph ibn ʿAwkal, on 8 April 1030, and is frequent in earlier letters addressed to the same merchant, some going back perhaps to the first decade of the century.[10] Even more remarkable is the fact that the Italian word *scala* for a plank used at the lading of a boat appears as an official term in an account prepared for Ibn ʿAwkal in Alexandria: 'For 100 bales $11\frac{1}{2}$ dinars (export dues have to be paid) while passing the *isqālā*.' The use of such a plank obviously was introduced by the Italians, and together with the technical improvement the term was taken over.

The European merchants were by no means confined to the seaports. The details about the market of the Rūm in Fusṭāṭ and the Dār Mānak, given above, are complemented by many direct references in letters. 'Keep your pepper, cinnamon and ginger,' writes a merchant from Alexandria, 'for the Rūm are keen solely on them and all of them are about to leave for Fusṭāṭ. They are only awaiting the arrival of two additional ships from Constantinople.' In another letter from Alexandria, the business correspondent in Old Cairo is advised to hold his date-palm fibre until the Rūm arrive from Damietta. In a report from Fusṭāṭ itself we read that the Rūm did not leave there a single piece of odoriferous wood (*ʿūd*). The Europeans normally travelled in groups, and we find 'some Rūm' visiting a Jewish business friend of theirs in his house in Fusṭāṭ.

The impact of the Europeans on the local market was equally (if not more) felt in Tunisia. Five letters from that country written in the second third of the eleventh century show that the price of pepper there depended on European demand, and in one case, payment was made in Sicilian and Pisan money (so that the merchant concerned had to pay an additional fee for the exchange). In Ascalon (as in Alexandria) Egyptian flax was bought by the Europeans when the Muslim merchants were unwilling to buy it because of its poor quality or when a state of war made its transport inland difficult. In the same, or another, Syro-Palestinian port, the Rūm paid an exorbitant price for *baqqam*, the Oriental red dye known as brazilwood. Potash alum (imported from Yemen or Upper Egypt) was another article repeatedly mentioned as sold to Europeans.

The products of the Rūm textile industry must have been extremely popular in the Muslim countries of the Mediterranean, as is evident from many dated marriage contracts and many others whose dates have not been preserved.[11] Every Jewish bride insisted on having a Rūm kerchief (*mindīl*, cf. Spanish *mantilla*), whether in Damascus in 956, or in Old Cairo in

[10] The business correspondence of Ibn ʿAwkal has been published by the present writer in *Tarbiz*, 36–8, 1967–9.

[11] When a wife received what was due to her, the marriage contract was torn up. Therefore in most fragments the date is not preserved.

1040, 1050, 1067 and later. Richer brides got a Rūm bed cover made of brocade or even a couch covered with the same precious material (references in documents dated 1031, 1034, 1050, 1064, etc.). Rūm chests, cupboards and bedsteads are among the furniture mentioned in the Geniza. Sicily exported cheese to Egypt and so did Crete. A ship from Amalfi brought, besides silk, the staple good of Sicily and southern Italy, honey to Alexandria, and the European winesellers, so prominent in that city, certainly carried the products of their native countries. Corals, a great article of export from the Mediterranean area to the countries of the Indian Ocean since Roman times, were collected partly on the Tunisian and partly on the European side. Consequently, both the Jewish merchants of Tunisia and the Rūm participated in this important trade. In one case, however—in a letter written around 1050—we read that the Rūm bought large quantities of coral in Tunisia. Since they could export to India solely via Egypt or Syro-Palestine, this means that already in this early period we find European merchants trading between one Muslim country (Tunisia) and another (Egypt or Syro-Palestine).

No Jewish Intermediaries between Christian Europe and the Islamic South. The way in which the Rūm merchants are mentioned in the Geniza papers leaves no doubt that all of them were European Christians. European Jews appear in the Geniza documents as wandering scholars, as pilgrims, as refugees or indigent people seeking help. Not a single Jewish merchant from southern France, northern Italy, Salonica or Constantinople has left his letters in the Geniza or is even mentioned there. Arabic speaking Jews occasionally visited cities such as Amalfi, Salerno or Constantinople, but such visits did not add up to wide-scale regular business relations the like of which existed with the Islamic extremities of the Mediterranean—Spain in the west and the ports of northern Syria in the east. The cultural and social ties between the Jews of southern France or Byzantium and those of Egypt and Palestine were rather close; in view of this, the absence or dearth of commercial relations is rather remarkable.

Diversity of Goods. Every overseas trader whose correspondence has been preserved to any extent was both an exporter and an importer. The diversity of goods handled by any one was astounding. Nahray ben Nissīm, a merchant of Qayrawān, who was active in Egypt from 1045 through 1096 and of whose correspondence and accounts about 280 items have come down to us, dealt with at least 120 different articles destined for overseas shipment. In addition, he was a merchant banker, engaged in changing, money lending and other banking business.[12] Still, some main items, or groups of items stand out as dominating the Mediterranean

[12] Nahray's correspondence forms the object of a Ph.D. thesis by Mr. M. Michael at the Hebrew University, Jerusalem. His banker's accounts were partly edited by me in *JESHO*, 9, 1966, pp. 28–66.

trade. The staple export of Egypt was flax, bought, as we have seen, by Europeans, but mainly going to the Manchester and Lancashire of the period, namely Sicily and Tunisia. The staple going in the opposite direction was silk, coming from Spain and Sicily, and having a standard price of two *dīnārs* per (Egyptian) pound, or rather of 20 *dīnārs* for 10 pounds. It was a commodity regarded as cash almost like gold. Rūm and Syrian cotton or North-African felt, as well as wool, hemp and other fabrics, like the fanciful seawool, were of secondary importance. Finished textiles came mainly from Tunisia and Sicily, but also from 'Rūm' (see above), and from Spain. There was, of course, the precious Egyptian linen, and the luxury products of Iran and, to a minor extent, of Iraq were traded as well. Hides and leather were also an important item of export from Sicily and Tunisia.

Second in quantity to the movement of fabrics, textiles and leather goods, but for many individual merchants first in economic rank, were the products of the Orient, re-exported from Egypt. They can be roughly divided into four main groups: Oriental spices, such as pepper, cinnamon, ginger and cloves (which were in demand in Europe not less than in the Islamic countries); aromatics, perfumes and gums, such as aloe, ambergris, camphor, frankincense, gum arabic, mastic gum, musk and betel leaves (one variety of ambergris came from the Atlantic Ocean); dyeing, tanning and varnishing materials, such as brazilwood, lacquer and indigo (one variety of indigo, as the name indicates, was grown in India; but indigo was grown at that time in large quantities in Egypt, as well as in Palestine, and many other dyeing and tanning materials were indigenous to the Mediterranean area, such as sumac and gall-nuts produced in Syria and saffron in Tunisia); finally, materials for jewellery and semi-precious stones, such as pearls, gems, carnelians, turquoises, onyxes and the like.

Metals, chemical and pharmaceutical products constituted the third group of articles prominent in the Mediterranean trade. Copper, iron, lead, mercury and tin came from or through Spain and other European countries. In the Mediterranean the Jews had almost no share in the iron trade, while they were prominent in this field in the export from India. Chemicals and pharmaceutical products moved East–West or West–East, depending on their country of origin. The chemicals most traded were alkali, alum, antimony, arsenic, bamboo crystals, borax, naphtha, sulphur, starch and vitriol. The products of the pharmaceutical industry, in which the Jews specialized, are too many to be specified here.

Olive oil (besides textiles) was the staple export of Tunisia, followed by soap and wax. The same products were exported, but in a far lesser volume, by Palestine and Syria, which sent also considerable quantities of honey abroad. Dried fruits were the speciality of northern Syria, and sugar that of Egypt. The Jews were prominent in the Egyptian sugar industry (in the sixteenth century they all but monopolized the sugar production of Morocco, from where they exported to England). Wheat, rice and other grains are frequently referred to in business letters, but seemingly as ordered or purchased for the households of the writers or their friends, not for commercial purposes. Whether there was no significant overseas trade in these foodstuffs, or whether the Jews had no share in this trade, needs to be clarified. In the turbulent 1060's we read that the coastal towns of Tunisia depended for their wheat supply entirely on import from Sicily.

Mention has been made above of coral. Other materials for cheap ornaments and trinkets, such as cowrie shells, tortoise shells, lapis lazuli, beads, 'pomegranate strings', were also great items of international trade, and so were different types of pitch and tar, as well as palm fibre, already referred to before as bought by the Rūm. Books, both Hebrew and Arabic, i.e., both religious and secular, were also an important item of international trade, Tunisia playing largely the role of exporter and Egypt that of importer. But bibliophiles were hunting after books everywhere.

Despite the enormous diversity of goods handled by individual merchants, it is evident that each had his specialities in which he was prominent. Thus, of the two merchants mentioned here by name, Ibn ʿAwkal, who had great means, specialized in luxury goods, such as choice textiles, crystal ware and costly pearls, the like of which were offered to sultans and the ladies of their harems. These things were beyond the reach of Nahray ben Nissīm, who, on the other hand (being himself a scholar) dealt also in books, an item never mentioned in Ibn ʿAwkal's correspondence, although the latter often had opportunity to pass on learned treatises from the Jewish academies of Baghdad to the Jewish communities of North Africa, serving as a middleman between both.

Money as a commercial commodity. The primary item in the export of the Muslim West to the Muslim East was gold *dīnārs* and silver *dirhams*, the former needed urgently for the trade with the Orient and the latter for circulation in Egypt itself, for little silver specie was coined in Egypt. On the other hand (and to a far lesser degree), 'silver', i.e., broken silver vessels and *dirhams* which had gone out of circulation, were sent to the West, where they were melted down and sold by the Jewish purveyors to the mints. Bars of gold and silver also were among the exports of the West to the East. The Geniza letters speak about the 'buying' and 'selling' of *dīnārs* and *dirhams* just as they do with regard to other commodities.

Sedentary and itinerant merchants. Some merchants, such as the great Ibn ʿAwkal, were completely sedentary. In all of the forty or so letters addressed to him between *ca.* 1000 and 1038 he is found in Fusṭāṭ, either in his office (presumably in his house) or in the *Dār al-Jawhar*, the Gem Bourse, one of the exchanges of the city, where he obviously had a second office. We should not imagine, however, that all of the great merchants were sedentary. Each of the four Tāhartī brothers (the most prominent of the approximately thirty merchant families from Qayrawān known to us during the first half of the eleventh century) is found at one time or another in Egypt, although two of the brothers were more mobile than the other two. Nahray ben Nissīm travelled much in his early years, first between Tunisia and Sicily and the East, and then between the capital of Egypt and the centres of flax-growing, where he gained that expert knowledge of the types of flax (twenty-two types are mentioned in the Geniza letters) and its processing for export, something which was indispensable for an accomplished merchant. In his later years he had his permanent seat in Fusṭāṭ, but travelled occasionally to Jerusalem and other Syro-Palestinian places, for, in addition to being a member of the Jewish academy of Jerusalem, he specialized in Syro-Palestinian money (in his capacity as money changer), and the most popular business maxim of the time was: 'A man present sees what a man absent can never see.' Finally, a high percentage of the eleventh-century merchants who have left us their records in the Geniza were outright commuters, staying during the winter in Sicily and Tunisia, and the following summer in Egypt, and often continuing on to the Syro-Palestinian coast and Jerusalem; others travelled regularly between Tunisia and Spain, or between Spain and Morocco, and Egypt and the Levant.

Travel and Seafaring. At the beginning of the eleventh century much of this traffic was overland. During the winter, when the sea was closed to shipping, three caravans left Qayrawān for Egypt. In addition, there was the Sijilmāsa caravan, setting out in Morocco for the East. We read also about the Damascus caravan leaving Qayrawān during the winter. The name for these caravans was *mawsim*, 'season', 'fixed date', because they seem to have had a rather fixed schedule, and fairs, also called by that name, were held before they set out and when they arrived. In the 1050's, when North Africa was flooded by the Bedouin hordes of the Hilāl and Sulaym, caravan traffic practically disappears from the Geniza letters. But even with regard to the first half of the century, this traffic is represented in the documents perhaps less than is warranted by its importance, the reason being that the Jewish travellers, because of the Sabbath rest, preferred to go by boat rather than overland.

Travel and transport, then, as far as the Geniza people are concerned, were mainly by sea, even between countries like Tunisia and Egypt, or Egypt and Palestine. Even for such a short trip as the one from Acre to Ramla, one would set out from Acre by boat to Jaffa and then continue on muleback to Ramla. Each and every aspect of seafaring is illustrated in the Geniza letters, and consequently a very extensive chapter is devoted to this subject in the forthcoming first volume of my book *A Mediterranean Society*. Here it suffices to state that while it was common for Muslims and

Arabic speaking Jews to travel in Christian ships during the twelfth century, during the eleventh century the proprietors of ships were Muslims (a few, very few, also local Christians), partly belonging to the ruling class, such as sultans (or ladies of the ruling houses), governors, generals and *qāḍīs*, partly powerful merchants. I have collected details of about 150 ships operating on the Mediterranean and the Nile, and it seems that many of these shipowners had their base in Tunisia. Sometimes the Jewish merchants had a double relationship with these shipowners, since they served both as transporters and customers, a relationship which sometimes was advantageous (one got a good and safe place for one's consignments on the ship) and occasionally dangerous (when a ship was seized by the government, inclusive of the cargo belonging to persons who had any business connections with the proprietor). While partnerships constituted the very base of international trade (see below), partnership in boats was exceptional—a fact which calls for comment. I am also at loss to explain why Jews did not own ships in the Mediterranean (with a few and doubtful exceptions). The Jews of Aden did (the references are from the twelfth century). When prominent Jewish merchants in Cairo are described by the term *nākhudā* (shipowner) around 1200, they have earned this title in the countries of the Indian Ocean, not in the Mediterranean.

The Organization of Trade. The most surprising aspect of international trade, as revealed by the Geniza records, is the prevalence in it of informal cooperation (called *ṣadāqa*, friendship, or *ṣuḥba*, companionship) between merchants living in different countries. The list of services rendered by business friends to one another is endless. First, a merchant had to deal with the shipments sent by his correspondent, namely to accept and then to sell them as profitably as possible, and, finally, to collect on them (which was quite a different undertaking). From the proceeds, payments often had to be made to specified persons. Then, local goods had to be purchased either according to a list provided or at the discretion of the buyer. Their dispatch within reasonable time and in seaworthy ships had to be arranged and supervised, something which was often, owing to the lack of shipping space, a most exacting task. Sometimes the goods had to be processed before being shipped: flax had to be combed, unbleached textiles bleached, pearls perforated and so on. For such transactions accounts had to be delivered, an activity, it seems, often more burdensome to the merchants than the operations themselves. Furthermore, business friends were expected to assist or to supervise other merchants working for their correspondent. Finally, travelling merchants usually carried with them goods of their business friends and supervised their transport.

The countless references to this relationship leave no doubt that it was based not on any monetary compensation, but on mutual service. 'You do for me at your end what I do for you in my place here.' We have called this aspect of Mediterranean trade surprising because it is at variance with the principle expressed in the Arabic maxim: '*taḥābabū wa-taḥāsabū*', 'be friends with one another, but make accounts with another'. I have not yet found this maxim quoted in the Geniza papers, but it certainly was applied, for exact accounts, detailed down to the *ḥabba* ($\frac{1}{72}$ part of a *dīnār*) used to be rendered even between brothers. The reason for this informal *ṣadāqa* is probably to be found in practical considerations, namely, that it was impossible to translate the exertions required on each side into ready cash. But I wonder whether this great institution of informal co-operation has not something to do with the ideas about friendship so extensively cultivated in Greek philosophy and so enthusiastically taken over by the Muslim teachers of ethics. More will be said about this point at the end of this section.

Merchants connected with one another by informal cooperation normally also concluded, year in year out, formal partnerships in several specific undertakings. Partnerships of different types and facets were the legal instruments for formal cooperation in both industry and commerce. Employment with a fixed salary, the normal relationship in our own society, was of little scope and importance, and so was investment of capital against fixed interest. Wages and interest were replaced in the Mediterranean society of the eleventh century, as known to us through the Geniza documents, by income from partnerships. There were two main types of contracts: in one, the contractors offered the various services in equal or unequal shares and partook of profit or loss in proportion to their investments; in the other, one or several partners contributed capital or goods or both, while the other, or others, did the work, in which case they received a smaller share in the profits, normally one-third, but did not participate in the losses. This latter form of partnership is akin to the European *commenda*, which is possibly derived from, or influenced by, its Muslim counterpart. The Jewish form of partnership, in which the agent received two-thirds of the profit, but was also responsible for losses, was not common in the Geniza period. The cases usually coming before Jewish courts were what they called Muslim partnerships. Since this institution pervaded the whole fabric of economic and social life, it became extremely developed and diversified. A preliminary report about it is contained in an article published by myself in *Islamic Studies*, Karachi, iii, 315–37, which is now replaced by the relevant chapter in *A Mediterranean Society*.

A special, and very important, case of partnership is represented by the *family companies*, formed by fathers and sons, brothers, uncles and nephews and even cousins. The origin of such companies was the mutual responsibility in which relatives were held, whether they liked it or not. These companies normally were loosely organized and did not engage the total capital possessed by the members, but sometimes they did and were also not limited in time. In any case, they seem to have been very effective. Most merchants appear in the Geniza papers as being connected in their dealings with one or more of their relatives.

With this, we have arrived at a most crucial point. While scrutinizing carefully the whole business correspondence from the eleventh century preserved in the Geniza, we come to the conclusion that at least 90 per cent of it originated in one single, closely knit group, which originally had its base in Qayrawān. Even members of the third generation of immigrants to Egypt or Palestine still were attached to this group. Thus, the informal cooperation or 'friendship', described by us as the basis of international trade, must perhaps be understood as a form of mutual help of compatriots, dispersed, owing to the eclipse of Tunisia, all over the Mediterranean area. It stands to reason that the Muslim merchants of Qayrawān and its seaport al-Mahdiyya cooperated in a similar way, and probably in a more grand manner, since many of them must have been shipowners, as we had opportunity to state. We find, then, on the southern shores of the Mediterranean, a merchants' community not dissimilar to those of cities like Amalfi, Pisa and Genoa, with the notable difference that the mercantile bourgeoisie of the Islamic world never became organized politically.

The Representative of the Merchants. Informal co-operation and partnerships of different sizes and types took care of most overseas business. But not everyone had a friend or could find a partner or was content to rely on either. The gap left by both was filled by the *wakīl al-tujjār*, the representative of the merchants. The Arabic language has a certain predilection for ambiguity. Just as *kātib*, literally scribe, can designate an all-powerful minister as well as a miserable clerk, or just as *jahbadh* may mean a treasurer or a low-grade accountant in a toll-house, thus *wakīl* may be used for a simple agent or for the bearer of that important office which we are now going to describe. A *wakīl tujjār* was a well-to-do merchant who, or whose father, had settled in a foreign country and served there as legal representative and business agent (against a commission) first for the people back home and then for anyone who confided in him. He kept a *dār wakāla*, or warehouse, where goods were stored and business was conducted. Some *wakīls* specialized in certain commodities. Others—it seems the majority—were as many-sided as the wholesale merchants were in general. He had some official standing, as is evidenced by the titles borne even by Jewish *wakīls* and the express statement that so-and-so 'has become *wakīl tujjār*'. In large cities like Fusṭāṭ, Tyre and Aleppo, there were several *wakīls* who were Jewish (besides those who were Muslim), and there was a *dār wakāla* even in a provincial town like Minyat Zifta. Often the office of the *wakīl* was connected with that of a Muslim judge, a superintendent of a port, or a powerful tax farmer. As far as we are able to trace the origin of Muslim and Jewish *wakīls* in Fusṭāṭ, we find that they originated in Mesopotamia and Syria on the one hand and in Tunisia and Morocco on the other. One can hardly escape the assumption that the office of the consul in the Italian settlements of the Levant was somehow connected with this ancient indigenous institution of the *wakīl al-tujjār*.

All in all it appears that interpretation and mutual influence were very much at work in the Mediterranean trade during the century preceding the Crusades. This process was furthered by the fact that little or no restrictions on the commercial activities of foreigners are evident during this period, at least on the Islamic side. The Mediterranean area gave the impression of a free trade area. Things being so, one wonders whether the exchange of goods and business techniques led to the travel of ideas and cultural contacts, especially as books (as we have seen) constituted an important item of export. As far as the Islamic world and the Jewish community is concerned, spiritual contacts between widely separated areas were often astonishingly close. The exchange of ideas between Christian Europe and the Islamic south, as far as it existed in this early period, has left no trace in the Geniza documents.

Eygptian Commercial Policy in the Middle Ages*

SUBHI LABIB

In the words of Pirenne, there is no event in the history of the world 'that can be compared to the rise of Islam in the seventh century in its universality and dramatic consequences. Within eighty years of the death of Muhammed (632), Islam extended from western Turkistan to the Atlantic Ocean. Christianity, which had embraced the entire Mediterranean coast, was confined to its northern shores. Three-quarters of the coastlands of this sea, once the focal point of Roman culture for the whole of Europe, now belonged to Islam.' Pirenne may also have been right in his theory that the Mediterranean became, in consequence of the rise of Islam, a cultural, political and spiritual dividing line between East and West. In the case of commerce, however, this was not so.

The history of the Medieval world to the west of India was in fact determined by the developments, interrelations and confrontations of three political and cultural powers: Islam, Byzantium and western Christendom. In spite of armed conflicts and cultural and spiritual differences, commercial relationships between these powers did not come to a standstill. If we are to be in a position to make a correct assessment of the commercial activity of the time, we must for one thing take into consideration the development of the West—the process of re-agrarianization and the dismantling of the great exchange economy which began in late antiquity, were intensified from the time of the barbarian invasions, and continued beyond the Carolingian period. In the agrarian society of Europe, trade, although it never wholly disappeared, played only a subordinate role. In the absence of western merchants, easterners took their place. Non-Arabic sources indicate that Greek and Syrian merchants dominated Mediterranean trade between the fifth and eighth centuries. They supplied western Europe with oriental goods not only from Byzantium, but also from further east: spices, foodstuffs, fine cloth and papyrus. Egypt was the main supplier of papyrus until the manufacture of paper seems to have been established following its spread in the tenth century. We cannot as yet say how far trade with the West was carried on by Egyptian merchants. For the Syrian and Greek merchants, Marseilles was the most important emporium until they lost their dominant position in the eighth century.

* The documentation for this survey will be found in my *Handelsgeschichte Ägyptens im Spätmittelalter (1171–1517)*, Wiesbaden, 1965.

Their place was taken by Jews as experts in long distance trade. Our only Arabic testimony from the ninth century informs us that these Jewish merchants, whom Ibn Khurdādhbih refers to as *Rādāniyya* (a term still not satisfactorily explained), carried on trade between western Europe, Byzantium and the Far East via Egypt and the Red Sea.

Another point is that we must not overestimate the significance of the Mediterranean for commercial intercourse in the early Middle Ages. For one thing, western Europe possessed no Mediterranean marine; furthermore, the inconclusive wars between Islam and Byzantium did not permit undisturbed trade. The result was inevitably a fall-off in commercial activity between East and West, and a trade which was based almost exclusively on the supply of luxury products to the ecclesiastical and secular notables of Europe. In fact, the West paid for its imports of Oriental goods in slaves, above all from the heathen Slav lands. These Slavs were a commodity very much in demand in the markets of the eastern Islamic lands, in the Near East, and in Islamic Spain. Finds of coins in the Baltic lands indicate the lively trade between East and West via the Russian rivers and the Baltic. The oldest Arabic silver coins brought to Russia and Northern Europe by this route date from the late seventh to the early eleventh centuries. Most of the coins of Islamic origin come from the area to the east of Iraq; coins from Egypt and the western Islamic world are rare. Besides Russians and Bulgarians, the Jewish *Rādāniyya* were also active as middlemen between Europe and the Orient along this route. Their travels took them as far as what is now Germany, to the Slav lands and to Itil, the capital of the Khazars, and from there they moved around the Caspian and Transoxiana to reach China. The weight of Islamic commercial activity lay not in Europe but in the regions of the Black Sea, in Byzantium and Trebizond, on the shores of the Caspian, and on the land routes through Asia. This was the meeting-place of Oriental merchants from Egypt, Syria, Iraq, Persia, Bukhārā and other parts of the Islamic world.

This brief survey shows the importance of the land routes for Islamic trade. They played a larger role than the sea route across the Mediterranean. There were moreover land routes through the Mediterranean coastlands leading from Spain via North Africa to the Sudan and Egypt and from there to the Far East. They were regularly used by Arab and also Jewish merchants.

In the early Middle Ages, Egypt did not yet occupy a central position in Islamic trade, which was orientated primarily towards Asia, and not towards Europe and Byzantium. In this period Baghdad was the commercial metropolis, and exerted a marked influence on the trade of Egypt. With the tenth century, however, began the decay of Baghdad. Even Baṣra, the gateway to the Indian Ocean and 'seaport of the world, goldmine of trade and capital', did not escape this fate. In this century the weight of Islamic commerce was gradually displaced from Iraq and the Persian Gulf to Egypt, the Red Sea, and the harbours of the Arabian Peninsula and the Indian Ocean. Merchants found it to their advantage to migrate to Aden, Oman or Egypt. In this way many left Baghdad and Iraq out of fear of disorders, insecurity and spoliation and turned to Egypt. Fusṭāṭ above all benefited from this development. Ships put in at this inland port not only from the Islamic lands but also from the Byzantine Empire and its territories in southern Italy and the Levant. Al-Maqdisī ascribed to the Fusṭāṭ of his time the same dominant position that had once belonged to Baghdad. In the tenth century, al-Kindī in his *Faḍā'il Miṣr* described Egypt as endowed by God with all manner of commodities and advantages: it was the emporium for Mecca and Medina, for Ṣanʿā', Aden, Oman, Shiḥr, India, Ceylon, China and many other lands. Perfumes, spices, precious stones and tools came by sea as far as Qulzum. Egypt also possessed important Mediterranean ports, emporia for Syria, Antioch, Byzantium and Rome, as also for the lands of the Franks, Sicily, the Maghrib, Cyprus and Rhodes. From these regions came slaves, silk, brocades, mastic, coral, amber, saffron, furs, gall-nuts and various metals, as iron, copper, silver, lead and tin, and finally timber. On these grounds al-Kindī asserted that Egypt was the centre of the trade of the time. In connection with this enumeration, al-Kindī gives a detailed account of the economy of Egypt, particularly of agriculture and the crafts.

Until 969, Egypt was nominally a province of the ʿAbbāsid caliphate in Baghdad, but it had in effect been independent since 868 under various dynasties of governors, and it carried on its own commercial relations with both the *Dār al-Islām* and the *Dār al-Ḥarb*. Under the Fāṭimids (969–1171) it was the centre of a universal empire, and the volume of its trade had increased. State fleets and the private ships of high dignitaries and merchants strengthened commercial links in the Mediterranean, above all with Sicily. Despite the political and religious rivalry between Cairo and Baghdad, commercial relations between the two great Islamic states were in no way interrupted. According to Ibn Ḥawqal, Egypt sent annually to Iraq textiles to the value of 20–30,000 *dīnārs* (wool and, above all, linen). At this time the commercial orbit of the Egyptian merchant extended as far eastwards as Bukhārā. Towards the end of the Fāṭimid period, the Egyptians erected a *Dār Wakālat al-Qāhira* for Iraqi and Syrian merchants who wished to set up offices in Cairo, or had regular commercial dealings there.

In contrast to this hospitality to Oriental merchants, there was no permanent colony of Byzantine merchants on Egyptian soil, either in the time of the Ṭūlūnids and Ikhshīdids, or in that of the Fāṭimids. A profitable seasonal trade was however carried on with the whole Mediterranean. Islam in no way forbade the commercial activities of Christian merchants on its soil as long as Islamic laws were not infringed. Arculf (about 670) remarks of the Alexandria of his time that it accommodated innumerable peoples within its walls. Many of its inmates seem to have come from Byzantium and its empire. Despite the Byzantine prohibition of visits to the coasts of Syria and Egypt, Venetian merchants put in at Alexandria in 828. Though there is no evidence to attest regular contacts between Venice and Egypt in this period, it is probable that this was not the only occasion on which Venetians visited Alexandria in the ninth century. In the tenth century, Frankish merchants had already advanced as far as Cairo, as is attested in our sources. Whether they had access to Jidda and the Red Sea, as did the Jewish *Rādāniyya*, is not certain. In the eleventh century too Frankish merchants strove eagerly to strengthen and widen their commercial contacts with Egypt. In the twelfth century their lively interest in commerce with Egypt had so increased that, for example, in 1154 (in the reign of the Fāṭimid Caliph al-Ẓāhir) Pisa concluded a trade treaty with Egypt in which, among other things, the Pisans were accorded a *funduq* in Cairo (in addition to their *funduq* in Alexandria). This privilege was however forfeited through Pisan participation in the Crusades aimed at the conquest of Egypt. In 1173 the Pisans obtained a new grant of privilege from the new ruler of Egypt, Saladin, and this became the basis of their subsequent position in Egypt. It was however confined to Alexandria. They were given no licence to acquire a *funduq* in Cairo, nor was this privilege accorded by Saladin to any other trading power of the *dār al-ḥarb*. In this way Saladin aimed to exclude western merchants from trade in the interior, above all Cairo. Saladin, as the protagonist of Islam, thus established the basic principles of the protectionist commercial policy which was to remain in force for the next three centuries. The attempt of the Crusaders under Reynald of Châtillon to penetrate the Red Sea area (1182–3) reinforced Saladin's conviction that the Franks wished to secure not only the Holy Land but also the commercial riches of the Orient. In a letter to the ʿAbbāsid Caliph, Saladin pointed out the danger to Islamic trade should the Franks succeed in seizing some point on the Red Sea, in addition to their foothold in Syria. This would threaten not only the pilgrim route to Mecca and Medina but also the activities of merchants in the Yemen, and especially of the Kārimīs in Aden. Saladin however added in the same letter that trade with the western Christians was in many ways advantageous to Islam, not least through the supply of strategic goods. If however the expulsion of the Franks from Syria were *jihād*, then preventing them from reaching the Red Sea and the Indian Ocean was also a sacred duty.

Saladin's action in excluding the unbelievers from the Red Sea, and thereby from the most important trade route between the west and the Far East, supported the rise of the Islamic Kārimī merchants, of whom we first hear in the eleventh century, and who were to acquire a special place in the Islamic mercantile community. This group of large-scale merchants was distinguished by its enterprise and competence, and soon attained wealth and influence in all important eastern markets and—through its considerable financing activities—in the field of politics too. *From the twelfth century, the Kārimīs and the Franks came by degrees to dominate the whole trade between west and east, and took over the place of the Christian and Jewish merchants of the Byzantine, Ayyūbid and Mamlūk states. Through commercial privileges obtained in return for military services to the Byzantine emperors, the Italians succeeded in eliminating Greek merchants almost entirely, while Saladin's support for the Muslim Kārimīs meant the end of the favoured position of the Coptic and Jewish merchants of Egypt.*

The failure of the Crusades from the time of Saladin is explained not only by political and military but also by economic and commercio-political factors. The supply of imported weapons and slaves to the army of Islam strengthened the resistance of the Ayyūbids and Mamlūks, and trade between the western Mediterranean ports and Alexandria filled the sultan's treasury. The prohibitions issued by the Curia were of no avail in this connection. Nor did Christian efforts to boycott trade with Alexandria and carry on commercial relations with the Far East via Central Asia succeed in shaking the hegemony of Alexandria. When Frankish rule in Syria was brought to an end in 1291, the Mongols in Iran replaced the Crusaders as the new enemy. However, through the efforts of the merchant Abū'l-Majd as-Sallamī, a definitive peace treaty was made with them (1323), their conversion to Islam having taken place in 1295. In 1322 the Egyptian army captured and destroyed the Armenian port of Ayās, and Egypt was able to drop the project of building up Latakia to an importance comparable with that of Alexandria in order to paralyse the Christian port of Ayās. In 1375 the kingdom of Little Armenia was finally destroyed, and 78 years later Constantinople fell to the Ottomans. By the end of the fifteenth century the Black Sea too had come under Ottoman rule. Thus almost all trade routes to the Orient were in Muslim hands, and Frankish merchants were dependent on the good will and co-operation of Muslim rulers.

Egypt's position in international trade was not secured only in the north. As far back as the eleventh century, when Fāṭimid power was as yet intact, disorders in Southern Mesopotamia and increasing insecurity in the Persian Gulf had proved to the advantage of Egyptian ports and commerce. The up-swing in Egyptian trade with Europe, systematically encouraged by the Fāṭimids through an intensified shipbuilding programme, and increasing influence in the Red Sea area, made Egypt's harbours the leading emporia of international maritime trade. As has already been mentioned, it was now Cairo and Alexandria, not Baghdad and Baṣra, which were among the most important emporia. Just as Hurmuz on the Persian Gulf was later to develop into an important commercial emporium, so likewise the position of Aden proved unshakable. Ibn al-Mujāwir speaks of merchants from Egypt, Iran, Ḥaḍramawt, Mogdishu, Zaylaʿ and Abyssinia who acquired large fortunes in Aden. Their goods came from China, India, Ethiopia, the Near East and the other lands of the Indian Ocean. The commonest forms of commercial association were the family company and the *commenda*. We know the biography of an Arabian merchant of the twelfth century, Abū'l-ʿAbbās al-Ḥijāzī, who spent forty years in China. He possessed a commercial fleet of twelve ships, which was lost in a storm on the Indian Ocean. Only one ship reached Egypt, and the rich cargo, which included porcelain and aloe wood, sold immediately. Abū'l-ʿAbbās soon re-attained great wealth, and imported goods from China, India, Abyssinia, Ceylon and the Indonesian Islands. There he posted his seven sons from seven different wives he had married during his long business life in the whole area. These sons of his had mastered the languages and business practices of the markets in question, whence they sent goods to their father in Egypt, receiving in return Levantine, Maghribī and Frankish goods.

Ayyūbid commercial policy in the Red Sea area, and particularly in the Yemen, was even more intensive than that of the Fāṭimids. The fiscal system and administration of the Yemenite ports were developed, and the rulers of the Yemen—a collateral branch of the Ayyūbids—erected splendid *funduqs* and *qayṣariyyas*. After the Ayyūbids, the Rasūlids ruled in the Yemen, theoretically as representatives of the Mamlūk sultans. However, disputes arose continually between Egypt and the Yemen, for the most part for the following reasons: the attempts of several Rasūlid rulers to extend their rule to the Ḥijāz, the omission of tribute payments to Egypt, the maltreatment and exploitation of merchants who put in at the Yemenite ports while trading between the Indian Ocean and the Red Sea. In such disputes the Kārimīs often appear as intermediaries between the conflicting rulers. It was not in their interests that these conflicts should be resolved by force. The Kārimīs also made large loans to the governments of both countries, acquiring power and prestige through this and through their role as emissaries of both sides. They applied to the Mamlūk sultan for the arbitration of their complaints against the rulers of the Yemen; an example is the Kārimīs who carried on trade between China and Egypt, and in 1304 complained against the illegitimate tax demands of the Yemenite ruler. Mamlūk Egypt was unable to achieve a definitive conquest of the Yemen. This would have required an Egyptian thalassocracy in the southern waters such as Egypt never seriously aimed at. Although the sea-worthiness of ships plying the Indian Ocean was always on the increase, no country or dynasty attempted to establish a thalassocracy upon it. This came only with the advent of the Western sea powers after the Portuguese discovery of the sea route to India.

As an example of the collision of Egyptian and Yemenite commerical interests in the area of the Indian Ocean, one may cite the rivalry between Egypt and the Yemen over trade with Ceylon which appears in our sources. A trade delegation from Ceylon which reached Cairo in 1283 mentioned Yemenite emissaries who had proposed a pact between Ceylon and the Yemen at the court of the king of Ceylon. Ceylon however had preferred to strengthen its relations with Egypt. The delegation stated that the king possessed 20 ships which he could send to Egypt laden with jewels, pearls, elephants, various textiles, brazil wood, bark and other wares. The Egyptian sultan would likewise be welcome to engage in commercial activity in Ceylon on his own account. The sources do not tell us whether or in what manner the sultan responded to this invitation. We do however know that the way in which Egypt affirmed her sovereignty over the Red Sea and her interests in the Indian Ocean was not the construction of a fleet for state commerce but the creation of a passport system. Every merchant who had a pass was under the immediate protection of the Egyptian sultan, and was guaranteed safe passage through the Red Sea, without danger to life or property. These passes indicate moreover the receptivity of the Egyptian markets. Merchants were assured that they could without hesitation import any quantity of Oriental goods into Egypt, that they would prosper, and that their establishments would be under Islamic protection. This section of the safe-conduct throws light on Egypt's intensive export drive: large quantities of imported spices and other wares were re-exported by the Kārimī merchants. The safe-conduct included a further pledge that foreign merchants would be well treated by the Egyptian fiscal authorities. At one point the document made reference to the slave trade. The import of slaves was welcomed not only across the Mediterranean but also through the Red Sea and from Central Asia. Slave traders were promised a higher rate of profit and accorded a remission of taxes. The sultan of Egypt stressed the supreme merit of importing *mamlūks* for the defence of Islam. This pass system remained in use up to the end of medieval times. Emissaries from the lands of the southern seas visited not only Egypt but also the Yemenite court. Gifts sent by the emperors of China and Ethiopia and by the Indian princes sought to advance the commercial interests of these countries on the Indian Ocean and in the Yemen. The various sources indicate that the Mamlūk sultans and the Chinese emperors showed a marked interest in mutual contacts. However, no permanent direct relations, such as existed between Egypt and India, arose between the two powers in the Middle Ages.

In the late Middle Ages a new market in international trade was opened to Egypt: the western Sudan region. The gold mines of Wādī al-ʿAllāqī were exhausted, but in 'Mali' Egypt secured a far more significant source of gold. Not just the caravan traders of North Africa, but all Islamic wholesale merchants of the Near East, were active in this market. Ibn Khaldūn in an informative passage directs attention to the significance of this trade. He states that in the year 1353 (754) 12,000 camels arrived in the Bilād al-Sūdān with goods from Egypt, and this apparently took place every year. According to Ibn Baṭṭūṭa, the sole occupation of the inhabitants of the city of Takadda (in the Bilād al-Sūdān) was the Egyptian trade. Merchants imported gold dust from the Sudan and had it minted in their own countries. The Sudan was attractive to merchants thanks to the peace and security which reigned over the vast area, and to the extremely low prices at which one could acquire land with rich gold output. Such was the honesty of the indigenous population that they would not touch the property of a 'white' (Arab) trader who died in their land.

Egyptian commercial policy, administration, the natural environment and the level of technological achievement constituted the framework of commercial activity. While the desert trade routes were firmly in the hands of the Arabs, maritime trade was limited for all peoples by technical factors. In the Mediterranean, travel by sea was confined to set times: in the early Middle Ages, as in Greek and Roman times, this sea was for nautical reasons not navigable in winter. In this season the sea was, in the Arabic idiom, 'closed'. The Venetians, Genoese and other Frankish peoples of the Mediterranean had to be content with a single voyage to the Islamic ports. After the invention of the compass—more precisely, the refinement of the already known, primitive compass—the Venetians and Genoese could make two voyages a year. This development took place at the end of the thirteenth or the beginning of the fourteenth century, and revolutionized the rhythm of sea travel in the later Middle Ages.

Navigation on the Indian Ocean was dominated by the Monsoon winds. From April to October the south-west Monsoon blows along the southern coasts of Asia and over the greater part of the Indian Ocean, while from October to April the north-west Monsoon blows. Ships navigated accordingly. The nautical sources of the later Middle Ages testify to the long experience which sailors had gained, thanks to which the voyage across the Indian Ocean between the Far East, Aden and the East African coast had lost many of its terrors.

The Egyptian administration did not confine its attention to the safety of the desert routes between Egypt, Syria and the Red Sea; the main roads in Egypt itself offered the travelling merchant security and relative comfort, except in times of dynastic change or rebellion. On the initiative of the state, and at its expense, inns (*khāns*) were set up along the main roads in Egypt. An interesting passage in al-Maqrīzī indicates that travel within

Egypt was fairly safe and comfortable; travellers in the reign of the sultan an-Nāṣir Muḥammad ibn Qalāwūn and under his successors could travel from Cairo to Aswān without having to stock up with provisions for the journey, since in each town and district there were inns in which they could obtain food and accommodation for themselves and their mounts. Even a woman could travel alone without any danger.

Being forbidden to carry on trade in Cairo itself, the Franks confined themselves to the commercial ports on the Mediterranean, above all Alexandria. This city thus became the Egyptian centre for the Mediterranean trade season, just as Cairo was for Oriental trade. While the duration of fairs in the interior was one to two weeks, the Alexandrian trade season lasted up to two months. Moslems, or rather native Egyptians, were free to take up accommodation where they pleased in the ports like Alexandria or Damietta, just as they could do in the interior. Foreigners, by contrast, had to take up accommodation in the *funduq* assigned to their country. Benjamin of Tudela remarks *à propos* of his stay in Alexandria that the Yemenites, Iraqis, Syrians, Byzantines, Turks and western Christian communities each had a *funduq* at their disposal, in which they transacted their business, stored their goods and had their living quarters. These *funduqs* were not extraterritorial enclaves on Egyptian soil, but buildings which the Egyptian government placed at the disposal of foreign merchants, the latter being responsible for their upkeep and extension. Thus the state reserved the right to close them at its discretion. It can be inferred from a contract of 1416 that Venetian or indeed Frankish merchants were permitted to rent shops outside their *funduqs*. In this document a native official attested that he had received 600 florins from the Venetian consul as the annual rent of a large shop situated near the entrance to the Venetian *funduq*. The Egyptian government also permitted foreign trading cities, in the first instance Venice, Genoa, Pisa, Barcelona and Marseilles, to maintain consular missions with their own jurisdictions. Freedom to trade was guaranteed, and the Egyptian sultans, by the terms of the treaties concluded with the western commercial powers, had no right of pre-emption. Nevertheless the sultans endeavoured to pay for the goods imported by Frankish merchants in part with state monopoly goods, above all alum. The seizure of goods was forbidden by law. The principle of individual responsiblity guaranteed that no one had to answer for another's offence. The right of salvage, which vested in the owners the right to the cargo of a wrecked or damaged ship, and indeed to the ship itself, was guaranteed to friendly nations by the sultan; and the right of reversion, whereby in the event of the death of a merchant on Egyptian territory his property was made over to his kindred, was assured. Frankish merchants could not be prevented from leaving Egyptian ports with their goods, even if a claim had been entered against them by a subject of the sultan, a merchant or a member of any other profession. A Frank might, however, be arrested on the order of the sultan or his officials. In times of good government it was not unknown for a *qāḍī* to be relieved of his office for unjustifiable action taken against a Frank.

A detailed description of the Egyptian market, with its mass of *funduqs*, *qayṣariyyas*, *wakālas* and large-scale trading establishments, would go beyond the limits of this paper. Here I shall merely attempt a characterization of its outstanding features. Alongside the 'daily market', i.e., the workshops and trading shops, there was the weekly market, the main regulator of the organized exchange of goods between town and country. Annual markets and fairs provided for exchange over longer distances, raised agricultural production, and strengthened commercial exchanges over the whole area of the country. As was normal in the world of the time, the annual markets were timed to occur in conjunction with much-frequented religious festivals, and located at the intersections of great maritime or terrestrial trade routes. In addition to the two great Islamic feasts, the dates of birth of several holy men were occasions for the activation of the local, periodic trade of Egypt. The most important Islamic fairs took place not in Egypt but in the Islamic Holy land at the time of the pilgrimage; for Islam permits and encourages commerce next after the performance of religious duties. 'There are no goods in the whole world,' writes Ibn Jubayr, 'which through this confluence of pilgrims are not to be found in Mecca.' Thanks to this development, Mecca was an important centre of marketing and exchange in the Islamic world, and played the role of a clearing house.

Of great significance for the medieval trade of Egypt was the establishment of *funduqs*, specialized large-scale commercial institutions and markets which virtually developed into stock exchanges. They dominated the townscape of the great cities. Cairo for example possessed at the time of the Crusades four *funduqs* for commercial exchange between Egypt and Syria. One of them was concerned with the import of oil from Syria. According to the sources, an oil trader who lived in the fourteenth century disbursed 20,000 silver *dirhams* for his oil imports, and a further 90,000 for other goods imported from Syria. In the Dār al-Tuffāḥ in Cairo, the wholsale fruit merchants of Egypt and Syria stored their goods—apples, pears, quinces, etc.—after having purchased them at the fruit market, the Funduq Qūṣūn. The Funduq al-ʿAnbar specialized in amber which was imported, not only from the Baltic region, and found a ready market in Egypt, for it was—and still is—a popular female ornament in the Egyptian countryside. In addition to Egyptian products, goods of Chinese, Indian, African, Western and Levantine origin were sold in the Cairene *funduqs*. The fur market of Cairo grew rapidly towards the end of the fourteenth century, for fur was in this period much in demand in male fashion. *Wālīs* and provincial governors would profit from this trade. Thus we hear for instance of a *wālī* and merchant who brought 300,000 garments of grey squirrel fur to sell on the Cairene market.

Scarcely a year after the failure of Reynald of Châtillon's expedition to the Red Sea, Taqī al-Dīn ʿUmar, a nephew of Saladin and his representative in Egypt, built the famous *funduq* for the Kārimī traders (Funduq al-Kārim) in Fusṭāṭ, the landing stage for the Nile ships. Soon after there sprang up Kārimī *funduqs* on the main trade routes from the Indian Ocean to the Mediterranean, in particular in Alexandria, Qūṣ, Aden, Taʿizz, Zabīd, Ghalāfiqa, Biʾr al-Rubāhiyya, Mecca and Medina/Jidda. The Sūq al-ʿAṭṭārīn or al-Buhār was presumably the centre of all the Kārimī trading in Alexandria.

Like Venice, Egypt was a commercial middleman, dealing less in the export of its own products than in the transit trade in foreign raw materials and manufactured goods. Pepper was the most important article in the trade of the Kārimī merchants, who sold it to the Venetians in Alexandria. Before the discovery of the Cape of Good Hope, the latter imported on average 1,150,000 pounds of pepper. At the same time, the slave trade was of great importance. After the conversion of the Slavs, slaves imported into Egypt originated for the most part in Asia and Africa. A few came from Northern Europe and the Baltic. In the late Middle Ages the Egyptian state was much concerned with the expansion of this trade. The main exporting region remained the Black Sea area. This was one of the motives which prompted Egypt to draw closer its ties with the Golden Horde and Byzantium. In a treaty between al-Ẓāhir Baybars and Michael Palaiologos, Egypt was conceded the right to lade two ships with slaves each year and sail them from the Black Sea through the Bosphorus to Egypt. Naturally their cargo did not suffice to meet the needs of the Egyptian court and army. Towards the middle of the fifteenth century, the numbers shipped annually to Alexandria from the Black Sea ports, above all Tana and Kaffa, were estimated at 2,000. In addition to slaves, iron, copper, gold, silver, arms, timber, grain and textiles were brought to Egypt by western merchants. Ships from the east, above all India, brought spices and drugs, precious stones, pearls, ivory, porcelain, dyestuffs, rare woods, muslin and cotton textiles. They returned home with gold, silver, copper, quicksilver, coral, rose water, linen, silk, camletts, taffeta and other wares. The main Egyptian products offered on the internal and external markets were: textiles, sugar, paper, leather, grain, flax, and other agrarian products, various foodstuffs, as fish of different kinds, including salted fish, poultry, salt, oil, dates, alum, carpets and metal goods.

In their prison in Cairo, the 'Frankish' prisoners made wine, which they sold on the native market. When the original building was demolished in 1343, the government permitted them to make wine in their new prison.

There was good reason for this tolerance; a by no means insignificant revenue of some 40,000 *dīnārs* per annum. Despite the religious prohibition, the breeding of pigs was of considerable commercial importance, especially in the export trade.

The government determined the level of taxation in accordance with its interests, the potentialities of the market, and its commercial policy, and not simply in accordance with the provisions of the Holy Law. This applied not only to Frankish or Byzantine merchants, but also to native and oriental merchants who reached Egyptian ports across the Mediterranean, the desert routes or through the Red Sea. Through meticulous bookkeeping, the customs authorities and the central government obtained an accurate picture of imports and exports, their provenance and owners. Even when ship owners and merchants were unable to pay their full export duties, the amount they owed was separately noted in the customs records. They received duplicates of these entries, and had to settle their debts in the following year.

We know from al-Maqdisī that customs dues were already high in Egypt before the Crusades. At the time of the Crusades, goods were so heavily taxed that the payment made on four ships' cargoes was itself equivalent to the value of a ship's cargo. The customs duty payable by Frankish merchants in accordance with the Holy Law was 20 per cent. In practice, however, import and export duties for friendly European commercial republics of the Mediterranean were reduced to 10 per cent for some wares. Thus Frankish merchants were in this respect in a more favourable position than native Islamic merchants.

Thanks to internal trade, towns of varying sizes flourished on the Mediterranean coast of Egypt, in the Delta and in the Nile valley; but they also had some influence on the form of external trade through their production and their highly developed handicrafts. Here too, within the framework of state commercial policy, specific fiscal stipulations had to be met. On entry into a town, each merchant was obliged to pay a *zakāh* of 5 *dirhams* for every 200 *dirhams* of his capital; after this he was free to trade unhindered in the town with his money and goods. If he left the town for commercial reasons more than four times, he had to pay the tax again; in this connection it is to be recalled that the fiscal year lasted only 10 months. The Kārimī, with his rather special commercial role, was subject to somewhat different stipulations. In each town in which he carried on business, he had to pay an annual *zakāh*.

Alongside this fiscal regime, which in the last analysis concerned foreign trade and large scale commercial enterprise, there existed a whole series of taxes on urban trading and markets which went under the name of *al-Māl al-Hilālī* (i.e., taxes reckoned on a monthly basis). The incidence of these taxes ranged from raw materials and natural products to small trading profits and manufactured goods. As in Roman times, taxes were farmed. The financial authorities often settled government debts by means of an assignation on the yield of some tax or other. Not uncommonly the *hilālī* taxes would be assigned in this way. These assignations were known as *suftajas*, and were in frequent use in the Islamic Orient, although our sources tell us little about them. The wish of the farmer or assignee to maximize his profit, and the constant financial straits in which rulers found themselves, encouraged over-exploitation and overloaded the economic life of the country. We have ample evidence on this point. Although the first Fāṭimids and later rulers attempted fiscal reform, the results were of short duration. This was because no fundamental transformation of the fiscal system was undertaken. Without free cities and legally competent guilds, it was impossible to determine unambiguously the fiscal liabilities of townsmen and merchants, and the way lay open to arbitrariness.

For political or commercio-political reasons, the Egyptian government would, in particular cases, concede to merchants, including foreign merchants, the privilege of exemption from taxation; they could not then be exploited by the fiscal authorities. Thus, for example, the merchant Abū'l-Majd al-Sallāmī deserved well through his efforts to bring about peace between Egypt and the Mongols in Iran (1323). When he returned to Egypt on the completion of his mission, the sultan entertained him and accorded him a trading licence to the value of 50,000 *dirhams* annually. By a further concession he did not have to pay tax on half of the goods which he handled. Merchants dealing in certain goods whose import was a matter of state interest were likewise given exemption from duty. Among them were the slave traders, who made a vital contribution to the maintenance of the army and the defence of the Islamic world. Al-Qalqashandī states that this concession related to slave traders everywhere in Egyptian territory. A slave trader might buy, sell, exchange, import or export goods to the value of the slaves he supplied to the sultan, so long as it was not a matter of prohibited goods. Thanks to al-Qalqashandī we are acquainted with the wording of such an exemption as accorded to the highly respected merchant Muḥammad ibn Muzalliq (1353–1444). The beneficiary was granted exemption from all fiscal liabilities within Egypt and Syria. An interesting list of the customs stations is given: Damascus, Aleppo, Tripoli, Ḥamā, Ṣafad, Ghazza, Ḥimṣ, Baʿlabakk and Qaṭyā. He was permitted to engage in tax-free commercial activity to the limit of 200,000 *dirhams*. The sultan accorded temporary tax exemption not only to merchants, but also to whole towns and villages which in consequence of severe economic or political crises could not meet their taxes and liabilities.

Egypt under Islamic rule was a centrally administered country, in which merchants and traders were organized into guilds for the defence and assistance of their members; they did not however possess a monopoly either of production or of buying and selling. The town, the uncontested social basis of Islam, was in the first instance a citadel of the faith, the seat of the governor, and the centre of an administrative area. Not only the governors of the early Islamic period, but also the caliphs of the Fāṭimid period and the sultans of the Ayyūbid and Mamlūk periods, considered it their right to engage in commercial activity, to create state monopolies and to effect requisitions when short of money. In medieval Egypt trade and state-political activity were not mutually exclusive. Rulers bought, sold, and filled their storehouses with native and foreign goods. I am thinking in the first instance of the Fāṭimid caliphs, who possessed several *funduqs* and shops and were at the same time the largest merchants, producers and consumers in the realm. High officials were also active in business life, and they, like the rulers, attempted to buy and sell at dictated prices. Tax evasion was anything but uncommon. The medieval history of Egypt shows repeated examples of *ṭarḥ* (forced sales), and their number grew ever larger with the passage of time. They were the doom of economic life in the fifteenth century.

Flourishing trade brought with it an increase in monetary exchange. This raised new problems, of which the most momentous was the rise in prices. Up to the fourteenth century, Egypt and Syria had hardly known deterioration of the monetary system, for they did not suffer from the Mongol assault as much as Iraq and Iran. Then, with the lucrative trade, prices began to rise. Thanks to its balance of trade, Egypt was free of dangerous inflation into the fifteenth century. The deterioration of the economic situation in that century was clearly discernible in the rise of prices. Towards mid-century, the price of bread had risen by 66 per cent, while the prices of manufactured goods had risen by as much as 500 per cent. Through this Egypt and still more Venice forfeited the high profit margins which had formerly accrued to them from the stability of prices in the Levant. At the same time the autarkic commercial policy of Egypt could not cope with the great rise in prices of this critical period. For in the fifteenth century, the Ottomans attempted to consolidate their power in the Near East and the Balkans. They threatened the position not just of Venice and Genoa but of Egypt too. Moreover, the 'wicked Franks' were eager to discover a new route to the spice-lands from Portugal. Egypt was no longer the main buyer of Sudanese gold from 'Mali and the Bilād al-Takrūr', for Frankish merchants had entered these markets. The Franks were now the chief suppliers of gold, silver and copper—above all the Genoese, Venetians and Catalans, on whose imports the Egyptian money market was now more or less dependent. Nevertheless a large part of this bullion was re-exported to the southern markets, India in the first place, in order to obtain the most sought-after wares for both Christian and Islamic Mediterranean markets.

The Mamlūk state in the fifteenth century had reached the same economic nadir from which the Roman Empire from the third century and the Byzantine Empire from the eleventh had been unable to recover. The heyday of Egyptian commerce was now over. In 1429, sultan Barsbāy monopolized the whole pepper trade, with the object of insuring a dependable source of revenue to meet the very high level of military expenses. The Kārimī merchants, who had from time to time relieved the financial straits of the sultans through loans and financial support, were obliged to make a gradual withdrawal. Jean Thenaud (1512) states that there were at that date in Cairo 200 large-scale merchants who possessed over two million pieces of gold each and that they hid this money for fear of the sultan and his officials. In a word, the conditions of business deteriorated more and more for European and Oriental merchants alike. This began with the world plague in the middle of the fourteenth century, which exterminated more than one third of the population of Egypt, continued with the rapid decline of manufacture and agriculture, and ended with the state monopoly of trade. Towards the beginning of the sixteenth century, the great upheavals of world history had a deep influence on the fate of Egypt. At this time the country had to face two enemies at one time: the Portuguese in the Indian Ocean and the Ottomans in the Near East. At this decisive moment for the traditional commercial policy of Egypt, the Ottomans in the name of the Holy War placed at the disposal of the Egyptians more than 2,000 men equipped with fire-arms. Their concern was however more to wrest from Egypt her hegemony over the Red Sea than to wage war against the Portuguese. The Italians, and above all the Venetians, were very much interested in close cooperation with the sultan, owing to the political and economic changes of the world situation in the sixteenth century. The Mamlūks however merely made capital out of their position without considering the consequences. They altogether overlooked the fact that a close military and political alliance with the Italian trading communes could have saved them from the pincer-grip from east and west.

In 1517 Egypt became a province of the Ottoman Empire. It is noteworthy that the Ottomans at first tried to continue the old Egyptian determination to monopolize the transit trade between Orient and Occident, although this monopoly had already been broken by the Portuguese. Moreover trade in the Egyptian interior was for a long time closed to westerners, and commercial activity in the Red Sea continued to be forbidden to them.

Sources for the Economic History of the Middle East

BERNARD LEWIS

THE economic historian, even more than his colleagues in other fields of historical inquiry, has a liking for documentary evidence—a marked tendency to prefer archives to annals and other literature. The historian will of course be aware of the insights, and even information that books can give him, and he will appreciate the relevance to his researches of the image of a society as reflected in the works of its authors and compilers. But whenever possible he will direct his main attention to the contemporary and immediate evidence or traces of historical events, in their original form, not as transmitted—and therefore transmuted—by a literary intermediary. The modern economic historian relies very largely on published and unpublished documentary and statistical materials. In the West, even the medievalist has at his disposal a mass of records, public and private, lay and ecclesiastical, central and local, on which to base his study of economic structures and economic change.

One of the classical difficulties of the historian of Islam is the lack of such evidence.[1] Without entering into the complex theoretical and philosophical problems of periodization, we may, for practical purposes, divide the history of the Middle East since the rise of Islam into three periods, defined by the availability and quality of documentary sources, and describe them by the neutral terms early, middle and late. In the late period, which in most areas begins in the nineteenth century and continues to our own day, our knowledge is enriched—if that is the right word—by the multifarious bureaucratic activities of the state and of other agencies. Research into the recent economic history of the Middle East can be based on material similar in form, if less so in content, to that appearing in other parts of the modern world, and can be pursued by similar techniques. Which parts, and which techniques, are for the researcher to determine, and it is possible that in time students of some Middle Eastern countries will develop a particular

[1] For discussions of archival and documentary sources for Islamic history, see *Jean Sauvaget's introduction to the history of the Muslim East: a bibliographical guide, based on the second edition as recast by Claude Cahen*, Berkeley and Los Angeles 1965, pp. 16–21; C. Cahen, 'L'histoire économique et sociale de l'Orient musulman', *Studia Islamica*, iii, 1965, pp. 93–115, especially 98 ff.; H. H. Roemer, 'Über Urkunden zur Geschichte Ägyptens und Persiens in islamischer Zeit', *Zeitschrift der Deutschen Morgenländischen Gesellschaft*, 107, 1957, pp. 519–38; S. M. Stern, *Fāṭimid decrees*, London 1964, p. 1 ff.; H. Ernst, *Die mamlukischen Sultansurkunden des Sinai-klosters*, Wiesbaden 1960 (with detailed bibliography); Muḥammad Aḥmad Ḥusayn, *Al-wathā'iq al-ta'rīkhiyya*, Cairo 1954, p. 58 ff.; *EI*², *s.v.* 'Diplomatic'.

technique of their own, analogous to those used by specialists in other regions where only published plans, reports and statistics are available, and where these pose distinctive problems of acceptance and evaluation.

The middle period, corresponding roughly to what European historians call early modern history, is also illustrated by archives, though of a different—an early modern—kind. The most important by far are the Ottoman archives, the existence and range of which in effect define this period. Apart from the major collections in Istanbul, there are others in Ankara and in a number of Turkish provincial cities. Archival collections, of varying types and sizes, have also survived in Egypt and Tunisia, and in some of the former Ottoman lands in Europe and Asia. The Ottoman archives have already given rise to a considerable literature, much of it concerned with economic matters; they also provide the basis of several papers presented to this colloquium.[2]

In other parts of the region the position is much less satisfactory. There are Ottoman records for those provinces of Persia and Transcaucasia which for a time were incorporated in the Ottoman Empire;[3] for the rest of Persia, no archives have so far come to light. Outside the areas under Ottoman rule or suzerainty, there is only one region for which archives are known to exist. This consists of the Muslim Khanates of Central Asia, incorporated in the Russian Empire between 1865 and 1887. State archives and some private archives, dating for the most part from the period immediately preceding the Russian conquest, were preserved by the conquerors, and contain data on land-tenure, taxation, and related matters.[4]

In addition to these, there are two other groups of archives, of considerable but unequal interest to the economic historian. The first, and smaller group, consists of records preserved among the non-Muslim communities

[2] Brief accounts of the Ottoman archives, with bibliographical guidance, will be found in *EI*², *svv*. 'Başvekâlet Arşivi' (by B. Lewis) and 'Daftar-i khāķānī' (by Ö. L. Barkan); S. J. Shaw, 'Archival Sources for Ottoman history: the archives of Turkey', *Journal of the American Oriental Society*, 80, 1960, pp. 1–12. Ottoman materials relating to Egypt and the Fertile Crescent are discussed in B. Lewis, 'The Ottoman archives as a source for the history of the Arab lands', *Journal of the Royal Asiatic Society*, 1951, pp. 139–55; S. J. Shaw, 'Cairo's archives and the history of Ottoman Egypt', *Report on Current Research, Spring 1956*, Middle East Institute, Washington 1956, pp. 59–72; *idem*, 'The Ottoman archives as a source for Egyptian history', *Journal of the American Oriental Society*, 83, 1963, pp. 447–52.

[3] B. Lewis, 'Registers on Iran and Âdharbâyjân in the Ottoman *Defter-i Khâqânî*', in *Mélanges Henri Massé*, Tehran 1963, pp. 259–63.

[4] For a brief account in English see M. Yuldashev, 'The State archives of XIX [*sic*] feudal Khiva', in *Papers presented by the Soviet delegation at the XXIII international congress of orientalists: Iranian, Armenian, and Central-Asian Studies*, Moscow 1954, pp. 221–30, where other Russian publications are cited. See further H. H. Roemer, 'Vorschläge für die Sammlung von Urkunden zur islamischen Geschichte Persiens', *Zeitschrift der Deutschen Morgenländischen Gesellschaft*, 104, 1954, p. 364 ff. The archives of the Sheikhs of Jūybār, edited by P. P. Ivanov, *Iz arkhiva Šeykhov Džuybary*, Moscow–Leningrad 1954, date from the sixteenth century.

within the Muslim world. These, by virtue of their coherence and institutional structure, often enjoyed a continuity lacking in the larger and more fragmented Muslim society, and were thus able to accumulate and preserve records over long periods of time. The best known are the Armenian monastery of Ečmiadzin and the Greek Orthodox St. Catherine's monastery in Mount Sinai, the documents of which have recently been studied and, in part, edited. Christian and Jewish ecclesiastical and communal archives exist in various centres, but have so far been little explored.[5] Published documents deal, among other things, with such familiar topics as the assessment and collection of taxes, land-tenure, and disputes of various kinds, usually over money or property.

The second, and very much larger group, consists of the archives of foreign governments, trading companies, religious orders, and other bodies that have been involved in or concerned with the Middle East—first in the Italian states, then Austria, Russia, the countries of Western Europe, especially Britain and France, and latterly also the U.S.A. These countries contain rich archive collections, almost all of which are freely open to researchers.

The Ottoman archives begin in the fifteenth century, and become really full in the sixteenth. For earlier periods of Middle Eastern history, and for areas outside the Ottoman Empire, there are, with certain limited exceptions, no archives at all.

This does not mean that there are no documents. Considerable numbers of documents have in fact survived, and may be found in public and private collections. But these collections are not archives; they are fortuitous assemblages of individual documents, discovered by chance and distributed haphazard, with no order other than that imposed on them by curators, editors, and historians. Their value may be very great, but it can never be the same as that of a genuine record office in which documents are preserved in their original form, order, and sequence, as they emerged from the work and served the needs of the institution that created them. Much of the value of such records lies in their comprehensiveness, continuity and cohesion. That such archives existed in medieval Islam is clear from the literary sources, but they have not survived. Archives are created and maintained for administrative use, not for the convenience of historians. The states of the medieval West survived and developed into the states of the modern West, and their archives, often still current, were preserved until a time when their historical importance was appreciated. This political continuity facilitated the survival of many other, local, institutions and the consequent conservation of their records. The church was another major

[5] The literature is reviewed by Roemer, 'Über Urkunden . . .', Stern, and Ernst. More recent publications include a group of articles, in Arabic, on documents in the St. Catherine's Monastery in the *Bulletin of the Faculty of Arts*, University of Alexandria, xviii, 1964.

element of stability and continuity, and the well-preserved and well-protected records of ecclesiastical offices and foundations are an invaluable source of information for the economic historian. The states of the medieval Middle East, with the exception of the Ottoman Empire, were destroyed, and their archives, ceasing to serve any practical purpose, were neglected, scattered and lost. Islam had no church, and the character of Islamic society did not favour the emergence of corporative bodies below government level, of such a type and of such duration as to produce and conserve records.

There are some exceptions to the statement, frequently repeated and generally accepted, that there are no archives for medieval Islamic history. The most important of these exceptions have already been mentioned—the archives of foreign and of minority institutions. These are naturally less plentiful than for the Ottoman period, but still contain much that is of interest. Italian and Spanish archives contain many documents relating to commerce, including a number in Arabic, which have received historically disproportionate attention from orientalists. Even the documents from St. Catherine's, reflecting the concerns of the monks and their dealings with the outside world, are not without economic interest. They include rulings from the Egyptian chancery on disputes between the monks and their Bedouin neighbours, who claimed a share of their lands and crops (wheat, barley and fruit), and replies to appeals from the monks for the remission of taxes, tolls and services.

Another exception is the pre-Ottoman material preserved in the Ottoman archives, most of it, unfortunately, in Ottoman copies or adaptations. Ottoman policy in a newly conquered province was usually very conservative and normally maintained, at least for a while, the existing fiscal and administrative practice. The Ottomans also recognized existing *waqf*, and the *waqf* registers compiled after the Ottoman conquest of Syria include many *waqfs* of the Mamlūk and even of the Ayyūbid period. The administration of *waqf*, together with other matters arising out of the application of the holy law, also gave rise to small groups of pre-Ottoman documents that have been preserved in the Ministry of *Waqf* and the court of personal affairs in Cairo.[6]

The European archives are often of considerable size and importance, but, in view of their external origin, are inevitably limited in the range of information which they can offer. Such Middle Eastern archives as survive, from the pre-Ottoman period, are vestigial and restricted, and have on the whole been of more interest for diplomatics than for history.

In the absence of genuine archives, the surviving documents, despite

[6] For an example, see Ḥasanayn Muḥammad Rabīʿ, 'Ḥujjat tamlīk wa-waqf', in *Al-Majalla al-taʾrīkhiyya al-Miṣriyya*, xii, 1964–5, pp. 191–202. See further Muḥammad Aḥmad Ḥusayn, *Al-Wathāʾiq*, p. 97 ff.

their non-archival character, acquire considerable importance. There are several categories of such documents; most of them come from Egypt, where the dry climate on the one hand, and a relatively high degree of political continuity on the other, favoured their preservation.

The first important group consists of some tens of thousands of miscellaneous documents and fragments, all but a few of them from Egypt, and written, for the most part, during the first four centuries of Islam. Some are in Greek, some in Arabic, some bilingual. A few are in other languages. They are known collectively as 'the papyri', from the material on which they are written, and the special branch of scholarship concerned with their study is called papyrology.[7] This terminology, as Professor Claude Cahen has remarked, is unfortunate, and conveys a somewhat misleading impression of the scope and purposes of these studies. 'In reality, papyrology, when it is concerned with mere deciphering, is a branch of palaeography; when interpretation is involved, it is exclusively a branch of history.'[8] In fact, there has been a tendency to make a distinction—which for the historian is of no importance—between documents written on papyrus and documents written on paper, and to neglect the latter; there has also been undue separation between the study of Greek and of Arabic papyri, even where both date from the Islamic period and deal with similar topics.

Despite these limitations, and some others arising from the predominantly philological character of scholarship in this field, the study of the papyri has already significantly altered the accepted view of early Islamic history. Many of the papyri are administrative and financial documents. A comparison of these with similar documents from the late Byzantine period shows greater continuity and less change than was previously believed; a comparison of the evidence of the papyri with juristic expositions reveals the latter to be schematic and anachronistic, and has led to a perhaps rather exaggerated reaction from the earlier habit of complete reliance on such sources.

In the work that has so far been done on the papyri, the main attention has been given to the workings of government—to such matters as provincial administration, the assessment and collection of taxes, land surveys and accountancy, the administration of justice, the recruitment, equipment and supply of the armed forces. Much of this has an obvious relevance to economic history. Documents relating to the navy, for example, include information concerning the employment of skilled and unskilled labour in the shipyards, the supply of timber, nails, ropes and other materials to them, and the provision of food for the sailors and workers. In addition, there are

[7] On the Arabic papyri, see A. Grohmann, *Einführung und Chrestomathie zur arabischen Papyruskunde*, vol. i, Prague 1954; *idem, Arabische Chronologie, Arabische Papyruskunde*, Leiden/Cologne 1966 (cf. the review by Claude Cahen in *Arabica*, xv, 1968, pp. 104–6), and, more briefly, Cahen–Sauvaget, pp. 16–18.

[8] Cahen–Sauvaget, p. 17.

numerous other papyri, of both official and private origin, dealing with the transfer of commodities by purchase, requisition or taxation, the employment of labour for wages or by *corvée*, and similar topics. After the pioneer work of Karabacek, Becker and Bell, published work on the papyri has, in the main, taken the form of editions, translations and evaluations of individual documents or groups of documents, with some work on administration, taxation, and law. The systematic use of the papyri by economic historians is still at a very rudimentary stage; given the unsystematic character of the evidence, and the arduous philological apprenticeship required for its study, this situation may well persist.

During the tenth century papyrus gradually went out of use, and was replaced, even in Egypt, by paper. Documents on paper, apparently of the same types as the papyri, have survived in considerable numbers. Not being papyri, these have been almost entirely disregarded by orientalist scholarship, and little is known about their range and content.

One important group of papers, also of Egyptian provenance, has received serious attention. These are the documents from the so-called *Geniza*, the repositories in which the Jews of Cairo placed written papers which were no longer required, to protect the name of God, which might occur in them, from desecration.[9] Leaving aside literary manuscripts and 'mere scraps', the number of whole documents and self-contained fragments in the *Geniza* has been estimated by Professor S. D. Goitein at about 10,000. These date mainly from the Fāṭimid and Ayyūbid periods, with a small number from Mamlūk times. There is in addition *Geniza* material of the Ottoman period, which has not so far been used.

Like the papyri, the *Geniza* documents are subject to certain limitations. They are not archival; they all come from Egypt—and they are further limited, by their Jewish provenance, to such matters as concerned the members of one religious minority. The first of these limitations, the non-archival character of the documents, is of major importance and severely restricts the use that can be made of data on such matters as prices and wages, in the *Geniza* as in the papyri. The other limitations, though serious, are less so than would at first appear. The papyri, largely of governmental origin and concerned with such very local matters as taxation and provincial administration, tell us little about conditions outside Egypt; apart from the very few papyri found in south-west Asia,[10] the best they can offer is comparative material, which may occasionally be of use in elucidating data

[9] On the *Geniza*, see S. D. Goitein, 'Geniza', in *EI*², where further references are given, and *idem*, *A Mediterranean Society: the Jewish Communities of the Arab World as portrayed in the documents of the Cairo Geniza*, vol. i: *Economic Foundations*, Berkeley and Los Angeles, 1967. A bibliography has been published by S. Shaked, *A tentative bibliography of Geniza documents*, Paris–The Hague 1964.

[10] At 'Awjā' al-Ḥafīr, and in the neighbourhood of Damascus and Sāmarrā. See Grohmann, *Einführung*, pp. 28–30.

obtained from other sources. The *Geniza* includes documents of governmental origin, but the greater and most valuable part, for the economic historian, is of private origin—business and family correspondence, accounts, receipts, contracts and other commercial documents, and legal deeds and reports of various kinds. The commercial and social relations reflected in these documents are by no means limited to Egypt, but extend westwards to the Mediterranean lands, eastward to India.[11] They provide fuller information on the life and activities of the commercial classes in medieval Egypt than is available from any other source.

No third group of documents, comparable in scale and importance with the papyri and the *Geniza*, has so far been brought to light. Many documents exist, however, of which only a small proportion have been studied. As in the earlier periods, Egypt is the richest source. Besides the papyri, large numbers of Egyptian documents written on paper, and dating from the tenth century onwards, are kept in public collections; some 28,000 are reported in Vienna alone.[12] These documents, said to be of the same general type as the papyri, have hardly been touched by modern scholarship. A small group of documents from Damascus, discovered by D. and J. Sourdel, include some deeds of sale dated 310/922–3, the title-deeds of an estate, dated 604/1207–8, and a letter announcing the restoration of property previously confiscated by the sovereign.[13]

After Egypt, Iran and the neighbouring lands in Transcaucasia and Central Asia provide the most important non-archival collections of documents. Original Persian documents from the pre-Mongol period are very few indeed. The earliest is a private letter from a Jewish merchant, written in Persian in Hebrew characters, possibly in the eighth century. It was found near Khotan. Others include a Judaeo-Persian law report of 1020 from Ahwāz, a deed for the sale of land, dated 501/1107, from the region of Khotan (?), and a group of six documents from Bāmyān of which one is dated 607/1211.[14] There are rather more documents from the period of the Il-Khāns and their successors, but it is not until the time of the Ṣafavids that we find them in any great numbers. Those that have already been found, in public and private collections in Iran and elsewhere, include many that deal with fiscal, commercial and other matters of economic interest.[15]

Besides all these, two other groups of documents have survived in the

[11] See S. D. Goitein, *Studies in Islamic history and institutions*, Leiden 1966, part III.

[12] Grohmann, *Einführung*, p. 56.

[13] Janine Sourdel-Thomine and D. Sourdel, 'Nouveaux documents sur l'histoire religieuse et sociale de Damas au Moyen Age', *Revue des Etudes Islamiques*, xxxii, 1964, pp. 1–25; *idem*, 'Trois actes de vente damascains du début du IVe/Xe siècle', *JESHO*, viii, 1965, pp. 164–85.

[14] V. Minorsky, 'Some early documents in Persian', *Journal of the Royal Asiatic Society*, 1942, pp. 181–94.

[15] See *EI*², 'Diplomatic iii' (by H. Busse), and the two articles by H. H. Roemer, cited above notes 1 and 4.

Middle East, because they were written on metal and on stone. Coins and inscriptions are available in great numbers, and have been extensively studied, by numismatists and epigraphers.[16] The documentary information inscribed on coins is inevitably meagre and repetitive, but even such modest data as the year and mint of issue can usefully contribute to the inferences drawn from the weight and metallic composition of coins, and from the place, quantity and company in which they are found. Probably the best known example is the series of hoards, containing many thousands of Muslim silver *dirhams*, that have been found in the countries around the Baltic. These coins come mainly from central Asian mints, and carry dates ranging from the turn of the seventh/eighth century to the early eleventh century. Until about the middle of the tenth century, the coins found in these hoards consist almost exclusively of Muslim *dirhams*. From the second half of the tenth century, the hoards include a growing proportion of other coins, Byzantine, West European, even Anglo-Saxon. Towards the middle of the eleventh century Muslim coins disappear entirely from these silver hoards. These hoards, together with similar finds in Poland and Russia, especially in the regions of Kazan and Kiev, on the one hand, and in Western Europe on the other, have given rise to a vast literature on the trade between the Muslim lands and the North.[17] The problem, as Professor Lewicki has remarked, is still anything but clarified.[18] The broader question of the relevance of numismatic evidence to the economic history of the Middle East is discussed in Dr. Ehrenkreutz's paper.

Islamic inscriptions are extant in great numbers, with a very wide range of countries and periods of origin. Their range of content is, however, disappointingly narrow. One of the greatest of Arabic epigraphers, Max van Berchem, remarked that almost all of them 'are centred on one of the two predominant ideas in the Muslim world: divine power and absolute political authority. On the one hand, the Koran, invocations, and pious phrases, confessions of faith, mystical allusions, and prayers for the dead; on the other hand, the names of the sovereign, his titles, exploits, and his perpetual praise.'[19] Though some of us may wish to dissent from the particulars of Van Berchem's formulation, we must surely agree with his conclusion, that the inscriptions of Islam have far less documentary value than those of Greek and Roman antiquity. 'In this world,' said Benjamin Franklin in a famous phrase, 'nothing can be said to be certain, except

[16] For a brief account, see Cahen–Sauvaget, pp. 52–7, and, on recent work, G. C. Miles, 'Islamic numismatics: a progress report', in *Congresso Internazionale di Numismatica: Rome 1961, Relazioni*, vol. i, pp. 181–92.

[17] See for example T. Lewicki, 'Il commercio arabo con la Russia e con i paesi slavi d'Occidente nei secoli ix–xi', *Annali. Instituto Universitario Orientale di Napoli*, n.s. viii, 1959, pp. 47–61, and J. Duplessy, 'La circulation des monnaies arabes en Europe occidentale du VIIIe au XIIIe siècle', in *Revue Numismatique*, 5e ser. xviii, 1956, pp. 101–63.

[18] Lewicki, p. 48.

[19] Cited in Cahen–Sauvaget, p. 52.

death and taxes.' The Muslim inscriptions may be said to reflect a parallel preoccupation with the two ultimate certainties, but differently expressed—as God and the government. It is at the point of contact or conflict between these two concerns that the inscriptions are most informative. Two groups of inscriptions are of particular interest to the economic historian. The first consists of the texts or summaries of *waqf* deeds, inscribed on pious foundations, to protect the service of God from the depredations of the state; the second deals with taxes, tolls and levies of various kind—usually in the form of the pious abolition of illegal taxes by a pious new ruler.[20] Though never, as far as can be seen from the record, reimposed, these illegal taxes are re-abolished with monotonous frequency. Between the papyri and the Ottoman archives, inscriptions provide the best documentary evidence concerning taxation. Also of interest are the inscriptions on metrological objects (weights, coin-weights, measure-stamps, vessel-stamps, tokens), and trade-marks or certificates on manufactured articles, especially textiles and metalwork.[21]

For the second and third of the three periods we have considered, the economic historian of the Middle East, apart from some problems of physical and linguistic access to documents, is not significantly worse off than his European colleague—indeed, he may find that the Ottoman archives offer material of a wealth and diversity not found elsewhere. For the first, or medieval, period, however, the documentary evidence available to him is very much poorer. In compensation, he has at his disposal a body of literary material of incomparable richness, 'larger perhaps than any other civilization has produced until modern times'.[22]

It would be pointless to attempt a survey of the literary sources for the economic history of the Middle East, which potentially include the whole vast literature of the area. It may, however, be useful to look at certain classes of writings, and to consider the type of information that they offer.

The first group of texts to be considered are those that deal directly and explicitly with economic questions, both theoretical and practical. The earliest prescriptive statements are in the Qur'ān itself, notably in the final pages of *Sūrat al-Baqara*. 'God has permitted buying and selling, and forbidden usury . . . O you who believe! Be pious towards God, and forgo what is owing to you from usury, if you are believers. If you do not do this, then expect war from God and the Prophet, but if you renounce (usury),

[20] For examples of both kinds see M. Sharon, 'A waqf inscription from Ramlah', *Arabica*, xiii, 1966, pp. 77–84; J. Sauvaget, 'Décrets mamelouks de Syrie, 3', *Bulletin d'Etudes Orientales*, xii, 1947–8, pp. 1–56.

[21] See for example G. C. Miles, 'Early Islamic glass weights and measures in Muntaza Palace, Alexandria', *Journal of the American Research Center in Egypt*, iii, 1964, pp. 105–113; *idem*, 'Egyptian glass pharmaceutical measures of the 8th century A.D.', *Journal of the History of Medicine and Allied Sciences*, xv, 1960, pp. 384–9, *idem*, 'Islamic numismatics . . .' (cited in note 16 above), pp. 188–9.

[22] Cahen–Sauvaget, p. 22.

your capital will remain with you, and you will neither inflict nor suffer injury.'[23] Other passages confirm the lawfulness of honest trading, and touch on such matters as fair weights and measures, debts, contracts, and the like.[24]

Qur'ānic approval of buying and selling is amplified in a large number of sayings, attributed to the Prophet and to the leading figures of early Islam, in praise of the honest merchant and of commerce as a way of life. Some sayings go further, and defend the more expensive commodities which the honest merchants sold—such as silks and brocades, jewels, male and female slaves, and other luxuries. 'When God gives wealth to a man,' the Prophet is improbably quoted as saying, 'He wants it to be seen on him.' Even more striking is a story told in an early Shī'ite work. The Imām Ja'far al-Ṣādiq, it is said, was reproached by one of his disciples for wearing fine apparel (a variant says: clothes from Marw), while his ancestors had worn rude, simple garments. The Imām is quoted as replying that his ancestors had lived in a time of scarcity, while he lived in a time of plenty, and that it was proper to wear the clothing of one's own time.[25] These and similar attempts to justify luxurious living mark a reaction against the strain of asceticism in Islam, and no doubt reflect the interests of the luxury trades.

As in many other fields, the earliest known Muslim work on economic ethics consists very largely of a collection of sayings attributed to the Prophet and the early heroes of Islam entitled *Kitāb al-Kasb*, 'On earning'; it was written by a Syrian of Iraqi *mawlā* ancestry called Muḥammad al-Shaybānī, who died in 804.[26] Shaybānī's purpose is to show that earning a livelihood is not merely permitted, but is incumbent on Muslims. Man's primary duty is to serve God, but to do this properly he must be adequately fed, housed and clothed. This can only be achieved by working and earning. Nor need his earnings be limited to providing for the bare necessities of life, since the acquisition and use of luxuries is also permitted.

Another point which Shaybānī is anxious to make is that money earned by commerce or crafts is more pleasing in God's eyes than money received from the government, for civil or military service. The same point is argued by al-Jāḥiẓ (d. 869) in an essay entitled 'In praise of merchants and in condemnation of officials',[27] and is echoed by many later writers. Jāḥiẓ

[23] Qur'ān, ii, 275 ff. Cf. iii, 125; iv, 159.

[24] Qur'ān, ii, 194, 276 ff., 282 ff.; iv, 33; vi, 153, lxii, 9–11.

[25] Abū 'Amr Muḥammad al-Kashshī, *Ma'rifat akhbār al-rijāl*, Bombay A.H. 1317, p. 249. For other similar stories see Goitein, *Studies*, pp. 224–5; cf. Max Weber, *The Sociology of Religion*, trans. E. Fischoff, London 1965, p. 263.

[26] The original text is lost, but the work survives in an abridgement, with refutation, by the author's pupil Ibn Samā'a (d. 847), entitled *Al-Iktisāb fi'l-rizq al-mustaṭāb*, Cairo 1938. It is examined in Goitein, *Studies*, p. 220 ff.

[27] An incomplete and somewhat garbled edition in *Iḥdā 'ashrata rasā'il*, Cairo 1324/1906, pp. 155–61; partial translation of the edition in O. Rescher, *Excerpte und Übersetzungen aus den Schriften des . . .* Ǧaḥiẓ, Stuttgart 1931, pp. 186–8. Cf. C. Pellat in *Arabica*, iii, 1956, p. 177.

stresses the security, dignity and independence of merchants in contrast with the uncertainty, humiliation and sycophancy of those who serve the ruler, and defends the piety and the learning of merchants against their detractors.

The discussion in ethical and religious terms of gainful employment, usually equated with commerce and crafts, was continued by a number of subsequent writers, occasionally in separate works, more frequently within the framework of more extensive treatises.[28] A tenth century encyclopaedic work of Ismāʿīlī inspiration includes a detailed survey of arts and crafts, classified in several different ways—by the materials they use, by the tools and movements they require and by 'rank'. Under the last heading crafts are divided into three main groups: The first, or primary group, provides basic necessities, and is subdivided into three subgroups—weaving, agriculture and building, providing the three basic needs for clothing, food and shelter. The second, or 'ancillary' group, consists of accessory and finishing trades, ancillary to the first. The third main group is concerned with luxuries such as silks, brocades and perfumes. A final cross-classification is by the 'merit' of the crafts, which may derive from their indispensability, as agriculture; their precious materials, as jewellery; their skilled workmanship, as the making of astronomical instruments; their public utility, as the work of bath-attendants and scavengers, or, finally, the nobility of the craft itself, as painting and music.[29]

It would be easy to assemble other traditions, and writings of ascetic tendency, that say just the opposite and condemn commerce and those engaged in it. It is, however, noteworthy that centuries before Christian writers were prepared to defend and define the ethics of commerce against ascetic criticism, Muslim writers were willing to do so, and that even a major theologian like al-Ghazzālī (d. 1111) could include, in his religious writings, a portrait of the ideal merchant and a defence of commerce as a way of preparing oneself for the world to come.[30]

Besides religious writings on commerce, there are others, of a more practical nature. The best known is the *Kitāb al-Ishāra ilā maḥāsin al-tijāra* (Indication of the merits of commerce) written in the eleventh or twelfth century by Abū'l Faḍl Jaʿfar b. ʿAlī al-Dimashqī. Greek

[28] On this literature, see W. Björkman, 'Kapitalentstehung und -anlage im Islam', *Mitteilungen des Seminars für orientalische Sprachen*, xxxii, 1929, p. 81 ff.; Sir T. W. Arnold, 'Arab travellers and merchants', *apud* A. P. Newton, *Travel and travellers of the Middle Ages*, London 1926, p. 92 ff.; 'Tidjāra' in *EI*[1] (by W. Heffening); Goitein, *Studies*, p. 220 ff.; Ann K. S. Lambton, 'The merchant in medieval Islam', in *A Locust's leg: studies in honour of S. H. Taqizadeh*, London 1962, pp. 121–30.

[29] *Rasā'il Ikhwān al-Ṣafā*, vol. i, Cairo 1928, pp. 210–26; cf. B. Lewis, 'An epistle on manual crafts', *Islamic Culture*, xvii, 1943, pp. 142–51. For an earlier consideration of the crafts see Jāḥiẓ, *Rasā'il*, ed. Ḥasan Sandūbī, Cairo 1352/1933, pp. 126–7.

[30] On Ghazzālī, see Arnold, pp. 93–4; Ann K. S. Lambton, 'The merchant . . .', p. 123 ff.

philosophic influences are already apparent in the tenth-century encyclopaedia, cited above. They appear again in al-Dimashqī's treatise, in a more specifically economic form—from Plato's *Politics*, Aristotle's doctrine of the golden mean and, in particular, the *Oikonomos* of the neo-Pythagorean 'Bryson'.

For al-Dimashqī, gain is a good thing for its own sake. Though he includes some theoretical and moralistic discussion, his main purpose is to provide practical guidance for merchants. He discusses, among other topics, the types, qualities and prices of merchandise, the roles of the three classes of merchants, the wholesaler (*khazzān*), the exporter (*mujahhiz*), and the travelling merchant (*rakkāḍ*), the dangers of fraud and waste, and various problems such as the appointment of agents, the obtaining of information about market prices, the fixing of prices, the delivery of goods, and financial and commercial administration.[31]

Even more practical are works dealing with specific problems. 'A Clear look at trade' (*al-Tabaṣṣur bi'l-tijāra*), probably written in ninth-century Iraq, discusses the qualities, values and ways of evaluating gold, silver, pearls and precious stones, scents and aromatics, textiles, skins and other commodities, and lists the goods imported from the provinces of the Islamic Empire and from foreign countries.[32] An eleventh-century author wrote 'On the purchase of slaves'—a sort of slave-trader's vade-mecum, with a classification of slaves by race and country of origin and much fascinating information on the slave-trade in all its stages. This work is also, incidentally, an important source for the history of Africa.[33] A common theme of the practical handbooks is the need for precautions against swindlers and fakers, whose methods are often described in fascinating detail. A thirteenth-century Syrian author devotes a whole book to the subject of trickery and fraud. Beginning with false prophets, spurious priests, thaumaturges, alchemists, astrologers, mountebanks and the like, the author goes on to discuss the distinctive malpractices of dishonest grocers, cooks, horse-copers, money-changers, physicians and other trades and professions.[34]

Farmers seem to have been less articulate—or less represented in book-writing circles—than merchants. There is, however, a literature on

[31] On al-Dimashqī see H. Ritter, 'Ein arabisches Handbuch der Handelswissenschaft', *Der Islam*, vii, 1917, pp. 1–91; C. Cahen, 'A propos et autour d'ein arabisches Handbuch der Handelswissenschaft', *Oriens*, xv, 1962, pp. 160–71. The text was published in Cairo in 1318 A.H.

[32] Jāḥiẓ (attrib.), *Al-Tabaṣṣur bi'l-tijāra*, ed. Ḥasan Ḥusnī 'Abd al-Wahhāb, *Revue de l'Academie Arabe de Damas*, xii, 1932, reprinted Cairo 1354/1935; French translation by C. Pellat, 'Ǧāḥiẓiana, I: le *Kitāb al-Tabaṣṣur bi'l-tigāra* attribué à Gāḥiẓ', *Arabica*, i, 1954, pp. 153–65. The attribution to Jāḥiẓ is almost certainly an error.

[33] Ibn Buṭlān, *Risāla fī shirā al-raqīq wa-taqlīb al-'abīd*, ed. 'Abd al-Salām Hārūn, in *Nawādir al-Makhṭūṭāt*, iv/16, Cairo 1373/1954, pp. 333–89. An English translation was prepared by the late Professor D. S. Rice.

[34] Al-Jawbarī, *Al-Mukhtār fī kashf al-asrār*, Cairo A.H. 1353.

agriculture, which deserves more attention than it has received. The earliest known work is the so-called 'Nabataean agriculture' (*al-Filāḥa al-nabaṭiyya*) written or translated into Arabic by Ibn Waḥshiyya in 291/904, and purporting to convey the agronomic knowledge of the pre-Arab inhabitants of Iraq. It was followed by a parallel compendium of Greek agronomy, *al-Filāḥa al-rūmiyya*, translated into Arabic from a Greek original. These and other, later, works deal with the different types and qualities of land, with agricultural implements and methods of work, with fertilizers, irrigation, animal and vegetable pests, and with the various problems of planting, tending and reaping crops, including cereals, vegetables, bulbs, fruits and flowers for perfume.[35]

Mining and metallurgy also received some attention. The South Arabian antiquary Ibn al-Ḥā'ik al-Hamdānī (d. 945) devoted a book to gold and silver, including a list of places from which they are obtained, with some information about the mines, and an account of the methods used in mining, smelting and assaying.[36] A thirteenth-century Egyptian mint official, Ibn Baʿra, deals more specifically with the use of gold and silver for coinage. Besides much technical detail, he also offers useful information on monetary matters.[37]

A very rich source of information on economic matters is the vast bureaucratic and administrative literature of medieval Islam. Written by civil servants for civil servants, these works vary from manuals dealing with the working of one office or official to immense encyclopaedias of bureaucratic usage and procedure. A major concern of these writers is of course finance—revenue, financial administration, expenditure. The information they offer is by no means limited to the financial activities of the state. Discussions of tolls and customs dues tell us something about trade and industry; works on the land-tax throw some light on agrarian conditions. To quote one rather striking example, an eleventh-century handbook of mathematics written for the use of tax-assessors in Iraq deals with problems of money, wages, and prices, with trade and manufactures (work in gold, gold thread, fine stuffs) and with both the technical and administrative aspects of irrigation.[38]

[35] On this literature see 'Filāḥa', in *EI*[2] (by various authors), where further references are given.

[36] D. M. Dunlop, 'Sources of gold and silver in Islam according to al-Hamdānī', *Studia Islamica*, viii, 1957, pp. 29–49. See further the materials collected by Ḥamd al-Jāsir in the review *Al-ʿArab* of Riyāḍ, ii, 1399/1968, p. 798 ff.

[37] A. S. Ehrenkreutz, 'Extracts from the technical manual on the Ayyubid mint in Cairo', *Bulletin of the School of Oriental and African Studies*, xv, 1953, pp. 423–47. The Arabic text of Ibn Baʿra's manual was published in Cairo in 1966.

[38] C. Cahen, 'Le service de l'irrigation en Iraq au début du XIe siècle', *Bulletin d'Etudes Orientales*, xiii, 1949–50, pp. 117–43; *idem*, 'Documents relatifs à quelques techniques iraqiennes au début du onzième siècle', in *Ars Islamica*, xv–xvi, 1951, pp. 23–8; *idem* 'Quelques problèmes économiques et fiscaux de l'Irâq Buyide d'après un traité de mathématiques' *Annales de l'Institut des Etudes Orientales*, x, 1952, pp. 326–63.

Taxation and the regulation of commerce also take up much space in another major branch of Muslim literature—that of the law. At one time the jurists were treated with excessive respect, and their statements taken as a sufficient description of the functioning of Muslim institutions. A reaction followed, in the course of which scholars remarked that lawyers in general are concerned with what ought to be rather than with what is, and that Muslim lawyers in particular are inclined to construct ideal systems which may have little to do with the real facts of life. Recent scholars have adopted a more balanced attitude, neither accepting the statements in the law books at face value, nor rejecting them out of hand. Muslim law has not been static; it has undergone a long and complex development. A careful scrutiny of juristic texts can produce valuable information on the changing conditions, pressures and influences to which the jurists were subject.[39] Another body of legal material, of considerable value, is the Jewish Responsa—the answers given by rabbis to questions put to them. Many of these deal with matters of economic interest—disputes arising out of trade, manufacture, employment, partnerships, tenancies, inheritances and the like. The Rabbinic Responsa are very rich for the Ottoman period, and by no means negligible for earlier times.[40]

Most other branches of the scientific and scholarly literature of the area are potentially relevant—military writings, chemistry and physics, religion—especially heresiography and hagiography, geography, even philology. Among the most important are works of narrative history and biography. The value of the chronicles is self-evident. Of special value are the numerous local histories, which frequently record in detail such things as floods, earthquakes, famine and plague, as well as scarcities and gluts, harvests, market prices, and other data of economic interest. Useful information, independent of the Muslim historiographic tradition, may also be found in the chronicles and other literature of the Christian populations under Muslim rule.[41]

Biography offers particular promise and interest. In the biographical appendices to the annals, in the largely biographical local histories, and in the biographical dictionaries arranged by centuries or devoted to certain professions and other groups, Muslim literature offers us a great treasure-house of information for social, cultural and economic history. The possible

[39] A notable example is Professor Schacht's studies on the use of *ḥiyal*, legal devices, to extend the sanction and protection of the law to transactions, such as lending on interest, which are strictly speaking outside it. See J. Schacht, *Introduction to Islamic Law*, Oxford 1964, especially p. 76 ff.; *idem*, 'Ḥiyal' in *EI*². On the special brand of legal writing concerned with the supervision of the markets, see 'Ḥisba' in *EI*².

[40] For an introduction to Jewish Responsa, see S. B. Freehof, *The Responsa Literature*, Philadelphia 1959; bibliography by Boaz Cohen, *Quntres ha-Teshubot*, Budapest 1930.

[41] For an example, see C. Cahen, 'Fiscalité, propriété, antagonismes sociaux en Haute-Mésopotamie au temps des premiers 'Abbasides, d'après Denys de Tell-Mahré', in *Arabica*, i, 1954, pp. 136–52.

contribution of these biographies to narrative history is obvious; less obvious, but far more important, is the cumulative value of these tens of thousands of life-histories, many of them of men of no great individual significance, in building up a picture of the society in which these men were born and educated, lived and died. In recent years, Western historians have made increasing use of the method of prosopography—that is, the approach to the study of historical phenomena through the examination and comparison of as many as possible relevant individual facts concerning as many as possible individual participants. This method, like any other, has its dangers and its limitations. It also has tremendous potentialities, especially for a society like that of Islam, where the mass of available biographical information goes far beyond the customary restricted oligarchies of power and privilege.[42]

Finally, there remains the vast mass of poetry and *belles lettres*, from which the historian can gather and piece together the countless fragments of information that he needs. The poet, in traditional Islamic society, often has an important public function. As panegyrist or satirist, he praises his patron, and abuses his enemies. In a sophisticated and literate society, without mass media, the poet produces versions of events and personalities that are vivid, memorable—and slanted. He is the propagandist, or, as we say now, the public relations officer and image-maker of the ruler. The political function of the poet—and the consequent political relevance of poetry—are well known. The economic uses of poetry are less explored. Two final examples, both from the Arabic Book of Songs (*Kitāb al-Aghānī*) must suffice. An Umayyad governor of Iraq, in the early eighth century, forcibly expropriated a piece of land, needed for the extension of the irrigation system. The famous poet Farazdaq, on behalf of the landowner, composed a poem attacking the governor and accusing him of oppression. The second story also comes from Umayyad times. A merchant went from Kūfa to Medina with a consignment of veils, and sold all but the black ones, which the ladies apparently did not like. He complained to a poet, who obliged him by composing some verses, in which he spoke of 'the beauty in the black veil'. The poem was set to music and sung all over Medina, every lady of refinement (*ẓarīfa*) bought a black veil, and the Iraqi merchant sold his entire stock. Thus, in a dark hour, with a black veil, the singing commercial was born.[43]

[42] On the biographical literature, see Sir Hamilton Gibb, 'Islamic biographical literature', and Ann K. S. Lambton, 'Persian biographical literature', *apud* B. Lewis and P. M. Holt, *Historians of the Middle East*, London 1962, pp. 54–8 and 141–51.

[43] Al-Iṣfahānī, *Kitāb al-Aghānī*, Būlāq, vol. xix, p. 18; third edition, vol. iii, p. 45.

England to Egypt, 1350–1500: Long-term Trends and Long-distance Trade

ROBERT LOPEZ—HARRY MISKIMIN—
ABRAHAM UDOVITCH

THE imaginative announcement of our conference spells a challenge which the writers of this joint paper have taken up boldly. We are asked to suggest leads for future research in what has been properly defined as an underdeveloped area of economic history: it will not be enough to use as working hypotheses such tentative generalizations as may be construed upon a handful of known Middle Eastern facts, unless we borrow concepts and assumptions from some of the more developed historical areas. Without minimizing the variables of geographic, political and cultural milieus, we are entitled to expect that fundamental trends of climate, population, and economic and social organization were not restricted to one of the major regions of Eurasia, but affected them all. At least, we must be prepared to assume that such international trade as may have existed in the Middle East was linked to trade conditions in other areas, and that basic changes in England, Italy, India and China had some repercussions on Middle Eastern commercial trends. With these guidelines in mind, we may explore the overall economic history of Eurasia at a period of accelerated change—namely, the late fourteenth and early fifteenth centuries—and endeavour to outline a general pattern. Clearly, such an undertaking within the scope of a few pages can produce no more than an over-simplified contour map; but while such a map will not tell us all we would like to know, it may add a dimension of knowledge which would be obscured by the immediate and overwhelming reality of minute detail.

I. THE FUNDAMENTAL OVERALL TRENDS

First of all, the fundamental trends. It is now generally agreed that almost everywhere in the Old World a multisecular age of steady economic and demographic growth came to an end in the fourteenth century; the crisis which then occurred was followed in the fifteenth century by a measure of readjustment and recovery, the size of which is a hotly debated question among western economic historians.

No doubt economic growth brings in itself the causes of its own saturation and exhaustion: it needs to be refuelled if the process is to continue indefinitely. Still, the fact that it came to a dead stop some time in the fourteenth century calls for explanations, of which many have been postulated.

It has been observed that a very long period of comparatively warm climate, prevailing over the entire temperate zone of the earth from the ninth to the thirteenth century approximately, was broken by a spell of cold and wet climate, during the fourteenth and fifteenth centuries. The message is written in the annual growth rings of the Californian trees and the tidal marks of the Caspian Sea, documented by the frequent recurrence of solid freezing in the Baltic Sea and the Suwa Lake of Japan, testified by failing harvests and retreating vineyards or corn fields in England and Poland. Farther south, it is true, changes seem to be less dramatic; here, there is no such disaster as the transformation of Greenland into a desert, and indeed increased rains may favour hitherto ill-suited crops, such as rice in the Po valley and sugar in the Greek islands; but excessive precipitations eroded the deforested highlands, and erected bars which prevented the flow of rivers into the sea. We are less informed on the subtropical and tropical regions, but there are indications that the Sahara, India, and perhaps Central America were afflicted by the opposite excess: there was unusual dryness, which caused serious famines, just as the unusual cold unleashed severe dearths in Northern Europe. Hunger also occurred in the middle area, but it was partly offset by the greater facility the ports of the Mediterranean had to import foodstuffs from surplus producing regions. As a matter of fact, there is no change of climate that has adverse effects in every region, but any change is everywhere a disturbing factor until agricultural methods adjust to it.

Malnutrition, in turn, probably diminished the resistance of the population to disease, especially to those illnesses which are normally confined to a restricted endemic area, but under certain circumstances may burst out in world-wide epidemics. The improvement of communication and long-distance travel that went with the prosperity of the thirteenth century made the transmission of disease easier. The Middle Ages tended to confuse all epidemics under a single name, plague; and it is neither possible nor indispensable for our purpose to distinguish the various strains, so long as we note a sudden, major flare-up of contagious disease. After a very long period of comparative immunity, chronologically coinciding with the period of warm climate, the frightful Black Death (mainly bubonic plague, here and there joined by cholera) swept through Asia, Africa and Europe. We can follow its progress step by step, from its incubation in Central Asia around 1338 to its eruption in India, 1342, its entrance in Italy, 1346, its capture of Portugal, 1348, its advance in Africa, 1351, and its conquest of Russia, 1352. Much worse, plague epidemics will hit the whole hemisphere again and again, throughout and beyond the fourteenth and fifteenth centuries. Nor are they the only mass killers; malaria, for many centuries reduced to minor importance rapidly gains ground and virulence as the mosquito-breeding swamps enlarge their surface. Those who are not killed by malaria remain nevertheless severely weakened. There are regions which lose more than half their population between 1350 and 1450: no region is entirely spared.

War, the third great scourge, cannot claim as many victims as famine and disease: medieval man did not have our efficiency in self-destruction. But its effects are particularly harmful for trade, as they make roads unsafe and divert capital and manpower from potential commercial investment. It does not seem necessary to list here the long- and short-range conflicts, from the Hundred Years War in the extreme West to the campaigns of Tamerlane in the centre and the expeditions of Yung-lo in the far East, which made the fourteenth century and, to a slightly lesser extent, the fifteenth especially war-ridden. Internal disorders and brigandage at many places increased the impact of foreign wars, as some of the largest states (Mongolian, Byzantine, Egyptian, French) collapsed and many smaller republics were torn by party struggle. Nevertheless, the unprecedented size of certain campaigns reflected the power and efficiency most governments had acquired by the end of the age of prosperity: in turn, the will to marshal the energies of the entire country in ever larger military efforts pushed fourteenth and fifteenth-century governments further towards relentless authoritarianism. This was not accomplished without opposition on the side of the middle and lower classes; but their resistance weakened at the same time as demographic growth and economic opportunities waned. Gradually, the comparatively open and democratic society of the age of prosperity froze into two widely separated compartments: at the top, the rich and powerful few; at the bottom, the hard pressed and degraded multitude.

It is an ill wind that blows nobody any good. The contraction of profitable agricultural space increased the productivity of what land was still profitable. Survivors of epidemics inherited the goods of the dead and asked for higher compensation for their work. War enriched some people, though investments in war cannot be productive for society at large. Hard times stimulated rational business. All through the fourteenth and fifteenth centuries we hear of desperate need for money and precious metals, of appeals to credit and requests for unbearable taxpayers' sacrifices. There is much complaint that one or another market is closing, that one or another area is ruined. But we also hear of new areas being opened, new mines being exploited, new alleys being found for profitable enterprise. The extravagant expenditure of the few is contrasted with the distressing poverty of the many. All this forms a complicated pattern which cannot be fully understood without coming down to some closer analysis.

We have singled out for special description three major regions and in each region, focussed on one country: England, a hitherto moderately developed area, about which a certain amount of statistical evidence is available to make our deductions fairly precise; Italy, the most developed area in the West, whose rich documentary material has not yet been adequately studied; and Egypt, where any analysis must be in the nature of tentative pioneering. It was our wish to include India and China in our paper as well; but we found it impossible at short notice to persuade a specialist to venture into these wildernesses of medieval economic history. What allusions to the latter countries may be made by the three writers of this joint report (Miskimin, for England; Lopez, for Italy; Udovitch, for Egypt) must be taken as working hypotheses based only on superficial information.

II. ENGLAND AND THE ECONOMY OF NORTH-WESTERN EUROPE

By the beginning of the fourteenth century, there is increasing evidence that the agricultural base of late medieval society had been pushed beyond prudent limits. The statistics for England assembled by Postan and Titow reveal a close correlation between increments in the price of grain and increases in the payment of death fees, and thus, by showing the impact of slight variations in grain production upon the death rate, make explicit the slender nature of the agricultural surplus.[1] More generally, the great European famine of 1315–17, which in some areas destroyed 10 per cent of the population, leaves no doubt at all regarding the fragility of the European agricultural structure in the early fourteenth century.[2] All over Europe, lands considered unsuitable for agriculture for centuries thereafter were pressed into service,[3] and one has the impression that during this period the rural economy was operating under conditions of near boom in which, except for an occasional run of particularly abundant harvests, market conditions greatly favoured the agricultural sector. Such a period of extended good harvests seems to have occurred during the second quarter of the fourteenth century, when grain prices fell to low levels in both France and England during the late 1330's and early 1340's.[4] This decline was only temporary, however, as prices recovered sharply during the late

[1] M. M. Postan and J. Titow, 'Heriots and Prices on Winchester Manors', *The Economic History Review*, 2nd series, xi, 1958–9, pp. 392–411.

[2] H. S. Lucas, 'The Great European Famine of 1315, 1316 and 1317', *Speculum*, v, 1930, pp. 343–77.

[3] W. Abel, *Die Wüstungen des ausgehenden Mittelalters, Ein Beitrag zur Siedlungs- und Agrargeschichte Deutschlands* (Quellen und Forschungen zur Agrargeschichte, I), Jena 1943; G. Duby, *L'Economie rurale et la vie des campagnes dans l'occident médieval*, 2 vols., Paris 1962; B. H. Slicher van Bath, *The Agrarian History of Western Europe, A.D. 500–1850*, London 1963.

[4] H. Miskimin, *Money, Prices, and Foreign Exchange in Fourteenth Century France*, New Haven 1963, p. 74.

'forties; indeed, famine conditions are reported in some areas of France in 1343 and 1344.[5]

By the middle of the fourteenth century then, the population of Europe appears to have been pushing against the vulnerable upper limits of agricultural production; indeed, it seems probable that those limits were themselves falling as a result of the over-exploitation of marginal lands.[6] At this juncture, the situation was sharply reversed; the demographic impact of the Black Death of 1348–9 and the subsequent recurrences of the epidemic to the end of the century converted a soil-hungry Europe into an economy where land was surplus and workers scarce. Labour was no longer available to cultivate the acreage which had been under the plough in the early fourteenth century, while the demand for foodstuffs had fallen sharply as a result of the loss of perhaps one-third of the pre-plague population, thus eliminating the need for the output of much of the formerly cultivated land. The cumulative response to such altered conditions was both rational and direct. Land rents fell, acreage was allowed to revert to forest or waste, wages rose reflecting the enhanced economic value of the worker, and the profits of the agricultural sector were diminished. Since the less productive and desirable land was in all probability allowed to lapse from cultivation first,[7] it seems likely that the average productivity of agricultural labour rose during the post-plague period; the rise in agricultural wages, evident at this time, is an indirect confirmation of this conclusion, as is the well-documented secular decline in grain prices which extends from the 1360's until well into the fifteenth century.[8]

Despite the presence of conditions favourable to an increase in the productivity of farm labour and the strong indications that, for the peasant, the terms of tenure softened while the size of holdings grew, it is far from certain that the agricultural sector was truly more prosperous after the plague. Prices of manufactured and luxury goods rose steeply, in contrast to the moderate decline in grain prices; the cost of agricultural implements in England in the second half of the fourteenth century, for example, was more than double the pre-plague level, and even higher when measured relatively against the sliding grain prices.[9] Confronted by falling prices for

[5] Marie-Josephe Larenaudie, 'Les Famines en Languedoc aux xive et xve siècles', *Annales du Midi*, 1952, pp. 29, 36. Helen Robbins, 'A Comparison of the effects of the Black Death on the Economic Organization of France and England', *Journal of Political Economy*, 36, 1928, p. 453.

[6] M. M. Postan, 'Medieval Agrarian Society in its Prime: England', *Cambridge Economic History of Europe*, vol. i, 2nd ed., Cambridge 1966, pp. 549–632.

[7] Postan, *ibid.*

[8] Slicher van Bath, *The Agrarian History*, pp. 137–44; Miskimin, *Money, Prices*, p. 74; L. Genicot, 'Crisis: From the Middle Ages to Modern Times', *Cambridge Economic History*, vol. i, pp. 679–87.

[9] H. Miskimin, 'Monetary Movements and Market Structure: Forces for Contraction in Fourteenth and Fifteenth Century England', *The Journal of Economic History*, xxiv, 1964, p. 484; Genicot, 'Crisis'.

its major product and by rising costs for the tools of production and other manufactured goods, both for luxury and for necessity, it seems clear that the agricultural sector was in effect experiencing a balance of payments crisis in its relationship with the non-agricultural segment of the late medieval world.[10] There are no adequate figures, but the laws of economics suggest that it is unlikely that urban dwellers would have been induced by lower prices to expand their *per capita* consumption of foodstuffs by a margin large enough to offset the loss of rural revenue caused by the adverse price pattern afflicting agriculture. Some contrary evidence regarding the prices of butter and meat suggests that consumers were enriching and adding more variety to their diet, but such substitution does not appear to have compensated for the loss of revenue from the major crop, grains.[11] As a result it seems probable that gold and silver were now less available to the agricultural sector, and that the towns, favoured by the new price structure, tended to attract the precious metals and to act as magnets drawing bullion into centres of urban concentration.

Now the towns suffered at least as heavily from the Black Death as did the countryside, but they did not experience to so great an extent the compensatory effects of a rise in the average productivity of labour. If anything, the reverse was true. The basic factor of production in medieval industry was the skilled artisan, working with relatively simple tools at tasks which demanded only a minor amount of capital investment. Under these circumstances, the consequence of a massive demographic catastrophe can only have been to reduce the technological competence of the urban population by raising the death rate, and raising it permanently through a series of recurrences, to a level that out-stripped the ordinary capacity of society to train its replacement labour to the old standard. Perhaps the most vivid illustration of this phenomenon may be borrowed from palaeography, where the intensified rate of substitution of one scribe for another during the plague years is directly associated with a deterioration in handwriting during the late fourteenth and early fifteenth centuries.[12] Irregularities multiplied and the old levels of clarity and accuracy were never completely restored. Whereas in agriculture, the use of fewer hands on better, or simply on more, soil, would have increased the average productivity of labour, in the towns the fewer hands lacked training which took years to acquire, while the greater *per capita* quantity of capital goods was not, under the conditions of medieval technology, a significantly strategic

[10] Miskimin, 'Monetary Movements'. I have discussed this question more fully here.

[11] M. M. Postan, 'The Trade of Medieval Europe: The North', *Cambridge Economic History of Europe*, vol. ii, Cambridge 1952, pp. 208–10. Slicher van Bath, *The Agrarian History*, pp. 139–44.

[12] See, for example, the series of wills enrolled in the Court of Hustings in London which provide a continuous witness to handwriting styles over the course of the fourteenth and fifteenth centuries.

element to have much effect on productivity. Productivity growth would have required that the increased capital be associated with considerable technological advance but, at least in the north, evidence for such an advance is simply lacking in the hundred years or so following the initial incidence of the Black Death. Trained labour remained the scarce resource; it could not immediately be replaced by the influx of former farm workers seeking the better living and higher wages of the urban centres.[13] When it takes seven years to train a man, the skill is in the man and not in his tools; what was lost could not be replaced by manpower alone.

Against the background of the scarcity of skilled labour, one must set the psychological impact of the over-riding presence of death and its role in structuring the demand for goods. The initial result of massive depopulation was a dramatic increase in the *per capita* wealth of the survivors; money, durable goods, gold and silver plate and expensive cloth remained to be divided among perhaps one-third fewer people than before. Life was short and uncertain and many people, first touched by luxury in the immediate post-plague period, opted for a higher standard of living, converting their new-found wealth into the joys of this world. In parallel with the simultaneous architectural development, the very style of life appears to have become flamboyant, reflecting at table and in costumes the same denial of constraint that is omnipresent in late Gothic building.[14] Matteo Villani, writing of Florence in 1351, puts the case succinctly: 'No sooner had the plague ceased than . . . since men were few and since by hereditary succession they abounded in earthly goods, they forgot the past as though it had never been and gave themselves up to a more shameful and disordered life than they had led before . . . and the common people by reason of the abundance and superfluity that they found would no longer work at their accustomed trades; they wanted the dearest and most delicate foods . . . while children and common women clad themselves in all the fair and costly garments of the illustrious ladies who had died.'[15] Such evidence of a shift to luxury in the south is reinforced by Boccaccio's introduction to the *Decameron* and by Sacchetti's late fourteenth century description of Italian fashion;[16] in the north, one can find similar comment on excess luxury in Chaucer's *Parson's Tale*: 'Alas! may men nat seen, as in oure dayes, the synful costlewe array of clothynge and namely in to muche superfluite or elles in to desordinat scantesse?'[17] The parson goes on to lament the 'cost

[13] May McKisack, *The Fourteenth Century, 1307–99*, Oxford 1959, p. 340.

[14] E. Panofsky, *Gothic Architecture and Scholasticism*, Cleveland 1961, p. 67.

[15] Quoted in Millard Meiss, *Painting in Florence and Siena after the Black Death*, New York 1964, p. 67.

[16] J. B. Ross and M. M. McLaughlin, *The Portable Medieval Reader*, New York 1950, pp. 169–70.

[17] F. N. Robinson, ed., *The Works of Geoffrey Chaucer*, 2nd ed., Boston 1957, p. 240: 'The Parson's Tale', lines 412–15.

of embrowdynge, the degise endentynge or barrynge, owndynge, palynge, wyndynge or bendynge, and semable wast of clooth in vanitee' and also the 'costlewe furrynge in hir gownes'. More substantial evidence, perhaps, than the testimony of a poet, heard indistinctly through the mouths of his characters, is the direct interest of the governments of France and England in the excess of consumption and luxury. In France, though without effect, Charles VII prohibited the use of cloth of gold, silver, or silk by the bourgeoisie.[18] In England, the Sumptuary Act of 1363 resulted from a petition from the Commons in 1362 asserting that excess consumption was destroying 'the wealth of the kingdom'; the act specifically limited over-indulgence in food and restricted by class the wearing of gold, silver, silk, embroidery, precious stones and furs.[19]

It would surely be an overstatement to assert that the immediate gratification of wordly desires was the primary, or even the most significant, response to pestilence. In many ways the church benefited from the intensification of the uncertainty of this life; a substantial segment of the population became more, not less, devout. Indeed, as in the case of the growing sects of flagellants and Spiritual Franciscans, now the expanding Fraticelli, overzealous piety sometimes challenged the established order within the church itself.[20] Appeals for true poverty, however, were not the only manifestation of religious enthusiasm; gifts to the church grew under a number of influences. The increased death rate automatically raised the level of bequests and testamentary legacies to the church; further, since the plague left many families without direct heirs, it is probable that the average amount of each bequest rose simultaneously with the actual number of bequests. In addition, the church as a major landowner profited in the short run from the sharp rise in the collection of heriots or death fees resultant upon the successive visitations of the plague; in the longer run, of course, the church suffered from the same decrease in agricultural revenues which afflicted other great landholders, but the initial result of the rise in the death rate was a concentration of liquid wealth in the hands of the clergy. What could the church do with these newly acquired funds? Many legacies specified the creation of chantries or were directly limited to consumption expenditures in the form of wax or vestments. In the case of free funds, however, several alternatives were available; funds could be used for construction or the fabric of the church; they could be spent for enhancing the glory of the church through altar decorations, stained glass, chalices, draperies, hangings, tapestries, and other ornamentation of both church and

[18] Francisque-Michel, *Recherches sur le commerce, la fabrication, et l'usage des étoffes de soie, d'or, et d'argent*, vol. ii, Paris 1853, p. 265 n. 2.

[19] F. E. Baldwin, *Sumptuary Legislation and Personal Regulation in England*, Baltimore 1926, pp. 46–51.

[20] Meiss, *Florence and Sienna*, p. 81.

clergy; funds could also be remitted to Rome or, for a time, to Avignon; or they could be hoarded.

Let us now reconsider our initial inquiry, the impact of a rising death rate upon the demand for goods. Both luxury consumption by the non-agricultural population and extensive investments in the ornamentation of churches would have exacerbated the already acute shortage of skilled craftsmen which followed the Black Death by causing a relative increase in the demand for their services. As a result, the wages of skilled artisans were considerably augmented[21] and some of the new demand for luxury, not satisfied domestically, was diverted to areas beyond northern Europe by economic necessity as well as in search of the exotic; the inevitable result of this demand was an increase in the export of money. Further, since the use of scarce labour in the production of domestic luxury proscribes its use for the manufacture of export articles, the potential foreign earnings of the northern economies were reduced.[22] Even in the exceptional and contradictory instance of the growing English cloth industry, the new earnings from the increased sales of cloth were not sufficient to compensate for the revenues lost on raw wool exports which plummeted after the mid-fourteenth century: between 1357 and 1400, the total annual foreign earnings from wool and cloth combined appear to have decreased by about £40,000.[23] The two aspects of luxury consumption, direct export of money for goods and the diversion of labour from the export trades, tended to cause money and bullion to flow from northern Europe. Luxury consumption merged with papal remittances in engendering an outflow of specie while diplomatic transfers, the interest paid to Italians on military loans, and direct military expenditures for such items as Milanese armour can only have reinforced the trend generated by the more purely economic forces at work in the late fourteenth century.

There are, of course, no surviving figures to enable us to calculate international payments accounts or to measure directly the flow of bullion in the fourteenth century, but there are several kinds of circumstantial evidence which, taken together, validate the hypothesis of a bullion drain from northern Europe. In the case of England, for example, we know that the silver mines had been exhausted by the early fourteenth century and that the chief source of new metal for the royal mints was imported foreign money, resmelted and struck into English coin.[24] Coinage figures, therefore,

[21] E. F. Jacob, *The Fifteenth Century, 1399–1485*, Oxford 1961, pp. 380–3; E. H. Phelps-Brown and Sheila V. Hopkins, 'Seven Centuries of Building Wages', *Economica*, 22, 1955; Genicot, 'Crisis', p. 689.

[22] See R. S. Lopez and H. A. Miskimin, 'The Economic Depression of the Renaissance', *The Economic History Review*, 2nd series, xiv, 1962, Graph V, p. 421 for statistical material on the decrease in foreign trade.

[23] Miskimin, 'Monetary Movements', p. 489.

[24] C. G. Crump and C. Johnson, 'Tables of Bullion Coined under Edward I, II, III', *The Numismatic Chronicle*, 4th series, xiii, 1913, pp. 200–45.

provide a guide to the balance of payments and it seems reasonable to interpret the tremendous decline in English mint output during the hundred years following the year 1362 as a clear sign of an unfavourable balance of payments; contemporary comments and complaints about the dearth of money certainly support this view.[25] In France, one may trace the same pattern of declining mint outputs during the late fourteenth and early fifteenth centuries,[26] while even a cursory survey of the *Ordonnances* of the French kings, couched in arcane language though they be, reveals a very pronounced shortage of bullion at the mints and consequently a shortage of coined money.[27] Similar problems appear in Flanders and Burgundy in the later fourteenth century.

Money, then, was in short supply throughout north western Europe in the hundred years following the plague, but where had it gone? I have already mentioned the church as one prominent route through which money was channelled away from the north. Direct reaction to this drain occurred in England in 1366 when Edward III at once prohibited the collection of Peter's Pence and the transfer of these revenues abroad; at a London monetary conference in 1381, John Hoo recommended that the papal collector be English and that ecclesiastical revenues be transferred only in the form of English goods; similar expressions of covetous national interest in clerical remittances may be found in English petitions and ordinances in 1376, 1384, 1399, 1409 and 1433.[28] In France, comparable complaint is widespread, but the most direct statement appears in the remonstrance which the Parlement issued against the royal edict of 27 November, 1461, abrogating the Pragmatic Sanction.[29] Here may be found an itemized statement of the present outflow of church funds, 300,000 *écus* per year, and the potential export of money, 2,800,000 *écus* per year, which would result from the abrogation of the Pragmatic Sanction. In Spain, between 1454 and 1458, the papal tenth amounted to two million marks; the period was referred to by contemporaries as the *evacuación de oro*.[30] It would appear to be no accident that the Rome branch of the Medici produced over 50 per cent of the total revenues of the bank during the early fifteenth century;[31]

[25] Miskimin, 'Monetary Movements'. During the period 1363–1464, the annual average English silver coinage drops to only 3·8 per cent of the level maintained in the period 1273–1322.

[26] Miskimin, *Money, Prices*, pp. 106–8.

[27] *Ordonnances des rois de France de la troisieme race recueillies par ordre chronologique*, Paris (Imprimerie Royale), vols. iii–xv.

[28] R. Ruding, *Annals of the Coinage of Britain and its Dependencies*, vol. ii, 2nd ed., London 1819, pp. 205, 210–11, 233, 236, 251, 271, 333.

[29] *Ordonnances des rois de France*, vol. xv, pp. 195–207.

[30] J. Vicens-Vives, *Historia social y económica de España y América*, vol. ii, Barcelona 1957, p. 91.

[31] R. de Roover, *The Rise and Decline of the Medici Bank, 1397–1494*, Cambridge 1963, p. 202.

the papacy was indeed a major drain on the metal supply of northern Europe.

In addition to direct transfers of money, however, the more conventional channels of commerce tended, through the medium of luxury consumption, to produce the same result; money left the north in search of goods, both the necessary and the exotic. Here again the Church made its presence felt. One of the more usual bequests made to the church in England was the assignment of a fixed portion of some income or rent for the purchase of candles or wax. Wax for ceremonial purposes had to be beeswax and this commodity was the speciality of the northern countries of the Hanseatic League; wax exports to Bruges from Livonia alone were worth 727 marks in 1356, a record figure reflecting the increased use of wax following the Black Death of 1348–9.[32] Of even greater monetary importance than the wax trade, the vastly increased consumption of fur during the fourteenth and fifteenth centuries greatly expanded one side of the trade between north-western and north-eastern Europe. By the time of Henry IV, ermine was in general use among the English nobility,[33] and at 14 ducats per hundred the skins of these animals were a substantial expenditure of the decreasing English monetary reserves, though not so grand in unit price as sable at 82 ducats or marten at 30 ducats per hundred.[34] The use of fur was not limited to the nobility, however; as an example of the scale of this trade, it is worth noting that in the year 1405, 450,000 pieces of fur worth 3,300 *livres gros* were exported from Riga to Bruges; the same ships carried 1,435 *livres gros* worth of wax.[35] It is no wonder, given a change in fashion favouring fur and a probable increase in the consumption of wax, that the English parliament in 1378–9 connected the import of fur with the acute monetary shortage and that, in 1381 at a monetary inquest, Richard Leyc blamed the excessive use of grocery and fur for the same phenomenon.[36]

Now if money was being exported toward the Hanse area, it is surprising that there is little comment upon its abundance in that region; indeed, there is a monetary shortage, parallel to that of Western Europe, in the period shortly after the Black Death.[37] Significantly, however, evidence from the Hanse towns also reveals a propensity for increased luxury consumption, and perhaps it is this factor which balances the increased inflow of money seeking the northern goods of fur, wax, amber, butter and other expensive commodities against an increased outflow of money in search of the Mediterranean luxuries carried over the north–south overland route, a commerce historically documented if statistically obscure. This pattern could explain the distrust of the Italians expressed by Hanseatic merchants

[32] P. Dollinger, *La Hanse: xiie–xviie siècles*, Paris 1964, p. 211.

[33] H. Norris, *Costume and Fashion*, London 1927, vol. ii, pp. 282–3.

[34] Dollinger, *La Hanse*, p. 291.

[35] *Ibid.*, p. 292.

[36] Ruding, *Annals*, vol. ii, pp. 220, 228.

[37] Dollinger, *La Hanse*, p. 83.

in 1397 and 1412; in the latter year, the Diet at Lunebourg prohibited further commercial activity by the Italians.[38] Despite such regulation, there was an increase in the commerce between the Hanse and the Nuremburg–Frankfurt–Mediterranean trading complex during the fourteenth and fifteenth centuries.[39] The hypothesis that this route drained precious metals southward from the Hanse is supported by a document of 1405 in which the merchants of Lübeck protest the sale of Mediterranean goods by the merchants of Nuremburg: 'they sell all kinds of articles . . . thread and silk, articles from Frankfurt as well as Venice . . . they also sell pearls and gold by the ounce . . . they sell more in one day than your merchants and bourgeois in a year.'[40] The continental termini of this north–south route were Milan, Genoa and Venice; even allowing for some provincial hyperbole, it would seem that there was an active and probably one-sided trade connecting the northern economy with the southern in such a way as to drain precious metals southward.

The taste for southern luxuries was not limited to the towns which comprised the Hanseatic League, however: the same desire for the exotic was apparently endemic to north-western Europe. The most obvious manifestation of this taste for luxury and display was the wearing of silk; the price of one ounce of fine black silk in London in 1419 was 2*s* 10*d*, roughly the equivalent to the wages earned by a London mason for six days' labour.[41] The use of silk was spreading rapidly during the fourteenth century and accelerated in the hundred-year period after the Black Death; the number of artisans in London connected with this trade increased correspondingly during the fifteenth century.[42] Further evidence of the taste for exotic imported goods may be found in the £5,650 cargo which a Venetian galley reported in London in 1421; it contained pepper, ginger, saffron, mace, cinnamon, rhubarb, silk, velvet, some of it embroidered with gold, damask, tartarine, and other luxuries.[43] The English parliament was not unaware of the impact of such consumption on the balance of payments; they requested import prohibitions against cloth of gold, silk, handkerchiefs, precious stones, and jewels, all Mediterranean in origin.[44] Richard Leyc did not neglect grocery, ivory and precious stones in his analysis of the outflow of bullion given at the monetary inquest of 1381.[45] He might also have added the expenditure, almost certainly intensified by the Hundred Years War, for the costly Milanese armour generally evident in medieval inventories.[46]

[38] Dollinger, *La Hanse*, pp. 238–9.
[39] *Ibid.*, pp. 279–83.
[40] Quoted in Dollinger, *La Hanse*, p. 513.
[41] M. K. Dale, 'The London Silkwomen of the Fifteenth Century', *The Economic History Review*, 1st series, iv, 1932–4, p. 330.
[42] *Ibid.*, p. 324.
[43] L. F. Salzman, *English Trade in the Middle Ages*, Oxford 1931, p. 422.
[44] Ruding, *Annals*, vol. ii, p. 220.
[45] *Ibid.*, p. 228.
[46] Salzman, *English Trade*, pp. 434–5.

In France, also, we find a widespread increase in the consumption of southern luxuries during the late fourteenth and early fifteenth centuries. From the fourteenth century on, French kings express distress over the export of gold in return for the luxury cloths, brocades and velvets sold by the Italians at Lyons and Champagne.[47] On 15 December, 1466, an edict of the well-informed Louis XI establishing the silk industry in France, directly, and I think rightly, connects the importation of cloth of gold and silk with a very large outflow of bullion from the kingdom.[48] Cloth, however, was but one among many imported luxuries and a short list of the desirable articles one might buy during this period would have to include the newly fashionable bracelets decorated with pearls,[49] Venetian buttons also ornamented with pearls,[50] diadems, one of which boasted 48 pearls and 33 diamonds,[51] book latches garnished with pearls and rubies from Alexandria,[52] and purses decorated with gold buttons from Cyprus and further graced by silk pendants.[53] In addition, ivory combs and mirror cases, delicately engraved in intaglio, became very popular during the later fourteenth and early fifteenth centuries.[54] By the end of the Middle Ages, Turkish camelot cloth was reportedly so widely available that its use was general even among the common people.[55]

The list of luxury cloths, ivories, jewels and spices could be multiplied almost endlessly during this period, while the range of goods could be greatly extended through the inclusion of such items as fruit, perfume, decorative coral and Turkish cotton. In the absence of more tangible statistical material, however, the value of such a catalogue lies chiefly in the impressionistic overview, thus afforded, of the massive influx into northern Europe of the high-priced, easily transported goods of Italy and the East. The evidence for an increase in the conspicuous consumption by northerners of Mediterranean foods is beyond dispute; so too is the evidence of monetary scarcity in the northern economy. The connection between the two is apparent and the causative mechanism creating the monetary shortage, northern money seeking southern goods, is not obscure despite the possible existence of certain leakages such as domestic hoarding or the retention of some of the exported money by the fur producing regions of north-eastern Europe. With due allowance for these minor complications, however, it seems clear that the increase in luxury consumption conjoined with altered political and religious influences to produce a massive export

[47] L. Boulnois, *La Route de la soie*, Paris 1963, p. 246.

[48] J. M. Comby, *Les Doctrines interventionistes en politique commerciale du XVe au XIXe siècle*, Paris 1930, p. 47.

[49] Henry-Rene d'Allemagne, *Les Accessoires du costume et du mobilier*, 3 vols., Paris 1928, vol. i, pp. 31–2.

[50] *Ibid.*, p. 56. [51] *Ibid.*, p. 68. [52] *Ibid.*, p. 107.

[53] *Ibid.*, p. 108. [54] *Ibid.*, vol. iii, p. 465.

[55] Francisque-Michel, *Recherches sur le commerce, la fabrication, et l'usage des étoffes de soie*, 2 vols., Paris 1852-4, vol. ii, p. 46.

of precious metals from north-western to southern Europe and the eastern Mediterranean. Northern coinage figures, where they exist, invariably reveal decreasing outputs in the century following the Black Death, while complaints regarding the scarcity of money rise in inverse proportion to declining bullion outputs.[56] All the evidence points to a drain of bullion toward Italy and the south, even the very bullionist legislation designed to end the overflow; the drain is not stopped by such legislation but the complicated measures for the evasion of the laws serve to point up the general nature of the problem. In England in 1409, an ordinance was passed to prevent the Italians from smuggling precious metals, concealed in shipments of other goods, out of the country;[57] in the first half of the fifteenth century, Bernardo Portinari, the Medici factor at Bruges, was employing this device to fulfil his obligation to transfer specie to the Italian home office.[58] Italians of this period appear to have valued northern money rather than northern goods and the Florentine galleys of 1466 do not appear to have been atypical; as a return cargo from the north-west, they carried a small quantity of wool, cloth, tin and lead and great a quantity of gold bullion, worth 40,000 ducats.[59]

As the fifteenth century progressed, the north became increasingly impoverished; trade figures declined and the economic troubles of the Renaissance worsened, but in the early stages of the slump, the concentration of wealth in the hands of a few had enabled the prodigal northerners to deceive themselves in the belief that their temporary and inherited affluence was a new and permanent order. It was the Italian merchant who first benefited from the extravagance of the northerner; it is only appropriate to yield the task of continuing the story of the travels of the lost northern wealth to an Italian historian.

III. ITALY

The extreme geographic diversity and political fragmentation of the Italian scene contrasts with the comparative uniformity of the English scene and leaves little room for generalizations. Still it seems safe to state that during the age of prosperity Italy became the most densely populated, urbanized and economically developed country in Europe, and on the whole maintained these characteristics throughout the age of crisis, although it was deeply scarred by the long-run adverse conjuncture.

The basic trends in agriculture were not unlike those of England, but

[56] Miskimin, 'Monetary Movements', *passim*.

[57] Ruding, *Annals*, vol. ii, p. 271.

[58] R. de Roover, 'La Balance commerciale entre les Pays-Bas et l'Italie au quinzième siècle', *Revue Belge de philologie et d'histoire*, 37, 1959, p. 384.

[59] R. de Roover, *The Rise and Decline of the Medici Bank, 1397–1494*, Cambridge, Mass., 1963, p. 150.

change was altogether slower and smoother.[60] While the demographic tide was mounting, pressure on the rural areas had been partly relieved by Italy's ampler opportunities for industrial and commercial employment. When it receded, the diminished pull of urban life to some extent offset the decline of agricultural manpower.[61] Deforestation had been the most serious consequence of land hunger, combined with the heavy demand for fuel and construction materials in an advanced economy. By the fourteenth century, it had brought about considerable erosion and silting of rivers; it also hampered the efforts at supplementing with leaves the fodder of Italy's inadequate meadows. Governments and economic writers expressed growing alarm at continuing deforestation, especially in the fifteenth century, but little was done to combat it, apart from planting live fences and increasing the number of vineyards and fruit orchards on painstakingly-built terraces.

At this point it is necessary to stress the already pronounced opposition between the North (chiefly the Po and Arno valleys), which was rainier, flatter and richer in commercial and industrial equipment, and the drier, stonier and more predominantly agricultural South. The latter region on the whole reacted to the fourteenth and fifteenth century crisis in a fashion more like that of England (or Spain, for that matter): certain villages were abandoned, and farming yielded to sheep raising (often by the wasteful method of transhumance, as the unpropitious soil and climate seemed to require) on wide stretches of inferior and not-so-inferior land. Only the more fertile parts of Sicily, Campania and Apulia kept producing grain, wine, oil and other crops for export. In the North, on the contrary, agriculture held its ground. Here and there, as in the Pistoia region, the highlands lost many inhabitants, but in the nearby Lucca highlands the intensive culture of chestnuts supported the population satisfactorily. The wet lowlands of Lombardy and Emilia reached a new peak of prosperity, at the very time the lower Arno valley became malaria-ridden. The word was getting round that average profits in agriculture would be higher and,

[60] P. J. Jones' essay in the new edition of the *Cambridge Economic History*, vol. i, and, still more, his Italian language survey in *Rivista Storica Italiana*, lxxvi, 1964, offer the best panorama of Italian agricultural history of the Middle Ages that one can build on such spotty and uneven preparatory studies as we now have; the Italian paper contains full bibliographical references. Among later works two excellent town-and-country monographs stand out: M. Berengo, *Nobili e mercanti nella Lucca del Cinquecento*, Turin 1965 (focusing on the sixteenth century, but with abundant references to the earlier period), and D. Herlihy, *Medieval and Renaissance Pistoia, 1200–1430*, New Haven, Conn., 1967.

[61] Here and hereafter, one can hardly overstress the necessity of disregarding very sharp deviations from the average, even within a small region, if one wishes to reach any kind of generalization: see, for instance, in C. Klapisch-Zuber and J. Day, 'Villages désertés en Italie', in the cooperative work *Villages désertés et histoire economique*, Paris 1965, both the opposite impact of the demographic crisis on the ratio between city and district population in such adjacent city-states as San Gimignano and Volterra (p. 438 n. 1), and the conclusion that, all told, there were relatively few deserted villages in Italy.

above all, safer than those of investments in commerce at a time when commercial risks were rising steeply. Modern historians disagree as to the size and significance of the reversion of commercial capital to agriculture during the fourteenth and fifteenth centuries; but it is certain that some reversion occurred, and that in many instances it resulted in increased productivity through technological improvement, especially in regard to terracing, irrigation, agricultural tools, and the introduction of more rewarding plants.

What matters most for the purpose of the present paper is the widespread conversion of subsistence farming and ordinary foodstuffs into specialized cultures for export. Lombardy increased the acreage of woad, largely destined for England; Abruzzo introduced saffron, mainly sold to German merchants; Liguria raised expensive oranges for the Northern rich; even Sicily tried its luck with sugar for the international market. Some other shifts in crops were mainly intended for the internal market, but reduced the need for imports: the diffusion of rice advantageously replaced much foreign grain; that of the mulberry tree supplied silk in lieu of, or in addition to Oriental silk; domestic wool could not fill the gap created by dwindling imports of the best English and Spanish wools, but competed with inferior French and African ones.

Granted that agriculture even in Italy was the occupation of an overwhelming majority, it was commerce, industry and finance that made Italy great.[62] They were probably the largest components of what we would call today her gross national product (since a great proportion of her farming was for subsistence), and certainly the chief sources of precious metals (since mines were negligible and deficits in certain basic agricultural staples offset surpluses in a few specialized sectors). And it is obvious that the crisis of the fourteenth century hit Italy doubly, because the reduced production and consumption of the internal market was compounded with the reduced demand and supply of foreign countries trading with her. Indeed, direct contact with some countries was at times almost entirely cut off: the collapse of the Mongol states barred China, then Central Asia, then Persia (and made communication with India harder); the Turkish advance hindered trade with what had been the Byzantine Empire; the Hundred Years War made parts of France inaccessible.[63]

[62] On the comparative importance of non-agricultural occupations see, for instance, the most recent general survey by the founding father of the Italian school of economic historians, Gino Luzzatto, *An Economic History of Italy from the Fall of the Roman Empire to the Beginning of the Sixteenth Century*, London and New York 1961. Surveys of trade and finance can also be found in two chapters, by R. S. Lopez and R. de Roover, in the *Cambridge Economic History*, vol. ii (soon to appear in a revised edition) and vol. iii; both contain bibliographies.

[63] The most recent, imaginative attempt at bringing together all aspects of the world-wide crisis of the fourteenth and fifteenth centuries is that of J. Glénisson, *Les découvertes*, Paris 1966.

How can we measure the effects of these and other adverse circumstances, while lacking preparatory studies on prices, wages, production, consumption and exchanges in each of the independent city-states that made medieval Italy as economically diversified as Europe is today? If both the total and the *per capita* volume of trade are directly related to the fall of the population during the mid-fourteenth century and its near-stabilization at a much lower level some time in the fifteenth, we would expect a sharp contraction followed by a long stagnation. This seems to be, in the main, what happened; but the pattern is blurred by innumerable local variables and blunted by all kinds of partially compensating elements. Above all, the Italian business men could draw on capital and experience accumulated during the age of prosperity; they showed themselves resilient enough to adjust their methods, modify their production and shift their markets to catch any favourable prospect.

Credit, both local and international, played in the Italian economy a far larger part than in that of north-western Europe. It was a great calamity that the last decades before the Black Death were marked by the successive failures of the most powerful Sienese and Florentine banks. Confiscations, royal insolvency, and defaults of north European debtors were largely responsible for the crash. In a growing economy, which had not accepted the possibility of limited liability, bank failures through overextension were frequent accidents, promptly offset by the growth of new banks. The outbreak of depression did not alter the general propensity to resort to credit when dealing with reliable parties, but retarded the incipient development of informal bills and endorsement, accelerated the drift of private capital towards conservative investments and the ever-hungry funded public debt, and prevented the formation of financial giants. Commercial interest rates, which had been considerably lowered in the last years of prosperity, remained too low, in the face of increasing risks, to prove very attractive. Not before the fifteenth century was there again in Italy an oversize bank, that of the Medici, whose capital, however, was slightly inferior to that of any one of the three major Florentine banks of the early 1400's (Bardi, Peruzzi, Acciaioli).[64]

The bearishness of credit placed a greater burden on cash payments, and these overtaxed transalpine sources. We have seen that England and France complained bitterly about the drain of their precious metals by Italy, but this was largely the counterpart of the drain from Italy into the Levant. At the initial period of the crisis, it was mainly silver that was absorbed by

[64] R. de Roover's studies on the Medici Bank, culminating in his *The Rise and Decline of the Medici Bank*, Cambridge, Mass., 1963, bring out most clearly this point which had been missed in the *Cambridge Economic History*, vol. ii, pp. 344–5, written when the capital data of the Medici bank were not available. Of equal importance, for the fourteenth-century banks, are the collected papers of A. Sapori, *Studi di storia economica*, 3 vols., Florence 1955–67.

Egypt and the western Mongol Khanates of Persia and the Golden Horde, where its value in terms of gold was higher than in Europe. The pull was so strong that around 1350, in spite of the *per capita* increase of coinage owing to the Black Death, the shortage of silver coins aroused alarm in Milan, Bologna, Florence and Lucca simultaneously. Then, as the post-plague inflated wages and spending sprees gave way to a long depression, the shortage eased; with the help of increased silver production in the Bohemian and Yugoslavian mines, most Italian states almost stabilized the weight and alloy of their petty coinage, which had been sinking ever since the beginning of the age of prosperity in the tenth century. The decline of the denier, however, resumed in the fifteenth century, for a variety of reasons among which the relentless growth of war expenditure by the Italian states may well have been the decisive one.[65]

No matter how hard pressed by economic and financial inflationary or deflationary urges, all governments of Italy felt committed to the preservation of a basic monetary standard: accordingly, the principal gold coin (florin, ducat, or the like) underwent very few and fleeting alterations ever since the first issuance of gold moneys in Genoa and Florence in 1252. Yet, in spite of gold imports from north-western Europe, a moderate production of central European mines, and more substantial amounts coming from Senegal, there are abundant indications that the supply of gold was at best barely adequate and often scarce. Granted that man's gold hunger is chronically insatiable, it is certain that trade with the Levant in the fourteenth and fifteenth centuries drained from Italy an ever growing amount of gold. No doubt Florence usually relieved the imbalance by pushing her cloth, Genoa did the same by selling slaves from the Black Sea and the Balkans, and Venice sold glass, timber and metals (especially copper); but these and other compensating factors became less adequate as time went on. Venice, which during that period outdistanced Genoa to become the paramount middleman of Europe in the Near East, was the principal pipeline for outgoing gold. Virtually every Venetian ship sailing to Egypt and Syria carried hard cash besides Western commodities, and by 1498 we hear of 200,000 ducats taken to Alexandria and 100,000 to Beirut by her merchantmen of that year. The year may have been exceptional, but only the need to export a substantial proportion of its output can explain why around 1423 the Venetian mint found it necessary to strike 1,200,000 ducats a year, whereas the Florentine mint shortly before the Black Death

[65] See especially C. M. Cipolla, *Studi di Storia della moneta*, Pavia 1948, and *Le avventure della lira*, Milan 1958, where he tones down to some extent the challenging but somewhat one-sided statements of his earlier book. On mining, J. U. Nef's chapter in the *Cambridge Economic History*, vol. ii, is still the best general view, but Yugoslavia's production is almost entirely overlooked; see, for instance, D. Kovačević, 'Dans la Serbie et la Bosnie medievales: les mines d'or et d'argent', in *Annales* (*Economies, Sociétés, Civilisations*), xv, 1960.

used to strike no more than 400,000 florins and the Genoese mint in 1355 struck 252,916 genoins exactly. This must have offset the inflow of gold, ultimately derived from northern Europe, and coming to Venice chiefly through Milan and other Italian centres.[66]

Inasmuch as the demographic trend between 1350 and 1500 spelled contraction and stagnation, the glitter of gold coming in from the North and flowing out through the South (and, no doubt, leaking all the while into Italian hands) might give the historians of Italy the impression of witnessing either a massive increase of *per capita* wealth in that country or a massive decrease of the purchasing power of the precious metal. Such an impression, in my opinion, would be wrong. What little we know about prices does not indicate any sharp rise—at any rate, not sharp enough to offset the diminution of people among whom the existing monetary stock and the continuing production of mines had to be divided. It would be much harder to calculate *per capita* wealth, and even if we could, the general average means little if it is not broken down according to classes and individuals. We know that in Venice, in 1379, no more than 2,128 heads of household (out of a total population of well over 100,000 inhabitants) had the minimum taxable capital of 300 pounds *a grossi*, while 31 of them had more than 20,000; in Florence, besides the small number of opulent families, were the more than two-thirds of the taxpayers who in 1399 paid taxes of less than one florin, or the 3,000 *miserabili* whose incomes in 1428 were too small to tax. These, and other figures from smaller towns, reflect a most unequal distribution of wealth. That inequality was greater than in the age of prosperity cannot be statistically proved, since we have hardly any figures for that period; but complaints on unemployment, stiffer requirements for admission to guilds, and the whole pattern of political evolution from comparatively open and democratic governments to frozen oligarchies and dictatorships, point that way. However, any conclusions we might be tempted to draw would depend on our own economic assumptions, since some people maintain that equal distribution constitutes an optimum for economic growth, whereas others argue that inequality is the mainspring of capitalistic progress.[67]

[66] H. Quiring, *Geschichte des Goldes* (Stuttgart 1948) is the most recent round-up of problems concerning gold; but it is of modest value, and its figures are based on inadequate and often questionable documentation. One still has to piece together the main trends from innumerable partial studies, some of which are quoted and discussed in R. S. Lopez, *Il ritorno all'oro nell'Occidente duecentesco*, Naples 1955 (the English summary, entitled 'Back to Gold, 1252', in *Economic History Review*, 1956, lacks the bibliographic references and most of the broader background). In particular, the Venetian mint output is quoted after Marin Sanudo's account of Doge Tomaso Mocenigo's financial report; the Florentine output, after Giovanni Villani, a contemporary chronicler; only the Genoese output is directly derived from the records of the mint.

[67] Unfortunately, there has been no attempt at gathering a systematic and critical series of prices in Italy over a long period; it would be imprudent to rely on the data of a pioneer

We are on safer ground if we pursue overall trends of production and trade, although the differences between one city and another forbid hasty generalizations. Let us take the 'big four' of medieval Italy, two seaports and two inland towns: Milan, Florence, Venice and Genoa. For the latter, we may use as a rough indication of the value of her sea trade the price paid by tax farmers who collected the main duty on incoming and outgoing goods. It had already significantly declined in the early fourteenth century; still if we quote to 100 the already reduced price paid in 1334, shortly before the Black Death, we see that it was more or less sustained until 1420, but fell below 50 in the mid- and late fifteenth century. A much sharper decline is indicated by taxes in the Genoese colony of Constantinople-Pera, from 100 in 1334 to 10 in 1423. As a matter of fact, Genoa made great and, on the whole, successful attempts at compensating for contracting markets in the Levant and Inner Asia by transferring a growing proportion of her investments to safer, if more underdeveloped regions of Europe, such as the Iberian peninsula, Hungary and Poland; but the total loss of her holdings in the Byzantine territory and the Black Sea could not be promptly absorbed. Florence, as we have seen, made only a slow and incomplete recovery in the financial field; the decline of what had been her major industry, cloth, is illustrated by the fact that, whereas before the Black Death her production had averaged 70,000–80,000 pieces yearly, in 1375 her wool workers vainly strove to force the masters of the craft to pledge a yearly production of 25,000 pieces. The steady but moderate progress of the silk industry and the relatively short ascendance of the Medici bank offered no more than partial compensation. Milan, for which no general figures of any kind are available, may have escaped the worst effects of the crisis thanks to a more active exploitation of her fertile agricultural district, and above all, through a boom of her famed armourers in times of great wars. It is impossible to measure economic trends in Venice, which persisted in betting on the old Levant routes while expanding on the Italian mainland; but her great historian, Gino Luzzatto, definitely states that she never recovered the prosperity she knew before the mid-fourteenth century.[68]

work by L. Cibrario, *Della economia politica del Medio Evo*, Turin 1839, and while there are some indications of rising prices in the fifteenth century, no proof of a sharp fall in the purchasing power of precious metals has so far been brought to light. See lately the debate Lopez–Miskimin–Cipolla in *Economic History Review*, xiv, 1962, and xvi, 1964, and compare the cautious remarks of Luzzatto, *An Economic History of Italy*, p. 129 ff. On the distribution of wealth, the few examples quoted in the *Cambridge Economic History*, vol. ii, p. 345, could easily be corroborated by similar ones culled from histories of municipal finances, of which there are a large number.

[68] On fifteenth-century Genoa there is a very thorough study by J. Heers, *Gênes au XVe siècle*, Paris 1961, but the fourteenth century is almost unexplored; see the short survey of R. S. Lopez, 'Market Expansion: The Case of Genoa', *Journal of Economic History*, xxix, 1964. The economic history of Florence, 1350–1500, is being renovated by

All local differences notwithstanding, it is possible to single out three general tendencies, which will make our remarks on money and precious metals more meaningful in terms of Asian trade.[69] First of all, a large proportion of the commercial profits still being made in Italy were sunk in war expenditure. Suffice it to consider that between 1377 and 1381 Venice took from her citizens, through compulsory loans, 107 per cent of their assessed fortune; between 1431 and 1441, she took another 288 per cent; nor were these the only contributions. Since the assessed value was approximately one-fourth of the actual value of taxpayers' assets, this means that the public debt swallowed more than one-fourth, then more than two-thirds of Venetian wealth. Even though part of the loans was eventually reimbursed while the remainder bore a modest interest, the sudden, recurrent withdrawal of such staggering sums must have harmed considerably all trades except the war trades.

Secondly, persistent economic inequality and the physical contraction of the market increased the already existing drift towards production of, and commerce in, luxury goods for a small elite. No doubt it is a common characteristic of all ages before the Industrial Revolution that business men and craftsmen find it more rewarding to strive for high profits from a small number of expensive goods than for low profits from a large volume of inexpensive ones. During the age of prosperity, however, the rising purchasing power of the lower classes had shortened the gap between luxuries for the few and necessities for the many. Not all gains in the general living standard were lost during the age of crisis, although it became necessary to lower the cost and quality of wares for mass consumption. Even the poorest Italians, for instance, had grown accustomed to wearing shop-made woollens instead of the skins and the homespun cloth that prevailed in the early Middle Ages. It is for their needs that sheep were raised in the central Italian mountains, cotton was imported from Syria, and workers of such smaller towns as Cremona and Pontremoli toiled at their looms. But luxury industries skimmed the best remaining opportunities of a generally contracting or stagnating business world.

---

a series of studies (mostly centring on social developments) by Sapori, Melis, Becker, Brucker, Martines and others too numerous for quoting; most of them, and the earlier bibliography, are listed in de Roover, *Medici Bank.* Milan is far less fortunate, but the main lines are sketched in Carlo M. Cipolla, 'L'economia milanese, 1350–1500', *Storia de Milano,* vol. viii, Milan 1962, which also supplies the meagre bibliography of the subject. Venice alone, among Italy's 'big four', is dealt with in a full, all-embracing book: G. Luzzatto, *Storia economica di Venezia dall'XI al XVI secolo*, Venice 1961, which ought to be supplemented by *Studi di storia economica veneziana* by the same author (Padua 1954). Another important collection of essays is that of F. C. Lane, *Venice and History*, Baltimore 1966.

[69] At this point it becomes impossible for this brief report to offer even the most elementary bibliography; we can only refer to the bibliographies of the general histories quoted at n. 62.

The refinement of the Italian Renaissance is too well known to require a long description. It reflected the growing sophistication of rich men who, more often than not, had not made but inherited their fortune; for the age of crisis was more successful in preserving the wealth of the wealthy than in offering enrichment to hard-working newcomers. There is the typical example of a Giovanni Rucellai, the descendant of a long line of wool traders and one of the first art collectors in Florence, who decided to withdraw from active business, for, he said, he got greater satisfaction from spending money than from gathering it. Even when it did not reflect a shift from active to contemplative life, luxury trade absorbed money and manpower which might have yielded greater results in the production of capital goods. It caused the silk industry to outstrip the once flourishing woollen industry, brocades to displace plain silk (and, in some instances, foreign tapestry to displace silk hangings), gold thread to be woven into dresses, costly jewellery and artistic furniture to become major components of Italian production and commerce. It also covered the tables of the upper bourgeoisie with all kinds of outlandish and expensive food and drink. Yet it is unlikely that the stress on conspicuous consumption led to an absolute gain in the output of luxury goods as compared to the age of prosperity. Though the silk trade relatively gained ground, Lucca, the major producer up to the fourteenth century, never equalled the production figures attained before the Black Death; Bologna, the second largest producer, complained of tightening opportunities and unrewarding prices as early as 1343. And though Genoa rose to prominence in the silk industry, increased her exports of the most expensive grades of alum for dyers, and sold oranges to northern customers at exorbitant prices, she could not prevent the total value of her sea trade from going down.

Luxury trade did not, of course, cater only for the Italian internal market, it probably became Italy's chief winner of gold and silver from northwestern Europe, although it also afforded new gains to Flemish painters and tapestry weavers and Hanse furriers who supplied the Italian rich. But the comparative ascendancy of luxury trade made Italy more dependent on the Levant and increased the drain of precious metals in that direction. This is the third general tendency which we wish to stress on account of its relevance to the economic history of Asia. Throughout the Middle Ages, European imports from the Orient had consisted mainly of luxuries, whereas European exports included a much larger proportion of cheap and bulky goods. Moreover, the military and economic developments of the fourteenth and fifteenth centuries augmented the cost of Oriental luxuries. Before the fall of the Mongol Empire, it had been possible for an enterprising Genoese to buy Chinese silk directly in Peking at the low price of eight *solidi* a pound (one-third of the price it would fetch in Genoa), and for a daring Venetian to obtain pearls in Delhi in return for a mechanical clock made in Venice or its territory; or, with a shorter and easier journey, the western Khanates of Persia and the Golden Horde offered the same commodities at slightly higher prices, and other luxuries of their own lands.[70] Again, before the conquests of the Ottoman Turks, the Italians traded without paying any duty in a large area of the Byzantine and Latin Levant, and obtained sugar, alum and many spices from their own colonies. All these advantages were lost as the frontier of European trade receded; it then became necessary to deal with the Turks, who exacted heavy tributes from Western merchants, and with the Egyptians, who sold Indian and Chinese goods at an exorbitantly increased price. Then the Genoese endeavoured to open substitute markets and grow oriental plants in the West, even if that meant paying more and settling for inferior quality. The Venetians clung to the Egyptian market, relying on their economic and military power as a weapon to resist against the harder and harder terms of the Kārimī merchants, then against the will of the state monopolies.[71] Their success, in this uphill fight, was at best moderate; but this part of the story will be told by the Islamic specialist who is responsible for the last part of the joint report.

IV. EGYPT

According to Maqrīzī, land, commerce and industry are the sources of all wealth.[72] In Egypt, during the period with which we are concerned, all the economic sectors which he enumerates experienced a serious decline. The figures from the Arabic sources quoted in the following pages are to be taken as orders of magnitude and not as precise quantitative indicators. Their cumulative force, however, leaves no doubt that the decline was considerable, and that it comprehended all levels of the economy.

By the fifteenth century, Egyptian agriculture had reached a state of severe crisis. In 1298, the land-tax (*kharāj*) of Egypt amounted to 10,816,584 *dīnārs*, in 1315 to 9,428,289, and shortly after the Ottoman conquest of Egypt in 1517 this figure had shrunk to 1,800,000. A census connected with the redistribution of fiefs in 1433–4 showed 2,170 villages as compared with 10,000 under the Fāṭimids in the tenth and eleventh centuries. A survey of 2,489 agricultural units in 1480 revealed that since 1375, 48 had fallen into complete ruin and 40 had suffered a diminution

[70] References in R. S. Lopez, 'L'extrême frontière du commerce de l'Europe medièvale', *Moyen Age*, 1963.

[71] For Western bibliography see the highly informative round-up of R. H. Bautier, 'Les Sources de l'histoire du commerce maritime en Mediterranée du XIIᵉ au XVᵉ siècle', and other papers in the transactions of the *IV Colloque International d'Histoire Maritime, Paris, 1959*, Paris 1962.

[72] *Ighāthat al-umma bi-kashf al-ghumma*, ed. M. M. Ziāda and Jamal ad-Dīn ash-Shayyāl, Cairo 1957, p. 84; tr. G. Wiet, 'Le Traité des Famines de Maqrīzī', *JESHO*, v, 1962, p. 82.

ranging from one-half to six-sevenths in their agricultural rent; only 11 units were fully prosperous, while the remainder were stagnating. The chronicles abound in references to deserted villages and to large tracts of land left uncultivated and untended, indicating a general depopulation of the countryside. This situation had apparently already reached serious proportions by the last quarter of the fourteenth century. As early as 1370 the Syrian legal scholar al-Subkī voiced strenuous objections to the practice of forcing Syrian and Egyptian farmers back to their land within a period of three years after they had left it. The contraction of the agricultural population continued well into the fifteenth century, and the attempts of several Mamlūk Sultans in the early fifteenth century to stem this tide proved futile. Scholars, both medieval and modern, concur that during the fourteenth and fifteenth centuries agricultural production progressively declined, and that the size of the crops and the extent of cultivated land diminished.[73]

Egyptian industry, with a slightly different chronology, and in a somewhat different manner, exhibits a similar trend. Egypt's textile industry was highly developed. Its products in the pre- and early Mamlūk period not only met the needs of internal consumption but were also an important export commodity. The great decline in the Egyptian textile industry seems to have begun in the late fourteenth century. According to an obviously exaggerated report of Ibn Taghrī Birdī, in a space of forty years, 1394 to 1434, the number of textile workers in Alexandria declined from 14,000 to 800. The Cypriot merchant, Piloti, who visited Egypt frequently during the first thirty years of the fifteenth century, says that before 1403 there were some 9,000 textiles *ateliers* in Alexandria, but that by his time (probably the 1430's) only a small number remained. By the mid-fourteenth century, sugar, another important traditional product of Egyptian agriculture and industry, entered upon a path of decline from which it never recovered. Of the sixty-six sugar refineries active in Fusṭāṭ (Old Cairo) in 1324, only nineteen were in operation at the beginning of the fifteenth century; the remainder had either been converted to other uses, or had completely fallen into ruin.[74]

Commerce followed agriculture and industry in decline. Data concerning the customs income from Qaṭyā, a toll station astride the main artery of Syrian-Egyptian trade, demonstrate this decline rather dramatically. In 1326 the revenue from goods passing through Qaṭyā was 1,000 *dīnārs* a day or approximately 350,000 *dīnārs* a year; in 1395/6, this had fallen to 8,000 *dīnārs* a month or 96,000 *dīnārs* per year and towards the end of the

[73] Ahmad Darrag, *L'Égypte Sous le Règne de Barsbay*, Damascus 1961, pp. 59–66; E. Strauss (Ashtor), 'Prix et salaires a l'époque mamelouke', *Revue des Etudes Islamiques*, xvii, 1949, pp. 50–1; Subhi Y. Labib, *Handelsgeschichte Ägyptens im Spätmittelalter*, Wiesbaden 1965, p. 419.

[74] Darrag, *op. cit.*, pp. 66–73; Labib, *op. cit.*, pp. 419–23, and sources cited there.

fifteenth century it had further diminished to a scant 8,000 *dīnārs* a year. Urban commercial activity possessed only a remnant of its former glory. In 1438 a contemporary said of the Mamlūk capital, 'present-day Cairo is not but an eightieth of what it once was'. Whereas this estimate might be somewhat exaggerated, it nevertheless reflects the extent to which the urban decline was palpable. Maqrīzī, whose lifetime spanned the most accelerated periods of decline, left an eyewitness description of the dilapidation of Cairo's commercial district. At the beginning of the fifteenth century, its twenty-two covered markets were in decrepit condition. On the central artery of the city, only traces remained of the 12,000 stalls once bustling with activity. The markets of Fusṭāṭ had suffered a similar fate. The only flourishing quarter was the port area which was the receiving point of grain coming into the city from the countryside and of the spices, precious stones and perfumes arriving from India. River traffic was also sharply down. Egypt's second city, Alexandria, never fully recovered from the pirate raids of 1365. Piloti tells us that in his times the city was almost abandoned. A house which in earlier times would have fetched a handsome price could hardly be sold for two ducats, and when a buyer was finally found, his interest was confined to removing marble and other salvageable material and shipping them to Cairo. By the mid-fifteenth century, two-thirds of the city was in ruins, and most commercial activity was concerned with foreign shipping and concentrated around the port and adjacent areas.[75]

The figures cited above should not be accepted uncritically, nor can they serve as the basis for any precise quantitative assertions. They do, however, clearly point to an absolute contraction of the Egyptian economy by the end of the fourteenth century and to an absolute quantitative decline of all its sectors.

How are we to explain so sharp and universal a decline? Maqrīzī attributes Egypt's economic difficulties to incompetent and corrupt administration, and to a debased monetary system in which copper coins predominated and coins of the precious metals were exceedingly rare.[76] Many modern commentators have taken Maqrīzī's views as their point of departure and have sought to attribute Egypt's economic decline to one or another feature of government policy. In very broad outline, the basic argument of what may be described as the current consensus explaining Egypt's economic decline runs as follows: The political unrest preceding and following the accession of the Circassian Mamlūks in 1382 resulted in internal turmoil and weakness. The loosening of state control encouraged increased bedouin encroachments on agricultural areas and on caravans

[75] Darrag, *op. cit.*, pp. 73–89, also p. 41; Labib, *op. cit.*, pp. 337–440; I. M. Lapidus, *Muslim Cities in the Later Middle Ages*, Cambridge, Mass., 1966, pp. 18, 30, 39.

[76] *Ighātha*, p. 82 ff.; trans., p. 81 ff.

resulting in the decline of rural goods production, the flight of the rural population, the loss of cultivated lands to the desert and a disruption of lucrative long-distance trade. The most disastrous consequence of internal Mamlūk dissension was the adverse effect on agricultural revenues which were their fundamental source of wealth. Diminishing agricultural revenues were in turn the ultimate source of urban economic problems, since these directly affected the level of income of the urban upper classes and exerted pressure for a variety of economically disruptive measures such as heavier taxation of urban commerce, confiscations, and forced purchases, all intended to buttress sagging Mamlūk incomes. This led to a descending spiral of urban economic decay to which our data on industrial and commercial decline bear such eloquent testimony.[77]

I submit that this analysis is an inadequate explanation both of the extent and the manifestations of Egypt's economic crisis. A number of questions are left unanswered. Since bedouin disruption of agriculture began as early as the 1330's, why are there no indications of any disastrous long-term consequences until much later in the fourteenth century? Similarly, oppressive exactions from both the urban and agricultural sectors were not novel features of Mamlūk rule. Why, then, in earlier periods, did these not lead to any pervasive and calamitous economic decline? The most important question left unanswered is: how did Egypt continue to feed itself in the face of diminishing agricultural production? If the area of land under cultivation and the absolute size of the agricultural harvest declined by a considerable percentage, and if the population remained relatively constant, we would expect a number of consequences to follow: either mass starvation, or a sustained inflation in the price of agricultural products, or both. Since we have no evidence that either of these occurred, nor of any continuing massive grain imports, we must conclude that demographic factors were at the root of Egypt's agricultural decline, and that smaller harvests were being produced by, and were feeding substantially fewer people.

While a number of scholars have posited a slow but steady demographic decline in Egypt beginning with the Islamic conquest and continuing to the time of Muḥammad ʿAlī in the early nineteenth century, this process was certainly accelerated in the mid-fourteenth century, becoming a significant, and indeed, a central factor in the history of the following century. The only population studies of this period are found in Ayalon's investigations of the Mamlūk army. These reveal a drastic reduction in the number of Mamlūks beginning in the late fourteenth or early fifteenth century. From an estimated 12,000 royal Mamlūks during the reign of Nāṣir Muḥammad (first half of the fourteenth century), their number fell to approximately 5,500 under Mu'ayyad Shaykh in 1417, and to about

[77] Cf. e.g., Lapidus, *op. cit.*, pp. 25–31; also, Darrag, *op. cit.*, pp. 57–8 and pp. 75–6.

4,000 in 1437 under Barsbāy.[78] Other segments of the Mamlūk army suffered a similar decline in numbers, so that 'most of the military expeditions concerning which Egyptian chronicles of the fifteenth century give details were carried out by two or three thousand, and sometimes, by several hundred Mamlūks'.[79] Whatever political and other factors contributed to the precipitate reduction in the size of the Mamlūk army, the decimations of the plague were undoubtedly the most important. The plague took a particularly heavy toll in Mamlūk ranks, since as imported foreigners their immunity was low and they were particularly vulnerable; it also decreased the population source in the Caucasus on which the Mamlūks drew for their manpower needs.[80]

The plague did not confine its devastations only to the Mamlūks. All strata of the Egyptian population suffered from the destructive impact of the series of plagues which visited Egypt during the latter half of the fourteenth and throughout the fifteenth centuries. Any recovery from the demographic inroads of these epidemics was made virtually impossible by their recurrence at intervals of between ten and twenty years.[81] Maqrīzī has left us a vivid description of the progress of what was probably the most costly outbreak of the plague, that of 1347–9. It made its appearance in Egypt in the autumn of 1347. By April 1348 it had spread throughout the country, attaining its height between November 1348 and January 1349, and finally subsiding in February 1349. During this year and a half it wreaked its havoc throughout Egypt from Alexandria in the North to the outskirts of Aswān in the South. In Alexandria, the plague carried off one hundred people each day, and at its height this number rose to two hundred. The royal *ṭirāz* factory was closed down for lack of workers; the markets and custom houses suspended operations for lack of merchants and travellers. The Delta areas were similarly afflicted. 'In Maḥalla the plague was so intense that the prefect (*wālī*) could find no one to come to complain to him; and the *qāḍī*, when approached by people to validate their wills, could, because of their small number, find no witnesses except after great exertion.' In the countryside, there was almost no one left to cultivate the land or collect the harvests. Fief-holders and their servants were forced to gather the harvest themselves. Even though they held out one-half of the harvest as a reward to anyone who would help, they could find no one to accept their offer. Because of the heavy toll taken from the

[78] D. Ayalon, 'Studies on the Structure of the Mamluk Army I', *Bulletin of the School of Oriental and African Studies*, xv, 1953, pp. 222–8.

[79] Strauss, 'Prix et Salaires', p. 49.

[80] D. Neustadt (Ayalon), 'The Plague and its Effects upon the Mamluk Army', *Journal of the Royal Asiatic Society*, 1946, pp. 68–70; cf. also Darrag, *op. cit.*, p. 59.

[81] For a partial list of the occurrences of the plague within the Mamlūk realm between 1350 and 1500, cf. *ibid.*, pp. 68–9, and L. Hautecoer and G. Wiet, *Les Mosquées du Caire*, 2 vols., Paris 1932, vol. i, p. 82.

army, fiefs rapidly passed from one person to another, changing hands as many as seven or eight times. Even artisans such as tailors and cobblers were falling heir to fiefs; and these latter mounted horses and donned military dress. Following the visitation of the plague, an expanse of land in Upper Egypt which was previously inhabited by 6,000 taxpayers contained only 116 who could pay taxes. In Cairo the number of daily deaths rose from 300 at the beginning of October 1348 to 3,000 towards the end of the month. Many streets were left only with empty houses, 'and the belongings of their occupants could not find a taker; and if a man inherited anything, it passed in one day to a fourth and a fifth party'. Survivors helped themselves to abandoned property, houses, furniture and money. Maqrīzī claims that in Cairo alone 900,000 people died, and that the figure would be doubled were it to include some of its suburbs and adjacent areas.[82]

While Maqrīzī's figures for Cairo are certainly exaggerated, his description is unequivocal in portraying the plague as a serious demographic blow to all parts of Egypt. At this stage of research, it is impossible to give any quantitative or comparative figures for the extent of the population decline. One can only say with certainty that it was considerable. In another of his works, Maqrīzī reports that in this period the Egyptian population declined by one-third. In view of almost identical European figures this would seem to be a reasonable estimate and, until more detailed and controlled studies are available, one which can be used for a working hypothesis.

Postulating a serious demographic decline in the mid-fourteenth century permits us to view the consequent economic decline in a new perspective. The causal relationship explaining the crisis can now be reversed. It was not rapacious Mamlūk policies which led to decline, it was rather the decline that was responsible for those policies. Demographic decline resulted in an absolute reduction of both urban and rural economic activity, thus accounting for a good deal, though not necessarily all, of the desolation described in our sources. Because of the uneven effects of the demographic decline on the price structures of the urban and rural sectors (to be discussed below), the Mamlūk ruling classes and the state generally, for whom agricultural revenues constituted the most important single source of income, were particularly hard hit. Higher urban prices and relatively lower agricultural profits impelled the government to squeeze the rural areas for more revenues and to intensify their taxation of, and expand their intervention into, urban commerce.

[82] Cf. Maqrīzī, *Kitāb al-sulūk*, ed. M. M. Ziāda, 2 vols., Cairo 1936–58, vol. ii, pp. 772–87; translation by G. Wiet, 'La Grande Peste Noire en Syrie et en Egypte', in *Études d'Orientalisme Dediées à la Mémoire de Lévi-Provençal*, 2 vols., Paris 1962, vol. i, pp. 368–80.

An imbalance between the agricultural and non-agricultural sectors of the medieval Egyptian economy was a permanent, built-in feature of the Mamlūk state. Foodstuffs and other raw materials poured into the major urban centres from the countryside, while only a slight trickle flowed in the other direction. The non-agricultural sector received no compensation for these imports since they constituted the tax revenues of the Mamlūk aristocracy and the incomes from endowment intended for the support of urban religious institutions.[83] It would, therefore, be inaccurate to speak of a balance of payments crisis between the two sectors similar to that experienced in post-plague Europe. Nevertheless, there is ample evidence that beginning with the latter part of the fourteenth century this imbalance became even more lopsided with consequences not entirely unlike those manifested in medieval Europe.

After several centuries of price stability, Egypt, beginning with the mid-fourteenth century, underwent what Ashtor has termed 'a price revolution'.[84] Prices and wages rose to hitherto unprecedented levels. Some scholars have connected this escalation in price level with the disappearance of silver coinage from Egypt and the excessive monetization of copper which provoked an inflation of prices quoted in its terms. If all that was involved was a translation of prices from one currency to another, we would expect a fairly uniform rise in the prices of all major categories of goods and services. Our data, however, show that the rise was anything but uniform.

While the price of wheat rose only 20 per cent during the reign of the Circassian Mamlūks, the price of bread rose 66 per cent. The difference is accounted for by an increase of 113–160 per cent in the wages of millers and bakers during the same period. Other agricultural staples, such as barley and beans, apparently increased in price as modestly as did wheat, while the wages of a simple urban worker rose 122 per cent from the end of the thirteenth century to the beginning of the fifteenth. Refined sugar, olive oil and honey rose in price as much as 100 per cent and more; the same was true of clothes and textiles. The discrepancy between the modest rise in the price of agricultural products on the one hand and the more severe rise in the price of industrial goods, urban wages and processed foodstuffs on the other, is consistent throughout our data.[85]

Any attempt to attribute the disparity in the rise of agricultural and non-agricultural prices to the ability of the state to control the agricultural sector more strictly than the urban market-place[86] must founder on the

[83] On this point, cf. Lapidus, *op. cit.*, p. 18.

[84] E. Ashtor, 'L'Évolution des Prix dans le Proche Orient a la Basse Époque', *JESHO*, iv, 1961, p. 16.

[85] Strauss, 'Prix et Salaires', pp. 68–90; Ashtor, 'Évolution des Prix', pp. 15–46; Lapidus, *op. cit.*, p. 31.

[86] Cf. Strauss, *op. cit.*, pp. 74–6.

fact that it was precisely the Mamlūks themselves who stood to lose most from lower agricultural prices. Indeed, some passages in Maqrīzī seem to indicate that the Mamlūks and their agents made deliberate attempts at artificially inflating agricultural prices by imposing successive increases in the land rent.[87]

Might it not be more plausible to assume that prices found their level on the basis of supply and demand, and that the disparity in question is more satisfactorily explained by a change in the structure of demand engendered by the effects of the great plague in urban centres?

There are good grounds for believing that in Egyptian towns, as in their European counterparts, the first generation of plague survivors benefited from an inheritance effect. With inheritances passing rapidly from one party to another, and with survivors helping themselves to the abandoned property of the deceased, the *per capita* wealth of urban dwellers increased.[88] In addition, the international spice trade, which for the preceding hundred years had by-passed Egypt, returned again to the Mamlūk realm in 1345[89] and provided a rich new source of urban wealth. These two factors apparently combined to generate an increased demand for goods and services, while the inelastic nature of the demand for agricultural products limited the transfer of the greater *per capita* wealth and revenues to the agricultural sector thus diverting a larger portion of income toward urban products.

The prosperity of urban workers and artisans during the economic crisis of the early fifteenth century is the one bright spot in Maqrīzī's otherwise consistently bleak description of its effects on the various classes of the Egyptian populace. He says: 'As for the sixth category, these are the artisans, wage workers, porters, servants, grooms, weavers, builders, labourers, and their like. Their wages multiplied many times over; however, not many remain, since most of them died. A worker of this type is not to be found except after strenuous searching.'[90] This passage bears testimony to the fact that even fifty years after the initial outbreak of the plague, and in spite of accretions to the urban population from rural migrations, the ranks of the urban workers were still too thin to meet the demand being placed on them. Immediately after the plague, the scarcity of artisans and workers is described in almost identical terms. Artisans and workers in all categories had almost totally disappeared. One could not find a water-carrier, a porter or a domestic servant, and the wages of a stable-boy rose from thirty to eighty *dirhams* a month. The authorities issued a proclamation ordering anyone with a trade or craft to resume its

[87] *Ighātha*, pp. 45–6, trans., pp. 48–9.

[88] Cf. Maqrīzī, *Sulūk*, vol. ii, pp. 780–5; trans., pp. 374–8; and Neustadt, *The Plague*, pp. 72–3, where an instance is cited in which the Sultan distributed a horse to each member of the army from the effects of the Mamlūks struck down by the plague of 1491–2.

[89] Cf. Lapidus, *op. cit.*, p. 24.

[90] *Ighātha*, p. 75, trans., p. 75.

practice; some had to be beaten to ensure compliance with this decree.[91] Might this not indicate that, as in Europe, the death rate outstripped the rate at which artisans could be trained and replaced to satisfy the increased pressure of demand?

Aside from artisans and urban workers, who were undeniably enjoying a higher standard of living and thus generating further demands for goods and services in the cities, the great merchants, who were the chief beneficiaries of the renewed and much expanded spice trade, were experiencing a period of great prosperity. Their prosperity is perhaps best epitomized by the claim of one Kārimī merchant ʿAṭiyya b. Khalīfa (d. 1424) that every *dirham* he invested brought him a return of six. Another Kārimī merchant Burhān ad-Dīn al-Maḥallī constructed, next to his palatial residence on the banks of the Nile, a *madrasa* costing fifty thousand *mithqāls* of gold, a sum equal to that spent by the Sultan Mu'ayyad Shaykh himself for the erection of the mosque bearing his name. Until their decline in the fourth decade of the fifteenth century consequent to the state's monopolization of the spice trade, individual Kārimī fortunes reached tens and hundreds of thousands of *dīnārs*.[92] There is no reason to doubt that the increased wealth of this class, as well as of those associated with the spice trade in more menial capacities, found its expression in increased demand for services and luxury goods.

The two urban classes most adversely affected by the relatively lower agricultural prices were the fief-holding Mamlūks and those members of the religious class who were the beneficiaries of rural *waqfs*.[93] Reduced Mamlūk revenues undoubtedly resulted in a decline of their patronage of urban services and products. However, this reduction was apparently more than compensated by the increased demand generated by other urban strata. It was to the profits of the urban market-place that the Mamlūks had to turn to recoup their dwindling revenues. Ultimately, the sustained urban inflation and their constant need for specie to meet state expenses for the acquisition of Mamlūks and for military expeditions, impelled them to increasingly blatant intervention in the urban economy in the form of taxes, confiscations and finally, in the 1420's and 1430's, to the late medieval equivalent of nationalization of the spice, sugar and other trades.[94]

Egypt's economic crisis was accompanied by a breakdown of its monetary system. Gold and silver currency became increasingly scarce, and copper coins predominated in internal circulation and on all levels of transactions. For Maqrīzī, the deterioration of its monetary system was the single most

[91] Cf. *Sulūk*, vol. ii, p. 786; trans., p. 380.

[92] Cf. Labib, *op. cit.*, pp. 402–4.

[93] Lapidus, *op. cit.*, pp. 29–30; and E. Ashtor, 'I Salari del Medio Oriente Durante l'Epoca Medievale', *Rivista Storica Italiana*, 78, 1966, pp. 321–49, which shows that while urban salaries were generally higher during the Circassian period, those of the members of the religious classes were comparatively lower.

[94] Cf. Darrag, *op. cit.*, pp. 146 ff., 222 ff.

important cause of Egypt's economic difficulties. As a panacea, he prescribed a return to the gold and silver standard and a relegation of copper coinage to the role that God and custom had ordained for it, viz., restricting it to petty transactions.[95] What Maqrīzī did not, and possibly could not understand was that Egypt's monetary problems were not the result of an unfortunate financial policy, but a manifestation of its unfavourable position in international trade.

A shortage of specie seems to have been a chronic, although manageable problem for Egypt beginning as early as the twelfth century under the later Fāṭimids whose silver coins were of consistently inferior quality.[96] Under the Ayyūbids in the early thirteenth century all metrological standards for the gold *dīnār* were abandoned and gold was minted in the form of stamped coin-ingots of irregular weight. The practice continued well into the Mamlūk period.[97] Silver *dirhams* replaced gold as Egypt's standard coinage, but gold, even though deprived of any metrological consistency, remained an important medium of exchange. By 1359 the shortage of specie apparently became fairly acute, for from that date, copper coins, which had hitherto passed by tale, were weighed for all transactions.[98] Silver was rapidly disappearing from circulation and the volume of copper emissions grew enormously. At the beginning of the fifteenth century, Maqrīzī writes concerning copper: 'The people of Egypt have no other currency, and no money except for it'.[99] It became the chief means of exchange for all commodities, and the standard for all wages, taxes and transactions. Lamenting this state of affairs, Maqrīzī wrote that copper 'causes the joy of the world to cease and its beauty to disappear, it leads to the diminishing of wealth and spoliation of its pleasures'.[100] The substantial silver emissions of Sultan Mu'ayyad Shaykh in 1412 and 1414 provided only temporary relief; several decades later the silver *dirham* gave way once again to copper *fulūs*.[101]

On its home territory, Egypt's irregular gold coinage was being progressively displaced by massive influxes of Italian ducats and florins. By 1400, according to Ibn Taghrī Birdī, these foreign coins became the principal and most sought after currency in trade 'in all the cities of the world such

[95] *Ighātha*, pp. 47 ff. and 81; trans., pp. 49 ff. and 79–80.

[96] Paul Balog, 'History of the Dirham in Egypt from the Fāṭimid Conquest until the Collapse of the Mamlūk Empire 358/968–922/1517', *Revue Numismatique*, series VI, iii, 1961, pp. 122–3.

[97] Balog, *op. cit.*, p. 132, and *idem*, *The Coinage of the Mamlūk Sultans of Egypt and Syria*, New York 1964, p. 40.

[98] Balog, 'I. A Hoard of Late Mamluk Copper Coins and II. Observations on the Metrology of the Mamluk Fals', *The Numismatic Chronicle*, series VII, ii, 1962, p. 273.

[99] *Ighātha*, p. 76; trans., pp. 75–6.

[100] *Ibid.*

[101] Balog, *Coinage of the Mamlūk Sultans*, pp. 9–10; William Popper, *Egypt and Syria under the Circassian Sultans*, University of California Publications in Semitic Philology, vol. 16, 1957, pp. 56–8.

as Cairo, Fusṭāṭ, Syria, Asia Minor, the East, Ḥijāz and Yemen'.[102] The extent and impact of this invasion of foreign gold can be gauged by the Mamlūk State's reaction. After more than a century and a half in which Egypt's gold issues had no connection to any ponderal system, Sultan Faraj, in an attempt to counteract the influence of the foreign coins, began, in 1401–2, to issue gold *dīnārs* at the canonic weight of 4·25 grams. A shortage of sufficient specie to sustain this reform and an apparent continued preference on the part of merchants and others for the lower weight but stable Italian gold coins led the same Sultan to institute a second reform in 1405–6. On this occasion he abandoned the traditional Islamic weight for the *dīnār* in favour of a lighter standard of 3·40 grams which approximated the weight of the *ifrantī* Italian gold coins. Because of its lower weight and gold content this *dīnār* did not gain the confidence of the Egyptian market and was soon superseded by the *ifrantī* coins. A somewhat more successful assault on the supremacy of the *ifrantī* was made by Sultan Barsbāy in 1425–6 and 1430 when he called all foreign coins into the mint, and reissued them as his own. These *ashrafī dīnārs* weighing approximately 3·45 grams of high quality gold remained current throughout the remainder of the fifteenth century, but did not displace the Italian coins which continued to circulate concurrently with the *ashrafī* and other Egyptian gold emissions until the end of the Mamlūk hegemony. Since it was Europe that served as Egypt's almost exclusive source of gold throughout the fifteenth century, any attempts at completely displacing Italian gold with native emissions were doomed to failure from the outset.[103]

Neither increased hoarding nor the alleged operation of Gresham's law provide an adequate explanation for Egypt's bullion shortage. Neither our literary sources, nor the *objets d'art* and hoards of the period which have survived can support the contention that a sufficient amount of gold and silver was withdrawn from circulation through a demonetization of specie to affect substantially the available supply. As for Gresham's law, it is doubtful that it had any applicability at all in the medieval Islamic monetary context. There is ample evidence showing that gold and silver coins of varying weight, quality and exchange rate circulated simultaneously for long periods of time, and that coins were individually weighed and evaluated for all important transactions. There is no observable trend of bad coins driving good ones out of circulation; rather, good and bad coins co-existed peacefully at their respective levels of value.[104] It was not, as

[102] Quoted in Popper, *op. cit.*, p. 47.

[103] Balog, *Coinage of the Mamlūk Sultans*, pp. 46–7; Popper, *op. cit.*, pp. 44–51; Darrag, *op. cit.*, pp. 91–107.

[104] Cf. the data collected by S. D. Goitein in 'The Exchange Rate of Gold and Silver Money in Fāṭimid and Ayyūbid Times', *JESHO*, viii, 1965, pp. 1–46; cf. also my remarks in *L'Occidente e l'Islam nell'Alto Medioevo, Settimane di Studio del Centro Italiano dī Studi Sull' Alto Medioevo*, XII, 2 vols., Spoleto 1965, vol. i, pp. 488–9.

some contend, the excessive monetization of copper which drove out silver and gold coins, but the shortage of gold and silver which led to the abundant monetization of copper.

Among the numerous factors contributing to Egypt's shortage of specie in the late fourteenth and fifteenth centuries, the most central was her persistent unfavourable balance of payment in international trade. By the thirteenth century, the Nubian gold mines were exhausted to the point that the gold extracted barely covered expenses. A lively and profitable trade with the western Sudan kept Egypt supplied with gold until the latter part of the fourteenth century, at which time this trade declined and the African gold was siphoned off toward Europe.[105] From that point on, the spice trade with Europe seems to have been Egypt's sole source of specie. At approximately the same time, nature seems to have conspired to deprive Egypt of several lucrative sources of foreign exchange. In the thirteenth century Egypt exported between five and thirteen thousand *qinṭārs* of alum annually. By the early fourteenth century her alum mines were exhausted, as were her emerald mines by 1359.[106]

While the source of Egypt's gold supply was contracting, there are no indications of a correspondingly significant decline in consumption of foreign products and luxury goods, or a parallel reduction in state expenditures for imports.

Throughout this period a variety of imported luxury wares were readily available in Egyptian markets. Indian crystalware and Chinese porcelain and ceramics were known and imported to Egypt throughout the Middle Ages. At the time of Maqrīzī, large quantities of European and Eastern textiles were to be found in the markets of Cairo and Alexandria. Not only did these imports directly aggravate an already serious balance of payments problem, but they also contributed in some measure to a decline of the indigenous Egyptian textile industry.[107] As an outstanding example of foreign luxury consumption one might point to the increased demand for furs from the Black Sea area which first becomes apparent around 1380. Fur trim on clothing became so fashionable at this time that as one writer put it 'there was hardly a Cairene who did not possess a fur'.[108] Some idea of the volume of the fur trade can be gleaned from the report of a single merchant who arrived in Cairo with a consignment of 300,000 fur garments.[109] When one considers that the price of choice skins sometimes ran into hundreds of *dīnārs*,[110] one can understand Genoa's willingness to

[105] On exhaustion of Nubian gold cf. Labib, *op. cit.*, pp. 312–13; on trade with the western Sudan, cf. *ibid.*, pp. 146–8, 271–2; Darrag, *op. cit.*, p. 92.

[106] Labib, *op. cit.*, pp. 313–15.

[107] *Ibid.*, pp. 311 and 316–17; Darrag, *op. cit.*, pp. 72–3, 155; Lapidus, *op. cit.*, pp. 33–4; Hautecoer and Wiet, *Les Mosquées*, vol. i, p. 77.

[108] Labib, *op. cit.*, p. 294.

[109] *Ibid.*; cf. also Darrag, *op. cit.*, p. 319.

[110] L. A. Mayer, *Mamluk Costume*, Geneva 1952, p. 23.

assign half its fleet in a conflict with Venice to protect its supremacy in conducting this profitable trade to Egypt from the Black Sea.[111]

A steady inflow of new slave manpower was an irreducible requirement of the Mamlūk system. These slaves were consumption items *par excellence*, generating no profitable return on the substantial investment required for their acquisition, training and upkeep. Strategic and political necessities superseded any purely economic considerations in the acquisition of expensive Tatar slaves imported by the Mamlūks from the Black Sea area. Very little compensating trade flowed northward from Egypt, so that even in the best of times this indispensable trade constituted a significant drain of Egypt's precious metal resources.[112] Any improvement in this respect resulting from the reduced number of Mamlūks in the fifteenth century was to a large extent vitiated by the particularly heavy toll which the recurrent plagues took in the Mamlūk ranks. Between 1348 and 1513, there were at least eighteen outbreaks of the plague of varying intensity.[113] The incidence of death among children and foreigners (a category which included Mamlūks) was especially high since they had not developed the same degree of immunity as had other population strata. 'The plague caused death among the Mamlūks, children, black slaves, slave-girls and foreigners',[114] is a dirge recurring with morbid frequency in the accounts of almost every epidemic. Fourteen hundred royal Mamlūks died in the plague of 1429; two thousand were carried away in 1476, and one thousand in 1497. One-third of all categories of Mamlūks are estimated to have perished in the plague of 1429, and one-half of the royal Mamlūks in the plague of 1459.[115] All these had to be replaced, and their replacements were equally vulnerable to recurring outbreaks of the plague. In the 1420's two thousand slaves were annually brought to the Cairo markets from the Black Sea area.[116] With the average price of a young Tatar varyingly estimated between fifty and one hundred and forty *dīnārs*,[117] this constituted an outflow of between one hundred and two hundred and eighty thousand gold *dīnārs* annually. When added to the substantial sums of gold flowing in the same direction to cover the consumption of furs, one can conclude that the Black Sea area was a major receptacle of Egypt's gold drain.

Throughout the fifteenth century, Europe was the only area with which Egypt maintained a favourable balance of trade. In the opinion of Ahmad Darrag, Egypt, at the beginning of the fifteenth century, was virtually

[111] Labib, *op. cit.*, pp. 331–2.
[112] For absence of compensating trade, Lapidus, *op. cit.*, p. 19.
[113] Cf. above, n. 81.
[114] Quoted in Neustadt, 'The Effects of the Plague', p. 70.
[115] *Ibid.*, pp. 70–1.
[116] Strauss, 'Prix et Salaires', p. 51; Labib, *op. cit.*, pp. 327–9; Darrag, *op. cit.*, p. 53.
[117] Strauss, *op. cit.*, p. 51; D. Ayalon, 'L'Esclavage du Mamelouk', Jerusalem 1951, pp. 6–9.

living only off the profits of the spice trade with Europe.[118] F. C. Lane has estimated that during the latter part of this century the Venetians were annually exporting from Alexandria 1,150,000 pounds of pepper and an approximately equal amount of other spices, aromatics and drugs. At an approximate price of twenty ducats per *qinṭār*, this comes to almost 250,000 ducats for pepper alone.[119] But only a fraction of this sum remained in the country. The spice trade was a transit trade. Spices were not indigenous to Egypt, but imported from India via the Red Sea and paid for in specie. Aside from the large quantities of oriental spices profitably resold to European merchants, a substantial amount was being consumed in Egypt itself. A wide variety of oriental spices were prominent ingredients of Arab cuisine, and were used not only for seasoning fish and meat, but for certain types of bread as well.[120] In his analysis of a hypothetical budget of a middle class person, Maqrīzī assumes that two out of the ten *dirhams* a member of this class earns daily would be spent on spices.[121] Internal consumption, therefore, made some inroads into the profits accruing from the spice trade. Egypt, then, was not merely a conduit funnelling Italian gold towards India, but was also contributing to this flow by its own internal consumption of spices and other imports from the Farther East.

We have no accurate, or even approximate figures for the amount of European and Egyptian gold that found its way to India. But our sources from the fifteenth century leave no doubt that the flow was constant and the amounts considerable. Nicola Conti, a Venetian traveller in India in the first half of the fifteenth century, reports that 'in some parts of anterior India Venetian ducats are in circulation',[122] and German sources, referring to the latter part of the century, report that ships would often leave Jidda, the Arabian entrepôt for the India trade, carrying with them one hundred thousand ducats in cash for the purchase of spices.[123] Thus, at least a good portion of the gold which began its long trek southward from Northern Europe in search of luxury products, travelling via Italy and Egypt, found its final resting place as additions to the already incredible gold accumulations of India.

[118] Darrag, *op. cit.*, p. 7; cf. also p. 106.

[119] F. C. Lane, 'The Mediterranean Spice Trade', *American Historical Review*, xlv, 1940, p. 587 n. 28, and *idem.*, 'Venetian Shipping During the Commercial Revolution', *ibid.*, xxxviii, 1933, p. 228. On the amounts of Italian gold flowing toward the Levant, cf. references in Strauss, *op. cit.*, p. 51.

[120] M. Rodinson, 'Recherches sur les Documents Arabes Relatifs à la Cuisine', *Revue des Etudes Islamiques*, xvii, 1949, p. 151 ff.

[121] *Ighātha*, p. 85; trans., p. 83.

[122] *The Travels of Nicolo Conti in the East in the Early Part of the Fifteenth Century*, trans. J. W. Jones, p. 30, in *India in the Fifteenth Century*, ed. R. H. Major, London 1857.

[123] Quoted in Labib, *op. cit.*, p. 393.

The Size and Value of the Iqṭāʿ in Egypt 564–741 A.H./1169–1341 A.D.

HASSANEIN RABIE

MAQRĪZĪ, who states that from Saladin's time onwards all Egyptian cultivated land had been assigned in the form of *iqṭāʿs* to the sultan, his *ajnād* and his *amīrs*, does not specify the method by which the individual shares were allotted, at that time, to the respective beneficiaries.[1] Nor is any mention made of this point by other historians of the Ayyūbid period, probably due to a lack of information about the Ṣalāḥī *rawk* ordered by Saladin in 572/1176. It is also possible that the Ayyūbid sultans prevented the officials of the *dīwān al-jaysh* (army office) from divulging this secret. The gist of the available information is that, when Sultan Lājīn came to power in the year 696/1296, he found that of the 24 *qīrāṭs* (*qīrāṭ* simply means $\frac{1}{24}$) constituting the cultivated land of Egypt, four were in the hands of the sultan including the royal *mamlūks*, ten in the hands of the *amīrs*, and the last ten in the hands of the *ajnād al-ḥalqa*, i.e., the non-*mamlūk* cavalry.[2] This proportion was changed as a result of the Ḥusāmī *rawk* in 697/1298, and the Nāṣirī *rawk* in 715/1315.

Relying on the *Ṣubḥ al-Aʿshā*, it can be said that the sultans used to distinguish three kinds of cultivated land conferred in the form of *iqṭāʿs* in terms of their yield in revenue. Land with the highest yield was assigned in the form of *iqṭāʿs* to the *amīrs* according to their rank, each receiving an *iqṭāʿ* consisting of one to ten villages. Land of the second category was conferred upon the sultan's *amīrs*. In rare cases, sultani *amīrs* had entire villages to themselves; in most cases there were two or more *muqṭaʿs* to one

[1] Maqrīzī, *Khiṭaṭ*, Cairo 1270/1853, vol. i, p. 97. A comparison of the main characteristics of the *iqṭāʿ* in the period under consideration with the main characteristics of European medieval feudalism shows that the *iqṭāʿ* system of the Ayyūbids and the Mamlūks was not derived from any of the various types of feudalism found in Western Europe. One is inclined to accept the view of Professor A. K. S. Lambton (*Landlord and Peasant in Persia*, London 1953, p. 53) that the circumstances which accompanied the rise and development of the *iqṭāʿ* system differed from those prevailing in Western Europe where feudalism took shape, and the results were consequently dissimilar. The writer will refrain from the use of European terms such as feudalism, fief, lord, etc.

[2] *Khiṭaṭ*, vol. i, p. 88; Maqrīzī, *Sulūk*, ed. Ziada, vol. i, pp. 841–2, tr. Quatremère, *Histoire des Sultans Mamlouks de l'Egypte*, vol. ii, ii, pp. 65–6; Ibn Taghrī Birdī, *Nujūm*, Cairo 1929–56, vol. viii, p. 92; Ibn Iyās, *Badāʾiʿ*, Cairo 1893–6, vol. i, p. 137; Gaudefroy-Demombynes, *La Syrie a l'Epoque des Mamelouks*, p. xl; Poliak, *Feudalism in Egypt, Syria, Palestine and the Lebanon*, London 1939, p. 24; Ayalon, 'Studies on the Structure of the Mamluk Army', *Bulletin of the School of Oriental and African Studies*, xv, 1953, p. 452.

village. Land yielding the least revenue was assigned to the *ajnād al-ḥalqa*, Bedouin tribes and others, each of the groups sharing a village. Unfortunately, there is no other evidence to support Qalqashandī's statement, which appears to point back to the Ayyūbid era.[3]

However, the size of a particular *iqṭāʿ* was dictated by the fact that *iqṭāʿs* of particular holders were scattered in different places and over a large area. It seems that it was the sultan's purpose to reduce the influence of the *muqtaʿ* in his *iqṭāʿ* lest he should proclaim independence or rebel. In five cases, there is evidence to prove that it was an Ayyūbid tradition later taken over by the Mamlūks to scatter particular *iqṭāʿs* in this way:

1. The *iqṭāʿ* of Tūrānshāh, Saladin's brother, consisted of many cities and villages in Upper and Lower Egypt.[4]

2. The *iqṭāʿ* of Taqī al-Dīn ʿUmar, Saladin's nephew, was scattered in many places in Syria and Egypt in 579/1183.[5]

3. The *tawqīʿ* (brevet of the *iqṭāʿ*) of Saladin's brother al-ʿĀdil, dated 580/1184–5 and preserved by Qalqashandī, indicates that his *iqṭāʿ* consisted of many villages in Egypt, Syria, the Jazīra and Diyār Bakr.[6]

4. Ibn Wāsil states that, while going to Damietta in Muḥarram 648/May 1250 to see the Muslims entering the city after the defeat of Louis IX, he passed Marṣafā which he described as 'one of the farms (*ḍayʿa*) forming part of the *iqṭāʿ* of Ḥusām al-Dīn Muḥammad ibn Abī ʿAlī (al-Hadhabānī)'.[7]

5. In his written *waṣiyya* (advice) to Tūrānshāh, Sultan al-Ṣāliḥ Ayyūb imputed to the Coptic clerks the intention of weakening the army and ruining the country. More details are found in the statement of Sultan al-Ṣāliḥ to the effect that the clerks would scatter the 1,000 *dīnār* (*jayshī*) *iqṭāʿ* of a *jundī* in five or six places, e.g., in Qūṣ in Upper Egypt, and Sharqiyya and Gharbiyya in Lower Egypt. In such a case the *muqṭāʿ* had to employ four or more *wakīls* (agents), so that no revenue was left to him, especially if he was absent at war. The sultan advised his son to grant adjacent *iqṭāʿs* in one or two places.[8]

[3] Qalqashandī, *Ṣubḥ*, Cairo 1919–22, vol. iii, pp. 457–8.

[4] *Tārīkh ibn Abī al-Hayjā'* (Maʿhad al-Makhṭūṭāt, Cairo, *Fā'* 16), vol. i, f. 177 r–v; Ḥanbalī, *Shifā' al-Qulūb* (MS. Brit. Mus. Add. 7311), f. 11 v; Abū Shāma, *al-Rawḍatayn*, ed. Aḥmad, Cairo 1962, vol. i, ii, p. 488; *Khiṭaṭ*, vol. ii, pp. 37–8; Maqrīzī, *al-Dhahab al-Masbūk*, ed. al-Shayyāl, Cairo 1955, pp. 70–1.

[5] Iṣfahānī, al-Barq al-Shāmī (Ms. Bodleian Marsh 425), vol. v, f. 120; *al-Rawḍatayn*, Cairo 1287/1870, vol. ii, p. 53; Ibn Wāṣil, *Mufarrij al-Kurūb*, vol. ii, p. 152; *Sulūk*, vol. i, p. 82, tr. Blochet, 'Histoire d'Egypte de Makrizi', *Revue de l'Orient Latin*, ix, p. 9; *Khiṭaṭ*, vol. ii, p. 364; Rabīʿ, *al-Nuẓum al-Māliyya fī Miṣr Zaman al-Ayyūbiyyīn*, Cairo 1964, pp. 28–9.

[6] *Ṣubḥ*, vol. xiii, pp. 146–7.

[7] *Mufarrij al-Kurūb*, f. 372 r; Rabīʿ, *al-Nuẓum al-Māliyya*, p. 36; Marṣafāi s nowadays in the Banhā district.

[8] Nuwayrī, *Nihāyat al-Arab* (MS. Dār al-Kutub, Cairo, 549 *Maʿārif ʿĀmma*), vol. xxvii, ff. 91–2; Nuwayrī copied the text of this *waṣiyya* from the original, cf. *ibid.* ff. 89–93. It seems that the *wakīl* (agent), the *muqtaʿs* assistant in the collection of taxes, was an important figure in the *iqṭāʿ*. Two unpublished documents from the Geniza

Unfortunately, Sultan Tūrānshāh, al-Ṣāliḥ's son, ruled only 71 days, and was supplanted by the Mamlūk sultanate. An increased dispersion of individual *iqṭāʿs* in Egypt and Syria over widely separated areas is observable in the Mamlūk period.

An alternative explanation of this phenomenon is that *iqṭāʿs* were allocated as they fell vacant (*maḥlūl*). They would not fall vacant in territorial blocks, but at random in different parts of the country.

The evaluation of the *iqṭāʿ* was based on what was called the *ʿibra*. Professor Cahen suggests that the *ʿibra* had existed since the advent of Islam and went back even further, perhaps, to Roman antecedents.[9] He also states that the term *ʿibra* used to be applied, in Muslim medieval administration, to the assessment of the fiscal value of a territory. But it is not always easy to see how it was established and what its connection was with the taxes actually levied.[10]

A description of the method by which the *ʿibra* was generally estimated can be found in the *Kitāb Mafātīḥ al-ʿUlūm* of al-Khwārizmī. It was based on the average revenue as arrived at by taking the revenue of the best and worst years, adding them and dividing by two, after allowing for changes in prices and occasional events such as wars, plague, etc.[11] Consequently the *ʿibra* of the *iqṭāʿ* was the average yearly revenue from the *iqṭāʿ*, at least theoretically. In practice, the *ʿibra* and the actual annual revenue from the *iqṭāʿ* had long ceased to coincide, a discrepancy which may have been quite considerable by the end of the period.[12] This can easily be shown, as Qalqashandī states that the *ʿibra* was useless because the actual revenue of an *iqṭāʿ* estimated at 100 *dīnārs jayshī* may have been higher than that of another *iqṭāʿ* estimated at 200 *dīnārs jayshī* or more.[13] Ibn al-Jīʿān also states that the passage of time, the devastation of most villages, the reconstruction of others and changes in the rate of exchange of the *dīnār* had made nonsense of the *ʿibra*.[14]

Collection (Cambridge U.L., T.-S. B. 39, F. 118 and F. 386) throw light on this office, one of them dated 7th Rabīʿ al-Awwal 644/23 July 1246. It is worth mentioning that there was a prejudice against Coptic clerks on the part of Muslim jurists and writers, probably because they resented their superior experience in financial matters; cf. C. Cahen: 'Histoire Copte d'un Cadi médiéval. Extraits du *Kitāb tadjrīd Saïf al-Himma li'stikhrādj mā fī dhimmat al-dhimma* de 'Uthmān b. Ihrāhīm an-Nābulusī', *Bulletin de l'Institut Français d'Archéologie Orientale du Caire*, lix, 1960, pp. 133–50; al-Asnāwī, *al-Kalimāt al-muhimma fī mubāsharat ahl al-dhimma*, ff. 6–14; Perlmann, 'Asnawī's tract against Christian officials', *Goldziher Memorial*, vol. ii, 1958, pp. 172–208; *id.*, 'Notes on anti-Christian propaganda in the Mamlūk Empire', *Bulletin of the School of Oriental and African Studies*, x, 1940–2, pp. 843–61.

[9] Cahen, 'L'Évolution de l'Iqṭāʿ du IXe au XIIIe Siècle', *Annales (Economies, Sociétés, Civilisations)*, viii, 1953, p. 46 note 3.

[10] Cahen, 'Le Régime des Impôts dans le Fayyūm Ayyūbide', *Arabica*, iii, 1956, p. 12.

[11] Khwārizmī, *Mafātīḥ al-ʿUlūm*, ed. Von Vloten, Leiden 1898, pp. 60–1.

[12] Cahen, 'L'Évolution de l'Iqṭāʿ', p. 46.

[13] *Ṣubḥ*, vol. iii, p. 442.

[14] Ibn al-Jīʿān, *al-Tuḥfa al-Saniyya*, ed. Moritz, Cairo 1898, p. 3.

The unit of calculation of the *ʿibra* was not the ordinary *dīnār*, but the *jayshī dīnār* (the army *dīnār*). Qalqashandī states that the *jayshī dīnār* was an arbitrary monetary unit, used by the officials of the *dīwān al-jaysh* in evaluating different *iqṭāʿs*.[15] It is worth mentioning that even before Qalqashandī, Ibn Mammātī described the *jayshī dīnār* as a fictitious *dīnār* whose value varied from one group to another. Thus in Ibn Mammātī's lifetime—before 606/1209—the *jayshī dīnār* used to be assessed as follows: for Turkish, Kurdish and Turkoman regulars at one gold *dīnār*; for the Kināniyya, the ʿAsāqila (from Ascalon) and other similar *ajnād* at $\frac{1}{2}$ gold *dīnār*; for naval service commanders and similar ranks at $\frac{1}{4}$ gold *dīnār*; for Arab auxiliaries, with certain exceptions, at $\frac{1}{8}$ gold *dīnār*.[16]

Ibn Mammātī also states the value of the *jayshī dīnār* as a specific combination of payments in cash and kind, namely $\frac{1}{4}$ gold *dīnār* and one *ardabb* of grain consisting of $\frac{1}{3}$ *ardabb* of barley and $\frac{2}{3}$ *ardabb* of wheat. That is to say, an *iqṭāʿ* with an *ʿibra* of 100 *dīnārs jayshī* was supposed to yield an average revenue of 25 gold *dīnārs* and 100 *ardabbs*, $\frac{1}{3}$ of which was barley and $\frac{2}{3}$ wheat.[17]

Qalqashandī, Ibn al-Jīʿān and al-Suyūṭī state that the value of the *jayshī dīnār* equalled $13\frac{1}{3}$ *dirhams* in ordinary currency.[18] Professor Cahen suggests that, since wheat was probably worth about $\frac{1}{2}$ gold *dīnār* an *ardabb* in the Ayyūbid period, and the *ardabb* of barley was half this price, one *ardabb* of grain in the proportion stated above was worth about $\frac{2}{5}$ of the ordinary *dīnār*, so that the *jayshī dīnār* was, in all, worth about $\frac{2}{3}$ of the ordinary gold *dīnār*. Professor Cahen insists that these figures are only approximate, as there seems to be little connection between the figures in the *Kitāb Tārīkh al-Fayyūm* by Nābulsī and this theoretical calculation, and that, in the Mamlūk era, the actual financial revenue diverged ever further from the initial estimate.[19] Poliak and Popper, relying on Maqrīzī's *Khiṭaṭ*, state that the value of the *jayshī dīnār* varied, at the time of the Nāṣirī *rawk* in 715/1315, from 10 to 7 *dirhams*, according to the *muqṭāʿs* rank.[20]

There are three reasons why these attempts to find a relationship between the *jayshī dīnār* and the ordinary *dīnār* can neither be confirmed nor refuted:

(*a*) The *jayshī dīnār* was a fictitious monetary unit, similar to the *qīrāṭ*,

[15] *Ṣubḥ*, vol. iii, p. 442.

[16] Ibn Mammātī, *Qawānīn al-Dawānīn*, ed. Atiya, Cairo 1943, p. 369; *Ṣubḥ*, vol. iii. p. 442; for the Kināniyya and ʿAsāqila cf. Gibb, 'The Armies of Saladin', in *Studies on the Civilisation of Islam*, p. 86, notes 25 and 26.

[17] *Qawānīn al-Dawānīn*, p. 369, note 9; Cahen, 'L'Évolution de l'Iqṭāʿ', p. 46; *id.*, 'Le Régime des Impôts', p. 12.

[18] *Ṣubḥ*, vol. iii, pp. 442–3; *al-Tuḥfa al-Saniyya*, p. 3; Suyūṭī, *Ḥusn al-Muḥāḍara*, Cairo 1321/1903, vol. ii, p. 191.

[19] Cahen, 'Le Régime des Impôts', pp. 12–13.

[20] *Khiṭaṭ*, vol. ii, pp. 218–19; Poliak, 'Some notes on the Feudal System of the Mamlūks', *Journal of the Royal Asiatic Society*, 1937, pp. 99–100; *id.*, *Feudalism*, p. 21; Popper, *Systematic Notes*, vol. ii, p. 109.

which is still in use in Egypt, especially among small landed proprietors. The value of the *qīrāṭ* differs according to time, area and the condition of the property. Thus, the real value of the *jayshī dīnār* differed from one year to another, and from one *iqṭāʿ* to another. As has already been pointed out, the value of the *jayshī dīnār* was indeterminate and varied for different people, according to their rank in the army.

(*b*) The rate of exchange of the gold *dīnār*, which was a component part of the *jayshī dīnār*, not only changed from one sultan's reign to another, but also, several times during the reign of a particular sultan.

(*c*) The prices of barley and wheat varied for many reasons, such as high or low Nile floods, wars, epidemics and even transport conditions; i.e., they could be dear or cheap, according to circumstances. Thus the value of the *jayshī dīnār* in terms of real money could be higher in a bad year or a year of famine when the prices of wheat and barley were high, than in a year of plenty, when they were low.

The reassignment of the *iqṭāʿs* took place after every *rawk*, i.e., cadastral survey of Egyptian cultivated land. Poliak has suggested that the concept of the *rawk* was of Mongol origin.[21] One might accept this as correct in the sense that the Mamlūk sultans imitated the Mongols in reassigning the *iqṭāʿs* after each cadastral survey of land under cultivation. But the opinion that the *rawk* as a method of surveying land and estimating taxes was introduced to Egypt by the Mongols does not seem acceptable for two reasons:

(*a*) Etymologically, the word *rawk* comes from the Coptic word *rōsh*, which means to measure the land by means of a rope. This Coptic word is possibly derived from the Demotic *rḫ̌* (*rukh*) which denotes land distribution.[22]

(*b*) It has been an old-established Egyptian custom, possibly going back to the days of the Pharaohs, to survey the land to assess the increase or decrease of cultivated land in order to adjust the taxes to be levied. The term *mukallafa* has been used in Egypt to denote a 'register of landed property'. The *māsiḥ* (surveyor) was the official who drew up *mukallafāt*, arranged—as Grohmann states—by villages.[23] In corroboration of these

[21] Poliak, 'Le Caractère Colonial de l'État Mamelouk dans ses Rapports avec la Horde d'Or', *Revue des Etudes Islamiques*, ix, 1935, pp. 239–41; *id.*, *Feudalism*, p. 23.

[22] Crum, *Coptic Dictionary*, p. 308. A. Gardiner, *Theban Ostraca*, Oxford 1913, p. 44, note 1; G. Mattha, *Demotic Ostraka*, *Publications de la Société Fouad I de Papyrologie. Textes et Documents*, vol. vi, 1945, p. 23; M. Lichtheim, *Demotic Ostraca from Medinet Habu*, The University of Chicago, *Oriental Institute Publications*, vol. lxxx, 1957, p. 53.

[23] *Qawānīn al-Dawāwīn*, p. 305; *Khiṭaṭ*, vol. i, pp. 86, 88; *Ṣubḥ*, vol. iii, p. 458; Grohmann, 'New discoveries in Arabic Papyri. An Arabic Tax-Account Book', *Bulletin de l'Institut Egyptien*, xxxii, 1949–50, p. 163; Dietrich (*Arabische Papyri*, Leipzig 1937, pp. 81–4) published a third/ninth-century papyrus which he described as a land tax register. He suggested that the columns of the latter represented not tax totals in *dīnārs*, but the number of *faddāns* planted with wheat or clover at successive dates, i.e., obviously a *mukallafa* fragment. It is worth noting that the eastern equivalent of the *mukallafa* in

remarks, it may not be amiss to give some data on the three main *rawks* carried out in Egypt before the Mongol invasions, although these fall outside the period considered in this paper. In the reign of Hishām, ʿUbayd Allāh ibn al-Ḥabḥāb, who was in charge of the finances of Egypt, initiated, after his arrival in Egypt in 105/724, a new land survey to which references are found in a papyrus dated 23 Rabīʿ al-Awwal 106/19 August 724 and recently published by Nabia Abbott. When Walīd ibn Rifāʿa became governor of Egypt in 109/727, both participated in the land survey and population census already initiated by Ibn al-Ḥabḥāb. During the reign of al-Muʿtazz, Ibn al-Mudabbir, then in charge of Egypt's finances, personally supervised a survey of Egyptian cultivated land in about 253/867–8; he subsequently increased the *kharāj* from one *dīnār* per *faddān* to as much as four. In the year 501/1107–8, both military and civilian *muqtaʿs* suffered from decreasing revenue from their *iqṭāʿs*. Following the advice of al-Maʾmūn al-Baṭāʾiḥī, al-Afḍal tried to solve the problem by a cadastral survey of the Egyptian land and a consequent reassignment of the *iqṭāʿs*.[24] Abū Ṣāliḥ the Armenian seems to have preserved in his book the data provided by the Afḍalī *rawk*. He states the number of Egyptian *nawāḥī* (districts) and *kufūr* (hamlets) in the provinces under the Fāṭimids, and also the revenue derived from most of their *iqṭāʿs*.[25] These data seem to have been of considerable assistance to Saladin in holding his Ṣalāḥī *rawk*, the first of three *rawks* which took place in the period under consideration.[26]

The Ṣalāḥī *rawk* was ordered by Saladin in the year 572/1176. It seems that Saladin intended this *rawk* to open a new era in the reassignment of the *iqṭāʿs* and the administration of Egypt. He chose Bahāʾ al-Dīn Qarāqūsh to supervise the work on the Ṣalāḥī *rawk*, the duration of which is not specified by the known sources.[27] One might infer from al-Fāḍil's *Mutajaddidāt* of Rajab 577/November–December 1181, and from what is quoted from al-Iṣfahānī in *al-Rawḍatayn* relating to the year 581/1185, that the Ṣalāḥī *rawk* directly influenced the reassignment of the *iqṭāʿs* for

Egypt was termed *qānūn al-kharāj*, cf. Lewis, art. *Daftar* in *EI*[2]; the *rawk* is denoted in Egypt by the term *fakk al-zimām*.

[24] Ibn al-Ḥabḥāb: Ibn ʿAbd al-Ḥakam, *Futūḥ Miṣr*, Leiden 1920, p. 156; Kindī, *Kitāb al-Wulā*, London 1912, pp. 75–9; *Khiṭaṭ*, vol. i, pp. 74–5, 98–9; *Ḥusn al-Muḥāḍara*, vol. i, p. 87; Nabia Abbott, 'A new papyrus and a review of the administration of ʿUbaid Allāh B. al-Ḥabḥāb', in *Arabic and Islamic Studies in Honor of Hamilton A. R. Gibb*, pp. 27–9. Ibn al-Mudabbir: *Khiṭaṭ*, vol. i, pp. 99, 103, 314; *Nujūm*, vol. i, p. 47; Dietrich, *Arabische Papyri*, p. 84. Al-Afḍal: *Nihāyat al-Arab*, vol. xxvi, ff. 81–2; *Khiṭaṭ*, vol. i, p. 83; al-Shayyāl, 'Ṭarīqat masḥ al-arāḍī wa taqdīr al-Kharāj fī Miṣr al-Islāmiyya', in *Dirāsāt fīʾl-Tārīkh al-Islāmī*, pp. 98–9; Rabīʿ, *al-Nuẓum al-Māliyya*, p. 13.

[25] *Tārīkh Abī Ṣāliḥ*, ed. B. Evetts, Oxford 1895, pp. 10–12 and the translation, pp. 15–18.

[26] The other two are the Ḥusāmī *rawk* and the Nāṣirī *rawk*.

[27] Dawādārī, *Durr Maṭlūb* (MS. Sara, Istanbul 2932, vol. vii), ff. 17 r, 39 r; *Khiṭaṭ*, vol. i, p. 101; *Ṣubḥ*, vol. iii, pp. 452–3; Rabīʿ, *al-Nuẓum al-Māliyya*, pp. 42–3.

a period of ten years or more.[28] It seems that the Ṣalāḥī *rawk* was the only *rawk* of the Ayyūbid period. This assumption is confirmed by the fact that, in his *waṣiyya* to his son Tūrānshāh, Sultan al-Sāliḥ Ayyūb advised him to base his estimation of the *ʿibra* on 'what it had been in Saladin's time'. It can therefore be assumed that the evaluation of the *iqṭāʿs* in the Ṣalāḥī *rawk* became the model for Saladin's successors.[29]

The Ḥusāmī *rawk*, held in the Mamlūk period in 697/1298, was instituted by Sultan Ḥusām al-Dīn Lājīn not only to reassign the *iqṭāʿs*, but also to investigate the deplorable condition of the *mamlūks* of those *amīrs* who had appropriated the *iqṭāʿs* of the *ajnād* under the pretext of *ḥimāya* (protection), so that confusion, disorder and looting in the *iqṭāʿs* could be prevented.[30]

The Ḥusāmī *rawk* was completed in less than eight months from Jumādā'l-Ūlā to Dhū'l-Ḥijja 697/March to October 1298, under the supervision of Mankūtamur, the vice-sultan, and other high officials.[31] The two main principles of that *rawk* were that *ḥimāya* was to be abolished, and the Egyptian cultivated land to be divided into 4 *qīrāṭs* for the sultan, *iqṭāʿ khāṣṣ*; 10 *qīrāṭs* for the *amīrs* and *ajnād al-ḥalqa*; one *qīrāṭ* to satisfy the complainants, and the remaining nine *qīrāṭs* to be conferred in the form of *iqṭāʿs* upon new troops.[32]

The Ḥusāmī *rawk* assigned the *iqṭāʿs darbasta*,[33] excluding the *jawālī*

[28] *Khiṭaṭ*, vol. i, pp. 86–7; *al-Rawḍatayn*, vol. ii, p. 62.

[29] *Nihāyat al-Arab*, vol. xxvii, f. 92.

[30] *Khiṭaṭ*, vol. i, pp. 87–8; for the *ḥimāya* cf. Cahen, 'Notes pour l'histoire de la Himaya', *Mélanges Louis Massignon*, vol. i, 1956, pp. 287–303; *id.*, articles *Ḍarība* and *Ḥimāya* in *EI*².

[31] *Nihāyat al-Arab*, vol. xxix, f. 100; Ibn Taghrī Birdī, *al-Manhal al-Ṣāfī* (MS. Bibliothèque Nationale, 2072 Arabe), vol. v, f. 55 r; al-Ṣafadī, *Nuzhat al-Mālik* (MS. Brit. Mus. Or. 6267), f. 58 r; Ibn Abī'l-Faḍā'il, *al-Nahj al-Sadīd*, ed. E. Blochet, Paris 1919–28, p. 437; *Nujūm*, vol. viii, p. 92; Ibn Taghrī Birdī, *Mawrid al-Laṭāfa*, ed. J. E. Carlyle, Cambridge 1798, p. 49.

[32] *Khiṭaṭ*, vol. i, p. 88; Sulūk, vol. i, pp. 841–4; tr. Quatremère, *op. cit.*, vol. ii, pp. 65–8; Gaudefroy-Demombynes, *op. cit.*, p. xl; Ibn Taghrī Birdī (*Nujūm*, vol. viii, pp. 92–3), quoting from an unknown source, states that 14 *qīrāṭs* were divided among the troops, 4 *qīrāṭs* went to the sultan, 2 to the complainants, and 4 to the newly recruited troops. For other divisions cf. Ibn Duqmāq, *al-Jawhar al-Thamīn* (MS. Bodleian, Digby Or. 28), ff. 120 v–121 r; the anonymous *Tārīkh al-Dawla al-Turkiyya* (MS. Cambridge U.L., Qq, 147), f. 21 r; *Badāʾiʿ*, vol. i, p. 137.

[33] *Darbast* is a Persian word which signifies 'completely or wholly'; Qalqashandī (*Ṣubḥ*, vol. xiii, p. 156) interprets the word *darbasta* in the same way, but the editor reads *karbasta*. The term *iqṭāʿ darbasta* was used in Egypt to denote assignment to one *muqtaʿ* of the right of collecting all taxes in the *iqṭāʿ*, including those collected for the sultan. In this sense, the *iqṭāʿ darbasta* is the antecedent and equivalent of the Ottoman *serbest tīmār* (free fief), cf. Ibn al-ʿAmīd, *Akhbār al-Ayyūbiyyīn*, ed. C. Cahen, *Bulletin d'Etudes Orientales*, xv, 1955–7, pp. 134–5; al-Manṣūrī, *Zubdat al-Fikra* (MS. Brit. Mus. Add. 23325, 11), f. 178, v; *Nihāyat al-Arab*, vol. xxix, f. 61; *Tārīkh Ibn al-Furāt*, ed. Q. Zurayq and N. ʿIzz al-Dīn, Beirut 1939, vol. viii, p. 123; *Sulūk*, vol. i, p. 770; tr. Quatremère, *op. cit.*, vol. ii, i, pp. 131–2; Lewis, 'Studies in the Ottoman Archives', *Bulletin of the School of Oriental and African Studies*, xvi, 1954, p. 483.

(poll tax) and the *mawārīth ḥashriyya*, which were collected for the sultan, and *al-rizaq al-aḥbāsiyya*, collected from the *waqf* lands for religious and charitable purposes.[34] The majority of the *muqṭaʿs* were dissatisfied with the provisions of the *rawk*. The contemporary historian Baybars al-Manṣūrī states that the Sultan Lājīn and his subordinates urged the *rawk* staff to bring it to a rapid conclusion. They actually surveyed only a part of the land, and the rest only symbolically.[35]

Al-Manṣūrī's statement is significant, because it is well known that the *ajnād al-ḥalqa* rebelled against the Ḥusāmī *rawk* which gave them only half of what they had before. Besides, the revenue of each new *iqṭāʿ* was insufficient to meet the expenses or duties of the *muqṭaʿ*. Some *ajnād* went in a body to Mankūtamur, asking him to increase their *iqṭāʿs*, to transfer them to the *amīrs*' service, or to release them entirely from military service. As the vice-sultan was severe, he imprisoned them, and threatened the *amīrs*. The reaction was that both the sultan and Mankūtamur were killed and, in the words of Maqrīzī, 'that *rawk* was the main reason of the collapse of [Lājīn's] state'.[36] The anonymous contemporary historian points to the Ḥusāmī *rawk* as the prime factor in the weakness of the Mamlūk army, especially the *ḥalqa*.[37] Ibn Taghrī Birdī ascribes it to the fact that no one obtained a satisfactory quantity. In reality, the injustice was even worse, as after Lājīn's murder, the nine *qīrāṭs* saved by the *rawk* were assigned to the *amīrs* only, disregarding the claims of most *muqṭaʿs*, which resulted mainly in a deterioration of the position of the *ḥalqa*.[38]

In ordering an Egyptian *rawk*[39] in Shaʿbān 715/November 1315, Sultan al-Nāṣir Muḥammad ibn Qalāwūn seems to have had several ends in view:

1. to survey the Egyptian land to estimate what was cultivated and what uncultivated, and determine the yields of the various taxes;
2. to abolish the taxes conferred as *iqṭāʿs*;
3. to cancel or decrease large *iqṭāʿs*;
4. to increase the sultan's *khāṣṣ*.

After Fakhr al-Dīn Muḥammad ibn Faḍl Allāh, *nāẓir al-jaysh* (chief of the army office), had prepared lists stating the area and *ʿibra* of each district, the sultan sent *amīrs*, clerks and land surveyors to all the provinces

[34] *Nihāyat al-Arab*, vol. xxix, f. 100; *Sulūk*, vol. i, pp. 844–5; tr. Quatremère, *op. cit.*, vol. ii, ii, p. 68.

[35] *Zubda*, f. 198 v.

[36] *Sulūk*, vol. i, p. 846; tr. Quatremère, *op. cit.*, vol. ii, ii, p. 69; *Khiṭaṭ*, vol. ii, p. 387.

[37] Zetterstéen, *Beiträge zur Geschichte der Mamlūkensultane in den Jahren 690–741 der Ḥiǵra nach Arabischen Handschriften*, p. 45.

[38] *Nujūm*, vol. viii, p. 95; Ayalon, 'Studies', II, p. 452.

[39] The *Shāmī rawk* took place by order of Sultan al-Nāṣir in various parts of Syria in the year 713/1313–14. Subsequently there were *rawks* in Tripoli in 717/1317, and in Aleppo in 725/1325, cf. *Nihāyat al-Arab*, vol. xxx, ff. 81, 105; al-ʿAynī, *Tārīkh al-Badr* (MS. Brit. Mus. Add., 22360), ff. 5 r, 16 v; Ṣāliḥ ibn Yaḥyā, *Tārīkh Bayrūt*, Beirut 1902, pp. 125–31; Zetterstéen, *op. cit.*, pp. 160–61; Ibn Ḥajar, *al-Durar al Kāmina*, Hyderabad 1929–32, vol. ii, pp. 170–1; vol. iv, pp. 354–5; *al-Nahj al-Sadīd*, p. 742; *Sulūk*, vol. ii, pp. 127, 264; *Badāʾiʿ*, vol. i, pp. 159, 164.

and districts of Egypt. In order to be in touch with these *amīrs*, Sultan al-Nāṣir himself went to Upper Egypt and spent about two months there. When each of the *amīrs* had completed his survey, he summoned the *shaykhs*, *dalīls* and *qāḍīs* (judges) of each village to examine the registers as well as the financial resources of the village, both in money and crops, its cultivated and uncultivated areas, its *ʿibra* and the *ḍiyāfa* (gifts) which were collected for the *muqṭaʿ*. Almost all the *amīrs* and their assistants carried out such a survey of the village lands, differentiating between the *iqṭāʿ* of the sultan, those of the *amīrs* and the *ajnād*, as well as *al-rizaq al-aḥbāsiyya*.[40] After the completion of the *rawk* Sultan al-Nāṣir turned to the *muqṭaʿs*. After having ascertained the name, origin and experience of each *muqṭaʿ*, he proceeded to the reassignment of the *iqṭāʿs*. It is to be ascribed to al-Nāṣir's personal merits that no *muqṭaʿ* returned the *mithāl* handed to him by the sultan, whose sense of justice is also proved by the fact that he forbade a *muqṭaʿ* to be recommended to him by any *amīr* in order to prevent favouritism.[41]

The changes made in the *iqṭāʿ* system and taxation by the Nāṣirī *rawk* were as follows:

1. Ten *qīrāṭs* of Egyptian land were set aside as *iqṭāʿ khāṣṣ* for the sultan, while the other 14 *qīrāṭs* were reassigned to the *amīrs* and the *ajnād* in the form of *iqṭāʿs*.[42]

2. Old and disabled *ajnād* were excluded from *iqṭāʿ* grants, the sultan allotting to each of them a pension of about 3,000 *dirhams* yearly.[43]

3. The *hadiyya* and *ḍiyāfa* (gifts) imposed on the *fallāḥīn*, and the *jawālī* tax were calculated in the *ʿibra* of each *iqṭāʿ*.[44]

4. All districts were exempted from arrears up to the end of 714/1315.[45]

5. *Al-Taqāwī al-sulṭāniyya* (seeds from the sultan), which were given to every *muqṭaʿ* on the conferment of the *iqṭāʿ* and were returnable in the event of his transfer elsewhere, remained the permanent property of the *iqṭāʿ* from which they could not be removed.[46]

6. Some villages were set aside to cover the costs of the maintenance of the sultan's retinue, while the pay of the civil officials came from other financial sources.[47]

[40] *Nihāyat al-Arab*, vol. xxx, ff. 90–1; *Nuzhat al-Mālik*, ff. 79 v–80 r; *Khiṭaṭ*, i, p. 88; *Sulūk*, ii, pp. 146–7; *Nujūm*, vol. ix, pp. 42–4.

[41] Zettersteén, *op. cit.*, p. 164; *al-Nahj al-Sadīd*, pp. 761–2; Ibn Kathīr, *al-Bidāya wa'l-Nihāya*, vol. xiv, p. 75; *Khiṭaṭ*, vol. i, pp. 90–1; *Sulūk*, vol. ii, pp. 154–7; *Nujūm*, vol. ix, pp. 51–5.

[42] *Khiṭaṭ*, vol. i, p. 90; Gaudefroy-Demombynes, *op. cit.*, p. xli.

[43] *Sulūk*, vol. ii, p. 156; *Khiṭaṭ*, vol. i, p. 90.

[44] *Khiṭaṭ*, vol. i, pp. 88–90; *Sulūk*, vol. ii, pp. 150–3; *Nujūm*, vol. ix, pp. 43–4, 50.

[45] *Nihāyat al-Arab*, vol. xxx, f. 91; al-ʿAynī, *ʿIqd al-Jumān* (MS. Dār al-Kutub, Cairo, 1584 *Tārīkh*), vol. xxiii, i, f. 55; *Sulūk*, vol. ii, p. 153; *Nujūm*, vol. ix, p. 49; for the arrears cf. Grohmann, 'New Discoveries in Arabic Papyri', pp. 164, 167.

[46] *Khiṭaṭ*, vol. i, p. 91.

[47] *Nihāyat al-Arab*, vol. xxx, f. 91; *ʿIqd al-Jumān*, vol. xxiii, i, f. 54; *al-Durar al-Kāmina*, vol. i, p. 359.

7. Taxes assigned in the form of *iqṭāʿs* were abolished.[48]

The Nāṣirī *rawk* had its advantages and disadvantages. First of all, it modified the very principle of the *iqṭāʿ* system of Egypt, limiting the *iqṭāʿs* to cultivated land only. It affected also the financial administration in Egypt not only within the first Mamlūk period, but also under the Circassians.[49] Figures found in the *Kitāb al-Tuḥfa al-Saniyya* indicate that the data provided by the Nāṣirī *rawk* were copied from its registers without modification until the end of the fifteenth century or even later.[50] Secondly, the Nāṣirī *rawk* minimized the influence of the great *amīrs* by decreasing and changing their *iqṭāʿs*. Thirdly, it afforded comfort to the inhabitants of the *iqṭāʿs* by abolishing heavy taxes.

As to the disadvantages of the Nāṣirī *rawk*, it may be said that it had two. First, the addition of the *jawālī* tax to the *ʿibra* of the *iqṭāʿ* was a grave mistake, since, by making it a local tax, it gave the Copts an opportunity to evade payment by moving from one village to another. Whenever the *muqṭaʿ* or his clerks demanded payment of this tax, they refused under the pretext that they were not permanent residents of the village. Naturally, the *muqṭaʿ* preferred to accept a part of the *jawālī* tax instead of nothing.[51] Secondly, each *iqṭāʿ* being scattered over many provinces of Lower and Upper Egypt, to a greater degree than before, the Egyptian army was weakened by the increase of *iqṭāʿ* expenses.[52] These increases appear to have been caused by the need to employ a separate agent and staff of clerks in each part of the *muqṭaʿ's* scattered *iqṭāʿs*. The cost of their salaries, as well as frequent dishonesty, decreased the revenue derived from the *iqṭāʿ*. Hence the *muqṭaʿ's* difficulties in fulfilling his military obligations, which were so great under al-Nāṣir's successors, that the *ajnād al-ḥalqa* resorted to *nuzūl* to have their *iqṭāʿs* changed to pay, or else accepted compensation. The prestige of the Mamlūk army suffered because so many non-military persons, such as pedlars and common people, held *iqṭāʿs*.[53]

[48] *ʿIqd al-Jumān*, vol. xxiii, i, f. 55; *al-Jawhar al-Thamīn*, ff. 130 v–131 r; al-Dawādārī, *al-Durr al-Fākhir*, ed. H. H. Roemer, Cairo 1960, p. 286; *Khiṭaṭ*, vol. i, pp. 88–9; *Sulūk*, vol. ii, pp. 150–2; *Nujūm*, vol. ix, pp. 44–7.

[49] *Khiṭaṭ*, vol. i, p. 91; *Nujūm*, vol. ix, p. 51.

[50] *Al-Tuḥfa al-Saniyya*, pp. 5, 6, 27, 39, 99, 106, 117, 125, 127, 129, 135, 138, 139; Poliak, *Feudalism*, pp. 22–3.

[51] *Nihāyat al-Arab*, vol. xxx, f. 91; *Khiṭaṭ*, vol. i, p. 90.

[52] *Khiṭaṭ*, vol. i, p. 90.

[53] *Khiṭaṭ*, vol. ii, p. 219; Gaudefroy-Demombynes, *op. cit.*, pp. xliv–xlv; Ayalon, 'Studies', II, p. 453; *id.*, 'The System of payment in Mamluk Military Society', *JESHO*, i, 1958, p. 45.

Histoire économique et Histoire des Classes sociales dans le Monde Musulman

MAXIME RODINSON

La tendance des historiens depuis un siècle environ à étudier avec de plus en plus d'attention l'histoire économique et sociale, à accorder de plus en plus d'importance aux faits économiques et sociaux dans la dynamique historique globale a fini, avec bien du retard, à se faire sentir dans le domaine de l'histoire du monde musulman. Certes, l'intérêt pour ces problèmes, dans ce domaine même, est ancien et, pour reprendre les mots de Claude Cahen, «Sylvestre de Sacy, Von Kremer, Van Berchem, Becker, Barthold, Mez, d'autres parmi les morts et divers parmi les vivants ont apporté à nos études en ce domaine des contributions dont moins que personne je contesterai l'importance».[1] Mais, depuis peu, depuis justement l'article-manifeste de Claude Cahen en 1955,[2] la tendance s'est accentuée vers des études plus nombreuses et plus spécifiques, vers une spécialisation plus poussée dans ces études et la présente conférence en est une marque non équivoque. On peut en espérer un développement encore plus grand des travaux particuliers. On peut s'attendre aussi à ce que les islamisants reconnaissent de façon plus généralisée l'importance de l'économique et du social pour la compréhension des problèmes historiques et structurels posés par la société musulmane à travers les âges. Ils finiront ainsi par rejoindre le point de vue auquel sont arrivés depuis déjà assez longtemps les historiens de l'Occident. L'évolution dans ce sens est des plus encourageante.

Nos connaissances vont donc s'accroître et se préciser. Il faut s'en féliciter, sans conteste. Pourtant, il est au plus haut point nécessaire, ce dont les spécialistes n'ont pas toujours conscience, que l'effort de compréhension accompagne l'accumulation des matériaux et l'élucidation des problèmes particuliers. Comme l'a fort bien dit encore Claude Cahen, «les documents dans une certaine mesure, on les trouve selon qu'on les cherche et on ne trouve pas ce qu'on ne cherche pas».[3] De même, les problèmes les plus particuliers ne peuvent être correctement posés — et par conséquent n'ont de chance de recevoir une solution valable — que s'ils sont bien situés dans un cadre conceptuel adéquat. La preuve en est qu'on a tiré des conclusions très différentes de documents identiques ou de même ordre à divers moments de l'évolution de l'historiographie européenne.

[1] *Studia Islamica*, 3, 1955, p. 97.

[2] 'L'histoire économique et sociale de l'Orient musulman médiéval', *Studia Islamica*, 3, 1955, pp. 93–115.

[3] *Ibid.*, p. 98.

Collecte des documents et des faits, élucidation des problèmes particuliers et effort de réflexion conceptuelle doivent marcher du même pas.

C'est dans cette perspective qu'ici je voudrais m'attacher à distinguer et à préciser des notions qui sont souvent confondues, tant par les historiens du monde musulman que par ceux de l'Occident chrétien, en essayant pourtant de montrer leurs rapports. Cette confusion constante n'est pas, me semble-t-il, sans conséquences néfastes. Il s'agit essentiellement des concepts d'histoire économique et d'histoire sociale.

L'histoire économique est celle à laquelle le plus d'attention a été accordée. Je me bornerai à la définir.

C'est en premier lieu l'étude, sur le plan historique, des évènements, des normes et des institutions proprement économiques. Il faut entendre par là ceux qui se rattachent à la production, à la circulation, à la répartition et à la consommation des biens et services quand ces fonctions visent à satisfaire les besoins de la société par la conjonction des efforts de ses membres.[4]

Ainsi on peut étudier les fluctuations de la production agricole ou industrielle, ses formes d'organisation: «enterprise» agricole ou artisanale à exploitation individuelle ou par les producteurs associés, selon les cas dirigée par le producteur individuel, des producteurs associés, des propriétaires non producteurs ou l'Etat. L'auto-consommation n'est justifiable de l'analyse économique que négativement, par l'évaluation de son poids respectif, de ses fluctuations par rapport à la partie des biens produits qui entre dans la circulation. La circulation et la redistribution se font à partir de prestations imposées au producteur, d'échanges bilatéraux immédiats entre producteurs ou de producteurs à intermédiaires, d'échanges par le marché enfin. On a donc affaire à des institutions comme les impôts (d'où l'étude nécessaire des finances publiques), les divers statuts de propriété, les contrats de répartition du produit entre propriétaires et producteurs ou les contrats de vente et d'achat, enfin le marché. D'autre part, l'échange peut se poursuivre entre intermédiaires: échange de produits, de moyens de production, de symboles de l'échange. D'où des institutions comme les associations de commerçants, les méthodes de circulation telles que les chèques, billets à ordre, etc. Enfin la distribution aux fins de consommation peut se faire par prestation ou par échange, par vente directe ou indirecte, par distribution gratuite. D'où des institutions comme les contrats de vente et encore, partiellement, le marché, etc.

On voit par là que les phénomènes économiques ont aussi des aspects qui se rattachent à d'autres systèmes de la vie sociale que l'économie, ainsi la technique et le droit. La technique agricole conditionne en partie

[4] M. Godelier, 'Objets et méthodes de l'anthropologie économique', dans *L'Homme*, 5, 1965, pp. 32–91, donne (p. 39) une définition qui doit être complétée evidemment par la mention de la conjonction des efforts. Cela apparaît d'ailleurs dans ses développements intéressants de la p. 45 par ex.

le volume des produits de l'agriculture disponible aux fins de prestation ou d'échange. Inversement d'ailleurs le mode de production, de circulation ou de répartition peut stimuler ou freiner le progrès de la technique agricole. L'étude économique statique ou dynamique, donc en particulier l'histoire économique, doit prendre en consideration, par conséquent, les aspects economiquement importants de divers phénomènes socio-culturels: techniques, relations juridiques, moeurs, esthétique, ideologie. Tout spécialement, les conditionnements réciproques sont à étudier.[5]

On voit l'importance et l'extension du domaine couvert par l'histoire économique. Tout islamisant, qui ne s'est pas borné à une étroite spécialité, sait que des travaux importants ont été publiés sur ces sujets, quoique en nombre très insuffisant assurément. Il est clair que l'histoire des groupes sociaux (et c'est ce qu'on entend en général par histoire sociale) a des rapports importants avec cette histoire économique au premier chef s'il s'agit de groupes sociaux définis selon des critères économiques, mais aussi quand les rapports entre groupes ont des aspects économiques. Il est difficile qu'il n'en existe aucun. Pourtant, il est clair aussi que l'histoire des groupes sociaux ne peut toute entière entrer dans les cadres de l'histoire économique définie ci-dessus. On sait aussi que cette étude est bien plus difficile, exige des vues synthétiques, embrasse une multitude de faits disparates. Il n'est pas étonnant qu'elle ait été bien moins cultivée. A côté des travaux importants de S. D. Goitein, on trouve peu à citer.

Les groupes sociaux qui ont une importance historique sont souvent désignés sous le nom de classes sociales quoique cette désignation soit contestée. Je ne puis évidemment tenter ici une analyse de la structure de la société musulmane suivant les groupes sociaux qui la composent. Cela doit être l'objet de multiples travaux convergents. Dans le cadre d'une communication méthodologique, je peux seulement essayer de définir, à un niveau très général, comment se pose le problème des classes sociales dans l'Islam pré-moderne.

Il a été dit que l'Islam ignorait le concept de classe et même que les langues musulmanes ne disposaient pas de mot pour définir ce concept. L'erreur est grande. Les sociologues qui ont avancé cette thèse veulent dire qu'il n'existe pas de mot qui corresponde au terme «classe» dans une acception sociologique précise. Mais alors on peut dire tout aussi bien cela du mot «classe» dans les langues européennes. Ils veulent aussi parfois indiquer que les associations étymologiques des termes arabes sont différentes de celles qu'évoque le mot latin *classis*. Mais l'emploi des mots n'est nulle part restreint par leur étymologie ou leurs associations sémantiques.[6]

[5] Ce tableau du domaine de l'économique est largement inspiré de Max Weber avec quelques divergences.

[6] Je me permets de renvoyer à mon article, 'Dynamique interne ou dynamique globale? L'exemple des pays musulmans', dans *Cahiers Internationaux de Sociologie*, 42, 1967.

Le terme choisi par l'arabe et le persan modernes pour designer la classe sociale est le mot *ṭabaqa*, mot dont la racine (empruntée peut-être à l'akkadien) se rattache à l'idée d'entassement, de couches superposées, racine contaminée d'ailleurs par une autre (présente en nord-sémitique et introduite de là en arabe sous la forme *dbq*), peut-être identique à l'origine, qui exprime l'idée d'adhésion étroite, de collage, d'engluement. Le choix n'est pas arbitraire. Le mot désigne en effet dès le Moyen Age des catégories d'individus avec l'idée de succession chronologique ou de gradation hiérarchique. Ainsi, comme il est bien connu, les générations de gens d'une même profession, des adhérents d'une même école, etc., d'où les nombreux ouvrages dont le titre commence par *ṭabaqāt*, «le livre des classes des . . .». Mais l'idée de catégories sociales hiérarchisées est aussi fréquente. Lorsque Muḥammad b. Aḥmad Abū'l-Muṭahhar al-Azdī dit au XIème siècle qu'il veut peindre «les moeurs des Baghdadiens dans la diversité de leurs *ṭabaqāt*» (ed. Mez, p. 1, l. 12), il pense à la multiplicité de ces catégories.

Cela est des plus clairs dans les passages suivants d'Ibn Khaldūn:

Les degrés d'honneur (*jāh*) sont distribués parmi les hommes et ordonnés selon une gradation régulière, de classe en classe (*ṭabaqa baʿda ṭabaqa*). Au sommet, ils s'arrêtent au rang des gouvernants au dessus desquels il n'y a pas d'autorité. Au plus bas, ils s'étendent jusqu'à ceux qui n'ont aucun pouvoir pour le bien ni le mal. Entre les deux se situent une foule de classes. . . .[7]

Et encore:

Chaque classe, parmi les habitants des villes ou des diverses zones du monde civilisé, exerce un pouvoir sur les classes qui lui sont inférieures et chaque membre d'une classe inférieure cherche un appui auprès d'un détenteur d'autorité de la classe qui lui est immédiatement supérieure.[8]

Un synonyme arabe de *ṭabaqa* est *ṣinf*, «espèce, sorte, catégorie» qui s'est spécialisé dans divers sens, notamment celui de «corporation». Son sens originel se rattache peut-être à l'idée de «bord», donc de «limite» et de délimitation. La synonymie avec *ṭabaqa* est posée au IVème/Xème siècle par le traité des synonymes de ʿAbd al-Raḥmān b. ʿĪsā al-Hamadhānī: «On dit: J'ai donné son dû à chaque *ṭabaqa* de gens et j'ai donné sa part à chaque *ṣinf* d'entre eux».[9] C'est le terme preféré par le turc moderne pour exprimer l'idée de classe sociale. On trouve encore le mot *zumra*, en turc *zümre*, à l'origine «bande de gens» et les mots exprimant la gradation: *martaba*, *daraja* «degré, rang». C'est ce dernier terme qu'emploie déjà le

[7] *Muqaddima*, éd. Quatremère, t. ii, p. 289; éd. Wāfī, t. iii, Le Caire 1379/1960, p. 909; trad. De Slane, t. ii, réimpr., Paris 1936, p. 339; trad. F. Rosenthal, t. ii, New York 1958, p. 328.

[8] *Ibid.*, éd. Quatremère, t. ii, p. 290 s.; éd. Wāfī, t. iii, p. 910; trad. De Slane, t. ii, p. 341; trad. F. Rosenthal, t. ii, p. 330.

[9] *Kitāb al-alfāẓ al-kitābiyya*, éd. L. Cheikho, 9ème éd., Beyrouth 1913, p. 222.

Coran (43: 31/32) pour exprimer l'idée des strates hiérarchiques de la société humaine.

On ne peut nier par conséquent que l'Islam classique ait eu conscience d'un certain classement en groupes sociaux en partie hiérarchisés. Ces groupes sociaux pourtant sont — à deux exceptions près — considérés comme fonctionnels et non comme statutaires de sorte que la hiérarchisation entre eux est conçue comme découlant de la hiérarchie socialement «naturelle» des occupations, non d'un statut acquis dès la naissance. En un sens — mais en un sens seulement — et avec la restriction sus-mentionnée — on peut dire donc dire que la société musulmane médiévale est une société sans classes.[10]

Cela est bien reflété par le droit musulman. Alors que le droit romain ou les droits coutumiers européens du Moyen Age partent d'une théorie du statut des personnes, le droit musulman part d'une théorie de la capacité. La capacité légale normale, celle du musulman libre, adulte et sain d'esprit, peut être diminuée par certaines circonstances. Mais il n'y a pas à la base un classement des personnes en catégories rigides dont chacune est dotée de son propre système de capacités.[11]

Une catégorie sociale se distingue par l'accumulation des incapacités enregistrées par le droit. C'est la categorie des esclaves. Mais il s'agit là d'un statut d'exception. «Le statut de base est la liberté» (*al-aṣl huwa'l-ḥurriyya*).[12] Il est assez parallèle en tant que tel au statut de la femme ou de l'aliéné. Quant au non-musulman, il est consideré comme extérieur d'une certaine façon à la société globale. Bref, la société musulmane est considerée comme englobant une masse de personnes égales en principe, mais où certaines particularités qui affectent des catégories de fait entraînent pour celles-ci des diminutions de la pleine capacité légale.

Une seule catégorie — en dehors de celle des esclaves — rappelle les catégories à statut de la société européenne médiévale. C'est la noblesse. Mais là encore, en théorie, cette catégorie reste une exception. Le fait de descendre du Prophète entraîne certaines qualités exceptionnelles qui désignent un individu pour certains privilèges extraordinaires et d'ailleurs d'une portée limitée. On sait qu'un de ces privilèges est la capacité exclusive à fournir un *imām* à la communauté, privilège nié par les Khâridjites.

Telle est la doctrine fondée sur l'égalité et la fraternité des croyants devant Dieu. Elle n'empêche nullement une stratification de fait. Mais

[10] Cf. H. A. R. Gibb, 'Government and Islam under the early ʿAbbasids, the political collapse of Islam', in *L'élaboration de l'Islam*, Paris 1961, pp. 115–27, notamment p. 119.

[11] Cf. J. Schacht, *An Introduction to Islamic Law*, Oxford 1964, p. 124 ss.; L. Milliot, *Introduction à l'étude du droit musulman*, Paris 1953, p. 221 s.; R. Brunschvig, 'Théorie générale de la capacité chez les Hanafites médiévaux', in *Mélanges Fernand de Visscher* [= *Revue internationale des droits de l'Antiquité*, 2 (1949)], pp. 157–72.

[12] Cf. R. Brunschvig, *'Abd* in *EI*², éd. française, t. i, p. 27.

elle a la conséquence importante que cette stratification n'est acceptée qu'avec réticence par le droit, n'est pas canonisée par la Loi sauf, partiellement, pour la classe des esclaves.

La stratification de fait, si elle n'est qu'à peine prise en considération par la théorie des relations juridiques, est naturellement constatée par la conscience sociale. On trouve mille expressions de cette constatation par les hommes de lettres, les philosophes, les administrateurs, etc. Les rapports entre les hommes sont gouvernés par cette stratification, constate Fārābī (mort en 339/950), en commençant son petit traité des rapports sociaux (*Risāla fī'l-siyāsa*):

> Nous avons voulu, dans ce traité, indiquer les lois des rapports sociaux (*qawānīn siyāsiyya*) dont le bénéfice s'étend à toutes les classes (*ṭabaqāt*) qui les utilisent dans leurs actions vis-à-vis de chaque groupe (*ṭā'ifa*) des gens de leur classe, de leurs supérieurs et de leurs inférieurs.[13]

Et il poursuit, non moins significativement:

> Chacun, lorsqu'il se replie sur soi-même et réfléchit à sa situation et à celle des autres, se situe à un rang (*rutba*) déterminé qu'il partage avec un certain groupe (*ṭā'ifa*). Il trouve au-dessus de son rang un groupe en situation plus élevée d'un point de vue ou de plusieurs et également au-dessous un groupe en situation inférieure d'une ou de plusieurs façons. . . . On tire avantage d'utiliser les règles de conduite sociale (*al-siyāsāt*) avec ces trois classes. Avec les plus élevés, on se hausse ainsi à leur niveau; vis-à-vis des égaux on acquiert quelque supériorité; par rapport aux inférieurs, on évite de s'abaisser jusqu'à leur bas rang (*rutba*).[14]

Les ethnies forment de grandes catégories d'hommes qui se situent suivant une hiérarchie donée. On sait que cette hiérarchie mettait au premier rang les Arabes avant la revolution ʿabbāside, non seulement du point de vue du prestige, mais en leur accordant des privilèges importants, en en faisant une caste dominante. La suppression de ces privilèges, l'égalisation théorique de toute la communauté des croyants, enregistrée par le droit religieux, laissa aux Arabes quelques prérogatives mineures, mais surtout un certain prestige social, très variable selon les lieux et les temps, différent aussi selon la position de l'Arabe concerné du point de vue des autres facteurs de hiérarchisation. La hiérarchie des ethnies était d'ailleurs envisagée différemment selon les membres de l'une ou de l'autre et on sait la vigueur de la polémique sur ces problèmes à l'époque ʿabbāside. Dans les divers Etats entre lesquels se fractionne la communauté, l'ethnie à laquelle appartient la famille gouvernante se trouve en général privilégiée en fait et jouit d'un prestige supérieur, au moins à un certain point de vue. L'appartenance ethnique fournit donc un critère de stratification,

[13] Fārābī, *Risāla fī'l-siyāsa*, ed. L. Cheikho, dans *Traités inédits d'anciens philosophes arabes* . . ., publiés . . . par L. Malouf, C. Eddé et L. Cheikho, 2ème éd., Beyrouth 1911, p. 18.

[14] *Ibid.*, p. 19.

délimitant une certaine aristocratie, pourtant stratifiée elle-même suivant d'autres critères avec des différenciations considérables.

L'hérédité intervient de façon plus restreinte pour délimiter une catégorie de descendants du Prophète ou encore de ses Compagnons. A l'époque ʿabbāside, ils ont certains privilèges, reçoivent des pensions, ont droit à la vénération publique. Mais cela n'empêche pas nombre d'entre eux de mener une vie assez misérable. A des époques postérieures, dans certains pays, certains de ces «nobles» purent tirer parti du culte croissant de leur glorieux ancêtre pour obtenir des privilèges bien plus importants et former une véritable aristocratie, non plus seulement théorique, mais effective.

De même, une certaine noblesse est constituée par les descendants des familles qui ont joué un rôle politique important: les chefs de tribus arabes, berbères, turques, kurdes, les grandes familles seigneuriales persanes etc.

La hiérarchie de prestige peut se conserver, même sans correspondre à une hiérarchie de pouvoir et de fortune, surtout quand elle est fondée sur le sentiment religieux. Mais elle n'équivaut à une véritable stratification que quand elle est consolidée par l'un des trois moyens de pouvoir suivants: la propriété foncière, la force militaire, l'argent — ou par plusieurs d'entre eux. Encore faut-il considérer que la force militaire ne se réalise en tant que force sociale que par l'un des deux autres moyens. En gros, par conséquent, la stratification repose sur la propriété foncière ou mobilière. Mais l'appartenance à une strate donnant des avantages économiques, si elle résulte de l'hérédité ou des efforts propres de chacun au niveau économique, peut être perdue par la contrainte de la force. Elle peut aussi être acquise par la force. On en bénéficie alors par l'appartenance à une strate en laquelle réside la force, fût-elle peu estimée en règle générale, comme celle des esclaves quand il s'agit d'esclaves-soldats appartenant à une certaine couche ethnique.

Il faut noter aussi que le terme de propriété foncière, employé ici pour faire court, est à prendre en un sens très large: il s'agit de droits, fondés juridiquement à une part du produit d'une terre quelconque, prélevée sur le fruit du travail du producteur direct, en bref d'un droit à l'exploitation du cultivateur, au sens marxiste du terme.

Pour les membres de la société musulmane qui essaient d'en comprendre la structure, la stratification est conçue comme fonctionnelle, d'autant qu'ils «oublient» d'y inclure la caste des esclaves — preuve d'ailleurs qu'à la différence de ce qui se passait en Grèce à l'époque d'Aristote, les esclaves ne jouaient pas un rôle *spécifique* tant soit peu important dans la production et la distribution. Ces auteurs partent de la théorie de la division du travail social reprise aux Grecs, insistant sur la diversité des besoins et l'inégalité des talents de chacun, ce qui impose cette division.

Dès lors, toute catégorie sociale, toute profession non immorales ont leur utilité. Les Ikhwān al-Ṣafā insistent ainsi sur l'utilité des balayeurs et boueux (I 220): s'ils s'arrêtaient une semaine seulement de travailler, une ville deviendrait inhabitable. Les grandes catégories sociales sont assimilées ainsi à des groupes fonctionnels. Déjà les Ikhwān al-Ṣafā parlent ainsi du souverain (*malik*) dont l'utilité est d'assurer le règne de la loi (*nāmūs*) et par là l'accomplissement des fonctions nécessaires au bon ordre de l'organisation spirituelle et temporelle (*ṣalāḥ al-dīn wa'l-dunyā*), vu la carence de la plupart des hommes de religion ou des philosophes en ce qui concerne l'application des règles qu'ils posent (I 223).

Ghazālī développe ces indications sur l'utilité des fonctions que nous appellerons tertiaires. Il classe les occupations en trois catégories. D'abord les producteurs qui assurent la satisfaction des besoins fondamentaux (nourriture, habitat, vêtement), soit en y travaillant directement, soit en fabriquant des outils pour le travail de ces industries primaires. Puis viennent les militaires qui protègent ce travail productif contre l'ennemi extérieur et contre les voleurs. Enfin ceux qui servent de coordinateurs[15] entre les deux premières catégories et leurs membres, notamment pour la perception et la redistribution des prestations nécessaires à la subsistance des non producteurs directs. Ainsi les fonctionnaires d'autorité (*ʿummāl*), les percepteurs, ceux qui assurent le cadastre, les spécialistes du droit et de la politique (*Iḥyā'*, Le Caire, 1352/1933, t. iii, p. 195 s. = livre xxvi § 5 = analyse G. H. Bousquet, § 108). On voit que Ghazālī, ici, justifie par une nécessité fonctionnelle la domination militaire qui commence alors à jouer un rôle capital.

Il est assez curieux que Ghazālī ne mentionne pas ici les commerçants. Il est naturellement conscient de leur rôle de coordination (*ibid.*, t. iv, p. 102 = livre xxxii, 2ème partie, 2ème *rukn* = analyse Bousquet, § 139 E). Il les classerait sans doute dans sa troisième catégorie.

Ibn Khaldūn a une classification plus brutale et moins idéologique des choses.[16] L'homme dépend de «moyens d'existence» (*maʿāsh*) qui lui fournissent les biens nécessaires à sa continuation dans l'existence et qui peuvent d'ailleurs se développer jusqu'à être des «moyens d'enrichissement» (*riyāsh*) quand leur produit dépasse ses besoins. Les moyens d'existence (ainsi que les quelques sources de biens gratuits qu'offre la nature) lui fournissent régulièrement des acquêts (*kasb*) qui, du point de vue de leur affectation, constituent un *rizq*, un fond de subsistance pour les dépenses en vue de ses besoins et de ses interêts. Ces diverses sortes de revenus sont acquis, soit par la confiscation de force (taxation et impôts),

[15] La traduction de l'expression *al-mutaraddidūn bayna'l-ṭā'ifatayn fī'l-akhdh wa'l-ʿaṭā'* par «les gens qui s'affilient aux deux premières catégories» dans l'*Analyse* de G. H. Bousquet (Paris 1955, p. 263) est certainement erronée.

[16] *Muqaddima*, éd. Quatremère, t. ii, p. 272 ss.; trad. De Slane, t. ii, p. 319 ss.; éd. Wāfī, t. iii, p. 893 ss.; trad. F. Rosenthal, t. ii, p. 311 ss.

soit par la collection des fruits de la nature, animaux terrestres ou marins (chasse et pêche), soit par la production primaire (agriculture et élevage), soit par la production secondaire (travail artisanal et industriel), soit enfin par l'échange (commerce). Oubliant la collection à cause de la minceur de son rôle, Ibn Khaldūn ne reconnaît comme moyens d'existence «naturels» que les métiers assurant la production (primaire ou secondaire) et son écoulement (commerce). Tout ce qui ne ressort pas à l'activité productrice est classé par Ibn Kahldūn comme non naturel, un peu à la manière des physiocrates. Cela ne signifie pas nécessairement qu'il en nie l'utilité, comme il appert de ce qu'il dit des fonctionnaires politiques ou religieux et de la nécessité absolue de l'Etat monarchique pour le fonctionnement harmonieux de la vie sociale.

La conception de la société musulmane comme société sans classes par les théoriciens du droit, son analyse comme consistant en catégories sociales fonctionnelles par les théoriciens qui l'on peut qualifier de sociologues ne sont nullement suffisants pour nous garantir que la société est réellement sans classes. Il s'agit de la conscience que les idéologues (ou du moins certains idéologues) ont de leur société et il est de règle que la réalité sociale soit déformée au cours de cette prise de conscience. Pourtant le contraste avec les conceptions que se font de leur société les idéologues des anciens Empires de l'Orient ou ceux de l'Occident médiéval par exemple a son intérêt. Il nous apprend que, même si les catégories sociales étaient plus ou moins fermées en fait (ce qui serait à vérifier), leur fermeture n'était pas institutionnalisée comme dans le cas des Etats de l'Europe féodale ou des castes de l'Inde. Cela est, en tout état de cause, très important.

On a vu, ci-dessus, qu'à côté de ces conceptions, il existait aussi l'idée très nette d'une stratification. Il est inutile d'alléguer des textes pour montrer qu'on avait conscience des trois dichotomies classiques bien mises en lumière par Ossowski: gouvernés et gouvernants, pauvres et riches, producteurs directs et «exploiteurs» au sens marxiste (c'est à dire non producteurs directs vivant d'un prélèvement sur les producteurs).[17] Mais des stratifications plus fines apparaissent. On le voit par les textes cités ci-dessus sur la hiérarchie de multiples strates ou *ṭabaqāt*. Cela apparaît aussi dans les textes étudiés par R. Brunschvig sur les métiers vils[18], y compris dans ceux émanant de juristes, qui s'efforcent de réhabiliter ces métiers. Il s'agit, il est vrai, de catégories exceptionnelles. Mais, le même auteur l'a montré, le concept se généralise quand les juristes traitent de la parité (*kafā'a*) entre époux dans le mariage et de l'honorabilité (*ʿadāla*) des individus dont le témoignage peut être accepté en justice. Surtout à

[17] Stanislaw Ossowski, *Struktura Klassowa w spoleczney świadomości*, Lódź, 1957; trad. all. *Die Klassenstruktur im sozialen Bewusstsein*, Neuwied am Rhein 1962, p. 38.

[18] R. Brunschvig, 'Métiers vils en Islam', *Studia Islamica*, 16, 1962, pp. 41–60.

propos des mariages, on classe les professions en inférieures, basses (*danīʾa*, *khasīsa*) et supérieures ou relevées (*rafīʿa*, *jalīla*).

Recoupant la notion de catégories fonctionnelles, en vertu desquelles tous les hommes sont égaux contribuant de façon complémentaire à la bonne marche de la société, existent, on l'a déjà vu, la notion de *jāh*, «rang honorifique» ainsi que la reconnaissance d'une hiérarchie économique par la richesse et aussi l'admission réaliste, par Ibn Khaldūn au moins, du fait qu'une position d'«exploiteur» peut être acquise par la force.

Cette dernière thèse équivaut à reconnaître que, dans un cas au moins — mais un cas très important — ce n'est pas la fonction, librement choisie, qui classe dans une catégorie privilégiée et hiérarchiquement supérieure, mais au contraire que l'appartenance (d'une manière ou d'une autre) à une caste détermine la fonction privilégiée.

De même, le *jāh* n'est pas déterminé uniquement par la fonction, mais les hommes classés à rang élevé dans la hiérarchie du *jāh* ont accès à des fonctions privilégiées. La fortune en particulier, selon Fārābī, à la haute époque ʿabbāside, ne peut servir à acquérir ce rang élevé. «Il convient à l'homme de consacrer tous ses efforts à conserver son propre rang. Lorsque se présentent à lui deux opportunités, l'une lui permettant d'accroître ses revenus (*manāfiʿ*), l'autre d'élever son rang, qu'il s'empresse de choisir celle qui lui est la plus propice pour élever son rang. En effet, un rang d'une certaine amplitude (*al-jāh al-ʿarīḍ*) fait nécessairement acquérir de la fortune tandis que la fortune ne permet pas nécessairement d'acquérir un rang donné.»[19]

C'est la même idée que développe Ibn Khaldūn qui y consacre une section de sa *Muqaddima*. La personne qui jouit d'un rang élevé (*ṣāḥib al-jāh*) bénéficie du travail gratuit des gens au dessous de lui, ce qui le rend vite très riche. «C'est dans ce sens que le pouvoir est un des moyens d'existence (*maʿāsh*).»[20]

Cependant la richesse peut, dans certains cas, faire accéder à un rang supérieur comme la pauvreté peut faire déchoir. Ici, tout spécialement, il faudrait tenir compte au maximum des situations historiques. Mez a mis en relief ce qu'il appelle les commérages (Klatsch) d'Ibn Rusta (fin du 3ème/9ème siècle) sur la basse extraction des grandes familles de son temps. Les Ashʿath seraient des descendants d'un cordonnier persan dont la tante avait épousé un riche juif sans enfants; les Muhallabides auraient eu pour ancêtre un tisserand persan; la maison de Khālid ibn Safwān tirerait son origine d'une paysanne de Ḥīra, tombée, enceinte, dans des mains arabes; la famille al-Jahm serait issue d'un esclave en fuite qui se serait attribué faussement une origine qurayshite; la maison princière

[19] Fārābī, ouvrage cité, p. 30.

[20] Ed. Quatremère, t. ii, p. 287 s.; éd. Wāfī, t. iii, p. 907; trad. De Slane, t. ii, p. 336 ss.; trad. Rosenthal, t. ii, p. 326 s.

d'Abū Dulaf viendrait d'un banquier chretien de Ḥīra; le maréchal de la cour al-Rabīʿ, ancêtre d'une influente famille de fonctionnaires aurait été un vaurien, fils naturel d'une esclave débauchée.[21]

De même, Ibn Khaldūn qui, en tant que sociologue, a reconnu l'utilité égale de tous les métiers, mais qui, en tant qu'aristocrate, a insisté sur le caractère méprisable des commerçants ordinaires, met à part les marchands dont le capital initial ne vient pas de la pratique du commerce. Ceux-ci ont pu bénéficier d'un coup de chance, par exemple d'un héritage. Ils n'ont pas été avilis par les pratiques commerciales et continuent à rester indemnes des défauts qu'elles entraînent en confiant à des agents appointés le soin de faire fonctionner leur firme. Ils sont ainsi protégés par leur *jāh* du soin de se livrer à ces pratiques. Leur fortune leur permet d'être associés à la couche des gouvernants (*ahl al-dawla*) et de gagner une situation fastueuse (*zuhūr*) et renommée parmi leurs contemporains.[22] Il est permis de se demander si une telle ascension n'était pas possible même aux marchands ordinaires pour peu que le style de vie qu'ils adoptaient, une fois parvenus à la grande fortune, ne les fasse pas trop mépriser par les aristocrates.

En bref, on peut considérer qu'à l'époque classique au moins la hiérarchie des catégories sociales se déterminait selon ce qu'Ossowski appelle une gradation synthétique, c'est-à-dire faisant appel à plusieurs critères différents conjugués. C'est aussi, visiblement, comme il découle notamment d'un des textes d'Ibn Khaldūn cités ci-dessus, une gradation à échelons multiples.

Mais beaucoup de sociologues modernes seraient d'accord pour refuser à ces catégories sociales le nom de «classes sociales». Ils ont de celles-ci des conceptions différentes, mais toutes modelées par les réalités de la société capitaliste européenne. Les définitions de la classe mettent toutes l'accent, comme le décèle clairement Raymond Aron, «sur ce qui crée la cohérence, l'unité globale ou totale, la communauté d'être ou de conscience d'un ensemble donné».[23] A travers des définitions hautement complexes comme celle de G. Gurvitch,[24] il indique à juste titre comme caractéristiques essentielles: 1° une «communauté objectivement saisissable (nature du travail, niveau des revenus) ou une communauté (. . .) des manières de pensée, des systèmes de valeur», 2° la «consistance à travers la durée de ces êtres collectifs»; 3° la «prise de conscience de ces êtres collectifs par eux-mêmes et (la) volonté propre à chacun d'accomplir une tâche».[25] Il faut

[21] Ibn Rusta, p. 207 s., ap. A. Mez, *Die Renaissance des Islams*, Heidelberg 1922, p. 151 s.

[22] *Muqaddima*, éd. Quatremère, t. ii, p. 305; éd. Wāfī, t. iii, p. 922; trad. De Slane, t. ii, p. 356 s.; trad. Rosenthal, t. ii, p. 344 s.

[23] R. Aron, 'La classe comme représentation et comme volonté', in *Cahiers Internationaux de Sociologie*, 38, 1965, p. 14.

[24] G. Gurvitch, *Le concept des classes sociales* (cours ronéotypé), Paris, Centre de documentation universitaire, 1954, p. 133; id., *Déterminismes sociaux et liberté humaine*, Paris 1955, p. 178, etc.

[25] R. Aron, *ibid.*, p. 14 s.

souligner ici que même un sociologue, qui a proposé une définition extrêmement précise et complexe de la classe sociale comme G. Gurvitch, insiste sur le fait que ses indications «ne mettent en relief que des caractéristiques tendancielles des classes, admettant $n+1$ degrés d'intensité variée».[26]

Or, on a pu voir ci-dessus que ceux qu'on peut appeler les sociologues de la société musulmane médiévale ne se sont pas contentés d'insister sur l'existence de multiples strates. Ils ont essayé de grouper celles-ci, pour reprendre certains termes de la définition de G. Gurvitch, en macrocosmes de groupements et d'individus ayant des fonctions sociales analogues et une position de prestige analogue dans les grandes lignes. Ces grands ensembles avaient assurément une «consistance à travers la durée», comme le montre la répétition de classifications grossièrement analogues et la récurrence des termes qui les désignent à travers les siècles. Il est hors de doute qu'ils tendaient à adopter des représentations communes, des opinions communes, comme le montrent notamment les indications des auteurs cités sur les qualités et défauts de leurs membres. Il est au plus haut point vraisemblable que ces opinions communes concernaient en particulier ce qui touchait de près ou de loin le partage du produit social et des avantages du pouvoir. D'autre part, ces «macrocosmes de groupements» étaient considérés par les gouvernants comme dotés au moins de réactions élémentaires communes, puisque la politique à leur égard suit certains grands principes au moins négatifs visant notamment à éviter certaines de ces réactions, telles que la révolte.[27]

Mais il semble rare qu'on puisse leur attribuer une conscience et une volonté communes sauf dans la limite de territoires très localisés et pendant des périodes restreintes. Il faudrait une enquête historique comparative très étendue pour aboutir là-dessus à des conclusions fermes. Mais l'impression que laisse une plus ou moins grande familiarité avec l'histoire islamique est plutôt que, lorsque des groupes d'intérêts et d'aspirations se présentent comme agents sur la scène de l'histoire, ils dépassent certes la plupart du temps en amplitude les groupes mineurs tels que celui que constituerait une profession donnée, mais ne s'étendent que très rarement à toute une strate majeure, accédant ainsi, par la conscience d'elle-même et la volonté commune, au statut de classe au sens des analyses sociologiques de la société moderne. Les divisions «verticales», par ethnies ou par communautés religieuses, recoupant les catégories horizontales, viennent jouer un grand rôle dans cette fragmentation, de toute évidence.

On peut refuser d'accoler aux grands groupes d'intérêts et d'aspirations

[26] G. Gurvitch, in *Cahiers Internationaux de Sociologie*, 38, 1965, p. 6.

[27] Cf. par exemple Niẓām al-mulk, *Siyāset-nāme*, ed. Ch. Schefer, Paris 1891, p. 144 s.; trad. Ch. Schefer, Paris 1893, p. 214 s.; trad. B. N. Zakhoder, Moscou–Leningrad 1949, p. 167 s.; trad. H. Darke, New Haven 1960, p. 170 s.

le terme de «classe», le réservant aux grandes strates unifiées de la société industrielle accédant à une conscience et à une volonté communes. Encore faut-il préciser que, même dans la société capitaliste moderne, cette conscience unifiée fait souvent défaut, que les strates sont souvent recoupées par d'autres divisions, au premier chef les divisions ethniques. On sait que les sociologues ont insisté là-dessus, particulièrement en ce qui concerne les Etats Unis où même l'observation commune distingue immédiatement, d'une part le manque de conscience de soi et de volonté commune de la classe ouvrière, d'autre part l'importance de la division verticale entre Blancs et Noirs qui vient recouper la stratification de classe.[28]

La complexité de la situation à laquelle on se trouve affronté ne doit pas, me semble-t-il, nous pousser à deux excès. D'une part, doter a priori les grandes catégories sociales déterminées par la position économico-juridique, que distinguent les sociologues indigènes, d'une conscience de classe et d'une volonté unifiées. D'autre part, négliger, contrairement à l'évidence historique, toute considération des groupes d'intérêt et d'aspirations, ne considérer ceux-ci comme agents ou patients historiques que lorsqu'ils sont réduits, par un processus de fragmentation extrême, à la dimension par exemple d'une profession. Surtout l'intérêt porté par les sociologues et les hommes politiques indigènes aux catégories sociales nous interdit de ne considérer comme protagonistes dignes d'intérêt dans la dynamique socio-historique que les ethnies ou les groupes distingués par le genre de vie (Bédouins et sédentaires).

Du point de vue terminologique, il est besoin d'un terme pour designer les macrocosmes de groupements sociaux qui dépassent l'envergure des groupes professionels, locaux, etc., et qui, fondés sur la fonction économique ou sociale, non sans croisements avec les critères de différenciation par l'origine ethnique, la communauté religieuse ou le genre de vie, peuvent être considérés comme relativement durables, comme ayant un stock de représentations communes, comme susceptibles de réactions communes. Dans des circonstances données, à des époques de tension, notamment, il n'est pas exclu que ces ensembles puissent accéder partiellement et temporairement à une conscience et à une volonté communes. Il me semble que le terme de «classe», seul disponible, peut parfaitement leur convenir à condition d'en élargir les définitions trop restrictives, souvent adoptées par les analystes de la société capitaliste contemporaine. Cet élargissement serait d'ailleurs intéressant même pour l'analyse de celle-ci. Il a été souvent pratiqué en fait même par ceux qui adhéraient théoriquement à une de ces définitions restrictives.[29]

On pourrait distinguer ainsi, dans la société islamique traditionelle, les

[28] Cf. St. Ossowski, ouvrage cité, *passim* et aussi, par ex., L. Reissman, *Class in American Society*, Glencoe 1959; trad. fr. *Les classes sociales aux Etats Unis*, Paris 1963.

[29] Notamment Marx. Cf. mon article cité ci-dessus n. 6.

paysans producteurs, les éleveurs tantôt opposés tantôt partiellement unis aux paysans, les petits producteurs urbains, artisans ou petits commerçants, le grand négoce capitalistique englobant en général l'activité financière, les esclaves domestiques, les esclaves de plantations, les militaires sur lesquels il faudra revenir, les fonctionnaires et les intellectuels et les hommes de religion plus ou moins confondus selon les lieux et les temps, les grands propriétaires fonciers, enfin la classe dirigeante qui concentre entre ses mains, suivant la caractérisation de Marx et de Tocqueville,[30] la puissance, le prestige et la fortune. Cette énumération n'est pas limitative. Elle suppose, on l'a dit, des croisements avec des divisions fondées sur d'autres critères. Ainsi les propriétaires fonciers de tel groupe ethnique formeraient une classe à part. Elle devrait être commentée de près, ce qui ne peut être fait ici, car, par exemple, la classe militaire peut être recrutée parmi les esclaves et voit en général son pouvoir assuré, comme on l'a dit, par sa constitution en classe privilégiée de propriétaires fonciers (le sens le plus large étant attribué au terme de propriété). Elle est plus ou moins associée au pouvoir ou peut le monopoliser selon les cas.

La classe dominante, quel que soit son recrutement originel, institutionalise sa domination, c'est-à-dire son pouvoir et les avantages qu'elle en retire, par le fait qu'elle monopolise la direction de l'Etat, qu'elle s'assure des avantages matériels, soit par le revenu de l'impôt redistribué en pensions, soit par des prestations imposées aux producteurs, soit enfin par une combinaison de ces deux modes d'«exploitation».

Une certaine mobilité sociale peut s'instaurer. Notamment l'accès des roguaes de l'Etat peut être assuré dans certaines conditions aux membres des autres classes, par exemple aux hommes de religion. Ils ne peuvent pourtant être considérés comme membres à part entière de la classe dominante que si cette élévation est consolidée par exemple par la dotation en propriétés foncières. Il faudra aussi considérer dans quelle mesure, ces dotations étant révoquables, l'élévation demeure précaire. D'autre part, la richesse acquise par le commerce permet en général l'accès à la propriété foncière. Il est important de savoir dans quelle mesure les propriétés acquises de cette façon permettent de participer au pouvoir de la classe dirigeante.

On voit comment cette mobilité se restreint. Les bénéfices du commerce se limitant, les possibilités d'en tirer parti pour une élévation sociale peuvent se réduire. A une certaine époque et dans certains pays, nous voyons aussi (notamment dans l'Etat mamelouk), la classe dirigeante se fermer, se constituer en caste, restreinte aux membres d'une couche socio-ethnique déterminée.

Les classes sociales, ainsi comprises, ne sont pas déterminées uniquement par les relations de production selon le schéma marxiste, encore

[30] R. Aron, article cité ci-dessus, p. 17.

durci par la conception léninienne des classes comme fondées uniquement sur la relation d'exploitation. D'ailleurs, il faut noter que Marx avait lui-même, à maintes occasions, tenu compte, dans ses études historiques, d'autres facteurs.[31] Pourtant les relations de production et l'exploitation jouent un rôle essentiel qu'il serait extrêmement erroné de nier ou même de minimiser. Les classes sont déterminées, comme l'ont fort bien vu les sociologues indigènes, par les exigences de l'organisation sociale totale où les impératifs de la production et de la redistribution jouent un rôle considérable, essentiel. Les autres clivages viennent recouper de façons diverses ce clivage fondamental du rôle fonctionnel dans l'organisation sociale totale; d'autre part, quel que soit le rôle de la classe dans l'organisation sociale et même si ce rôle n'est pas fondamentalement un rôle économique, elle se voit attribuer une part donnée dans la distribution du produit social, une part distribuée selon certaines règles de nature juridique, mais qui lui assignent une certaine place dans le système économique de production et de redistribution des biens. Les clivages ethniques ou autres peuvent augmenter ou diminuer cette part, ils peuvent surtout donner droit à telle ou telle fonction qui elle-même donne droit à telle ou telle espèce de revenu, mais toujours on en revient à la jouissance d'une part donnée.

L'évolution sociale passe par des phases contrastées. Il y a des phases où la production et la répartition du produit social sont, de manière durable et institutionalisée, distribuées entre des classes déterminées. Le fonctionnement régulier du mécanisme social peut provoquer alors une certaine mobilité social, c'est-à-dire le déclassement et le reclassement d'un certain nombre d'individus. Il peut même aboutir à l'ascension globale ou au déclin global de certaines classes, c'est-à-dire à des variations dans la part de pouvoir et d'avantages sociaux dont elles jouissent.

A d'autres moments, essentiellement lors de conquêtes, il se produit un remplacement brutal, total ou partiel de certaines classes par d'autres; c'est-à-dire que telle ou telle fonction, tel ou tel droit à une part donnée du produit social se trouvent affectés à de nouvelles couches. La fréquence de ces mutations brusques a certainement joué un grand rôle historique en empêchant une classe donnée, celle des commerçants dont un fonctionnement régulier, stable a tendance à accroître constamment le pouvoir, de réaliser une ascension continue comme dans l'Occident chrétien.

Y a-t-il lutte de classes? Il y a au moins compétition permanente, insatisfactions latentes pour le moins d'un côté et, de l'autre, préoccupation d'assurer la continuation et le fonctionnement régulier d'un système avantageux. Comme il n'existe pas de mécanisme par lequel les aspirations et les intérêts des diverses classes pourraient exprimer leurs revendications, certaines classes sont poussées parfois à la révolte brutale. Celle-ci est

[31] Cf. mon article cité ci-dessus, n. 6.

souvent idéologisée sous la forme d'une dénonciation des tares et vices de la classe dirigeante, essentiellement du point de vue de l'attitude religieuse. Mais aucun organisme ne vient déterminer un programme de revendications seculières autre que le remplacement du chef de la communauté et de la couche dirigeante. Aucune modification structurelle n'est, sauf exceptions, envisagée.

L'histoire sociale est l'histoire de la compétition, des vicissitudes des classes entendues dans le sens défini ci-dessus par rapport au pouvoir et à ses avantages.

On voit qu'elle a des rapports certains avec l'histoire économique, mais qu'elle est loin de s'y réduire.

C'est pendant les phases de développement régulier qu'elle en est le moins distincte. Les variations des agrégats économiques à la disposition des diverses classes jouent alors un rôle capital en accroissant ou en diminuant leur force de pression. Pourtant, même alors, l'intervention de la force pure, les décisions politiques, etc., peuvent modifier de façon importante le jeu des seuls facteurs économiques. Notons toutefois qu'elles ont souvent tendance à se traduire en termes économiques.

Pendant les phases de bouleversement au contraire, l'efficace propre de l'économie le cède en importance aux effets de la force brutale, de la contrainte politico-militaire. Mais il ne faut pas oublier que même alors les exigences de la production et de la redistribution restent primordiales.

On peut voir par ce qui a été dit que les rapports de l'histoire économique et de l'histoire sociale sont complexes, que ce serait par conséquent une grave erreur que d'identifier l'une et l'autre, de réduire l'une à l'autre.

L'histoire sociale, si on entend par là l'histoire des grands groupes sociaux et de leurs rapports, dépend fondamentalement des nécessités primordiales de l'activité economique. Ces grands groupes en effet sont déterminés en grande partie par les exigences de la production et la nécessité d'existence d'un mécanisme quelconque de circulation et de répartition. Ils dépendent ainsi de l'économie, mais en un sens seulement, il est vrai en un sens fondamental. Il ne faut pas oublier, d'autre part, que certains de ces grands groupes sont déterminés plus largement par les nécessités de l'activité sociale totale dans une culture donnée. De même, les catégories sociales determinées par les relations de production, d'échange et de répartition sont définies souvent par des règles juridiques qui codifient elles-mêmes une situation résultant d'évènements de nature politique ou découlant d'exigences idéologiques.

L'histoire économique ne peut être réduite à décrire le mécanisme fondamental de la production, de l'échange et de la redistribution, substructure générale de la vie sociale, car ce mécanisme est resté le même dans ses grandes lignes pendant des millénaires. Les variations de volume des agrégats économiques (production agricole et artisanale au premier chef) dépendent de facteurs techniques, de facteurs politiques et sociaux (conquête, dévastations, déportations, législation augmentant ou diminuant les prestations, etc.). Il en est de même pour l'histoire des institutions économiques qui dépend dans une très large mesure de l'histoire sociale.

Cependant, des variations très importantes dans le volume des agrégats économiques, par exemple une augmentation considérable de la production industrielle ou au contraire une diminution drastique, peuvent entraîner des conséquences d'une importance énorme dans le domaine de l'histoire sociale, par exemple un réajustment des relations entre classes. Mais une telle «révolution», si elle est d'une importance capitale, ne se produit que rarement.

On voit combien il est équivoque de parler du rôle de l'économie, de discuter là-dessus sans affiner et éclaircir les concepts. Il faut distinguer au premier chef le mécanisme fondamental de la production, de la circulation et de l'échange et les autres phénomènes économiques. Selon qu'on parle d'un domaine ou de l'autre, les problèmes se présentent de façon très différente, notamment quand on parle des relations avec l'histoire sociale.

Les islamisants ont tout intérêt à prendre conscience de ces distinctions nécessaires et de la façon dont, dans les grandes lignes, se dessinent les rapports de divers phénomènes sociaux. Il est par exemple néfaste de penser qu'une étude poussée d'histoire économique résoud à elle seule des problèmes d'histoire sociale. Il ne faut pas croire que l'importance primordiale du mécanisme économique fondamental se transmet à tous les phénomènes économiques. D'autre part, on ne doit pas penser que l'étude historique d'une classe sociale soit sans importance pour la compréhension de l'évolution économique.

PART TWO

The Sixteenth to Eighteenth Centuries

Conference on the Economic History
of the Middle East
4–6 July 1967

Résolution

En vue du grand nombre des registres de recensements ottomans dont l'importance a été démontré dans le rapport de Monsieur le Professeur Ö. L. Barkan, lors de la conférence d'histoire économique du Moyen Orient (le 4 à 6 juillet, 1967 à Londres) et qui sont conservés non seulement dans les archives de la Turquie mais dans bien d'autres pays, la conférence juge bien utile d'attirer l'attention de la Commission pour les sources ottomanes au sein de l'Association d'Etudes Sud-Est Européennes, attachée au Comité International des sciences historiques sur la nécessité d'effectuer un travail avec la coopération de plusieurs spécialistes sur les registres en question. La première chose à faire, c'est d'élaborer et de publier dans un proche avenir un catalogue d'ensemble de tous les registres de recensements qui existent à présent éparpillés dans de différents pays. Ce catalogue facilitera dans une large mesure les efforts des spécialistes dans le domaine de l'histoire économique de l'Empire Ottoman.

Introductory Remarks

M. A. COOK

It is not accidental or arbitrary that the papers in this section are mainly concerned with the Ottoman Empire in the sixteenth century. This concentration reflects the survival in Istanbul (and to a lesser degree elsewhere) of a vast body of archival material generated by the activities of a highly centralized state. No comparable archive survives for any other pre-modern Middle Eastern state, and the archives of the Ottoman Empire itself for the seventeenth and eighteenth centuries are less informative, because the work of a less centralized administration. Not much of the potential of this archival source has as yet been realized. The contribution of European Orientalism has been fairly small, partly for the very straightforward reason that it is only comparatively recently that most of the material has become accessible to scholars, and partly because Orientalism has tended to remain a philology in the classical tradition, that is to say one whose skills are best employed in dealing with a paucity of evidence. Much more has been done by historians in Turkey and the Balkans, but here again most of the effort is fairly recent.

In what follows I have not attempted to comment on the papers of Mr. Parry and Prof. Davis. Mr. Parry's paper is a valuable collection of data on the provenance of Ottoman war materials, and it contains many facts which will interest economic historians; but it is not primarily an attempt to answer questions about economic history, and the context from which it derives its meaning is rather that of its author's extensive researches into Ottoman military history. Prof. Davis's paper also stands apart from the rest, in its concern with a later period and in its primary orientation towards the commercial history of England. These are not, however, the reasons for my offering no comment on it. The lucid account which Prof. Davis gives of the problem of the decline of the Levant trade, of what previous research (much of it his own) has established, and of what future research might seek to discover, achieves a level of complexity which makes such evidence as might be gleaned from studies in Middle Eastern sources seem jejune and irrelevant. It is perhaps doubtful whether the Ottoman documents of the period will ever throw much light on Prof. Davis's problem, and certainly the questions he addresses to the Middle Eastern experts were in no danger of being answered at the conference.

Prof. Barkan's paper is an account of his important researches into the Ottoman fiscal surveys of the fifteenth and sixteenth centuries. These are primarily listings of adult males—it is usually possible to distinguish heads of households, but there is no information from which the composition of the population by age or sex could be determined. The interest of the data thus lies mainly in the indication they give of the approximate size of the population at various times. Here the paper contains a number of additions to the figures given in Prof. Barkan's earlier articles.[1] He does not however offer an assessment of the reliability of the data; nor does he attempt to account for the population growth which they indicate, or to identify the economic or social consequences of this growth.[2]

Mme. Cvetkova's paper, with its characteristically impressive documentation, describes the way in which the Ottoman government sought to ensure the supply of mutton to the capital and the army. With mutton, as with grain, the state opted for coercion rather than a free market. The mode of coercion was not however the same in both cases. The essence of the *celep* system described by Mme. Cvetkova was not the extensive coercion of a whole market familiar from studies of the grain trade, but the intensive coercion of a few thousand wealthy individuals, the imposition of a liturgy. Why there should have been this difference is not immediately obvious, and the paper does not enlarge on the initial observation that the system was engendered by the specific conditions present in the Ottoman Empire.

Prof. İnalcık's paper is among other things an interesting account of the contribution of the state to the economic infrastructure. That this is to be seen as investment for fiscal returns—more economic activity means more taxation—is in general a matter of inference, but the fiscal rationale is explicitly developed in the remarks of Selman Reis on trade and revenue in the Red Sea. The state was of course frequently deflected from the pursuit of fiscal rationality—witness the enormous losses in revenue from the silk trade incurred during the Persian wars, the political criteria applied in allocating to western merchants access to Ottoman markets, perhaps also the underwriting of the monopolistic interests of the guilds as the price of administrative control. But the interesting question is whether the degree of fiscal rationality displayed by the Ottoman government was exceptional, and this needs to be considered in a comparative context, such as Prof. İnalcik invokes when he contrasts the abilities of Ottoman and European statesmen in the manipulation of the economy. Here, in Prof. İnalcık's view, the comparison comes out very unfavourably to the Ottomans. It is, however, only fair to the Ottomans to point out that this

[1] See below, p. 163, note 1. Readers familiar with the second of the two articles there cited should note the following additions: (i) Table 2 (but not the data for Anadolu); (ii) the figures for the growth of the Balkan and Syrian populations given on pp. 169–70; (iii) Table 4.

[2] His views on the consequences are briefly presented in 'The Social Consequences of Economic Crisis in Later Sixteenth Century Turkey', in *Social Aspects of Economic Development*, Istanbul 1964. The paper which I submitted to the conference under the title 'Population Pressure in the Ottoman Empire, 1450–1600' is not included in this volume, as it is merely a summary of a book which I hope to publish shortly.

judgement rests on a more flattering assessment of the modernity of the European sixteenth century than many would now adopt.

Many Islamic societies have had problems arising from the concurrent use of lunar and solar calendars. Just what these problems are in any particular case depends on the uses to which the two calendars are put. Dr. Sahillioğlu's rather intriguing paper deals with the case of the Ottoman administration in the fifteenth to eighteenth centuries. The usual practice here was to collect revenue by the solar calendar and disburse it by the lunar calendar. This gave rise to two problems which it may help to distinguish. The first was an accounting problem, and it was resolved by an accounting convention (the *sıvış* year). The second was a more embarrassingly real problem. The Janissaries in particular were paid once a quarter by the lunar calendar; this meant that every eight years or so the government was faced by a solar year—a revenue year—in which not *four* but *five* quarterly payments fell due. The choice of evils which then confronted a government which had not saved in advance to meet the extra payment is well set out by Dr. Sahillioğlu, and he has certainly established that it played a part in some of the many disturbances to which the Ottoman political system was subject.

That it has not been possible to present these papers in terms of any overall framework is perhaps hardly surprising in a volume of this kind. But it does also convey something about the present state of the field—that it is still a rather disorganized one in which the activities of scholars lie few and far between. Perhaps the creation of a periodical devoted to Ottoman studies will in the near future do something to raise the level of interaction between the currently dispersed efforts of historians working in different parts of the field. Even more, the full publication of Prof. Barkan's researches into population history may establish a structure of hypotheses relating to secular change in the later fifteenth and sixteenth centuries in terms of which much that is now disorganized and dispersed may begin to acquire a more central significance. Such a development could make the field a very interesting one.

Research on the Ottoman Fiscal Surveys

ÖMER LÛTFİ BARKAN

1. *Periodic and general surveys of the entire empire*

As I have indicated elsewhere in some detail,[1] the most precious possession of the Turkish archives is the great series of registers in which were entered the results of the surveys of population and taxable resources which, until the beginning of the seventeenth century, were carried out every 30 or 40 years in accordance with a long-established administrative tradition.

These registers (*defter-i hâkani*) contain in the first instance a listing of the empire's adult male population; the entry for each person states his father's name, his legal status, the duties and privileges of his economic or social position, and the extent of his land. The registers also give much information regarding land use (arable, orchard, vineyard, rice-paddy), the numbers of mills, beehives, etc., and the estimated fiscal value of these sources of revenue. Moreover, the information contained in the registers is not confined to an agrarian inventory. There is information on the revenue from customs duties, markets, official weighing scales (with their locations, regulations and the volume of transactions effected), fisheries and mines. The registers make it possible to establish the precise distribution of revenue as between imperial domain, military fiefs (*timar*), pious foundations and private property. In effect the registers were a cadastre of fiefs and other land in which was entered the status of each fief with a summary statement of its tenurial history.

The reason why these surveys were carried out relates to the administrative organization of the empire. The great majority of Ottoman civil and military functionaries were not paid from the central treasury of the empire but accorded the right to enjoy the revenue from certain taxes in a given area. At the beginning of the sixteenth century the fief holders alone numbered some 38,000 and were in receipt of more than half the empire's revenue; moreover, the sum allocated to military fiefs increased over the sixteenth century with the rising number of timariots. The successful operation of this system required detailed information on the empire's various sources of revenue and the changes which they underwent. Only

[1] 'Les grands recensements de la population et du territoire de l'empire Ottoman et les registres impériaux de statistiques', *Revue de la Faculté des Sciences Economiques de l'Université d'Istanbul*, ii, 1940; 'Essai sur les données statistiques des registres de recensements dans l'Empire Ottoman aux XVème et XVIème siècles', *Journal of the Economic and Social History of the Orient*, i, 1957; *EI*² *s.v. Daftar-i Khāḳānī.*

in this way was it possible to keep a check on the relationship between the value officially assigned to a fief (in the registers and the *berat* issued to the beneficiary) and the amount of revenue actually accruing to the beneficiary. Furthermore, in the period of economic expansion when the population was growing, surveys carried out at frequent intervals made it possible for the state to keep its registers up to date and thus profit from new sources of revenue. In the seventeenth century, however, the central government no longer possessed either the authority or the will to carry out these surveys effectively in consequence of the prevailing anarchy in the empire's administration. The disordered state of the fief system in any case rendered the activity pointless.

2. *The state of preservation of the registers*

On the completion of a new survey, the obsolete registers containing the results of the previous survey were deposited in the archives of the *Defterhane*. For the most part they were later mislaid or destroyed, principally in the course of being moved from one depository to another in the last century. Nevertheless there remain almost a thousand volumes in various libraries and archives in Turkey and elsewhere, above all in the Başbakanlık Arşivi, Istanbul.

Some of the extant registers date from the reigns of Murad II (1422–51) and Mehmed the Conqueror (1451–81); these contain references to even earlier registers which have been lost. There is also a complete collection of registers containing the results of the last surveys carried out in the empire. These date primarily from the reigns of Selim II (1566–74) and Murad III (1574–95), with the addition of a few surveys carried out at a later date in such provinces as Crete on its conquest from the Venetians or the Morea on its reconquest. This collection is now kept in the archives of the Tapu ve Kadastro Umum Müdürlüğü in Ankara. The number of detailed (*mufassal*) registers in this collection is 254; most of these volumes measure 15 × 42 cm. and contain about 300 leaves. Some are as large as 21 × 58 cm., are 7·5 cm. thick, and weigh 6·5 kg. Each province (*sancak*) is covered on average in two to three of these volumes.

3. *Current research*

Following the publication of my earlier studies drawing attention to the historical importance of these registers, the Turkish Historical Society asked me to prepare a full-scale study of them. This study will contain a detailed catalogue of the surviving registers. It will present the results of my research on the methods by which the surveys were executed, the way in which the registers were compiled, and the palaeographic problems which they raise. I shall give an account of the peculiarities of the administrative and fiscal system of the Ottoman Empire, and in the light of this explain the functions of the various kinds of register which were in use. In short, my study will contain all that is needed to facilitate the use of these registers. In addition, the study will include a first presentation of the demographic data contained in these registers for a period comprising the early years of the reign of Suleyman the Magnificent (1520–30). On the basis of the almost complete series of registers extant for this period, I shall attempt to give a quantitive account of a number of aspects of the economic and social structure of the empire in the early sixteenth century. This account will be illustrated by graphs and maps.

What are the results of these first researches into the demographic data of the registers? I am arranging them in a series of tables of greater or less uniformity covering the entire empire. The most important types of table are the following:

(i) A first group covers a category of the population referred to as the *ʿavarız haneleri*, that is those households liable to pay the tax known as *ʿavarız* which was levied in the empire at irregular intervals. This category covers those who, lacking any inherited or acquired privilege in virtue of which they could claim exemption from the tax, constituted the mass of the Ottoman population. The tables relating to this category of the population present the primary information on the demography of the empire. They show the composition of the empire's population by religion (Muslim, Christian, Jew) or way of life (townsman, peasant, nomad). Furthermore, within these main lines of division the population can be subdivided by marital status (head of a household or bachelor for Muslims, head of a household, bachelor or widow acting as head of a household in the case of Christians and Jews). This information is of great value when one comes to estimate the size of the total population.

(ii) The second category consists of those who for one reason or another enjoyed the privilege of exemption from the payment of *ʿavarız*. They fall into two groups: (*a*) The first comprises the grand dignitaries of the empire who represented its military and ruling classes. The study of their numbers and distribution is of great help in understanding the social and administrative structure of the empire; it shows us exactly how many military and other fiefs and fief-holders (*zaʿim*, *sipahi*) there were, and where in their fiefs the fief-holders usually lived. This category includes the *sancak beyleri* (the military and administrative governors of the *sancaks*), the kadis, the *medrese* teachers, the leaders of caravans, the commanders of garrisons and their subordinates, but also many more humble subjects of the empire who served the state as falconers, grooms in the imperial stables, and members of the minor military organizations (*voynuks*, *yörüks*, *müsellems*, *Tatars*, etc.). (*b*) The second group comprises a long list of persons exempted from *ʿavarız*: the servants of religious institutions, members of illustrious families whose services to the empire in war or religion had been confirmed by imperial firman, persons engaged in the performance of duties imposed by the state such as miners, the guardians of defiles and mountain passes, those who watched and repaired the bridges and the roads, those responsible for tending the horses, water-buffaloes and camels of the sultan, and those who supplied salt-petre, arrows, timber for the navy, and other materials of war. To this list may be added those who, by reason of old age or infirmity, were not in a position to make a living and so were unable to pay taxes. These were the old, the blind, the dumb, the paralysed and the insolvent.

These registers are not simple enumerations of households or tax-payers. In the first place, they constitute a systematic census of the entire population of the empire (excluding only Egypt, North Africa and the Ḥijāz) executed in a statistical spirit with a wealth of details, and for this reason their value from the point of view of historical demography is very great. Secondly, the registers contain the results of a detailed agricultural census covering arable land, fruit trees, vines, mills, pasture land, beehives, and all kinds of agricultural products with numerous data on the approximate volume of production and its yield in revenue.

4. *A comparison*

In comparison to the material available to demographic historians elsewhere, the Ottoman registers constitute a very impressive source. Historians of medieval Europe give the impression that properly demographic sources come into existence only from the thirteenth century in southern Europe and from the fourteenth in the north.[2] This material, however, arises not so much from true censuses as from enumerations carried out in exceptional circumstances for fiscal or military purposes. This makes it difficult to use. It often turns out that, for example, only those possessing more than a certain minimum amount of property or those capable of bearing arms were registered in a given city. In other cases the only index of the size of the population is the number of households, and we have to make an arbitrary guess at the value of the multiplier, which varied with time and place. Moreover, as a result of the territorial fragmentation of the feudal period, these enumerations consist only of partial and heterogeneous data among which it is hard to establish any basis for comparison. Thus there is in a sense no lack of demographic material for medieval Europe; what is missing is results derived from censuses carried out over large territories at regular intervals using uniform procedures and covering the whole population. The surveys which took place in England in 1086 and in France in 1328 are rare and exceptional.

It might be supposed that the Ottoman Empire would be an unlikely place to find such materials. The empire had no well-established landed

[2] IXe Congrès International des Sciences Historiques, Paris 1950, *Rapports*, p. 56.

or racial aristocracy, gave no encouragement to municipal autonomy, and lacked any organization comparable to the Catholic Church with regard to the registration of births, deaths and marriages. Consequently it has no familial, municipal or religious archives. Equally one might expect the execution of regular censuses of the population for the purpose of obtaining demographic statistics to be a practice developed in Western Europe in modern times, and thus belonging to an evolutionary stage which the Ottoman Empire had not reached. However, it has to be remembered that, even if the statistical spirit is a modern Western development, the eminently centralized Oriental monarchies of the past were compelled for administrative and financial reasons to carry out frequent censuses according to methods which were already well-advanced.

The Ottoman registers do in fact contain the results of systematic censuses of the population uniformly executed, repeated at regular intervals, and covering large areas of the empire. The data are genuine statistics intended to provide information which was basic to the whole administrative and financial organization of the empire.

5. *The growth of the Ottoman population in the sixteenth century*

Using the two fairly complete collections of registers referred to above that for the early years of the reign of Suleyman the Magnificent (1520–30) and that for the reigns of Selim II and Murad III (1566–95), it is possible to obtain a statistical account of the empire's population at two different periods and to establish what changes had taken place in the interval, in particular the amount by which the population had grown. This project has not however been completed as yet. In the interim, I give some sample figures relating (i) to the size of the urban population, and (ii) to certain provinces of the empire.

(i) Naturally the growth of the population in a number of the larger towns is not a precise index of the growth of the population as a whole. There may have been increasing urbanization and some evacuation of the countryside in favour of the towns, above all in times of social and economic crises; and a redistribution of the population in favour of certain parts of the empire could render any inference of this kind misleading. We are however in the sixteenth century and in the Ottoman Empire. The urbanization of the period of industrialization is still in the future, and the movement of population is strictly controlled under a regime of attachment to the soil. Thus with certain qualifications one can accept the hypothesis that in this period the growth of the urban population was closely related to the growth of the total population, and assume the proportion to be the same in each case. Table 1 shows the amount of this increase for some typically Ottoman cities and towns.

To obtain the total populations from the numbers of households given

TABLE I. *Population of the principal cities and towns at various dates*

City or town	Before 1520	1520–1530	1571–1580	After 1580
Istanbul	97,956 (1478)	400,000(?) (?)	700,000(?) (?)	—
Aleppo	67,344 (1519)	56,881	45,331	46,365
Damascus		57,326	—	42,779 (1595)
Bursa	—	34,930	70,686	
Edirne	—	22,335	30,140	—
Amid	—	18,942 (1541)	31,443	—
Ankara	—	14,872	29,007	
Athens	—	12,633	17,616	
Tokat	17,328 (1455)	8,354	13,282	21,219 (1646)
Konya	—	6,127	15,356	—
Sivas	3,396	5,560	16,846	—
Sarajevo		5,632	23,485	—
Monastir	2,645	4,647	5,918	—
Skoplje	4,974	4,631	9,867	—
Sofia	—	3,899	7,848	—
Total for 12 towns	—	142,562	271,494	—

in the registers, I have used a multiplier of 5. Since, moreover, certain military groups, the Janissaries, the servants of the imperial court and the empire's slave population were excluded, I have raised the figures by 20 per cent in the case of Istanbul and 10 per cent elsewhere. It must be admitted that these are only assumptions and may in some cases be misleading. With this qualification, we can for the moment infer from the table the following results:

(*a*) In comparison to the size they have attained at the present day, the cities and towns of the Ottoman Empire in the sixteenth century represented concentrations of population on a very small scale, with the one exception of Istanbul. However, the order of size indicated in the table is in line with what we find elsewhere in the Mediterranean in the same period.[3]

[3] The population of Venice stood at 100,000 inhabitants in 1509, and had only reached 175,000 in 1575. Similarly the population of Naples and Milan from the end of the fifteenth century stood at 100,000 inhabitants each, while that of such major Italian cities as Rome, Florence, Bologna and Verona must have remained at about 50,000. The other

(*b*) Leaving aside the Syrian cities of Aleppo and Damascus, the population of which decreased in the sixteenth century, the Ottoman urban population grew continuously. Thus the population of the former capital of Bursa, a typically Ottoman city, doubled between 1520–30 and 1570–80. Similarly, if we leave aside Istanbul and the two Syrian cities, the population of the remaining twelve towns and cities given in the table increased on average by 90 per cent. This may be compared with the figure of 84 per cent for the increase in the urban population elsewhere in the Mediterranean.[4]

(ii) I have also attempted to calculate the growth of the population in selected provinces; the results are given in Table 2.

The table shows the steeply upward trend of population growth in the provinces selected. In addition I have calculated the increase to be 71 per

TABLE 2. *Population of selected provinces at two periods*
(*A* = 1520–30; *B* = 1570–80)

Province		Muslims: Settled	Muslims: Nomad	Christians	Jews	Total	% increase
Anadolu	A	388,397	77,268	8,511	271	474,447	41·7
	B	535,495	116,219	20,264	534	672,512	
Karaman (Konya, Akşehir, Kayseri, etc.)	A	117,863	25,654	3,127	—	146,644	82·8
	B	214,952	39,617	13,448	11	268,028	
Zülkadriye (Kırşehir, Mar῾aş, etc.)	A	18,185	48,665	2,631	—	69,481	62·6
	B	70,368	38,497	4,163	—	113,028	
Rum-i Kadîm (Amasya, Tokat, Canik, etc.)	A	90,839	8,672	6,551	—	106,062	79
	B	145,715	25,724	18,177	27	189,643	
Rum-i Hadis (Trabzon, Kemah, Malatya, etc.)	A	24,914	305	50,757	—	75,976	54
	B	58,957	160	58,146	—	117,263	
Total	A	640,193	160,564	71,577	271	872,610	59·9
	B	1,025,487	220,217	114,198	572	1,360,474	

towns did not even exceed 10,000. See F. Braudel, *La Méditerranée et le Monde méditerranéen a l'époque de Philippe II*, Paris 1949, p. 268; IXe Congrès International des Sciences Historiques, Paris 1950, *Rapports*, p. 65.

[4] See note 3.

cent for a large part of the eastern Balkans (the *sancaks* of Gelibolu, Vize, Edirne, Çirmen, Silistre, Niğbolu, Vidin, Sofya, Köstendil and Selanik) and 55 per cent for Syria. Thus the Ottoman Empire participated fully in the well-known growth of population which characterized the Mediterranean countries in the sixteenth century.

6. *The religious composition of the population*

To give the reader an idea of the range of demographic information to be found in the surveys, I give in Table 3 a break-down of a number of urban populations by religion. The figures relate simply to the number of households entered in the registers (cf. Table 1).

TABLE 3. *Religious composition of the principal urban populations*, circa 1520–35

City or town	Muslims	Christians	Jews	Total
Istanbul	9,517	5,162	1,647	16,326 (1478)
Bursa	6,165	69	117	6,351
Edirne	3,338	522	201	4,061
Ankara	2,399	277	28	2,704
Athens	11	2,286		2,297
Tokat	818	701		1,519
Konya	1,092	22		1,114
Sivas	261	750		1,011
Sarajevo	1,024	—		1,024
Monastir	640	171	34	845
Skoplje	630	200	12	842
Sofia	471	238		709
Salonica	1,229	989	2,645	4,863
Serres	671	357	65	1,093
Trikkala	301	343	181	825
Larissa	693	75		768
Nicopolis	468	775		1,343

It is surprising to note that, even in the most unlikely places, there is a marked Turko-Muslim majority. This state of affairs must be due in part to the coercive resettlements of population effected by the government.[5] At the same time it is notable that the Muslims who lived in these towns were not, as has been thought, exclusively officials or soldiers in an army

[5] See my article 'Les déportations comme méthode de peuplement et de colonisation dans l'Empire Ottoman', in *Revue de la Faculté des Sciences Economiques de l'Université d'Istanbul*, xi, xiii, xv, 1953.

of occupation. This is shown by the few registers in which the livelihood of the persons listed is stated. The following examples illustrate the participation of Muslims in the urban economy:

(i) According to a census carried out in 1546, of the 1,427 households in Sofia, 1,171 were Muslim, 168 were Christian, 52 were Jewish and 36 were foreign, of Ragusan origin. Of the 1,171 Muslim households, 626 were headed by craftsmen (saddlers, tanners, cobblers, dyers, weavers, blacksmiths, armourers, etc.). Only 247 heads of households were soldiers, officials, men of religion or in receipt of pensions. The rest were probably agriculturalists. The 168 Christian heads of households included 110 artisans and traders; in 58 cases no information is given.

(ii) In 1546 again the town of Skoplje consisted of 1,004 Muslim, 216 Christian and 32 Jewish households. Of the 1,004 heads of Muslim households, 434 were officials, soldiers and men of religion, and 14 were entered as old or infirm. The rest consisted entirely of craftsmen and traders.

(iii) In 1454, of the 355 Muslim heads of households entered for the town of Larissa, 217 were craftsmen. In the same period, the town of Trikkala contained 255 Muslim households of which the heads of 121 were entered as craftsmen.

(iv) In 1478, not a single Jew yet lived in Salonica. Of the 837 Muslim households mentioned at this time, 584 were entered as craftsmen. By contrast, the occupation of 282 Christians is not indicated; this suggests to me that they were simply cultivators of the soil.

7. *The fertile crescent*, circa *1570–90*

Finally Table 4 shows the population of a number of Arab provinces as given in surveys carried out between 1570 and 1590. The figures refer to households.

TABLE 4. *Population of certain Arab provinces* circa *1570–90*

Province	Muslims		Christians	Jews	Total
	Settled	Nomad			
Halep	81,203	47,454	3,386	233	132,276
Trablus	34,316	4,698	11,768	307	51,089
Şam	86,369	4,062	7,867	2,068	100,186
Bagdad	39,379	24,619	4,035	603	68,636
Basra	13,464	6,197	—	—	19,661

Les *Celep* et leur Rôle dans la Vie Economique des Balkans a l'Epoque Ottomane (XVᵉ–XVIIIᵉs.)

BISTRA CVETKOVA

L'ORGANISATION de l'approvisionnement d'Etat et public constituait un important élément de la politique économique du pouvoir turc dès le début du développement de l'Empire Ottoman. Les besoins sans cesse plus pressants de son appareil militaire et l'accroissement progressif, à partir du XVIᵉs., de ses forces combattantes, engagées dans des guerres continuelles sur trois continents, motivèrent la prise de toute une série d'initiatives et de mesures visant à garantir l'approvisionnement constant et abondant de l'armée en produits alimentaires et munitions.

D'un autre côté, l'Empire devait faire face à de sérieux problèmes liés au développement des grands centres urbains de l'Empire, où étaient concentrés de nombreux organes de l'administration osmanlie, de garnisons et de représentants de l'aristocratie féodale.

La solution de ces problèmes, engendrés par les conditions spécifiques en présence dans l'Empire Ottoman, avait imposé la prise de différentes initiatives, dont l'aspiration des autorités osmanlies de profiter surtout des possibilités de l'activité commerciale libre. A cet effet elles instaurèrent plusieurs limitations et monopoles concernant les échanges commerciaux, ainsi qu'un sévère régime de contrôle exercé par les nombreux intendants et autres organes d'approvisionnement. Or, les mesures prises n'arrivaient pas toujours à régler avec succès les questions de l'approvisionnement, ce qui forçait le pouvoir à recourir de plus en plus souvent, surtout à partir du XVIᵉs.' au système des achats obligatoires de l'Etat de produits alimentaires et de munitions, connus sous les noms d'*iştira* et *mubaya'a* (*mukayese*).

Les céréales formaient le principal objectif de ces achats.[1] Comme on le sait, la question de l'approvisionnement régulier en blé des provinces de l'Empire occupait une place importante dans les initiatives économiques des milieux gouvernementaux turcs. Cette question a d'ailleurs déjà fait l'objet à plus d'une reprise et à des degrés différents d'études plus spécialisées.[2]

[1] Ce problème était commun et très important pour tout le monde méditerranéen au cours du XVIᵉs. Cf. F. Braudel, *La Méditerranée et le Monde méditerranéen à l'époque de Philippe II*, Paris 1949, p. 283; nouvelle édition, Paris 1966, t. i, pp. 517–48.

[2] L. Güçer, *XVI–XVII Asırlarda Osmanlı İmparatorluğunda Hububat Meselesi ve Hububattan Alınan vergiler*, Istanbul 1964. Cf. pour plus de détails B. Cvetkova, *Izvănredni danăci i dăržavni povinnosti v bălgarskite zemi pod turska vlast*, Sofia 1958.

Non moins importantes étaient aussi les fournitures de viande et de bétail. De nombreuses sources attestent que durant de siècles l'Etat ottoman avait déployé de soins particuliers en vue de s'assurer de fournitures massives surtout de menu bétail (agneaux, moutons et chèvres) pour l'alimentation de l'armée et de la population des grandes villes. Cette pratique a été conservée jusqu'à la fin du XIX^e^s. entre autre aussi pour la raison que les habitants musulmans en Turquie préféraient la viande du mouton à tous les autres produits alimentaires locaux.

Les fournitures d'Etat de menu bétail ne pouvaient avoir lieu qu'en présence d'un élevage de moutons bien développé dans les vastes provinces de l'Empire et, plus spécialement, de ses provinces balkaniques. Les conditions climatiques du Sud-Est européen ont été de tout temps favorables à l'élevage de menu bétail. Déjà au cours des premiers temps de son établissement le pouvoir ottoman s'était empressé d'incorporer ce secteur de l'économie populaire dans la sphère de son système fiscal. Ainsi, au XV^e^s., un impôt spécial et général frappant les moutons (*ʿadet-i ağnam*)[3] vint accroître la liste des principales institutions fiscales de l'Etat. D'autre part, sur la foi de certaines données, par endroits les milieux gouvernementaux ottomans encourageaient par différents moyens l'élevage des moutons, sans doute pour la raison bien simple, que cette activité constituait une précieuse source de revenus. Ainsi, dans son *mülk* du village de Drianovo le grand vizir Kasım pacha avait consenti, par des actes législatifs spéciaux, des allégements fiscaux à une certaine catégorie de la population locale s'occupant de l'élevage de moutons. Durant deux années ces personnes étaient exonérées de *harac* et de l'impôt sur les moutons.[4] Probablement par suite de ce régime protectionniste et d'après les données du rôle des contribuables du milieu du XVI^e^s. le village de Drianovo se distingue par le développement de son élevage—22 moutons par l'exploitation familiale dûment imposée de *resm-i ağnam* au profit du *vakif* établi par Kasım pacha.[5]

L'importance de la place que l'élevage des moutons occupait dans l'économie des terres balkaniques, respectivement dans les terres bulgares est confirmée de manière éloquente aussi par les informations sur l'activité commerciale pendant les XVe–XVI^e^s. Le menu bétail était un article courant dans les échanges commerciaux sur les marchés.[6] De leur côté, la

[3] Sa plus ancienne réglementation se trouve dans le code de Mehmet II. Cf. F. Kraelitz-Greifenhorst, «Kānūnnāme Sultan Mehmeds des Eroberers. Die ältesten osmanischen Straf- und Finanzgesetze», *Mitteilungen zur osmanischen Geschichte*, I, p. 29. Pour l'institution elle-même cf. H. Hadžibegić, «Porez na sitnu stoku i korišćenje ispaša», *Prilozi*, viii–ix, 1958/59, pp. 63–109.

[4] Cf. l'acte du statut de Drianovo dans le registre de la Section orientale auprès de la Bibliothèque nationale «Kiril i Metodi»—Sofia, OAK 217/8, f. 10b.

[5] OAK 217/8, f. 8a–10b. Pour plus de détails cf. B. Cvetkova, «Novi arkhivni iztočnici za agrarniya režim v Severna Bălgariya prez načalniya period na turskoto vladičestvo», *Izvestiya na Dăržavnite Arkhivi*, vii, pp. 314, 337.

[6] Les taxes et les droits perçus sur les marchés intérieurs lors des transactions ayant

laine et les peaux de mouton, de chèvre et d'agneau étaient les principales marchandises destinées à l'exportation.[7]

Il est incontestable que la colonisation de groupes de la formation de *yürük* a grandement contribué au développement de l'élevage de moutons dans les provinces balkaniques. Profitant de leur statut spécial que le pouvoir suprême leur avait accordé en récompense de leur participation aux corps auxiliaires de l'armée turque, les *yürüks* et, à partir du XVII[e]s., aussi les *evlâd-i fâtihân*, étaient devenus de riches éleveurs dans le pays.

L'organisation de l'approvisionnement en menu bétail sous l'incessant contrôle des autorités avait conduit à la création, sur un vaste plan, de toute une catégorie sociale, dite les *celep*, à laquelle incombait l'obligation de cet approvisionnement. Le rôle et la place de cette intéressante institution dans la vie économique de l'Empire ottoman au cours du XIX[e]s. sont relativement bien connus par la science.

L'origine et la nature de cette institution des *celep* et plus spécialement le rôle qu'elle a joué dans les provinces balkaniques pendant les XVe–XVIII[e]s. sont moins connus[8] et attirent à juste titre l'attention des chercheurs dans ce domaine. Toute une série de documents, surtout de registres fiscaux consacrés à cette catégorie de contribuables dans les terres bulgares, nous fournissent d'amples données aptes à élucider plusieurs problèmes dans ce domaine. Malgré le caractère forcément limité de point de vue régional de ces matériaux, on peut en faire des analyses et des conclusions valables non seulement pour le caractère de l'institution des *celep* en Bulgarie pendant les XVe–XVIII[e]s. mais aussi pour les terres balkaniques et même pour l'Empire ottoman pris dans son ensemble.

Le fait que dans les Balkans et, plus spécialement en Bulgarie, des fonctions de *celep* étaient chargées surtout des personnes issues de la population asservie non-musulmane, pose plusieurs questions concernant la place et le rôle de ces couches sociales aisées dans le développement des peuples balkaniques durant l'époque de leur Renaissance nationale.

Plusieurs documents datant de la deuxième moitié du XVI[e]s.[9] élucident

---

pour objet achat-vente de moutons, chèvres ou agneaux constituaient d'importantes sources de revenus. Cf. les dispositions législatives chez B. Cvetkova, «Kăm văprosa za pazarnite i pristaništnite mita i taksi v nyakoi bălgarski gradove prez XVI v.», *Izvestiya na Instituta za istoriya*, xiii, 1963, pp. 204–5.

[7] Durant de longs siècles les commerçants de Doubrovnik achetaient et exportaient de la Bulgarie d'importantes quantités de kordovans, de montonins, etc. Cf. I. Sakăzov, *Stopanskite vrăzki meždu Dubrovnik i bălgarskite zemi prez XVI i XVII stoletiya*, Sofia 1930, pp. 115–17, 151, 155.

[8] Pour le métier de *celepkeşan* au XVIe–XVIII[e]s. on ne trouve que de notes éparses dans l'historiographie. H. W. Duda, *Balkantürkische Studien*, Wien 1949, pp. 92–6; H. A. R. Gibb et H. Bowen, *Islamic Society and the West*, London–New York–Toronto 1957, vol. i, part II, pp. 34–5; P. Miyatev, «Nyakolko turski dokumenti ot XVI v. po prodovolstvieto na sultanskata voyska c ovce ot bălgarski selišta», *APPr.*, i, 1938, No. 1, pp. 130–5; B. Cvetkova, *Izvănredni danăci*, pp. 95–6, 101.

[9] De toute probabilité l'institution de *celepkeşan* a été introduite déjà au XV[e]s. Ce fait est

le rôle important joué par la catégorie des *celepkeşan* dans les fournitures d'Etat en moutons, surtout aux moments de grande tension militaire.[10] Les autorités ne cessaient d'exiger de ces pourvoyeurs de très grandes quantités de menu bétail, destinées surtout aux besoins de l'armée.

Les sources dont nous disposons permettent d'établir avec précision quelles sont les couches sociales desquelles étaient issues les personnes formant la catégorie de *celepkeşan*, ainsi que quels sont leur statut, leur appartenance nationale et les fonctions qu'elles remplissaient.

On sait qu'au XIX^e^s. les *celepkeşan* appartenaient à des milieux plus aisés. Des nouvelles données datant du XVIe–XVIII^e^s. appuyent cette constatation et nous autorisent à la préciser encore davantage. Ces données montrent qu'un certain bien-être matériel était une condition indispensable pour être incorporé à la catégorie des *celepkeşan*. Ainsi, un registre officiel des *celepkeşan* de 1576 note, à côté de chaque nom de six personnes de Plovdiv, que cette personne est aisée et que, par conséquent, elle devrait être inscrite au nombre des *celepkeşan*. Le texte laisse entendre, que ces personnes s'efforçaient de se soustraire à cette obligation particulière, en alléguant comme raison qu'ils étaient enregistrés comme *kırklu*.[11] Or, la note souligne que d'autres pauvres gens pouvaient être classés comme *kırklu*, tandis que les six personnes dont il s'agit sont, selon l'usage, tenues d'être *celep*.[12] Encore une note explicative de l'enregistrement central du fisc nous offre d'autres détails sur la situation aisée des *celepkeşan*. La personne Piri Mustafa, figurant au nombre des *celepkeşan* de Tatar-Pazardžik est mentionée comme étant le capitaine en chef des bateaux qui, probablement, assuraient le trafic fluvial sur la Maritza en aval de Pazardžik. En outre, il possédait des rizières dont il cédait même une partie en métayage à d'autres personnes. Ce même Piri était propriétaire de 4,000 moutons.[13] Au sujet de *celepkeşan* Hasan, fils de Mustafa, ce même registre note qu'auparavant il avait été timariote. A cause de l'inexécution de ses obligations militaires, il fut dépossédé de son *timar*. Par la suite il se fit usurier et amassa richesse et biens immeubles, raison pour laqualle il fut porté sur le registre des *celep*.[14] Les données d'un *ʿarz* du kadi de Sofia du XVI^e^s. sont très significatives de ce point de vue. Cet *ʿarz* révèle les efforts que le *celep* Guéorgui Vaskov de Sofia a fait afin de se soustraire à l'augmentation injuste des fournitures en moutons qui lui incombaient. Par suite

attesté par un firman qui exonère expressement les mineurs de Siderocapsa du service *celepkeşan*. N. Beldiceanu, *Les actes des premiers sultans conservés dans les manuscrits de la Bibliothèque nationale à Paris, I*, Paris 1960, p. 138, No. 48.

[10] Cf. A. Refik, *Türk idaresinde Bulgaristan (973–1275)*, Istanbul 1933, p. 8, No. 3, p. 10, No. 8, pp. 13–14, No. 13, pp. 26–7, No. 36; *Dokumenti za bălgarskata istoriya* (hereafter *DBI*), vol. iii, Sofia 1940, No. 6, p. 3, No. 11, p. 5, No. 40, pp. 17–18; Gl. Elezović, *Iz carigradskih turskih arhiva, muhimme defteri*, Beograd 1950, No. 194, p. 229.

[11] C'est-à-dire obligés de payer annuellement 40 aktchés pour le service des stations (*menzil*).

[12] Fonds 95, inv. 23, fol. 81b.

[13] *Ibid.*

[14] Fonds 95, inv. 23, fol. 82a.

d'une confusion entre son nom et le nom d'une autre personne il était dénoncé auprès des autorités respectives d'avoir fait faire pour son propre usage lors du mariage de son fils un bonnet d'or empanaché, des sandales d'argent et d'autres habits précieux. On prétendait que tout cela prouvait sa situation matérielle bien aisée et que le *celep* en question pouvait être chargé d'une obligation plus importante qui portait sur 150 moutons au lieu de 100 moutons que G. Vaskov était tenu de livrer à l'Etat jusqu'à ce moment. Toutes ces données démontrent que l'aisance matérielle était le critère principal pour déterminer le nombre des moutons que les *celep* devaient livrer à l'Etat.[15]

L'insuffisance de données contrecarrent dans une grande mesure les efforts visant à élucider dans sa plénitude la question de l'appartenance sociale des *celepkeşan*. L'analyse des quelques registres *celepkeşan* accessibles des archives turques de Sofia nous permettent de systématiser les données comme dans la table en face.[16]

En dehors des professions mentionnées dans la table, les documents mentionnent aussi des personnes occupées à d'autres métiers; vendeurs de bois, vendeurs de couteaux, pêcheurs, cardeurs de laine, chameliers, verriers, charpentiers, chaudronniers, passementiers, fabricants de fontes (*koburcu*), armuriers, chandeliers, selliers, fabricants de bonnets en toile, vendeurs de cotton, bijoutiers, marchands de *halva*, fariniers, potiers, meuniers, marchands de foulards, prêtres, marchands de lattes, tailleurs de souquenilles, marchands de kouskous, barbiers, marchands de cuillers, étameurs, marchands de sorbets, cardeurs de cotton, marchands de fil, feutriers, *tuzcu* et autres personnes de catégories à charges spéciales.

Ce qui, de ces données systématisées, attire tout de suite l'attention, c'est la circonstance que la plupart des *celep*, donc ce registre indique le métier,

[15] Istanbul, Başvekâlet Arşivi, Kepeci 222 (*ruus* 127) 927.720. Je dois toutes ces données au Dr. H. Sahillioğlu qui a eu la gentillesse de me les procurer d'après les copies des documents dont il disposait lors de la conférence à Londres.

[16] Registre de 1576 (Fonds 95, inv. 23, deux fragments de registres pour les *kaza* Yenidjé Karassu et Drama. Fonds 95, inv. 70 et Drama *kaza*, XVIes. I, B.2. Elevage). Les deux documents sont sans doute de la deuxième moitié du XVIes. Enfin pour les besoins de cette étude on a compulsé encore un autre registre de ce genre, relatif aux *kaza* de Varna, Nikopol, Šumen, Razgrad et Provadia, datant de 1573 (Fonds 20, inv. 261, a, b, v, g, d). En utilisant la table, il faudrait tenir compte du fait que: (*a*) la table est dressée à partir de l'enregistrement de 23 *kaza*, comprenant 7931 *celep*. (*b*) les indications de métier et condition sociale sont données surtout pour les *celepkeşan* des milieux urbains. Ainsi à Sofia, d'un total de 207 *celepkeşan* turcs, 135 sont désignés comme artisans, commerçants et usuriers, tandis que parmi les 91 Bulgares, 53 sont consignés comme exerçant aussi de semblables professions (Fonds 93, inv. 23, fol. 47b–50b). A Varna d'un total de 9 *celepkeşan* musulmans et 42 non-musulmans, 6 figurent comme artisans ou commerçants et 2 *celepkeşan* sont seulement des fonctionnaires (Fond 20, inv. 261b). De plus, il est peu certain que le préposé à l'enregistrement a consigné de pareilles données pour chacun des noms de *celep*. Il s'en suit donc que nos déductions ne sauraient être absolument catégoriques. (*c*) la table ne mentionne rien de professions qui, selon les registres, ne sont exercées que d'un ou de deux *celep*.

Possesseurs de moutons				Possesseurs de moutons (jusqu'à)			
Profession	Musulmans	Non musulmans	Total	25	50	100	plus de 100
Tisserands de bure	13	6	19	3	14		
Charretiers	4		4		3	1	
Quincailliers (*ahtar*)	9		9	2	4	3	
Epiciers	19	1	20	8	10	2	
Commerçants	10	6	16	6	8	1	
Sandaliers	1	3	4	2	1		
Toiliers	4	1	5		5		
Teinturiers	10	3	13	1	11		
Tanneurs	38		38	9	22	6	1
Ferronniers	9	1	10	5	3	2	
Tailleurs	10	18	28	17	11		
Boulangers	7	3	10	7	3		
Bouchers	9	3	12	1	10	1	
Orfèvres	12	13	25	13	9	2	1
Pelletiers	4	14	18	7	10	1	
Scribes	5		5	1	3	1	
Cabaretiers		5	5	2	3		
Tisserands d'objects en poil de chèvre	3	5	8	3	4		
Maréchaux-ferrants	6		6	3	3		
Savetiers	2	6	8	3	5		
Prêteurs d'argent (usuriers)	7		7		2	4	2
Savonniers	11		11	3	8		
Bourreliers	14		14	4	10		
Conducteurs de troupeaux	1	3	4		4		
Vend. de soieries	6	3	9	3	6		
Fauconniers	2	3	5	2	2	1	
Chefs de bergers (*kethuda*)	3	3	6	3	3		
Forgerons	1	9	10	3	6	1	
Bergers	9	7	16	11	5		
Hommes de guerre (*akıncı*)	8		8				

provenaient de milieux s'occupant de commerce (commerçants, épiciers, bouchers, boulangers), puis des artisans dont les produits faisaient l'objet d'une forte consommation, vu qu'ils avaient à satisfaire les besoins quotidiens de la population (beaucoup de peaussiers, fourreurs, tailleurs et couturiers, bourreliers, forgerons, tisserands, savetiers, savonniers). Connaissant le caractère de la production artisanale à cette époque, il n'est pas douteux que les artisans mentionnés n'aient été en même temps commerçants et vendeurs des produits de leur travail. Le nombre des orfèvres est relativement élevé et il serait juste de supposer qu'ils disposaient de moyens pécuniaires considérables ainsi que de métaux précieux.

Un fait particulièrement important est de trouver parmi les *celepkeşan* des prêteurs d'argent, bien qu'en nombre modeste, et qu'ils tiennent à la disposition de l'Etat un plus grand nombre de moutons, cent, voir plus de cent. Ce sont là des indications que les *celepkeşan* respectifs possédaient un grand nombre de moutons. Il est évident qu'ils employaient l'argent que leur rapportaient leur métier de prêteurs ou d'usuriers, à organiser l'élevage en gros des moutons. On en trouve d'ailleurs la confirmation dans la note déjà citée au suget du prêteur d'argent Hasan, fils de Mustafa.[17] Le groupe des bergers, relativement plus nombreux, ne doit pas nous surprendre, bien entendu. Parmi les *celepkeşan* nous trouvons aussi quelques fonctionnaires de l'administration ottomane: notables, chefs militaires locaux, douaniers, inspecteurs en chef, pages officiels ou gens de l'entourage et de la suite des dignitaires ottomans, etc.

Toutes ces données et les faits que nous venons de rapporter suggèrent des suppositions, sollicitent certaines déductions. Sans aucun doute les *celepkeşan* se dessinent encore au cours du XVIe s. comme couche sociale plus aisée. De plus, autant que les données bien insuffisantes tirées de ces registres nous permettent de l'établir, du moins pour les agglomérations plus grandes, les *celepkeşan* provenaient surtout des milieux qui représentaient le capital commercial et usuraire,[18] ou bien qui disposaient de moyens pécuniaires plus considérables du fait qu'ils tenaient un poste dans l'administration ottomane ou appartenaient à la classe dirigeante ottomane. En recrutant ses *celep* précisément dans ces milieux, le gouvernement ottoman, conscient de ses intérêts économiques primordiaux, orientait leurs moyens pécuniaires, amassés surtout grace à leur activité de commerçants-usuriers et d'artisans, vers l'organisation plus intense de l'élevage et du commerce des moutons.

Considérant tout ce qui précède on peut admettre, non sans quelque

[17] Fonds 95, inv. 23, f. 82a.

[18] A ce sujet on ne saurait ignorer le fait que, selon les données des registres datant du XVI^e^s. et d'autres documents émanant des *sicil* (registres des kadis) du XVII^e^s., la catégorie des *celepkeşan* comprenait aussi pas mal d'Arméniens et de Juifs dont on sait qu'ils appartiennent à la catégorie des commerçants-usuriers et des artisans (cf. Fonds 95, inv. 23, fol. 21b).

raison, que déjà au cours du XVIe s., le capital commercial-usuraire participait dans une certaine mesure à l'organisation du ravitaillement de l'Etat et de l'approvisionnement public.

Pour pouvoir tenir les *celepkeşan* sous son contrôle direct et constant, le gouvernement ottoman avait eu recours, comme du reste pour les autres catégories spécialés de la population, aux enregistrements périodiques généraux. Des documents dressés à l'occasion de pareils enregistrements ont été conservés chez nous. Ce sont en particulier des registres (*defter*) datant des années 70 du XVIes. où figurent les noms des *celepkeşan* des divers districts (*kaza*). Chaque nom y est accompagné d'indications en chiffres concernant les moutons que le *celepkeşan* respectif est tenu de livrer à la réquisition de l'Etat.[19]

Le service de l'enregistrement était confié aux kadis locaux, aidés par les organes administratifs. A l'époque de la stabilisation de cette institution, chaque nouvel enregistrement offrait l'occasion d'y inclure un nombre considérable de «nouveau» *celep*, personnes que les autorités dépistaient entre deux enregistrements consécutifs, comme capables de s'acquitter des obligations de *celepkeşan*. Une circonstance retient ici notre attention; on remarque souvent que beaucoup de ces «nouveux» *celepkeşan*, c'est-à-dire nouvellement inscrits sur le registre, ont des garants[20] dont les noms figurent également sur le registre. De toute évidence il s'agit ici d'une mesure de précaution, prise par les autorités pour se garantir des fournitures sûres et opportunes, en engageant non seulement la responsabilité des *celepkeşan*, mais aussi celle de personnes supplémentaires.

Au cours des inspections périodiques des *celep* enregistrés, tous les changements intervenus dans l'étendue de leurs obligations en raison de leur situation matérielle, étaient portés au registre. Cette pratique nous est révélée par une lettre du sultan, datant du XVIes., adressée au kadi respectif. Il appert de ce document, qu'un *celep* dont l'obligation envers l'Etat, inscrite au registre, portait sur 150 moutons s'était présenté à la cour du sultan. Or, il s'y déclare être insolvable, demandant en même temps la formulation d'un ordre en conséquence. Des *celep* de confiance et compétents et d'autres experts furent chargés de vérifier ses dires. Il fut constaté que le solliciteur était vraiment pauvre, ayant de surcroît une nombreuse famille à charge; qu'il n'était pas en mesure de livrer 150 moutons. Selon leur estimation on ne pouvait le charger que d'une obligation de 50

[19] Il est hors de doute que le nombre de moutons, indiqué dans les registres respectifs en regards des noms de chaque *celepkeşan*, ne désigne pas le nombre de bêtes que celui possède. On en trouve la confirmation dans la remarque expresse, citée déjà à un autre propos, figurant sur l'un des registres et disant que la personne Piri Mustafa possède 4,000 moutons, alors qu'il est tenu de livrer 200 moutons seulement comme fourniture d'Etat (cf. Fonds 95, inv. 23, f. 81b).

[20] Cf. p. ex. Fonds 95, inv. 70. Ici les cautions inscrites ne sont que des Turcs. Sur le registre de 1576, une note dit que les habitants du village sont cautions de deux *celepkeşan* du village de Osenovlak, district de Sofia (Fonds 95, inv. 23, f. 54a).

moutons à fournir annuellement à l'Etat.[21] Ordre fut donné en conséquence si l'état de fait était réellement tel, de réduire à 50 moutons l'engagement de l'homme, en trouvant une autre personne plus aisée qui assumerait, par dévolu, l'engagement de livrer les cent moutons que le *celep* insolvable n'était pas en état de fournir. Comme on le voit, nonobstant les modifications qu'on se voyait parfois contraint d'apporter aux obligations de tel ou tel autre *celep*, les autorités se laissaient toujours guider par la considération de ne pas réduire le volume des fournitures d'Etat. Dans d'autres cas, de semblables modifications du statut des *celepkeşan* se faisaient à l'époque de l'enregistrement même, lorsqu'un changement constaté dans la situation matérielle du solliciteur les justifiait. De pareils cas ont été inscrits lors de l'enregistrement en 1576, dans le district de Kjustendil. Ainsi, au sujet du *celepkeşan* Petre Miniu, du village de Stemnik il est dit, que d'aprés les renseignements donnés par le kadi de Kjustendil, il se serait ruiné et ne pouvait donc plus faire face à ses obligations de *celepkeşan*. Vu cet état de choses, il fallait demander sa radiation des listes et son remplacement par une autre personne.[22] Au village de Zlosica, situé dans la même région, trois personnes sont portées sur la liste. Il est noté à leur sujet, que le kadi de Kjustendil devait prendre la résolution de les radier des listes, puisqu'ils n'étaient plus bons à faire face aux obligations de *celep*[23].

Or, il paraît que pour être inscrit dans la catégorie des *celep*, on devait se conformer aussi à d'autres conditions, qu'il est difficile d'éclaircir en raison de la pénurie des sources. Si l'on considère le fardeau et les responsabilités des obligations assumées par les *celep*, il convient d'admettre, qu'on ne pouvait affecter à ce groupe des personnes appartenant à d'autres catégories de la population jouissant d'un statut spécial, et qui avaient aussi leurs obligations envers le gouvernement, surtout dans les cas où ils étaient engagés dans les corps auxiliaires de l'armée ottomane. C'est à de pareilles raisons que se référent les *voynuk* du district de Sofia en 1575, lorsqu'on tenta de les enrôler comme *celep*. Le gouvernement avait déjà prévenu les autorités, que les *voynuk* et leurs fils ne pouvaient pas être enrôlés comme *celep*[24] Or, si nous confrontons les données du document cité, avec les renseignements provenant d'autres sources, il nous faudrait reconnaître que ce régime n'était pas toujours observé, meme à l'égard des *voynuk*. Ainsi, au temps de l'enregistrement en masse de 1576, à Sofia, six personnes de la catégorie des *voynuk* avaient été inscrites comme *celep* et chargées de fournir en tout 285 moutons.[25] En présence de ces données, il faudrait croire qu'en pratique, on inscrivait sur les listes des *celepkeşan* aussi des gens appartenant à d'autres catégories à obligations spéciales.

[21] Manuscrit de la Bibliothèque Nationale de Paris — Fonds Turc 85, f. 56b.

[22] Fonds 95, inv. 23, f. 4b, 9a.

[23] *Ibid.*

[24] Refik, *op. cit.*, No. 30, p. 23; *DBI*, t. iii, No. 28, p. 13.

[25] Fonds 95, inv. 23, f. 50b.

Ceci est corroboré par le fait que les registres que nous venons d'analyser, mentionnent les noms de *doğanci*, *atmacaci*, *yuvaci* (engagés dans l'élevage et le dressage de faucons de chasse destinés à la cour du sultan), des *tuzcu* (qui fournissaient le sel nécessaire aux besoins de l'Etat), qui y figurent comme *celep*. La présence d'*akıncı* au sein de la catégorie des *celep* est explicable, vu qu'avec la restriction de l'expansion ottomane ces corps de troupes d'attaque avaient perdu leur importance.[26]

Le développement de l'institution des *celepkeşan* est marqué par la place prépondérante assignée aux *yürük* et le rôle que ceux-ci y jouèrent. Il n'y a pas de doute que le gouvernement s'efforçait de tirer parti de l'activité économique coutumière des *yürük*, au profit de ses besoins de ravitaillement, lorsque ces gens n'étaient pas engagés par leurs obligations militaires. Ainsi, dans le grand registre des *celepkeşan*, datant de 1576, on relève les noms de 200 *yürük*, membres de 35 *cemaʿat* des districts de Plovdiv, Pazardžik, Sofia, Berkovica et Samokov[27], qui y figurent comme *celep*.

Des indications que nous avons pu recueillir il appert que les *yürük* pareillement aux *voynuk* s'efforçaient de réduire le fardeau de leurs doubles obligations au cas où ils étaient inscrits comme *celepkeşan*, c'est-à-dire de se soustraire au service militaire. Ainsi, en 1579, les *yürük* du groupe Tanrıdağ refusèrent de partir en guerre en raison de leur enregistrement comme *celep* et, forts de cet argument, insistaient à être radiés du nouveau registre, où ils figuraient comme *eşkinci*.[28]

Il paraît que plus tard, ces doubles obligations, déjà différenciées, étaient traitées à part lors de l'enregistrement. Ceci apparaît clairement d'un registre de 1720, relatif à l'institution *evlâd-i fâtihân* (autre variété de l'institution *yürük*). Dans les registres dressés sur l'ordre du vizir Hasan pacha, le statut des *evlâd-i fâtihân* était révoqué dans les districts de Dojran, Radovište, ʿAvrathisar, Salonique, Karadağ, Vranja, Sarıgöl, Bitolia, Džuma-Pazar, Florina, Prilep, Yenidže-Vardar et les personnes bénéficiaires de cette révocation étaient réinscrites sur le registre des obligations de *hane* (logement). Lors de la guerre de 1128/1129 (1715 à 1717), les charges d'*evlâd-i fâtihân* furent rétablies. Mais l'enregistrement manquait d'exactitude et il fallut définir clairement et distinguer ceux qui seraient chargés d'obligations militaires, des autres qui avaient à s'acquitter des obligations de *celepkeşan* ou de celles de *hane*.[29] Il est donc clair que les obligations *eşkinci* (de servir dans l'armée) des *evlâd-i fâtihân* ne cumulaient pas avec celles des *celepkeşan*.

Les registres du XVIᵉs., parvenus jusqu'à nous, nous permettent de

[26] A ce sujet v. Gibb et Bowen, *op. cit.*, vol. i, part I, p. 56.

[27] Fonds 95, inv. 23.

[28] M. T. Gökbilgin, *Rumeli'de Yürükler, Tatarlar ve Evlâd-i Fâtihân*, Istanbul 1958, p. 51, n. 4.

[29] Fonds 156, inv. 58, Registre de 34 pages daté du 11 cemazi II, 1132.

jeter aussi un peu de lumière sur un sujet, aussi intéressant qu'important: celui de l'appartenance ethnique des *celepkeşan*. Selon des évaluations approximatives, faites sur la base de ces registres et portant sur une grande partie des territoires bulgares de cette époque, le rapport entre *celepkeşan* musulmans et non-musulmans est le suivant: pour 13 districts de la Bulgarie du Sud et de l'Ouest, environ 3,743 non-musulmans font face à 1,429 Turcs et 233 *yürük*; pour 7 districts de la Bulgarie du Nord-Est—585 non-musulmans contre 1,565 Turcs, enfin pour le district de Yenidže-Karasu—33 non-musulmans contre 102 Turcs. Il faut remarquer que la majeure partie de ceux qui, dans la pratique courante de l'enregistrement ottoman, sont inscrits dans la catégorie non-différenciées des «non-musulmans» sont en fait des Bulgares. Il n'y a que certains milieux urbains où des Juifs, des Arméniens et des Grecs, à en juger par leurs noms, sont inscrits sur le registre, alors que dans le district de Yenidže-Karasu 14 personnes des 33 non-musulmans sont probablement des Grecs. Parmi les musulmans, qui sont exclusivement Turcs ou *yürük*, il en est par-ci, par-là (surtout dans la région des Rhodopes et en Bulgarie du Nord-Est[30]) qui sont des Bulgares convertis à l'islamisme. Le plus souvent ceux-ci sont inscrits avec mention de leur sobriquet bulgare ou de surnom ʿAbdullah.

La supériorité numérique des musulmans dans les territoires de la Bulgarie du Nord-Est explicable par la colonisation relativement plus massive d'éléments turcs, conjuguée à l'islamisation de la population autochtone de ces contrées. En revanche, pour l'ensemble des 14 districts de la Bulgarie occidentale, la Thrace, les Rhodopes et le littoral de la mer Egée, les Turcs sont en nombre supérieur dans les seuls districts de Plovdiv, Pazardžik et Yenidže-Karasu. En partant de ces données on pourrait admettre que le ravitaillement en bétail ou institution des celep, se trouvait avant tout aux mains des Bulgares dans une considérable partie des terres bulgares. C'est de ces milieux bulgares que, déjà à partir du XVI^e^s., se dégagent et se constituent ces couches plus aisées de la population bulgare qui, s'affermissant avec le temps, se font enfin valoir dans la vie politique et sociale au cours du XIX^e^s.

Il conviendrait d'accorder quelque attention au caractère des obligations qui pesaient sur les *celepkeşan*. Il a été déjà dit que l'affectation principale des *celep* était de fournir un nombre déterminé de moutons aux services d'approvisionnement de l'Etat. Il est difficile de désigner le critère qu'on choisissait pour déterminer le chiffre de ces fournitures obligatoires dont s'acquittaient les *celepkeşan*. Il est des indications qui pourraient nous renseigner sur ce sujet. Ainsi, le *celep* Piri Mustafa de Pazardžik, déjà

[30] A ce sujet v. B. Cvetkova, «Za poselištnite i demografski otnošeniya v nyakoi severoiztočni rayoni na Bălgariya prez XV–XVI v.», *Izvestiya na Narodniya muzey v Kolarovgrad*, iii, 1965, pp. 43, 52; B. Cvetkova, «Za stopanskiya oblik i feodalnite zadălženiya na nyakoi selišta v Rodopite i priležaštite rayoni prez XV–XVII v.», *Rodopski Sbornik*, i, 1965, pp. 49–51.

mentionné, qui possédait 4,000 moutons, était engagé envers l'Etat pour une livraison de 200 moutons, c'est-à-dire de vingt fois moindre. Si pareille proportion semble assez peu réelle on pourrait, sans exagération, admettre comme chiffre d'orientation un rapport moyen et plus normal de 1 : 10. Prenant ce rapport comme point de départ, nous pourrions reconstituer le nombre approximatif de moutons que possédait chaque *celepkeşan*. Ceci nous permettra, à son tour, de nous faire une certaine idée, d'aprés les données des registres concernant les *celepkeşan*, quel serait le rapport approximatif entre les gros éleveurs de moutons et ceux moyens et petits. Un sommaire des renseignements numériques relatifs aux *celepkeşan* de la Bulgarie du Nord-Est, pour les années 70 du XVIes. (c'est-à-dire une région où l'élevage de moutons est très développé) nous donne les chiffres suivants: d'un total de 1,565 *celepkeşan* turcs et 585 non-musulmans, 906 étaient inscrits avec l'obligation de fournir pour les besoins d'Etat jusqu'à 25 moutons, 1,114—jusqu'à 50, 120—jusqu'à 100, enfin seulement 8 personnes étaient obligées de livrer au-delà de cent moutons.[31] Par conséquent, le nombre prédominant est celui des éleveurs moyens qui possédaient des troupeaux comptant de 500 à 1000 moutons. Les petits éleveurs formaient, après eux, le groupe le plus nombreux. Une analyse des données relatives aux *celepkeşan* de la region des Rhodopes, constituée par les districts de Plovdiv, Pazardžik et Razlog, données valables pour l'année 1576, nous donne à peu près le même résultat.[32]

Ainsi qu'il appert des données documentaires des dernières décades du XVI[e]s., les plus fortes livraisons de moutons étaient faites par les *celepkeşan* des régions de Plovdiv (très riche région d'élevage de moutons), de Sofia et de nombre de districts des terres bulgares du Sud-Ouest.

En connexion avec ce qui précède, il ne serait pas sans intérêt de connaître quel était le nombre et la proportion des moutons livrés par les Turcs et par les non-musulmans. Dans les terres bulgares occidentales et en Thrace, au cours de l'année 1576, 3,743 Bulgares—*celepkeşan*—étaient chargés de livrer 131,846 moutons, alors que les Turcs (y compris les *yürük*) au nombre de 1,662 étaient obligés de fournir 57,265 moutons. En Bulgarie du Nord-Est, le tableau est quelque peu différent. Ainsi, l'analyse des données relatives au district de Šumen, fortement affecté par la colonisation turque et l'islamisation de la population autochtone, indique environ 295 *celepkeşan* turcs obligés de livrer 10,705 moutons et 151 non-musulmans (presque tous Bulgares) chargés de fournir 5,725 moutons.[33] Cependant, ces

[31] Fonds 20, inv. 261a, b, v, g, d.

[32] Fonds 95, inv. 23, v. Table détaillée chez. B. Cvetkova, «Za stopanskiya oblik», pp. 49–51.

[33] Fonds 20, inv. 261d. Il va sans dire que cette proportion ou l'élément turc est prédominant n'était pas aussi prononcée dans les districts de la Bulgarie du Nord-Est. Ainsi, dans le district de Provadija, les Turcs avaient à livrer 9,500 moutons, alors que les Bulgares, assez nombreux ici, devaient fournir 6,080 moutons (Fonds 20, inv. 261g).

données n'infirment pas la constatation, faite déjà à propos des chiffres cités, relatifs à 13 districts englobant la majeure partie des terres bulgares à cette époque, notamment que les *celepkeşan* bulgares avaient à s'acquitter de la plus grande part des fournitures de moutons destinées à satisfaire aux besoins de l'État, dont étaient chargées les terres bulgares. Les *celep* enregistrés s'acquittaient de leurs obligations soit individuellement, soit en collectivité. Il est fréquent de voir les noms de deux ou trois *celep* figurer ensemble dans le registre, suivis par la mention du nombre total de moutons qu'ils sont tenus de livrer. Parfois le registre indique aussi la quote-part de la livraison qui revient à chacun d'eux, d'autres fois une pareille indication fait défaut. Souvent, ces associés étaient père et fils, ou des frères, ce qui fait penser au caractère héréditaire du service de *celep*. Parfois des veuves de *celepkeşan* figurent au registre, ce qui veut dire qu'elles continuaient à assumer les obligations de leurs maris.

Toujours en connexion avec leur principale obligation de fournir par contrainte des moutons pour les besoins de l'Etat, les *celepkeşan* étaient parfois envoyés aux armées.[34]

Les données documentaires datant du XVI^e^s. ne nous donnent pas une raison suffisante de penser que *celepkeşan* et *celep*, ces termes par lesquels on désignait les personnes chargées des fournitures de moutons pour les besoins de l'Etat, s'adressent à des individus dont les fonctions et l'affectation étaient différentes.[35] Il est possible que cette différenciation soit intervenue plus tard. En tous cas, la législation du XVI^e^s.[36] est catégorique sur la participation des *celepkeşan* au commerce de menu bétail, voire même de gros bétail.[37] En effet, on y trouve des ordonnances précises visant l'achat de moutons de la part de *celep*.[38] Il y a bien plus, un décret vers 1522–1523 prévoit des mesures propres à faciliter les *celep* de Roumélie dans leurs achats de moutons. A cause de la concurrence que faisaient des spéculateurs en achetant des moutons de boucherie, et qui empêchait les *celep* de conclure leurs achats, l'administration suprême ordonna: jusqu'à ce que les *celep* n'aient pas acheté une quantité suffisante de moutons, il est interdit

[34] Cf. p. ex. ordre datant de 1566, adressé aux kadis de Čirmen, Stara Zagora, etc. (Elezović, *op. cit.*, No. 1206, III, p. 336).

[35] En effet, les registres des *celepkeşan* portent en regard de quelques noms aussi l'indication de *celep*. Considérant que ce surnom est donné aux *celepkeşan* enregistrés, on pourrait admettre que le préposé à l'enregistrement ait voulu distinguer le *celepkeşan* du *celep*. Quoiqu'il en soit, nous sommes enclins de penser qu'il s'agit ici d'un sobriquet, plutôt que d'une indication de fonctions plus spéciales.

[36] Cf. p. ex. Bibliothèque Nationale de Paris, Fonds Turc 85, f. 109b à 110a. V. B. Cvetkova, «Kăm văprosa», pp. 201, 219, 221; B. Cvetkova, «Za režima na stopanskata, obmyana meždu rumănskite i bălgarskite pridunavski zemi prez XVI v.», in *Bălgaro-rumănski vrăzki i otnošeniya prez vekovete, Izsledvaniya, v.I* (*XII–XIX v.*), Sofia 1965, p. 133.

[37] Fonds Turc 85, f. 110ab.

[38] H. Hadžibegić, «Kanun-nama sultana Sulejmana Zakonodavca», *Glasnik Zemalskog Muzeja u Sarajevu*, 1949–50, pp. 334–5.

aux spéculants d'en acheter.[39] D'autres sources mentionnent qu'en 1591, des *celep* turcs ont acheté 24,500 moutons dans la région de Černovic et de Sučava.[40]

Des documents datant d'une période plus récente disent en termes précis que les *celep* achètent des moutons qu'ils livrent ensuite aux autorités.[41]

La circonstance que les *celepkeşan* s'occupaient de moutons, leur permettait aussi d'exercer d'autres métiers. Ainsi, les habitants des villages de *celep* Černevo et Arnautkjoj, dans la région de Ruse, s'occupaient, selon des données datant de 1714, à abattre du bétail et à ramasser du suif et du beurre fondu pour l'approvisionnement de l'Etat.[42]

Ayant tout intérêt à s'assurer les services opportuns et constants des *celep*, l'administration suprême mattait tout ses soins à préserver ceux-ci d'une surcharge d'impôts et de l'arbitraire fiscal. Ainsi, le code de Soliman Ier contient déjà des ordonnances visant à préserver les *celep* et les bouchers d'un double payement de l'*ʿadet-i ağnam*. Ces ordonnances préviennent les dites catégories de personnes de se nantir de *hüccet* certifiant le payement du *ʿadet-i ağnam* s'ils achètent des moutons avant le mois d'avril (c'est-a-dire avant le terme de perception de cet impôt). S'ils ne peuvent pas se nantir d'un pareil document, ils n'auront lors de l'achat, qu'à en rabattre le prix sous prétexte du payement imminent de l'impôt sur les moutons.[43]

Une suite de violations de la part des autorités, qui eurent lieu en 1522–1523, provoquèrent la promulgation d'un firman exprès, adressé aux *sancakbeys* de la Roumélie et aux kadis, à l'occasion de la plainte portée par quelques *celep* du district de Vranja. Ceux-ci se plaignaient qu'étant enregistrés comme *celep*, ils conduisaient des moutons et d'autres bêtes à Constantinople. En cours de route ils s'arrêtaient en divers lieux, mais en les quittant, les gens des *sancakbeys*, des voyvodes, des *subaşı*, des spahis et d'autres encore les appréhendaient, se saisissaient aussi de leurs bergers sous prétexte qu'ils avaient traversé leurs terres et leurs ponts, et exigeaient d'eux le payement de *otlak resmi*, *eğrek hakkı* (taxe de troupeau), *deştibani* (taxe de garde champêtre), *ispençe* et autres impôts. En conséquence, l'administration suprême interdit les molestations illicites des *celep* enregistés, par l'exigence de pareilles taxes, moutons, agneaux et chevaux pour l'exécution de corvées. En outre, il a été signalé que les gens des *sancakbeys* et des voïvodes se rendaient dans les districts et y tourmentaient la population par des actes arbitraires. Ils dépouillaient les *celep* de leurs chevaux, de leurs vêtements, de leur outillage agricole. Au passage de leurs troupeaux, ils leurs imposaient un droit de péage et percevaient 200 à 300

[39] Fonds Turc 85, f. 90b–91a.

[40] J. Nistor, *Handel und Wandel in der Moldau bis zum Ende des 16 Jahrhunderts nach den Quellen dargestellt*, Czernowitz 1912, p. 159.

[41] BNS, Registre du kadi de Vidin 46, f. 47a, doc. II.; Elezović, *op. cit.*, No. 80, p. 43.

[42] *DBI*, vol. iii, No. 80, p. 37.

[43] H. Hadžibegić, *op. cit.*, p. 335.

aktchés par troupeau, au lieu de 25 aktchés, comme par le passé. Après avoir percu une fois l'octroi (*baç*) sur les moutons des *celep*, ce même octroi était exigé une seconde fois lors de l'achat des moutons. A part cela, les *celep* signalèrent qu'il arrivait à des moutons de tomber malades. Le troupeau s'arrêtait quelque part, sans entrer dans aucun champ, mais malgré cela les paysans des villages voisins l'empêchaient de s'arrêter. De même, les *celep* se plaignaient des difficultés qu'on leur faisait en les empêchant de parquer leurs moutons en des lieux affectés à cet usage dans le passé. Ils étaient opprimés par les spahis qui tardaient à percevoir leurs dîmes à temps et, plus tard, au lieu de les percevoir en nature, ils les réclamaient en argent, à des prix supérieurs à ceux du marché. Ils leurs imposaient la taxe de l'*ispençe* à raison de 32 aktchés au lieu de 25 et les forçaient à leur apporter du bois et du foin. Le pouvoir suprême interdit sévèrement tous ces procédés arbitraires à l'égard des *celep*.[44] Un firman daté du 28. V–6. VI. 1550 ordonne au kadi de Sofia de couper court aux exactions fiscales à l'égard de deux *celep* du village Bogrofča, district de Sofia. Les deux *celep* s'étaient plaints des autorités locales de les avoir surchargé d'impôts, les empêchant de cette manière de remplir leurs obligations de *celep*.[45] D'après les témoignages de documents de la fin du XVIIIe et du début du XIX^e^s. des mesures de ce genre protègent les *celep* et les bergers qui amènent des troupeaux de la Moldavie à la capitale pour accomplir l'obligation habituelle imposée au prince de la Moldavie. Les vizirs, les *beylerbeys*, les *zabits* et les *iş erleri* tout le long du chemin allant de la Moldavie jusqu'à Constantinople sont prévenus des nombreuses exactions, que les *celep* et les bergers subissaient souvent en traversant le Danube. Ils étaient surchargés de lourdes obligations fiscales: on leur imposait un *baç*, une taxe pour la traversée des champs (*toprak baştı*), une taxe pour le passage (*müruriye*). Le sultan ordonne aux autorités ci-mentionnées de ne pas causer des difficultés pareilles aux *celep* et aux bergers en question.[46]

Souvent, les ordres du sultan du XVIII^e^s., par lesquels les *celep* étaient aussi requis de participer aux approvisionnements de l'Etat en menu bétail, ordonnaient de ne pas exiger des *celep*, tout au long de leur route jusqu'à Constantinople où ils devaient conduire le bétail, le payement d'octroi contraire à la loi et aux coutumes, ni de taxes de voyvodes et de *subaşı* sous prétexte que leurs moutons foulaient la terre de leurs possessions.[47]

Le ramassage et l'expédition des fournitures des *celepkeşan* se faisaient selon un ordre établi et déterminé. De même que pour toutes réquisitions de provisions et de vivres, un *mübaşir* exprès, porteur de l'ordre du Sultan, était dépêché de Constantinople. Avec son assistance, les kadis vérifiaient,

[44] Fonds Turc 85, f. 90b–91a.

[45] *Die Protokollbücher des Kadiamtes Sofia*, bearb. von G. Gălăbov, édit. H. Duda, München 1960, No. 9, p. 11.

[46] M. Guboglu, *Catalogul documentelor turceşti*, vol. ii, Bucureşti 1965, No. 1132.

[47] Cf. p. ex. Registre du kadi de Sofia 16, p. 11, doc. III; 25, p. 12, doc. III.

en personne, le nombre des *celepkeşan* et celui des moutons qui étaient dus[48] selon les registres respectifs. De leur côté, les kadis informaient le pouvoir central par *iʿlâm* de l'organisation des fournitures des *celepkeşan*. Ensuite les moutons étaient ordinairement remis aux *sürüci*, désignés pour les mener au lieu de leur destination. Les moutons achetés étaient alors emmenés par les *sürüci* jusqu'aux stations (*menzil*) les plus proches du camp, si la fourniture était faite en temps de guerre pour les besoins de l'armée, ou bien jusqu'à la capitale, si elle était destinée à approvisionnement de la cour ou de la population urbaine. Dans ce dernier cas les moutons étaient remis au *koyun emini* (intendant de la cour préposé aux viandes de mouton) ou bien au *kasapbaşi*.[49] Très souvent, lorsque le passage à l'abattoir n'était pas imminent, les troupeaux de moutons étaient concentrés dans des pâturages d'hiver ou des plaines pâturables destinées à cet effet. Il y avait de ces pâturages près de Čorlu, et dans la région de Plovdiv aux environs du village de Kečidere, dénommés pâturages de Sari, Youn et Delak pinari ou dans la forêt entre Viza et Midia.[50]

Après avoir remis la fourniture au lieu de destination, les *sürüci* en recevaient une pièce justificative pour acquit. Il est intéressant de noter que parmi les *sürüci* on mentionne fréquemment la présence de non-musulmans.[51] De toute évidence, la population des terres balkaniques conquises prédominait dans le système de ravitaillement de l'Etat en moutons.

Les obligations dont le gouvernement ottoman chargeait les *celepkeşan* n'étaient pas, sans doute, des plus légères. Les livraisons par contrainte de menu bétail acheté à des prix bien plus bas que ceux du marché, leur retour périodique, les difficultés de rassembler et d'élever ces bêtes, etc., causaient de graves soucis, surtout aux petits éleveurs. Le fardeau de ces obligations explique-t-il aussi les fréquentes tentatives des *celepkeşan* de se soustraire à leurs devoirs. Ainsi, une note consignée dans le registre de 1576, fait savoir que douze Bulgares — *celepkeşan* — du village de Košarevo, district de Radomir se cachaient, raison pour laquelle ils avaient été réinscrits sans changement, comme dans l'ancien registre. Ils s'étaient comportés de la même manière aussi par le passé. Par ailleurs, le seul *celep* bulgaro-mahométan du même village, qui fut présent, n'avait pas livré le nombre de moutons qu'on exigeait de lui.[52]

Au reste il ne manquait pas de renseignements témoignant de l'inexécution en masse des fournitures à terme fixe.[53] Ces actes d'insoumission aux

[48] Cf. *DBI*, vol. iii, No. 6, pp. 3–4; No. 9, p. 5; Refik, *op. cit.*, No. 3, p. 8.

[49] Cf. p. ex. Refik, *op. cit.*, No. 6, pp. 9–10; *DBI*, vol. iii, No. 9, p. 5; A. Refik, *Hicrî on ikinci asırda Istanbul hayatı* (*1100–1200*), Istanbul 1930, No. 184, p. 154, etc.

[50] Refik, *Türk idaresinde . . .*, No. 36, pp. 26–7; No. 35, pp. 25–6; *DBI*, vol. iii, No. 40, pp. 17–18, No. 38, p. 17; Elezović, *op. cit.*, No. 1270, III, p. 343.

[51] BNS, Constantinople–Defterhane, I. K. Fournitures d'Etat 9 cemazi II 1084.

[52] Fonds 95, inv. 23, f. 41a.

[53] *DBI*, vol. iii, No. 40, pp. 17–18; Refik, *op. cit.*, No. 36, pp. 26–7; No. 13, pp. 13–14, etc.

ordres des autorités pouvaient s'expliquer, jusqu'à un certain degré, par la circonstance que le bien-être plus prononcé des *celep*, dont les services constituaient une nécessité urgente pour les autorités, suscitait chez eux un esprit d'indépendance et d'insoumission.

Sans doute ces soustractions des *celep* à leurs obligations causaient de sérieuses difficultés aux autorités. Malgré tout, le gouvernement ne cessait de recourir au service des *celep* aussi pendant les XVIIe et XVIIIes.[54]

La plus grande quantité de menu bétail, dont disposaient les *celep* et la possibilité qu'elle leur offrait d'en vendre sur le marché libre, les incitaient à préférer le commerce aux fournitures obligatoires d'Etat, lesquelles étaient relativement mal payées. Les autorités s'efforçaient de toute façon à limiter ce commerce indépendant des *celep*, au profit du ravitaillement public organisé. Un firman adressé aux vizirs des contrées de l'aile moyenne, de gauche et de droite en Roumélie, ainsi qu'à d' autres fonctionnaires, en 1757, laisse nettement percer cette préoccupation.

Il y est dit, en effet, que les personnes de la catégorie des *celep*, les rayas et autres commerçants des villes et des villages amenaient constamment à Constantinople leurs moutons pour les y vendre sur le marché libre, sans que les *kasapbaşı* aient à intervenir dans ces tractions. Or, l'administration suprême s'efforce de placer sous son contrôle cet afflux de moutons et prévient les autorités d'user de fermeté en faisant diriger son cours sur la capitale pour le ravitaillement de sa population. Les *celep* et autres éleveurs de moutons ne doivent pas retenir leurs moutons dans les pâturages et plaines pâturables, parce que le printemps approche et c'est la saison propice au marché des moutons. Le *kasapbaşı* prendra en main propre l'achat par contrainte de ces troupeaux, en payant à l'avance les patrons qui auraient amené leurs moutons à Constantinople.[55] Le document ne dit mot des prix auxquels se feront ces achats, prix du marché ou prix fixés par l'Etat. Quoiqu'il en soit, il est hors de doute que le commerce libre des moutons des *celep* ou autres éleveurs était restreint et contrôlé par les autorités.

Les conflits surgissant sur ce plan entre les *celep* et les autorités dataient encore du XVIes. Du témoignage d'un firman daté du 23.1.1594, les *celep* allaient à la rencontre des troupeaux arrivant à Constantinople pour le ravitaillement et, aux portes de la ville, les répartissaient selon leur bon gré. En conséquence les cuisines du sultan n'obtenaient pas de viande de bonne qualité. Il est ordonné que dorénavant, dès l'arrivée aux portes de la ville de moutons venant de Roumélie, ceux-ci seront vendus avec le concours de l'*emin* des cuisines du sultan. La répartition des bêtes entre les *celep* aura

[54] Registre du kadi de Sofia 159, p. 11, doc. I; Registre du kadi de Vidin 46, f. 45a, doc. II.

[55] Registre du kadi de Sofia 16, p. 11, doc. III; v. ordre d'un contenu pareil du 6–15. IV.1756, dans le Registre du kadi de Sofia 159, p. 34, doc. I.

lieu à partir de là, de sorte qu'aucune vente ne se fasse en dehors de ce procédé. Les moutons vendus illicitement seront confisqués au profit du trésor.[56]

Or, les *celep* s'efforçaient toujours de tourner les restrictions administratives, pour des raisons d'enrichissement personnel et autres. Ainsi, en 1714, les villages de *celep* Černevo et Arnautkjoj, district de Ruse, recelaient le suif et le beurre fondu, recueillis des bêtes abattues, pour pouvoir en obtenir un meilleur prix. De cette manière, le ravitaillement de Constantinople en produits de ce genre en souffrait. En conséquence, le kadi de Ruse est requis de découvrir les produits recelés en effectuant des recherches dans les maisons et les caves, de les vendre au prix courant, à des marchands de beurre; les provisions devront être transportées du port le plus proche, par bateau, à Constantinople, aux fins d'y être vendus.[57]

Toutes ces possibilités de commerce libre et de diverses spéculations, existantes dès le XVIes., malgré les restrictions imposées par les autorités, créaient des conditions propices pour les *celep* et, en général, les gros éleveurs de s'enrichir et d'amasser des fortunes considerables. De riches éleveurs se désignent parmi eux, dès la fin du XVIIIe et surtout au XIXes., qui réorganisèrent sur des principes capitalistes l'élevage des moutons, les productions de lait et de viande ainsi que la transformation de la laine.[58]

Malgré tous les efforts, monopoles, interdictions et restrictions, bien qu'il eût de plus en plus recours au marché libre pour équilibrer son ravitaillement, le gouvernement ottoman organisait avec des difficultés toujours croissantes les fournitures de moutons pour les besoins de l'Etat. Lors de ses achats, le gouvernement se heurtait toujours davantage aux difficultés que lui suscitaient toutes sortes de spéculateurs et d'acheteurs en vert qui avançaient aux rayas des sommes sur les achats à venir, conclus à des prix supérieurs à ceux offerts par l'Etat. Pour parer à cette concurrence, le gouvernement ordonnait à ses agents officiels préposés aux achats (*saycı*), d'avancer à la population le montant des sommes qu'elle avait déjà reçues de la part de spéculateurs.[59]

Plus d'une fois, l'administration suprême s'était vue obligée de rappeler aux autorités locales de ne souffrir ni retards, ni soustractions de la part des *celep* et autres éleveurs qui laissaient les troupeaux, destinés aux besoins de

[56] A. Refik, *Hicrî onbirinci asırda Istanbul hayatı (1000–1100)*, Istanbul, 1931, No. 31, p. 16.

[57] *DBI*, vol. iii, No. 80, p. 37.

[58] Cf. A. Neyčev, «*Dželepi i beglikčii*», *Yubileen sbornik po minaloto na Koprivštica*, Sofia 1926, pp. 523–34; H. W. Duda, *op. cit.*, pp. 94–6. A. Matkovski, *Gurčin Kokalevski (1775–1863). Prilog kon prašanjeto za sozdavanjeto na selska stočarsko-trgovska buržoazija vo Makedonija*, Skopje 1959, pp. 125–34.

[59] Un firman par exemple dans ce sens a été adressé en 1742 au prince roumain Mihail. En tant que vassal du sultan il était tenu de prendre des mesures contre les boyars, les spéculateurs et autres, qui empêchaient les *celep* et les *saycı* d'acheter des moutons en Valachie pour le ravitaillement de la capitale. En dépit des ordres précedents ces spéculateurs avancaient aux rayas des sommes sur les futurs achats des moutons. M. Guboglu, *op. cit.*, p. 243. V. aussi Registre du kadi de Sofia 25, p. 12, doc. III, 30 *bis*, p. 104, doc. I; 165, p. 8, doc. I; Vidin-*muhafiz*, I. Fournitures d'Etat 13 cemazi II, 1198.

l'Etat, paître dans les plaines le long des routes et entravaient de cette manière l'approvisionnement de la capitale.[60]

Il est probable que les difficultés et les embarras auxquels se heurtaient les autorités en organisant l'achat par contrainte de moutons, les retards apportés à l'exécution des fournitures, les arrérages et les tentatives systématiques des *celep* de se soustraire à ce régime, aient en fin de compte amené le gouvernement à introduire le payement en numéraire de l'équivalent des fournitures obligatoires des *celep*, dit *celepkeşan bedeli.*[61] Cependant l'imposition de ce versement ne saurait guère être considérée comme une étape nouvelle dans l'évolution du service de *celep* et des réquisitions de *celep*, vu que ces réquisitions continuent d'être en usage simultanément et parallèlement au *celepkeşan bedeli*. Il est plus probable que celui-ci ait été créé pour satisfaire à certaines nécessités pratiques, soit dans les cas où l'administration se trouvait en difficulté de réaliser ses fournitures, ou bien lorsque ces fournitures étaient exécutées en quantité suffisante pour satisfaire aux exigences du moment. On rencontre des données sur le *celepkeşan bedeli* déjà au début du XVII^e^s. Les revenus de cette imposition étaient de nouveau assignés à l'achat de moutons pour ravitaillement public, que les autorités réalisaient par l'entremise de commerçants privés. Le montant total de l'impôt *celepkeşan bedeli* était fixé en proportion du nombre des moutons de *celepkeşan* que devait livrer un district déterminé, à en croire le témoignage de la plupart des documents datant des XVIIe et XVIII^e^s. Cela revient à dire, que l'impôt ne devait probablement être perçu que des *celepkeşan* dans le district respectif, au lieu de leur obligation de livrer à l'achat d'Etat un nombre déterminé de leurs moutons.[62]

L'imposition se faisait selon différents systèmes. Le plus souvent c'était sous la forme de contre-valeur équivalente à chaque mouton *celepkeşan* payable en numéraire. Le montant en était fixé à raison de 48 aktchés par mouton, dont 36 aktchés couvraient l'impôt même, 8 étaient percus comme taxe *gulâmiye* et 4 comme rémuneration des fonctionnaires percepteurs (*vech-i maʿaş*).[63]

La répartition de cet impôt se faisait parfois par *hane*. En 1768–69

[60] Cf. p. ex. Registre du kadi de Sofia 159, p. 11, doc. I, p. 15, doc. I; 16, p. 11, doc. III; 6, f. 37b, doc. I, etc.

[61] Dans son exposé de 1687 sur l'organisation intérieure de l'Empire Ottoman l'ambassadeur de France à Constantinople (Girardin) affirme que les obligations imposées aux *celepkeşan* ont été remplacées par un impôt payé en espèces. Cette transformation s'est produite à l'époque où l'Empire s'agrandissait afin «d'épargner des frais pour les longs voyages». D'après les renseignements de l'ambassadeur français son revenu total remontait à 200,000 écus par an. A la lumière de ces données la perception de l'impôt en espèces parait avoir été générale (v. Paris, Archives du Ministère des Affaires Etrangères, série Mémoires et documents, Turquie, I, f. 55b).

[62] Registre du kadi de Sofia 312/1, f. 24a, doc. I, f. 24b, doc. II.

[63] Cf. Registre du kadi de Sofia 306, f. 9a, doc. I; 309-*bis*/1, p. 3, d. II; 312/8, f. 17b, f. 20b, d. II; 166, p. 49, doc. III; Registre du kadi de Ruse R/2, f. 18b, I, 50b, I, 51a, I; R/51, f. 40a, I, 47b, I; R/7, f. 47b, I; R/8, f. 59a, II; R/37, f. 12a, II.

l'impôt *celepkeşan bedeli* incombant au district de Sofia, fut réparti d'après ce procédé, entre 162½ *hane*. Chaque *hane* était requise de verser 16 piastres et 33 paras. Pendant le premier quart du siècle, ce district comptait un nombre plus élevé de *hane*, 224 en tout, dont chacune devait verser 11 piastres et 32 paras comme contre-valeur équivalente des 5,812 moutons qui devaient être livrés.[64] Dans d'autres cas ce même impôt était payable d'après le procédé *maktu*ʿ, c'est-à-dire sous forme d'une somme globale.[65]

La perception du *celepkeşan bedeli*, comme du reste beaucoup d'autres impôts, surtout au XVIIIᵉs., était cédée à ferme.

Il ne faudrait pas oublier, bien entendu, que l'affermage de cet impôt, comme c'était d'ailleurs le cas de bien d'autres institutions fiscales, ne s'est guère révélé bien avantageux à la régularité des rentrées du *celepkeşan bedeli*.[66] Or, cela suscitait à son tour, sans aucun doute, des difficultés aux autorités, lors des fournitures de menu bétail pour les besoins publics et de l'Etat. Selon toute probabilité, c'est aussi en raison de ces circonstances que les livraisons en nature, par les services des *celep* ou moyennant achats généraux, ont toujours retenu leur importance jusqu'à une époque très avancée.

Nos recherches, effectuées surtout à partir de matériaux documentaires inédits, mettent en évidence que l'institution des *celep* dans l'Empire ottoman date d'une époque assez reculée et joue, sans contredit, un rôle considérable dans la vie économique de l'Etat.

L'analyse des sources montre qu'une bonne partie des *celep* étaient des personnes entretenant des attaches avec le capital commercial et usuraire, qui, moyennant le système *celepkeşan*, participaient à l'organisation du ravitaillement d'Etat. Par ailleurs, il est hors de doute que dans la majeure partie des terres bulgares de l'époque, le métier de *celepkeşan* se trouvait surtout aux mains de Bulgares dont la plupart étaient éleveurs de moutons.

[64] Registres du kadi de Sofia 166, p. 49, doc. III; 306, f. 13, doc. I. Des renseignements de ce genre suggèrent que le *celepkeşan bedeli* est devenu peu à peu une obligation de toute la population, et non seulement des *celepkeşan*. Les sources assez confuses ne nous permettent pas d'en arriver à des déductions là-dessus.

[65] Registres du kadi de Ruse R/7, f. 47a, doc. II; R/38, f. 47a, doc. II, f. 48b, doc. I, etc. *Evreyski izvori za obštestveno-ikonomičeskoto razvitie na balkanskite zemi prez XVII v.*, t. ii, Sofia 1960, pp. 290–2. D'après des renseignements puisés aux registres de kadis au XVIIᵉs. les Juifs de Sofia qui, lors de l'enregistrement général de 1576 avaient été inscrits pour une obligation de livrer 1200 moutons de *celepkeşan*, en 1611/12 avaient été chargés de payer la taxe *celepkeşan bedeli* pour 1,400 moutons. Le percepteur de cet impôt communique qu'ils ne peuvent payer que pour 1,200 moutons (*Die Protokollbücher* . . ., No. 834, pp. 240–1). Il est évident qu'en l'occurrence cet impôt n'était pas exigible selon le procédé *maktu*ʿ.

[66] A ce sujet voir pour plus de détails B. Cvetkova, «Otkupnata sistema (*iltizam*) v Osmanskata imperiya prez XVI–XVIII v. s ogled na bălgarskite zemi», *Izvestiya na Instituta za pravni nauki*, xi, 2, pp. 216–18; B. Cvetkova, «Recherches sur le système d'affermage (*iltizam*) dans l'Empire ottoman au cours du XVI–XVIII s. par rapport aux contrées bulgares», *Rocznik Orientalistyczny*, xxvii, 1964, pp. 111–32.

Exerçant le métier d'éleveurs et du fournisseurs de moutons, les *celep* étaient en temps, au XVI^{e}s. déjà, marchands de menu bétail.

L'origine et l'évolution de cette institution surtout dans les Balkans, où l'élevage bien développé existait depuis des siècles, étaient tout à fait conformées aux directives fondamentales de la politique économique du gouvernment: exploiter au maximum les ressources naturelles de pays conquis, en vue de satisfaire à ses propres intérêts fiscaux et à ses problèmes de ravitaillement qui étaient d'une importance vitale pour l'entretien de l'appareil militaire complexe de l'Empire.

Il est indubitable que l'engagement des *celepkeşan* des terres bulgares à participer aux entreprises d'Etat du ravitaillement en menu bétail, appuyé du régime protectionniste que le gouvernement ottoman s'efforçait de leur assurer, suscitèrent dans les milieux bulgares la formation de couches sociales plus aisées et saillantes qui s'affirmèrent, petit à petit, au cours des siècles. Cependant les moyens pécuniaires que les *celep* en gros amassaient au XVIe et XVII^{e}s., grâce au commerce de menu bétail et aux fournitures d'Etat, n'étaient toujours pas employés à réorganiser l'élevage des moutons sur un plan capitaliste. Ils étaient plutôt investis dans de nouveaux achats de bétail et, dans ce sens, leur importance ne dépassait pas le cadre du rôle habituel d'un capital commercial, voire usuraire, dans les conditions du système féodal ottoman. Il est vrai que, à partir de la fin du XVIII^{e}s., certains changements aurent lieu sous ce rapport, toujours est-il que, tout au long du XIX^{e}s., le service des *celep* garda son caractère d'institution féodale rattachée aux nécessités d'ordre fiscal de l'Empire Ottoman.

Le temps aidant, l'influence des *celep* prit de l'ampleur en même temps qu'une importance sociale considérable à l'époque de la Renaissance bulgare.

English Imports from the Middle East, 1580–1780[1]

RALPH DAVIS

POPULAR and governmental attitudes towards trade, whether in the twentieth century or in the sixteenth, are nearly always concerned with exports; foreign trade is associated with the notion that national power and prosperity come from exporting as much, and importing as little as possible. Of course these are not sophisticated views, but they have always been widespread and influential ones. Following them, writers on the history of different branches of trade are much inclined to confine their discussion to export trade, implicitly adopting the assumption that this is what traders have been concerned with. But of course merchants were never conscious servants of national interest, whether rightly or wrongly conceived; they were guided by their own interest, seeking their profit in both import and export, or, if they found it profitable to do so, concentrating most of their commodity traffic in one direction and remitting money (coin, bullion or bills of exchange) the other way.

The trade of each merchant, of each nation, and of Western Europe as a whole with the Middle East depended in a special way on the capacity to absorb imports of Middle Eastern goods. There were no regular facilities for transferring money by means of bills of exchange to or from Europe. While money could be, and was, taken into the Ottoman Empire to pay for excess imports to various European countries, it was never taken out of the Empire in payment for European goods. The Ottoman Empire forbade the export of coin; and, probably more important, the purchasing power of silver was generally greater in its territories than in Europe, so that it was more profitable, as well as safer, to bring home goods rather than coin.[2]

[1] From the point of view of English trade statistics, 'the Levant' was the area covered by the Levant Company's monopoly. This was the Ottoman Empire and, until late in the seventeenth century, Venice and its dependencies. But, except for a time in the matter of currants (see note 26) neither Venice nor the Greek lands of the Ottoman Empire were of any significance to English trade. I have therefore used the terms 'Levant' and 'Ottoman Empire' interchangeably. The Middle East I have taken to be the Ottoman Empire in Asia and Egypt, together with Persia and Arabia. Normally, produce of all this area on its way to Europe came through Levant ports; normally English Middle East trade has the same meaning as English Levant trade. But there were brief periods when English trade with Persia and southern Arabia was, for special reasons, carried on across the Indian Ocean or through Russia, and I have commented on this in appropriate places.

[2] The greater purchasing power of silver throughout Asia accounts for the continuous drain from Europe in all recorded history, well illustrated in the seventeenth and eighteenth centuries by the vast silver exports of the English and Dutch East India Companies.

Thus a high demand in Europe for Levant goods could be paid for, if European goods were not acceptable in return, by sending out coin; but the opposite situation could not be dealt with in a similar way. If the Middle Eastern demand for his goods was high, the European exporter could not simply send out goods and get cash in return. He had to make sure that his home market (or an accessible market in another European country) could absorb Levant goods, since goods were the only possible returns for his exports. In practice, this offered little difficulty to most European merchants. Over a long period of time, Italians, French and Dutch regularly bought far more in the Levant than they sold there, and balanced the account by remitting coin and bullion. But the English merchants' experience was a different one, for they were usually able to export goods sufficient to pay for all their import needs, and there were times when a real problem emerged of finding goods to be returned home in exchange. The ultimate decline in the English Levant trade is more obviously related to the failure of English demand for Levant goods than to decline in exports to the Levant.

I

The first English traders who made their way by sea directly to the Levant, soon after 1580, had little interest in the produce of the Middle Eastern lands themselves. They came with two objects, the relative importance of which is hard to determine. One was to find a way into eastern markets to which English cloth had previously gone by overland routes (now blocked by the Netherlands revolt against Spain); the other, to secure to themselves a share of the import to Europe of the drugs, pepper, spices and dyestuffs of Indonesia. These goods were the original basis of their import trade.[3] But almost simultaneously with the opening of this trade with the Levant, English seamen were being despatched to seek out the Portuguese route to the Indies by way of the Cape of Good Hope.[4] This was a more difficult task; but when the pioneers had opened the way, and the first East India ships returned to England in 1603—less than twenty years after the Levant Company factors settled themselves in Istanbul and Smyrna[5]—the Levant route was doomed as a way for the transit of Far

[3] The earliest recorded consignments from the Levant, in 1587–8, were dominated by indigo and nutmegs and other spices from further east; but they already included Levant cotton and galls in considerable quantities (T. S. Willan, 'Some Aspects of English Trade with the Levant during the Sixteenth century', *English Historical Review*, lxx, 1955, p. 399). By 1620–1, the next year for which figures are available, indigo and spices were only trivial elements in Levant trade (A. M. Millard, 'The Import Trade of London, 1600–1640', unpublished London Ph.D. thesis, 1956).

[4] The first English attempt at the Cape route to the East was Fenton's disastrous voyage of 1582–3; James Lancaster's voyage of 1591–3 penetrated to Indonesia, though he barely returned alive; and Lancaster led the successful first trading fleet of the East India Company in 1601–3.

[5] Professor Wood and Dr. Chaudhuri have shown that the East India Company was

Eastern goods to England.[6] But the English traders in the Levant had already found that the Middle East itself produced goods that were saleable in England, and consequently the total value of imports was maintained despite the falling away of the transit trade.

During this early period of the trade down to 1620, the English sent coin or bullion to the Levant from time to time, because they could not sell sufficient goods to pay for all they wanted. But after 1600 English merchants found that for the first time English woollen broadcloths could be sold in the Levant in competition with Venetian cloth.[7] The export soared during the following decades, and after the early 1620's it became the English boast that they earned their Levant imports entirely by the sale of cloth. These imports were largely of raw silk, to serve an English industry which must have expanded at a prodigious rate, though some of the silk was re-sold on the continent.[8] The expansion of cloth export continued, was checked in mid-century by the English Civil War and the unsettled conditions that followed it, and burst out after 1660 into a great export boom. The problem now was to find goods to bring home, since the proceeds of exports could not be returned in money. Consequently, a variety of other commodities appeared in the import trade, and silk, though still imported in growing quantities, came to account for little more than a third of the total.

But this was a temporary phase. The import of each of these new commodities began to fall off, at various dates between 1680 and 1730. Silk imports continued to grow during most of this half-century, and the variety which had been present in the trade for some decades slowly disappeared; by 1730 silk accounted for nearly four-fifths of the import trade. On the other hand, new difficulties in exporting arose and for a time outran any decline in the total demand for imports. The great expansion of cloth exports after 1660 had been stimulated by French withdrawal from the Levant trade in the middle decades of the seventeenth century; it lost its strength in the 1680's when French trade began a rapid recovery, and in consequence, during many of the years between 1680 and 1718 coin had to be sent out to the Levant to pay for an import surplus.[9] But as the fall in

established, and financed in its early days, largely by Levant merchants who feared the effect on their own trade of the Dutch penetration to Indonesia (A. C. Wood, *History of the Levant Company*, Oxford 1935, p. 31; K. N. Chaudhuri, *The English East India Company*, London 1965, pp. 11–12.

[6] The Levant Company ledgers show that in 1626, 1643 and 1644 pepper imported to England by the Cape route was re-exported through the Mediterranean to Turkey!

[7] R. Davis, 'England and the Mediterranean, 1570–1670', in F. J. Fisher, ed., *Essays in the Economic and Social History of Tudor and Stuart England*, Cambridge 1961, pp. 119–24.

[8] Exports to Turkey 'is chiefly returned to us in silk, the other commodities of those countries being gross goods and of small consequence in comparison' (Levant Company Court Minutes, 15 September 1639).

[9] The Levant Company banned the export of coin in 1718; after it lifted the ban in 1744 little coin was sent to the Levant.

English demand for Levant goods gathered momentum, the balance between imports and exports was restored. Still later, from the middle of the eighteenth century, English demand for Levant silk began to fall away rapidly, and the Middle East could offer nothing that adequately replaced it. The total value of the English Levant trade now fell away, and made no real recovery until quite new conditions emerged in the nineteenth century.

II

Almost from the earliest years, silk predominated in English import trade from the Middle East. Around 1600 it supplemented the transit trade; in the middle and later decades of the seventeenth century it was the most important among a number of imported commodities; by the middle of the eighteenth century it was sustaining the trade almost alone.

England had practically no silk industry in the sixteenth century; silk fabrics and most silk trimmings were imported from France or Italy. The opening of direct trade with the Levant sources of raw silk, and the immigration of refugee artisans from the Low Countries in the last years of the century, combined to transform the scale of the industry. Considerable silk imports first appeared in the 1590's and may have included Middle East silk,[10] in the early decades of the new century imports grew rapidly, and by the 1620's silk, now coming almost entirely from the Levant, had become the largest of raw material imports to England.[11] Though other sources of silk came to be important during the seventeenth century, the Middle East remained the principal English supplier for well over a hundred years.

The Middle Eastern silk that came to England—and Europe—in the seventeenth century was produced in Persia. High quality silk (sherbassee) came from Ghilan, the south-eastern coast of the Caspian Sea; and ardasset, a poorer grade, from its western shore. The normal routes to Europe passed through the Ottoman Empire—by Erzerum or by Kermanshah and Baghdad to Aleppo or, in smaller quantitities, to Smyrna. Vast quantities of English cloth were sent by native merchants from Aleppo to Persia in exchange. From time to time routes were interrupted by Turco-Persian war, and then the English and Dutch East India Companies seized the opportunity to open Persian trade along the alternative route, by the Persian Gulf, the Indian Ocean and the Cape of Good Hope.[12] But

[10] *Historical Manuscripts Comm., Salisbury Mss.*, vol. iv, pp. 574–5.

[11] Millard, *op. cit.* Some of the silk taken in exchange for cloth in Levant markets was not brought to England, but was sold at Leghorn on the way home (*The Turkey Merchants and their Trade Vindicated*, 1720).

[12] Silk, with its high value in relation to bulk, could bear the cost of roundabout transport routes. In the 1560's, before there was an English trade through the Mediterranean, some silk was brought from Persia across Russia to Archangel, and then to England (T. S. Willan, *The Early History of the Russia Company*, Manchester 1956, pp. 58–62,

when the frontiers were open, Persian silk returned to its regular Levant routes.

The greatest—and as it turned out, the permanent— interruption of the Persian silk trade resulted from the weakness of government there at the beginning of the eighteenth century, leading up to civil war in 1717, and Russian and Turkish invasion in 1722–4. These disasters laid waste much of the silk-producing area and broke the trade routes with Turkey, and were followed by a period of Turco-Persian hostility, at times flaring up into war, which hindered the re-opening of these routes.[13] European merchants in Aleppo and Smyrna, facing what they thought to be a temporary interruption to the supply of Persian silk, turned their attention to silk-producing areas closer at hand. The Anatolian valleys round Brusa and Tokat, the northern part of the Syrian coastal plain and the Orontes valley near Antioch, and Cyprus, all had a considerable and long-established silk production. They served the weavers in the cities of the Ottoman Empire, especially Aleppo, Homs, Damascus and Cairo. Syrian silk was known in Europe,[14] and indeed was marketed at Marseilles well back in the seventeenth century,[15] yet English trade in it was evidently inconsiderable when compared with that in Persian silk. Presumably before the civil wars in Persia, Persian silk was cheaper, allowing for the difference in quality.[16] When the suspension of Persian supply compelled the English merchants to buy Syrian silk as a temporary expedient, they quickly found it was quite acceptable in England, filling many of the uses of sherbassee, though recognized to be of poorer quality. Moreover, it was obtainable in the quantities they needed, though whether Syrian production was expanded to meet European needs, or European demand took silk from the looms of the Syrian artisans, is not clear. By 1730 much the greatest part of Syrian production was going down to the ports for export to Europe, yet its price was little higher than in the days when it served only local needs.[17] The anticipated recovery in Persian silk supplies never came; there were odd years between 1724 and 1750 when caravans came in with good supplies of sherbassee, but they were increasingly unreliable and met only a little of the

---

146–55). In the 1740's this route was used again, when prolonged Anglo-French war made the Mediterranean passage dangerous and costly.

[13] There was intermittent fighting between 1730 and 1736, and again between 1743 and 1746.

[14] As early as 1621 Thomas Mun refers not only to Persian silk but also to 'the fine rawe-silk, made in Soria' (J. R. McCulloch (ed.), *A Select Collection of Early English Tracts on Commerce*, London 1856, p. 14).

[15] See the price lists beginning in 1680 in P. Masson, *Histoire du Commerce Français dans le Levant au XVII siècle*, Paris 1896, pp. xx-xxi.

[16] Unfortunately there are no regular statistics of relative price movements of Persian and Syrian silks during the decisive first quarter of the eighteenth century.

[17] Brusa and Tokat silk, however, was generally bought by the Syrian artisans, except in periods of exceptionally acute European need reflected in very high prices.

European demand for Levant silk. Yet the total supply of silk from the Levant was fully maintained; there was an almost complete turnover from Persian to Syrian silk in no more than a decade after 1717. English silk imports from the Levant did not fall in quantity at any stage of the transition, and the London and Amsterdam markets quickly adjusted themselves to dealing in the new qualities.[18]

Thus the cutting off of Persian silk supplies, which might have been expected to ruin the English Levant trade, had only a limited effect. But other and more serious blows were soon to fall.

The East India Company not only traded, when it could, in Persian silk; it also brought Bengal silk, and later China silk, to England. During most of the seventeenth century the quantity was small, for Bengal silk was of poor quality. From the beginning it was an acceptable substitute for ardasset, but for a long time it had little effect on the much more important trade in sherbassee. But the situation was changing after 1700. Bengal silk was being improved in quality as the English grip on Bengal tightened, and the East India Company's agents gradually acquired some control over the handling and presently over the production of the silk. Moreover, Antioch and other Syrian silks were of rather poorer quality than sherbassee, and therefore more closely threatened by Bengal. Syrian industry seems to have been prosperous in the middle decades of the eighteenth century (until 1758) and rising artisan demand for silk in Aleppo and Damascus was reflected in a tendency for prices to rise in the 1740's and 1750's. So the market for Syrian silk became increasingly affected by the arrival of Bengal silk in England, and the situation markedly worsened when big supplies from China began to arrive, for the first time, after 1752.

Far better silks than those of Persia, Syria or Bengal were produced in Italy. These were used for making high quality silk fabrics for clothing and furnishings. But during most of the seventeenth century the English silk industry was confined to making ribbon, thread, buttons and stockings, for which the poorer—but much cheaper—Levant silk was adequate. The home market for these was firmly secured well before 1700, and the further expansion of the silk industry, which continued at a good pace, depended on extending it into branches hitherto dominated by the French and Italians—making broad fabrics—under the guidance of the new wave of religious refugees coming in from France after 1680. Because Levant and Bengal silks were generally too poor for making these (though Levant silk could sometimes supply the shute or weft)[19] the eighteenth-century development of the industry was reflected in a growing import of Italian

[18] Antioch silk first appears in 1718 among the varieties of silk whose prices at Amsterdam are recorded in N. W. Posthumus, *Nederlandsche Prijsgeschiednis,* Leiden 1943.

[19] 'Turkey silk is in general too coarse to be used for the warp' (*House of Commons Journals,* xxv, 1749, p. 996).

rather than Levant silk. Thus, although the silk industry as a whole continued to grow, Bengal and Levant silk were fighting to supply the side of it that was nearly stationary. So long as the competition from Bengal silk was intermittent, and its quality compared rather badly with that of Levant silk, the latter retained its hold on a large part of the cheap end of the silk market. The rising cost of Levant silk in the 1750's worsened its competitive position, and Bengal and China silk were imported in larger quantities. Later in the century English demand for all these poorer kinds of silk actually began to go downhill, as changes in English fashion—the turn to cotton and worsted stockings, and to metal buttons—destroyed important sections of the market.[20]

English Silk Imports
(thousands of lbs. of 24 ozs.)

	Total	Levant	India and China	Other (mostly Italy)
1663, 1669 av.	366	264	1	101
1721–5 av.	639	240	84	315
1741–5 av.	555	145	116	294
1761–5 av.	844	113	73	658

III

The expansion of England's cloth export to the Levant during the seventeenth century outran the capacity of the English economy to absorb Middle Eastern silk. Already, in the 1630's, Levant silk was sometimes sold at Leghorn on the return voyage from the Levant, or re-exported from London; but the growth of Italian silk production, and the economic depression of Italy and Central Europe in the middle decades of the century cut away these possibilities. The English merchants had to find other Middle Eastern goods which could be sold in some quantity in England or Europe. They found a number of such things, and for a few decades after 1660 the character of the import trade was transformed as silk became simply the leading item among a variety of imports, and the prospect of great and long-continuing expansion of the Levant trade opened itself. But this prospect soon began to fade. After 1680 these various imports came under a variety of influences which caused them, in some cases rapidly and in others gradually, to fall away. No doubt the slow decline of cloth exports, under the pressure of French competition, had a tendency to depress the

[20] There is an extensive discussion of the eighteenth-century silk trade in R. Davis, *Aleppo and Devonshire Square*, London 1967, chaps. viii and ix.

general value of imports; but when these were badly wanted they were paid for in coin. A particular reason, arising from conditions of European or local demand, or of world supply, can be seen for the decline in the import of each particular Middle Eastern commodity.

Cotton was the only Middle Eastern product other than silk which had real importance in English trade before the middle of the seventeenth century. It first came from western Anatolia, through Smyrna, but in the eighteenth century there was some development in the trade from Syria (through the port of Acre) and from Cyprus. Imported at first for candle-wicks, cotton soon began to be used with other fibres for making cheap cloths, and a new branch of industry, parallel with but much smaller than silk manufacture, was established in England. Cotton is recorded among the earliest Levant cargoes of 1587–8,[21] and consignments built up to a substantial level which was maintained all through the seventeenth century. But the Levant lost its position as sole supplier to the little English cotton industry. The British West Indian islands, settled from the 1620's onward, began to produce cotton, and by the end of the century they were expanding their supply faster than the English demand was growing. In the first half of the eighteenth century the import from Turkey declined, slowly and with temporary recoveries, in the face of this competition.[22]

A second Turkish product, also handled through Smyrna, was mohair yarn. This was an extremely valuable textile yarn, spun in the villages of central Anatolia from the hair of the Angora goat.[23] It began to come to England in considerable quantities in the 1630's, chiefly for making buttons and buttonholes, and was to some extent substituted for the cheapest Persian silk, ardasset.[24] The trade grew rapidly in importance, so that at the end of the century it was second only to silk. But by this time a change of fashion was beginning to diminish its importance; metal buttons were coming into use even among the well-to-do. The principal function of mohair yarn was therefore gradually lost during the eighteenth century, and the English import fell away heavily, though it did not entirely disappear.

The third important Levant product brought to England was galls, from the region of Mosul and Diyarbekir. Galls (growths on certain kinds of trees, especially oaks) were used in conjunction with some types of red and black dyes, and also for making ink. They were imported in great

[21] Willan, *op. cit.*, p. 399.

[22] Statistics of English cotton imports from various sources, 1696–1780, are given in A. P. Wadsworth and J. de L. Mann, *The Cotton Trade and Industrial Lancashire*, Manchester 1931, pp. 520–1. The rapid expansion of the cotton industry after 1770 led to a sharp growth of cotton imports in which the Levant took some part. But this was far from sufficient to replace the decline in silk, and was very much smaller than the growth of French cotton import from the Levant (see p. 204 *infra*).

[23] The Turkish government forbade the export of unspun hair.

[24] C. King, *The British Merchant* (1743 edn.), pp. 192–3.

quantities in the second half of the seventeenth century, but within a very few years after 1700 the trade had fallen away to small proportions. The reasons for its decline are not clear. Certainly an alternative to galls was found in sumach (a product of the western Mediterranean) and there was some substitution; and it is possible that imports of galls, at their peak, were partly for re-export.

The earliest records of the Levant trade show great shipments of dried fruits, but for a long time these were entirely currants from the Greek islands and mainland, which do not concern us. By the middle of the seventeenth century, however, currants, figs and raisins from the coastal regions of Anatolia were being sent out through Smyrna, and this trade expanded rapidly during the succeeding thirty years, making Smyrna, for a time, the seat of the largest English merchant settlement in the Levant. But the basis of this trade was always precarious, for the Ottoman government was opposed to it. It was legalized, but on a very restricted scale, when the Levant Company secured new capitulations from the Porte in 1675; and this was in fact the death of the trade, for after a few years the Ottoman government started to enforce the restrictions with great rigidity. The fruit trade therefore fell away rapidly in the 1680's.

Many other Middle Eastern commodities, such as goat and camel hair, dyestuffs and drugs, textile fabrics and carpets, were brought to England in small quantities. Only one of these, coffee, is worthy of special notice. Coffee, the growth of southern Arabia, came through Cairo and Damietta, and provided the only substantial English trading link with Egypt. Arabian coffee was also brought to England by the alternative Indian Ocean route, and the Egyptian trade fluctuated violently. But coffee production was extended by European settlers, to Java under Dutch guidance, and to the West Indies where the French became large producers. After a period of growing competition, these supplies swamped the market in the 1730's. The coffee trade through Cairo collapsed, and a few years later the French were actually selling West Indian coffee in Syria and Egypt.

The import to England of almost all the principal Levant products, therefore, reached a peak in the last quarter of the seventeenth century and then began to fall away—rapidly in some cases, as with galls, slowly in others, such as mohair yarn. The fruit trade was checked by the action of the Ottoman government; mohair yarn and perhaps galls lost their market because of changes in English needs; cotton, coffee, many minor drugs and dyestuffs, and in the end silk, met competition from further afield and succumbed before it. The Levant, which in 1680 had been nearly a monopolist supplier of a number of important English needs, became of less and less significance to English commerce and to English industry.

English Imports from the Levant[25]
(thousands of £s)

	1621, 1630, 1634 av.	1663, 1669 av.	1699–1701 av.	1722–4 av.	1752–4 av.
Raw silk	73	172	219	274	81
Mohair Yarn	9	45	32	40	13
Cotton and cotton yarn	25	28	25	12	20
Galls	5	58	13	7	1
Fruit[26]	65	79	5	4	11
Coffee[27]	—	—	3	3	—
Other	72	39	17	16	26
Total	249	421	314	356	152

IV

England was not, of course, alone among western countries in trading with the Ottoman Empire; but in the seventeenth and eighteenth centuries it was consistently one of the two largest traders by sea, and for several decades in the middle of the seventeenth century was much the largest.

Italian cities, and above all Venice, had been the traditional suppliers of the West with eastern goods; and Venice, which had survived the opening of the Cape route by the Portuguese, and even expanded its import of Asian goods through the Levant at the end of the sixteenth century, was quickly driven from the transit trade when the Dutch and English entered the Indian Ocean after 1600. Venice also had a great import of Levant silk in the 1590's, supplying much of central Europe as well as the industry in Venice itself. This silk trade fell away very heavily in the first years of the new century, and never recovered; by 1620 it was negligible, for Holland and England were supplying much of Europe with eastern silk.[28] The whole of the Levant trade of Venice presents, in fact, a similar picture;

[25] 1621–34 from A. M. Millard, *op. cit.*; 1663–9 from BM Add. MSS. 36785; 1699–1774 from PRO Customs Ledgers (Customs 3). The totals depend on official valuations, which vary both absolutely and in relation to the true value of commodities; but the general relationship between the importance of different commodities is reasonably well indicated.

[26] The import figures before 1699 include Greece in the Levant totals, and nearly all the fruit in the early seventeenth century was Greek currants. No other commodity came from Greece in any quantity.

[27] Though coffee imports are small in the representative years used here, there were many years during the first third of the eighteenth century in which coffee imports were in the range £20,000–£30,000.

[28] D. Sella, *Commerci e Industrie a Venezia nel Secolo XVII*, Venice 1961, pp. 111–13.

from its position of dominance Venice's trade fell within a single generation to small proportions, and despite some recovery late in the seventeenth century, Venice was never again among the chief traders with the Levant.[29]

The Dutch appeared in the Levant in force after 1612, and developed a considerable import—chiefly of silk and mohair yarn—from Smyrna. Being much more heavily committed than the English to Indian Ocean trade, they were more persistent during the seventeenth century in trying to bring Persian silk to Europe by that route. Moreover, from the beginning of the century they were sending Bengal and Chinese silk home. The Bengal import became a large one, and consequently they ceased to have a solid basis for their Levant trade as the English did.[30] Only during a few years around 1650, when England was wracked by political struggles, was the Dutch trade on a large scale, and it declined rapidly after 1660.

France was the only country whose seaborne trade with the Levant rivalled England's in the seventeenth and most of the eighteenth century. The French had earlier developed an immense Levant trade, and made themselves the chief rivals of Venice; but war and civil war greatly damaged the industries in France on which this trade depended, and French trade fell to small proportions during the middle decades of the seventeenth century.[31] It was this vacuum that English—and for a short period, Dutch—traders filled with success. The whole situation was changed when political stability was restored, commerce and industry recovered, and French traders, returning to Levant trade in the last quarter of the seventeenth century, rapidly overtook the English.

From the time of this recovery, French trade with the Levant shows some important parallels with the English, and some differences. France, like England, found better suppliers of a number of commodities it had once imported from the Levant. Thus French silk imports, which had been considerable in the first decades of the eighteenth century, slowly fell away because alternative sources of supply appeared.[32] Coffee imports, which had been much larger than the English, collapsed when the West Indian crop flowed in. Imports of mohair yarn continued to expand for a long time, but turned down after mid-century.

Yet the French Levant trade grew rapidly in the eighteenth century, continuing to expand when the English trade had gone into decline. This buoyancy depended mainly on an enormous growth of the trade in a single

[29] On the general decline of Venice and its trade, see *Aspetti e Cause della Decadenza Economica Veneziana nel Secolo XVII*, Venice 1961.

[30] K. Glamann, *Dutch–Asiatic Trade, 1620–1740*, Copenhagen 1958, pp. 123–4.

[31] On French Levant trade, see L. Bergasse and G. Rambert, *Histoire du Commerce de Marseille*, vol. iv, Paris 1954; R. Paris, *Histoire du Commerce de Marseille, Le Levant*, Paris 1957; and P. Masson's two works cited in note 15 above and note 32 below.

[32] The French silk industry, far larger than the English, depended mainly on French and Italian silk; Levant silk was only a marginal supplement to these. See P. Masson, *Histoire du Commerce Français dans le Levant au XVIII Siècle*, Paris 1911, pp. 445–6.

commodity, cotton. In 1700 cotton was simply one among the many products which France took from the Levant, and was much less important than silk; the trade grew steadily, and by 1785 cotton accounted for nearly half the greatly increased total of French imports from the Middle Eastern lands. Right down to the 1780's the French cotton industry was much larger than the English, for it was growing throughout the century, whereas the English industry made its tremendous advance only in the last quarter. Though France, like England, imported rapidly increasing quantities of cotton from the West Indies, its total needs were so great that they changed the form of French Levant trade.[33] The maintenance of French demand for Levant goods, especially for cotton, should be given as high a place as the successes of French cloth export, in explaining how the French Levant trade came to surpass the English.

Principal French Imports from the Levant, 1700–1789[34]
(millions of *livres*)[35]

	1700–2 av.	1750–4 av.	1785–9 av.
Textile materials			
Silk	2,416	2,095	1,638
Cotton	1,528	5,684	12,792
Mohair Yarn	639	1,835	1,437
Camel Hair	137	914	1,021
Galls	170	488	853
Saffron	33	250	504
Textile manufactures	385	1,715	2,430

V

In the long history of European trade with the Levant, English participation was only a late episode. For many centuries the Levant had been the source—whether as producer or as middleman—from which Europe secured all its supplies of eastern goods. Having survived the competition of the Portuguese Cape route, the Levant transit trade was destroyed by the much more energetic English and Dutch exploitation of that route. But

[33] P. Masson, *op. cit.*, pp. 432–40.

[34] Adapted from R. Paris, *op. cit.*, pp. 504–41. The Levant trade included trade with the Greek mainland and islands, which was important to France. Omitting corn, wool and some minor items, which came mainly from Greece, the total value of the trade was approximately: 1700–2, 7 million *livres*; 1750–4, 13 million; 1785–9, 23 million. A small part of the cotton import came from Greece.

[35] The value of the *livre* in terms of English money varied considerably, but after a heavy fall in value in 1718 it was generally worth about tenpence.

the Levant was not merely a place of transit. Along with parts of North Africa, it was the nearest seat of production of many products which, for reasons of geography and climate, were not easily produced in Europe. But the same skills and knowledge which had taken the Portuguese round the Cape were slowly opening the whole world to European traders, and parts of it to European settlers. Already, by the early sixteenth century, Europe was taking its sugar from Atlantic islands rather than Mediterranean ones, its best red dyestuff from central America rather than the Mediterranean shores. This process was extended. The advantages of one region over another as provider of the more exotic products of the soil have rarely been examined historically; it is not clear why West Indian cotton was better (or cheaper) than Syrian; why Canaries sugar was cheaper (or better) than Cretan; why Bengal silk was cheaper, and Italian silk better, than the silks of Antioch and Cyprus. There may be individual reasons which would provide an adequate particular explanation in each case.

But a general question which requires an answer from the historians of the Middle East is why this area, which produced so many things for which demand was growing rapidly in eighteenth-century Europe—silk, coffee, cotton, for example—so easily lost its place as the leading supplier of them, and in some cases was driven from the market completely. Was there a general deficiency of enterprise in the Ottoman Empire, which held back its subjects from taking advantage of favourable demand conditions in Europe? Did government and local oppression create insuperable difficulties, especially among non-Muslims? Or, on the other hand, was growing population and local demand pressing on agricultural surpluses, and on the land area available for market crops? Were monetary influences tending to push up prices; did the general price level feel the effect of the long-continuing inflow of silver from Europe? (Or did most of this silver flow out again eastwards?) Is the whole view of relative decline in trade with Europe an illusion; a decline in seaborne trade alone, accompanied by an expansion of trade over Europe's land frontiers with the Ottoman Empire? (The replacement of the Dutch lion dollar by the Imperial dollar as a general circulating medium, in the second half of the eighteenth century, provokes thought along this line.)

These are questions which can only be answered by those with detailed knowledge of economic and social conditions within the Middle East itself. But the facts are clear. Venice, which had lived largely by Levant trade, dwindled into insignificance. The Levant accounted for half the trade of France in the late sixteenth century; for a twentieth of it in the 1780's. It was never so important to England, but in several decades of the seventeenth century about a tenth of the total of English trade was carried on with the Levant; by the 1770's the Levant accounted for no more than 1 per cent. Western Europe's trade with Turkey lagged far behind the general expansion of the western economies, of western commerce, even of western commerce in the produce of warm lands. The Levant, which in the fifteenth and sixteenth centuries had been indispensable to Europe, was by the middle of the eighteenth century struggling to compete with other, better equipped suppliers in filling only a small corner in the needs of Europe.

The Ottoman Economic Mind and Aspects of the Ottoman Economy

HALİL İNALCIK

I. THE RISE OF THE OTTOMAN COMMERCIAL CENTRES

It was a deliberate policy of the Ottoman government that was primarily responsible for the development of Bursa, Edirne (Adrianople) and Istanbul, successive Ottoman capitals between 1326 and 1402, 1402 and 1453 and from 1453 onwards, into major commercial and industrial centres. The measures which the Ottomans took to this end varied.

Following a very old tradition of Middle Eastern states, the Ottoman government must have believed that merchants and artisans were indispensable in creating and developing a new metropolis. It used every means to attract and settle them in the new capitals. By granting tax exemptions and immunities the imperial government encouraged them to come and settle or in a summary fashion forcibly exiled them to the capital.

After the conquest of Constantinople Mehmed II made every effort to convert the ruined city into a real metropolis, the seat of a universal empire, and in his policy of settlement he gave central importance to bringing into the city merchants and artisans. He was furious when in the fall of 1453 he learned that well-to-do people in Bursa did not comply with his order to come and settle in Istanbul. In 1475 after the conquest of Caffa a group of rich merchants were exiled and settled in Istanbul in a district where they numbered 267 families in 1477. With the same end in view he encouraged the Jews in Europe to migrate to his new capital and their number reached 1,647 families in 1477. When later under Bayezid II the Ottomans welcomed an exodus of Jews from Spain, Italy and Portugal who were settled in the main ports of the empire the idea was always that their commercial activities would bring prosperity to these ports. Jews made up an important part of the population of Istanbul in the sixteenth century (by 1535, 8,070 families) and turned Salonica into one of the most developed commercial and industrial centres of the empire. In 1554 the house of Nasi, the Ottoman Fuggers, came and settled in Istanbul under the special protection of Suleiman I. The method of forcible settlement was used by Selim I who drove to Istanbul about 1,500 merchants, artisans from Cairo and Tabriz.

In rebuilding the Ottoman cities and regenerating commerce and the economy, the construction of *ʿimarets,* each a complex of religious and commercial institutions, played a decisive part. Always established as a pious foundation, an ʿ*imaret* consisted of religious and charitable institutions such as mosque, *medrese*, *mekteb*, hospice and hospital on the one hand and mercantile establishments such as *bedestan* (*bezzazistan*), caravanserail, *han*, covered bazaars, market places on the other. The latter group was designed to provide for the expenses of the former. As in classical Islamic cities, the bazaars and industries of an Ottoman city developed around the *bedestan*, which was a building serving as a stronghold in the centre of the city to store and guard the precious merchandise as well as the fortunes of the ordinary citizens. It was also employed as the city hall for important transactions and exchange. Many Ottoman towns owed their development into commercial centres to their having a *bedestan*. In the seventeenth century Evliya Çelebi divided the Ottoman cities into those with a *bedestan* and those without it. Similar complexes were also built on the important trade routes and later on gave rise to thriving cities.

Caravanserails, *hans* and *zaviyes* in the cities or on the routes completed the system, which was designed to facilitate the caravan trade and make the trade routes converge on the capital city. The interesting point was that the state took a keen interest in promoting it. In 1459 Mehmed the Conqueror convoked the high dignitaries to his presence and required them to build ʿ*imaret*-cities wherever they liked in Istanbul. Thus the main districts of Turkish Istanbul came into being with their monumental religious institutions as well as bazaars and *hans*. On the other hand the *bedestan* and ʿ*imaret* which Minnet-oğlu Mehmed Beğ built at the beginning of the fifteenth century at Tatar-Pazarcığı became the nucleus of the thriving city with the same name in Bulgaria. The *uc-beğis* like Minnet-oğlu were responsible for the building of several provincial towns. The state encouraged such foundations, especially by granting property rights on the lands which were to be made *waqf* for them. It should be noted that in most cases such land was *mawāt*, waste or abandoned land, and the founder of the ʿ*imaret* undertook to bring it under cultivation. The usual procedure was as follows: the founder came to the Porte with a project, saying that if such and such lands with property rights were granted, he would revive them by settling there people who were sometimes the founder's slaves and by building dams and digging canals; and the revenues of the land were to be assigned as *waqf* for the upkeep of the ʿ*imaret*. Thus such projects gave rise to commercial centres and to the creation of new farm lands and villages in the countryside. Incidentally, the letters of Rashīd al-Dīn give examples of such projects in Iran under the Ilkhānids. The idea goes back apparently to ancient Iran as reflected in *Siyāsatnāmes* and Ṭabarī's account of the Sassanian kings. The state's main concern was to extend the sources of revenue for the treasury.

Zaviyes of dervishes, with the obligation of sheltering travellers in the cities and on the routes, were established on the same principles and must be considered as part of the same system. In early Ottoman history they played a pioneering role in Turkish settlement in the newly-conquered lands, and many Turkish villages in western Anatolia and the Balkans came into being around *zaviyes*. On the original *waqf* lands granted by the Sultan, the dervishes themselves or their slaves provided labour to bring them into cultivation.

When in the late fifteenth and sixteenth centuries most of the *waqfs* of *zaviyes* lost their original function, they were returned to the state's ownership. These reforms caused widespread social and political reactions in the empire. But it is interesting to add that when Suleiman I wanted to bring back prosperity to the major trade route from Iran to Erzurum, it was found necessary to restore the *zaviyes* on this route.

To come back to the rise of commercial centres in the Ottoman empire, it can safely be said that the Ottomans tried to bring about a route system around their capital cities, and that many of their conquests were motivated by the desire to take control of certain trade routes.

II. THE OTTOMANS AND THE TRADE ROUTES

With the fall of the Mongol Ilkhānid empire in Iran in the early fourteenth century, and the rise of the Ottomans in western Anatolia, the political, and subsequently, the commercial centre of gravity gradually shifted to western Anatolia. Concomitantly there was a change in the pattern of commercial routes. Bursa, which until the end of the fourteenth century was both the political and commercial centre of the Ottoman domains that stretched from the Euphrates to the Danube, became the most important trading city of Anatolia. It was the hub of the Anatolian commercial network. The former emporia of western Anatolia, such as Palatia, Altoluogo (Ephesus) and Smyrna, had already fallen under Ottoman control in 1391, and were now linked to Bursa. Caravans arriving from Iran now reached these seaports by way of Bursa. Moreover, by extending his domains eastwards as far as Erzincan, through Amasya and Tokat, Bayezid I (1389–1403) took control of this caravan route. Iranian silk caravans began to penetrate overland as far as Bursa. In the fifteenth century the cities of Amasya and Tokat, located on this route, became the most important political, economic, and cultural centres in Anatolia after Bursa.

The Ottomans did not neglect the trade routes in the southerly direction. In 1391 Bayezid I incorporated into his domains Antalya and Alanya, the principal ports of entry in southern Anatolia for Indian and Arabian goods. The main overland route followed by this trade was the ancient Aleppo–Adana–Konya–Istanbul road that cut diagonally across Anatolia. Complete Ottoman hegemony over this route that connected Bursa with the southern countries was established in 1468 when the Ottomans put an end to the Karamanids.

Muslim traders could now come to Bursa from Iran and Arabia in complete security. In addition, European traders from Venice, Genoa and Florence operating from Istanbul and Galata, which had been the most important centres of the Levant trade, now found Bursa the closest market in which they could purchase eastern goods and sell European woollens. This situation must have been apparent quite early, for Ibn Baṭṭūṭa mentioned, around 1330, that Orhan was considered the richest of the Turcoman sultans in Anatolia, and as early as 1352 the Genoese had concluded a commercial agreement with the Ottomans. At the end of the fourteenth century Schildtberger compared Bursa's silk industry and trade to that of Damascus and Caffa. He noted that Iranian silk was sent from Bursa to Venice, and to Lucca, which was then the centre of the European silk industry.

Bursa's development stemmed primarily from the Iranian silk trade. The silk industry in Europe experienced a great expansion in the fifteenth century, and Bursa became the international market place for the raw material upon which that industry depended, the esteemed silk of Astarābād ('Strava' in Italian) and Gīlān in northern Iran. J. Maringhi, the representative in Bursa of the Medicis and other Florentine houses, noted in 1501 that every year numerous silk caravans arrived in Bursa from Iran. In his letters is reflected the anxiety with which the merchants awaited the arrival of those caravans, and the eagerness with which the goods were bought in sharp competition. The rewards were handsome, for in Italy each *fardello* (about 150 kgr.) fetched seventy to eighty ducats profit. About a thousand silk looms in Bursa consumed five *fardelli* of silk a day. The price of silk rose constantly, fifty *akça* in 1467, seventy in 1488, and eighty-two in 1494. An average caravan brought about two hundred *fardelli* of silk. The table below gives the value of customs receipts from silk in Bursa for various years:

Year	Gold Ducats
1487	120,000
1508	100,000
1512	130,000
1521	40,000
1523	50,000
1557	70,000

The sudden decline after 1512 is a result of the wars with Iran. Although an upward trend is discernible after the peace of 1555, the level is far below that of the fifteenth century.

Even after Istanbul became the capital of the empire, Bursa continued to flourish as a principal trade centre of the empire for another century. Her rival in the silk trade, Aleppo, had been of importance for a long time. The silk caravans from Iran would arrive at Aleppo by way of Erzurum, following the Euphrates valley, or more often along the Tabriz–Van–Bitlis–Diyarbekir–Birecik route. In 1516–17 the Ottomans assumed control of these routes and of the Aleppo market as well. As a result, all outlets for Iranian silk open to Europeans were now in Ottoman hands. Not content with control of the outlets, the Ottomans attempted in the sixteenth century to place the north Iranian centres of silk production, such as Shīrvān and Gīlān, directly under their own domination.

Iranian silk, however, was not the only item traded in Bursa. Musk, rhubarb and Chinese porcelain assumed an important place among the merchandise coming to Bursa from China and Central Asia. Iranian merchants sought to take back with them mainly European woollens, precious brocades and velvets, and especially gold and silver specie, since it was scarcer and had a higher value in Iran.

A description of the diagonal land route from Damascus to Bursa in 1432 has been left to us by the noted traveller Bertrandon de la Broquière. He had joined in Damascus a three thousand camel caravan of pilgrims and merchants returning from Mecca. The Turkish group in the caravan included many notable men and was placed by appointment of the sultan under a merchant of Bursa. De la Broquière reached Bursa after a journey of some fifty days. There he found Florentine as well as Genoese merchants from Pera who were interested in buying spices.

Goods in transit on this caravan route tended most often to be merchandise light in weight and expensive in price, such as spices, dyestuffs (indigo and gum lac), drugs, and textiles. This caravan trade was totally in the hands of Muslim merchants. Among them was Abū Bakr, a substantial merchant of Aleppo, who in 1500 had brought to Bursa a shipment of spices worth 4,000 gold ducats, and Mahmud Gavan of India who in the 1470's annually sent his commercial agents to Bursa with Indian merchandise. In 1481 some of his agents even passed over the Balkans to trade textiles and other goods.

About 1470 Benedetto Dei, a Florentine, was able to claim that his fellow citizens could provide in Bursa not only cotton and wax, but also spices. From the reports of Maringhi we know that spices were exported to Italy from Bursa, however small the quantity. In 1501 he wrote to his associate in Florence that he had consigned three sacks of pepper to him, and if he wanted, he could send more. As it turned out, however, the difference in price between Bursa and Florence was not large enough compared to the profits obtainable in the silk trade. Maringhi wrote in 1503 that the price of pepper might go up to twenty-seven gold ducats a *kantar* (about 56 kilos) in Pera if new supplies did not arrive. The official price in Edirne in 1501 was only eighteen gold ducats a *kantar*. Connected with this crisis, of course, was the fact that at this time the Portuguese had already circumnavigated Africa and had begun to transport spices by sea. Antwerp received its first shipment of spices over this new route in 1501.

Selman Reis' famous report of 1525 demonstrated how the Ottomans reacted to the threat. In his report he tried to emphasize how easy it was for the Ottomans to wipe out the small Portuguese garrisons from their fortified posts on the Indian Ocean in order to re-establish the traffic between India and the Red Sea and thus to restore the state's revenues accruing from the spice trade in Egypt. He suggested the necessity for the Ottoman government to extend its rule over the Yemen and Aden, which would give it complete control of Indian trade. He further added that these conquests would bring to the Ottoman treasury hundreds of thousands of gold pieces and jewels every year as tax revenue. The port of Aden, he said, was visited by fifty or sixty ships every year and the tax revenue of this trade amounted to 200,000 gold ducats a year. He further argued that Sawākin, the rival of Aden, and Jidda would yield a huge amount of revenue for the Ottoman treasury if the Ottomans established their control there. Interestingly enough all his arguments to persuade the Ottoman government to take action against the Portuguese related to profits for the treasury. This is not the place to discuss the Ottoman struggle against the Portuguese in the Indian Ocean. It is now an established fact that the spice trade through the Middle East continued to be as important as before all through the sixteenth century.

Contemporary Venetian observation on Suleiman's policy of making Istanbul the centre of the world spice trade needs comment. It was a fact that half of the spices reaching Cairo and Damascus were conveyed to the Turkish markets, especially to Bursa and Istanbul, and from these cities it was re-exported to the Balkans and to the northern frontiers via Akkerman, Kilia and Caffa. On the other hand when in 1562 the English negotiated with the Shah of Iran to establish a direct trade route through the Caucasus and Russia, the Ottoman diplomatic mission then in Qazvīn insinuated that the Ottoman government would consider it a sign of hostility. But none of these attitudes was actually translated into a well-defined policy on foreign trade or the economy of the empire which could be compared to what we find in the same period in the West. The benefits of the state treasury and the needs of the internal market seem to be the only concern of the Ottoman government. In the late sixteenth and early seventeenth centuries the deterioration of Ottoman finances and increase of various duties and exactions at the ports of arrival were among other causes of the rising prices of Indian goods and Persian silk in the Ottoman markets which made the

English and Dutch intensify their efforts to establish direct relations with India and Persia.

The wars with Persia in the sixteenth century seriously affected the silk trade and had profound repercussions on the economies and finances of the two countries. The first stage began with Selim I's imposition, as a weapon of war, of a commercial blockade. He intended to prevent the Persians from acquiring war materials, silver and iron, and, by forbidding the trade in silk, to reduce the Shah's income from dues, one of his main sources of revenue. But the blockade had no effect, since most merchants began using the routes through Aleppo and Iskenderun. Thereupon Selim I resorted to more violent measures. Arab, Persian and Turkish merchants with stocks of Persian goods had their goods confiscated. The silks and cloths of all Persians at Bursa were confiscated and listed, and the merchants themselves were transported to Rumeli and Istanbul in 1515. The import and sale of Persian silk was forbidden. Anyone proved to have sold silk was fined its value. When Suleiman I came to the throne he released the merchants and restored their goods or paid them compensation. Nevertheless the ban on the import of and trade in silk by Persian merchants was maintained for a time. This blockade had important effects: it increased state control of the sale and distribution of silk; the scarcity and high price of silk obliged many merchants and weavers to go out of business; instead of Persian and Turkish merchants, Armenians began to gain control of the trade; and finally the government encouraged the production of silk within the Ottoman empire. When the silk routes were reopened under Suleiman, the industry again became dependent on Persian silk, and there was a new expansion in the trade and manufacture of silk. Yet in this reign too, during the wars with Persia, the Ottoman government imposed restrictions on the movement of gold and silver currency into Persia: the consequent shortage of silk harmed the Bursa industry and led to a fall in the revenue derived from it. In the ensuing period of peace the silk trade flourished again, but in the long period of war from 1578 to 1639 silk became an important political weapon for each side. As early as 1579 the Ottoman revenue from the trade had been halved, and the Ottomans again imposed a strict control on the export of gold and silver. In 1586 the shortage of silk had left three-quarters of the looms of Bursa idle, and the quality of the fabrics produced had begun to decline. The peace of 1590 extended Ottoman sovereignty over the silk-producing regions of Ganja and Shīrvān north of the river Kura. In the following year the ruler of Gīlān, Aḥmad, attempted to exchange Persian for Ottoman protection. The restrictions on the export of gold and silver caused an acute shortage of currency in Persia. Before Shah ʿAbbās launched his counter-attack in 1603, he sought means (no doubt at the suggestion of the Sherley brothers) to export Persian silk direct to Europe, via the Indian Ocean, whereby the English would escape the need to pay customs in the

Ottoman empire and the Shah would deprive his enemy of a rich source of revenue. In 1610 he sent an embassy to Lisbon and exported 200 loads of silk by sea, hoping to prove that this route was cheaper. When the attempt to make an agreement with Spain failed, the Shah turned to England, and in 1617 Sir Thomas Roe opened negotiations with the Shah. Of the 3–4 million gold pieces which Persian silk cost annually, England undertook to pay two-thirds in goods and one-third in coin. In order to maintain control of it, the Shah made the silk trade a state monopoly and forbade the export of silk to Turkey. The Ottomans and Venice—the two states most affected—watched these developments with anxiety. In 1619 and 1622 consignments of silk were indeed sent to England by sea. After the Ottoman-Persian peace of 1618, Persian silk was again exported to Aleppo, Bursa and Foça. Shah ʿAbbās's policy was not followed by his successor, who abolished the state monopoly of silk, and the use of the Indian Ocean route did not develop as was expected mainly because England was reluctant to provide the gold and silver currency required for it. Nevertheless in 1633 the Venetians were concerned at learning that English merchants were buying large quantities of silk at Bandar ʿAbbās. In 1664 the French too were attempting to divert the Persian silk-trade through the Persian Gulf and Surat.

The Ottoman government often used the trade privileges which it granted as a political asset. The grain of western Anatolia, Thrace, Macedonia and Thessaly was vitally important for feeding Venice and the cities of Northern Italy. In his excellent study M. Silberschmidt demonstrated how Bayezid I (1389–1403) in his relations with Venice could influence Venetian diplomacy by regulating grain export. Showing himself generous by letting Venice export grain from his dominions, Mehmed II (1451–81) kept Venice unsuspecting about his intentions before the siege of Constantinople.

It can be said that the capitulations were often granted on political considerations rather than economic. It was true that the Ottomans could not do without European cloths, an indispensable luxury for the higher classes, English tin and steel, and especially bullion on which the finances of the empire relied. So I think there is some exaggeration in saying that the Ottoman empire was economically self-sufficient. But it was equally true that from the outset, when the Ottomans favoured the Genoese against the Venetians by granting the capitulations of 1352, down to those granted to England in 1581 and to Holland in 1612, the Ottomans believed that they were favouring and supporting the friendly nations against the hostile ones by giving them trade privileges. I think one should first consider changes in Ottoman political attitudes to understand the fluctuations in the trade of a particular western nation in the Levant. Also it must be added that the extension of the capitulations to the western nations was very beneficial for the Ottoman economy in the sixteenth century, for such a policy kept the Levant markets alive and enabled the Ottoman Empire to compete successfully with other routes for the trade in spices and silk. In the early seventeenth century it was argued in England that the Levant Company was more important than the East India Company. The English capitulations were granted just at the time when England renewed its attempts to set up a trade route through Russia, the Caucasus and Iran to Ormuz. The fact that the Ottoman market consumed a large amount of cloth made a great difference for the English who were trying to pay for oriental goods with as little bullion as possible. It was along the same line that Naʿīmā, the Ottoman chronicler of the early eighteenth century, wrote: 'People in this country must abstain from the use of luxury goods of the countries hostile to the Ottoman empire and thus keep currency and goods from flowing out. They must use as much as possible the products of native industries . . . One may argue that such a policy might result in a decrease in the customs revenues, but one must not forget that if foreign merchants spend the money they earn by selling their goods here to buy what they need of Ottoman products, the money remains within the country. Moreover duties are paid more than once on these transactions. The European merchants import woollen cloths and buy for export wool, mohair, alum, gallnuts, potash and other goods, and pay for them at Smyrna, Payas, Ṣaydā and Alexandria with shiploads of silver and gold. This money is spread over the country, especially in Ankara, Ṣaydā, Tripoli and the Lebanon. But the Muscovites sell us expensive furs but purchase nothing in the Ottoman dominions and keep the money for themselves. Also we spend so much for Indian goods but Indians purchase nothing here. As a matter of fact they have nothing to buy here. Consequently incalculable fortunes are amassed in India. The same can be said about the Yemen from which we import coffee.' It is interesting to note that Naʿīmā avoided mentioning among the goods exported to Europe wheat, cotton, textiles and hides the export of which in the traditional thinking of the Ottomans was not desirable as they were necessities for the internal market.

In peace as in war the Ottoman government forbade the export of certain goods. In the list were usually included cotton, wax, leather, hides, grain. The idea was to protect the domestic market and prevent scarcity and higher prices.

III. THE OTTOMAN GOVERNMENT AND THE GUILDS

The attitude of the Ottoman government towards the guilds and domestic commerce is of particular interest in understanding the Ottoman economic mind.

The Ottoman guild system (called *esnaf*, *hirfet* or *lonca*) was actually a continuation of the *akhī* organization with this difference that the independent and powerful position of the guilds in the thirteenth and fourteenth centuries weakened under the centralist system of government of the Ottomans.

Let us first have a glance at the internal organization of an Ottoman *hirfet:* the number of *ustas* (from *ustādh*, master-craftsman) was limited. They elected from among themselves a council of control known as 'the Six', *Altilar*, who were, in descending order, the *shaykh*, spiritual head, the *kâhya* (from *katkhudā*), the *yiğit-başı*, *işçi-başı* and two *ehl-i hibre*, experts. The local kadi would confirm the election and register the result in his official *sicil*. The Sultan's diploma was to be obtained for the *kâhya*, actual leader and representative of the *hirfet* as was the *akhī* in earlier times. The principal duties of this council were to ensure that regulations concerning the quality and prices of manufactured goods were enforced, to carry out the examinations for promotion from apprentice (*şagird*) to journeyman (*kalfa*, from *khalīfa*) and from journeyman to master, to issue licences (*icaze*), to investigate and settle disputes and malpractices in the guild, to represent the guild in dealings with the government, and most important of all to prevent competition and underhand practices in the employment of workmen and in the buying of stocks. In carrying out these duties the *kâhya*, usually acting as the principal officer, the *yiğit-başı*, and his assistant the *işçi-başı*, would investigate complaints and make a report to the *ehl-i hibre*, on the basis of which they made the final decision. The guild co-operated closely with the government, and if there was any resistance to the decision of 'the Six', the latter could call upon the local state officers to enforce it. The regulations of the guild were confirmed by the Sultan, so becoming an *ihtisab* law, and as such, their application became the responsibility of the kadi. The work-people were divided into three main groups: *kuls* (slaves), *şagirds* (apprentices) and *ecirs* (wage-earners). The masters sold their products at specified shops in the market and were not permitted to sell their goods elsewhere. When one branch of a *hirfet* expanded, its members could easily form themselves into a new *hirfet* but the Sultan's diploma for recognition was required.

The government's control of a guild was carried on through various agents such as the local kadi, the *muhtesib* and various *emins*, agents of the Sultan. In Istanbul in certain professions the *kâhyas* had first to obtain a high official's certificate to get the Sultan's diploma. For example, the chief architect at the Porte was authorized to give such certificates to *kâhyas* elected by the guild of architects. The government usually respected the decision of the guild. There are indeed many instances in which the guilds imposed their own choice instead of a *kâhya* favoured by the local authority.

The disputes in a guild or between guilds or malpractices and deviations from the rules often made the government interfere in the affairs of the guilds. Almost without exception the Ottoman government adopted the views of the guilds about new trends against the rules. In the thriving cities of Bursa and Istanbul masters working outside the guilds and cheaper production to meet growing demand for goods at popular prices appeared to be the two principal threats against the guild system. Usually the guild denounced them at the Porte as working without licence and producing defective goods in violation of the regulations. The government interfered in favour of the guild and tried to restore the old regulations apparently without great success. A firman reduced the number of looms weaving brocade from 318 to 100 in 1564 but a new inspection in 1577 found 268 looms still working. Measures were taken to prevent hoarding of raw material. A special market or hall was assigned for each major item such as wheat, butter, honey, cloth, silk, leather and it was brought, weighed, taxed and then distributed to the representatives of the *hirfets* there. For the necessities such as wheat and meat for the Istanbul market the government established a close supervision from the producer in the provinces down to the retailers in Istanbul in order to provide a regular and sufficient supply of these goods and eliminate speculators. For purchase on a large scale in the provinces the government appointed rich persons, sometimes without their consent. The strict regulation and close control of domestic trade and industry was dictated, as seen above, by the government's major concern to meet the needs of the population at normal prices. Under the Islamic *ḥisba* rules the community was to be protected from unjust practices in the market. Especially in a city like Istanbul where a shortage or abnormally high prices of basic goods might rouse the military and the common people against the government all this was of vital importance with far-reaching political implications. We have also seen above how concern over scarcity and high prices made the government forbid the export of certain goods and thus affected foreign trade. In general the export of goods was not something desirable. When not forbidden, goods for export were subject to customs duties as high as those for import.

Conclusion

The Ottoman economic mind was closely related to the basic concept of state and society in the Middle East. It professed that the ultimate goal of a state was consolidation and extension of the ruler's power and the only way to reach it was to get rich sources of revenues. This in turn depended on the conditions making the productive classes prosperous. So the essential function of the state was to keep in force these conditions.

The society is, in this philosophy of state, divided into the ruling class who are not engaged in production and consequently pay no taxes and the subjects who are engaged in production and pay taxes. The latter is subdivided into city-dwellers engaged in commerce and industry and peasants engaged in agriculture. In the Middle Eastern state the belief prevailed that the peace and prosperity of the state depended on keeping the members of each class in their own place. It was such a concept of state and society that was prevalent in the minds of the *kuttāb*, actual administrators in a Middle Eastern state formulating all the measures to be taken. It called for an economy and economic organization the ultimate aim of which was to increase the state revenues as much as possible without impairing the prosperity of the subjects and to keep the traditional organization of the society from alteration.

By developing commercial centres and routes, encouraging people to extend the area of cultivated land in the country and international trade through its dominions, the state performed basic economic functions in the empire. But in all this the financial and political interests of the state were always prevalent and the Ottoman administrator could never have realized within the political and social system in which he lived the principles of a capitalistic economy of the Modern Age; while Europe, equipped with the knowledge and organization of such a system, came to challenge the Middle Eastern empire of the Ottomans.

Materials of War in the Ottoman Empire

V. J. PARRY

THE material of war assigned to an Ottoman army in the field or to an Ottoman fortress on the frontier of the empire was varied and complex in character. Documents relating to the campaign against Vienna in 1683 list in detail the *âlât-i âhen*, i.e., implements of iron, requisitioned from the mines at Samokov in Bulgaria and elsewhere: picks, shovels, hammers, axes, mattocks and also nails of diverse kinds—e.g., *meteris kazması, ferhadi lağım kazması, bir yüzlü balta, iki yüzlü balta, kassa mismar kuhle, mismar mertek, mismar nazlı mertek, mismar orta sayış, mismar zağra, mismar lofça, mismar tahta* and the like (Grzegorzewski, docs. no. 2 and 30).

On their conquest, from the Ottomans, of the Hungarian fortress Alba Regalis (Székesfehérvár, Stuhlweissenburg) in 1688 the Christians acquired, *inter alia*, a large number of guns (*colombrine, falconetti, moschettoni, schioppi di Gianizzeri*), quantities of lead and of quick-match (*miccia*, i.e., *fitil*), bombs, grenades, chests of musket and pistol balls, new cartridge cases, powder-horns, small leather sacks (for gunpowder), instruments (*siringe*) for extinguishing fires in time of assault, hooks, pikes, hoes, shovels, gun-carriages, carts, axle-trees of iron, waggon-wheels *alla Turca*, timber, anvils, bellows, nails, cables, ropes, stores of cotton, sandbags made of animal hair, copper cauldrons (including one full of *olio Petroglio*), pitch, etc. (Zenarolla, 99–105; cf. also Fekete, *Siyāqat-Schrift*, i, 692–8: a list, dated 1643, of the munitions then at the Ottoman fortress of Egri (Erlau) in Hungary).

A list of the spoils which fell to the Christians after their defeat of the Ottomans at the battle of Peterwardein in 1716 includes lead, hand-grenades of metal, quick-match, saltpetre, horseshoes, camel and ox hair, sheepskins, halberds, scythes, cotton, Janissary powder-flasks, bellows for heating cannon-balls, munition carts, waggon-jacks of wood, anvils, cannon and mortars, buffaloes, camels, drag-ropes, etc. (*Mon. Hung. Hist., Scriptores*, xxvii, 585–6).

Often the source references are brief and incomplete. There is mention, for example, of (*a*) wood drawn from the forests of Ada (Ada Bazarı) and used to make stocks for the muskets of the Janissaries (Uzunçarşılı, ii, 13, note 2); (*b*) timber from the forests of 'Resina' and 'Iskente' in Moldavia—a hard, fine, striped wood called in Turkish 'Sarma Agagdzi' and employed, in the Crimea, for the butts of muskets (Peyssonel, i, 114–15); (*c*) timber for the artillery waggons (*top ʿarabaları*), which came from the region of

Požega and of Sirem, the Roman Sirmium (Uzunçarşılı, ii, 99); (*d*) 'li schioppi lunghi che si fabricano in Algier e si chiamano Sciemete' (? cf. Ar. *shamāta*, 'a loud noise')—i.e., long guns imported from Algiers (Minadoi, 350); (*e*) *iplik* (*pamuk ipliği*?—cotton yarn) destined for the *cebe-hane* (armoury) of the Janissaries and levied from the *eyalet* of Haleb, i.e., from the province of Aleppo (Uzunçarşılı, ii, 14, note 1); (*f*) felt cloth for the artillery horses—*top ʿarabaları beygirleri* (Uzunçarşılı, ii, 99); (*g*) hemp from the lands along the southern shore of the Black Sea (Peyssonel, ii, 91, 120; Pertusier, 156) and also from Wallachia and Moldavia (Peyssonel, ii, 187, 198; Businello, 96); (*h*) ox fat and ox hides from Wallachia (Businello, 96); (*i*) fine clay for cannon moulds from 'les Eaux Douces' near Istanbul (Silihdar, i, 481; Râşid, i, 205–6; Hammer, *Histoire*, xi, 313); (j) rice supplied to the Ottoman armies and grown under state control along the rivers Maritsa, Karasu, Vardar and Salambria (*EI*², *s.v. Filāḥa*); (*k*) *naft* from Kirkūk in Iraq (Refik, *Madenleri*, 43; cf. also Evliya Çelebi, v, 201: *naft ve katranlı paçavra*, i.e., a reference to petroleum and tar).

On a number of themes the sources offer data of much interest, as the examples listed below will make clear:

(1) *Transport Animals*: There is frequent mention of the animals used in large numbers by the Ottoman army. Wallachia and Moldavia were an important source of the draught horses (*bargir*) often employed to haul the Ottoman artillery (Peçevi, ii, 152; Refik, *İstanbul Hayati* (*1553–1591*), 6; cf. also Silihdar, i, 365 (*alay topları ʿarabalarının bargirleri*), ii, 773; Naʿima, i, 99, iv, 204; Evliya Çelebi, v, 486). Some of the horses came from Transylvania (Hurmuzaki, ii/1, 229–30: *onerarios equos*).

In addition to horses, the Ottomans made use of oxen and buffaloes to pull their guns and waggons (oxen: Giese, i, 74 (*her bir topa niçe yüz çift öküzler*), Naʿima, iv, 206; buffaloes: Peçevi, ii, 411; Evliya Çelebi, v, 136 (*top çeken camusları*), 579 and vii, 204; Naʿima, iv, 204). At times in the course of a campaign beasts of burden like oxen and buffaloes might be hired (*ücret ile*) from the peasants of a local area (Naʿima, i, 99: buffaloes requisitioned from the district around Egri; also iv, 206: oxen hired from the *reʿaya*). Evliya Çelebi (iii, 40) notes that large numbers of *camus* were reared for the service of the Sultan in the region of Cilicia. Marsigli (ii, 64) names, for oxen, Thrace, Bulgaria and Wallachia and, for buffaloes, Bulgaria, Thrace and Greece as important sources of supply.

The sources refer less frequently to other kinds of animal. Peçevi (ii, 411) mentions camels and mules belonging to the state (*balyemez top kalʿe-yi gob çeken camus ve miri üştür ve esteri*); cf. also Marsigli, ii, 63–4, on camels and mules—the latter, raised mainly in Asia Minor, being the subject of his highest praise. A document preserved in the archives at Istanbul (*Mühimme* 5, no. 405, p. 166: dated 1565) orders the Beğlerbeği of Baghdad to hire, from the Arabs of the desert lands, camels for the transport to Aleppo of gunpowder made at Baghdad (*Bağdad'dan işlenen ve toplanan barutu Halebe göndermek için Ebu Rîş'den ücretle develer tedarik etmesi ve Halebe göndermesi için Bağdad Beğlerbeğine hüküm*). The name 'Abū Rīsha' (cf. al-ʿAzzāwī, Ta'rīkh al-ʿIrāq, iv, 242 ff.) is mentioned also in a European travel account relating to the years 1598–9 (*Trois Relations*, 107: 'Aborice est Roy des Arabes qui demeure ordinairement en Mesopotamie—Il avoit un grand haras de chameaux de plusieurs milliers'. This encounter with 'Aborice' occurred near 'Raccha' on the Euphrates: *ibid.*, 106).

(2) *Gunpowder*: (*a*) *Charcoal*: Much of the Ottoman Empire, e.g., various regions of Asia Minor and of the Balkans, had an abundance of timber and therefore of charcoal—a substance in common use for domestic purposes as well as for the making of gunpowder. The sources mention charcoal more often in relation to unusual than to normal circumstances—i.e., in relation to areas of the empire (above all the Arab lands) where trees were lacking and where other resources had to be found in order to meet the need for charcoal. A certain amount of information can be drawn from accounts of Asia Minor, Syria and Egypt dating from the years a little before and a little after 1800. Charcoal was made in one region of Asia Minor from 'Kara-gatch' (*kara ağaç*: black tree), an expression which the Turks used for trees not bearing fruit (Arundell, ii, 59). It was also obtained, again in Asia Minor, from oak trees: 'una specie di cerreto, detto Palmut (Turk. *palamud*), o sia Quercus-Aegylops' (Sestini, 85). Some charcoal was manufactured in the Lebanon from the willow tree (Seetzen, i, 204) and in Syria from the poplar tree (*ṣafṣāf*—Burckhardt, 250). The Arabs of the Sinai desert used for charcoal not the normal Arabic word *faḥm*, but the expression 'habes'; their charcoal came from the roots of the shrub 'rethem' and also from 'mimosa (seyal)' and from 'tamaris' (Burckhardt, 483, 623; *Description*, xvi, 184–5). As to Egypt—charcoal was made there from the tamarisk, the acacia and from the lupin, this latter being esteemed the best for gunpowder (*Mémoires sur l'Egypte* (*Années VI & VII*), 34–9 *passim*; *Mémoires sur l'Egypte* (*Années VII-IX*), iii, 47, 86 and iv, 4, 51–2; *Description*, xvii, 76, 261, 264; Seetzen, iii, 381; Shaw, *Ottoman Egypt*, 277–8). Also available are several documents relating to the preparation and dispatch of charcoal for use in such mines as Keban, Argana (Ergeni) and Ispiye in Asia Minor (Refik, *Madenleri*, 26–34).

(*b*) *Sulphur*: The mention of sulphur is infrequent. A number of references attest to its presence in the lands around and adjacent to the Dead Sea (Scholz, 130, 133; Irby and Mangles, 467; Seetzen, i, 305, 311–12, 358, 421, 423 and ii, 302, 336, 337, 352). Sulphur is also named in connection with the region of Van (*Mühimme* 112, no. 135, p. 62 (dated 1571): Erciş and Ahlat). Two documents of 1570 reveal that some sulphur was obtained from the *Hakkâri beği Zeynel* (Refik, *Madenleri*, 7) and that supplies of sulphur came also from Iran (Refik, *Madenleri*, 7: *ve Kızılbaş vilâyetinden Ercişe kükürd toprağı gelür*; *Mühimme* 14, no. 1063, p. 740: *Erciş kârhanesinde işlenen kükürt Irandan geliyor ve buna kara kükürt deniliyordu*). The island of Melos also contained deposits of sulphur (Savary des Bruslons, v, 1044; Ferrières-Sauveboeuf, ii, 226). Moldavia too supplied some sulphur (Businello, 96). The sources of more recent date mention sulphur as an article of normal commerce imported into Syria and Egypt from Venice and Trieste (Morana, 23–4; *Mémoires sur l'Egypte* (*Années VI & VII*), 34).

(*c*) *Saltpetre*: The Ottomans had no lack of saltpetre. It was to be found in numerous areas of their empire. Egypt was rich in this essential constituent of gunpowder (Evliya Çelebi, x, 494 (the province of Buḥayra: *ve her kuralarında güherçile maʿdeni hasıl olur*); also van Egmont and Heyman, i, 194–5 (the province of 'Saide'). Cf. in addition, Barkan, *Kanunlar*, 356–7, 368–9). The main centres of production were, in Upper Egypt, 'Dehechneh' and, in Lower Egypt, old Cairo (*Description*, xvii, 252–3). At old Cairo the saltpetre was refined first through boiling in water and then 'en employant pour mucilage des blancs d'oeuf' (Seetzen, iii, 381; *Mémoires sur l'Egypte* (*Années VI & VII*), 34–9).

Saltpetre was also plentiful in Syria, especially in the regions of the Ḥawrān and of the Leja (Burckhardt, 102, 111, 114–15, 214, 216, 217, 250; Seetzen, i, 305, 311). It existed, too, in Palestine (Heyd, 137–8: Hebron) and in the Lebanon (Seetzen, i, 204). The saltpetre of Syria was, however, perhaps too moist to be of the highest excellence (Alberi, i, 146: report of Domenico Trevisano, 1554. Cf. also *L'Illustre Orbandale*, 113).

Iraq also had an abundance of saltpetre. There were no less than fourteen gunpowder 'factories' at Baghdad alone (*Mühimme* 22, no. 476, p. 244: dated 1573). Basra, likewise, was rich in saltpetre (Parsons, 156). As to Asia Minor—saltpetre was available there in numerous localities, amongst them Niğde, Malatya, Laranda, İçel and Van (Refik, *Madenleri*, 7–18 *passim; idem*, *Aşiretleri*, 28, and *İstanbul Hayati* (*1553–1591*), 109; also Evliya Çelebi, iii, 191 (Bor, in the *sancak* of Niğde) and Kinneir, 114–15).

The chief centre in the Crimea was Karasu, which handled saltpetre obtained from the Tatar Shirin (Peyssonel, i, 15, 140–1). 'Sorocca' in Moldavia was also a source of saltpetre (Raicevich, 102–3; Nistor, 167). Of the Balkan lands in general it will suffice to note here that saltpetre existed in the areas around Thessalonica, Philippopolis (Plovdiv), Monastir, Skopje and Temesvár and also in the Morea, e.g., in the Troezenia region there (Evliya Çelebi, v, 554, vii, 202; Peyssonel, ii, 169; Marriott, 213; Refik, *Madenleri*, 8–9; *Firmans Impériaux*, 109 (no. 348); *Documents Turcs* (Macedonia), iii, 92, iv, 125; Svoronos, 269–70).

(3) *Quick-match*: The quick-match (*fitil*, *fitil otu*) in use amongst the

Janissaries and the other Ottoman forces armed with arquebuses was of 'cotton retors' (Montecuculi-Crissé, iii, 31) impregnated with a combustible such as sulphur. Cotton itself was available from Egypt and Syria (cf. Uzunçarşılı, ii, 14, note 1: a reference to *iplik* (? cotton yarn, i.e., *pamuk ipliği*) from the *eyalet* of Haleb). There are references also to *fitil* made from *ketan*, i.e., flax (Evliya Çelebi, viii, 469), but it would appear that it did not burn well (*Firmans Impériaux*, 50–1 (no. 161, dated 1811): supplies of *fitil* for the Ottoman artillery having failed to arrive from Egypt, 'on a cherché a suppléer a son absence avec du lin égyptien pour les canons balyemez, mais celui-ci ne s'allume pas facilement comme la meche égyptienne'). The sources mention other varieties of *fitil*. Arab tribesmen in the region near the Dead Sea used for their match-lock guns a *fitil* woven from the fine silk-like filaments of a plant named 'Asheyr', i.e., *ʿushār*, the apple of Sodom—the quick-match obtained from this plant burned freely and, according to one account, did not need impregnation with sulphur (Burckhardt, 392; Irby and Mangles, 450; cf. also, on this plant, Norden, iii, 29). There is, in addition, a reference to a particular kind of *fitil* used in the lands around the northern shore of the Black Sea: 'dans ces Steps on trouve aussi une espèce d'herbe, dont les Turcs et les Tartares se servent pour faire leurs meches' (Manstein, *Mémoires Historiques sur la Russie*, 181: *sub anno* 1736).

(4) *Lead*: The Ottomans carried to war large quantities of lead (*kurşun*). One main use of this metal was for musket and pistol bullets. Sometimes ammunition made from lead was cast at the mines (cf. Anhegger, i, 148, 149, ii, 298: orders (dated 1566) to the mines at Kučanja and Rudnik for the manufacture of lead bullets). It was also the custom, however, to distribute to the soldiers bars of lead, which could be cut into small fragments of an appropriate size (Marsigli, ii, 15). The ores of lead, e.g., galena (lead sulphide), often contain silver—hence the fact that the silver mines of the Ottoman Empire were, in general, the chief centres for the production of lead. Among the more notable of these mines were Srebrnica and Olovo in Bosnia (this latter a source of 'plumbum dulce' or soft lead), Rudnik, Novo Brdo, Kratovo and Kučanja in Serbia (the last-named, with other mines like the Bosnian Srebrnica, well known amongst the Christians for its 'plumbum durum' or hard lead—the 'Raczenpley', i.e., lead from Serbia, mentioned in Dernschwam, 254) and also Siderokapsa (Sidre Kapsa) in Greece (Anhegger, i, 133–7, 147–67, 178–204; Uzunçarşılı, *Kıbrıs Fethi*, 285). Lead was obtainable from silver-bearing ores in Asia Minor, e.g., at Gümüşhane, 'Boulgarmaden' in the Taurus, and Bozkır (İnan, *Aperçu*, 40, 42, 68), and from iron and copper deposits at Keban and Argana, i.e., Ergeni (Sestini, 84, 90 ff.). The archives at Istanbul contain documents ordering supplies of lead from the *Hakkâri hakimi Zeynel Beğ* (*Mühimme* 14, no. 646, p. 457, with the date 1570, and

Mühimme 18, no. 22, p. 99, dated 1572). There was also lead available to the Ottomans as an article of commerce—e.g., at Thessalonica the English merchants sold lead refined to a high degree of purity (Beaujour, ii, 16–17).

(5) *Iron*: This metal was employed to make articles which, although not instruments of war, might yet serve the purposes of war—e.g., anvils, horseshoes, nails, picks, shovels and the like. It was also used to make guns and weapons. There were iron mines of note around Banja Luka, Kamengrad, Fojnica, Kreševo and Vareš in Bosnia; at Rudnik and in the Kopaonik area of Serbia; in north-west Macedonia and in the district of Eğridere; amongst the Rhodope mountains and also in Thrace (Samokovcuk); in addition, Pravište, near Kavalla, in Greece and Samokov in Bulgaria were likewise iron centres of great importance (Anhegger, i, 138–46, 148–50, 168–73, 204–6, 210–11 and ii, 306–8; Evliya Çelebi, v, 438, 565 and vi, 128; Refik, *Madenleri*, 9, 16–17; İnan, *Aperçu*, 41, 42; Uzunçarşılı, *Kıbrıs Fethi*, 266, 268, 269; *L'Illustre Orbandale*, 113). One source indicates that some iron ('fers de Siberie') reached the Ottoman Empire via Taganrog and Azov on the northern shore of the Black Sea (Pertusier, 158). Iron was also available in Asia Minor—e.g., from Bilecik (Refik, *Madenleri*, 4), Keban (Sestini, 83, 84), 'Pendirachi' (*L'Illustre Orbandale*, 113), Kiği (*Tarih Vesikalari*, xi, 325–7; Refik, *Madenleri*, 15, 21, 46) and elsewhere. A certain amount of iron was to be found, moreover, in the Lebanon (Volney, ii, 400–1; Seetzen, i, 145, 188 ff.; and Brocchi, iii, 187–94, 283–4: Seetzen and Brocchi give full accounts of the actual methods used to mine and smelt the iron ore). Le Comte Turpin de Crissé, commenting on a passage in the *Memoires de Montecuculi*, notes that 'le fer en Turquie est peut-être moins aigre et plus liant qu'il ne l'est en Hongrie ou dans l'Autriche et les autres Etats de l'Empereur' (Montecuculi-Crissé, iii, 92). The channels of trade also brought much iron to the Ottomans—through Holland and Livorno, through Carinthia and Resina (Beaujour, ii, 17, 78–9; Pantz, 81; Svoronos, 230). The more important centres produced not only raw iron, but also munitions of war, e.g., cannon balls (Uzunçarşılı, ii, 47 (*badoluska güllesi*), 48 (*şâhî, miyâne ve kolonborna yuvarlaği*), 72–88 *passim*; also *EI*², *s.v. Bārūd*, 1063). Seetzen mentions that at Damascus the making of cannon balls was in the hands of people called 'Hauawîny'—*Hawāwīnī* (Seetzen, i, 312). Often, in order to overcome difficulties of windage, the Ottomans wrapped their cannon balls in sheepskins, thus making the fire of their guns more accurate (Montecuculi-Crissé, iii, 138: 'ils enveloppent leurs boulets de peaux de moutons . . . afin de rendre plus justes les coups, qui souvent ne le sont pas à cause du vent qu'on donne au boulet').

(6) *Copper*: Copper was in much demand for the manufacture of domestic utensils (plated with tin). It had also a most important role in the making of cannon. Deposits of copper ore existed in the Balkans, e.g., at Kratova

and at Majdanek in Serbia (Evliya Çelebi, v, 564; Anhegger, i, 163, 168); also in Bosnia and in the Banat of Temesvár (Refik, *Madenleri*, 49–50; Anhegger, i, 137; Born, 25, 27). The main supplies of copper came, however, from Asia Minor, above all from such mines as Kure, Argana (Ergeni) and Keban (*Tarih Vesikaları*, i, 262–82; Refik, *Madenleri*, 9–10, 37, 45–6; Browne, 493; Peyssonel, ii, 68, 78, 82–3; Sestini, 83, 90). At Trebizond, in the eighteenth century, ingots of copper amounting to 12,000 quintals and more are said to have been loaded each year on a warship of the Sultan for transport to Istanbul (Peyssonel, ii, 78). Production was being hindered, however, through the growing lack of fuel. One account states that copper ore was carried by camel a seven days' journey to Tokat, where adequate supplies of fuel were to be found for the smelting; also that production of copper at mines like Argana (Ergeni) on the road to Diyarbekir depended on the haulage of charcoal over a distance of a hundred miles. The same source estimates the yield of copper from the mines in eastern Asia Minor at about 3–4 million okkas, i.e., 3,750–5,000 tons, in 1799 (Hawkins, 302 ff., 306). Some copper passed into the Ottoman lands through Hungarian towns like Szolnok, Vács and Debreczen, where Christian, Jewish and Muslim merchants came into contact. At times the amount of metal involved was not inconsiderable—as much as 882½ *másza* (quintals) of copper in one series of transactions dating from 1559 (Fekete, 323, 330; Blaskovics, 66). Austria, in the course of the eighteenth century, abandoned its old restrictions on the export, to the Ottoman territories, of metals like copper and iron (Beer, 26–7; Srbik, 401–2, 410).

(7) *Tin*: The Ottomans had a constant need of tin, a metal which could be combined with copper to form bronze—and bronze was used to make cannon. Some tin came into Muslim hands, it would seem, from Transylvania through the town of Szolnok during the sixteenth and seventeenth centuries (Fekete, 323). Tin from England—in the years around 1800—was sold in considerable quantities at Thessalonica. In time of dearth tin might be secured from Spain (a soft tin of American provenance) or else from the Bohemian (Schlakenwald) and Saxon (Altenberg) mines (Beaujour, ii, 14–15).

A continuing source of military supply was the illicit traffic in contraband of war flowing from the Christian to the Muslim world. The canon law of the Christian Church had long forbidden trade with the Infidel in materials useful for war. A clause of the papal bull *In Cena Domini* threatened with excommunication all Christians who carried to the Muslims horses and arms, iron, tin, copper, sulphur, saltpetre and the like, also the ropes and timber indispensable in naval affairs (*Bulla In Cena Domini*, 1527 (pontificate of Clement VII): 'equos, arma, ferrum, filum ferri, stannum, aera, bandaraspatam, aurichalcum, sulfur, salnitrum, et omnia alia ad faciendum artelarias opportuna . . . necnon funes et alia rei nauticae necessaria lignamina'. Cf. also Raynaldus, *Annales Ecclesiastici*, xviii, 294 (a bull of Eugenius IV, dated 1444, against the transport of war material to the Ottoman Turks) and, in general, Pfaff, 'Abendmahlsbulle', *passim*). A decree emanating in 1544 from the Archduke Ferdinand of Austria declares to be illegal all traffic with the Ottomans in victuals, fire-arms, gunpowder, saltpetre, lances, armour, cuirasses, iron, tin and lead (*Codex Austriacus*, i, 248–9: 'Proviant, Büchsen, Pulver, Saliter, Spiess, Härnisch, Pantzer, Eisen, Zinn, Bley gearbeitet oder ungearbeitet und wass in Summa zu der Währ und Proviantirung dess Feinds dienstlich ist'). These prohibitions, often renewed, had little effect—the flow of munitions into the Ottoman Empire continued unabated despite all that Austria could do and despite the efforts of Spain, the Pope and the Knights of Saint John at Malta to seize the well-armed vessels which took the contraband through the Mediterranean to the harbours of the Levant.

One document, dated 1517, notes that 'miera 100 di stagno' had reached the Turks 'de ponente', i.e., from the west and that a ship at 'Syo' had on board 'miara 25' of the same metal (Sanuto, *Diarii*, xxv, 146). The Pfalzgraf bei Rhein, on pilgrimage to Palestine in 1521, encountered a vessel flying the flags of France and Genoa and laden, so it was said, with contraband of war for the Muslims (*Deutsche Pilgerreisen*, 395).

The English in particular—and later the Dutch also—created for themselves a lucrative trade with the Ottomans in war material. An English ship is mentioned at Livorno in 1573 with a cargo of tin, broken bells and ingots of lead (Braudel, 479: 'deux barils d'étain travaillé . . . 37 tonneaux de cloches brisées, 5 cloches entières, 380 pains de plomb'). The ambassador of France at Istanbul, de Germigny, notes in 1580 that the English brought to the Porte much steel, broken images, bronze and brass for the casting of guns (Charrière, iv, 907, note 1: 'grande quantité d'acier et pièces d'images rompues, d'airain et laiton pour fondre artillerie'). The broken bells and images came, of course, from the churches despoiled in England during the course of the Reformation.

Bernardino de Mendoza, the ambassador of Spain at London, informed his master Philip II in 1579 of an English vessel bearing 20,000 crowns' worth of bar tin to the Levant (*C. S. P. Spanish (1568–1579)*, 706). Again, in 1582, de Mendoza told Philip II that the English sent large amounts of tin and lead which the Ottomans bought 'almost for its weight in gold, the tin being vitally necessary for the casting of guns and the lead for purposes of war' (*C. S. P. Spanish (1580–1586)*, 366).

The cargo of an English ship taken at Melos in 1605 contained 700 barrels of gunpowder, 1,000 arquebus barrels, 500 mounted arquebuses, 2,000 sword blades and a barrel full of ingots of fine gold (*C. S. P. Venetian (1603–1607)*, 326; cf. also the references given in *EI*², *s.v. Bārūd*, 1063). Diego de Haedo observes (*Topographia*, 19r) that the English carried to

North Africa much contraband of war, including iron, lead, tin and copper ('hierro, plomo, estaño, cobre, peltre, polvora, y paños de toda suerte'); also, from Marseilles, quantities of sail-cloth, iron, steel, saltpetre, gunpowder, sulphur, pitch and the like ('cotonias para velas, hierro, azero, clavaçon, salitre, polvora, alumbre, azufre, pez'). A letter which the Lords of the Council sent in 1624 to the English ambassador at Istanbul, Sir Thomas Roe, complains about the smuggling of tin from England to the Levant (Roe, *Negotiations*, 253–4). There is mention, too, of a 'bertone inglese' in 1651, said to have had on board 250 iron guns ('bombarde di ferro') which were unloaded at night and handed over to the 'capitan del mare', i.e., to the Kapudan Pasha of the Ottoman fleet (Dujčev, *Avvisi*, 159).

Documents from the archives at Marseilles give some information about the movement to the Levant—under royal licence—of copper and steel (to Tripoli and Beirut in Syria, 1572) and also of tin (English, acquired at Rouen, and German, obtained at Lyons) in 1553, 1556, 1571, 1582–91 (*Marseille*, iii, 516–21). A French vessel was at Istanbul in 1645 with a cargo which included 'polvere e miccio', i.e., gunpowder and quick-match (Dujčev, *Avvisi*, 32). As for the Dutch—it is said of them that one of their cargoes unloaded at Smyrna contained 30,000 bombs (Scheither, 75).

The illicit traffic was not confined to the raw materials of war. It embraced also the sale of arms, e.g., arquebuses, pistols and muskets. One Ottoman document refers to a *muḥtasib* of Ṣafad in Palestine who obtained fire-arms from the *Dār al-Ḥarb* and sold them to the Arab tribesmen (Heyd, 82–3). There is mention, too, of *dalyan tüfenkler*, i.e., Italian muskets (Evliya Çelebi, v, 115, 205; vi, 322 (*dalyan karabina çarhlı boylu tüfenkler*); vii, 246; viii, 491; x, 328, 330, 402). Some of these guns came—at least in the eighteenth century—from the arms factories at Brescia in northern Italy (Beaujour, ii, 94–5). The methods employed to transmit weapons of this kind to the Ottomans must have been varied indeed. One account states that Hungarian merchants concealed forbidden wares, including arms, in the driving seat ('in den Kutschersitzen') of their waggons (*Geschichte der Stadt Wien*, iv, 532–3).

The notes assembled here offer no more than a brief and incomplete outline of a complicated—and most important—subject. It is no doubt the archives at Istanbul which will yield, in due course, answers to most of the problems adumbrated in this paper.

BIBLIOGRAPHY

Die altosmanischen anonymen Chroniken, ed. F. Giese, Teil I, Berlin 1922; Peçevi, *Tarih*, Istanbul A.H. 1381–3; Evliya Çelebi, *Seyahatname*, iii, v, vi (Istanbul A.H. 1314–18), vii, viii, x (Istanbul 1928–38); Silihdar, *Tarih*, Istanbul 1928; Na'ima,

Tarih, Istanbul A.H. 1281–3; Râşid, *Tarih*, Istanbul 1282; *Mühimme Defterleri* (references which I owe to the kindness of Mr. Turgut Işıksal, of the Başvekâlet Arşivi at Istanbul); J. Grzegorzewski, *Z Sidżyllatów Rumelijskich epoki wyprawy wiedeńskiej Akta Tureckie* (*Archiwum Naukowe, Dział I.*, vi/I), Lwow 1912; Ahmet Refik, *Anadoluda Türk Aşiretleri* (*966–1200*), Istanbul 1930; *idem*, *Osmanlı Devrinde Türkiye Madenleri* (*967–1200*), Istanbul 1931; *idem*, *İstanbul Hayatı* (*1553–1591*), Istanbul 1935; *Tarih Vesikaları*, i/4 (1941) and ii/2 (1943); I. H. Uzunçarşılı, 'Kıbris Fethi ile Lepant (İnebahtı) *Muharebesi*', in *Türkiyat Mecmuası*, iii, 1935; *idem*, *Osmanlı Devleti teşkilâtından Kapukulu Ocakları*, ii, Ankara 1944; Ö. L. Barkan, *XV ve XVI inci asırlarda Osmanlı Imparatorluğunda Zirâi Ekonominin Hukukî ve Malî Esasları, Cild I, Kanunlar*, Istanbul 1943; L. Fekete, *Die Siyāqat-Schrift in der türkischen Finanzverwaltung* (*Bibliotheca Orientalis Hungarica VII*), i, Budapest 1955; ʿAbbās al-ʿAzzāwī, *Taʾrīkh al-ʿIrāq*, iv (1534–1638), Baghdad 1949; M. Sanuto, *I Diarii*, xxv, Venezia 1899; H. Dernschwam, *Tagebuch einer Reise nach Konstantinopel und Kleinasien* (*1553/55*), ed. F. Babinger (*Studien zur Fuggergeschichte*, 7), München 1923; G. T. Minadoi, *Historia della Guerra fra Turchi e Persiani*, Venice 1594; Diego de Haedo, *Topographia e Historia General de Argel*, Valladolid 1612; *Trois Relations d'Egypte et autres Memoires curieux*, Paris 1651; *L'Ilustre Orbandale*, Lyon 1662; J. B. Scheither, *Novissima Praxis Militaris*, Braunschweig 1672; G. P. Zenarolla, *Operationi di Leopoldo Primo, Imparatore de' Romani sempre Augusto sotto l'anno 1688*, Vienna 1689; *Annales Ecclesiastici . . . auctore Odorico Raynaldo, Tomus XVIII*, Coloniae Agrippinae 1694; *Codicis Austriaci . . . Pars Prima* (— *Secunda*), Vienna 1704; L. F. Marsigli, *L'Etat Militaire de l'Empire Ottoman*, La Haye and Amsterdam 1732; *The Negotiations of Sir Thomas Roe*, London 1740; *Memoires de Montecuculi . . . avec les Commentaires de M. le Comte Turpin de Crissé*, Amsterdam and Leipzig 1770; J. A. van Egmont and J. Heyman, *Travels through . . . Asia Minor . . . Syria, Palestine, Egypt*, 2 vols., London 1759; J. Savary des Bruslons, *Dictionnaire Universel de Commerce*, v, Copenhague 1765; I. Born, *Travels through the Banat of Temesvár, Transylvania and Hungary in the year 1770* (trans. R. E. Raspe), London 1777; Le Général de Manstein, *Mémoires Historiques, Politiques et Militaires sur la Russie* (*1727–1744*), Amsterdam 1771; P. Businello, 'Nachrichten', in C. W. Lüdeke, *Beschreibung des Turkischen Reiches, Zweyter Theil*, Leipzig, 1778; M. de Peyssonel, *Traité sur le Commerce de la Mer Noire*, 2 vols., Paris 1787; D. Sestini, *Viaggio da Constantinopoli a Bassora*, Yverdun 1786; C. F. de Volney, *Voyage en Syrie et en Egypte* (*1783–1785*), 2 vols., Paris 1787; J. Raicevich, *Osservazioni Storiche, Naturali e Politiche intorno la Valachia e Moldavia*, Napoli 1788; Le Comte de Ferrières-Sauveboeuf, *Mémoires Historiques, Politiques et Géographiques*, 2 vols., Paris 1790; F.-L. Norden, *Voyage d'Egypte et de Nubie*, 3 vols., Paris 1795–8; G. A. M. Morana, *Relazione del Commercio d'Aleppo ed altre Scale della Siria e Palestina*, Venice 1799; F. Beaujour, *Tableau du Commerce de la Grèce*, 2 vols., Paris An VII–VIII; *Mémoires sur l'Egypte publiés . . . dans les Années VI et VII*, Paris An VIII; *Mémoires sur l'Egypte publiés dans les Années VII, VIII et IX*, vol. 3, Paris An X, and vol. 4, Paris An XI; *Description de l'Egypte*, 2nd ed., Paris 1821–9; W. J. Browne, *Travels in Africa, Egypt and Syria* (*1792–1798*), 2nd ed., London 1806; A. Parsons, *Travels in Asia and Africa*, London 1808; J. M. Kinneir, *Journey through Asia Minor, Armenia and Kurdistan* (*1813–1814*), London 1818; J. M. A. Scholz, *Reise in . . . Egypten, Palästina und Syrien* (*1820–1821*), Leipzig and Sorau 1822; J. L. Burckhardt, *Travels in Syria and the Holy Land*, London 1822; C. Pertusier, *La Bosnie considérée dans ses rapports avec l'Empire Ottoman*, Paris 1822; C. L. Irby and J. Mangles, *Travels in Egypt, Nubia, Syria and Asia Minor* (*1817–1818*), London

1823; J. Hawkins, 'On the Produce of the Copper Mines of Europe and Asia and particularly those of Armenia', in *Transactions of the Royal Geological Society of Cornwall*, iii, Penzance, 1828; F. V. J. Arundell, *Discoveries in Asia Minor*, 2 vols., London 1834; G. B. Brocchi, *Giornale delle Osservazioni fatte ne' Viaggi in Egitto, nella Siria e nella Nubia*, 5 vols., Bassano 1841–3; U. J. Seetzen, *Reise durch Syrien, Palästina, Phönicien, etc.*, ed. F. Kruse, 3 vols., Berlin 1854–5; *The letters of J. B. S. Marriott*, ed. G. E. Marindin, London 1914; J. von Hammer, *Histoire de l'Empire Ottoman*, trans. J.-J. Hellert, xi, Paris 1838; E. Alberi, *Relazioni degli Ambasciatori Veneti al Senato, serie III*, vol. I, Firenze 1840; E. Charrière, *Négociations de la France dans le Levant*, 4 vols., Paris 1848–60; *Monumenta Hungariae Historica: Scriptores*, xxvii, Budapest 1875; *Deutsche Pilgerreisen*, edd. R. Röhricht and H. Meisner, Berlin 1880; *Calendar of State Papers, Spanish, 1568–1579* (London 1894) and *1580–1586* (London 1896); *Calendar of State Papers, Venetian, 1603–1607* (London 1900); E. de Hurmuzaki, *Documente privitóre la Istoria Românilor*, ii/I (1451–1575), Bucuresci 1891; A. Beer, 'Die österreichische Handelspolitik unter Maria Theresa and Josef II', in *Archiv für österreichische Geschichte*, lxxxvi/I, Vienna 1898; H. von Srbik, *Der staatliche Exporthandel Österreichs von Leopold I bis Maria Theresia*, Vienna 1907; *Geschichte der Stadt Wien*, iv (ed. A. Mayer), Vienna 1911; I. Nistor, *Handel und Wandel in der Moldau bis zum Ende des 16. Jahrhunderts*, Czernowitz 1912; K. Pfaff, 'Beitrage zur Geschichte der Abendmahlsbulle vom 16. bis 18. Jahrhundert', in *Römische Quartalschrift für christliche Altertumskunde und für Kirchengeschichte*, xxxviii, Freiburg im Breisgau 1930; A. von Pantz, 'Die Innerberger Hauptgewerkschaft (1625–1783)', in *Forschungen zur Verfassungs- und Verwaltungsgeschichte der Steiermark*, vi/2; *Recueil de Firmans Impériaux Ottomans addressés aux Valis et aux Khédives d'Egypte (1597–1904)*, Cairo 1934; I. Dujčev, *Avvisi di Ragusa. Documenti sull' Impero Turco nel sec. XVII e sulla Guerra di Candia* (*Orientalia Christiana Analecta*, no. 101), Rome 1935; L. Fekete, 'Le Commerce à Bude au temps des Turcs', in *Nouvelle Revue de Hongrie*, lv, Budapest 1936; Afet İnan, *Aperçu Général sur l'Histoire Economique de l'Empire Turc-Ottoman*, Istanbul 1941; F. Braudel, *La Méditerranée et le Monde Méditerranéen a l'époque de Philippe II*, Paris 1949; R. Collier and J. Billiard, *Histoire du Commerce de Marseille, iii (1480–1599)*, Paris 1951; J. Blaskovics, 'Ein Schreiben des Ofener Defterdār Muṣṭafā an den Hatvaner Mauteinnehmer Derwīš Baša', in *Charisteria Orientalia*, edd. Tauer, Kubícková and Hrbek, Praha 1956; N. G. Svoronos, *Le Commerce de Salonique au XVIIIe siècle*, Paris 1956; *Documents Turcs pour l'Histoire Macédonienne (1809–1817)*, iii, Skopje 1955; U. Heyd, *Ottoman Documents on Palestine (1552–1615)*, Oxford 1960; S. J. Shaw, *The Financial and Administrative Organisation and Development of Ottoman Egypt (1517–1798)*, Princeton, New Jersey, 1962; *EI*[2] *s.v.v. Bārūd, Filāḥa, Ḥarb, Ḥiṣār.*

Sıvış Year Crises in the Ottoman Empire*

HALİL SAHİLLİOĞLU

A complex fiscal year which combines the solar and the lunar years was used by the Ottomans through the centuries. The solar year was more functional for revenue collecting, the lunar year for expenditures. These two kinds of years differ by eleven days in length. Ottoman finance officials and astrologers were aware of this difference, and that from time to time this might cause problems. Nevertheless, they seem to have decided that it was not important, since the daily revenues and expenditures of the treasury balanced. In the leasing of state farms and possessions, they added the rent of the additional eleven solar year days to the price of the *iltizam* (farm) under the name of *tefâvüt-i şemsiyye*. To make up the above-mentioned difference and to balance the budget, they registered the revenues on the basis of a lower exchange rate and the expenditures on a higher one, calling the fictitious income *tefâvüt-i hasene ve guruş*. Such measures, however, did not solve the basic problems of budgetary deficits in Ottoman finance. These deficits, as in other Islamic societies that have had budgets with dual characteristics, paved the way to crises, explained in this paper, which contributed to the decline and downfall of the Empire in its financial aspects. Although the difference between the two calendars and the corrections and adjustments periodically made has not escaped the attention of some scholars,[1] the repercussions of this phenomenon on the financial, military, social and monetary life of the Ottoman Empire have not yet been studied.

The Astronomical Reality

The earth completes its path around the sun in a solar year which is 365 days, 5 hours and 39 minutes.

The lunar year, which comprises 12 lunar months of 29 and 30 days alternating regularly, is 354 days, 8 hours and 48 minutes.[2]

There is approximately 11 days' difference between the solar and the lunar year (the former being longer) which when multiplied by 32 totals 352 days or almost another lunar year. Hence, 97 solar years constitute a lunar century, introducing a difference of about 3 per cent between the two systems.

* Translated by Dr. İlter Turan.

[1] A. N. Poliak, *Feudalism in Egypt, Syria, Palestine and the Lebanon 1250–1900*, London 1939. See his explanation of the *taḥwīl-i sinīn*, pp. 21–2.

[2] Başbakanlık Arşivi, Istanbul (hereafter BA), Cevdet, Maʿarif no. 3081, statement of the Chief Astrologer (Müneccimbaşı) to the *Divan*.

The Historical Reality

Islam, which was born into a society that used the lunar calendar, accepted that tradition and continued it. In the territories over which Islam expanded and in which Islamic states were established, the usage of a lunar chronology was also adopted. Since the starting date for this calendar was taken as the year of Mohammed's migration from Mecca to Medina (the *Hicre*), this calendar is referred to as *hicrî*.

Being members of the Islamic community, the Ottomans abided by the Islamic tradition and employed the *hicrî* calendar. Events were recorded, imperial rescripts (*fermans*) were issued, and financial activities were carried on, all utilizing the lunar calendar. The usage of the Christian solar calendar was limited to imperial letters sent to Christian kings and to treaties and agreements signed with them, until the *Tanzimat*. Although other calendars began to be used during and after the *Tanzimat* in government offices, the *hicrî* calendar was not completely abandoned until the founding of the Turkish Republic.

Economic Necessity

Nevertheless, there seems to have been no conflict over the use of the *hicrî* calendar between the state and its subjects; in the basically agricultural economy of the Ottomans, the income of the subjects, and the revenue of the state which was based on this income, were both dependent on the seasons and hence on the solar calendar. It was essential that the state await the creation of this income before it could tax it. Seasons affected not only agriculture but also trade and hence customs revenues and even mining operations. During winter, in many places, mining was completely halted, overland trade and revenue from it declined because of the roads being closed by snow. Similarly maritime trade and the revenue from it was lively only in the seasons which permitted seafaring.[3]

Particularly in the case of the provinces of Anatolia and Rumelia which, not having budgets of their own, were dependent on the central fiscal system, revenues reserved for the Ottoman treasury were sent twice a year at *Nevruz* (11 March) and the beginning of August. Provincial tax-farm inspectors (*nâzır*, *müfettiş*) were held responsible for the remission of revenue in *Nevruz* and August. The dates for the collection of taxes which did not come under the authority of the provincial tax-farm inspectors (*mukataʿa müfettişleri*) were announced by imperial rescript (*ferman*) to the authorized collectors at various times.

[3] BA, Maliyeden Müdevver no. 17898, *Akhâm Defteri*, p. 105, decree sent to the governor of Basra (14 May 1697) in response to a letter stating the reasons for the need to employ a solar year for the budget of Basra.

During the Ottoman Period, although the revenues were a function of the seasons and the solar year, treasury expenditures were quite frequently made on the basis of the lunar year. For example, one of the major items of expenditure, the *ʿulûfe* or payment of the troops, was made quarterly. This meant that the troops would be paid four times in a lunar year (see Figure 1). Each quarter was named after the first letters of the months comprising it, thus *Masar* (*m-ṣ-r*) after *Muharrem*, *Safer*, *Rebiʿülevvel* was the name of the first quarter, *Recec* (*r-j-j* for *Rebiʿülâhar*, *Cümâdelûlâ*, *Cümâdelâhar*) of the second, *Reşen* (*r-sh-n* for *Receb*, *Şaʿban*, *Ramazan*) of the third, and *Lezez* (*l-dh-dh* for *Şevvâl*, *Zilkaʿde*, *Zilhicce*) of the fourth.

The Budget and the Fiscal Year

Of course, neither were all the expenditures of the treasury made according to the lunar year, nor were all its revenues collected on the basis of the solar year. Some taxes were levied and collected according to the lunar year and the tax-farms were leased for a *tahvil*, generally a period of three lunar or solar years.

If a state, whose revenue is received in part on a lunar year and in part on a solar year basis, is to prepare a budget, on what system should it base the budget? If it chooses the solar year in accordance with the creation and the taxation of income, it behaves logically from the revenue angle. But, assuming that the daily revenue and expenditures were equal, it would meet the problem of an eleven day revenue surplus at the end of the year. If, on the other hand, it organizes its budget according to the lunar calendar because of its expenditures, it would not be able to establish a balance between its revenues and expenditures because the *hicrî* year would fall further behind every year by eleven days.

Ottoman Budgets

Up to the *Tanzimat*, one cannot speak of an Ottoman budget in the modern sense of the term. That is, there was no estimation of the expenditures to be met, no identification of the sources from which the revenues to meet these expenditures would come, no authorization of the collecting and spending of revenue, and certainly no question of the approval of a legislative body. The brief tables showing the revenues and expenditures of the treasury drawn up before the *Tanzimat* are not real budgets, but abstracts from account books recording the amounts actually received and expended by the central treasury and the amounts that were collected and spent within given localities. They are more in the nature of a final inventory or balance sheet. However, since they show the revenues and expenditures on an annual basis, they will be referred to as budgets from here on.

Ottoman budgets of the sixteenth century are solar year budgets.[4] They were calculated for a period of a solar year which began on *Nevruz* (New Year, 11 March of the Julian Calendar) and ended on the same date the following year.

The budgets of the seventeenth century are unspecific as to what fiscal year was used. In fact, for a long time in this century, summary accounts for incomes and expenditures were not calculated. That the budget of Tarhuncu (Grand Vizier 1652–3) is accorded much importance and is generally looked upon as the first Ottoman budget must be for this reason. The currently published budgets of this century, those of 1070–1 (1660–1) and 1079–80 (1669–70) do not indicate which calendar was used, in contrast to the similar budgets of the sixteenth century. However, some yet unpublished budgets belonging to the end of the century indicate that they were calculated for a lunar year starting at the beginning of *Muharrem* and running to the end of *Zilhicce*.

Defining the Solar Year in Terms of the Lunar Year

The Ottoman fiscal organization used the solar year and its months in cases where this proved necessary, for example when tax-farms (*mukataʿa*) were leased or sometimes even when revenues and expenditures were calculated. It is also certain that they were familiar with the Christian calendar, although they never used it and encountered difficulties in defining the solar year. Whenever they defined the solar year, they expressed the beginning and the end of it according to the *hicrî* calendar. If we examine the budget of the fiscal year 1547–8 published by Prof. Ömer Lütfi Barkan, we see that it begins on the *Nevruz* that coincides with the 19 *Muharrem* 954 A.H. and ends on the *Nevruz* which coincides with the 30 *Muharrem* 955 A.H.

If we want to refer to the fiscal year in a single *hicrî* date, we would, like the Ottomans, define it as the fiscal year 954 A.H., since it began on the *Nevruz* of 954. However, since the lunar and the solar year do not contain the same number of days, we would have to make a correction in this solar-lunar calendar every 33 years. As has been pointed out above, the eleven days' difference between the two systems produces one additional lunar year in every 32 solar years. Therefore, for 32 budgets there will be 33 lunar years. Since no budget will be made for this 33rd year, it will be discarded or skipped. Let us look at an example.

[4] Ömer Lütfi Barkan's articles in *İktisat Fakültesi Mecmuası*:
1. 'H. 933–934 (M. 1527–1528) Malî yılına ait bir Osmanlı Bütçesi', 15, 1954;
2. 'H. 954–955 (M. 1547–1548) Malî yılına ait bir Osmanlı Bütçesi', *ibid.*;
3. 'H. 974–975 (M. 1567–1568) Malî yılına ait bir Osmanlı Bütçesi', 19, 1958;
4. 'H. 1070–1071 (M. 1660–1661) Tarihli Osmanlı Bütçesi ve bir mukayese', 17, 1956;
5. 'H. 1079–1080 (M. 1669–1670) Malî yılına ait bir Osmanlı bütçesi ve ekleri', *ibid.*

If the budgets preceding the budget of 954 were available, they would bear the following dates:

1546–7 budget between *Nevruzes*: 7 *Muharrem* 953–19 *Muharrem* 954
1545–6 „ „ „ 26 *Zilhicce* 951–7 *Muharrem* 953

Sıvış or 'Skip Year'

If we wanted to express these two fiscal years in terms of a *hicrî* lunar-solar calendar, the first would be referred to as 953 A.H. and the second as 951 A.H., and the lunar year 952 would have been skipped. The Ottomans called this a *sıvış* (skip) year.

When tax-farms were leased, if the solar year was taken as the basis, a method similar to the above was followed, and corrections of years were made periodically. For example, the *mukataʿa* of the port of Akkerman, which used to be auctioned at the beginning of March, was auctioned in 984 A.H. (1577) for 4,975,000 *akçes* for three solar years. It would be auctioned again at the beginning of the March of 1580. However, the March of 1580 corresponds not to 987 but to 988. Hence, the year 987 needed to be skipped. It was in fact skipped, and the concession was again auctioned for three years for 5,155,000 *akçes* in 988. The procedure was repeated after three years in 991 A.H. (1583), but the port was leased for four solar years for 3,666,666 *akçes* this time (see Figure 4a).

As the examples indicate, both in the calculations of the summary income-expenditure accounts and in the leasing of tax-farms and state possessions, it was necessary to make calendar adjustments. Since the auctions took place not only at the beginning of March, but also at the beginning of May and August, both the *sıviş* year and the adjustment to be made varied according to each case.

Because the *sıvış* years of 1255 A.H. and 1288 A.H. were not skipped through forgetfulness or negligence, the *sıvış* year 1328 also could not be skipped; thus was introduced a difference of two years between the standard Ottoman calendar and the fiscal year. Since the discrepancy would increase regularly in the future, Ahmet Muhtar Paşa during the budgetary discussions of 1328 A.H. prepared a project for a *hicrî* solar year which he presented to the *Meclis* (Assembly) along with a statute relating to government offices.[5]

Sıvış Year Crises

Was it really sufficient to make adjustments in the calendar by advancing the *hicrî*-solar year by one from time to time so that it corresponded

[5] *Tarih-i ʿArabî denilen hicrî-i kamerî 1256 senesinden beru bilâ inkitâʿ devâm edegelen malî sene tarihinin tanzim ve ıslahına dâir nizamnâme*. See also: Faik R. Unat, *Hicrî Tarihleri Miladî Tarihlere Çevirme Kılavuzu*, Ankara 1959, pp. xiv–xv.

to the *hicrî* year? Or did the yearly deviations of the fiscal year mark the beginnings of crises, since revenues were received on the basis of a solar year, whereas expenditures were made on the basis of a lunar year?

As was indicated above, in the sixteenth century accounts were closed on *Nevruz*, and a balance sheet was abstracted from the *Ruznâmçe* (tax journal) and other documents used in the accounting system. The fiscal year, being a solar one, is longer than the lunar year according to which expenditures were made. Hence, in each solar year parts of two lunar years and in *sıvış* years parts of three lunar years are to be found. This can be seen in Figure 1.

The figure gives the years and the months between 1643 and 1677. Each *hicrî* quarter has been marked against the Christian month to which it corresponds, the four quarters for which the troops were paid being distinctively marked.

1054 A.H. is a *sıvış* year and, therefore, it will be skipped and 1645 A.D. will correspond to the fiscal year 1055 A.H. As may also be seen from the figure, the expenditures of 1055 will have started before the March of 1645. Those of 1056 will start eleven days before the revenues of 1646 A.D. are received. However, since the first quarterly payment is due sometime after the year 1646 has started, no problems are created. This would continue until the year 1062 A.H. But, since the lunar year comes eleven days earlier every year, the differences would add up so that the first quarterly payment of 1063 A.H. would have to be made before the revenues for that fiscal year (1653 A.D.) began to come in.

From the figure, it can be seen that in 1653 A.D. not only the *ʿulûfe* (pay) of 1063 A.H. will be paid, but also the first *ʿulûfe* of 1064 A.H. This is because the four payments of 1063 A.H. and the first payment of 1064 A.H. (as well as part of the second quarter) fall within the year 1653 A.D.

The expenditures of 1070 A.H. will start six months before the revenues for that year are received. In the same fashion, expenditures for 1079 A.H. will start being made nine months before the revenues are collected. The expenditures of 1087 A.H. will have to be made one year in advance. It is essential, according to this line of argument, to reserve the revenue received in 1677 A.D. for the expenditures to be made in 1087. How then, will the revenues to be spent in 1088, a *sıvış* year, be found?

Alternatives

In the 33rd budget, logically speaking, there are no revenues to be used to finance the needs of that year. In other words, there is a deficit equal to one year's revenues. If the government had made no previous plans to meet the deficit, if no measures had been taken or they had proven insufficient, a very severe financial problem would be unavoidable. It is possible to save an amount equal to expenditures of eleven days during each budget year, and pay five *ʿulûfes* in the eighth year, as was done in 1063–4 A.H. (1653–4 A.D.), in order that no trouble may arise. Thus, by making five payments every eight years in a thirty-three year period, the problem could be alleviated. If no such savings are made, or conditions do not allow it, the first payment of the eighth year after the *sıvış* year could be postponed three months, that of the fifteenth/sixteenth year six months, and so on, until there is a delay of a year by the next *sıvış* year. If the government can resist the pressure of those who are paid on an *ʿulûfe* basis, then the payment of the latter can be withheld until the funds necessary to make such a payment are found.

If savings totalling the one year's *ʿulûfe* had not been realized, the government would be faced by the following choices:

(*a*) to double taxation for the thirty-third budget or to make up the deficit by levying new taxes,
(*b*) to engage in borrowing,
(*c*) to devalue the currency,
(*d*) to search for new sources of revenue through conquests,
(*e*) to resort to a combination of the above, depending on the urgency of the situation.

The Ottomans had an 'Inner Treasury', the holdings of which may be looked upon as positive savings. Although the Inner Treasury will be referred to later, it may be appropriate to mention here that the savings of the Inner Treasury were used under certain conditions to pay the postponed *ʿulûfe*. It is difficult to say, however, whether the yearly savings of the Inner Treasury covered the 3 per cent divergence between the revenue and expenditure schedules. It is a fact that even when the Empire was at its zenith, the payments were postponed. If the postponement amounted to two, three, or, as in the case of *sıvış* years, four payments, the recipients rebelled. As a consequence of such uprisings, treasurers and Grand Viziers were dismissed or even executed and sultans were dethroned. Under such conditions, the rebels were successful in establishing dictatorial rule for short periods.

The payment of the postponed *ʿulûfe*, which assumed the utmost importance after such rebellions, and which was made possible by the devaluation of the currency, the imposition of new taxes, and other means, had repercussions through the whole economy. The people and peasants, who were called upon to pay more than their limited resources could bear, engaged in migrations, and some took to the mountains as bandits or joined the *Celâlî* risings against the government.

Devaluations of the currency had the expected consequences, and helped spread the crises to all sectors of the economy. Conflicts between civil servants and merchants, a rising cost of living, profiteering, black market activities and domestic unrest followed one another.

If the calendars are carefully studied, especially those years in which the beginning of the revenue and expenditure years coincided (i.e. *sıvış* years), then the symptoms of crisis can be found. The cumulatively worsening financial problem caused a popular explosion which used any event as a pretext, generally when *Muharrem* (the beginning of the expenditure year) coincided with January, i.e., when *ʿulûfe* was again delayed for another three months. The consequences of these crises have already been mentioned. However, the financial difficulties arising from the *sıvış* year were felt less during the rise of the empire than during its stagnation and decline, when the dislocation and collapse they caused in the economy was great and deep.

We shall try to demonstrate that similar crises took place every thirty-two or thirty-three years during the history of the Ottoman empire, particularly in the period 1640–1740.

The Interpretation of Ottoman History in terms of Sıvış Year Crises

Sıvış year analyses not only provide the key to explaining and interpreting many events in Ottoman history, but also provide a tool of analysis for the history of other Islamic societies which had a two-calendar fiscal system.

If one asks when the Ottomans began to feel the effects of the *sıvış* year crises, it may be answered that these began to be felt when the *ʿulûfe* became an increasingly important part of the budget, or, to put it more clearly, when the economy began to assume the characteristics of a money economy. At a time when the government gave *timars* (temporary land grants in return for military obligation) to the troops, or when a barter economy prevailed, *sıvış* year crises would not have taken place. Although the history of the Ottomans up to the fifteenth century is not yet well known, it may be supposed that *ʿulûfe* was relatively insignificant. During the last years of Murad II, it is estimated that there were only 5,000 Janissaries in an army of 125,000, the remainder being soldiers with *timars*.[6] Even this 5,000 should be considered significant, however, since the Grand Vizier Lütfî Paşa (in office 1539–41) felt compelled to say, while the Empire was at its peak, that 'finding pay for 15,000 soldiers was a real achievement'.[7]

Crises During Sıvış Years

The events of Ottoman history during *sıvış* years are as follows:

Sıvış Year 852 A.H. or Revenue Year 1448 A.D.

The events occurred before the *sıvış* year was reached. The troops, whose

[6] Halil Inalcık, *Fatih Devri Üzerinde Tetkikler ve Vesikalar*, Ankara 1954, p. 57.

[7] Lutfî Paşa, *Asafnâme*, Istanbul 1326.

pay was six months in arrears, had not put up much resistance against the Hungarian and Serbian forces which had entered Ottoman territory during the winter of 1442. The Sultan, who was upset about the army and saddened by the death of his son, abdicated in favour of his young heir, Mehmed II. The latter's first accomplishment was to devalue the currency and thus make up the budgetary deficit and pay the troops. The *akçe* weighed 1·181 gr. (260 *akçe* = 100 *dirhems*) in 835 A.H.[8] (1431–2 A.D.). The first coin issued by Mehmed II the Conqueror weighed 1·012 gr.

The dissatisfied army did not hesitate to become the tool of various statesmen who struggled to stay in power during the reigns of Murad II and Mehmed II. On the instigation of the Grand Vizier Halil Paşa, some soldiers raided the home of Şehabüddin Paşa and caused him to take refuge in the palace of the young ruler Mehmed. The disorders which began with a political motive later took a different turn and were exploited to demand higher pay. The city and the covered bazaar were set on fire by the mutineers, who gathered on a hill called Buçuk Tepe and announced that they would support an heir who was favourably disposed towards Byzantium, should they not be granted pay increases.[9]

Unfortunately, no information has been found on the social consequences of this event, which is registered in chronologies as the first rebellion caused by postponed payments made in devalued currency.

Mehmed II, who ascended the throne in 1451 upon the death of his father and at a time when the beginning of the *hicrî* year coincided with the beginning of January, implying a three month delay of the *ʿulûfe*, devalued the *akçe* by 0·48 grams. Each time arrears in payment arose, we observe devaluation by the Conqueror.

The Conquest of Istanbul furnished a new source of income and mitigated the financial pressure.

886 A.H. or 1481 A.D.

The death of the Conqueror also coincides with a *sıvış* year. During this year, the sultan had crossed into Anatolia for a campaign, the destination of which was unknown. The *akçe* had again been devalued and the turning in of the old *akçes* in return for new ones was made mandatory. An added income of 60 million *akçes* was expected as a result of this move.[10]

A rebellion broke out immediately after his death in which the Grand Vizier Karamanî Mehmed Paşa (in office 1477–81) was murdered because his policy of devaluation had not been approved by the army. The rebels established a Janissary junta which lasted for seventy days. Bayezid II was

[8] Oruç bin Âdil, *Tevârih-i âl-i Osman*, Hanover 1925, p. 49.

[9] Halil İnalcık, *op. cit.*, p. 92.

[10] Halil Sahillioğlu, 'Bir mültezim zimem defterine göre xv. yüzyıl sonunda osmanlı darphane mukataʿalari', *İktisat Fakültesi Mecmuası*, 23, 1962–3.

given the throne after this interregnum with the stipulation that he would not resort to devaluation.[11]

Information on the social consequences of the crisis is not available.

919 A.H. or 1513 A.D.

The dissatisfied army supported Selim in his revolt against his father. Bayezid II abdicated in favour of his son. Although no devaluation took place, a reissuing of coins was resorted to.[12]

The conquest of Syria and Egypt was instrumental in reducing the financial pressure. Both the allocation of new *timars* and receipt of new revenue made it possible for the government to avoid financial difficulties for some time to come.

Difficulties, however, continued in newly conquered areas.[13] Suleiman the Magnificent was in fact compelled to send his Grand Vizier Ibrahim Paşa (in office 1523–36) to conduct reforms there in 1531.[14]

It is also known that Selim borrowed before he went on his expedition.[15]

953 A.H. or 1546 A.D.

The budget of 1546–7 has been published by Ö. L. Barkan.[16] In order to make a comparison possible, the figures for the preceding year, which is a *sıvış* year, are also given in this budget.

69,839,477 *akçes* are credited to the 1546 budget from the *sıvış* year budget; in other words, there is no deficit: 86,889,845 *akçes* are credited to 1547 and 1546, implying another surplus for that year.

If the budget is examined closely, it may be seen that an extraordinary tax was imposed in 1545 which had secured a revenue of 8,620,773 *akçes*. In 1546 also, 1,779,100 *akçes* were collected through an extraordinary tax.

Whereas the total revenue of the treasury was 241,711,834 *akçes* during the *sıvış* year, it had dropped to 198,887,294 *akçes* in 1546.

It should be added that the budget was operating at a deficit, although a budgetary surplus was witnessed in these years. The expenditure of the central budget reached 171,997,449 *akçes* during the *sıvış* year of 1546 and 111,997,449 *akçes* for 1547. The revenue of the central system, received from the provinces of Anatolia and Rumelia during the same years, was 135,402,022 *akçes* in 1546 and 94,543,349 *akçes* in 1547. Thus deficits of

[11] *Ibid.*

[12] *Ibid.* For this reason, Anatolian mints which were leased for 200,000 *akçes* in normal times had been leased for 7 million *akçes*.

[13] Gaston Wiet, *Journal d'un Bourgeois du Caire, Chronique d'Ibn Iyas*, Paris 1960, index *s.vv. Monnaies* and *Prix*.

[14] Ö. L. Barkan, *XV ve XVI inci Asırlarda Osmanlı Imparatorluğunda Zirâi Ekonominin Hukukî ve Mâlî Esâsları*, vol. i, *Kanunlar*, Istanbul 1945, the *Kanunnâme* of Egypt prepared as a result of the reform of Ibrahim Paşa at pp. 354–87.

[15] Âlî, *Nasihatü'l-Mülûk*, Süleymaniye Library, Fatih MS. no. 3525, f. 125 v.

[16] See note 4.

36,470,335 and 17,454,694 respectively were incurred. These were covered by the surplus revenues deriving from the newly conquered provinces of Egypt, Syria, Diyarbekir and Baghdad.

Rüstem Paşa was made Grand Vizier in 1544 to solve the financial problems. He was successful in filling the treasury of the palace as well as that of Yedikule with *akçes* but only through extraordinary taxes and at the price of the collapse of the imperial economy.[17]

Six or seven years after the *sıvış* year in 1552, the gold coin was devalued, since an additional quarterly payment would be needed soon. Whereas, in 1479, during the reign of Mehmed II, 129 *sultanîs* (gold coins) were made from 100 *miskals* of gold, now 130 *sultanîs* were made. Thus the weight of each *sultanî* went down from 3·559 gr. to 3·545 gr.[18]

The struggles between the heirs to the throne took place at this time. Hordes of farmers had evacuated the villages and migrated into the towns, and some had taken to the mountains and practised banditry under the name of *levends* as a consequence of Rüstem Paşa's fiscal policies.[19]

986 A.H. or 1578 A.D.

Expeditions to Iran were made preceding the crisis. Unfortunately, these did not prove to be similar to those of the Conqueror against Istanbul and Selim against Syria and Egypt, which were brief and yielded immediate results. They took a long time and further weakened the treasury of the state which was already weak.

The weight and the standard of silver coins like the *akçe*, *pâre* and *şahî* could not be preserved. Even the state mints engaged in issuing defective, lighter coins of lower metal content. A devaluation was carried out in 1584 by minting 800 *akçes* from 100 *dirhems* of silver as opposed to the previous 450. This caused the price of gold coins to rise from 60 to 120 *akçes*. Just as an attempt at stabilization was being made in 1586, the first and most spectacular Janissary revolt in Ottoman history took place; in it the governor of Rumelia, the treasurer and the superintendent of the mints were murdered because the *ʿulûfe* had been paid with *akçes* of a lower standard.

In the fiscal year 1581, the deficit of the central budget reached 56,255,462 *akçes*, despite the fact that extraordinary taxes had supplied an additional income of 75,934,596 *akçes*.[20] Even the surpluses of the provincial budgets could not eliminate the deficit, which with their help fell to 727,870 *akçes*.

New taxes caused a decline in population in Anatolia and Rumelia, and were one of the main factors in popular participation in the *Celâlî* risings

[17] *Kitâb-i Mustetâb*, Süleymaniye Library, Fatih MS. no. 3514, f. 39 v.
[18] *Kanunnâme-i Mısır*, Paris, Bibl. Nat. MS. Turc no. 82, f. 51 v, 52 r.
[19] See note 17.
[20] BA, Maliyeden Müdevver no. 893.

which occupy the first half of the seventeenth century. These rebellions paved the way for further decline in the revenues, and so led to increased deficits, and eventually resulted in a new devaluation of the *akçe*.

After the Persian Wars (1578–88), the Grand Vizier Sinan Paşa admitted that revenues were one-third less than the expenditures.[21]

1021 A.H. or 1612 A.D.

This date marks the closing of the second stage of the Persian Wars and the signing of the peace. The only important events in Anatolia are the *Celâlî* rebellions.

In 1607 the income of the treasury for the first six months was	204,273,747 *akçes*
Expenditure for the same period was	202,973,744 *akçes*[22]
The revenue of the 1608 budget was	503,691,446 *akçes*
The expenditure was	599,191,446 *akçes*[23].

The deficit in 1608 was approximately 19 per cent of the budget, despite a grant of 78 million *akçes* from the Inner Treasury. In this year, 95·5 million *akçes* were paid to the frontier troops stationed on the eastern and the western borders of the Empire.

It should be pointed out here that in the years that are close to the preceding *sıvış* year, there are only the quarterly payments of one year. In other words, if a number of payments are delayed, then the deficit is even greater than it appears at first sight.

The rate of exchange of the *akçe* exhibited remarkable stability during the *sıviş* year. The price of gold went up only as late as 1616 and stabilization was resorted to when an additional quarterly payment had to be made.

The delayed *ʿulûfe* caused the Hotin Expedition (1621) to end as a failure, and brought the army to oppose the Sultan Osman II (1617–22), leading eventually to his forced abdication and later murder. A Janissary junta dominated the politics of the country for a long period thereafter.

Budget deficits during this era caused the Inner Treasury to go bankrupt, and some metal objects in the Palace were melted down to mint coins. Just prior to the next *sıviş* year, relative stability was achieved through the conquest of Baghdad (1637) and through the efforts of a capable Grand Vizier.

1054 A.H. or 1644 A.D.

The murder of the Grand Vizier Kemankeş Kara Mustafa Paşa in 1644 and the extravagant spending of the insane İbrahim (1640–8) caused the deficits to assume dangerous magnitudes, finally paving the way for the

[21] Sinan Paşa, *Telhisât*, Süleymaniye Library, Esad Efendi MS no. 2236, f. 52 r.

[22] BA, Kepeci no. 3398.

[23] BA, D. BŞM. 1017.12.15.

latter's deposition and murder and the accession of his son Mehmed IV as a child. During the childhood of the new Emperor, the *harem* and the Janissary Ağas dominated the formation of government policy. In this period, the deficits of the treasury were made up by additional taxes and by the collection of the normal taxes one or two years in advance.

The burden of the taxes resulted in internal migrations by the peasants and their participation in popular rebellions.

The delayed *ʿulûfe* payments were made in devalued *akçes*, paving the way for yet another Janissary revolt in 1656 in which many statesmen were hanged on the plane-tree in front of the palace. A revolt of the small merchants, which resulted in the dismissal of the Grand Vizier Melek Ahmed Paşa (in office 1650–1) because the government had attempted to distribute lower valued *akçes* among them at an overvalued exchange rate, followed the Janissary affair.

1088 A.H. or 1677 A.D.

We know that in 1669 (when a third quarterly payment was about to be postponed before a year's would be at the *sıvış* year) the expenditures of the treasury were 637,206,348 *akçes*, whereas its revenues, including the 122 million *akçes* collected through an extraordinary tax, were only 612,528,960 *akçes*.[24] How the deficit was met is not explained in the budget, but another source relates that a grant of 142 million *akçes* was made from the Inner Treasury that year for current expenditure.[25]

It may be useful to give a brief account of the Inner Treasury here: There were two Ottoman treasuries: the Outer Treasury, the revenue and the expenditures of which correspond to those of the budget, and which was controlled by the Grand Vizier, and the Inner Treasury, dependent on the Outer Treasury but controlled by the Sultan personally. The surpluses of the Outer Treasury were recorded as revenue for the Inner Treasury and as an expenditure of the Outer Treasury. Conversely, the sums loaned or granted to the Outer Treasury by the Inner with the consent of the Sultan were treated as revenue by the former.

Generally, the Sultan resisted allowing advances to be made to the Outer Treasury unless the need for such sums was very urgent. It may be that the Inner Treasury was originally established as a measure to meet the *sıvış* year crises, but this purpose was soon forgotten and it began to be administered as the private treasury of the Sultan. The budgetary surplus of Egypt was automatically turned over to the Inner Treasury. Apart from this, when the Sultan thought that excessive sums had accumulated in the Outer Treasury, he would take them into the Inner Treasury to prevent extravagant spending. Among the other regular sources of income of the Inner Treasury was the revenue from the Baghdad customs, and from

[24] See note 4.

[25] See note 26.

the possessions of high officials subject to confiscation or reverting to the state in the absence of an heir.

The following table shows the sums transferred to the Outer Treasury from the Inner prior to and after the *sıvış* year in question. The period includes the first and second expeditions to Poland (1672–6), the expeditions to Czehryn and Russia (1678–81), the famous Austrian expedition which included the defeat at the gates of Vienna (1682), and the deposition of Mehmed IV in 1687.[26]

Years	Withdrawals from Inner Treasury *akçes*	Repayments to Inner Treasury *akçes*
1081 (1670–1)	49,440,000	24,015,000
1082 (1671)	30,930,000	11,940,000
1083 (1672)	36,500,000	7,371,000
1084 (1673–4)	161,962,773	43,159,311
1085 (1674–5)	84,000,000	13,544,700
1086 (1675–6)	99,039,590	17,397,500
1088 (1677)	141,968,677	—
1089 (1678)	146,087,980	42,000,000
1090 (1679–80)	127,852,120	12,000,000
1091 (1680)	86,169,130	—
1092 (1681–2)	110,857,980	18,000,000
1093 (1682, first half)	9,702,195	2,530,200
1093 (1682, second half)	120,960,012	—
1094 (1683)	251,832,000	90,000,000
1095 (1684)	255,209,760	—
1096 (1685–6)	301,922,280	—
1097 (1686–7)	389,950,056	—
1098 (1687–8)	111,581,648	—

The table indicates the nature of the funds made available to the Outer Treasury from the Inner. These were credits, not grants, and they were made available only through the Grand Vizier's and the Treasurer's guarantees.

The amounts accumulating in the Inner Treasury had enabled the Ottoman Empire to survive various crises through the centuries. Only after the Empire had lost the possibility of resorting to the use of the Inner Treasury in the 18th century did it begin to engage first in domestic, then in foreign borrowing. In contrast, outside borrowing in Europe had started as early as the Hundred Years' War, and the bankruptcies of the era of Philip II had become famous despite the wealth that was brought over from the New World.

[26] BA, Maliyeden Müdevver nos. 15846 and 20739 (registers of treasury accounts).

Had the plan of Merzifonlu Kara Mustafa Paşa to conquer Vienna been successful, it would have relieved the Empire from financial pressures during the *sıvış* year, just as the conquest of Egypt had done in the sixteenth century, and would have helped mitigate the damage and financial dislocation. The failure of the Vienna Campaign, however, not only worsened the crisis, but also made it less likely for an expansionist, imperialistic policy to be employed to alleviate the problem. In the years succeeding the failure of the Vienna Expedition, the domestic financial resources of the Empire reached a point of near-exhaustion and state revenues declined because of territorial losses, while the number of paid military positions, which had been increased through the years, could not be cut down; this created a heavy burden on the budget. The collected and uncollected revenues of the state, its expenditures and the yearly deficits after 1690, may be traced in the following table:

Years	Income		Expenditure	Balance
1102 (1690–1)	coll.	565,751,408	812,878,365	−247,126,957[27]
	uncoll.	281,947,388		
1103 (1691–2)	coll.	818,188,665	929,173,910	−110,984,245[28]
	uncoll.	284,148,424		
1104 (1692–3)		?	?	−262,217,191[29]
1110 (1698–9)	coll.	1,148,250,641	1,211,379,266	− 63,560,888[30]
	uncoll.	117,450,000		
1113 (1701–2)		1,182,327,378	1,070,460,505	+111,866,873[31]
1114 (1702–3)	coll.	1,060,277,518	?	? [32]
	uncoll.	70,816,246		

In the fiscal year 1103 (1691–2), with some exceptions, the income from territories subject to invasion was estimated to be 70,701,801 *akçes*. The uncollected income from state farms and possessions which could not be leased because of war and other reasons would have been approximately 90,620,559 *akçes*. If one adds to this other uncollected revenue, it is seen

[27] BA, Kepeci 2313.

[28] *Seferler olmayub Asitane ve Edirne'de ikamet olundukça hazine-i ʿamirenin iradından masarif-i mukarreresi bir senede 2,219 kise ile 34,245* [= 110,984,245] *akçe izdiyadı olub ve sefer-i hümayun içün işbu sene 1103'de tahsili ferman olunan akçelerden maʿada mühimmat-i seferiyenin tekmili içün iktiza eden dahi 4,721 kise ve 5,620* [= 236,055,620] *akçe olub ki bu cümle bir senede 6,940 kise 39,865* [= 346,939,965] *akçe iraddan masraf ziyade olur* (BA, Maliyeden Müdevver no. 12603; a *kise* is 50,000 *akçes*).

[29] Belediye Kitaplığı, Belediye Yazmaları 0.4. This budget is a copy containing a number of errors; in what appears to be the original (BA, Maliyeden Müdevver no. 5033) the totals for expenditure have not been computed.

[30] Although the revenue totals have been computed in this budget, the equivalents for some of the expenditure items have not been given, and thus totals for these have not been computed. The figure given for expenditure was calculated by myself. BA, Kepeci 2324.

[31] BA, Kepeci, 2324.

[32] BA, Kepeci 2326.

that uncollected revenue accounted for 35·7 per cent of the total national revenue of the state.

The crisis which was anticipated in 1687 did not come until the first payment of the next 33-year period was postponed. Then the army—with promotions refused, maintenance insufficient, and five quarterly payments in arrears—revolted, marched to Edirne, dethroned Mehmed IV and placed Süleyman II on the throne. The administration of state affairs remained in the hands of a group of rough soldiers for some time after.[33]

Since the cash holdings of the Inner Treasury had diminished rapidly, it became necessary in 1685 to melt down the gold and silverware in the treasury. As a result, *şerifîs* (gold coins) worth 2,693,000 *akçes* and *pâres* and *akçes* (silver coins) worth 65,853,177 *akçes* were issued, creating new business for the mint which had been inactive for a long time.[34] The *akçe* was revalued at the same time, 12·5 *akçes* now weighing one *dirhem* (0·256 gr. each) in contrast to the 14 old *akçes* of 0·229 gr. each. However, the importance of the *akçe*, the oldest Ottoman coin, had by this time become minimal, and it was replaced to a great extent by the Egyptian silver *pâre*. At this date, the *pâre* was a 70 per cent silver coin weighing 0·769 gr. When Mehmed IV was deposed, its weight was lowered to 0.738 gr., although the percentage of silver was kept the same. The content of gold coins was adjusted after 1640. Although the imperial rescripts (*fermans*) are not clear, it is understood that coins which had been made from pure gold up to this year began to contain 96 per cent gold and weighed 3.527 gr.

The most important development during this crisis period is a copper coin inflation which lasted for three years, beginning soon after the accession of Süleyman II. The *mangur* (copper coin), which weighed half a *dirhem*, was treated as if it were equal to a silver *akçe*, seventeen of which weighed one *dirhem* (0·188 gr. each). The use of the *mangur* was however abolished since the difference between its metal and exchange value invited many domestic and foreign counterfeit producers to strike coins. The first inflation by emission had been made possible in Turkey at this time through the introduction of the screw press into the mint, making possible higher production than could be obtained with the old hammering method.[35]

Another interesting observation for this period, particularly the relatively peaceful interval between 1699 and 1711, is that the Empire, whose prospects and chances of solving the crises through conquest grew dim, attempted to create wealth and increase state revenue by industrialization. After the construction of a modern mint, various attempts to erect a

[33] *Silahdar Tarihi*, vol. ii, p. 273 f. *Raşid Tarihi*, vol. i, p. 496 f., vol. ii, p. 15.

[34] BA, Maliyeden Müdevver no. 4028 (accounts of the Mint).

[35] The method of making coins with a screw press was employed between June 1690 and September 1691 to produce 558,873 kgs. of *mangur*.

broadcloth factory were made. But the Empire had fallen behind in this area as in others—and the western nations which were competing among themselves for the Turkish market naturally would not support Turkish industrial development and did in fact work to hinder it.[36] The only attempt at westernization which the West seems to have supported was the introduction of the printing press. The ambassadors in Istanbul helped İbrahim Müteferrika who installed the first printing press in Turkey.

1121 A.H. or 1710 A.D.

No uprising took place because of postponed payments during this *sıvış* year. In the preceding period of thirty-three years, a rebellion had taken place at the time when three *ʿulûfe* payments began to be delayed until the beginning of the solar fiscal year. The Grand Vizier had then instigated a revolt of the soldiers in order to reduce the power of the Şeyhülislâm, who had begun to dominate the political scene. An outcome of this event in which the soldiers were used as tools for political purposes was the murder of the Şeyhülislâm and the deposition of Mustafa II. The first thing that the rebels demanded from Ahmed III, who had just acceded, was the payment of the delayed *ʿulûfe.* In order to fulfil this demand, short-term domestic borrowing was resorted to, since the treasury was empty. On this occasion, the French Ambassador is known to have commented: 'Le Grand Seigneur doit commencer la paye le 13 de ce mois, on a assemblé six million avec toutes les peines du monde et le commerce en est devenu languissant, ce sera pour donner trois payes d'un quartier chacune'.[37] Ambassador Feriol's letter also indicates that three payments of the *ʿulûfe* had been postponed. However, from the last volume of Silahdar's history, which has not yet been published, we learn that the *ʿulûfe* was paid twice within the same quarter, as can be seen in Figure 3. This shows the timing of the postponement of the *ʿulûfe* between 1703 and 1721. The bottom line shows the dates on which payments were due. The top line, on the other hand, shows the dates on which payments were actually made. If there had been no arrears, the figure would have consisted of vertical columns. But because of the delay in payments, the columns incline to the right at angles depending on the length of the delay. There were rebellions in the first quarter of the 33-year period following the *sıvış* year, in 1717, 1718 and 1719. The three quarters in the figure which are marked with horizontal lines pertain to provincial soldiers whose *ʿulûfe* was seven quarters in arrears. They also attempted a rebellion.

From this *sıvış* year on, the Ottoman Budget shows that the formation of taxable wealth in terms of both the solar and the lunar year began to be

[36] Paris, Archives Nationales, Aff. Etr. B 1, no. 384, French ambassador Feriol's letters dated 4 and 18 July 1703.

[37] *Ibid.*, letter dated 4 November 1703.

attended to. For example, the budget of 1122 (1710–11) was broken down not only in terms of the departments of the treasury, as had been the case in the seventeenth century, but also according to the divisions of the solar and lunar years. The distribution of the revenue into the lunar and solar months during the year in question is as follows (see Figure 4b):[38]

Lunar year		Solar year	
Months	*Akçes*	Months	*Akçes*
1. *Muharrem*	276,170,230	*Mart* (March)	339,427,824
2. *Safer*	6,000	*Nevruz* (21 March)	3,112,816
3. *Rebiʿülevvel*	100,000	*Abril* (April)	2,100,000
4. *Rebiʿülâhar*	285,188	*Ruz-i Hızır* (St. George's day, 23 April)	6,199,800
5. *Cümâdelevvel*	—	*Mayıs* (May)	616,000
6. *Cümâdelâhar*	1,293,885	*Haziran* (June)	3,000,000
7. *Receb*	2,968,882	*Temmuz* (July)	120,000
8. *Şaʿban*	530,303,409	*Ağustos* (August)	1,072,000
9. *Ramazan*	94,714,329	*Eylûl* (September)	8,052,000
10. *Şevval*	444,400	*Kasım* (November)	65,920
11. *Zilkaʿde*	3,254,400	*Zekevris* (December)	818,932
12. *Zilhicce*	10,943,780	*Yenar* (January)	5,421,480
		Şubat (February)	12,063,540
Total	920,484,103		382,070,312

Of the total revenue of 1,302,554,415 *akçes*, approximately 30 per cent was formed and collected on the basis of the solar year. That the crisis this year was light may be explained by this reason. This also accounts for the fact that at other times a year's *ʿulûfe* did not always fall behind.

Using the same line of reasoning, it is possible to explain and interpret many events in Ottoman history in terms of the 11 days' difference between the lunar and the solar year, but the above analysis should be sufficient as an introduction.

Conclusion

In the Islamic countries the budgets of which have dual characteristics, it is possible to speak of *sıvış* year crises among the many other cyclical crises encountered by any society. To interpret Islamic History through *sıvış* year crises is, I believe, not only possible but would also yield interesting results.[39]

[38] BA, Kepeci no. 2326.

[39] The Turkish version of this paper published in *İktisat Fakültesi Mecmusaı*, 27, 1969, contains transcriptions of a number of documents which are not included here.

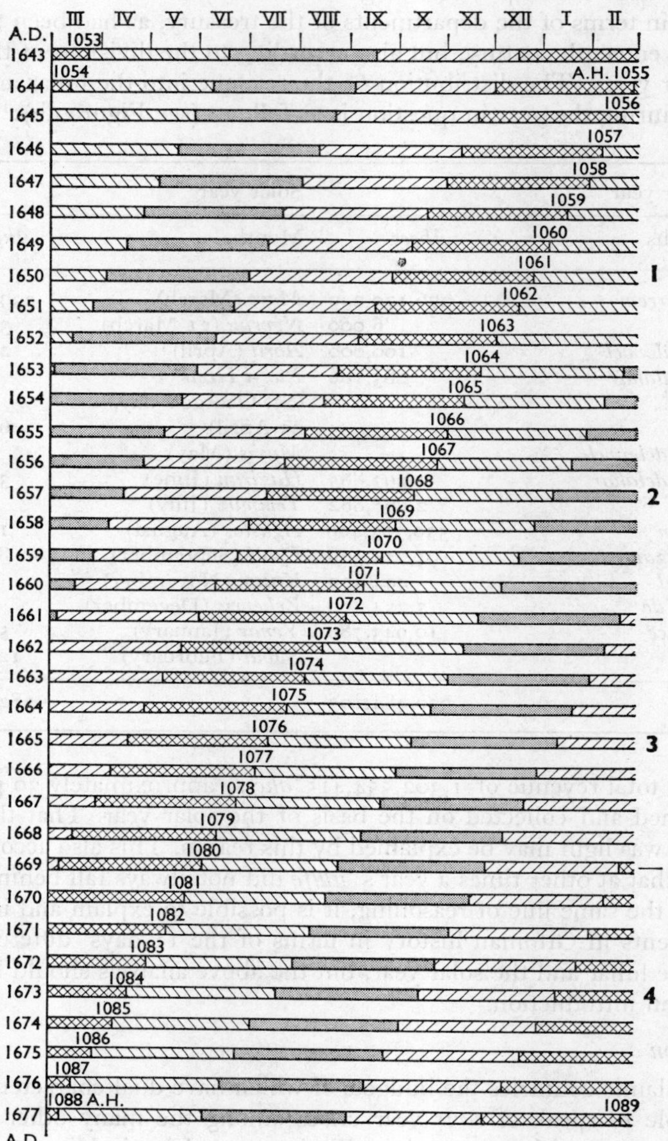

FIG. 1. *Diagram to elucidate the postponement of ʿulûfe payments, showing the generation of a sıvış year in consequence of the progression of the expenditure year with respect to the revenue year*

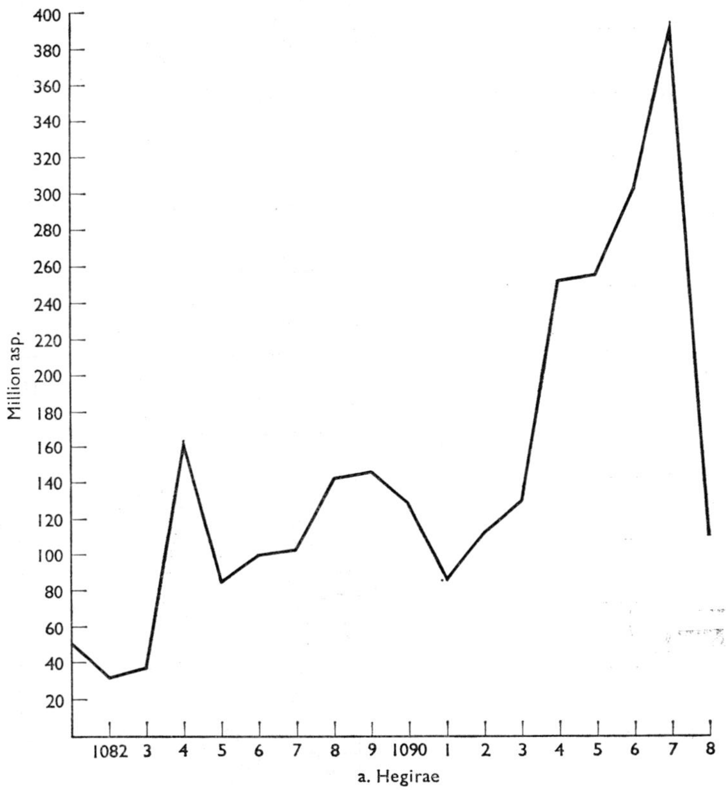

FIG. 2. *The decline of the holdings of the Inner Treasury*, 1081–1098 *A.H.* (1670–1687 *A.D.*)

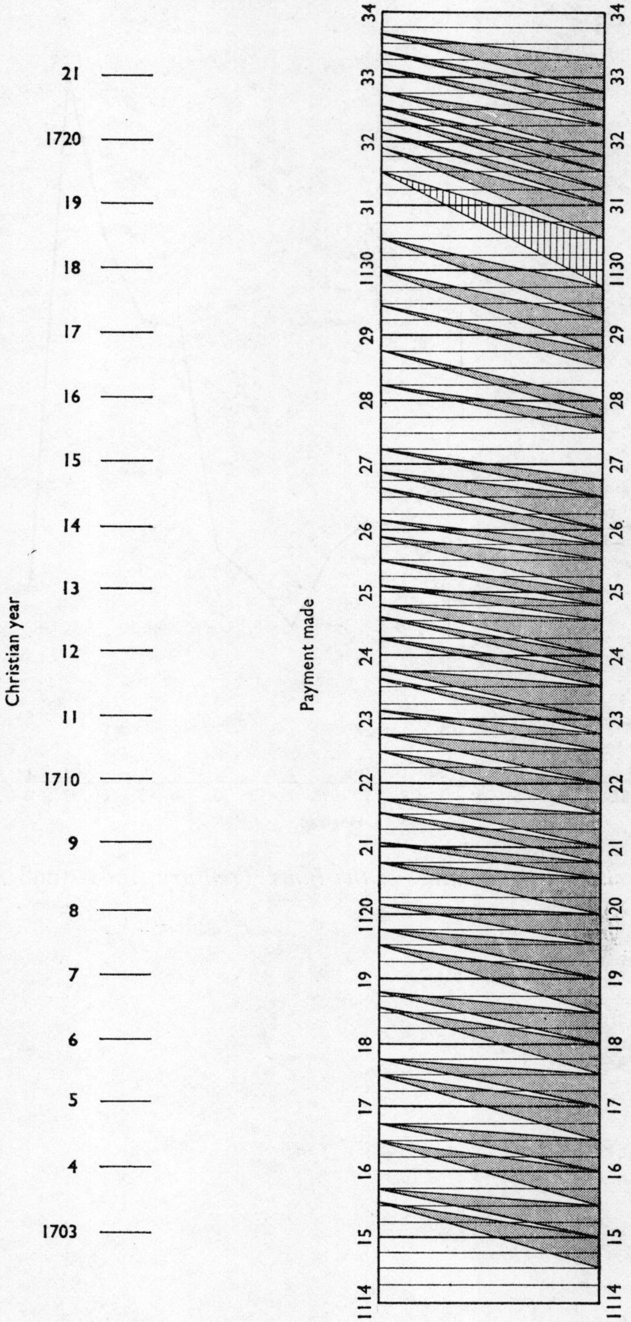

FIG. 3. *A graph showing the dates on which payments fell due and the dates on which they were actually made*, 1114–1134 *A.H.* (1703–1721 *A.D.*)

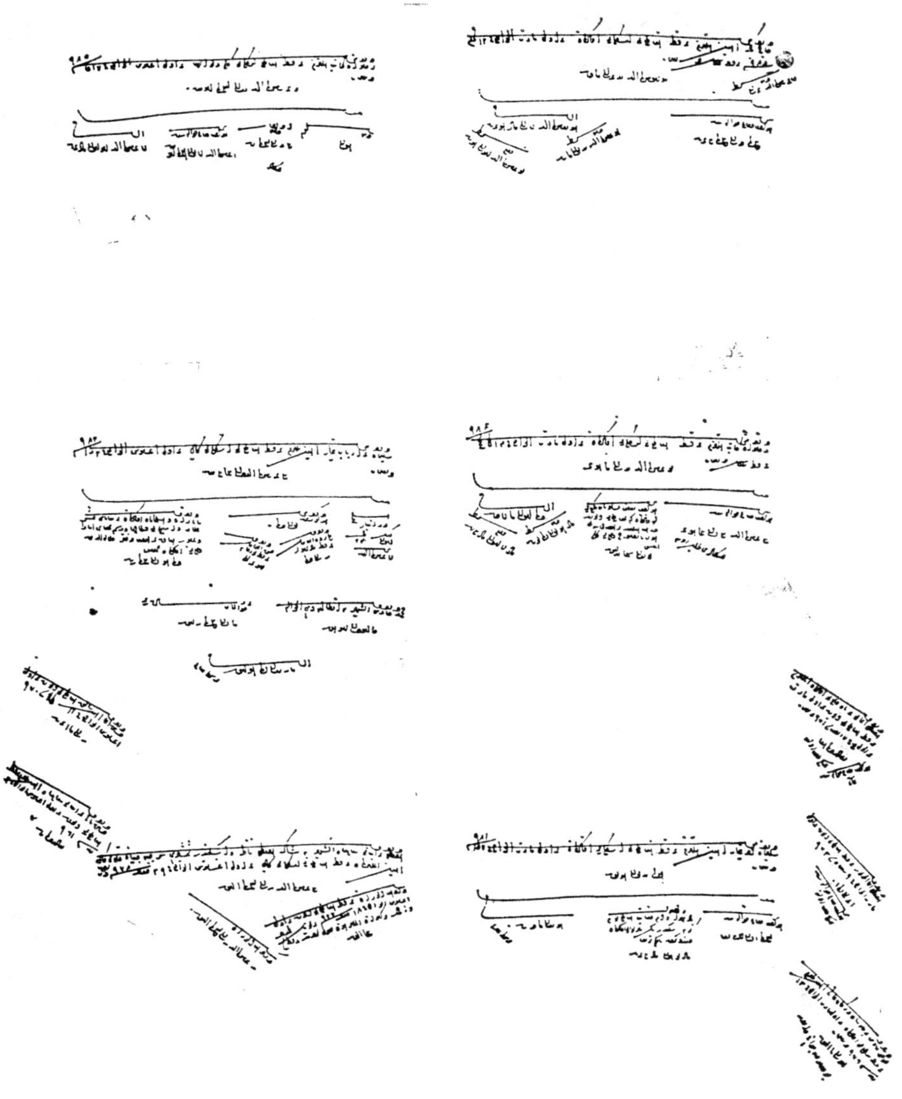

FIG. 4a.

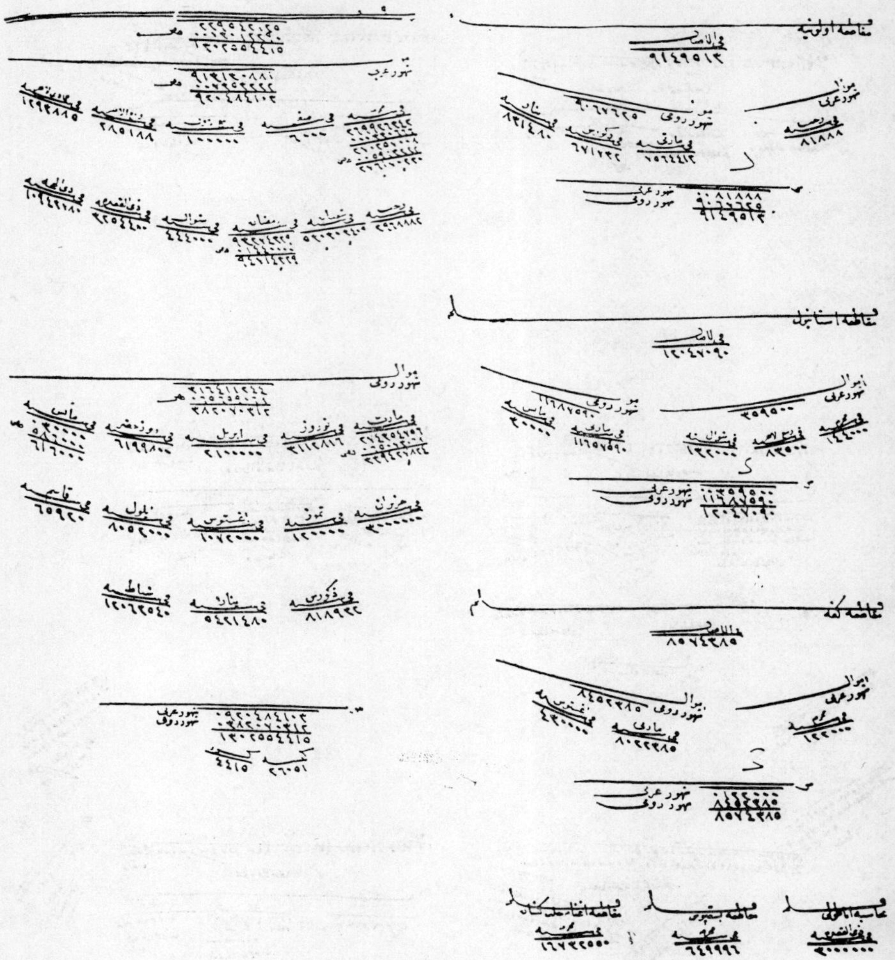

FIG. 4b.

PART THREE

The Nineteenth and Twentieth Centuries

Introductory Remarks

HOSSEIN MAHDAVY

THE papers in this part were not planned to relate to any special theme in the economic history of the Middle East. In fact the notion of the Middle East as a homogeneous region whose economic history could profitably be studied was seriously challenged in the course of the conference. All the same, the participants in the conference were keenly aware of the relative economic decline and stagnation of the Middle Eastern countries in modern times, and their attempts at explaining the continued backwardness of these countries often betrayed their deep concern over the present economic conditions prevailing in the area.

The twelve papers in this part can be grouped under four headings. Six papers are concerned with sources, methodology and the role of social and ideological factors in economic history. One paper offers an overall view of the economic history of the Middle East during the period 1815–1914 and compares it with that of Japan and India. Three papers deal with the oil industry and two of the oil-producing countries (Iraq and Iran), and finally two papers concentrate on Egypt's economic development. Egypt and Iran also receive some attention in the first group of papers. Syria, Lebanon, Saudi Arabia, Kuwait and the Gulf Sheikhdoms receive only passing attention. On a sectoral or industrial basis, the list of omissions could be long. In view of the dominance of the agricultural sector in the region, an analysis of the agricultural and agrarian problems of the region and their relation to the long-run growth prospects of the area could have been of some interest. On a different level, a more direct and explicit analysis of the role and the effects of imperialism in the economic under-development of the Middle East might have proved highly stimulating. However, it has to be remembered that the conference was offering not an inventory but only a sample of the kind of research that is currently being undertaken in the field.

Among the first group of papers, Dr. Abdel-Malek argues that economic history should be used together with other social sciences in an integrated manner to explain the totality of a social phenomenon rather than certain limited aspects of it. He divides economic history into three different types: (i) histories of economic ideas and systems; (ii) histories of the economic development of countries or regions; and (iii) histories of specific fields of activity or industry. The second and the third types in his view dominate the economic history of the Middle East and other under-developed regions. Seldom are movements of economic ideas taken into account in the less-developed regions since the economic ideas of the vanguard countries of Europe and North America are considered sufficient or good enough for other countries. But the heterogeneity of the nation-states within the three continents of Asia, Africa and Latin America rules out any simple and unified application of Western theoretical frameworks to these countries. An easy way out has been a factual, mostly descriptive approach to such countries with little historical background or analysis. International comparisons of national income calculations belong to this category. This approach has little explanatory content for understanding the more interesting aspects of a social phenomenon. A different approach has been to make certain assumptions about the interrelation between, say, oriental religion and modern economic activity, and then to let the behaviour of *Homo Islamicus* conveniently fill in the explanatory gaps left by the more statistical studies of the first type. A third approach, which Dr. Abdel-Malek espouses, combines the use of modern analytical tools with social analysis set in historical perspective. The typical problems which can be tackled in this way are those of economic development in different countries, of the interrelation between past history and present development, and between ideology and socio-economic structure. To understand a stagnant society trapped for centuries in poverty, disease, ignorance and a traditional form of government one must turn to in-depth historical and sociological analysis—rather than to platitudinous statements about the oriental mind or to dubious statistical time series. In this way, Dr. Abdel-Malek believes, we may be able to get at the nerve-centre, a kind of national will or 'implicit ideology' of a country—a specific *national* socio-historical structure. He suggests that we should study history not as a record of events, but as a sequence of socio-economic formations, trying to distinguish the persistent features which form the central nucleus or the 'kernel' of any particular historical tradition. Though this nucleus of beliefs, customs, ideas and systems of thought is of the utmost importance, the concepts of change, transformation and evolution are of equal interest and related to the persistent kernel: for in the course of time the kernel itself may be modified by such nodal elements of change as technology, institutions and ideology.

The specific case Dr. Abdel-Malek has in mind for the application of his analysis is Egypt. He seems to suggest that the seventy centuries of centralization in a compact hydraulic society such as Egypt cannot be considered accidental. The state has always controlled the Nile and for most of the time the available land along it too. This geo-political situation provided the state with a formidable apparatus as well as a kind of ideology. After the 1952 revolution, the traditional centralization was buttressed by state capitalism—a phenomenon not to be confused with socialism. Since this centralism is itself subject to change—because of both infrastructural and ideological changes—the future, argues Dr. Abdel-Malek, need not follow a linear projection of past trends—socialism may yet come about in Egypt, via its own specific national route.

However sympathetic one may intuitively feel towards this national set of beliefs and traditions of which Dr. Abdel-Malek speaks, one may find it difficult to identify this 'kernel' or to make much use of it as a scientific concept. The Nile in Egypt, as the geographer in Saint Exupéry's *The Little Prince* would say, is eternal enough. But so are the other rivers in the Middle East, Asia and in the rest of the world. What perhaps Dr. Abdel-Malek is trying to stress is not so much that national characteristics may prevent theorizing about factors that are believed to cut across national boundaries, but rather that such general theories may have to be modified when applied to such special cases as Egypt. But since discontinuity with the past is considered possible and within the scope of human action, these national kernels—even when easily identifiable—need no longer be as significant or as awesome a parameter as may appear at any given time.

Mr. Chevalier's paper is concerned with the social framework of the agrarian economy in the Near East at the beginning of the nineteenth century. Mr. Chevalier uses the case study approach (Mount Lebanon), but he is clearly interested in more than the case itself: he sees possibilities of generalizing his thesis so as to encompass a considerable part of the Near East (though not a clearly demarcated one). His main hypothesis is that the social organization prevailing then in Lebanon differed fundamentally from the kind of social system that existed in Europe before the industrial revolution. Such concepts as 'fief', 'feudal', 'seigneur' and the like belong to a different system of culture and a different frame of mind.

To consider the Near Eastern reality and to develop its appropriate concepts and vocabulary, Mr. Chevalier suggests that we should look at the family and its interaction with a given set of natural resources and technology as the key elements in our approach. For him, family relations arising from the necessity of regeneration, and social relations stemming from a given combination of technology and resources coupled with the necessity of production for survival, interact on each other to determine the behaviour of a group which is both a family and a productive unit. From the village upward, the same socio-political structure based on family relations can be detected, and the impact of outside forces such as the impact of the West can be evaluated only within the framework of a historically determined social organization.

The factors that Mr. Chevalier has thus underlined—the family, resources and technology—are undoubtedly of some importance in explaining some of the dissimilarities of social organization in the West and the Near East. But to accept their significance does not furnish us with any *theory* of social development and change. Family relations—of sorts—, technology and natural resources—of sorts—are found in all societies. Why then the differences? And if the differences are due to different combinations of these factors, what is the mechanism of this interaction and what are its dynamics?

Mr. Ashraf's paper is concerned with historical obstacles to the development of a bourgeoisie in Iran. The author argues that no bourgeoisie has—until very recently—developed in Iran, either because of state capitalism under the display of total power of a despotic ruler, or because of the submission of this same despotism to foreign colonial powers which frustrated the development of an independent bourgeoisie. The assumption here is that the emergence of a bourgeoisie is the norm and its absence a deviation of sorts which requires explanation. To account for this deviation Mr. Ashraf relies heavily on Marx's notion of asiatic society and Weber's concept of patrimonial government. The thrust of the argument is that the undifferentiated unity of town, country and the tribal areas, with the Shah and his agents controlling the economic life of the three, left little opportunity for the development of private initiative and the generation of structural conflicts that could ultimately have led to evolutionary changes within society. The author traces out a propensity towards bureaucratic capitalism and bureaucratic landlordism during the Ṣafawid and Qājār periods and then extends his analysis to Reza Pahlavi's rule during 1921–41. The constitutional revolution of 1905–7—recognized at least as a quasi-bourgeois movement—is perhaps too summarily disposed of and the description of the rapid growth of a modern bourgeoisie after the mid-1950's while both asiatic society and foreign economic domination of Iran have been in full swing, casts some doubt on the potency of the obstacles. The concepts of asiatic society and patrimonial government themselves need further elaboration and elucidation. How do these kinds of societies and governments come about and how do they dissolve or disappear? Can they remain completely static for centuries and fail to develop their own internal mechanism of checks and balances?

Professor Hershlag's paper deals with the problems of using economic history in choosing appropriate growth models for the Middle East. The neglected economic history of the Middle East, he laments, has been told in terms of chronology and pragmatism. Lack of adequate data, abundance of non-quantitative factors, as well as indecision about methods have been behind this approach. What are these indecisions? There are first differences of approach *within* economic history, and then the problem of using the results in economic forecasting and planning. He contrasts the methods of the traditional—mainly the German—school of economic history with those of the so-called New Economic History. The former sees economic growth as a sequence of socio-economic *stages*, through which all countries have to pass, whereas the latter is more concerned with statistical or economic verification of specific hypotheses usually concerned with the contribution of various *factors* to economic growth. He does not see much use in the application of stage theories to the Middle East since most of the countries of that region would appear to have got stuck in the second Listian stage of improving agriculture, increasing commerce and rising manufacture. He is more optimistic about an initial disaggregation of the problems and intensive study of a number of specific issues along the partial lines of the New Economic History, so that a more meaningful reaggregation could perhaps be achieved later. Except in the case of Israel, he is wary of the national development plans—some fairly sophisticated from a purely mathematical point of view—which have cropped up during the last decade or so, with emphasis on the investment rate as the crucial factor and a 7 per cent increase in GNP as their common goal. He stresses, with some justification, that under the particular circumstances prevailing in the Middle East, the quality of the human factor and the efficiency—or rather the lack of it—of government machinery seems to be more pertinent than capital investment: conspicuous investment, he feels, can be as damning as conspicuous consumption.

The errors, the pitfalls and the gaps are thus well indicated and an outline of action for the future suggested. There seems little that can be done in the meantime to relate the feverish planning activities of the Middle Eastern countries to the historical realities—or even the present realities—of their environment. It would have been interesting to have considered how similar problems have been handled in the Soviet part of the Middle East, the economic performance of which is believed to be superior to that of the rest of the area. The Soviet Middle East would certainly be less of an atypical case than that of Israel, from which Professor Hershlag feels the other countries of the region can learn so much.

Mr. Owen's paper surveys the attitudes of a number of high-ranking British officials in Egypt during the 1882–1922 period towards the development of the economy and describes the effects of some of the policies pursued by them. The claim is that although such officials as Cromer, Gorst and Kitchener were administrators rather than economists or political philosophers, nevertheless their approach to development revealed some uniformity of basic principles either stemming from the conventional wisdom of the age or imposed by the nature of the Egyptian economy and its specific problems—the Nile, the importance of agriculture, etc. What were these principles? That the government should not interfere in economic matters except for public works, that private enterprise should be encouraged, that whereas agriculture may receive some assistance, industry and education should not receive direct government protection and help. As new problems and crises arose, they improvised and modified their policies, but the basic approach remained the same.

A difficulty encountered throughout the paper is the fluidity of the 'attitudes' which are being studied. No clearcut distinction is made between the personal beliefs of the administrators, their official policies, the policies of the British government, the so called 'conventional wisdom' of the age, and the internal logic and mechanism of imperialism. Britain was after all a great imperial power, and the British officials in Egypt were only administrators, not oriental potentates. Whatever autonomy they may have had, they certainly could not have worked against the basic interests of the Empire—as their persistent failure to give any protection to local industries demonstrated. Even if these administrators had read Marx instead of Mill, they would still have found it difficult to behave much differently under the same set of circumstances. The saving grace is that probably the attitudes of the administrators in Egypt were not very much different from those of their political superiors at home, so that in effect we are dealing with the ideology of an imperial power with respect to the development of the 'natives' and their land.

Dr. Yapp's paper evaluates the India Office records as a possible source for the economic history of the Middle East. Students of the field will find themselves indebted to Dr. Yapp for a readable—almost enjoyable—guide to the voluminous material related to four centuries of British commercial, imperial and diplomatic interests in the Middle East. From the sixteenth till the nineteenth century these records are almost unparalleled in importance. Hardly any of the Middle Eastern countries has any systematic record and, with the exception of Russia, no other foreign power has been in a position to acquire and accumulate the wealth of information that the British East India Company and the British government have gathered and stored.

But Dr. Yapp's paper is more than a simple guide to a bulky and dispersed source. It analyses the material and, with a healthy dose of scepticism, cautions the student against some of the dangers of plunging into the 'sources' without having a prior theoretical frame of reference. We are reminded that the criterion for preserving records was mainly their value for further office use, not for later historiography. Reporting and recording —periodic destructions apart—were often intermittent. Nor was the quality of reporting at all even. Occasional brilliance was mingled with cases of illiteracy, lunacy, or outright dishonesty. And perhaps most important of all, we are asked to bear in mind that the records are not a disinterested collection of facts about the economy of the Middle Eastern countries. These records are primarily concerned with British interests and the formation of British policy in the region. However, Dr. Yapp maintains that in the course of centuries, as British involvement extended from commercial domains to predominantly political fields, and as the centres of policy, as far as British interests were concerned, shifted upward from Bombay to Calcutta and from Calcutta to London, more and more interest was shown in the overall *economic* conditions of the Middle Eastern countries. To control a region effectively, the British government needed information and (as perhaps the most efficient imperial administrative machinery the world had ever known) they obtained it. One of the interesting aspects of Dr. Yapp's paper is that, like the sources under review, it provides some insight into the economics and processes of information-gathering on the part of the British government as well as the economies of the countries of the Middle East.

Professor Issawi's paper pioneers a bird's eye view of the economic history of the Middle East from 1815 to 1914 and compares it with that of Japan and India. His task even for the Middle Eastern part of it alone is an unenviable one. He has to overcome two almost insurmountable problems: the heterogeneity of the region, and a question raised by Professor Fisher at the conference: how does one explain why things don't happen? Professor Issawi tries to overcome the first difficulty by dividing the region into two parts: the Mediterranean Middle East and the Persian Gulf–Red Sea Middle East, but little analytical use is made of the subdivision and the bulk of the argument runs, in uncertain terms, about the Middle East in general. The second problem presents a more formidable challenge, in spite of Professor Issawi's heroic attempt to muster any and every argument to account for the Middle East's lack of rapid development.

The initial approach is to set up a *general pattern* for the transformation of all non-European countries in response to the gradual integration of various regions into a world-wide economy based on Western Europe, and then to determine how the Middle East diverged from these patterns. The patterns are manifold: increase in population, expansion of agricultural output, shift from subsistence crops to cash crops, decline of handicrafts, increase in disparity of wealth and income and predominance of foreigners as agents of change and entrepreneurial activity.

The population of the Arab countries apparently increased at a higher rate than those of Asia and Africa (especially those of Japan and India) and hence, argues Professor Issawi, an unusually large share of the increment in income achieved was swallowed up by population growth. But it is not clear why the increase in population did not result in the expansion of markets and output. And then there is the counter-example of Iran, whose population, if anything, remained the same or declined; and yet her pattern of growth (or the lack of it) wasn't much different from that of the rest of the Middle East.

The Ottoman Empire and even more so Egypt received enormous amounts of foreign capital. But, claims Professor Issawi, the capital was *misused*. This is more or less true of the public sector debts; but in Egypt more than one half of the capital inflow was channelled into the private sector, and presumably not altogether wasted. From the point of view of the inflow of foreign capital and development of transportation facilities, Iran and Egypt were again at opposite poles, and yet their fates were not much different. Iran had little foreign capital and no railways, Egypt had plenty of both (in fact, we are told, the highest mileage per unit of inhabited area in the world). The same story is repeated with foreign trade. The Middle East as a whole did not match the general world advance in international trade, but Egypt's average was probably higher and Iran's certainly lower than the world average. It is thus not clear what conclusions can be drawn. A hint of more potent explanatory factors is offered when the *composition* of trade and the *nature* of expansion in agricultural output is discussed. Japan's exports already contained a good proportion of manufactured goods while agricultural commodities and raw materials constituted the bulk of the Middle East exports. In agriculture, the increase in output in the Middle East was achieved mainly through the extension of the area under cultivation, Egypt being the notable exception. It is in this way that differences of technology and organization of production are introduced into the argument. This aspect is more openly discussed when the hiatus between the decline of handicrafts and the development of modern industry is being described. However, there is a tendency to exaggerate both the initial importance of the handicrafts and the extent and the duration of the hiatus ('deindustrialization'). Handicrafts often suffered at the hands of small local manufacturers as well as from imports of European commodities. The educational factor is raised by contrasting the astronomical illiteracy rates in the Middle East (this time Egypt included) with the virtual eradication of it in Japan by 1914, and by comparing Japanese and Indian universities and technical institutes with the more recently founded and anaemic universities of the Middle East. The entrepreneurial argument is introduced by claiming that the pre-1914 development was achieved 'almost entirely by foreigners and members of minority groups'. As Professor Issawi admitted in the course of the discussions, he had indeed underestimated the natives.

Finally, three underlying factors are introduced as basic to the patterns described: proximity to Europe, the social and political backwardness of the Middle East, and the nature of foreign economic and political control. The notion of proximity, if used in the physical sense (contiguity), has only meaning for the Mediterranean part of the Middle East, and if used in an economic or political sense it probably lost much of its significance with the improvement in (and reduction in costs of) transportation and communications. India and the Far East were not adjacent to Europe and yet they were not spared. The socio-political 'backwardness' of the area according to Professor Issawi meant that it had neither an efficient government nor a native bourgeoisie, so that the process of capitalistic development was left to the Europeans and the minorities—by-passing the Moslems and inhibiting the growth of a Moslem entrepreneurial and bourgeois class. At times, the argument comes dangerously close to an Islamic theory of underdevelopment. Finally, though imperialism is not mentioned by name, the beast is nevertheless well described and given credit for its share of mischief-making. The Middle East, we are told, had the worst of two worlds: neither the complete independence of Japan, nor the complete colonization of India with its partial beneficial effects (though some Indians would violently disagree with this doctrine).

When all is said and done one still wants to know why the Middle East was socio-politically backward, why it submitted to imperialism for so long a period, why it failed to educate its people, emulate or adapt modern technology, industrialize earlier, etc. Any answer to such questions may involve excursions into other fields of social studies as well as a considerable amount of counter-factual reasoning. But the questions seem legitimate enough.

Dr. Hasan's paper offers an example of the 'vent for surplus' type of development generated by foreign trade that Professor Issawi had claimed to be the general pattern for the Middle East. But whereas the oil exports were viewed by the latter as a second chance for the Middle East, the former considers them as but another stage in turning Iraq into a 'dependent' economy. Dr. Hasan first describes how agricultural exports acted as an 'engine of growth' during the 1869–1914 period, increasing faster than population, income and imports. This expansion was made possible by the utilization of Iraq's surplus tribal lands and nomadic population. However, the technology of this commercial farming was not superior to the kind of agriculture already practised in the country—the *shaykhs*, the town notables, the bureaucrats and officers who increasingly appropriated the tribal lands, were interested in maximizing their rents rather than in the total value of agricultural output. Thus in spite of a long-term price differential in favour of pastoral production and in spite of the decline in agricultural productivity, agriculture continued to expand at the expense of pastoral production: the tribal pastures were rent-free and therefore of no interest to the rentier *shaykhs*.

In spite of its shortcomings, the great expansion in output and exports did result in higher incomes—however unequally distributed—in higher savings and in more capital formation, especially in urban construction. The facilities provided for foreign trade—transportation, security, financial institutions—had some external effects for domestic production and trade, and the rise of imports—even of the more luxurious kind favoured by the *shaykhs*—was instrumental in developing new tastes and in encouraging people to work harder in order to satisfy their wants. Thus from 1918 onwards, after a long delay during which the local handicrafts had suffered greatly, there began a process of urban development and beginnings of industrialization, mainly of an import-substituting nature. The increase in the size of the urban population (and hence the size of the market) and since the 1930's greater protection for local industries—rather than customs revenue maximization—have also been important factors in boosting Iraq's industrial growth; but nonetheless on the eve of the 1958 revolution the industrial expansion was not capable of exploiting fully Iraq's manpower and natural resources (other than oil).

The oil sector of the economy begins to assume an increasing importance from the 1950's: imports and oil revenues show a high degree of correlation, the income elasticity of demand for imports is calculated to be greater than unity, the non-oil exports have become an insignificant proportion of national income, and oil revenues finance over 90 per cent of the total imports and provide about a third of Iraq's national income. Iraq thus seems to have completed the shift from dependence on cereal exports to dependence on oil exports. However, the new situation is more precarious according to Dr. Hasan, since less than 5 per cent of the value of exports is spent locally on wages and materials, and few linkages exist between the oil sector and the rest of the economy. Nor does he feel that the tendency towards increasing dependence on oil has been counter-balanced by the land reform and industrialization policies adopted since the 1958 revolution. It is of course possible that the policies adopted may have been inadequate or inappropriate; but it may also be the case that the difficulties of receiving sudden large quantities of foreign exchange with little opportunity cost from the domestic economy are more deep-rooted and require special analysis and remedial action.

The paper dealing with Iran as a case of a Rentier State adopts the line of reasoning that the oil exporting countries are faced with a number of serious problems as well as exceptional prospects. These countries could have been studied within the framework of the 'enclave' economies perhaps until the early 1950's: the export sector having no effect on the rest of the economy. However as the result of major political upheavals in the two largest countries of the area (nationalization of the oil industry in Iran and of the Suez Canal in Egypt) most of the countries in the area began to receive much larger rental payments for the exploitation of their natural resources. The magnitude of the amounts involved and the effects these payments have had—through government expenditures—on the economies of the region justify considering the 1950–6 period as a kind of discontinuity, a watershed in the economic history of the Middle East.

Governments receiving large oil revenues have first the choice of spending or saving these resources. If the temptation to use these resources for internal security or for other current government activities is resisted, and if the investment projects are not altogether worthless, the very utilization of these resources, unless carefully planned, creates certain structural problems within the country. Imports are 'cheap' and therefore can be liberally indulged in, and since physical commodities constitute the bulk of imports, the services component of government and private outlays has to be provided domestically—hence the expansion of the services sector. And if somehow one suspects that the oil industry over the next few decades or so will reach its peak, stabilize and then decline, the long term prospects of the oil-producing countries may be that of a large lop-sided services sector, providing little opportunity for the mass of the people to receive the kind of technological training and organizational framework required for long-run growth. The transformation curve between the oil and the non-oil sectors being almost angular, the increase in oil production results in higher welfare only through the exchange of oil for imports of non-oil commodities. Since the oil sector cannot be relied upon to grow indefinitely, the question of expanding the non-oil sector becomes the crucial question. To materialize the externalities associated with industrialization, it may be advisable to resort to direct subsidization of industries that generate employment or have considerable domestic inter-industry linkages. Should subsidization and provision of basic facilities fail to bring forward from the private sector the rapid pace of industrialization required, direct government investment in interlinked industrial complexes may be the best alternative, especially if the acute problem of income distribution is also to be faced. This contrasts with little government planning or the use of protective tariffs and monopolistic advantages granted to specific local or foreign interests.

Professor Mikdashi's paper is concerned with the profitability of the Middle East oil ventures. He first shows that though it is difficult to obtain reliable data concerning oil prices, costs and profits of the oil industry, it is not by any means impossible: it only takes time and effort. Secondly, he demonstrates that application of different criteria for calculating the profitability of the oil industry will lead to different judgments about the performance of various oil ventures in the Middle East. He is specifically interested in the application of the Discounted Cash Flow criterion. The method involves the application—to historical figures—of the rate of return criterion used for the evaluation of investment projects. The main advantage claimed for the criterion is that it differentiates between the time profiles of returns on oil investments. In Iran, the oil industry began to show returns almost immediately, whereas in Iraq, about a decade had to pass before they accrued. Consequently, the rate of return turns out to be much lower for Iraq than for Iran. The usual shortcomings of the rate of return criterion apart, Professor Mikdashi is quick in pointing out the main problem with the application of the Discounted Cash Flow to projects that have not terminated their operations, for the calculation of the imputed terminal market value of a venture—which must remain somewhat arbitrary—can affect the rates considerably. What would have been the terminal value of the Anglo-Iranian oil venture just before nationalization, just after it, and since the 1953 *coup d'état*?

A more basic problem which is touched upon but not elaborated in the paper is whether the profitability of crude oil exports can be determined independently of the integrated operations of the oil industry. The oil companies would claim that such a study is impossible; Professor Mikdashi feels it is not. If the latter's approach is accepted, then some of the results must be described as 'stunning'. For instance, the average annual rate of return for the Iranian oil consortium during 1954–64 is calculated to be about 70 per cent. One wonders whether any country in the West would have allowed a major industry—especially if dominated by foreign interests—to make profits of this magnitude. Professor Mikdashi may have revealed some of the economic reasons for the deep-rooted resentment against the oil companies in the Middle East as well as having opened the way for the application of modern concepts of investment theory to the oil industry.

The two papers dealing with Egypt are in a sense complementary. Messrs. Mabro and O'Brien in their joint paper examine the structural transformation of the Egyptian economy during the 1937–65 period, and draw attention to the increasing role of government intervention and planning, as of 1954, in bringing about this transformation. Dr. Amin shows in detail how the Egyptian development plans and programmes have been financed during this latter period.

The basic transformation Messrs. Mabro and O'Brien speak of is the change from the vulnerable cotton-exporting economy of the earlier decades of this century to something more complex in recent times. The rapid pace of development, especially since 1957, has inevitably been accompanied by some of the 'expected' structural changes. However, taking into account the qualitative aspect of these changes, the authors argue that the Egyptian economy is still oriented towards agriculture and heavily dependent on imports. Whatever industrialization has taken place is based on the processing of agricultural commodities for consumption purposes. The policy of import substitution has had only partial success since the imports of intermediate goods and raw materials have in part been replacing the declining imports of finished consumer products.

But despite such shortcomings rapid growth has occurred, and an effort is made to discern the determining factors. The high rates of growth in the 1950's and early 1960's show some correlation with the moderate increase in the ratio of gross investment to Gross Domestic Product. However, the capital/output ratio implicit in the regression results turns out to be unusually low. A more important factor contributing to rapid growth (and which can also explain the low capital/output ratio of the regression study) is indicated in both papers: Egypt has achieved much of her growth by changing the *composition* of her investment, shifting considerable resources from housing into industry, transport and agriculture. This is a lesson that almost all Middle Eastern countries need to bear in mind. Dr. Amin's paper shows how this has been achieved: through the expansion of the public sector and the dynamism of the nationalized enterprises. Another point which again can be detected in both papers is that Egypt has been using up its reserves and obtaining foreign grants and aid to import both capital goods and food materials to an extent wholly incommensurate with her export capabilities. This leaves Egypt with an apparent dilemma of either reducing her rate of growth in the future or making the kind of accommodations with foreign powers that for political reasons she would rather avoid. The dilemma can probably be taken by the horns by still better use of her resources (especially her manpower resources) and by a more efficient organization of her productive system. Furthermore, both agriculture and the capital goods industries are bound to respond to some of the heavy investments of the past decade. And as Professor Lewis indicated in the course of the discussions, the effects of non-economic factors on the economic performance of a country must not be ignored. Religious feelings and wars, political education and psychological factors could produce results—for better or worse—that would not be explained by investment figures and foreign exchange availability alone.

The conference ended on the whole on an optimistic note: not so much because any immediate breakthrough in the economic problems of the Middle East could be sighted, but rather because it was hoped that the demonstrated fruitfulness of the first conference would encourage some of the countries in the region as well as research institutions abroad to devote more time and effort to the study of the economic history of the Middle East. The economic histories of Europe, the USA, the Far East and more recently that of India have received considerable attention from economists and economic historians alike. The Middle East is the obvious next field if the circle is to be completed. However, it may only be too characteristic of the problems of the Middle East that few of the national universities offer courses in their own country's economic history, let alone in that of the region as a whole.

Sociology and Economic History: an essay on mediation

ANOUAR ABDEL-MALEK

ECONOMIC historians working on the Middle East—and more so perhaps on its modern period—have been submitted, for a generation or a little more, to the impact of the complex range of factors of change which has been remoulding the hitherto remote fields of the social sciences (including economic history) and regional studies, understood as the study of the underdeveloped 'Three continents' (including the Middle East). From the methodological viewpoint—which can only be of a generally valid, scientific, type, not of the more restricted regional one—we have to question the uses and limits of economic history, not *per se*, but within the general framework of the social sciences; this analysis will have to bear upon the field under study—i.e., the modern Middle East, with special reference to Egypt—with its specific features, yet within the broader framework of Asia, Africa and Latin America.

Such inadequacy as is currently perceived in the field of modern Orientalistic studies has been mainly ascribed to the inadequate training and equipment of specialists in the 'modern'-type disciplines.[1] I would rather suggest that the central problem is that of a restricted vision of the problem. For methodology is but the prospecting head of different social philosophies as related to concrete reality.

I. ECONOMIC HISTORY AND NATIONAL DEVELOPMENT

The science of economics, or political economy as we know it today, retains but little of what classical figures, such as Plato and Aristotle, or a founding father, such as Ibn Khaldūn, contributed to it. The starting point is currently admitted to be the transition period between feudalism and capitalism in Europe, between scholasticism and *The Wealth of Nations*. The rise of mercantilism and the coming of age of industrial capitalism had to tackle problems such as: the rationale of (apparently) economic obstacles to progress; the role of different factors in economic activity; the finality of this activity; the quest for moral and political justifications for this activity, etc.

[1] Cf. *University Grants Committee: Report of the Sub-Committee on Oriental, Slavonic, East European and African Studies*, H.M.S.O., London 1961. Latin America remains outside the scope of this report, as the linguistic factor (Spanish, Portuguese) obviously does not hinder research. Yet the nature of the problems is similar to those of Asia and Africa.

The happy pastoral interlude of the Physiocrats contrasts sharply with Adam Smith's work in 1776. A new socio-economic formation—capitalism—was seeking its way; a new class—the bourgeoisie and, later, the industrial sector of the bourgeoisie—was fighting ahead and finally coming to power with the victory of the French revolution.

Economic analysis, or economic history? This question raised by *The Wealth of Nations* came again to the fore with *Das Kapital* (1867–94). The narrow specialist's approach to the various fields of political economy and the rising social sciences was compelled to recant: here were two towering works that combined economic history, economic analysis, social analysis and philosophy.[2] Their aim was not descriptive but interpretative: of the *Homo economicus,* as an entity, by Smith; of social causation and the dynamics of human history, not just fact-finding and the rearrangement of evidence, in Marx's work. And yet, positivism was beginning to emerge as the logical sequel to empiricism and the dominant philosophy of the nineteenth century. Twice in modern times, and in the field of economics proper, Oscar Lange's thesis was thus illustrated, viz., that 'the existence and development of a scientific economic knowledge depends on the existence of a social class that would be interested to know really the economic relations and the laws that govern those relations, a class whose aspirations express themselves in a progressive ideology, an ideology that unveils reality'.[3]

The rise of the historical school (W. Roscher, B. Hildebrand, K. Knies, etc.) as from 1843, and the work of Richard Jones, nearly coincide with the beginnings of economic history, then understood as the history of economic ideas.[4] A brief survey of a century's work in the field of economic history shows that, under this title, three different types can be distinguished: (i) histories of economic ideas and systems; (ii) histories of the economic evolution, or development, of a single country or group of countries; (iii) histories of a specific field of economic activity (industry, transport, etc.).

Economic history relating to the 'Three continents', including the Middle East, recent as it is, lies within the field of the second type, sometimes with openings towards the third. Very seldom has a serious effort been made to analyse the movement of economic ideas and relate them to the general stream of the history of thought. Colonial countries, it was thought, could not evolve an autonomous body of theoretical thinking, let alone of economic theory. Broadly speaking, this was the situation obtaining in the major ex-colonial countries, for obvious reasons, till the 1930's. It is

[2] A. W. Small, *Adam Smith and modern sociology*, vol. i, pp. 235, 238, in H. Becker and H. E. Barnes, *Social thought from lore to science*, 3rd ed., New York 1961, vol. ii, pp. 523–6.

[3] *Economie Politique*, French trans. by A. Posner, Paris 1962, vol. i, p. 379.

[4] E. Roll, *A history of economic thought*, revised ed., London 1962, pp. 11–17, 303–18.

therefore important to elucidate the nature of the work achieved by the general body of classical European and North-American economic historians, so as to put the work of their colleagues on ex-colonial countries in general, and the Middle East more particularly, in proper perspective.

The basic postulate of economic history, and indeed of all the social sciences, is that of the universal validity of patterns and concepts evolved in the advanced capitalist countries of Europe and North America. Clearly, the world did not consist of similar units. But differences were generally thought to be amenable to rationality, which would secure their 'normal' development, according to the model set by the vanguard countries. This basic postulate comes, it will be seen, from the general humanistic social philosophy and, perhaps more, from the evolutionary philosophy which entered the field of social studies during the late nineteenth century. It was reinforced by the tacit assumption that what was good for the best could not possibly fail to be a guiding-line for the rest of the world, i.e., the colonial countries: Europeo-centrism, came gradually to take the place of evolutionary humanism, as colonial countries came to the fore in their struggle for national liberation. The concentration of academic life and institutions in the Western world, late in the nineteenth century, led quite naturally to the strengthening of this tendency. Centres for specialized scientific education; libraries; publishing and the press; the leading thinkers and professors—such were the major elements of thought and action which contributed to assert the universalist postulate in the field under study. The whole conceptual framework of the social sciences was, and remains broadly to this day, Western in its origins and orientations. And this trend, in the field of economics, was much reinforced by the leading economic role of the major capitalist countries in world politics, by the creation of the world economic market and the forced integration of the colonial and dependent countries into it, by the hegemony of the West over that market. Traditional cultures and religions of a non-European type continued to obtain in the majority of the world; only in the field of economic activity were most peoples and countries compelled, at it were, to go the path of the West.

Asa Briggs has recently pointed to the fact that 'it is primarily through the development of 'sub-histories' that theory has been injected into history. Economic history provides one of the best examples.' The main influence is Marx's, followed by Max Weber. 'The theories will rest on "concepts", "frameworks" and "techniques of thinking": when the historian begins to study a particular problem he will start with these as with the data.'[5] This 'two-way traffic between history and economics' has been developing with growing intensity in (normal) works of economic history

[5] 'History and society', in *A Guide to the social sciences*, ed. N. Mackenzie, London 1966, pp. 33–53 (38–9).

and theory; and specialists have found it necessary to co-operate with anthropologists, sociologists, psychologists and other social scientists. For the problems to be studied gradually appeared as complex totalities, rather than split phenomena. Here lies the source of social history, as a discipline, which was soon to supersede traditional historiography, notably in France, with Marc Bloch's school of the *Annales*.

Economic change, its rate, type and scale; economic growth and stagnation; economic welfare; economic development and social values—how did these theoretical notions and concepts fare when applied by economic historians to the 'Three continents'?

The nature of the problems encountered, first. They seem to lie within two different fields:

(i) The type of economic milieu. Everything goes to suggest that we have to deal with heterogeneous units and this at several levels. We are familiar with the 'two sectors' in underdeveloped, or developing, economies, i.e., the traditional and the modern, the archaic and the developed, forward-looking.[6] We now can see how 'economic development' can be combined with 'economic backwardness', though much remains to be explored if we are to rise to the level of meaningful analysis.[7] The contrast between old nation-states (Egypt, China, Persia, Turkey, etc.) and other types of 'national formation', including the so-called 'new nations' and the problem of artificial colonial frontiers, have put to question the operational concept of the 'Third World'.[8] The image of large devastated areas, cornered by famine and death, looms large in manifestoes, counsels and guerillas and is coming to be accepted as part of our contemporary human condition.

Heterogeneity—and not only dichotomy. Not a combination of old and new, but, as a consequence of complex diverging factors active throughout the social texture of these countries, a basic unwholeness, a fundamental disquiet, trouble and strife. *Homo economicus* could never be dreamt of in that realm of mankind.

(ii) And yet, in spite of this basic structure, chaos is being pushed aside, in a steady and decisive way, in the old nation-states; and the will to do so can be observed in the other categories. What is it, then, that makes for cohesiveness in spite of heterogeneity?

[6] Literature from autochthonous social scientists abounds, especially from Latin America, viz., the work of Raul Prebisch, Celso Furtado, etc., and the recent issue of *Partisans*, nos. 26–7, c. 1966, devoted to 'L'Amérique Latine en marche'; etc.

[7] Cf. the gathering of theses and discussions, especially those of T. Balogh and H. Myint, in *The teaching of development economics*, ed. K. Martin and J. Knapp, London 1967; and the General Introduction by C. Issawi to *The economic history of the Middle East, 1800–1914, a book of readings*, Chicago and London 1966, pp. 3–13.

[8] Cf. A. Abdel-Malek, 'La vision du problème colonial par le monde afro-asiatique', *Cahiers Internationaux de Sociologie*, xxx, 1963, pp. 145–56, and 'Sociologie du dévelopment national: problèmes de conceptualisation', *Revue de l'Institut de Sociologie*, 1967, pp. 63–78.

Specialists and public opinion alike in the West are gradually coming to realize that—beyond economic disparities and incoherence—there lies a whole stratum, deeply entrenched, of beliefs, customs, ways of living, ideas and systems of thoughts, a will-to-be, a collective, national, will at that. And, if this national will has clearly to be made explicit and forcefully set forth, its mainstay—the nerve-centre, as it were, of this depth-structure—can be accurately labelled 'implicit ideology',[9] the largely hidden part of the iceberg, far beyond statistics, surveys, polls and the like—far more wholesome, a submerged socio-historical specific national structure that no social analyst can afford to neglect or underestimate. This will be, then, my working hypothesis, which this essay is trying to illustrate.

Meanwhile, we can proceed and, after the problems, consider the nature of the work achieved by economic historians in the field under study:

(i) A first set of books and studies provide factual surveys, mainly descriptive, sometimes analytical. And, in this last instance, analysis is usually set against a sketchy 'historical background', unless it starts with general assumptions about Oriental religion in relation to economic activity. Under the influence of Colin Clark, a whole trend of economic thought has tried, and still is trying, to evaluate the economic development of ex-colonial countries with a unified set of statistical, mathematically-regimented criteria, particularly international 'comparisons' of national income calculations:[10] accountancy and econometrics have resolutely pushed aside historicism and ignored the problems of specific national characteristics.[11]

(ii) Studies set against the 'historical background' usually start with general postulates about the interrelation between Oriental religions and modern economic activity. Underdevelopment and prospects for the future are explained in terms of permanent structural units and learned considerations about *Homo Islamicus*, etc., are propounded to fill the gaps left inevitably by work done under (i).

(iii) There is, however, a third group of studies, which has developed recently, trying to combine the use of modern analytical tools with social analysis set in its historical perspective. The problems which are being tackled are, mainly, those of discontinuity, heterogeneity and the specific character of economic development in different countries of the 'Three continents': the interrelation between past history and present development; between ideology and socio-economic structure; the reasons for the uneven evolution of different countries; the role of voluntarism and political activism etc.

[9] This concept has been refined and applied recently by M. Rodinson, especially in his *Islam et capitalisme*, Paris 1966.

[10] E.g., on the basis of the purchasing power of the U.S. dollar in 1924–33.

[11] J. Weiler, 'Le passage de l'analyse à la sociologie économique', in G. Gurvitch, *Traité de sociologie*, Paris 1962, vol. i, pp. 357–82 (370–2); he mentions the similar criticism by J. Nef.

Hypotheses are being formulated which provoke considerable theoretical discussions and are also geared to guide future practical activity. In both fields—theory and action—the work of this group now under way aims at putting the universal and the particular—science and national development—in a historically correct relationship, at the same time meaningful and efficient.

II. THE USES OF SOCIOLOGY

It has recently been argued with much force by Raymond Aron that the dividing line between the two sociologies—Western and Soviet, liberal-bourgeois and Marxist—is now in process of being replaced by a new cleavage, between the empiricist-experimental and the theoretical trends.[12] And though it seems that Marxist sociological writing stands more within the realm of theoretical sociology, major works by prominent Western-liberal sociologists (with R. Aron himself at the forefront) suggest that the two divisions inter-cross in many sectors and cases.

Clearly, if classical economic history, and its application to the 'Three continents', lends itself to severe criticism for lack of theoretical insight into the *nationalitarian* process, such help as we are now seeking from sociology cannot be derived from its empirical-experimental sector. In fact, the theoretical sociology to which we now turn is not a philosophical digression on society, but, in a very precise way, the conceptual elaboration of sociological findings within the framework of history.

Marx and Weber, albeit in highly different ways, lead the way. And our generation, so different from their age, witnessing the appearance and growth of socialist states and the upsurge of national movements and revivals in the ex-colonial world, has evolved a body of sociology which is gradually coming to be recognized as more adequate than the hitherto prevalent schools and categories. Perhaps even more so in our specific field of study, so rich in new, non-classical, disruptive, disquieting, phenomena. Because of its scope of vision, eagerness and penetration, let alone other classical scientific criteria, C. Wright Mills' *The Sociological Imagination* (1959) has appeared to a great many social scientists and non-specialists alike as a turning-point in the intellectual history of our time; and, for those working on the new problems raised by the profound transformations under way, as an inspiration and guide in method. Three points need concise discussion:

(i) Sociology has been currently regarded as two things at a time: a vision of things; a specialized body of study bearing on social institutions, material and spiritual. The first element—a vision of things—is now taking shape. 'The sociological imagination enables us to grasp history and biography and the relations between the two within society,' by asking three

[12] Cf. his introduction to *Les étapes de la pensée sociologique*, Paris 1967, pp. 9–22.

types of questions: '(1) What is the structure of this particular society as a whole? What are its essential components, and how are they related to one another? How does if differ from other varieties of social order? Within it, what is the meaning of any particular feature for its continuance and for its change? (2) Where does this society stand in human history? What are the mechanics of its change? What is its place within and its meaning for the development of humanity as a whole? How does any particular feature we are examining affect, and how is it affected by, the historical period in which it moves? And this period—what are its essential features? How does it differ from other periods? What are its characteristic ways of history-making? (3) What varieties of men and women now prevail in this society and in this period? And what varieties are coming to prevail? In what ways are they selected and formed, liberated and repressed, made sensitive and blunted? What kinds of "human nature" are revealed in the conduct and character we observe in this society in this period? And what is the meaning for "human nature" of each and every feature we are examining? . . . These are the kinds of questions the best social analysts have asked . . .—and they are the questions inevitably raised by any mind possessing the sociological imagination. For that imagination is the capacity to shift from one perspective to another—from the political to the psychological; from examination of a single family to comparative assessment of the national budgets of the world; from the theological school to the military establishment; from considerations of an oil industry to studies of contemporary poetry. It is the capacity to range from the most impersonal and remote transformations to the most intimate features of the human self—and to see the relations between the two.'[13]

I have quoted at length, as this first draft of the 'sociological imagination' cuts through nearly all the problems raised in section I, and clearly shows the spirit in which it is proposed to use sociology to overcome the difficulties now encountered by classical economic history.

(ii) The main point—once agreement is reached about the interrelation between the different social sciences, and their respective sub-divisions—is: how to integrate the historical dimension into social studies?

We are familiar with Ferdinand Braudel's distinction between the three levels of history: short-range micro-history at one end, faced by long-range structural history at the other; and between them, intermediate medium-range history ('conjoncturelle'). In his view, the second one unites history with sociology.[14] How could middle-range history, which is here our main concern, fail to show traces of this earlier symbiosis? Hence the wide audience of Wright Mills' thesis that 'history is the shank of social

[13] New York ed., 1959, pp. 6–7. J. Berque's approach to Arab studies has opened new perspectives for specialists by the use of what I would call 'prospective intuition'.

[14] 'Histoire et sociologie', in G. Gurvitch, *op. cit.*, vol. i, pp. 83–98.

study'—directly derived from Marx—and his conception that 'all sociology worthy of the name is "historical sociology" '.[15] For this intimate connection between history and sociology, several reasons are put forward that apply to all societies: 'In our statement of what-is-to-be-explained, we need the fuller range that can be provided only by knowledge of the historical varieties of human society.[16] . . . A-historical studies usually tend to be static or very short-term studies of limited milieux. . . . Knowing that what we are studying is subject to change, on the simplest of descriptive levels, we must ask: What are the salient trends? To answer that question we must make a statement of at least "from what" and "to what". . . . Long-term trends are usually needed if only in order to overcome historical provincialism: the assumption that the present is a sort of autonomous creation.' A second thesis follows: If 'historical change *is* change of social structures, of the relations among their component parts', it follows that the social scientist, 'when he compares, becomes aware of the historical as intrinsic to what he wants to understand and not merely as "general background" '.

The third thesis is grounded in Marx's famous 'principle of historical specificity'. Could it mean that the past dominates and shapes both the present and the future? T. B. Bottomore has recently stressed the fact that the whole range of national phenomena (as well as the bureaucratic rationalization of society) remained unknown until Weber.[17] Marx's principle would therefore refer 'first, to a guide-line: any given society is to be understood in terms of the specific period in which it exists', and second, 'that within this historical type various mechanisms of change come to some specific kind of intersection'. But Wright Mills moves further, as he discovers Marx's ignorance of the scope and significance of the national process: 'It is, of course, quite clear that to understand a slow-moving society, trapped for centuries in a cycle of poverty and tradition and disease and ignorance, requires that we study the historical ground, and the persistent historical mechanisms of its terrible entrapment in its own history. Explanation of that cycle, and of the mechanics of each of its phases, requires a very deep-going historical analysis.' The reference here is to Asia, Africa and Latin America; but also, in some ways, to North America: 'It is only by comparative studies that we can become aware of the *absence* of certain historical phases from a society, which is often quite essential to understanding its contemporary shape. . . . A retreat from history makes it impossible—and I choose the word with care—to understand precisely the most contemporary features of this one society which is an historical

[15] For a survey of this subject as a particular field of sociology in the nineteenth century classical style, cf. H. E. Barnes, *Historical sociology: its origins and development*, New York 1948.

[16] It is significant that the two phenomena selected by C. Wright Mills should be the role of the army and nationalism (*op. cit.*, p. 146).

[17] 'Sociology', in *A guide . . .*, pp. 79–94 (87–8).

structure that we cannot hope to understand unless we are guided by the sociological principle of historical specificity.'[18]

(iii) Historical specificity should not lead to immobility and stagnation. 'We must often study history in order to get rid of it. . . . Rather than "explain" something as "a persistence from the past", we ought to ask, "why has it persisted?"' Hence, 'it is very often a good rule first to attempt to explain its contemporary features in terms of their contemporary function'.[19] For history, conceived as a non-revocable condemnation, can block the way to evolution, and render 'the present as history', in Paul Sweezy's very apt word, simply non-existent, as the present would be but a contemporary image of the historical past. 'The national mould of historical composition encourages the use of stereotypes, including stereotypes about national character': here lies the danger of Weber's 'ideal types', as Asa Briggs forcefully points out.[20]

Typology, and its application to the whole ex-colonial world: a veiled racialism. In place and lieu of this static approach, the principle of historical specificity, precisely as it introduces the notion of history, directly leads to the concepts of evolution and change; and these, in turn, require the tools of criticism. The central questions, as regards the present, become: 'why?'; and, as the future is concerned: 'how?'

How are we to conceive then the principle of historical specificity in the light of the sociological imagination for our specific purpose, i.e., economic history?

(i) Dealing, as we are, with a part of the world with a very old historical tradition of ethnic existence, and sometimes national cohesiveness, our first aim should be to study in depth the long history of these countries. Not as a record of events but a sequence of socio-economic formations. We should then try to discover those features that appear to be persistently present, distinguish carefully their shapes and the degree of their impact during different historical stages, and reach at what would appear to be the central nucleus, the *kernel*, of any particular historical tradition, i.e., the historical specificity of a given society.

(ii) This central nucleus is to be conceived as a factor of both continuity and change. Its influence on continuity is much greater and direct: in the final instance, this central nucleus is the very texture of national continuity. When it comes to change, the interrelations are more complex. That central

[18] This case is argued, *inter alia*, by both A. Briggs and T. B. Bottomore in their contributions already quoted.

[19] All quotations are taken from ch. 8 ('The uses of history') of C. Wright Mills' work (pp. 143–64).

[20] A. Briggs, *op. cit.*, p. 49; cf. A. Abdel-Malek, 'L'orientalisme en crise', *Diogène*, 44, 1963, pp. 109–42; and I. Sachs, 'Du Moyen-Age à nos jours: Européo-centrisme et découverte du Tiers-Monde', *Annales*, xxi, 1966, pp. 465–87; etc. The apex of this typological approach is to be found in J. Austruy's books.

nucleus which makes for such persistent stability can only be viewed as giving the basic framework within which a certain limited range of patterns of change can take place.

(iii) Change, transformation, evolution—these are the key concepts and the general tone of modern scientific historical studies. Such changes as take place within the basic framework of any given historical specificity cannot but leave their mark on the basic framework itself. And this means that, by acting in a conscious, persistent, powerful manner on nodal elements of change (such as technology, institutions, the structure of social relations, at times, even more so, ideology), on such elements as appear to be the most vulnerable to modification and wide public acceptance of this modification, there is reasonable hope that the basic framework itself, the *kernel* of the historical specificity of a given society, can be, in its turn, slowly modified.

Neither change, any change, in a uniform, cosmopolitan, way—the hegemonic dream of the leading industrial societies— nor immutable stagnation, at which ethno-racial typologies inevitably point. Rather, a specific range of possibilities and ways of transformation.

III. EGYPT'S PAST UNTO PRESENT AND FUTURE

Let us now consider how these two series of considerations could be brought to bear upon certain concrete and reputedly complex problems of the modern economic history of Egypt. Reference will be made to a select number of studies to illustrate the analysis, and to help to detect significant questions which lie ahead.

A first problem is that of the transition from feudalism to capitalism. It is noteworthy that this problem, which belongs to the classical tradition of economic history, has only recently been raised under the impact of the ideological discussions around the nature of the Egyptian revolution—and not through autonomous academic channels. Social thinkers and political cadres alike had to assess the nature of Egyptian society around the Second World War, in order to frame an image of the future that was feverishly being sought by the national movement. Could it be that Egypt was predominantly a 'feudal' society for which a national capitalist, bourgeois democratic, revolution could be assigned as a national aim? Or was feudalism but a relic from the past, hence opening the path for more radical advances, perhaps even to socialism?

The economic system before 1952 was heavily based on agriculture. The ruling class and groups belonged, with few exceptions, to different sections of the landed aristocracy. Culture and traditions, the role of religion, the quality of inter-personal relations, the condition of women tended to confirm this backward, 'agrarian' pattern. Political denunciations of the overt or tacit alliance between the Egyptian ruling groups and imperialism naturally centred around the notion of the *iqṭāʿiyyīn*, i.e., big landowners, or 'feudal' landlords as they were, and could at first sight be called, led by the ex-royal family. Several radical groups adopted this definition of Egypt's economic and social system, in spite of their difference of outlook and programme: the M.D.L.N., one of the main communist organizations, as well as the Free Officers. By and large, public opinion and the press did not fail to concur; and there were several instances of this theme being used in the universities and learned circles. After the 1952 *coup d'état*, it became possible to describe the agrarian reform as tantamount to the liquidation of feudalism and the launching of the new, modern, phase in Egypt's economic and social history. The industrialists, in their turn, seized on this thesis to claim their share in the control and management of the economy and the State, pointing out that both the bourgeois-democratic and the socialist revolutions could be averted, the main thing, i.e., the destruction of 'feudalism' and the shift towards industrialization having been achieved. Economic history—mainly in the form of vulgarized essays and articles—took a curious shape of total discontinuity: a gap remained half-hidden, that of Egypt's social and economic history from Muḥammad ʿAlī till 23 July 1952.

The discussion of 'feudalism' started around 1944–6, only some years after the publication of A. E. Crouchley's pioneer work on *The economic development of modern Egypt* (1938). In 1944, two economic histories of Egypt were produced, one by Muḥammad Fahmī Lahīṭa, the other by Rāshid al-Barāwī and Muḥammad Ḥamza ʿUlaysh. By then, discussion was starting seriously in the Marxist political-cultural centres of Cairo and Alexandria. The adoption of what was then the classical Marxian periodization of socio-economic formations,[21] as applied to Egypt, could not but reveal that, at least since the institution of private landed property under Saʿīd, and, still more, with the integration of Egypt into the world economic market precipitated by British rule from 1882, the whole socio-economic structure had shifted to a new level, i.e., capitalism, with its two (Marxian) characteristics of production for the market and wage labour. 'Feudalism' could no more be said to be the system obtaining in Egypt; and al-Barāwī's formulation, under the influence of the Left at that time, can be considered as the first academic admission of this trend of thought,[22] which has gained official (national) recognition with Ḥusayn Khallāf's analysis of moderniz-

[21] Primitive classless society, slavery, feudalism, capitalism, socialism and communism. The gradual publication of Marx's *Grundrisse der Kritik der Politischen Ökonomie* (Berlin 1953) has stimulated discussion around pre-capitalist economic formations of the non-European type, among them the so-called 'Asiatic mode of production'. Cf. E. Hobsbawm's illuminating introduction to K. Marx, *Pre-capitalist economic formations*, London 1964, pp. 9–65.

[22] *Al-taṭawwur al-iqtiṣādī fī Miṣr fi'l-ʿaṣr al-ḥadīth*, Cairo 1944, pp. 27–8. Leading centres at the time were 'Dār al-Abḥāth al-ʿIlmiyya' and 'Lajnat Nashr al-Thaqāfa al-Ḥadītha'.

ation in 1962.[23] The main work was done, however, during the years 1956–8, and greater attention given to the forms of transition from Oriental feudalism to capitalism, since Muḥammad ʿAlī, by a group of Marxist historians and theoreticians, the most important for our present purposes being Ibrāhīm ʿĀmir.[24] A more sophisticated and relaxed study of the same problems was undertaken independently by Ch. Issawi and G. Baer, with basically similar conclusions.[25]

Not 'feudalism'; but then, if capitalism, of what type? The current formulation to define the immense and still very heavy legacy from the era of the great decay was 'relics of feudalism'. The aftermath of Suez stimulated research in two directions.

(i) The nature of Egyptian capitalism. Clearly, in Egypt as in other colonial countries, slowly emerging from underdevelopment and foreign domination, monoculture and 'export-oriented economy' (Ch. Issawi) contributed to shape a distorted version of Western capitalism. The very heavy predominance of the agrarian sector did not mean 'feudalism': it meant, however, that the other sectors—industrial, commercial, financial—were lagging behind. Therefore, the economic system prevalent in modern Egypt (from Ismāʿīl till 1952) could be described broadly speaking as 'backward capitalism of the colonial type with a prominent agrarian sector'.[26] This definition could help to interpret the course of development, as from the 1930's, i.e., the struggle of the industrial and financial sectors of Egyptian capitalism to gain access to the power of decision in economic matters, with the aim of reshaping the whole power-structure at the top in the final analysis. It could also help to interpret the economic history of Egypt under the new regime—from the agrarian reform to the massive nationalization of the modern sectors.

(ii) The second topic required much deeper insight, this time in the domain of sociology. How could it be that a society tightly integrated to the world economic market since the 1860's could present such a vast arsenal of 'feudal relics' at mid-twentieth century? A first explanation could be supplied by the greater persistence of the ideological factors as compared to the material ones (the 'infrastructure'). In the specific case of Egypt, a second explanation was suggested by studying one of the items of its historical specificity. The central, hegemonic, persistent, role of State religion, as

[23] *Al-tajdīd fī'l-iqtiṣād al-Miṣrī al-ḥadīth*, Cairo 1962, pp. 431–41.

[24] *Al-arḍ wa'l-fallāḥ, al-mas'ala al-zirāʿiyya fī Miṣr*, Cairo 1958. Other studies with special attention to this field by Shuhdī A. al-Shāfiʿī and F. Jirjis. The whole discussion has been studied in A. Abdel-Malek, *Egypte, société militaire*, Paris 1962, pp. 15–91.

[25] C. Issawi, *Egypt at mid-century*, New York 1954, ch. 2 and 3; G. Baer, *A history of landownership in modern Egypt 1800–1950*, London 1962; A. A. I. el-Gritly's *The structure of modern industry in Egypt*, Cairo 1948, starts from a slight historical background, in sharp contrast with his very interesting *Al-sukkān wa'l-mawārid al-iqtiṣādiyya fī Miṣr*, Cairo 1962.

[26] This is the formulation adopted in *Egypte, société militaire*.

ideology, meant that one could expect a similar situation in less important fields of ideology and culture, in the sociology of everyday life to which reference was made above. And this greater persistence was in turn reinforced by the exceptional intensity of ethnic and national unity obtaining in Egypt. Differences with, for instance, India—as regards the degree of integration into the world economic market and that of ethnic and national unity—could and should be clearly seen by economic historians and observers, seeking to find the diverging paths of the interrelation between the universal and the specific-particular cases.

The second main problem is that of socialism. The history of the creation and growth of the public sector is impressive, from 1957 to 1963, and onwards. Mass-media have tended to obscure figures provided by government sources: estimates for the 1962–3 Budget put the private sector's contribution at 65.8 per cent thus leaving only 34.2 per cent to the public sector; plan targets for 1964–5 indicate that the expected value added was 1.538 million pounds from the private sector, as against 375.7 million from the public one. Meanwhile, i.e., between 1963 and today, nearly 80 per cent of industry, transport and commerce have been brought into the public sector, and by 1970 the bulk of agricultural output will be achieved within the framework of the producers' co-operatives.[27]

Three years ago, summing up twelve years of economic development, I wrote thus: 'The Egyptian economy appears as a mixed economy. It is still in many ways capitalistic: the land remains nearly untouched by nationalization: the public sector, though under the direction of managers (technocrats) is still ruled by the market and (public) profit incentive; and planning, and foreign aid particularly, tend to strengthen this pattern, at least in the short run. It is a relatively fast-growing economy with a central State-capitalistic sector (the public sector) of unusual proportions: but every new wave of nationalization, while it weakens the power of private capital, only provides more solidly entrenched positions and power to the technocrats.'[28] A more critical estimate had just been propounded by Hassan Riad.[29] And the careful study of Patrick O'Brien, in spite of its subtitle, chooses 'the term centralized market economy (as) more revealing than vaguer adjectives like planned and socialist'.[30]

[27] The first figure is from 'The U.A.R. Budget estimates 1962–63', *National Bank of Egypt Economic Bulletin*, xv, 1962, pp. 108–25; the last item is from P. O'Brien, *The revolution in Egypt's economic system, from private enterprise to socialism 1952–1965*, London 1966, pp. 325, 317.

[28] A. Abdel-Malek, 'Nasserism and socialism', *The Socialist Register 1964*, pp. 38–55 (44).

[29] *L'Egypte nassérienne*, Paris 1964.

[30] *Op. cit.*, p. 316, and also: 'As a document, the First Five-Year Plan suggests, however, that almost all economic activity is centrally planned, but as implemented Egyptian planning includes no more than investment expenditure by the public and private sectors and the allocation of foreign exchange' (p. 319).

These three estimates, as well as the recently published work of several specialists, all revolve about the key notion of centralization. I have tried to show that seventy centuries of centralization had not been limited to the economic sphere in that most compact of all 'hydraulic societies': the State controlled the Nile and, till the second half of the last century, owned the land; it had to concentrate a powerful apparatus in its hand, because of the geo-political situation of Egypt; and ideological homogeneity, often pointing to theocracy, is clearly perceptible throughout, from the Pharaohs to Sunnī Islam, including the Coptic era. Here, in this symbiosis, lies the central nucleus, the *kernel*, of Egypt's historical specificity. And from here, any analysis of its economic history should proceed and provide a rational, meaningful, interpretation, pointing to the future. Over-centralization is not in itself socialism. The central, hegemonic, role of the State does not constitute by itself a collectivist socio-economic formation. Neither is it any more a free market economy.

The approach to these two select problems of modern economic history has centred around the relationship between ideology and the economic structure, and the analysis of the short-term evolution related to the century-long historical specificity of Egyptian society. Ideology and historical specificity appear, thus, in the case of this exceptionally old nation-state, as factors of the first magnitude—what Louis Althusser recently called '*surdétermination*'[31] in another context; and these two factors themselves appear, in the final instance, to be shaped by the geographical and economic conditions which have put their indelible stamp on Egyptian history from its very beginning till today.

And yet, this very sociological approach to economic problems can throw light on some possibilities for a non-utopian future. The role-to-be of this over-centralization, in all spheres of social life, suggests at least two possible courses:

(i) The first one would be to use such a tradition to accelerate the building up of an even more powerful leading economic sector, as a spearhead to development. It would be interesting to study closely the impact of the world economic crisis (1929–32) on the Egyptian economy and society; the shift to the right and the imposition of the dictatorial rule of Ismāʿīl Ṣidqī against the Wafdist masses was coupled with protective tariffs for nascent industry and a whole policy designed to favour national capital, especially its industrial and finance sectors. But it could be argued reasonably that Egypt's present regime has already gone a very long way in this latter direction, and that the main obstacles to further economic development lie in the deeply entrenched 'new class', and the bureaucratic, veiled sabotage of a wide array of government organs to the social dynamics—objective and not ideological—of the present national-radical policy. And

[31] *Pour Marx*, Paris 1965, pp. 85–128, 206–24.

it would be highly unrealistic to dream of a change in the very nature of the state that would enhance the role of the peasantry, the working-class and the radical intellectuals in a decisive way.

(ii) The second course belongs to medium-range history. The nodal point would be the very texture of Egyptian society itself with its majority of *fallāḥs*. Here lies the crux of the matter, as it does in the 'Three continents'. Underdevelopment, poverty and illiteracy are still much greater in the countryside than in the cities, though notable progress has been realized since 1952. But the formidable efforts required to develop Egypt cannot be restricted to the technological and state levels; they require mass-mobilization of the people; and this mobilization, if it is not to take an ugly form, cannot be put to effect in a rational, humane, manner unless carried out by institutions and organs emanating from the peasantry itself. Such appears to be the true meaning of the Kamshīsh affair (April 1966) and its sequels.

(iii) Attention should be drawn, finally, to the profound transformation of the socio-economic terrain itself, both at the level of infrastructure (economic institutions, living conditions of the working people), and ideology (the deep impact of the adoption of socialism as a national programme and ideology, in spite of vagueness and distortions). The intermediate level in the sociological pyramid—i.e., the state apparatus and the 'new class'—on the other hand, appears to be much more static; intentions are hardly coupled with action, for we are here at the very heart of the problem of power.

The 'principle of historical specificity', heavy as it is bound to be in such cases, is not, however, a stumbling block. Analysis shows its cohesiveness to be dynamic. And though the potential range of change variables is limited as regards future history—including economic history—for the near future, the dialectics of Egyptian society, never dormant, have been at work in an intensified manner since 1939-46.

History, from curse to promise: such could be the uses of the sociological imagination.

L'Evolution des Structures du Financement du Développement Economique en Egypte de 1952 à 1967

SAMIR AMIN

On partagera la période des 15 années 1952–1967 en deux sous-périodes, respectivement 1952–1958 et 1959–1967, les années 1957–60 correspondant aux changements politiques importants que l'on connait.

I. PERIODE 1952–1958

LES RESULTATS DE L'ANALYSE[1]

L'évolution des investissements bruts pour la période 1953–58 est retracée ci-dessous:

	1953	1954	1955	1956	1957	1958
Etat[2]	32	41	47	51	56	56
Entreprises[3]	38	43	65	66	39	67
Constructions immobilières	47	47	47	46	48	48
Total (millions LE courantes)	115	131	159	163	143	171

L'investissement brut, qui représentait en moyenne pour la période de 1945-52 environ 13 pour cent du produit intérieur brut, s'élève progressivement pour atteindre 17 pour cent en 1959.

[1] Sources: Samir Amin, *Bulletins de l'ODE*, 1959–60, no. 94, 104, 105, 106, 107/108–110; *L'Egypte Contemporaine*, no. 297–299, *L'Economie et les Finances de la Syrie et des pays arabes*, no. 20, 22; les «Flux monétaires et financièrs en Egypte 1948–1958», ouvrage (en arabe) publié au Caire en 1959.

[2] En gros équipement administratif et social et infrastructure (gros travaux publics d'irrigation et voies de communications).

[3] En gros investissements directement productifs.

1. *Le modèle général de financement*

Il se présente comme suit:

	1953	1954	1955	1956	1957	1958
Epargne des ménages	59	82	71	71	43	49
Epargne publique	17	14	7	12	30	37
Autofinancement des entreprises	25	26	38	38	23	37
Autofinancement des institutions financières	8	9	8	10	13	15
Déficit extérieur	8	0	35	32	34	33
Total (millions LE courantes)	117	131	159	163	143	171

— Epargne publique: comprend l'épargne courante des Administrations stricto sensu et l'autofinancement de certains Organismes publics (Chemins de Fer — Postes — Canal de Suez). On remarque que cette épargne décroît jusqu'en 1956 (croissance des dépenses courantes publiques plus rapide que celle des recettes fiscales), puis remonte grâce à la nationalisation du Canal de Suez dont les recettes sont désormais reversées au Trésor.

— Autofinancement des entreprises: l'ensemble des investissements directement productifs (investissements des enterprises) a été en moyenne de 47 millions dont 28 d'autofinancement (revenus non distribués des Sociétés et financement par les entrepreneurs individuels). La proportion, voisine de 60 pour cent, est grossièrement stable durant la période étudiée.

– Autofinancement des institutions financières: les réserves des Assurances et Organismes publics d'épargne passent graduellement de 7,3 pour cent des moyens locaux de financement en 1953 à 10,9 pour cent en 1958.

— Déficit extérieur: depuis 1955 voisin de 35 millions.

— Epargne spontanée des ménages: obtenue par solde (le chiffre de 1954 semble un peu aberrant), de l'ordre de 50 millions semble-t-il, c'est-à-dire sensiblement équivalente aux constructions immobilières.

2. *Financement des investissements publics*

Les investissements publics comprennent:

— les investissements de l'Etat (équipement de base).

— les prises de participations de l'Etat dans les entreprises du secteur public.

Ces investissements publics qui représentaient 12 pour cent de l'investissement brut pour la période 1945–52, augmentent progressivement durant la période étudiée pour atteindre 38 pour cent en 1958.

Leur composition et leur financement a évolué comme suit:

Total (millions LE courantes)	1953	1954	1955	1956	1957	1958	1959
Composition							
Investissement de l'Etat							
Equipment de base } Autres[4] }	32	41	47	51	56	56	61
Participations	—	3	3	5	4	7	33
Total (millions LE courantes)	32	44	50	56	60	63	94
Financement							
Epargne publique[5]	17	14	7	12	30	37	40
Financement par les institutions spécialisées	1	3	3	3	4	5	6
Financement par le Trésor	14	27	40	41	26	21	48

On constate:

— Que de 1953 à 1956 la charge du financement par le Trésor augmente au fur et à mesure que les investissements de l'Etat augmentent et que l'épargne administrative diminue.

— Qu'à partir de 1957 les recettes du Canal, désormais nationalisé, parviennent à alléger la charge du Trésor mais qu'à partir de 1959 le montant des participations s'élève si brutalement (conséquence des nationalisations et de la mise en route du Plan d'industrialisation) que le déficit à charge du Trésor devient à nouveau très important.

3. *Développement du marché monétaire et financier*[6]

1. L'augmentation régulière (freinée en 1957–8 mais qui a repris à partir de 1959) des concours du Trésor à l'Administration et à l'économie constitue la raison principale du développement du marché monétaire et financier.

L'apport des Institutions financières spécialisées au Trésor étant demeuré modeste (4 mls en moyenne et 4 mls encore en 1958), celui du public étant négligeable, c'est la Banque Centrale qui a pris en charge la majeure partie du financement du Trésor (23 mls en moyenne par an pour la période 1953–58).

Ce financement inflationniste du déficit public a été accompagné d'un déficit extérieur sensiblement équivalent (24 mls par an pour la période étudiée).

[4] En gros de 1953 à 1958, 2 millions par an (Chemins de fer et Postes).

[5] Epargne administrative courante, autofinancement des Organismes publics traditionnels (Chemins de fer, postes), et du Canal de Suez.

[6] Voir les tableaux d'opérations financières joints, tab. I à IV.

L'amélioration de la situation ou cours des années 1957–58 (réduction des concours de la National Bank of Egypt au Trésor à 13 mls en 1957 et 8 mls en 1958) a été de courte durée. A partir de 1959 le mouvement reprend.

2. L'augmentation du volume de l'activité des Institutions spécialisées a été régulière et passe d'une dizaine de millions vers 1952–53 à une trentaine de millions à la fin de la période étudiée (moyenne annuelle de la période: 17 mls).

Cette augmentation provient en partie seulment de la croissance rapide des ressources d'autofinancement (réserves mathématiques des Assurances et des Organismes publics d'épargne) qui passent de 8 à 15 mls. Les concours de la Banque Centrale, en augmentation continue (sauf en 1958, année pour laquelle des concours extérieurs exceptionnels ont été obtenus), sont venus compléter la progression des ressources propres.

L'apport des Institutions spécialisées au Trésor a pu ainsi augmenter légèrement. Mais il est demeuré, comme nous l'avons déjà dit, modeste. Aussi on peut dire qu'en gros ce sont les entreprises qui ont bénéficié le plus de l'augmentation des concours des Institutions specialisées: ces concours qui s'élèvent à 5 mls en moyenne pour la période de 1953–58, négligeables au début de la période, ont atteint respectivement 18 mls et 14 mls en 1957 et 1958.

3. Le gonflement du marché monétaire caractérise également l'évolution de cette période. Comme on l'a vu, le financement par crédits bancaires inflationnistes, faible au début de la période étudiée, devient très important en 1958. Les concours des Banques à l'économie, de l'ordre de quelques millions au début de la période étudiée (du même ordre de grandeur que les stocks) passent à 32 mls en 1958 (moyenne 1953–58: 14 mls). Comme évidemment les dépôts bancaires ont augmenté moins vite les concours de la Banque Centrale au marché monétaire, nuls ou même négatifs avant 1953, ont atteint 15 mls en fin de période.

4. La cause essentielle de l'inflation a donc été les besoins du Trésor pour financer le déficit administratif et le développement économique, accessoirement (en 1958) la politique de crédits bancaires inflationnistes (situation exceptionnelle de l'année 1958). La nationalisation du Canal de Suez en 1956 a allégé les tensions inflationnistes en donnant aux finances publiques une aisance nouvelle. Mais à partir de 1959 de nouvelles tensions réapparaissent par suite de l'élargissement du secteur public.

Toutes ces tensions inflationnistes ont pu être supportées grace à une assez forte préférence pour la liquidité: augmentation annuelle moyenne des billets et dépôts des ménages et des entreprises: 19 mls. Cette préférence, exceptionnellement élevée en 1957 (augmentation des monnaies: 47 mls) a permis l'équilibre de cette année très particulière. En 1958 l'augmentation de la circulation monétaire est réduite à 5 mls.

4. *Evolution du modèle général du financement*

Même à la fin de la période le rôle du marché monétaire et financier demeure modeste.

En effet la presque totalité de l'épargne privée spontanée (80 pour cent en moyenne pour la période 1953–58) est consacrée à la construction immobilière. Le reste est généralement conservé liquide, les souscriptions du public aux émissions de valeurs mobilières étant encore très modestes (et semblent en décroissance: 4 mls en 1958 contre 7 mls moyenne de la période).

La part de l'autofinancement dans le financement des investissements des entreprises demeure forte (59 pour cent en 1957, 39 pour cent en 1958) bien qu'en décroissance à partir de 1958 (60 pour cent pour la moyenne 1953–58) par suite de la mise en route de nombreux projets nouveaux prévus au Plan.

Le complément était traditionnellement apporté dans des proportions sensiblement équivalentes (12 pour cent environ des investissements) par les banques, les institutions spécialisées et le public. En 1958 la participation du public diminue au profit de celle des banques. A partir de 1959 le Trésor est devenue le pourvoyeur principal de fonds, dans le cadre de la nouvelle politique (nationalisation de l'ensemble de l'économie).

5. *La contrepartie de la circulation monétaire en Egypte* 1948–1958

L'analyse du bilan différential des banques permet d'établir l'évolution de la contrepartie de la circulation monétaire en Egypte de 1948 à 1958 (tableau ci-dessous).

Ces derniers chiffres pour 1957 et 1958 diffèrent de ceux des 2 tableaux joints III et IV pour des raisons de méthodologie: la définition des dépôts dans ce dernier tableau comprend les dépôts des Institutions financières, retranchés des concours des Banques à ces Institutions dans les tableaux financiers joints, de même que les billets de banque dans le dernier tableau comprennent ceux détenus dans les caisses du Trésor et des banques, Banque Centrale exceptée, alors que les tableaux financiers joints la même rubrique ne comprend que les billets de banque détenus par les agents non financiers.

Mais évidemment l'interprétation donne les mêmes résultats et le mouvement à long terme ne fait pas de doute: l'augmentation quasi régulière de la circulation monétaire durant la période 1948–58 a été due pour l'essentiel aux concours inflationnistes de la Banque Centrale au Trésor (256,8 mls pour l'ensemble de la période). Le facteur déflationniste majeur a été le déficit de la balance extérieure, sensiblement égal (242,5 mls).

Le niveau de la préférence pour la liquidité des ménages et des entreprises a entraîné une augmentation de la circulation monétaire de l'ordre de 45 pour cent en 10 ans (157,7 mls dont 77,1 mls pour les billets de banque et 80,6 mls pour les dépôts).

	1948	1949	1950	1951	1952	1953	1954	1955	1956	1957	1958
Billets de Banque	+16,4	+12,3	+17,8	+28,8	− 0,5	−28,0	− 1,8	− 2,2	+41,1	+ 1,3	− 8,1
Dépôts	+26,5	−13,0	+ 3,2	−27,7	− 8,0	+22,1	+21,4	+16,9	+ 3,4	+15,6	+20,2
Total Monnaie et quasi monnaie	+42,9	− 0,7	+21,0	+ 1,1	− 8,5	− 5,9	+19,6	+14,7	+44,5	+16,9	+12,1
Contrepartie											
Avoirs extérieurs	−13,1	+ 0,3	− 7,4	− 7,4	−59,7	− 9,8	− 1,8	−34,6	−40,9	−35,0	−33,1
Concours au Trésor	+37,9	−21,9	+11,1	+32,5	+55,7	+ 7,5	−15,5	+44,1	+71,7	+32,9	+ 0,8
Concours à l'Economie	+18,1	+20,9	+17,3	−24,0	− 4,5	− 3,6	+36,9	+ 5,2	+13,7	+19,0	+44,4

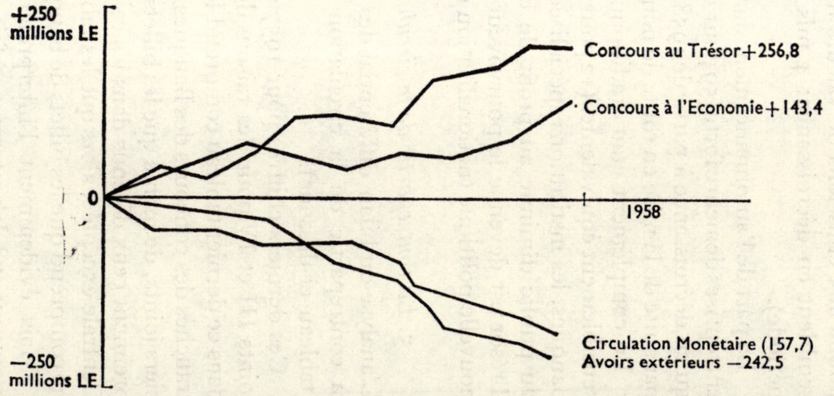

Le système bancaire a fait face spontanément à cette demande de monnaie et le montant de ses concours à l'économie lui a été sensiblement égal (143,4 mls).

II. PERIODE 1959–1967

On envisagera successivement le modèle de financement proposé par le Plan 1960–65 (A); puis l'évolution probable effective des dernières années (B).

A. LES STRUCTURES DE FINANCEMENT ENVISAGEES PAR LE PLAN QUINQUENNAL 1960–65[7]

1. *L'équilibre général envisagé par le Plan 1960–65*

	1959–60	1964–65	Indices	
Production	1 224	1 717	140	
+Imports	248	245	100	
−Exports	235	302	120	
	1 237	1 661	135	
Consommation finale				
Ménages	975	1 236	127	125
Administrations	58	72	124	
Formation brute de capital				
Entreprises	115	245	212	172
Administrations	80	97	121	
Ménages	9	9	100	

(millions LE valeur 1959)

Production: taux de croissance très fort envisagé: 7 pour cent soit par tête (emploi: indice 117): 3,7 pour cent (doublement du revenu par tête en 20 ans.)

Investissements:

— Effort global: la part des investissements devait passer de 16,7 pour cent à 20,5 pour cent de la production.

— Efficacité des investissements prévue:

Coefficient de capital:

Augmentation de production prévue: 483 mls.

Investissements 5 ans 1959–60 à 1963–64 selon le Plan: 1 385 mls d'où k = 2,9

[7] Voir les 2 tableaux économiques d'ensemble joints, tab. V et VI.

— Orientation des investissements: réduction prévue de la part des investissements administratifs au profit des investissements des entreprises (de 56 à 70 pour cent du total).

Consommation:

Restriction de la consommation prévue.

Productivité (production par tête): indice 120

Consommation par tête: indice 113 (population: indice 112) donc en gros seulement 60 pour cent des gains de productivité consommés, le reste étant réservé à l'investissement.

Balance extérieure:

Très forte amélioration prévue: maintien des imports à leur niveau de base, mais avec structure nouvelle (moins de biens de consommation finale et de matières premières et davantage de biens d'équipement) et parallèlement forte progression des exports de marchandises, notamment des nouvelles productions industrielles (doubler) et des recettes du Canal de Suez.

D'où retournement de balance déficitaire en 1959–60 à fort excédent prévu en 1964–65.

2. *La Répartition*

A. Au niveau des Entreprises

Le compte agrégé d'exploitation — affection des entreprises donne les lignes générales de l'évolution envisagée pour la répartition:

	1959–60	1964–65	Indices	
Production[1]	1 238	1 739	140	
Recettes extérieures[2]	5	7		
Total (millions LE valeur 1959)	1 243	1 746		
Revenus de l'Etat:				
Fiscalité[3]	226	291	130	144
Bénéfices Ent. Etat[4]	34	81	234	
Revenus de la population				
Salariés	409	549	134	131
Revenus des E.I.	450	576	128	
Dividendes[5]	7	10	160	
Transferts divers[6]	12	19	128	
Revenus retenus	112	225	200	

Notes:

[1] Si on considère les Institutions financières (Banques, Assurances, Organismes Publics d'épargne) comme des entreprises la production est ici le total algébrique production du T E E, intérêts et assurances nets.

[2] nettes des dépenses extérieures.

[3] nettes des subventions d'exploitation.

[4] partie des dividendes payés par les entreprises.

[5] nets des dividendes reçus par les entreprises.

[6] nets.

Commentaires

— Revenus de l'Etat:

L'hypothèse du Plan (maintien du système fiscal actuel) donne un allègement de la charge fiscale globale des entreprises.

Charge de la fiscaliteé indirecte: de 13,7 pour cent à 12,6 pour cent de la production (de 11,4 pour cent à 11 pour cent du total production + imports).

Charge de la fiscalité directe: de 10,5 pour cent à 8,9 pour cent du revenu brut d'entreprise.

Les nationalisations devaient entraîner une très forte augmentation des bénéfices du secteur public reversés à l'Etat. S'y ajoute la progression des bénéfices du Canal.

De sorte que l'ensemble des revenus reversés à l'Etat est à un indice légèrement plus fort que la production.

— Par contre tandis que les revenus distribués par les entreprises à la population ne sont qu'à l'indice 131, les revenus retenus sont à l'indice 200.

Donc:

Production par tête: indice 120 (production: 140 et emploi: 117)

Revenus distribués par tête: 112

Donc 60 pour cent des gains de productivité distribués.

Les revenus retenus comprennent évidemment les revenus non distribués des societés et le financement par les entrepreneurs individuels.

B. La redistribution par l'Etat

— Evolution des recettes de l'Etat:

	1959–60	1964–65	Indice
Recettes fiscales	265	335	126
Revenus des Entreprises publiques	34	81	234
Total (millions LE valeur 1959)	299	416	140

De même que pour la charge fiscale sur les entreprises, le maintien des taux du système fiscal actuel allège la charge fiscale globale sur les ménages (qui passe de 2,4 à 2,2 pour cent des ressources des ménages).

Au total la charge fiscale devait diminuer de 19,5 pou rcent du produit intérieur brut à 17,8 pour cent.

Mais compte tenu des revenus du secteur public, malgré cet allègement de la charge fiscale (qui, dans la mesure où l'économie est nationalisée perd sa signification), l'évolution des recettes publiques devait être parallèle à celle de la production.

— Evolution des dépenses administratives.

Les dépenses courantes devaient passer de 253 mls à 326 mls (indice 129) de sorte que l'épargne publique devait être doublée: passer de 47 à 90 mls.

Donc politique d'austérité.

La composition de ces dépenses courantes, sauf l'augmentation des intérêts de la dette, ne devait pas beaucoup changer.

	1959–60		1964–65	
	Chiffre	%	Chiffre	%
Salaires	129	53	165	52
Consommations courantes	58	24	72	23
Dépenses extérieures	28	12	31	10
Intérêts dette publique	7	3	19	6
Transferts sociaux	19	8	30	9
Total[8] (millions LE valeur 1959)	242	100	316	100

C. Revenus et dépenses des Ménages

Evolution envisagée:

	1959–60	1964–65	Indices	
— Revenus de la population				
Salaires	554	732	132	132
Revenus des entrepreneurs individuels	450	576	128	
Divers	42	69	164	
— Touristes étrangers	23	30	130	
Total (millions LE valeur 1959)	1 069	1 406	132	
— Dépenses:				
Biens et Services[9]	990	1 266	128	127
Salaires domestiques	16	18	122	
Tourisme à l'extérieur	11	11	100	
— Fiscalité	26	31	119	
— Epargne	26	80	308	

Donc hypothèse que la propension à l'épargne sera relevée dans de très fortes proportions: de 2,50 pour cent du revenu de la population à 5,8 pour cent — Cohérence de cette très forte épargne spontanée des ménages avec les objectifs sociaux du Plan (distribution moins inégale)?

[8] Subventions d'exploitation exclue (traitée en fiscalité négative).
[9] Y compris intérêts et assurances.

3. *Le Financement*

Il n'est pas envisagé dans les documents du Plan de tableaux de financement.

— Pour 1959–60 le tableau d'ensemble des comptes de patrimoine se présente en effet simplement comme suit:

	Ressources					Emplois			
	Entr.	Adm.	Mén.	Extér.	Total	Entr.	Adm.	Mén.	Extér.
Investissements					216	115	80	9	
Epargnes locales	112	47	26						
Aide extérieure (nette)				23					
Opérations diverses		8				5		7	
Subventions d'équipement	71				71		71		
Prêts					101	63	5	10	23
Emprunts		101							
Total (mls LE)	183	156	26	23	—	183	156	26	23

Ce tableau ne fournit pas les éléments nécessaires pour préciser le modèle de financement: il y manque une décontraction des entreprises (financières et non financières) et un éclatement des soldes de prêts et emprunts.

La comparaison avec notre tableau financier 1958 est assez malaisée pour les raisons suivantes:

— Notre concept d'Etat est plus large que celui de l'Administration au sens classique de la Comptabilité.

L'augmentation des investissements administratifs (1958: investissements de base de l'Etat, concept plus large que les investissements administratifs: 49 mls — 1959–60: investissements administratifs: 80 mls) s' explique par la mise en route des travaux du Haut Barrage.

— La totalité des constructions de logements était portée par nous au compte des Ménages (48 mls en 1958). Ce dernier chiffre ne s'élève qu'à 31 mls en 1959–60, d'après les documents du Plan (réduction de la construction voulue), dont 9 mls seulement portée au compte des Ménages (construction pour le logement personnel du propriétaire, notamment dans les zônes rurales), le reste étant porté au compte des entreprises.

Le modèle de financement 1959–60 semble néanmoins différer assez considerablement de celui relatif à 1958.

— L'épargne spontanée des ménages demeure à un niveau faible:

Excédant de l'épargne des Ménages sur les constructions immobilières	
Moyenne 1953–58	13 mls
1958 (exceptionnel):	2 „
1959–60	10 „

— L'augmentation de l'épargne publique (austerité + augmentation des recettes de Suez), est très nette: de 38 mls en 1958 à 47 mls en 1959–60.

Mais les besoins du financement public ont augmenté dans de très fortes proportions:

1958:	— besoins du Trésor		49 mls
	— Financement:		
	Epargne publique	38 mls	
	Emprunts	11 mls	
1959–60:	— besoins du Trésor		156 mls
	FBCF administrative	80 mls	
	Subventions d'équipement	71 mls	
	Remboursements de prêts (extérieurs)	5 mls	
	— Financement		
	Epargne publique		47 mls
	Divers		8 mls
	Solde: emprunts		101 mls
	dont:		
	Aide extérieure	23 mls	
	Recours au marché monétaire et financier	78 mls	

Donc le recours au marché monétaire et financier est multiplié par 7 environ.

— Comment le marché monétaire et financier a-t-il pu faire face à cette demande du Trésor?

Grâce à l'excédent des entreprises (très forte préférence des entreprises pour la liquidité).

Ressources:		
	Revenus retenus	112 mls
	Subventions d'équipement	71 „
		183 „
Emplois:	Investissements	120 „
	Solde disponible	63 „

Modèle évidemment curieux (raison de la forte préférence des entreprises pour la liquidité?)

— *Pour 1964–65*

— Les besoins de financement du Trésor devaient demeurer, comme en 1960, à un niveau très élevé.

Besoins du Trésor:	
Investissements administratifs	97 mls
Subventions d'équipement	63 „
Remboursements d'emprunts	11 „
	171 „
Epargne Publique	90 „
Solde à financer	81 „

Comment devait être financé ce solde?

— Pas par l'extérieur puisque paradoxalement on prévoyait un *excédent* de la balance extérieure (41 mls).

— Ce devait être financé par:

les entreprises: modèle analogue à celui de 1959–60: excédent des ressources (revenus retenus et subventions d'équipement) sur les investissements: 38 mls.

les ménages: excédent de leure épargne spontanée sur leurs investissements: 71 mls (soit environ 7 fois plus élevé qu'en 1959–60).

Il s'agissait d'un modèle peu réaliste (resumé dans le tableau cidessous). L'évolution effective probable montre d'ailleurs que les choses se sont passées d'une toute autre manière.

Modèle de financement prévu par le Plan pour 1964–65

	Ressources					Emplois			
	Entr.	Adm.	Mén.	Ext.	Total	Entr.	Adm.	Mén.	Ext.
Investissements						245	97	9	
Epargne locale	225	90	80						
Apport extérieur net				−41	359				
Opérations diverses		5				5		3	
Subventions d'équipement	63				63		63		
Prêts					117	38	11	68	
Emprunts		76		41					
Total (mls LE)	288	171	80	0		288	171	80	0

B. L'EVOLUTION EFFECTIVE PROBABLE DE 1959 A 1966

1. *Données disponibles*

A. Situation monétaire

	1959	1960	1961	1962	1963	1964	1965
Concours au Trésor	24	66	39	55	128	87	77
Concours à l'Economie	29	−39	46	46	−10	44	−4
Avoirs extérieurs nets	−29	−15	−26	−57	1	−16	−13
Total: circulation monétaire	24	12	59	44	119	115	60

(millions LE courants)

Le graphique ci-dessous montre que ce modèle d'évolution 1959–65 est désormais différent de celui qui caractérisait la période précédante 1948–58. Le tirage sur les avoirs extérieurs étant devenu impossible après la liquidation de ceux-ci à partir de 1962 et l'endettement extérieur à court terme se faisant de plus en plus difficile, l'inflation va se manifester ouvertement après cette date; les concours du Trésor entrainant désormais une augmentation parallèle sensiblement équivalente de la circulation monétaire.

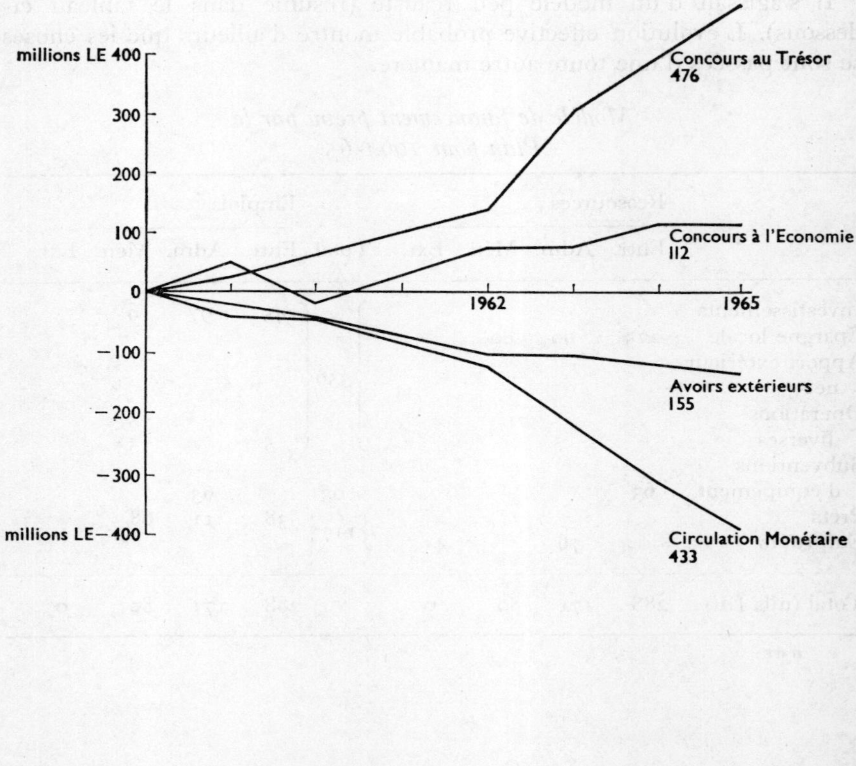

B. Balance des paiements

	1959	1960	1961	1962	1963	1964
Recettes:						
Exports	167	204	165	145	229	228
Canal de Suez	44	50	51	54	71	78
Recettes diverses	50	45	33	28	94	64
Aide extérieure en capital (nette)	11	11	34	81	94	111
Réduction des avoirs extérieurs (nets)	29	15	26	57	−1	16
Total	301	325	309	365	487	497
Dépenses:						
Imports	242	261	246	300	409	405
Dépenses publiques	28	25	31	28	28	37
Dépenses diverses	31	39	32	37	50	55

(millions LE courants)

C. Finances publiques

Ensemble des budgets des services publics et du secteur productif d'Etat.

	1959–60	1960–61	1961–62	1962–63	1963–64	1964–65	1965–66
Dépenses	511	700	780	970	1 079	1 184	1 206
Recettes	445	541	550	728	774	828	957
Déficit	66	160	229	243	305	356	249

(millions LE courants)

2. *Etablissement d'un tableau de financement approximatif probable pour 1964–65:*

(*a*) Les éléments connus de ce tableau sont ceux fournis par la situation monétaire (les concours à l'économie: 25 millions, étant ventilés entre secteur public et autres entreprises, voir ci-dessous; les monnaies étant ventilées entre entreprises et Ménages), la balance extérieure (aide extérieure en capital: 110 mls), enfin l'analyse des finances publiques.

(*b*) L'analyse des finances publiques nous indique le déficit global à charge du Trésor, qui, pour la moyenne des années fiscales 1964–65 et 65–66, aurait été de l'ordre de 300 millions: recettes publiques totales fiscales, parafiscales et bénéfices des entreprises publiques reversés au budget: 900 millions, dépenses publiques totales de fonctionnement, d'équipement administratif, subventions et prêts budgetisés au secteur public: 1200 millions.

Si l'on admet comme hypothèse les charges mêmes du Plan pour le Trésor: investissements administratifs, 100 mls; subventions et prêts d'équipement aux entreprises, 65 mls; les dépenses courantes se seraient élevées à 1035 mls, à ventiler (selon des proportions inconnues) entre les dépenses administratives de fonctionnement (935 mls?) et les subventions d'équilibre aux entreprises publiques déficitaires (100 mls?).

Le déficit total, connu (300 mls), ayant été couvert à concurrence de 110 mls par l'aide extérieure et à concurrence de 80 mls par les concours bancaires au Trésor il reste 110 mls qui ne peuvent représenter autre chose que des concours bancaires aux entreprises publiques.

Recettes publiques totales			900 mls
Dépenses publiques totales			1 200
Dépenses courantes:			
Administratives	935	1 035	
Subventions d'équilibre au secteur public	100		
Dépenses en capital:			
Investissement adm.	100	165	
Financement des invest. du secteur public	65		
Déficit global			300 mls
Couverture du déficit:			
Aide extérieure			110 mls
Concours bancaires			
au Trésor			80 ,,
aux Entreprises publiques			110 ,,

L'equilibre du compte des administrations exige alors un financement «résiduel» du Trésor par les Entreprises.

Charges du Trésor:	
Déficit public courant	135 mls
Investissements administratifs	100 ,,
Financement du développement	65 ,,
Total	300 ,,
Couverture:	
Aide extérieure	110 mls
Concours bancaires au Trésor	80 ,,
Solde: financement du Trésor par les entreprises	110 ,,

(*c*) Le tableau de financement 1964–65 ci-après peut alors être établi. Nous l'avons fait pour 2 hypothèses concernant les investissements des entreprises: 245 mls (objectif du Plan); et 145 mls (justification plus loin).

L'équilibre comptable n'est compatible avec l'ensemble des données analysées ci-dessus qu'à la condition que l'épargne d'entreprise atteigne 315 mls dans la première hypothèse et 215 mls dans la seconde.

	Ressources						Emplois				
	Entr.	Inst. Fin.	Adm.	Mén.	Ext.	Total	Entr.	Inst. Fin.	Adm.	Mén.	Ext.
Investissement						355 ou 255	245 ou 145		100	10	
Epargne locale	315 ou 215		−135	55							
Apport extérieur					125						
Aide extérieure en capital			110			110					110
Financement public	65					65			65		
Situation monétaire											
Monnaie		90				90	45			45	
Concours bancaires											
au Trésor			80			80		80			
aux Entreprises publiques	110					25		110			
aux autres entreprises	−85							−85			
Avoirs exter. nets		15				15					15
Finance du Trésor (résiduel)			110				110				
Total (millions LE courantes)	400 ou 300	105	165	55	125		400 ou 300	105	165	55	125

Caractéristiques du modèle de financement effectif probable pour 1960–65

(1) Le Plan avait prévu une forte épargne administrative qui aurait été affectée au développement (90 mls en fin de Plan). En fait nous avons en fin de Plan un déficit public courant de 135 mls. Sources du déficit: dépenses administratives courantes et déficits des entreprises publiques, mais dans quelles mesures respectives? Cela n'est pas connu.

(2) L'apport extérieur net prévu par le Plan devait être négatif en fin de Plan, les remboursements de prêts extérieurs devant l'emporter sur le flux des prêts nouveaux. Ce remboursement rapide des prêts extérieurs n'a pas été possible. L'apport extérieur net en fin de Plan demeure très

TABLEAU I. *Opérations financières 1958 (détail)*

	Ressources														
	Entreprises				Institutions financières										
							Banques		Autres Institut.						
	ETAT	ODE	MISR	Autres	Trésor	NBE	ODE	Autres	ODE	Autres	ODE	Ménages	Administrat.	Extérieur	Total
F.B.C. des agents															} 172,5
Epargne brute des agents	15,4	5,0	6,9	12,5			2,5	1,0	2,7	17,7	1,6	45,1	25,9	36,2	}
1. *Liquidité et semi-liquidités*															
11 – Billets de banque								0,5				8,0			8,5
12 – Dépôts 121 des agents non fin.				2,5			15,8		0,6	3,3					22,2
122 des Inst. fin.						4,6	0,2	3,0							7,8
13 – Dépôts au Trésor					2,7										2,7
14 – Dépôts du Trésor						5,9	3,6	3,0							12,5
2. *Concours des Institutions financières*															
21 – Concours de la NBE															
211 aux Banques Commerc.							2,0	11,6							13,6
212 aux autres Inst. Fin.									2,4						2,4
22 – ,, des banques commerciales		6,5	3,3	22,4											32,2
23 – ,, à l'ODE											8,2				8,2
24 – ,, des autres Inst. Fin.		2,3	0,5	2,8								5,5	5,9		17,0
3. *Concours du et au Trésor*	10,6				0,1										10,7
4. *Crédits divers (non bancaires)*		6,5										2,0			8,5
5. *Valeurs mobilières:*															
51 – Bons du Trésor et obligations publiques					13,3		3,0	1,1							17,4
52 – Autres valeurs mobilières		7,7	1,8	0,2	0,7		0,5	0,6	1,9			0,1			13,5
6. *Or, devises et Crédits extérieurs*						33,1			7,5						40,6
Total (millions LE courantes)	26,0	28,0	12,5	40,4	19,8	43,6	27,6	20,8	15,1	21,0	9,8	60,7	31,8	36,2	

TABLEAU I. *Opérations financières 1958 (détail) (suite)*

	Emplois													
	Entreprises				Institutions financières									
						Banques			Autres Institut.					
	ETAT	ODE	MISR	Autres	Trésor	NBE	ODE	Autres	ODE	Autres	ODE	Ménages	Administrat.	Extérieur
F.B.C. des agents	24,0	27,0	7,7	33,2					6,9	0,2		48,0	25,5	
Epargne brute des agents														
1. *Liquidité et semi-liquidités*														
11 – Billets de banque						8,2	0,3							
12 – Dépôts 121 des agents non fin.		1,0	2,8					9,4				9,0		
122 des Inst. fin.									2,3	5,5				
13 – Dépôts au Trésor				2,7										
14 – Dépôts du Trésor					12,5									
2. *Concours des Institutions financières*														
21 – Concours de la NBE														
211 aux Banques Commerc.						13,6								
212 aux autres Inst. Fin.						1,6				0,8				
22 – ,, des banques commerciales						4,1	20,0	8,1						
23 – ,, à l'ODE						2,0	6,2							
24 – ,, des autres Inst. fin.									4,9	12,1				
3. *Concours du et au Trésor*					4,3					0,1			6,3	
4. *Crédits divers* (non bancaires)	2,0		2,0	4,5										
5. *Valeurs mobilières*														
51 – Bons du Trésor et obligations						14,1			1,0	2,3				
52 – Autres valeurs mobilières											9,8	3,7		
6. *Or, devises et Crédits extérieurs*							1,1	3,3						36,2
Total (millions LE courantes)	26,0	28,0	12,5	40,4	16,8	43,6	27,6	20,8	15,1	21,0	9,8	60,7	31,8	36,2

ODE: Organisme de Développement Economique (Etat)
NBE: National Bank of Egypt
FBC: Formation brute de capital

TABLEAU II. *Opérations financières 1952–58 (moyenne)*

	Ressources									Emplois							
		Instit. financières									Instit. financières						
	Entre-prises	Trésor	NBE	Banques	autres	Ménages	Etat	Extérieur	Total	Entre-prises	Trésor	NBE	Banques	autres	Ménages	Etat	Extérieur
F.B.C. des agents									} 146 {	47				3	47	49	
Epargne brute des agents	28			1	11	60	22	24									
Liquidités:																	
Billets			4						4						4		
Dépôts				14	1				15	7					8		
Concours des & aux Inst. fin.																	
Concours au Trésor		28							28			23	1	4			
,, aux Banques				2					2			2					
,, aux Inst. spécial.					5				5			5					
,, du Trésor	2						24		26		26						
,, des Banques	14		2						16				16				
,, des Inst. spécial.	5					2	3		10					10			
Crédits divers						2			2	2							
Souscriptions du public	7					2			9		2				7		
Avoirs et dettes extérieurs			24						24								24
Total (millions LE courantes)	56	28	30	17	17	66	49	24		56	28	30	17	17	66	49	24

TABLEAU III. *Opérations financières 1957*

	Ressources									Emplois							
		Instit. financières									Instit. financières						
	Entre-prises	Trésor	NBE	Banques	Autres	Ménages	Etat	Extérieur	Total	Entre-prises	Trésor	NBE	Banques	Autres	Ménages	Etat	Extérieur
F.B.C. des agents									140	41				7	48	44	
Epargne brute des agents	24				14	66	16	20									
Liquidités:																	
Billets			8						8						8		
Dépôts		8		25	6				39	29					10		
Concours des & aux Inst. Fin.																	
Concours au Trésor		18							18			13		5			
,, aux Banques			15						15				15				
,, aux Inst. spécial				1	23				24			24					
,, du Trésor							26		26		26						
,, des Banques	25								25			21	4				
,, des Inst. spéc.	18					3	2		23					23			
Crédits divers						2			2	2							
Souscriptions du public	5								5						5		
Avoirs et dettes extérieurs			35						35				7	8			20
Total (millions LE courantes)	72	26	58	26	43	71	44	20		72	26	58	26	43	71	44	20

Tableau IV. *Opérations financières 1958*

	Ressources									Emplois							
		Instit. financières									Instit. financières						
	Entre-prises	Trésor	NBE	Banques	Autres	Ménages	Etat	Extérieur	Total	Entre-prises	Trésor	NBE	Banques	Autres	Ménages	Etat	Extérieur
F.B.C. des agents									} 172	69				6	48	49	
Epargne brute des agents	27			3	22	46	38	36									
Liquidités:																	
Billets						8			8			8					
Dépôts		3		6	4				13	4					9		
Concours des & aux Inst. Fin.																	
Concours au Trésor		1		11					12			8		4			
,, aux Banques				14					14			14					
,, aux Inst. special.			1		2				3				3				
,, du Trésor							5		5		5						
,, des banques	32								32			4	28				
,, des Inst. special	14					5	6		25					25			
Crédits divers:						2			2	2							
Souscriptions du public	2	1		1					4						4		
Avoirs et dettes extérieurs			33		7				40				4				36
Total (millions LE courantes)	75	5	34	35	35	61	49	36		75	5	34	35	35	61	49	36

TABLEAU V. *Tableau économique d'ensemble 1959–60*

	Ressources									Emplois							
	entreprises			admin.		ménages				entreprises			admin.		ménages		
	E	A	C	A	C	A	C	extérieur	Total	E	A	C	A	C	A	C	extérieur
Opérations sur biens & services	1224							248	1472			115	58	80	975	9	235
Opérations de Répartition																	
Intérêts	23					4		3	30	17			7		3		3
Salaires						554			554	409			129		16		
Cotisations sociales, assurances	21	3				10			34	11	5		6		12		
Prestations, Pensions						13			13				13				
Fiscalité				265					265	167	68	1			25	4	
Subventions d'exploit.	10								10				10				
Recettes et dépenses extérieur	11					23		45	79	6			28		11		34
Dividendes, Revenus Entrep. Etat		11		34		6		1	53		52						1
RBE		680							680	680							
Transferts divers		11			8	8			27		19	4				4	
Revenus des entrepren. individuels						450			450		450						
Opérations de financement:																	
Revenus retenus			112						112		112						
Epargne publique					47				47				47				
Epargne des ménages							26		26						26		
Subventions d'équipement			71						71					71			
Prêts et Emprunts					101				101			64		5		10	23
Total (millions LE courantes)	1290	705	183	299	156	1069	26	296		1290	705	183	299	156	1069	26	296

E Exploitation A Affectation C Capital

TABLEAU VI. *Tableau économique d'ensemble 1964–65*

	Ressources									Emplois							
	entreprises			admin.		ménage		exté-		entreprises			admin.		ménage		exté-
	E	A	C	A	C	A	C	rieur	Total	E	A	C	A	C	A	C	rieur
Opérations sur biens et services	1717							245	1962			245	72	97	1236	9	302
Opérations de répartition																	
Intérêts	30					6		12	47	25			19		3		
Salaires						732			732	548			165		18		
Cotisations sociales, Assurances	46	5				22			73	27	7		12		27		
Prestations, pensions						18			18				18				
Fiscalité, parafiscalité				335					335	216	85				31	3	
Subvent. d'exploitation	10								10				10				
Recettes & dépenses exté.	15					30		50	95	8			31		11		45
Dividendes, Rev. Entrep. Etat		17		81		10		1	109		108						1
R B E		991							991	991							
Transferts divers		15				13			34		29	5					
Revenus des entrep. indiv.						576			576		576						
Opérations de financement																	
Revenus retenus			225						225		225						
Epargne publique					90				90				90				
Epargne des ménages							80		80						80		
Subventions d'équipement			63						63					63			
Prêts et Emprunts					76			40	117			38		11		68	
Total (millions LE valeur 1959)	1817	1028	288	416	170	1406	80	347		1817	1028	288	416	170	1406	80	347

élevé: 125 mls. Les imports de biens d'équipement étant de l'ordre de 120-130 mls en fin de Plan,[10] et ces biens d'équipement représentant environ 50 pour cent de la formation brute de capital (le reste étant constitué de travaux et constructions), le volume le plus probable des investissements effectivement réalisés serait de l'ordre de 250 mls, l'apport extérieur en assurant donc le financement de 50 pour cent.

(3) L'épargne d'entreprise est devenue la source essentielle de financement local. Comment cela a-t-il été possible? Sans doute grâce aux pratiques monopolistiques en matière de prix du secteur public.

Conclusions

Le régime nouveau de l'Egypte a réalisé depuis 1952 des transformations structurelles importantes. Jusqu'en 1956 celles-ci n'ont pratiquement touché que l'agriculture (réforme agraire); à partir de 1957 les nationalisations, d'abord limitées aux capitaux britanniques et français, puis étendues en 1960 à l'ensemble de l'industrie, du commerce et des institutions financières, ont modifié la physionomie et les modes de gestion économiques du pays. Le premier Plan — 1960–65 — devait assurer son démarrage au nouveau système économique.

Le taux de croissance élevé prévu par le Plan (7 pour cent l'an) supposait des investissements importants et efficaces. Par ailleurs le financement devant être local, le Plan était fondé sur des hypothèses sous-jacentes d'un optimisme extrême: maintien des imports à un niveau très bas (ce que contredit les exigences de l'industrialisation d'un petit pays dans le cadre du marché mondial), croissance immédiate et forte des profits du secteur public, austérité administrative, amélioration de la productivité sans augmentations de salaires etc. . . .

L'évolution effective a démenti ces hypothèses: le Plan a été financé par l'extérieur (50 pour cent) et l'inflation. Les pratiques du secteur public, en masquant les déficiences de gestion, rendent difficile l'analyse de l'origine de l'inflation. En fait il y a lieu de penser qu'à la fois les objectifs d'austérité n'ont pas été respectés et que la gestion des entreprises publiques a été a l'origine de déficits graves. L'inflation qui en est résultée, malgré l'aide extérieure massive reçue par l'Egypte, a sans doute gêné la réalisation des objectifs physiques qui se sont avérés, dans ces conditions, trop ambitieux.

[10] N.B.E. Bulletin 1966 no. 1 tab. 3/4C.

Historical Obstacles to the Development of a Bourgeoisie in Iran

AHMAD ASHRAF

I. ECONOMIC HISTORY AND EPOCHAL ANALYSIS

THE processes of development in the 'Third World' are of great concern to historical sociologists and economic historians. However, despite the great interest displayed by the founding fathers of sociology in the nineteenth century in similar questions, and despite their historical orientation and liking of historical periodization, present day sociologists tend to be uninterested in both this subject matter and this orientation. In this respect they have lagged behind economists and economic historians interested in questions of development.

Following in Marx and Weber's tradition of social-economic science the objective of this paper is to demonstrate the importance of historical analysis for a deeper understanding of the problem of economic development. From the outset the basic question will be the proper use of history to construct the historical processes of development both in the past and the future.

Historical sociology gives us a structural view of a total society and its historical development. It also directs us into the principle of historical specificity which should be taken as a guide-line in understanding and explaining socio-economic phenomena and their development.

This principle of historical specificity, used as a rule of enquiry and reflection, leads to an analysis of the trends of a certain era as well as to the discovery of processes by which that era comes into being and is transformed into another. On exactly the same basis a model of the sub-stages of development of a specific society can be constructed. The advantage of following such a procedure is that it forestalls superficial and premature generalizations beyond the confines of a specific epoch, whilst at the same time, it leaves the question of a general theory of social change open. Further since from this theoretical perspective both thought and action are historically conditioned, we regard human nature and man's conceptualizations of the human condition (scientific as well as literary and philosophical) as specific to each era. Thus we are cautious towards economic and sociological concepts of an unhistorical character.[1]

[1] See for example C. W. Mills, *Images of Man: The Classic Tradition in Sociological Thinking*, N.Y. 1960; *id., The Sociological Imagination*, N.Y. 1959, especially his article

The division of Persian history into periods is a matter of controversy. A review of the relevant literature will reveal four different interpretations of the historical evidence.

The first of these consists of attempts made by Soviet Iranologists to divide the historical development of Persian society into four stages: primitive communes, slavery, feudalism and bourgeois society.[2] Thus, according to this theory, the Median, Achaemenian and Parthian periods represent a typical stage of slavery.[3] The Sāsānid period is categorized as an incipient stage in the development of feudalism,[4] the period of the caliphs as 'underdeveloped feudalism' brought about by the expansion of the state lands;[5] and in the Saljūq period we witness the growth of feudalism proper.[6] The Mongol Invasion is dubbed as a stage of 'nomadic feudalism'.[7] For the highly centralized state system created in Persia under the Ṣafawids, the term 'centralized feudalism' is used,[8] whilst the nineteenth century is thought to be a period of the disintegration of feudalism in a situation of colonial penetration.[9] Finally, the present century's history is interpreted and analysed in terms of the rise of a 'national and dependent bourgeoisie'.

Although the Soviet historians have illuminated the area of Persian history, their preconceived theoretical commitments distorted their portrayal of the course of historical developments in Persia. The existence of slavery and the ensuing stage of feudalism is doubtful and the Soviet historians have been unable to verify the unilinear theory of historical developments in Iran. Consequently they have been unable to substantiate the development of slavery and feudalism from the standpoint of the specificities of social and economic formation in those eras.[10]

A second approach has been introduced more recently by those who

on 'Uses of History', pp. 143–64; *id., The Marxists*, N.Y. 1961; I. L. Horowitz, *The New Sociology*, N.Y. 1964; M. Stein and A. Vidich, *Sociology on Trial*, N.Y. 1964; M. Weber, *Methodology of the Social Sciences*, N.Y. 1949.

[2] 'All peoples travel what is basically the same path. . . . The development of society proceeds through the consecutive replacement, according to definite laws, of one socio-economic formation by another.' O. Kunsined ed., *Fundamentals of Marxism–Leninism*, London 1961, p. 153.

[3] See N. V. Pigulevskaya, A. U. Yakubovsky, I. P. Petrushevsky, L. V. Striyeva, A. M. Belnitsky, *Tārīkh-i Īrān az Dawre-yi Bāstān tā Pāyān-i Ṣade-yi Heždahum*, 2 vols., translated by K. Kishāwarz, Tehran 1346/1967, pp. 5–67 (hereafter T.I.). See also I. M. Diakonov, *Tārīkh-i Mad*, translated by K. Kishāwarz, Tehran 1344/1965; M. M. Diakonov, *Āshkānīyān*, translated by K. Kishāwarz, Tehran 1344/1965.

[4] T.I., pp. 68–149. [5] *Ibid.*, pp. 150–237. [6] *Ibid.*, pp. 238–324.

[7] *Ibid.*, pp. 325–418 and 419–90; see also B. Vladimirtsov, *Le Régime Social des Mongols: le Féodalisme nomade*, Paris 1934; V. V. Barthold, *Turkestan down to the Mongol Invasion*, London 1928; I. P. Petrushevsky, *Kishāwarzī va Munāsabat-i Arḍī dar Īrān-i 'Ahd-i Moghūl*, translated by K. Kishāwarz, Tehran 1345/1966.

[8] T.I., pp. 491–529 and 530–96. [9] *Ibid.*, pp. 597–664.

[10] See for example M. A. Khonji, 'Tārīkh-i Mad va Manshā-yi Naẓariyye-yi Diakonov', in *Rāhnumā-yi Kitāb*, Shahrīyār-i 1346 (October 1967), appendix, pp. 1–36; see also A. Ashraf, 'Niẓām-i Āsīyā'ī yā Niẓām-i Feodālī', *Jahān-i Naw*, 1346/1967 nos. 5–7, 8–10 and 11–12.

have attempted to revive Marx's concept of an 'Asiatic mode of production'. According to this view the early tribal communities of the Orient (together with a few other societies) by-passed the stages of slavery and feudalism and developed into 'Asiatic societies'. For Marx this type of social system exhibited special characteristics. Of the relationship between town and country he said:

'Asiatic society is a kind of undifferentiated unity of town and country (the large city, properly, must be regarded merely as a princely camp, superimposed on the real economic structure).'[11]

He also pointed out that, in the vast dry territories of the East, the need for water-works, irrigation systems and other large-scale communal facilities creates a superior central organization and gives rise to a historical stage in which overall unity suspends itself over real communal unity and in which, as a consequence, private ownership of the means of production is absent.[12]

Wittfogel, whose *Oriental Despotism* revived the issue after nearly a century, focuses almost completely on the question of the vital role of the water supply in the Orient. Working on the basis of Marx's theory of Asiatic society and Max Weber's ideal type of oriental patrimonialism, he has formulated three overlapping key concepts, 'hydraulic civilization', 'agromanagerial society' and 'oriental despotism'; however, the weakness of this attempt lies in the fact that, instead of undertaking research on Persian history, Wittfogel has rather casually cited examples from the work of other historians to support his conclusions.[13]

The third and fourth interpretations consist of, on the one hand, the work of those scholars who claim that the socio-economic system of the East more or less resembles that of the feudal West,[14] and on the other hand those who stress the differences between the feudal system and Persia's historical institutions.[15] These latter stress the differences between the

[11] K. Marx, *Pre-Capitalist Economic Formations,* edited with an introduction by E. Hobsbawm, N.Y. 1964, p. 78.

[12] K. Marx, 'British Rule in India', *New York Daily Tribune,* 15 June 1853; also 25 June and 8 August 1853; see also Marx to Engels 2.6.53 and 14.6.53 and Engels to Marx 6.6.53.

[13] K. Wittfogel, *Oriental Despotism,* New Haven 1957.

[14] See for example E. Herzfeld, *Archaeological History of Iraq,* London 1935; also *Iran in the Ancient East,* London 1914; N. Adontz, *L'aspect iranien du servage,* Bruxelles 1937; A. Christensen, *L'Iran sous les Sasanides,* Copenhagen 1944; C. Cahen, 'L'évolution de l'*iqṭā'* du IX au XIII siècle', in *Annales* (*Economies—Sociétés—Civilisations*) 1953; A. Ben Shemesh, *Taxation in Islam,* vol. i, Leiden 1958, pp. 62–4.

[15] See for example C. H. Becker, *Islamstudien,* vol. i, Leipzig 1924; A. K. S. Lambton, *Landlord and Peasant in Persia,* London 1953, pp. 53–74; see also her excellent reflections, 'The Evolution of the Iqṭā' in Medieval Īrān', in *Journal of the British Institute of Persian Studies,* v, 1967, pp. 41–50; A. Poliak, 'La Féodalité islamique', *Revue des Etudes Islamiques,* 1936, pp. 247–65; Fr. Løkkegaard, *Islamic Taxation in the Classic Period,* Copenhagen 1950; see also B. Brandage, 'Feudalism in Ancient Mesopotamia and Iran', and R. Coulborn, 'The case of Iran', in R. Coulborn ed., *Feudalism in History,* Princeton 1956.

urban structures of Persia and the West, or the expansion of trade and the growth of a money economy or the persistent and important element of bureaucracy and the bureaucratic nature of land tenure in Persian society. Whilst the former are close in some respects to the views of Soviet historians, those who hold the latter view come close to the analyses of Wittfogel, Marx and Weber.

Of all the various schools of thought it is those who see the structural differences between the pre-modern history of Persia and the pre-modern history of the West who are most aware of the historical obstacles to the development of a modern bourgeoisie in that country. Both Marx and Weber were acutely concerned with this problem. For Marx, 'The Asiatic form necessarily survives longest and most stubbornly. This is due to the fundamental principle on which it is based, that is, that the individual does not become independent of the community, that the circle of production is self-sustaining, unity of agriculture and craft manufacture etc.'[16] Thus the theoretical absence of property in Asiatic Society masks the tribal or communal property which is its real base. Asiatic systems may be 'centralized or decentralized, more despotic or more democratic in form, and variously organized. Where such small community units exist as part of a larger unity, they may devote part of their surplus product to pay the costs of the larger community, i.e., for war, religious worship, . . . irrigation, . . . communication.'[17] The closed nature and undifferentiated unity of agriculture and craft means that the cities of the Asiatic epoch hardly belong to the real economic structure, expanding 'only where the location is particularly favourable to external trade, or where the ruler and his satraps change their revenue (surplus product) against labour, which they expend as labour funds'.[18] Marx concludes that the Asiatic system resists disintegration and economic evolution more stubbornly than any other historical system because its characteristics 'make it resistant to disintegration and economic evolution, until wrecked by the external force of capitalism'.[19]

In Weber's view, patrimonialism, particularly in its oriental manifestation, differs in several significant aspects from the pure type of western feudalism.

'Patrimonial government is an extension of the ruler's household in which the relation between the ruler and his officials remains on the basis of paternal authority and filial dependence. Feudal government replaces the paternal relationship by a contractually fixed fealty on the basis of knightly militarism'.[20] It is in this respect that Weber makes his sharp distinction between the 'fief' and the 'benefice'. The former predominated in the

[16] Marx, *Pre-Capitalist Economic Formations*, pp. 77–8.
[17] *Ibid.*, pp. 33–4. [18] *Ibid.*, p. 71. [19] *Ibid.*, p. 38.
[20] R. Bendix, *Max Weber: an Intellectual Portrait*, N.Y. 1960, p. 359.

Occident and the latter in the Orient. Whereas feudalism gave rise to a consolidation of the feudal nobility amongst the fief holders, oriental patrimonialism meant that the landed notables could not develop into a cohesive social class. The feudal ruler was more bound by the rules of tradition and the power and status of the nobility, whereas in the patrimonial regimes the arbitrary decision of the despot prevailed. Weber is in agreement with Marx that, in this situation, the emergence of a bourgeoisie and the development of modern capitalism is severely obstructed even though a strongly centralized, patrimonial regime is often dependent on trade. The reason lies in the fact that 'the important openings for profit are in the hands of the chief and the members of his administrative staff'.[21] Further 'under the dominance of a patrimonial regime only certain types of capitalism are able to develop. It leaves room for a certain amount of capitalist mercantile trade, for capitalistic organization of tax farming, and the sale and lease of offices, for the provision of supplies for the state, for the financing of wars and, under certain circumstances, capitalistic plantations and other enterprises.'[22] The main historical obstacles to the development of a bourgeoisie under patrimonial regimes according to Weber are a 'traditional attitude to economic activities', 'arbitrariness in financial activities' and the lack of 'a basis for the calculability of obligations and of the extent of freedom which will be allowed to private acquisitive activity'.[23] Moreover, 'insofar as productive enterprises are directly administered by the governing group itself, the development of capitalism is thereby directly obstructed'.[24]

But let us turn from general interpretative models to the specific historical characteristics of Persian society. These can be listed as follows:

(*a*) The superimposition of a traditional bureaucratic machinery (patrimonial and Asiatic) over the real economic structure of the urban, rural and tribal communities. These were operated from the town or 'princely camps' of the Asiatic patrimonial ruler and his staff.

(*b*) The result of this first feature was that a traditional bureaucratic capitalism and bureaucratic landlordism developed.

(*c*) It seems that the coexistence of the trichotomous social system of urban, rural and tribal communities had important consequences for each individual system and for the social system as a whole.

(*d*) The fluctuation of the whole social system between centralization and decentralization. Centralization was always advocated by powerful Shahs and their bureaucrats who constituted an important stratum in the machinery of despotic domination and who had an idealized view of

[21] M. Weber, *The Theory of Social and Economic Organization*, N.Y. 1947, p. 355.
[22] *Ibid.*, p. 357.
[23] *Ibid.*, p. 355.
[24] *Ibid.*, p. 355. See also A. Ashraf, 'Jāmiʿeshināsī-yi Siyāsī-yi Max Weber', in *Sukhan*, nos. 10, 11, 12, 1346/1968.

centralized government. During such periods of strength on the part of the political centre huge public works such as the construction of roads, irrigation systems, caravanserais and so on were undertaken. Moreover, there was a tendency towards the development of bureaucratic capitalism and the expansion of state lands.

(*e*) The lack of a western type of aristocracy, and the dispersion of the landed nobility.

(*f*) The arbitrary rule of the despot over every group and stratum of the society.

(*g*) The peculiar structure of numerous urban communities, and the existence of a money economy and traditional capitalism.

Following these characteristics we can now cite three important objective obstacles to the growth of an independent western type of bourgeoisie in Iran. Firstly, the rise of strong Shahs and a centralized political authority meant that capitalistic activities became dependent on the state and the ruling group. Secondly, the existence of powerful tribal groups, the frequency of tribal invasions and the dominance of the tribes in the countryside during times of weakness on the part of the central power, inhibited the growth of stable commerical activities. Thirdly, colonial penetration, followed by the decline of the traditional bourgeoisie and the *aṣnāfs*, gave rise to a dependent 'bourgeoisie'.

The period selected for this study stretches from the age of the Ṣafawids to the modern era. The Ṣafawid period is of significance for various reasons. It is contemporary with the colonial expansion of Europe, it is a typical period of Asiatic patrimonial despotism, it evidences the growth of trade, industry and bureaucratic capitalism, and is considered as the period of the unification and revitalization of Persia, and finally, in a sense, it is considered as the golden age of the Shīʿite *ʿulamā* and the agents of trade and industry. Following the Ṣafawids we witness a typical period of tribal chaos and the fall of trades and crafts.

The Qājār period is important because it shows the collapse and disintegration of an Asiatic patrimonial system in a situation of colonial penetration. The Riḍā Shah period evidences several serious attempts at the revival of the Asiatic patrimonial system, which fails to achieve total success. More recently there has been rapid growth of bourgeois activities. However, the forces of history are still at work, the patrimonial nature of political domination over the whole society obstructs the development of a modern bourgeoisie in Iran.

II. THE GROWTH OF TRADITIONAL CAPITALISM AND ASIATIC PATRIMONIAL DESPOTISM UNDER THE ṢAFAWIDS

The founders of the Ṣafawid Dynasty were the charismatic leaders of the Ṣūfī and Shīʿite sects, the major carriers of their charismatic orders being the Turkoman tribes—the Qizilbāsh.[25] The routinization of charismatic domination was realized in the establishment of the Ṣafawid Dynasty and was in accordance with the material and ideal interests of the tribal rulers.[26] It is in this sense that 'the beginning of the dynasty can be represented, not inaccurately, as a third wave of the eastwards movement of the Turcomans'.[27] Thus the Qizilbāsh *amīrs* were the major ruling elements throughout the sixteenth century.[28]

However, at the turn of the century, the foundations of power were partly transformed into the patrimonial staffs of Shah ʿAbbās I and his successors. In this way the centralized Asiatic patrimonial domination of the Ṣafawids was established.[29] The members of this dynasty—particularly ʿAbbās I—changed the land appropriation policy to minimize a quasi-feudal tendency which had been increased by granting the *suyūrghāl* in the previous period.[30] They limited the appropriation of the new *suyūrghāls* and attempted to set back the appropriation of *tuyūl* to the original temporary bureaucratic nature of the *iqṭāʿ* of earlier periods. Following this policy the state lands, the crown lands, and the *waqf* lands were expanded at the expense of the *suyūrghāls* and private lands.[31] Consequently, the bureaucratic network and the functional significance of its members increased rapidly—again particularly under Shah ʿAbbās I.[32]

This monarch utilized all the familiar methods of Oriental despots to establish a situation of total power in his territory.[33] He levelled the aristocracy, in order to unify the kingdom. He crushed the Qizilbāsh

[25] V. Minorsky, *Tadhkirat al-Mulūk: a Manual of Ṣafavid Administration*, London 1943 (hereafter T.M.), p. 12; T.I., pp. 500–3.

[26] *Ibid.*, p. 502.

[27] T.M., p. 188; see also Lambton, *op. cit.*, p. 106; T.I., pp. 507–8.

[28] *Ibid.*, p. 507; T.M., pp. 14–16.

[29] *Ibid.*, pp. 16–18.

[30] The *suyūrghāl*, which was granted under the Mongols and their successors, was, to some extent, like the 'fief'. However, the centralizing tendency already realized under Ghāzān Khān and Aḥmad Aq-qoyunlu—the Ṣafawid predecessors—was contradictory to granting *suyūrghāls* and limited the practice. Minorsky says, 'In the article on Aḥmad Aq-qoyunlu completed in January 1942, Professor Petrushevsky used practically the same sources as myself and came to the same conclusions on the purport of the centralizing tendency of the government directed against the fief-holders' (V. Minorsky, *Iranica, Twenty Articles*, Tehran, 1964, pp. 224–41 (p. 241); see also Petrushevsky, *op. cit.*, pp. 72–4; Lambton, *op. cit.*, pp. 197–211; T.I., pp. 469–75, 478–88; Lambton, 1967, *op. cit.*, pp. 48–50).

[31] T.I., pp. 510–11, 551, 557–9, 581; Lambton *op. cit.*, pp. 105–28.

[32] For a good account of the despotic character of Shah ʿAbbās I, see N. Falsafī, *Zindagānī-yi Shāh ʿAbbās-i Awwal*, Tehran 1334/1955, vol. ii, pp. 77–211, and vol. iii, pp. 119–200.

[33] T.I., pp. 543–6 and 556–64.

troops, the old families and the clergy, by recruiting Georgian slaves who were baseless in the country and were his own personal dependants.[34] Chardin says 'il n'y a point de noblesse en Perse, non plus que dans tout l'Orient, et l'on n'y porte de respect qu'aux charges, aux dignités, au mérite extraordinaire, et particulièrement aux richesses'.[35]

The patrimonial recruitment of the staff and its development is manifested in a list of high officials under Shah Ṭahmāsb and Shah ʿAbbās I, presented in the *ʿĀlamārā-yi ʿAbbāsī*,[36] and under Shah Ṣafī presented in the *Khuld-i Barīn*.[37] During the time of Shah Ismāʿīl and Shah Ṭahmāsb, high officials were recruited from the tribal ruling families who constituted the foundation of the patrimonial authority.[38] However, under the despotic rule of Shah ʿAbbās I, new developments toward the consolidation of political domination took place. Patrimonial recruitment of the *amīrs* surpassed that of the tribal *khāns* and also included the *amīrs* who were *ghulāms* (slaves) of the court.[39] Minorsky concludes that 'consequently 20 per cent of the high administration had passed to new elements owing their rise not to their origin but to personal merit and the confidence of the Shah . . . these important statistics reflect the situation at the death of Shah ʿAbbās I (A.D. 1619) who so profoundly changed the foundation of Ṣafawid power. Under his grandson Shah Ṣafī the changes go still deeper.'[40]

Further, under Shah ʿAbbās, the system of army recruitment was changed; he 'diminished the number of tribal forces and side by side with them created new troops, armed with up-to-date weapons and fully dependent on the central government'.[41] His army comprised 44,000 permanent troops raised and paid by himself, and 77,000 of the old tribal forces. The *amīrs* of the new troops were appointed from the Georgian and Armenian slaves of a private household distinguished by devotion to His Majesty.[42]

To summarise, he created a strong army from the non-tribal population, reduced the power of the tribal leaders, split up and resettled some, and consolidated central administration. As a result, a traditional 'bureaucratic landlordism'[43] and a traditional 'bureaucratic capitalism' became highly

[34] T.M., p. 16; T.I., pp. 551–6 and 581–90.

[35] Chardin, *Voyages du Chevalier Chardin*, Paris 1811, vol. v, pp. 224–5, cited in T.M., p. 16. [36] Iskandar Munshī, *ʿĀlamārā-yi ʿAbbāsī*, 1314/1935, pp. 104–24 and 761–7.

[37] *Khuld-i Barīn*, appendix to the *ʿĀlamārā*, 1317/1939.

[38] T.M., p. 15; T.I., p. 507.

[39] T.M., pp. 17–18. [40] *Ibid.*, p. 18. [41] *Ibid.*, p. 30.

[42] See *ibid.*, pp. 30–6; T.I., pp. 544–6, 556; Chardin, vol. v, pp. 292–332; P. Della Valle, *Viaggi*, Brighton 1843, pp. 476, 759–68; Ḥasan-i Rumlu, *Aḥsan al-Tawārīkh*, Sedon 1931, p. 368.

[43] Under Abbās I and his successors a bureaucratic landlordism developed. In the expanding state lands and crown lands opium, tobacco, barley and fruits were cultivated. According to the authors of the *Tadhkirat al-Mulūk* and Olearius, the Shah possessed the best and most numerous cattle in the land. See T.I., pp. 564–70.

developed. The theoretical absence of property was utilized in order to extend an iron control over the basic means of production in the rural, tribal and urban communities. Together with his *amīrs* he superimposed his bureaucratic machinery over the real economic structure of these communities and ruled from the cities which were his 'princely camps'.

Following from his major economic policy of establishing an Asiatic patrimonial type of state capitalism, Shah ʿAbbās created a network of state-controlled commerce and industry. He commenced certain monopolies and royal industries and protected local industry and trade through various measures. The construction of roads, caravanserais, official postal services, and customs houses was instrumental in his policy. The *amīrs* were responsible for providing all facilities and for protecting the caravans against the raids and lootings of gunmen; otherwise they were compelled to compensate for stolen merchandise.[44]

The foreign economic policy of Shah ʿAbbās was to encourage European countries to buy Persian manufactures and raw materials on the one hand, and to reopen the trade routes between the East and West through Persia on the other. He sent commercial envoys to France, England, the Netherlands and Denmark and began active political and commerical relations with these countries at the turn of the sixteenth century. He gave concessions to Dutch and British companies to increase their trade with Persia and to expand the export of Persian manufactures and raw materials to Europe and the Far East.[45]

To prevent the flight of liquid resources from the country he encouraged his people to pray at the tomb of Imām Riḍā in Mashhad and prohibited them from going to Mecca and Medina. He also took a firm hand against the Banyans, a group of Hindu money dealers, whose activities were disastrous to the Iṣfahān economy.[46]

In this period exports comprised silks, brocades, carpets, camel wool, some precious stones, tobacco and dried fruits. The most important article was silk whose yearly export amounted to 22,000 bales, each weighing 276 pounds.[47] Imports consisted of copper, steel, musical instruments, curtains, velvet, paper trays, gold, silver and coins.[48]

The import of the last item reveals that at the time the balance of trade was in Persia's favour, although the money collected by the royal treasury was hoarded and hardly ever appeared in circulation. This predisposition was also exhibited by the rich money dealers and merchants.[49]

[44] See for example T.I., pp. 551–6; R. Z. Ṣafawī, *Īrān-i Iqtiṣādī*, vol. ii, Tehran 1309/1930, p. 78; B. Parizi, 'Jazr va Madd-i Siyāsat va iqtiṣād dar ʿaṣr-i Ṣafawiyye', in *Yaghmā*, no. 2, 1346/1967, p. 62, and no. 3, pp. 121–2.

[45] Ṣafawī, *Īrān-i, Iqtiṣādī*, p. 61; T.M., pp. 19–20; Parizi, *op. cit.*, no. 2; T.I., pp. 551–6.

[46] Chardin, vol. iv., p. 64.

[47] *Ibid.*, p. 162; T.I., pp. 577–9.

[48] Chardin, vol. iv, pp. 162–6; Ṣafawī, *op. cit.*, pp. 70–3; T.I., pp. 579–80.

[49] Chardin, vol. i, p. 64; Muḥammad Muḥsin, *Zubdat al-tawārīkh*, p. 208.

The general rise of prosperity stimulated the growth of the cities of the kingdom, but of the central areas. Since it was ʿAbbās the Great's policy to develop the central cities at the expense of the conquered areas, it was mainly the cities that were the favourites of the Shah which benefited.[50] The most important cities during this period were Iṣfahān, Tabrīz, Kāshān, Yazd, Bandar ʿAbbās, Hamadān, Qazvīn, Mashhad, Ardabīl and Barfurūsh respectively.[51]

Among them, Iṣfahān, Tabrīz and Kāshān were of the utmost importance. All travellers to Kāshān reported its prosperity and commercial significance. G. Ducket who 'went up to Kashan in 1573 reported it to be a town that consisteth altogether of merchaundise, and the best trade of all the land is there, beyng greatly frequented by the merchuntes of India'.[52] J. Cartwright called it in 1600 'the very magazeen and warehouse of all the Persian cities for stuffes'.[53] Sir T. Herbert in 1627 said, 'This noble city is in comparison not less than York or Norvich, about 4,000 families being accounted in here.'[54] The population of Tabrīz at this period was estimated to be 550,000. It contained 15,000 houses, 15,000 shops, 250 mosques and 300 caravanserais. 'There are the fairest Basaars that are in any place of Asia, . . . their vast extent, . . . their largeness, . . . and the vast quantities of merchandise with which they are filled.'[55]

Iṣfahān, the new capital city, was reconstructed under Shah ʿAbbās I. It had been, for centuries, the most famous industrial and commercial city in Persia. Nāṣir Khusraw, the celebrated traveller who visited the city in 1052, reports that 'the money dealers have a special bazaar in which 200 of them work'.[56] In this period it was the most active industrial city in the whole country, and its bazaar expanded rapidly. As it was the centre of patrimonial capitalism, many state-controlled monopolies and industries were located there. The population of Iṣfahān increased from 80,000 in the late sixteenth century to 600,000 in the middle of the seventeenth century.[57]

The structure of the urban community in this period consisted of the Shah at the peak, his family, his staff, the tribal chiefs and the ʿ*ulamā* who together constructed the ruling class. The middle rank bureaucrats come next. The prosperous merchants and large manufacturers, the craftsmen, and finally the lumpenproletarians are respectively located in the downward hierarchy of the urban social and economic class system.[58]

[50] T.I., pp. 551–2.

[51] *Ibid.*, p. 373; Ṣafawī, *op. cit.*, pp. 74–5.

[52] G. N. Curzon, *Persia and the Persian Question*, London 1892, vol. ii, p. 13 (hereafter P.Q.).

[53] *Ibid.*, p. 13.

[54] *Ibid.*, p. 13; H. Narāqī, *Tārīkh-i ijtimāʿī-yi Kāshān*, Tehran 1345/1966, p. 132.

[55] P.Q., vol. ii, p. 250; see also V. Minorsky, *Tārīkh-i Tabrīz*, trans. A. Karang, Tehran 1337/1958, pp. 55–7; Iʿtimād al-Ṣulṭān, *Mir'āt al-Buldān*, Tehran 1294, vol. i, pp. 554–61.

[56] Nāṣir-i Khusraw, *Safarnāme*, Tehran 1335/1956, p. 123.

[57] T.I., p. 554.

[58] T.M., pp. 12–23.

Trades and crafts were developed concomitant with the expansion of the cities in the century. Various strata of artisans loosely organized into the numerous *ṣinfs* were highly active in the cities of central Iran in general and in Iṣfahān in particular. The fact that the historical sources of the period talk more than the previous ones about the *aṣnāfs* is not accidental. For their functional significance was elevated in the context of patrimonial domination.[59]

Each *ṣinf* consisted of the loosely differentiated ranks of *ustādkār*, *khalīfe* and *shāgird*. The *ṣinf* had to certify the technical competence of the *ustādkār*, and a special ceremony was held for the announcement of the *ustādī*. Each had an elective *ra'īs* who had to be officially recognized by the city authorities. In general, the people of every neighbourhood, village and *ṣinf* elected a person amongst themselves, and granted him a certificate and a salary. Then the *naqīb* (deputy town chief) stamped the document, and finally the *kalāntar* (town chief) issued an official certificate for him. The elected and recognized *ra'īs* is the representative of the association for meeting the economic needs of government.[60]

The *aṣnāfs* had the right of administering their internal affairs, but they were subjected to the supervision of the city authorities. The *ustāds* of each *ṣinf* had their own meetings.[61] In the first three months of the year the *kalāntar* would hold a meeting with all the *ra'īses* at his house, where he assigned the share of the total taxes to be paid by each collectivity. Some of the *aṣnāfs* paid their taxes in cash and others in kind (the produced commodities).[62]

There was no autonomous municipality in this period. The head of the city or *kalāntar* was appointed by the Shah. He was rarely appointed from the merchants, the only exception being the *kalāntar* of Julfa who was elected from among the prosperous Armenian traders of the town.[63]

Aṣnāfs had a close relationship with the Ḥaydarī and Niʿmat-allāhī

[59] See for example Du Mans, *Estate de la Perse en 1660*, Paris 1890, pp. 195–211; Chardin, vol. iv, pp. 95–151; T.I., p. 570; T.M., p. 20.

[60] According to the *Tadhkirat al-Mulūk*, 'the *Kalāntar* appointed the *Kadkhudās*, contributed to the reportation of taxes among the guilds, formulated the desiderata of the latter' (T.M., p. 148). See also E. Kaempfer, *Amoenitatum exoticarum*, Lemgoviae 1712, p. 141; T.I., p. 571. In Weber's view 'patrimonial rulers frequently resort to the organization of associations that are held collectively responsible for the performance of public duties . . . all village residents . . . guilds and other occupational associations are held jointly responsible . . . for the political and economic obligation of each' (*Max Weber*: *An Intellectual Portrait*, p. 337).

[61] According to the author of the *Tadhkirat al-Mulūk*, 'the guilds held some professional meetings, but Chardin, IV, 93, asserts that the guilds never met and that their organization was quite loose' (T.M., p. 148); the Soviet authors of the *Tārīkh-i Īrān* are in agreement with the former view (p. 571).

[62] *Ibid.*, pp. 571–2.

[63] *Ibid.*, p. 572. However, Minorsky maintains that 'Most probably both had to be chosen from among the local notables, though we know nothing of the system of their election' (T.M., pp. 148–9).

Dervishes who were highly influential in Persian cities in the seventeenth and eighteenth centuries.[64]

We may conclude that trades and crafts were subject, like the Byzantine guilds and the Mamlūk *aṣnāfs*, to rigorous external state control. Though internally more democratic and loosely organized, the *aṣnāfs* were not like their counterparts in the West, spontaneous and autonomous corporations. The *kadkhudā* or the head of the *ṣinf* was appointed to his position by the Shah or *kalāntar* of the town. On his election he had to be recognized by the dependent city authorities. He administered his *ṣinf* by the help of *rīsh-safīds*, whose intermediary position caused them to consider the interests of merchants and craftsmen; but they were not the spokesmen of their independent interests against the huge and powerful Asiatic patrimonial machinery. The Shah and *kalāntars* through their *muḥtasibs*, or market supervisors in the bazaars, firmly controlled the daily activities of the *aṣnāfs*.[65]

The *aṣnāfs* combined their economic function with political, social and religious ones, and could benefit from a certain amount of corporal autonomy. However, the Asiatic authority used the *kadkhudās* and *rīsh-safīds* by assigning the administrative and tax-collecting positions to them, and thus created serious barriers to the independent development of the *aṣnāfs*. Although the *aṣnāfs* played an important role in the social and economic life of the city, they had no voice in the machinery of the Asiatic type of power system and in the life of the country as a whole.

The main function of the *kadkhudās* was tax collecting and calling on the craftsmen to do corvées for the Shah. As Minorsky says, 'they possessed elected representatives but the latter's competence seems to have been rather restricted except in the case when they had to call up their guildsmen for carrying out corvées for the King'.[66] Those guilds which were exempt from these corvées had to pay a levy called *kharāj-i Pādishāh*. The construction workers were exploited the most. They had to build palaces for the king and the *amīrs* without receiving any pay, and usually during the corvée activities had to live at their own expense.[67]

The prosperous traders, as in other Islamic cities, were rich, powerful and esteemed people. They were supported by the Shah and his *amīrs* who utilized them for their commercial enterprise.[68] They were active as wholesalers, international traders, brokers, money dealers and so on. Although they advanced their wealth, power and status in this period, they found themselves in all of their activities intimately linked and subordinated to the Asiatic patrimonial domination. Shah ʿAbbās I and his bureaucratic agents established a firm control over property, labour

[64] T.I., p. 571.
[65] T.M., p. 149.
[66] *Ibid.*, p. 20; Chardin, vol. iv, p. 93.
[67] *Ibid.*, pp. 20–1; Chardin, vol. vi, p. 119.
[68] T.I., pp. 551, 576.

and materials. Consequently, the prosperous traders functioned as the Shah's semi-bureaucratic agents. Shah ʿAbbās established a registration office in each of the major caravanserais to keep a record of all commercial transactions through his official agents: the *kārvānsarāydārs*.[69]

Shah ʿAbbās selected a chief from the merchants and appointed him as *ra'īs al-tujjār* to act as a liaison for their banking, diplomatic and fiscal duties to the state.[70]

Shah ʿAbbās monopolized the silk trade through firm state control. The state monopoly agents collected the silk from the provinces and stored it in the state warehouses, to supply the inputs of state factories and to sell the surplus in foreign markets. The merchants who were engaged in the silk trade were all the agents of the state. Shah ʿAbbās appointed the Armenians of Julfa as the silk traders whose function was similar to that of Kārimī spice traders in the Mamlūk state in the cities of Egypt and Syria. The Armenian silk traders expanded their commercial activities into other items of commerce and were sent to foreign countries as official envoys. They expanded their trade to the West as well as to the East. They also functioned as state bankers and money dealers in the Bazaar of Iṣfahān. The Armenians of Iṣfahān usually travelled to foreign lands and traded with the liquid wealth of the state or that of the ruling class elements.

Shah ʿAbbās, the royal family and his *amīrs* gave direct employment to the Armenians because of their extensive manufacturing and trading activities. About 60 *nouveaux riches* existed amongst the Armenian merchants, who accumulated from 60,000 to 200,000 *tūmāns* in cash.[71]

The state installed the largest factories in the country.[72] There were about 32 royal workshops with approximately 150 workers each. The annual expenditure of the workshops was approximately 350,000 *tūmāns*. This was the largest enterprise in the whole country and the total expenditure approximated to half of the royal revenues.[73] These state factories

[69] *Īrān-i Iqtiṣādī*, p. 80.

[70] Chardin says that a *ra'īs al-tujjār* existed in all the cities (Chardin, vol. v, p. 262 and T.M., p. 149). According to Minorsky 'The T.M. says nothing about *Malik at-tujjār* who probably was elected by the merchants themselves' (T.M., p. 149); Le Brun says 'The chief of the merchants had to decide on mercantile proceedings and also inspected the weavers and the tailors of the court' (cited in T.M., p. 149).

[71] See for example T.M., pp. 19–20; Chardin, vol. iv, p. 167; Du Mans, *op. cit.*, p. 183; T.I., p. 576.

[72] Minorsky says, 'In the absence of capitalistic industry, Safavid kings, similarly to their predecessors and contemporaries, had to secure production of certain necessaries and objects de luxe at the work-shops of their own household. Many of these *buyūtāt* were simply domestic departments, such as the kitchen, scullery, various stores, stables, kennels, etc.; there were, however, some *buyūtāt* which were run like real state-owned manufactories. Our source mentions a weaving mill, two tailoring departments, the Mint consisting of seven departments, the Arsenal, etc.' (T.M., p. 29).

[73] Chardin counts 32 workshops, whereas the author of the *Tadhkirat al-Mulūk* counts 33 workshops. See Chardin, vol. vii, pp. 329–34; T.M., p. 30.

produced silk and wool carpets, wool and cotton materials, velvet and brocades. They also produced the best copper handicrafts, watches, china, leather and guns. They were in a good position to export Persian goods to the European countries.[74]

As Minorsky says, 'the Shahs are now the largest capitalists; they amass goods in their *Buyūtāts*, they attract and court European merchants, they use their Armenian subjects as their trading agents for disposing of the chief exportable commodity, namely silk'.[75]

Although economic conditions prospered in Persia, and all the historical sources evidence the growth of traditional capitalism during the rise of centralized patrimonial domination, and the country was able to resist the European colonial forces at the incipient stage of their expansion, the total situation was not favourable for the development of an independent bourgeoisie and ensuing modern capitalism in Persia. The trichotomy of urban, rural and tribal communities with the superimposition of the oriental patrimonial authority over the real economic structure of all three community types, and their undifferentiated unity created serious barriers to set in motion structural conflicts and dissolution of the whole system and its evolution toward the other societal type.

Traditional attitudes of the patrimonial staff and the traders, the non-rational practice of hoarding by treasury and money dealers, the disposition towards luxurious living and resulting corruption set strict limits to the development of rational economic activities, modern capitalism and a western-type bourgeoisie in Iran. These conditions prevented the sustained growth of traditional capitalism as well. Minorsky casts doubt on the expansion of capitalistic enterprise and says 'the amount of Persian trade could not be called vast'.[76] The fall of the Ṣafawids and ensuing tribal chaos is an example of the situation which impedes the development of trade and industry.

When Āghā Muḥammad Khān rose to power, total chaos and insecurity was predominant throughout the country. The tribal leaders 'had become accustomed to revolt and plunder, and were reluctant to submit to any kind of authority; the countryside had been ruined by repeated pillage. Security on the roads was virtually non-existent and commerce had greatly declined.'[77]

III. TRADE AND INDUSTRY IN A SITUATION OF WESTERN PENETRATION

The Asiatic system of Persian society and its ruling class surrendered to the West's colonial power and to its ensuing penetration in the middle

74 See for example *Īrān-i Iqtiṣādī*, pp. 73–4. 75 T.M., p. 14. 76 *Ibid.*, p. 20.

77 Lambton, *op. cit.*, p. 134; Sir John Malcolm, *History of Persia*, London 1820, pp. 182–3.

of the nineteenth century. After the Iranian-Russian War of 1828, the ill-fated military expedition to Herat in 1855, and finally the Anglo-Iranian War in 1856, Persia lost its independence and moved into a semi-colonial situation in the modern world.

This peculiar type of 'contact' between the West and Persia has taken place through the process of Western penetration and through direct contacts between Western agents, i.e., the representatives of the colonial ruling class and power élite on the one hand, and the major Persian structural forces on the other. The peculiarity of this total situation is due to the rivalry of the two great powers in maintaining the collapsing political community in Persia. Moreover, the rulers were forced to accept a policy of balancing irresistible pressures within the new situation. As a result Persia did not enter into a formal colonial situation but survived as a buffer state between the expanding Russian appetite for the South and the British policy of the defence of India. Following their so-called 'special interest' the two colonial powers arrived at a general agreement to divide the country into zones of influence.[78]

The rivalry of the two powers intensified during the last quarter of the nineteenth century and their political goals merged with economic ones. This new economic policy is what Dr. Keddie has judiciously called 'concession-hunting' by the two powers in Persia. 'In general, concession-hunting in Iran was a game of speculators and adventurers, out for quick profits, whose wits were matched against those of wily courtiers and the Shah, who equally wanted as little trouble as possible.'[79]

Britain's principal objectives in this period were to establish and expand British trade, and to defend her possessions in India. The main goal of Russia was 'to extend her territorial possessions as far into Persia as was feasible, while laying the foundations for a contest with Great Britain for the commercial and political domination of Persia'.[80]

The major economic concessions may be summarized as follows:

A maximum 5 per cent customs duty for imported goods was extended to other European countries under the 'most favoured nation' clause of the treaty with Russia. Immunity from road-tolls and internal transit taxes which were collected from Persian merchants was given to foreigners. A comprehensive country-wide monopoly of railway construction, mining, and banking was given to a British subject, Baron de Reuter. A concession went to Britain to organize the Imperial Bank of Persia with a monopoly

[78] See for example Curzon, *Persia and Persian Question*, vol. ii, pp. 554–85; R. Greaves, *Persia and the Defence of India*, London 1959; R. Cottam, *Nationalism in Iran*, Pittsburg 1964; M. Shuster, *The Strangling of Persia*, London 1912; *Khāṭirāt-i Colonel Kasakowski*, trans. by A. Jalī, Tehran 1344/1965.

[79] N. Keddie, *Religion and Rebellion in Iran, the Iranian Tobacco Protest of 1891–1892*, London 1966, p. 7.

[80] J. Upton, *The History of Modern Iran*, Cambridge 1961, p. 7.

in issuing currency and another to Russia to establish the Banque d'Escompte, an agency of the Russian Ministry of Finance which functioned as a political instrument. A railroad concession from Julfa to Tabrīz, and a Caspian Sea fisheries monopoly were granted to Russia. A British subject obtained a tobacco concession and another the D'Arcy concession. Persia also received loans with disastrous conditions, in various forms, from the two powers, and finally granted the right of capitulation to the colonial powers.[81]

Although the total power of the Shah diminished, as against the powerful tribal chiefs and the agents of the colonial powers, his absolute power and that of his ruling elements over traders and craftsmen remained intact. The Shah still conceived of himself as an Asiatic despot with an absolute right resulting from the Asiatic patrimonial principle that everything—the land, the people and their property—were his possessions. 'The Shah is thus, in fact, the government—the nation. All are his servants—his slaves; to be raised into his affluence and favour at his pleasure, to be degraded and destroyed at his caprice, without remonstrance or appeal.'[82] Thus the atmosphere of autonomous commercial activities which existed in the medieval European towns and which contributed to the precapitalist formation of a bourgeoisie was conspicuously lacking in Persia.

This situation of total power discouraged the British bourgeoisie—the investors and merchants—from risking their lives and fortunes in Persia. The British government pressed Nāṣir al-Dīn Shah for a life and property decree. Finally the Shah announced an important proclamation which was drafted by Amīn al-Sulṭān with Wolff's assistance on 22 May 1888. The life and property decree is of the utmost significance, because it is a leading idea of the Western bourgeoisie and was instituted to protect British traders and investors.[83] Ostensibly it was not the Persian bourgeoisie who benefited from this proclamation, but British adventurers.

British endeavours for the so-called purpose of 'strengthening' Persia were designed to make her resist Russian pressures and attract British speculators and adventurers to step into the Persian economy. Contrary to the assertions of the British authorities and Salisbury's statement in his note to the Lord of Commissioners of the Treasury in 1889,[84] British economic activities were neither intended to promote the independent economic development of Persia, nor as a latent function did they have

[81] See for example Curzon, *op. cit.*, vol. ii, pp. 528–85; Greaves, *op. cit.*; M. Jamālzāde, *Ganj-i Shāygān*, Tehran 1335/1917, pp. 100–16; E. N. Yeganegi, *Recent Financial and Monetary History of Persia*, N.Y. 1934, ch. ii on 'The History of Foreign Politico-Economic Influences in Persia', pp. 15–46.

[82] J. Fraser, *Historical and Descriptive Account of Persia*, N.Y. 1834, p. 222.

[83] See 'Correspondence Respecting the Issue of a Decree by His Majesty the Shah of Persia for the Protection of Rights of Property in Persia', *British Parliamentary Papers* cix, 1888 (C. 5434).

[84] See 'Foreign Office to Treasury', 2 July 1889 (F.O. 60/50).

such a consequence. Russian and British economic activities in Persia, though fruitful in the dissolution of Asiatic society, were disastrous for the independent economic development of this country.

The history of Persia in the nineteenth century evidences the mounting economic interest and commercial activities of the two colonial powers. The act of 1889 which established consular control over British subjects in Persia was 'the natural outgrowth of the increasing numbers of British subjects who resided in Persia as a result of the banking activities, the opening of Karun, the operation of telegraph lines, and the mining explorations'.[85]

The increasing economic interests of Russia and Britain in Persia gave rise to the growth of commercial activities in the country and moved its economy to the orbit of nineteenth-century colonial expansion. However, the growth of economic activities in Persian cities was of a specific type and had paramount consequences. While in the early nineteenth century the commerce of the country was very limited in its extent and the balance of trade was in favour of Persia, and while we can find some manufactured goods among the articles of export,[86] the situation was reversed at the turn of the century.

'In fifteen years from 1873 to 1883, the value of the imports and exports of Bushire increased by about 5,000,000 rupees. In a period of ten years from 1878 to 1888, the trade of Bandar Abas increased to a similar extent. In 1874 the customs of Bushire were farmed for 40,000 tomans, in 1889 for 99,000 tomans, in 1874 those of Bandar Abas for 30,000 tomans, in 1889 for 53,000 tomans, in 1874 those of Lingah for 6,500 tomans, in 1889 for 12,000 tomans. This growth is by no means exhausted, but that the total value of Anglo-Indo-Persian trade by the Gulf may be expected to attain much larger dimensions in the future.'[87] The exports from Persia to Russia and the imports from Russia were estimated at about £1,164,968 and £881,920 respectively in 1889, which shows a rapid increase compared to the early nineteenth century.[88]

Though British trade with Persia increased in the late nineteenth century and in the early twentieth century, it did not exceed half of the Russo-Persian trade. Over half of the foreign trade was in the hands of Russian firms; British agencies had only one-quarter of foreign trade in the early twentieth century.[89] Regarding the balance of trade in this period, it is not in favour of Persia either in general or in the trade with Britain

[85] Greaves, *op. cit.*, p. 175; see also 'Foreign Office to Law Officers of the Crown', 7 May 1889 (F.O. 60/518), and Wolf to Salisbury, no. 3, Consular, 30 March 1889 (F.O. 60/518).

[86] James Fraser estimated the total amount of exports and imports as about one million and a quarter sterling in the early nineteenth century, see J. Fraser, *op. cit.*, p. 211.

[87] Curzon, *op. cit.*, vol. ii, p. 572.

[88] *Ibid.*, p. 580.

[89] Jamālzāde, *op. cit.*, p. 9.

and India in particular. In the early twentieth century the exports of Persia to England and to India were approximately one-fifth of its imports from those areas.[90] D'Allemagne reports in 1907 the mounting increase in Persia's foreign trade with the total import of 200,153,000 and export of 162,153,000 francs.[91]

The growth of trade in the late nineteenth century gave rise to an increase in the urban population in the commercial cities of Persia and the capital city of Tehran. The population of Tehran doubled in the second half of the nineteenth century. According to Iʿtimād Salṭane 2,000 miles of roads, 100,000 shops and 600 caravanserais were constructed during the reign of Nāṣir al-Dīn Shah.[92]

Western penetration, which was achieved through colonial policy and superior technology, destroyed the Persian manufactories which were important during the Ṣafawid period. As a result European manufactured goods superseded Persian local products on the one hand, and the export of raw materials replaced that of manufactured materials on the other. The nineteenth century evidences the decay of industrial activities in the cities of Iṣfahān, Kāshān, Tabrīz, Yazd, Kirmān and Mashhad.[93]

Flandin, who visited Kāshān in 1840, reports that the import of British materials had destroyed the large factories of Kāshān. The practice of dumping which is possible for large foreign traders who have local tax immunities and low customs duties has systematically caused the decadence of Persian industry.[94] Iṣfahān, which was famous in manufactured materials is now the consumer of 'manufactured cotton goods, almost wholly from Manchester and Glasgow'. And 'of the exports whose value and bulk are both greatly inferior to the imports, the principals are: opium, tobacco, cotton, almonds and rice.[95]

Curzon reports that in Yazd 'silk weaving was formerly the chief local industry, the mulberry being cultivated in great abundance in the neighbourhood; and as many as 1,800 factories, employing some 9,000 hands, were in the middle of the present century engaged in the business. This has however declined, and its place has been taken . . . by the cultivation of the poppy, 2,000 chests of the opium extracted from which are now said to leave Yazd annually.'[96] He also points out that 'in the middle ages Kerman possessed a great reputation for the manufacture of arms; but this, like that of Meshed is a thing of the past'.[97]

[90] *Irān-i Iqtiṣādī*, p. 159.

[91] H. D'Allemagne, *Safarnāme-i az Khurāsān tā Bakhtiyārī*, trans. Faraḥ Washī, Tehran 1335/1956, p. 102.

[92] Ṣāniʿ al-Dawle, *Ma'āthir al-Āthār*, Tehran 1306/1888, p. 90.

[93] *Tārīkhche-yi Sīsāle-yi Bānk-i Millī-yi Īrān*, Tehran 1338/1959, p. 3.

[94] E. Flandin, *Safarnāme-yi Eugene Flandin dar Īrān, 1840–1841*, trans. Ṣādiqī, second ed., Tehran 1324/1945, p. 107.

[95] Curzon, *op. cit.*, vol. ii, p. 41.

[96] *Ibid.*, pp. 211–12.

[97] *Ibid.*, p. 245.

Not only were the traditional manufactories destroyed in the new situation, but the various attempts of the independent Persian bourgeoisie to establish itself failed for two basic reasons. Firstly the resistance of the Asiatic type of social, economic and political order with all the impeding factors of the Ṣafawid period, and without its advantages. Secondly, there was the intervention of the colonial powers on behalf of their bourgeois elements. Two major examples of genuine endeavour amongst the Persian bourgeoisie for independent growth are the establishment of new factories and the creation of a local and national banking enterprise.

Jamālzāde reports that 30 major factories which were installed in the later Qājār period were closed partially due to the intervention and competition of the foreign companies.[98] For example a modern sugar-cane factory, which was installed in 1899 by Amīn al-Dawle, and whose products were of better quality than Russian sugar, finally went bankrupt as a result of Russian dumping practices.[99]

Another example is the failure of Persian money dealers and traders to establish an independent local and national banking system in their country. Persian money dealers were active in local markets up to 1888. The Imperial Bank of Persia, which had the monopoly of issuing currency and other concessions, concomitant with the activities of the Banque d'Escompte, an agency of the Russian Ministry of Finance, dominated the money market of Persia and limited the activities of the local money dealers. Persian money dealers and traders made several attempts to organize independent banks, but failed due to the imposing power of the two colonial banks. The failure of the Persian bourgeoisie to create the National Bank of Iran at the time of the first Majlis is a dramatic story.[100] Moreover, five other relatively large corporations failed due to the same reasons.[101] The growth of trade, the decay of local manufactories and the failure of the independent bourgeoisie gave rise to the emergence of a dependent bourgeoisie in the late Qājār period. Powerful foreign firms opened up their offices or appointed representatives in the major commercial cities of Persia in this period. Curzon reports that six large British firms were active in the British zone of influence.[102] 'A good deal of trade is done by native merchants; but the bulk of mercantile transactions passed through the hands of what may indisputably be described as English firms, whose activity here is in pleasing contrast with the apathy that has been displayed in other parts of Central Asia.'[103] Consequently many prosperous Persian traders were converted into the agents of

[98] Jamālzāde, *op. cit.*, pp. 93–5.

[99] *Ibid.*, p. 99.

[100] *Ibid.*, p. 100; *Tārīkhche-yi Sīsāle-yi Bānk-i Millī-yi Īrān*, p. 54; 'Bānkdārī dar Īrān', *Bānk-i Markazī Bulliten*, no. 1, 1340/1960, pp. 1–9.

[101] Jamālzāde, *op. cit.*, pp. 98–9.

[102] Curzon, *op. cit.*, vol. ii, p. 573.

[103] *Ibid.*, p. 41.

Russian and British commercial firms and lost their independence. The predominance of the two colonial banks over the Persian money market, the apathy of the Asiatic rulers toward the local bourgeois elements in a situation of decentralized patrimonialism, and the intervention of the two powers to protect the interest of their traders and investors, forced Persian traders to work with the foreign firms to survive.[104]

One of the important characteristics of the bourgeoisie in this period is their tendency to seek for landownership in order to achieve status and power. The sale of state lands and crown lands, in this period, gave them an opportunity to invest their liquid funds in land. This should be taken as another obstacle to the development of an industrial bourgeoisie in Persia.

The Constitutional Revolution of 1905, which was a quasi-bourgeois movement, was partially due to accumulated discontents amongst the Persian traditional bourgeoisie and the petty-bourgeoisie in this period. However, it was defeated in a society in which the particular Asiatic patrimonial system and strong tribal forces were predominant. In the first Majlis the ideas of revolution were still in the air and its active elements were in the foreground. Thus, 22 per cent of deputies represented the petty-bourgeoisie and 15 per cent represented the mercantile bourgeoisie, while the landlords constituted only 8 per cent of the total representations. In the second Majlis the petty-bourgeoisie was moved out from the scene, for ever. The proportion of the mercantile bourgeoisie also gradually declined in the Qājār period of Majlis life.[105]

To epitomize the major developments in this period we may say that both bureaucratic landlordism and bureaucratic capitalism collapsed during the Qājār period. Finally the abolition of the *tuyūl* by the first Majlis transformed the administrative nature of land tenure into the institution of private property.[106] All the advantages of the Asiatic system of total power for the growth of trade and industry in the Ṣafawid period were absent, whilst all its disadvantages for the rise of an independent bourgeoisie were present. The rapid growth of the trade and the failure of traditional manufactures and the independent bourgeoisie gave rise to the emergence of the dependent bourgeoisie on the one hand, and increasing petty-bourgeois activities in trade, diminishing the importance of the industrial petty-bourgeoisie, on the other.

[104] K. Khusrawī, *Bourgeoisie dar Īrān*, Tehran University, Memo. 1344/1965.

[105] Shāji'ī, *Numāyandegān-i Majlis-i Shūrā-yi Millī dar Bīst-u Yak Dawre-yi Qānūnguzarī*, Tehran 1344/1965, pp. 185–9.

[106] For an account of the collapse of state landlordism in this period see N. Keddie, *The Historical Obstacles to Agrarian Change in Iran*, Claremont 1960. See also Lambton, *op. cit.*, pp. 152–6, 178.

IV. THE REVIVAL OF CENTRALIZED ORIENTAL PATRIMONIALISM AND STATE CAPITALISM IN THE RIḌĀ SHAH PERIOD

The reign of Riḍā Shah may be divided into two phases, the first lasting from the *coup d'état* of 1921 and his coronation in 1925 to 1930, and the second from 1931 to 1941. He revitalized the Asiatic system of power in the former period and established state capitalism in the latter. It was in the second period that the difficulties arising from the world depression and foreign trade problems made the Shah fulfil his Asiatic patrimonial mission by extending state intervention in all facets of the economic life of the country.[107] We may find a good statement on his policy in the following official remarks which mask and rationalize 30 centuries' tradition of patrimonial intervention in economic enterprise: 'The weakness and incapability of individual initiatives which has been proved since the World War, has forced all countries to abandon the Laisser-Faire policy and compelled all governments to take an active part in the economic life of their countries. Our country has also followed this universal trend, and the government of Iran has directly or indirectly controlled 33 per cent of the imports and 49 per cent of the exports through the state monopolies'.[108] However, we should notice the hiatus between the planned economic policy following the Great Depression in the sphere of Western legal-rational domination and the state controlled economy in the sphere of arbitrary and non-rational authority of Persian patrimonialism.[109]

Serious action in this direction was set in motion by a law declaring a monopoly on foreign trade in 1930,[110] which was supplemented in 1932 and partially revised in 1936 and 1941. Following this direction the government created 17 companies by 1935 for the implementation of the law. Consequently the state controlled the major part of foreign trade and possessed the largest trading companies in the country. As well it acquired an increasing degree of central control over the financial affairs of the

[107] See for example A. Banani, *The Modernization of Iran, 1921–1941*, Stanford 1961; Lambton, *op. cit.*, pp. 131–93; H. Makkī, *Tārīkh-i Bīstsāle-yi Īrān*, 3 vols., Tehran 1324–26/1945–47.

[108] *Bānk-i Millī-yi Īrān Bulletin*, no. 9, December 1936, p. 6.

[109] As Professor Charles Issawi expounded in a session of the Conference, we can understand the situation vertically and horizontally. He means by the former the historical forces at work and by the latter the contemporary necessities. The fact that the nature of political domination in this country has been the fusion of traditional patrimonialism and legal rational authority, since the Constitutional Revolution of 1905, may help us to understand the situation more deeply. However I do believe that the force of tradition has played an important part, and consequently patrimonialism has assimilated the legal rational apparatus into its own framework up to the present time. The fact that the government lays emphasis on 25 centuries of patrimonial domination for the legitimation of political authority is of the utmost significance to understand the situation from within.

[110] *Majmūʿe-yi Qawānīn-i Mawḍūʿe* (8th Majlis), pp. 171–93.

country, and the volume of state financial activities grew rapidly, particularly in the second phase of Riḍā Shah's reign. For example, the estimated state revenue in 1924 was under 237 million rials, while it had rapidly risen to over 3,613 million rials in 1941.[111] In April 1927, the Majlis passed a law for the establishment of the Bānk-i Millī-yi Īrān, and the right of issuing notes was withdrawn from the Imperial Bank and transferred to this bank, which functioned as a central state bank as well as a state commercial bank.[112]

Another state initiative in the Asiatic tradition was in road construction. Riḍā Shah raised the already active Road Department into an independent Ministry of Roads in 1930. Road construction activities extended the carriage roads from 1,286 miles in 1921 to 16,000 miles in 1938.[113] Several attempts such as tariff exemption for trucks and buses were also made to encourage the use of motor vehicles. The import of motor vehicles and spare parts increased four times from 1927 to 1936.[114] There were about 25,000 motor vehicles in Persia in 1941. However, the master project of the Shah's transportation and communication programme was the Trans-Iranian Railway. The project was carried out mainly by Western contracting companies with the assistance of a few Persian companies.[115] Finally, 850 miles of railway with a total cost of 2,552 million rials, which was raised by the tax on tea and sugar, were constructed in the later period of Riḍā Shah's reign.[116] As a result of these construction activities, a group of contractors emerged as a part of the Persian bourgeoisie. Over ten of the contracting companies of this period have survived up to the present time and are registered among the leading contractors.[117]

Serious attempts to industrialize the country were taken in the period lasting from 1934 to 1940. Priority in these projects was given to light industries, largely to make Persia less dependent on imported goods. By 1941 about 200 plants, that might be considered as industrial establishments, existed in the country. Out of these, 30 large factories directly owned by the State were the largest establishments in their particular trades, and some of them had a monopoly of production.[118] Private enterprise was subordinated to the large establishments of the state and functioned under the firm control of the Ministry of Mines and Industry.

The total number of workers in these 200 plants may be estimated at 50,000 to 60,000. About 120 factories employed from 30 to 100 workers, about 10 had from 100 to 500, and some 15 large plants, including some of the textile factories in Iṣfahān and Tabrīz, had 500 to 1,000 workers. The

[111] *Ibid.*, 5th, pp. 316–23, 12th, pp. 528–33.
[112] See for example *Bānk-i Millī-yi Īrān Bulletin* from 1933 to 1940.
[113] *Bānk-i Millī-yi Īrān Bulletin,* July 1938, p. 211. [114] *Ibid.*, p. 212.
[115] *Ibid.*, February 1933, p. 29. [116] *Ibid.*, May 1940, pp. 82–91.
[117] *Ṣūrat-i Paymānkārān-i Sāzmān-i Barnāme dar Barnāme-yi Sewwum,* April 1967.
[118] See for example *Bānk-i Millī-yi Īrān Bulletin* from 1933 to 1940.

largest factories at this time were the state arsenal with 2,300 employees, and the state tobacco plant with 3,300. The most important industry was textiles, which employed half of the total industrial labour force. Consequently state-owned industry employed almost 40 per cent of all workers in these factories and possessed 80 per cent of the largest plants. If we add the number of workers in the state-owned railway system and the mines, the percentage of government workers would rise to 60 per cent.

The most important state-owned factories were sugar refineries, textile factories, cement plants, arsenals and tobacco factories. The total output of 8 sugar refineries which started their operation from 1931 to 1937 increased from 2,300 tons of sugar-cane in 1932 to 33,000 tons in 1940. Over 4,000 workers were employed in these plants. A cement plant started operation in 1934 and its total annual output increased from 25,000 tons in 1934 to 70,000 tons in 1940. The plant employed about 1,000 workers. The government installed 4 modern textile factories which started their operations from 1930 to 1937 and employed about 8,000 workers by 1940.

The most important area for private initiative was the textile industry. Some 20 large textile plants were created or extended in this period. These private factories employed about 35 per cent of industrial workers by 1940. The total number of wool spindles was increased from 2,000 in 1925 to 7,920 in 1930, and to 25,548 in 1940, and that of cotton spindles from 3,842 in 1921 to 16,142 in 1930, and to 200,000 in 1940. However, the spindles of the state-owned factories are included for the period from 1930 to 1940.[119]

Regarding bureaucratic landlordism, the trend of its transformation into private landownership, which was begun during the earlier period, was intensified in this period. The institution of private landed property was well established and received a solid legal basis. The Shah himself confiscated a good portion of prosperous villages and became the largest landowner in the country. Although he demolished the power of tribal chiefs and large landowners and scorned their aristocratic tendencies in the 'Asiatic' tradition, he strengthened and established the institution of private landownership. Not only were 57 per cent of Majlis deputies in this period landowners (and half of the deputies who were also government employees were from this class), but the higher echelons of the military, the public bureaucracy, and successful businessmen were incorporated into the landowning class.[120]

[119] The figures in this section are basically estimated from the following sources: *Bānk-i Millī-yi Īrān Bulletin* from 1933 to 1940; *Āmār-i 'Amalkard-i Ṣanāyi'-i 'Umde-yi Kishwar*, Wizārat-i Kār, 1326/1947; *Persia*, in Geographical Handbook Series, London 1945, pp. 457–64.

[120] See N. Keddie, *The Historical Obstacles to Agrarian Change in Iran*, Claremont 1960; Lambton, *op. cit.*, pp. 181–93; Shāji'ī, *op. cit.*, pp. 174–205.

As far as the development of the bourgeoisie in this period is concerned, we should examine various strata of this class. As we have already demonstrated, private initiative in the fields of banking, transportation, mining and construction was dominated by state activities and no strata of the bourgeoisie developed in these areas. Although in the areas of trade and industry, state capitalism subordinated entrepreneurial initiative, the middle strata of bourgeois elements intensified their activities in these fields and grew in numbers and economic prosperity. In this period the hiatus between the traditional bourgeoisie who resided in the bazaar and the modernized elements who left the bazaar behind physically or mentally, was intensified. The latter strata could easily work with bureaucratic elements and the Western bourgeoisie. These strata supported the Riḍā Shah regime and manifested eagerness for dependent bourgeois activities.[121] Whilst the industrial petty-bourgeoisie lost its functional importance in both periods, the petty-bourgeois traders grew rapidly.

V. A NOTE ON RECENT DEVELOPMENTS

In the recent period, which begins in the mid-1950's and continues to the present time, the resumption and rapid increase in oil revenues which was followed by the growth of small industries, foreign capital investments, private banking enterprises, transportation firms, local and foreign trade, brought about structural change in the society. The social order and security, which were maintained by the use of absolute force in this period, were partially designed to attract both domestic and foreign capital for investment. Consequently, the modern bourgeoisie entered into the infantile stage of its development and grew rapidly within a decade. As regards state capitalism, by adopting the Western capitalistic model for development, the major economic policy of the government became the development of private enterprise. However, a community of interest has been established between the higher echelon of bureaucracy and the economic élites. Without the coalition with these elements, the wealthy bourgeoisie would lose its power and probably its prosperity.

Because the increasing oil revenue is instrumental in the maintenance of the absolute economic and political power of the government, the economic policy of the state, formulated by the modernized patrimonial staff, has vital consequences for all sectors of private enterprise, such as the support of local industries, the attraction of foreign investment and the allocation of money to contractors.

We may epitomize the recent development of the Persian bourgeoisie as follows:

(*a*) The industrial bourgeoisie grew rapidly in this period. Private firms

[121] H. Makkī, *op. cit.*, vol. iii, p. 395.

possess 12 large industrial establishments, each of which employs over 1,000 workers. The remaining 4 large factories of this type belong to the state.[122] The number of commencement permits issued for industrial establishments increased rapidly from 55 permits in 1956 to 596 in 1965.[123] There were over 300 private industrial companies which employed over 100 workers in 1963.[124]

(*b*) The industrial and mercantile dependent bourgeoisie has also developed in the past decade. The amount of foreign private investment increased from $414,313 in 1956 to $12,763,340 in 1966.[125] In banking activities 8 mixed banks were established by Persian and Western investors with a total paid-up capital of $25,000,000 in this period. However, the main area in this respect is the oil industry.

(*c*) In regard to banking, 10 private companies with a total paid-up capital of $12,400,000 were created in this period by leading economic and bureaucratic élites and have been highly successful in their enterprise. They usually utilize the former bureaucratic élite for their executive positions.[126]

(*d*) The number of contracting companies increased rapidly from 52 firms in 1953 to 500 in 1967, including 100 leading contractors who are either former bureaucratic élite members or have a coalition with these elements.[127]

(*e*) Bourgeois activities in transportation enterprises also show rapid development in the past decade. Persian agencies of the international airlines, a few boat lines and several large truck-operating companies have been established. The number of truck-holding companies possessing more than 20 trucks has reached 50 firms, including 10 companies which have over 100 trucks at the present time.[128]

We may conclude that the Persian bourgeoisie is still in its formative period. Though it has gained functional significance, wealth, prestige and power in the past decade, it is not an independent, powerful force in this country and is still dependent on the bureaucratic machinery which carries the burden of the centuries of 'Asiatic' tradition of total power.[129]

[122] *Shānzdah Kārkhāne-yi Buzurg-i Kishwar*, Wizārat-i Iqtiṣād, Tehran 1343/1964 p. 8.

[123] *Report on Commencement and Operation Permits for Industrial Establishments in 1965*, Ministry of Economy, Tehran, p. 41.

[124] *Rāhnumā-yi Maʿādin va Kārgāhhā-yi Buzurg-i Ṣanʿatī-yi Īrān*, Wizārat-i Iqtiṣād, 1964, pp. 178–99.

[125] *Central Bank*, unpublished.

[126] *Ibid.*

[127] *Ṣūrat-i Paymānkārān-i Sāzmān-i Barnāme*, Tehran 1346/1967.

[128] Interview with the authorities of the Union of Truck Holders.

[129] A research project on the recent development of the Persian bourgeoisie is being carried out under the supervision of the present author at the Institute for Social Research of Tehran University. The present paper is a historical background to this research.

Les Cadres Sociaux de l'Economie Agraire dans le Proche-Orient au Début du XIXe Siècle: le cas du Mont Liban

DOMINIQUE CHEVALLIER

L'ÉTUDE d'une économie n'est pas séparable de l'explication de la société qui la régit, l'organise et lui demande subsistances et biens matériels. Savoir comment une économie orientale réagit, au XIXe siècle, au contact de l'économie européenne qui commence à connaître le dynamisme industriel, c'est premièrement se demander comment une société orientale peut se comporter en fonction de l'organisation de ses éléments constitutifs. Une société réagit en effet selon ses propres critères à une action qui s'exerce sur elle de l'extérieur. Quels sont ceux qui déterminent la vie sociale et individuelle dans le cadre économique du Proche-Orient?

Pour répondre à cette question, quelques exemples seront pris dans le milieu humain qui s'est constitué dans la montagne libanaise.[1]

Les minorités confessionnelles, au premier rang desquelles se trouvaient alors la communauté druze et la communauté maronite, n'avaient pu vivre et se développer dans cette zone refuge que dans la mesure où des circonstances historiques et économiques leur permirent de mettre en œuvre certaines techniques pour exploiter les conditions naturelles. Il faut donc d'abord rappeler brièvement quels sont les possibilitiés et le genre d'activité agricole dans cette région.

La chaîne du Liban est bien arrosée à une latitude où l'eau est déjà rare. Elle forme en bordure de la Méditerranée une barrière nord-sud qui retient l'humidité venant de l'Ouest, et les précipitations hivernales, s'accumulant en neige sur les hauts plateaux calcaires, permettent à l'eau de s'emmagasiner dans leur masse et d'être restituée au cours de la saison estivale sèche.

Les meilleures terres arables sont situées là où le climat est aussi le plus sain. Séparées du littoral par de fortes pentes arides et caillouteuses qui rendent la circulation difficile et par conséquent forment une défense contre les incursions, elles ont été dégagées par l'érosion entre 500 m. et 1200 m. d'altitude, et elles ont été aménagées par l'homme en terrasses de culture qui s'étagent le long des versants.

Ces champs étroits et pierreux ne donnent qu'une médiocre production céréalière. Comme en d'autres montagnes méditerranéennes, leur utilisation

[1] Le mot «Liban» sera utilisé ici dans son sens géographique pour désigner la chaîne montagneuse qui s'étend du nahr el-Kabîr, au nord, au Lîṭânî, au sud.

la plus rentable, celle qui a permis de faire vivre et travailler une population relativement nombreuse, a été trouvée dans les cultures arbustives: mûrier, olivier, vigne et arbres fruitiers. Mais pour que celles-ci aient pu être étendues, il a fallu que leurs produits — soie, huile, fruits et dérivés — pussent être vendus hors de la montagne, afin que ses habitants eussent en échange de quoi acheter dans les plaines les céréales nécessaires à leur alimentation. Le Liban ne produisait en effet, dans les premières décennies du XIXe siècle, que pour environ quatre ou cinq mois de sa consommation annuelle en grains.

Les montagnards n'ont donc pu mettre en valeur les ressources naturelles de ce massif qu'en pratiquant des échanges avec les plaines, les villes et les ports de Syrie, c'est-à-dire en participant à l'activité du marché ottoman et à ses relations méditerranéennes.

La position économique du Liban et son rôle politique dans le Proche-Orient s'affirmèrent dans l'ouverture commerciale sur l'Europe, la circulation monétaire qui en résulta, et le renforcement des liens avec la chrétienté occidentale qui agissaient aussi sur les forces morales et matérielles des communautés chrétiennes rattachées à Rome, des Maronites notamment, par la venue des missionnaires et la protection de la France. Grâce à la commercialisation de sa soie et de son huile dans l'Empire ottoman et surtout grâce à la vente aux marchands marseillais trafiquant dans les échelles de Syrie, la montagne fut un lieu de thésaurisation de l'argent jusqu'au dernier quart du XVIIIe siècle. Corancez, consul de France à Alep au début du XIXe siècle, notait que: «L'abondance de ce métal parmi les montagnards, et les trésors que Gézar a tirés des émirs, prouvent également que la balance du commerce est tout en faveur de ceux-ci.»[2]

Cette remarque souligne la relation qui existait entre l'accumulation métallique réalisée dans la montagne grâce au commerce, et la satisfaction des exigences fiscales du gouverneur d'Acre, Jazzâr Pacha, à la fin du XVIIIe siècle.

Expression d'abus locaux qui se développaient avec l'affaiblissement du pouvoir central de Constantinople, ces exigences et la possibilité de les satisfaire n'en étaient pas moins le signe de la dépendance du Liban à l'égard de l'autorité ottomane. Les montagnards ne pouvaient en effet participer aux courants commerciaux animant le marché ottoman et y réaliser un gain, que dans la sujétion à l'égard de la Porte, ne serait-ce que parce que les agents de celle-ci contrôlaient les plaines, les routes et les débouchés dont ils avaient absolument besoin pour se procurer leur nourriture et écouler leur production. L'observation de Corancez est encore sur ce point perspicace:

«Inattaquables dans leurs pays, ils [les habitants du Liban] y font seuls

[2] [L. de Corancez], *Itinéraire d'une partie peu connue de l'Asie Mineure*, Paris 1816, p. 153.

la loi. Mais forcés à retirer du pays qui les entoure une partie de leur subsistance, ils en dépendent au moins pour cet objet. Aussi la Sublime Porte les regarde-t-elle comme ses sujets. On a déjà vu qu'ils lui paient un miri ou tribut annuel. La perception de ce tribut et le droit d'investir, chaque année, les princes qui commandent dans la montagne, droit qui n'est plus qu'une simple formalité, voilà quels sont les actes de cette souveraineté . . . Ces émirs perçoivent le miri, dont ils tiennent compte aux pachas d'Acre et de Tripoli. Ce tribut est aujourd'hui exactement payé. La nécessité des communications avec Beïrout, Seyde, Tripoli et Acre, est la raison de cette exactitude.»[3]

Ces conditions ne faisaient pas toujours du «droit d'investir» un émir chargé de recueillir le tribut au nom du Sultan une formalité aussi simple qu'à l'époque où écrivait Corancez; même si le choix du personnage était imposé par les coutumes et les réalités sociales locales, ce droit se présentait comme une nécessité pour lui comme pour la Porte, puisqu'il s'agissait de lui attribuer une autorité ou de la confirmer en lui déléguant une parcelle du pouvoir souverain. Tout au long de sa carrière (1788–1840), et à travers des fortunes diverses, l'émir Bachîr II Chihâb dut solliciter, pour se maintenir, la confirmation de sa charge auprès du pacha d'Acre, puis après 1831 auprès de Moḥammad ʿAlî et d'Ibrâhîm Pacha, et prit finalement le chemin de l'exil en 1840 lorsqu'elle lui fut retirée définitivement par le Sultan.

L'originalité de ces imbrications, entre les conditions économiques et l'exercice du pouvoir, tient à la structure de la société où s'organise l'exploitation de la terre. Il faut donc savoir en quoi l'économie agraire du Liban coïncide avec un système de parenté, une organisation sociale, des traditions juridiques et une armature confessionnelle pour former un tout cohérent utilisé — et ainsi aidé ou maintenu dans ses formes institutionnelles jusqu'au début du XIXe siècle — par le pouvoir ottoman se manifestant par sa fiscalité.

Il ne peut s'agir dans le cadre de cette communication que de proposer un certain nombre de suggestions.

La mise en valeur du terroir villageois repose sur la petite exploitation parcellaire que commandent le relief, la faible dimension des champs en terrasses, l'outillage, et la tradition de l'organisation du travail agricole et des rapports sociaux dans le Proche-Orient méditerranéen. Mais la parcelle cultivée par un agriculteur et sa famille, qu'il dispose du sol ou qu'il soit métayer, reste soumise à l'effort général d'une collectivité paysanne.

Tapissant le Liban en un magnifique panorama, les terrasses de culture offrent la meilleure illustration de chef-d'œuvre réglé en commun pour

[3] *Id.*, pp. 157–8. Et il ajoute: «Aussi est-ce la plus forte ambition des émirs de reprendre Beïrout ou un autre point important sur la côte. Ce débouché une fois assuré, leur indépendance en serait le gage.»

garantir le travail de chaque participant. L'ensemble que forme leur construction en niveaux successifs et horizontaux, a été élaboré suivant la disposition du relief, et il ne tient que par la solidité de chaque élément: le bon entretien de la murette et du sol de chaque terrasse est indispensable à la conservation de celles qui s'étagent en amont et en aval. La terrasse est également soumise aux servitudes de passage, et fréquemment à l'assolement obligatoire et aux usages de partage des eaux d'irrigation. Elle ne peut jamais être complètement individualisée tout en favorisant la distinction de la parcelle.

La pratique de cette solidarité de travail est commandée par les modes d'organisation sociale qu'oriente à la base le système de parenté.[4] La relation familiale où s'ordonne le renouvellement de l'espèce, et la relation sociale qui naît de la production des biens pour assurer la subsistance de l'individu, agissent l'une sur l'autre pour définir le comportement d'un groupe qui est à la fois familial et producteur. Ce sont les liens familiaux qui, par leur importance fondamentale, soulignent le pouvoir de la culture sociale dans la vie du centre de connexions humaines et de coordination du travail qu'est le village.

Au Liban, les fonctions culturelles déterminantes qui procèdent de structures généralisées dans le Moyen-Orient arabe — et dont le monde bédouin fournit un modèle privilégié parce qu'adapté à la fragmentation des groupements imposée par l'existance nomade —, sont supportées par une économie agraire et de vieilles populations rurales. L'avantage donné au mariage avec la fille de l'oncle paternel, *bint al-ʿamm*, et le constant regroupement des lignées en deux partis, traits qui sont spécifiques de la culture arabe, caractérisent les rapports sociaux à l'intérieur du village libanais, quelle que soit la confession de ses habitants. La préférence endogamique qui assure une forte cohésion au groupe familial par un repli sur lui-même, et la perpétuelle opposition de deux éléments — individus ou groupes — dans la vie sociale, s'accompagnent d'un autre caractère de la structure des sociétés arabes: le cloisonnement des groupes et leur juxtaposition. Sans vouloir chercher ici les origines de cette structure, il faut observer que des hommes de confessions différentes mais de langue arabe, tels les Druzes et les Maronites, agissent conformément à une configuration culturelle identique, même si dans l'une et l'autre communauté des usages, comme l'union endogamique par exemple, peuvent éventuellement n'avoir pas la même fréquence statistique.

Dans toutes les communautés libanaises, les époux s'appellent

[4] La bibliographie sur les relations de parenté dans les pays arabes est assez abondante; mais, après R. Murphy et L. Kasdan («The Structure of Parallel Cousin Marriage», *The American Anthropologist*, 61, 1959), la question a été récemment reprise par J. Cuisenier, «Endogamie et exogamie dans le mariage arabe», *L'Homme*, ii, no. 2, 1962, pp. 80–105, et par J. Cuisenier et A. Miquel, «La terminologie arabe de la parenté», *L'Homme*, v, n⁰ 3–4, 1965, pp. 17–59.

couramment entre eux «fils» et «fille de mon oncle paternel». Qu'il s'agisse de la désignation de la vraie cousine parallèle, de celle d'une cousine paternelle éloignée, ou d'une simple formule de relation affectueuse, le vocabulaire courant rappelle que la cohésion, la solidité et la pérennité de la famille ne sont conçues que dans l'union à l'intérieur de la parenté agnatique. La prépondérance masculine qui s'affirme dans cette conception et cette pratique, s'exprime dans l'utilisation de la seule généalogie patrilinéaire; l'ensemble des parents mâles du côté paternel est appelé *ʿaṣab*, qui a aussi le sens de «nerf», et par un de ces pléonasmes chers à la pensée populaire arabe on dit — je l'ai entendu chez des Maronites du Liban — que «le fils de l'oncle paternel fait partie du *ʿaṣab*», *ibn al-ʿamm min al-ʿaṣab*.

D'autre part, le douaire, *mahr*, que le marié doit verser au père de la femme qu'il épouse, est relativement important lorsqu'il prend une femme à l'extérieur de son groupe; ce mariage se traduit donc par une perte matérielle pour la famille qui prend la femme — et évidemment par un gain pour celle qui la donne. Au contraire dans le cas d'une union endogamique, le douaire peut être très faible, sinon nul, mais les biens, comme les femmes, restent à l'intérieur du groupe agnatique — même si c'est aux dépens de l'intérêt personnel et immédiat de l'oncle paternel cédant sa fille à son neveu. Il faut ajouter que l'autorité et les responsabilités familiales qu'assure ou que renforce le mariage avec la fille de l'oncle paternel, ne peuvent que contribuer au maintien des biens de la lignée.

Deux faits fondamentaux et complémentaires caractérisent donc la pratique de l'endogamie: le cloisonnement du groupe familial par rapport aux autres groupes, et sa relative stabilité économique dans la mesure où n'interviennent pas de profondes modifications démographiques ou commerciales.

L'exogamie n'en existe pas moins comme autre terme d'une alternative, terme qui permet au groupe de s'ouvrir sur l'extérieur. Les unions exogamiques représentent une proportion plus ou moins variable du nombre des mariages; elles donnent au groupe le moyen de se procurer d'autres femmes, ou en en cédant de recevoir des biens, et par là de resserrer des liens d'intérêt, d'en nouer de nouveaux et de conclure des alliances avec d'autres groupes.

Mais ce qui compte dans ces pratiques matrimoniales, c'est la consolidation du groupe. Ainsi le mariage avec la fille de l'oncle maternel, normalement exogamique, ne peut être isolé de ce contexte en raison de la consistance qu'ont déjà donnée à la famille des liens intérieurs enchevêtrés.[5]

[5] Il faudrait d'ailleurs préciser le rôle joué par la parenté maternelle pour celui qui cherche à s'imposer contre la domination de la parenté paternelle. Par exemple, contre l'émir Yûsuf Chihâb qui est le cousin parallèle de son père et qui exerce le pouvoir dans la montagne, le jeune et pauvre émir Bachîr Chihâb acquiert fortune et alliances en épousant, en 1787, la riche veuve d'un oncle maternel de Yûsuf; peu après, les circonstances aidant ses intrigues, il succède à celui-ci.

L'exemple du village druze de ʿAmmâtûr[6] montre que les mariages se nouent essentiellement à l'intérieur des lignées ou entre lignées réunies sous le nom d'un aïeul commun plus ou moins mythique, pour sans cesse affermir la cohésion familiale — sans que, le plus souvent, on puisse probablement distinguer parmi ces liens perpétuellement renoués si les mariages se font entre cousins du côté paternel ou du côté maternel.

Deux familles principales, les Abû Chaqrâ et les ʿAbd aṣ-Ṣamad, contrôlent la vie de ce village qui est un marché assez important du Chûf au début du XIXe siècle. Chacune d'entre elles se réclame d'un ancêtre plus ou moins légendaire; mais, comme ailleurs dans les pays arabes, cette référence à une commune origine permet aux membres du groupe de se sentir «familialement» solidaires, et ils traduisent ce phénomène en généalogies masculines qui se transmettent le plus souvent par voie orale et peuvent être ingénieusement créées ou déformées. Par là même, les deux groupes «familiaux» majeurs du village ont pu en fait s'agrandir ou se régénérer en adoptant des groupes mineurs, étrangers ou déchus.[7] Chacune de ces familles «élargies» se partage en effet en quatre lignées; cette branche familiale — appelée *bayt* ou *jîb* — est désignée elle aussi par le nom d'un ancêtre, mais, de par sa nature et sa dimension plus réduite, elle a une consistance beaucoup plus réelle. Sa cohésion recouvre l'organisation du travail agricole: le partage des eaux d'irrigation se fait entre chaque *jîb*; c'est donc la lignée qui fait valoir les droits de ses membres. En outre, à l'intérieur du village, ceux-ci habitent dans le même quartier, *dâr* ou *ḥâra*, formé d'une agglomération protectrice de maisons; les cérémonies sociales et religieuses tels que les mariages et les enterrements s'y organisent en commun, et sont autant d'occasions d'exprimer la vitalité de la lignée et par conséquent pour l'individu d'affirmer la valeur de son identité.

Faisant un sondage indicatif et sans donner de détails par lignée, W. R. Polk a relevé que sur 189 mariages de la famille ʿAbd aṣ-Ṣamad, 16 seulement ont été contractés avec des familles d'autres villages, 11 avec la famille Abû Chaqrâ, et un seul avec une famille druze de basse condition, et encore pas avant le XXe siècle. Dans la famille Abû Chaqrâ, sur 187 mariages, 24 ont été contractés avec des familles d'autres villages et 11 avec la famille ʿAbd aṣ-Ṣamad. Bien entendu, il n'y a aucun mariage avec les paysans chrétiens venus s'installer dans ce village druze. Les deux principaux

[6] W. R. Polk, *The opening of South Lebanon, 1788–1840*, Cambridge, Mass., 1963, pp. 175–89.

[7] Ibn Khaldûn avait souligné cet aspect de la *ʿaṣabiyya*, de cette tendance au groupement solidaire: «Lorsque les fruits des liens du sang sont assurés, c'est comme si ces liens existaient effectivement. Car, qu'une personne appartienne par le sang à tel ou tel groupe, cela n'a aucun sens, ce qui importe c'est d'être soumis aux mêmes lois, et de subir le même sort que l'ensemble des membres du groupe, c'est-à-dire d'être comme soudé à eux.» Cité par M. Talbi, «Ibn Ḫaldûn et le sens de l'Histoire», *Studia Islamica*, xxvi, 1967, p. 89.

groupes familiaux de ʿAmmâṭûr s'équilibrent ainsi en protégeant leur consistance par la reprise incessante de leurs relations matrimoniales internes; par là ils maintiennent leurs biens et leur «rang», et donc aussi leur rôle dirigeant dans le village. Ce point est socialement très important: il y a peu de mariages avec des femmes d'autres villages; il n'y a pas de mariage, avant le XXᵉ siècle, parmi les familles druzes pauvres qui vivent dans la dépendance mais en marge de deux groupes principaux; mais il n'y en a pas non plus avec les familles druzes de haut rang, et notamment pas avec les Janblâṭ qui occupent la position prééminente dans le Chûf.

Cet exemple fait ressortir deux éléments importants du mode d'organisation sociale: 1° la population d'un village se partage en deux factions que conduisent deux familles principales; 2° il existe aussi une hiérarchie sociale des groupes familiaux, hiérarchie qui s'appuie sur l'étendue des terres contrôlées et sur l'autorité exercée.

Le premier point est conforme à la tendance générale chez les peuples arabes à toujours se regrouper en deux camps; l'expérience en a été frappée en dicton: «Moi et mon frère contre le fils de mon oncle paternel, moi et le fils de mon oncle paternel contre l'étranger.»[8] Les individus qui se définissent par rapport à des groupes cloisonnés et juxtaposés les uns aux autres, «ne peuvent s'identifier autrement que par couple, que par rapport à autrui».[9] S'identifier par rapport à un autre, s'unir à celui-ci pour s'opposer à un autre encore plus éloignée, sont les termes constants de tous les regroupements; c'est par des seuils qui se définissent à leurs limites, que des groupes distincts entrent en relation. Dans un sens inverse, tout groupe constitué — en dehors du couple familial — porte en lui les éléments de sa division bipolaire. Tout se fait par rapport à une unité souvent garantie par son cloisonnement et se définissant par rapport à une autre entité; tout se fait donc aussi par rapport à une constante dualité aux différents niveaux de la construction sociale.

Le second point appelle une remarque préalable qui découle des traits envisagés plus haut: les formes de la hiérarchie socio-familiale sont adaptées à la dimension biologique que comporte nécessairement un groupe qui,

[8] C. Landberg, *Proverbes et dictons de la province de Syrie, section de Saydâ*, Leyde-Paris 1883, p. 63.

[9] R. Cresswell, «Le concept de structure au Proche-Orient», *Travaux et Jours*, n° 20, 1966, p. 56. J. Cuisenier (*art. cit.*) suggère que cette dualité a pour point de départ l'opposition entre deux frères dont l'un se marie dans le sens de l'endogamie et l'autre dans le sens de l'exogamie, cette opposition se retrouvant à tous les niveaux du groupe agnatique. Contre cette théorie et les invraisemblances numériques auxquelles elle conduit, on a notamment fait remarquer qu'un homme, chez les musulmans polygames, peut contracter à la fois un mariage avec sa cousine parallèle et un mariage avec une femme venant d'une autre lignée (J. Chelhod, «Le mariage avec la cousine parallèle dans le système arabe», *L'Homme*, v, n° 3–4, 1965, pp. 126 et 164–73). Il n'en reste pas moins que la dualité dans les relations entre individus et entre groupes, dans le cadre du cloisonnement du groupe et de sa définition par rapport à un autre, est particulièrement bien sentie et marquée dans un système de parenté qui sert de référence et d'identification sociales à chacun.

dans sa formation et son existence, se veut une famille repliée sur elle-même pour mieux se perpétuer et définir l'identité de ses membres. Ce qu'il y a de plus malheureux pour un individu, c'est d'être sans origine, *min dûna 'aṣl,* donc méprisé;[10] il ne se sent concerné par un groupe que parce qu'il y est intégré en tant que «fils d'Un Tel». La référence familiale s'impose donc au départ pour qu'un homme se reconnaisse engagé dans une entité sociale, toujours distincte d'une autre et juxtaposée à elle; cette référence fixe donc d'elle-même certaines limites aux groupes, et c'est par rapport à elle qu'ils organisent les possibilités qu'ils ont d'entrer en relation les uns avec les autres.

Les familles principales des villages qui protègent jalousement leur fonction, leurs biens et leur rang, occupent une position intermédiaire. Sous elles, se trouvent des catégories déshéritées qui ont une faible consistance du point de vue du groupe familial, et qui sont doublement méprisées pour leur origine incertaine et pour leur pauvreté. Mais ces milieux forment les éléments les plus mobiles de la population. Ce sont eux qui sont les premiers à se déplacer lorsque la misère et la recherche de terres les y contraignent, notamment en période d'expansion démographique. Celle-ci qui a surtout été forte dans la communauté maronite, est aussi un motif d'appauvrissement et de mise en cause des lignées villageoises en provoquant de nouvelles divisions, de nouveaux regroupements, et en suscitant des migrations. Les paysans maronites qui se sont répandus, depuis les XVe–XVIe siècles, des régions élevées du Liban septentrional vers le Kesruwân puis vers les régions druzes, ont ainsi animé, à partir de nouvelles possibilités économiques et d'une augmentation de leur nombre, des mouvements migratoires d'où résultèrent des déséquilibres démographiques et territoriaux entre les communautés confessionnelles, et une saturation humaine de la montagne atteignant un point critique dans la première motié du XIXe siècle. A cette époque, cet essor démographique constitue une situation nouvelle qui coïncide avec les nouvelles manifestations de l'impact occidental.

Au-dessus des groupes familiaux villageois, sont établies des familles de rang plus élevé dont la forte consistance interne s'appuie sur une autorité territorialement plus étendue. L'action et les décisions des membres de ces familles dirigeantes restent étroitement soumises aux règles des relations de parenté, puisque ces familles tendent à être les mieux structurées pour conserver ou consolider, à l'abri des traditions, leur influence et leurs richesses sur un territoire qui regroupe plusieurs villages. Entre les groupes familiaux de niveaux sociaux différents où les liens du sang sont pratiquement inexistants, il s'institue des rapports de voisinage et de clientéle qui s'expèriment dans les responsabilités fiscales assumées par les familles dirigeantes à l'égard du pouvoir, et par conséquent dans

[10] C. Landberg, *op. cit.*, p. 56.

les obligations coutumières exercées vis-à-vis des familles villageoises, mais dont les dispositions de base retrouvent les nécessités et les formes de la mise en valeur agricole de la région. L'établissement des rapports socioéconomiques est défini dans les «associations» de métayage,[11] la nature des impositions et la répartition des prélèvements fiscaux.

Ces rapports sont en outre souvent garantis ou renforcés par la solidarité communautaire. C'est un phénomène majeur: par-delà les cloisonnements et les hiérarchies des groupes, la société cristallise la conscience de sa spécificité dans une transcendance religieuse qui s'incarne dans la communauté confessionnelle. Il a donc été presque naturel pour les familles dirigeantes de chercher à identifier leur fonction avec au moins les intérêts temporels de la communauté à laquelle elles appartiennent; c'est ce qu'ont visé de grandes familles druzes et, à leur suite et par imitation de leurs formes sociales, de grandes familles maronites du Kesruwân et du Matn dans le Liban central. Cette conjonction souligne que la force matérielle d'une communauté confessionnelle tient à la structuration de ses cadres, sociaux ou religieux, au nombre de ses membres et à l'importance de leur activité économique. Le rôle des grandes familles et l'armature confessionnelle assurent à la communauté druze et à la communauté maronite, à partir d'origines différentes, une forte solidité agraire qui les distingue d'autres communautés, notamment chiites. La solidarité confessionnelle obéit d'ailleurs aux réflexes sociaux les plus profonds; dans la multiplicité des communautés religieuses issues du Christianisme et de l'Islam, le rassemblement confessionnel est limité aux dimensions humaines de la communauté qui, coexistant avec d'autres communautés, s'identifie encore par rapport à elles selon différents degrés allant, pour les minoritaires, de la place à maintenir par rapport à la position prééminente de la communauté du sultan et de la majorité sunnite, à la définition de règles liturgiques par rapport aux tendances voisines.

D'où ce retour à l'essentiel: la communauté elle-même ne peut être formée que par un ensemble d'entités juxtaposées et hiérarchisées en clientèles. Ainsi les répercussions des affrontements internes des familles dirigeantes, de l'opposition entre le parti yazbakî et le parti janblâṭî entre lesquels leurs membres se partagent, sont à la mesure de l'étendue de leur influence, des liens de dépendance économique qui se sont établis avec les groupes villageois. D'autre part, ces rivalités touchent à la politique gouvernementale en raison du pouvoir social de ces familles et du rôle fiscal qu'elles assument à l'égard des représentants de la Porte ottomane; car l'Etat ne peut se manifester qu'en passant par cette hiérarchie et cette juxtaposition de groupes où les événements particuliers et généraux se répercutent, du niveau le plus élevé au plus bas ou inversement, en

[11] Sur les contrats de métayage: D. Chevallier, «Aux origines des troubles agraires banais en 1858», *Annales Economies—Sociétés—Civilisations*, xiv, 1959, pp. 44–51.

obligeant les individus à se regrouper par rapport à des coalitions politico-familiales ou confessionnelles.

Les relations socio-économiques font en effet des familles dirigeantes les intermédiaires naturels et obligés de l'Etat parce que la fonction fiscale qu'elles sont aptes à remplir, est fondée sur leur emprise sociale, économique et politique. Ce point fixe exactement la nature des intérêts réciproques: l'Etat ne peut se passer de ces familles pour se faire reconnaître, et en même temps elles ont besoin de lui pour garantir leur supériorité par la parcelle de pouvoir qu'il leur délègue pour être responsables du fisc sur un territoire.

Le cadre territorial où s'exerce l'action des familles dominantes, est le district dont l'appellation, *muqâṭaʿa*, se confond avec la charge fiscale qu'il représente. Cette organisation est particulièrement bien marquée dans la zone méridionale et centrale du Liban, le *ḥukum Jabal ach-Chûf wa Kesruwân* des chroniqueurs locaux, «le gouvernement des Druzes» des voyageurs et des consuls européens, qui dépend du pachalik de Sayda. De longue date, des familles druzes ont fondé leur force sur une base territoriale et, dans les régions maronites placées dans «le gouvernement des Druzes», les relations entre grandes familles et familles villageoises ont suivi le même type de hiérarchie.

Selon une définition qu'a donnée Claude Cahen pour une période bien antérieure mais qui reste en gros valable pour le Liban au début du XIXe siècle, les *muqâṭaʿât* sont des «districts dont un notable assume vis-à-vis du fisc l'impôt à un tarif forfaitaire».[12] Toutefois, au Liban, cette responsabilité n'est pas assumée par un notable mais par une famille notable dont les membres portent conjointement le titre de *muqâṭaʿaji*. C'est parce qu'ils appartiennent à une famille hiérarchiquement supérieure dans un ensemble de familles, parce qu'ainsi ils contrôlent plusieurs villages, que les *muqâṭaʿaji*-s peuvent occuper la place d'intermédiaires entre l'Etat et les paysans.

La coïncidence entre la puissance sociale des notables (*aʿyân*) et leur fonction fiscale se manifeste dans les titres qu'ils portent. Celui de «cheikh» — parfois d'«émir» — définit le rang supérieur de leur famille, et par conséquent indique aussi qu'ils sont à la tête d'une clientèle de groupes familiaux; le titre de *muqâṭaʿaji* définit leur fonction à l'égard de l'autorité ottomane, et donc aussi la nature du pouvoir que celle-ci leur délègue pour percevoir le *mîrî*. Pour être efficace, la concession fiscale s'appuie

[12] C. Cahen, «Notes pour l'histoire de la ḥimāya», *Mélanges Louis Massignon*, Damas 1956, t. i, p. 296. Voir aussi du même auteur le compte rendu du livre de Løkkegaard dans *Arabica*, i, 1954, p. 351, et «L'évolution de l'iqtâʿ du IXe au XIIIe siècle», *Annales Economies—Sociétés—Civilisations*, vii, 1953, pp. 25–52.

Sur la valeur du terme *muqâṭaʿa* pour l'administration centrale ottomane: H. A. R. Gibb et H. Bowen, *Islamic Society and the West*, vol. i, part I, pp. 132–4, et part II, pp. 21–2.

sur un état de fait — la supériorité acquise par une famille sur plusieurs groupes familiaux villageois — et par là même elle le consacre; corollairement, le prestige et la fortune d'une famille dominante ne se maintiennent que par la parcelle de pouvoir qui lui est déléguée pour qu'elle puisse remplir son rôle fiscal. L'administration ottomane a consolidé une hiérarchie socio-familiale en l'utilisant pour imposer un pays difficile d'accès non seulement par son relief, mais par le cloisonnement des groupes.

Si les pachas doivent passer par cette structure sociale pour faire valoir indirectement leur autorité — ce qui est d'ailleurs conforme à l'esprit et aux méthodes de l'administration ottomane —, le paiement du tribut n'en est pas moins le meilleur signe d'allégeance à la Porte. La charge fiscale théoriquement temporaire qu'implique le titre de *muqâṭaʿaji*, témoigne aussi que la notion et le fait de la propriété éminente du sultan sur les terres labourées sont bien affirmés au Liban.

A l'échelon le plus élevé de la hiérarchie socio-familiale, la famille des émirs Chihâb fournit ceux qui sont responsables devant le gouverneur de la province du versement de l'impôt de «la Montagne», et y exercent par conséquent l'autorité la plus étendue. La force de l'émir Bachîr, la durée de son pouvoir, ont tenu en bonne partie à sa capacité à lever les taxes — donc à satisfaire les demandes du pacha afin de conserver sa fonction — avec l'aide de ses proches qu'il plaça souvent dans les fonctions occupées jusqu'alors par des *muqâṭaʿaji*-s, après avoir écarté ceux-ci ou restreint leurs responsabilités.

Cette politique a visé à faire entrer tous les groupes libanais plus directement dans sa clientèle, à renforcer ainsi son autorité au-delà des perpétuelles rivalités divisant les familles dominantes y compris la sienne. Mais par là elle a contribué à ébranler la hiérarchie établie en affaiblissant les *muqâṭaʿaji*-s.

Cet affaiblissement est aussi matériel, dans une période que ponctuent le ralentissement du commerce extérieur à cause des événements européens à la charnière des deux siècles, puis une reprise, après 1825, qui souligne le nouveau déséquilibre s'instituant entre l'économie occidentale et l'économie orientale. Les augmentations d'impôts qui ont été exigées à partir de Jazzâr Pacha, avec le concours de l'émir Bachîr, ont fort probablement entraîné une diminution des réserves monétaires du Liban. Il y a eu ainsi, à la fin du XVIIIe siècle et au début du XIXe siècle, une déthésaurisation d'origine fiscale, avant même que le renouvellement du commerce de l'Europe s'industrialisant provoque une très forte hémorragie de métaux précieux par les ports du Levant, dans les années 1830 et 1840.[13]

[13] Sur les sorties de monnaies et métaux précieux dans les années 1830 et 1840: D. Chevallier, 'Western Development and Eastern Crisis in the Mid-Nineteenth Century', dans W. R. Polk et R. L. Chambers, *The Beginnings of Modernization in the Middle East*, Chicago 1968.

Ces faits économiques s'ajoutent aux conséquences de l'augmentation démographique pour diminuer la puissance réelle des familles dominantes, tout en les rendant par compensation plus exigeantes, et pour accroître la gêne et le mécontentement des paysans. Après l'exil de l'émir Bachîr, le rétablissement du contrôle de la Porte en 1840, et la perte du pouvoir par la famille Chihâb, les réactions des *muqâṭaʿaji*-s ne font que souligner la mise en cause du système de la *muqâṭaʿa* que déterminent, sous l'effet de l'action européenne, la modification des méthodes et de la nature des échanges commerciaux, et la politique de réforme du gouvernement turc.

Ce sont les éléments qui sont liés au pouvoir de l'Etat, à sa fiscalité — elle-même définie par un certain stade économique et une certaine forme d'organisation sociale —, qui sont les premiers atteints lorsque commencent à se modifier des rapports économiques et l'attitude du gouvernement. Mais, si la hiérarchie socio-familiale est ainsi ébranlée, la structure sociale spécifique, celle des groupes cloisonnés et juxtaposés, demeure. Le rôle des familles villageoises dans les mouvements paysans du milieu du XIXe siècle le montre bien.

C'est sur une société dont l'expérience historique est très différente de celle de l'Europe que l'impact occidental agit au XIXe siècle. Probablement est-ce parce que les relations entre la culture occidentale et la culture orientale ont été depuis lors soumises à la prépondérance de la première, que bien des confusions sur la nature de cette société et de ses réflexes ont été entretenues jusqu'à nos jours.

L'organisation du Proche-Orient au début du XIXe siècle se distingue nettement de celle qu'a connue l'Europe occidentale avant la révolution industrielle. Des mots tels que «fief», «féodal», «seigneur» . . . portent des notions qui correspondent à un tout autre système, à une toute autre culture, à un tout autre esprit, que celles qui permettent de définir et d'expliquer les réalités du Proche-Orient. Il est donc temps de se débarrasser d'un vocabulaire inadapté à l'analyse de ces réalités, car son emploi a déjà trop souvent conduit à des contresens.

Pour étudier les «changements» qui surviennent à partir du XIXe siècle, il faut en effet savoir par rapport à quoi ils se font. Il ne suffit pas de déterminer ce qui provoque ces changements par l'extérieur, et à quel rythme ils se font; il est d'abord nécessaire de repérer sur quel milieu, sur quelles structures ils agissent, pour comprendre ensuite comment celles-ci se comportent. C'est cette question qui a retenu notre attention dans la présentation de cadres sociaux par rapport auxquels l'action des faits économiques doit être interprétée.

Il est en effet impossible de négliger la nature et les motifs des réactions humaines dans leur spécificité sociale et leur adaptation à un mode de vie agraire. Au XIXe siècle, sous l'aiguillon de mutations provoquées par une action extérieure, devant l'irruption d'un autre temps, les sociétés du Moyen-Orient réagissent suivant les nécessités, les habitudes et les possibilités que leur offrent les cadres où elles se sont historiquement construites.

The Role of Foreign Trade in the Economic Development of Iraq, 1864–1964: A Study in the Growth of a Dependent Economy

MOHAMMAD SALMAN HASAN

I. INTRODUCTION

THE stages of economic growth, the position of external payments, and the roles of foreign trade, are still controversial subjects in the field of the recent economic history of the underdeveloped countries and of their economic development policies. Some light might be shed on this subject by examining the economic development of Iraq during the past hundred years.

The recent economic history of Iraq seems to fall into three distinct phases or states of development. In the first place, there was the state characterized by the failure of the immediate leap from a subsistence economy to a modern economy, during the 1817–68 period in general and during the governorship of Dāwūd Pasha, 1817–31, in particular. Dāwūd Pasha introduced the first modern munitions factory, textile plant, water-oil-pump, printing press and school to Iraq, which he attempted to govern independently of the Sublime Porte at Constantinople and of the British Residency at Baghdad. But this attempt proved to be abortive owing to the rising forces of foreign economic expansion and penetration in Iraq.

Secondly, there came the stage of transition from a subsistence economy to a foreign-trade oriented economy, during the 1869–1951 period, during which the backward economy of Iraq adjusted itself to the forces of the world market and became increasingly dependent upon it. It is, perhaps, necessary to point out that the 1939–51 sub-period might be considered as a prelude to the rise of the following phase of development.

Finally, the stage of the transformation of the Iraqi economy into an oil-export economy has reigned supreme from 1952 onwards, in spite of the development of the counter-forces of land reform and industrialization that have been introduced since the 1958 Revolution.

In the course of the past hundred years, the Iraqi economy found itself in three distinct phases with regard to its external trade and payments position. First, the export trade acted as an 'engine of growth' during the 1869–1914 period, as it generally increased faster than population, income and imports. Secondly, there came the phase where import substitution set the pace during the 1918–51 period. Finally, unbalanced economic growth and structural inflation seem to characterize the oil-export economy especially since 1951.

Perhaps it is the central theme of this paper to examine the various roles of foreign trade in the development of the Iraqi economy. Theoretically, four specific roles and one general role of foreign trade between the advanced and the backward economies have been distinguished.

In the first place, the deficiencies of the home market, either in total demand or in the response of important sectors, explain why it usually falls to foreign trade to give an economy that upward twist which sets it on the development road. Thus the growth of the export trade is supposed not only to contribute to the extension of the market, but also to the expansion of total output through the utilization of surplus productive capacity of land and labour, to specialization in the production of the commodity in which the economy enjoys comparative cost advantages, to the consequent division of labour with its improved skill and productivity, and ultimately to a rise in the productivity of land and labour.

Secondly, the common result of the extension of the market and the increase in productivity, themselves the consequences of the growth of the export trade, is increase in output and income. Out of greater output, more should be saved and invested. Thus the growth of foreign trade stimulates capital accumulation, and ultimately accelerates the rate of economic growth.

Thirdly, the growth of the import trade creates new tastes and patterns of consumption which are thought to stimulate new energies for work, and a new willingness to make the best use of available resources and to bring forth new techniques and better knowledge, which direct domestic saving into productive investment, so that extra income may become available to buy the new goods.

Fourthly, the growth of foreign trade is said to have generated external economies. It also stimulates home industries, as the facilities created for the export industries, such as communications, training facilities and engineering services, are also available for the home industries, which are also induced, through the competitive market process, to introduce innovations designed to increase their productivity.

Finally, there is the question of whether these four specific roles of foreign trade in economic development have raised backward economies to the level of self-sustained economic growth or frozen their economic structure and pattern of production at a stage which make them chronic export economies dependent upon the vicissitudes of the world market.

Section II of this paper will examine the growth of the 'export-propelled' sector; while Section III will deal with the 'import-propelled' sector of the economy. The major changes in the structure of the economy as a whole are discussed in Section IV; while Section V is devoted to the study of the growth of economic dependence on the oil-export economy.

II. THE GROWTH OF THE EXPORT TRADE, THE EXPANSION OF AGRICULTURAL PRODUCTION AND THE DECLINE OF AGRICULTURAL PRODUCTIVITY

The basic characteristics of the growth of the Iraqi export trade, during the period 1864–1958, may be described as follows: first of all, its more rapid expansion in the early period up to the First World War than in the interwar period; it rose from £147,000 per annum in 1864–71 to £2,960,000 in 1912–13, a twenty-fold increase, whereas it rose more slowly to £3,629,000 per annum in 1933–9, or by one-quarter only. These export trends were consistent with and largely explicable by the nineteenth-century secular expansion in world income and trade and the Great Depression of the interwar period.

Secondly, the expansion in the Iraqi export trade up to the First World War was due much more to the growth of the quantity of exports than to any significant rise in their prices; while the later and slower growth of exports was due rather more to the decline in the export prices than to any fall in the quantity of exports.

As to the period 1940–58, the quantity of agricultural exports continued to rise absolutely, despite the fall in their prices relatively. On the other hand, pastoral exports suffered from a decline in their quantities, despite the relative improvement in their prices.

Thirdly, although pastoral exports (especially wool) and agricultural exports (especially dates) were of more or less the same importance in the total value of exports during the 1860's, the relative position of agricultural exports steadily improved, sometimes amounting to as much as four-fifths, but becoming responsible for three-fourths of the total value of exports from the 1930's to the 1950's.

Fourthly, the direction of the Iraqi export trade shifted increasingly away from Middle Eastern markets to Indian and European markets; so much so that the share of European markets rose from under one-third in the 1860's to the point at which the markets of Great Britain and its Empire only bought from one-half to two-thirds of Iraqi exports just before the First World War. The Middle Eastern markets, which accounted for as much as two-thirds during the 1860's, absorbed one-quarter of Iraqi exports on the eve of the First World War, and during the 1930's, and only one-fifth during the 1950's.

Fifthly, with the shift of the Iraqi export trade towards the world capitalist market, there developed many foreign and local trading firms which handled the export of dates and grain. But the keen competition between them led to the development, especially in the interwar period, of the monopoly by the British Andrew Weir Co. of the dates and barley export trade later in the Second World War and in the postwar years. This tendency to concentration in the export trade was accompanied by rising rates of trading profits, from about 8 per cent on the eve of the First World War to around 50–60 per cent during the postwar years.

The nineteenth-century secular growth in world, and especially European, income and demand for foodstuffs and raw materials, facilitated by the development of modern transport (especially the opening of the Suez Canal in 1869 and the launching of steam navigation in the Tigris in 1861), widened the market for Iraqi produce. Producing for export did not have the same disadvantages as producing for the home market. It did not depend on demand growing appropriately in other sectors of the economy. Nor did it depend on effective demand at home. The deficiency of the latter was due to the low productivity of the relatively sparse population of Iraq.

The rising European demand for foodstuffs and raw materials provided outlets for surplus productive capacity in Iraq. Although the Iraqi population was sparse relative to resources, over one-third of the people consisted of largely 'unproductive' nomadic tribes. The gradual growth of modern means of transport rendered their dependence on the camel-caravan trade increasingly precarious. On the other hand, the slow development of law and order, through the slow but definite growth of governmental control, made plunder an unprofitable means of livelihood. The nomadic population of Iraq constituted, therefore, a large potential supply of labour for pastoral and agricultural production. This became available for productive employment, quite apart from the natural increase of population.

During the 1860's, only a limited proportion of the grazing and cultivable areas was actually used. The cultivated area was probably well under 150,000 *dūnums*. The surplus capacity of land was due to the relatively low level of productivity and demand of the urban population, lack of adequate means of transport, the absence of security of tenure, the high tax rates and the oppressive methods of collection and last, but not least, the great risk imposed by the hungry, plundering nomads. There were also the twin problems of flood control and irrigation.

Thus the expansion of European demand for Iraq's produce of wool, dates and grain was satisfied by the utilization of Iraq's surplus productive capacity of land and labour. The economic process whereby the surplus productive capacity was used for the satisfaction of the rising European demand took the form of a decline in subsistence agriculture and pasture, and an expansion of commercial production for exports. This transformation was made gradually possible and increasingly profitable essentially by the change-over from tribal landownership to the *tapu* or private land system. Thus, the *mīrī* or state land fell from about four-fifths during the 1860's to about 60 per cent during 1933–58 period. But the arable proportion of the *mīrī* land was rather small, as it did not exceed five million *dūnums*. *Tapu* land rose from about 20 per cent during the 1860's to about 30 per cent on the eve of the 1958 Revolution, while the remaining 10 per cent consisted of waste lands and religious endowments.

The rise of modern transport and the development of law and order pushed both tribesmen and *shaykhs* towards grazing or cultivation. The increasing foreign demand for pastoral and agricultural produce provided an alternative to nomadic life. Nomads who were no longer in a position to rely on the camel or plunder for their livelihood, but were still subject to the discipline of tribal organization regarding the relations between the followers and their leaders, had no alternative but to follow their *shaykhs* into settlement on the land.

Shaykhs, town notables and bureaucratic officials and officers found it in their interest to settle tribes on the land, which they gradually acquired at a nominal price over the head of the cultivators. In this way the tribal system was transformed into the system of private landownership. They became landlords, entitled to a substantial share in the crops which they sold to merchants; the latter marketed the surplus agricultural produce—the *tapu* crop share—in the towns and abroad. The share of landlords in agricultural produce increased in proportion to the expansion in production, the transformation of tribal into *tapu* landownership, and the decline of subsistence relative to commercial agriculture—but, above all, in proportion to the growth of exports and the development of law and order which made practicable the effective appropriation of the *tapu* crop share.

The expansion of foreign demand for Iraqi produce provided an alternative to nomadic life and made the extension of cultivation profitable. The interaction between foreign demand and the local surplus capacity of land and labour resulted in the growth of the rural population, the growth of agricultural output and exports and an increase in government revenues from agriculture and livestock.

This agricultural expansion followed a simple pattern. It rose rapidly from the 1860's till the 1920's, apart from the decline ensuing from the ravages of the First World War; but the high rate of growth tapered off as a result of the Great Depression. Despite the variation in the rate of growth, the absolute expansion in agricultural production is unmistakable. Throughout this period (from the 1860's to 1950's) grain production rose by about 1 per cent per annum and that of dates slightly more. The area under cultivation extended fairly rapidly, from probably less than 100,000 *dūnums* in the 1860's to about 1,613,000 *dūnums* in 1913, to 9,258,000 *dūnums* during the Second World War, and then to about 16 million *dūnums* during the 1950's. This means that the agricultural area increased ten times after the First World War, or doubled every five years. The over-all growth of exports was undoubtedly higher than the expansion of production or the extension of cultivation, increasing at around 2·7 per cent per annum.

The rapid growth of the Iraqi export trade was accompanied by an increase in the proportion of the cultivated area falling under the control and ownership of tribal *shaykhs*, who received a substantial share of the crop as rent. This surplus agricultural produce was channelled into exports on an increasing scale, because the absentee landlords developed urban consumption, without any saving habits and even with contempt for business or investment acumen. Apart from their relatively minor expenditure on housing and domestic servants, their bulk of the income was spent on consumption imports. Thus, up to the end of the Second World War, two-thirds of the value of imports almost invariably consisted of such consumer goods as food, drink, tobacco, textiles, clothing and household requirements. During the postwar period, the expenditure of *shaykhs* on ostentatious consumption imports fell as a proportion of total imports, but increased in absolute value. No significant change is to be observed in the pattern of expenditure of tribal landlords, except in the construction of urban buildings and the acquisition of real estate in the main towns, especially Baghdad, up to the Revolution of 14 July 1958.

The expenditure of the greater part of the proceeds of surplus agricultural produce on consumption meant that there was very little investment in maintaining, let alone improving, the fertility of the soil, flood control, and the quality of seed. Nor were the peasants induced to accumulate and invest in the land, even if they had been in a position to do so, as the fruits of such developments would have had to be shared with the absentee landlords. What there was of investment in opening new canals was largely undertaken by the peasantry or the government. It was only when there was a shortage of labour that the *shaykhs* made advances to tribal cultivators.

Nor did the government have adequate finances to control the floods and radically improve the system of irrigation and drainage, as the agricultural revenue was hardly sufficient for the requirements of the current expenditure of the government. Even when financial resources became available after 1952, the prevailing semi-feudal system militated against the formation and execution of a well-co-ordinated irrigation and drainage policy which would increase agricultural production in proportion to agricultural investment expenditure.

Thus flood control and irrigation projects put into operation by the government, partly during the interwar period but mainly during the

1958 Revolution, have had a necessarily limited impact on agriculture as a whole. Equally limited were the improvements in cultivation and irrigation introduced by urban landowners, especially the small and medium proprietors in the north and around Ḥilla and the small-holders of the date plantations of Basra. But the rise of various groups of merchant-tractorists, especially in Mosul, facilitated the increase in wheat production during the rainfall years of the postwar period.

The greater part of the agricultural area remained, therefore, to be cultivated with traditional instruments of production. Nor had agricultural methods undergone any significant change, despite the efforts of the Government Demonstration farms in Baghdad. Thus, up to the 1958 Revolution agriculture remained at the mercy of floods—the last and most devastating took place in 1954—droughts, and locusts, with the urbanized *shaykhs* uninterested in the improvement of the land and the government subject to their influence and therefore unable to undertake land reform, while the majority of the peasantry were illiterate, unhealthy and underfed and the productivity of the land was on the decline.

The growth of the Iraqi export trade stimulated the expansion of agricultural and pastoral production. This was not, however, accompanied by any significant improvement in the methods and instruments of production. Indeed, the introduction of pump-driven irrigation, the specialization in barley production for export and the limited extension of cotton and flax, fruits and vegetables, did not even off-set the effects of increasing salination of the soil. Thus, average grain yields actually declined from 225 kilos per *dūnum* during the 1920's, to 187 kilos in the 1930's, and further to 143 kilos in the 1950's.

The growth of foreign demand which spurred the expansion of commercial production in agriculture, as shown by the rising ratio of exports to production and correspondingly in the relative decline in subsistence economy, did not help to raise the productivity of the land, which was actually falling, as the system of irrigation, the method of production and the economic and cultural level of the peasantry had not undergone any radical change.

The declining productivity of the land and the growth of rural population more rapidly than production—the rate of growth of the former was twice as high as that of the latter—resulted in a fall in the output per head of the pastoral and agricultural population. Thus the annual output of grain fell from 1,000 kilos per head of the rural population in the 1880's, to 560 kilos during the 1930's and further to 505 kilos during the 1950's.

The increasing effective share of the landowners in a relatively declining agricultural production meant a fall in the standard of life of the Iraqi peasantry. This was reflected, among other things, in the increasing indebtedness of the peasantry and the rising rural exodus to the towns.

The declining agricultural productivity, and the falling income of the peasantry, are characteristics of the phenomenon of rural underdevelopment, which led, on the one hand, to the intensification of rural unemployment—and on the other hand to a large-scale rural exodus. The active population in the rural areas rose from about 1,399,000 in 1947 to about 1,814,000 in 1957, while the number of persons employed in agriculture increased from 748,000 to 852,000 respectively. This indicates that the increase of the active rural population was four times as great as the increase in the number of peasants actually employed in agriculture. Accordingly, the number of unemployed peasants rose from 651,000 in 1947 to about 962,000 in 1957, or by 311,000 during the decades between the two population censuses, or at the rate of 31,100 per annum. The figures for the rural exodus also increased from 300,000 persons during the period up to 1947 to about 450,000 during the decade up to 1957, or from 25,000 persons per annum before 1947 to about 45,000 persons annually up to the 1958 Revolution.

Thus, despite the growth of the Iraqi export trade, the extension of agricultural and pastoral land, the rise of agricultural and pastoral production, the transformation of subsistence into commodity production and exchange in the agricultural sector, it was the appropriation of agricultural land and its surplus produce, which amounted to about fifty million Iraqi dinars or 17 per cent of the National Income during the 1950's, by tribal *shaykhs*, town notables and bureaucratic officials and officers and their expenditure of it mainly on consumption imports, that hampered the growth of domestic saving and investment to the high levels required by the national economy to take off into self-sustained economic growth.

III. THE GROWTH OF THE IMPORT TRADE AND THE EXPANSION OF URBAN ECONOMIC ACTIVITY

Turning to the 'import-propelled' sector of the Iraqi economy, the basic characteristics of the growth of the import trade may be described as follows: in the first place, during the period 1864–1914, its rate of growth was about 5 per cent annually, rising absolutely from ID.290,000 in 1864–71 to ID.3·5 million in 1912–13, a twelve-fold increase. It also increased to ID.7·6 million in 1933–9. Its expansion was considerably enhanced during the postwar period, and it amounted to ID.92 million in 1952–8.

Secondly, the changes in the import values of tea and sugar were mainly due to changes in quantity. The early increase in the import values of textiles was also due to increase in quantity, while the fall in their values during the interwar period was due to the fall in their prices. The rise in the import values of tea and sugar was entirely due to the rise in their prices, while both price and quantity increases contributed to the rise in their value during the postwar period. This also holds good for textiles during the Second World War and postwar periods.

Thirdly, the position of productive imports rose from about one-quarter of the total value of the import trade during the 1860's to about two-fifths during the 1930's; while the position of the consumption imports accounted for about two-thirds of the value of the import trade up to the Second World War, and then fell to about one-half of it during the postwar years.

Fourthly, the direction of the Iraqi import trade shifted very sharply from Middle Eastern to European markets. The share of the advanced economies rose from an insignificant proportion before the opening of the Suez Canal to as much as 70 per cent (of which 49 per cent was due to British suppliers) of the total value of the import trade on the eve of the First World War. While the share of the capitalist world in the Iraqi import trade continued to expand, rising to one-third in the case of Britain and from 9 per cent to 15 per cent in case of the U.S.A., that of the Middle East was below 10 per cent during the 1950's.

Fifthly, the shift of the Iraqi import trade towards Western and especially British markets transformed its organization. Iraqi commission agents became importers on their own account. Foreign firms, especially British, formerly engaged only in the Iraqi export trade, turned to the import trade. The tendency towards concentration in the import trade was enhanced. The number of tea and sugar importers fell from 50, including four large foreign firms during the 1930's, to 16, including three large foreign firms, during the 1950's. The number of textile importers fell from 167, including nine local firms and three foreign firms, to about 47 importers respectively. The import of medical drugs was confined to ten firms, the automobile trade to four firms, and the whole of the chemicals trade was concentrated in I.C.I. This concentration of the import trade, also observable in the capital-goods import market, manifested itself in the rising trading profits, absolutely and relatively. During the 1930's, the trading profits of foreign firms transferred abroad amounted to ID.450,000 annually, which accounts for the relatively high profit margins on their share in the Iraqi import trade. This rate of profit rose variously from 25 per cent to 50 per cent of the value of the import trade carried on by foreign firms, during the postwar years; and sometimes, as in the case of I.C.I., it rose to 500 per cent of the relevant import trade.

Both the rising demand of the *shaykhs* and of the mercantile sections of the urban population for consumption imports, and the declining productivity and income of the Iraqi peasantry, limited the size of the home market and hindered industrial development and led to the concentration of urban economic activity on commerce and buildings, over most of the period of our study.

The rapid growth of consumption imports, which accounted for 13 per cent of the value of the import trade in 1864–5 rising to 66 per cent in 1933–39 and then falling off to 49 per cent in 1952–7, destroyed the handicraft industries, especially woollen textiles, by reason of unfair competition due to the prevailing 'open door' commercial policy. Thus, the number of handloom weavers in Baghdad declined from 3,500 in 1866 to about 120 in 1934.

On the other hand, the expansion of the export trade required the development of such processing industries as date-packing, wool-pressing, cotton ginning, etc. The rise of the processing industries compensated, to some extent, for the loss of income and employment previously generated by the handicraft industries whose annual value of production, estimated at T£350,000 in the 1880's, sharply declined under the pressure of manufactured imports. Alongside this went on the expansion in the processing industries; for example, the annual capacity of the wool pressing industry rose from 30,000 bales during the 1880's to 180,000 bales during the 1930's.

Moreover, the expansion of urban employment and the growth of investment in the towns tended to extend the size of the urban market for manufacturing industries. While the urban population of Iraq increased at a rate of about 2 per cent per annum during the period 1867–1939, then at about 4 per cent during 1947–57, the rate of increase in the value of productive imports rose from about 5 per cent prior to the Second World War to 9 per cent between 1946–51 and 1952–8. This means that the rate of growth of productive imports was two-and-a-half times as high as the rate of growth of the urban population. Thus productive imports per head of the urban population rose from one-quarter of a dinar in 1864–5, to one-and-a-half dinars per annum in 1933–9 and to about nine-and-a-half dinars in 1941–6 and further to about eighteen dinars in 1952–8.

The increasing rate of urban economic investment, as measured by the rise in productive imports per head of the urban population, indicates the improvement of urban productivity and income. One consequence of this was the expansion of demand for domestic agricultural and animal products; another was continuous increase in the demand for consumption imports, especially by feudal and mercantile classes in the towns. Accordingly, the value of consumption imports per head of the urban population rose from one-half of a dinar per annum in the 1860's, to three dinars during the decade preceding the First World War, to about four dinars during the 1930's, to twelve dinars in 1946–51, and further to seventeen-and-a-half dinars in 1952–8.

The growth of urban economic investment reflected the development of urban economic activity, especially in the field of commerce, domestic and foreign, the field of real estate and buildings and land markets and their speculations. But it also reflected the delayed industrial development, which started with the establishment of some modern consumer goods industries during the 1930's, and the growth of some other import substituting industries, both of consumers' and producers' goods, during the 1950's.

The superiority of the growth of commercial and urban building activity over industrial growth was manifested in the distribution of employment and profits in the towns. A comparison of the occupational distribution returns of the 1947 and 1957 censuses shows that the number of persons engaged in trade and services rose from 471,000, or 35·7 per cent of the national labour force, to 674,000 or 37·5 per cent of it. By contrast, the number of persons employed in the industrial sector rose from 96,000 or about 7 per cent of the national labour force, to 264,000 or 15 per cent, during the same period. This means that the rate of increase of employment in the commercial sector was about 20,000 persons per annum, while its counterpart in the industrial sector amounted to 17,000 persons per annum during the decade preceding the 1958 Revolution. As to the distribution of gross profits accruing outside the agricultural and oil sectors, the share of commerce and real estate activities accounted for 75 per cent of the total, while that of the industrial sector did not exceed 12 per cent of it during the 1950's. Thus the industrial sector continued to occupy a secondary position in the national economy, as its contribution to the National Income did not exceed 8·3 per cent per annum during the 1953–8 period.

The growth of machine-made imports ushered in the decline of the local handicraft industries, especially those producing textile goods. The relatively lower costs and prices of imported goods also stood in the way of rapid industrial development, which requires, among other things, protection against unfair foreign competition. Thus the development of consumer goods industries lagged behind for thirty years, as the handicraft industries declined during the first decade of the present century, while the rise of the import substituting industries was held up until the 1930's. The development of other consumer goods industries, such as vegetable oil extraction, beer, etc., and of the producers' goods industries, mainly cement, was also held up for about twenty years, as the demand for products emerged and expanded during the 1930's, but this domestic production started only during the postwar years.

The concentration of commercial policy on the maximization of customs revenue during the 1861–1927 period made for the perpetuation of the phenomenon of industrial underdevelopment. The increasing foreign borrowing of the Ottoman Empire and the consequent financial burdens resulted in the pursuit of a perverse commercial policy which encouraged imports and discouraged domestic production. Later, the increasing need for revenue naturally did not result in adequate emphasis being put on the protection of home production.

Apart from the role of foreign oil investment and the transfer of oil profits abroad, and the industrial policy of the Development Board, the fundamental explanation for the phenomenon of industrial under-development is that the main source of potential domestic saving, namely the proceeds from the surplus agricultural produce, accrued mainly to absentee landlords who were lacking in habits of saving and investment, and full of contempt for business acumen.

Further, the relatively small urban savings tended traditionally to be invested in trade, where profits were comparatively high, rather than in industry, where greater risks were involved. Borrowing for trading purposes was also less difficult and less costly than for financing new industrial projects.

But in the meantime, the expansion of the Iraqi import trade created new tastes, stimulated new energies for work and a new willingness to make the best use of available resources, so that extra income became available to buy the new goods. This was especially true of a large number among the mercantile community during the interwar period. However, mercantile profits constituted a relatively small proportion of the total value of trade and the agricultural surplus produce. This meant that, over the greater part of our period, the Iraqi mercantile community acquired the entrepreneurial skills, but lacked the necessary capital for industrial investment.

Since the late 1930's, the size of the national market has expanded steadily, by reason of the growth of urban population and the rise of urban income. After 1927, commercial policy acquired a new emphasis on the protection of national production, under the pressure of the national commercial and industrial bourgeoisie, which meant the reservation of certain parts of local markets to domestic industrial production. However slow the accumulation of mercantile profits and capital might have been, with the passage of time they increased slowly but sufficiently for the establishment of certain consumer goods industries which met a significant proportion of domestic demands for cheap textiles, cigarettes and soap during the 1930's. Later their production rose further; and new consumer goods industries were set up and their share of national consumption increased, so much so that they produced 90 per cent of cigarettes, 83 per cent of beer, 80 per cent of soap, and 75 per cent of vegetable oil on the eve of the 1958 Revolution. The production of building materials, especially of cement and bricks, expanded not only to meet rising domestic demand, but also for export to neighbouring countries.

From the 1930's to the 1950's industrial growth was enhanced by the emergence of new developmental elements in the field of commercial policy, such as the new imposition of low tariff rates on productive imports to the extent of exemption on an increasing scale, the imposition of high tariff rates on unnecessary consumption imports, the raising of tariff rates on imports which had substitutes in domestic production. But the real impact of these measures was limited by the fact that this tariff policy was not sufficiently backed up by quantitative controls.

Yet this industrial growth, which could not meet the whole requirements of the domestic market, was unable to employ the supply of labour becoming available, and to exploit fully the raw materials other than oil. This means that the phenomenon of industrial underdevelopment continued despite the expansion of urban economic activity. The expenditure of the bulk of the surplus agricultural produce on consumption imports made for the low proportion of investment in the national income. Even as late as 1950, total annual gross investment in fixed capital did not exceed ID.17 millions, and net investment amounted to eight million dinars. This means that gross investment was 10 per cent, and net investment only 5 per cent, of national income. It is almost certain that net investment was less than 5 per cent of national income up to the 1950's, when it rose with the expansion of oil production and revenues on an increasing scale. Consequently, the phenomenon of industrial underdevelopment reigned supreme, and the problem of urban unemployment remained acute. The active urban population increased by 484,000 persons between 1947 and 1957, or by 48,400 per annum, while urban employment increased by 370,000 persons, or by 37,000 per annum, during the same period. This implies that the rate of increase of active urban population was 22 per cent higher than the rate of increase in employment. Thus, the number of unemployed in the towns rose from about 291,000 persons in 1947 to 405,000 persons in 1957, or 11,400 persons per annum.

IV. THE TRANSFORMATION OF THE ECONOMIC STRUCTURE

Side by side with the role of foreign trade in the absolute growth of rural population, accompanied by the decline of the agricultural productivity of land and labour, and in the expansion of both the total and average economic activity of the urban population, there also occurred a significant transformation in the structure of the Iraqi economy. Throughout the period of the past hundred years, Iraq was adjusting her traditional economic structure to a world market made accessible by new and improved forms of transport and profitable by the expansion of world demand for primary products.

The essential features of economic structure are made up of the patterns of production and consumption, the composition of exports and imports and the pattern of employment and activity.

The study of changes in the pattern of production and exports reveals three discernible changes over the period of our study. On the one hand, there was the relative decline of pastoral and comparative rise of agricultural production and exports. On the other hand, there came the change-over from the export of agricultural and primitive industrial products to the export of primary products of foodstuffs and raw materials up to the 1950's. Owing to the decline of the handicraft industries and to the delayed growth of modern industry, Iraq was able to export only a small proportion of its production, prior to the 1958 Revolution. Finally, the development of both commercial agriculture and modern industry involved the decline of subsistence economy and the growth of money and exchange economy.

The decline in the importance of pastoral production and exports relative to agricultural production and exports calls for an explanation. During the 1860's, these two sectors occupied more or less the same position. At the outbreak of the Second World War, agricultural exports accounted for three-quarters of the total value of exports and pastoral exports accounted for the remainder. On the eve of the 1958 Revolution, the value of agricultural exports rose to 77 per cent of the total value of the export trade (except oil), while the value of pastoral exports rose to about 16 per cent and the remainder, which accounted for 7 per cent, represented industrial exports. One of the factors economists would look for is whether or not there were any long-term price differentials in favour of agricultural production. But our study of the differences in the trends of the 'average values' of agricultural and pastoral exports indicates that they were, on the whole, of no great consequence, and in any case these price differentials moved in favour of wool, hides and skins rather than of dates and grain.

However, the degree of profitability of a branch of economic activity does not depend only on relative prices, but also on relative costs. Neither price differences nor differences in the degree of precariousness of natural conditions of agricultural and pastoral production were significant factors in explaining the relative decline of pastoral and rise of agricultural activity. It was the pastoral and agricultural *shaykhs* (or their agents) rather than the shepherds and peasants who decided on the relative profitability of pasture and agriculture. Iraq supplied only a small proportion of world demand for pastoral and agricultural products, with the sole exception of dates, and thus had to take world prices as given. In general, it was the transformation of rent-free tribally-owned grazing lands into rent-paying *shaykh*-owned lands which made agriculture relatively more profitable than pasture for *shaykhs*. The large and increasing share of the landowners in agricultural produce relative to their share in pastoral produce induced the *shaykhs* gradually to settle their tribes on the land. This tendency was also enhanced by government policy favouring the settlement of nomadic and pastoral tribes. Apart from supporting the government objective of controlling these tribes, this policy cannot be separated from the government's interest in the potential increase in its revenue from taxes on agriculture relative to pasture—as animals would be driven off more rapidly than agricultural produce—nor from the potential decrease in the cost of maintaining law and order among the otherwise ferocious tribes. Further, land policy, under the British occupation of the Mandatory Regime, depended on a new and basic factor, i.e., the development of a class of large landowners, both tribal and urban, which became the local social basis of foreign political and economic power.

So much for the relative decline of pastoral and rise of agricultural production and exports. It is sufficient to indicate briefly the changes in the pattern of production and exports; namely, the decline of handicraft industries and the disappearance of their export products, the emergence, however slowly, of consumer goods industrial production for import substitution, the growth of producers' goods industries, however delayed, for the satisfaction of the requirements of the building and construction industry, and the beginning of the export of manufactured goods, on the eve of the 1958 Revolution.

During the 1860's, Iraq exported to her neighbours such primitively manufactured products as silk piece-goods, boots and shoes, soap, etc. But the decline of the Iraqi handicraft industries, under the pressure of foreign competition at home and in neighbouring markets, made for the disappearance of these export products. Thus Iraqi exports were confined to primary products on the eve of the Second World War. The reason is obviously two-fold: first, the substitution of the cheaper European manufactures by domestic consumers and foreign importers of Iraqi products; secondly, the persistence of the phenomenon of industrial underdevelopment, with the consequence of small scale of activity and prices not yet competitive with those of modern industry, except during the 1950's when small-scale exports of some manufactures took place. Iraqi industrial exports accounted for 4–7 per cent of the export trade and consisted mainly of cement, which amounted to about half-a-million dinars and of cigarettes which amounted to quarter of a million dinars.

Both of these changes in the pattern of production and export—the rise of agricultural relative to pastoral production and exports, the disappearance of the handicraft industries and their exports and the ultimate emergence of industrial production and exports—reflect the other major transformation, namely, the decline of the natural economy depending on production for direct consumption or barter and the expansion in the scope of money exchange depending on commodity production and money as means of exchange, with the development of division of labour, primitive capital accumulation, private ownership of the means of production, the growth of exchange between town and country, and the formation of a national market. The development of a money exchange economy is shown by the rising ratio of exports to rural production. Thus, the ratio of date exports to production rose from one-third in the 1860's to three-quarters prior to the First World War; to two-thirds, prior to the Second World War, and to 69 per cent during the 1950's. The ratio of grain exports to production also rose, though less rapidly, from 6–10 per cent in the 1890's, to 10–15 per cent in the 1930's. The increase was confined to the rising ratio of barley exports to production, as it rose to 44 per cent, while that of wheat fell off and that of rice remained stable during the postwar years. The growth of the money economy is also reflected in rise of money wages paid to workers in modern industry replacing the wages in kind received by the apprentices of the former handicraft industry. Under this economic system, communal landownership was largely transformed into private ownership by a class of landowners consisting mainly of tribal *shaykhs*, urban notables and bureaucratic officials and officers, up to the promulgation of the Land Reform Law No. 30 in September 1958. Capital—commercial, real estate and industrial—had also been accumulated, however slowly, by the rising middle class. The peasantry remained almost entirely landless, and the working class without capital.

The principal changes in the pattern of consumption and imports reflected, for the greater part of the period of our study, the conditions of the urban population. The food of the peasantry retained essentially its traditional character, with the exception of the introduction of tea and sugar during the interwar period, but their consumption became substantial only in the 1950's. The clothing produced by the handicraft industry was substituted by cheap calico from imports and from the local industry during the 1950's.

But the pattern of consumption of the urban population, especially in the principal cities of Baghdad, Basra and Mosul, became increasingly rich and diverse, mainly in proportion to the increasing share of tribal and urban landowners in the surplus agricultural produce, to the share of the commercial bourgeoisie in the profits of trade and real estate, and to the increase in the profits of the industrial bourgeoisie. Not only did the consumption of meat increase, but vegetables, fruit, sweets and liquor also became widespread, especially amongst the *shaykhs* and the mercantile sections of the population. Modern housing and furniture came very much into vogue from the 1930's. In addition, the use of luxurious motor cars by the upper income groups, and of ordinary motor cars by the middle classes became widespread. On the other hand, the consumption by the other sections of the urban population of cheap textiles, tea and sugar also increased, especially during the 1950's and 1960's.

Moreover, imports of capital equipment, raw materials and semi-finished manufactured goods were also rising. This in turn reflected the expanding economic activity among the urban population. Thus, the value of productive imports per head of the urban population increased from a quarter of a dinar per annum during the 1860's to about ID.18 on the eve of the 1958 Revolution. This increase in the rate of growth of productive imports reflected the growth of urban investment, especially in commerce and real estate, at a rate insufficient for rapid industrialization and full employment.

All these long-term changes in the pattern of production, consumption and trade would no doubt be appropriately manifested in changes in the structure of employment and economic activity, were there adequate data on the occupational distribution of the Iraqi population. The long-term changes in Iraq's population may, however, broadly indicate the major shifts in the pattern of employment. Furthermore the occupational distribution of the population, as shown by the 1947 and 1957 censuses, indicates some important changes in the pattern of economic activity and level and structure of employment.

The long-term changes in the pattern of Iraq's population and employment may be seen in the absolute and relative decline of her nomadic population, the absolute and relative growth of her rural population up to 1930, the decline in the relative position of this part of the population afterwards, and, finally, the absolute growth but relative constancy of the urban population till 1930, with the later rise in the relative position of this component of the population.

The nomadic population declined from nearly half a million, accounting for as much as 35 per cent of Iraq's population in 1867, to under one-quarter of a million, accounting for only about 7 per cent in 1930, and to about 66,000 or 1 per cent of total population in 1957. The fall in the nomadic population provided part of the necessary labour for the expansion of rural production.

On the other hand, the rural population rose from just over half a million, accounting for about two-fifths of Iraq's population in 1867, to nearly two and a half millions, accounting for as much as 68 per cent of the total population in 1930, when its relative position began to decline. It rose absolutely to 3·7 millions, and fell off relatively to 58 per cent of the total population in 1957. This was partly due to the increasing rural exodus to the towns. The 'over-all' exodus, from the whole of the countryside to all towns, might be estimated at 45,000 persons per annum, while the 'partial' exodus, from some rural areas, such as ʿAmāra, to the principal commercial and industrial towns, might be estimated at about 16,000 persons per annum during the period 1947–57. On the other hand, the relative decline of rural population was due to the growth of urban population in Iraq.

Finally, the urban population expanded from the relatively high figure of nearly one-third of a million in 1867 to over three-quarters of a million in 1930, each accounting for one-quarter of Iraq's population in both years. After 1930, the urban population grew both absolutely and relatively. The relative constancy of the urban population before 1930 was, probably, due to the relative increase of town population consequent upon the growth of merchandise trade, and the processing industries, being more or less off-set by the comparative decrease in population owing to the decline of the extensive handicraft industries. After 1930, the urban population rose absolutely and relatively to 1·9 million or 38 per cent in 1947, and then to 2·6 millions or about 41 per cent in 1957. This later rise of the urban population was no doubt due to the emergence of consumer goods industries, the growth of building activity during the 1930's, the expansion of these activities and the establishment of new consumer and producers' goods industries, and the expansion of oil production during the 1950's.

The analysis of the changes in the occupational distribution of population during the decade preceding the 1958 Revolution shows that the proportion of the population occupied in the agricultural sector of the national labour force began to decline slightly. It rose absolutely from 748,000 in 1947 to 862,000 in 1957, and declined relatively from 57 per cent to 48 per cent. Socially, the agricultural sector consisted of two principal classes: the class of tribal and urban landowners, and the class of landless and poor peasants. The number of landowners did not exceed 168,000, 98 per cent of whom owned less than one-third of the area of agricultural holdings, while 2 per cent of them owned two-thirds of this area, according to the 1958–9 Census of Agriculture and Livestock.

It also seems that the population occupied in the industrial sector rose both absolutely and relatively, from 96,000 persons in 1947 to 263,000 in 1957, or from 7 per cent to 15 per cent respectively. Socially, the industrial sector also consisted of two main classes: the industrial class and the working class. The size of the young industrial capitalist class becomes partially clear from the number of industrial firms belonging to the Iraqi Federation of Industries, each of which possessed capital of not less than ID.10,000: they numbered 184 firms, and the total capital was valued at ID.46·5 millions on the eve of the 1958 Revolution. On the other hand, to arrive at the size of the working class, we have to add 90,000 workers employed in transport and communications in 1957, and 88,000 workers toiling in various private and public services and other activities which would bring up the total number of workers to 442,000 persons on the eve of the 1958 Revolution.

Finally, the population occupied in the commercial and service sector rose absolutely and relatively, from 471,000 in 1947 to 774,000 in 1957, or from 35·7 per cent to 37·5 per cent respectively.

In 1957, the number of persons engaged in domestic and foreign trade was about 90,000 persons (of whom 8,600 were of the business class and 58,000 were working on their own account). The public service (excluding education) employed 150,000 persons (about 91,000 of them were workers) while the educational service alone employed 10,000 persons and the professional and technical services returned 39,000 persons. If the number of persons engaged in transport and communications and in the non-commercial services were excluded, the remainder of total employment in the territory sector would represent the real estate and commercial middle class. Both of these strata of the bourgeoisie expanded remarkably. In Baghdad alone, the number of real estate owners who entered into commercial transactions for the purpose of profit amounted to about 4,000 persons, who realized ID.6–9 millions per annum as profits on real estate transactions during the 1950's. The number of persons engaged in real estates services (such as real estate agents and others) amounted to 5,000 persons during the same period. As to the commercial strata, the number of registered members of the Baghdad Chamber of Commerce (founded about 1911) rose from about 288 persons in 1926–7 to 3,439 persons in 1957–8. With the establishment of chambers of commerce in most of the principal towns, especially in Basra (1928) and Mosul (1947) and in various other towns during the postwar period, the total membership of these chambers increased to 9,423 registered merchants on the eve of the 1958 Revolution.

The main characteristic of the structure of the Iraqi bourgeoisie—agricultural, real estate, commercial and industrial—is that it is mixed in the sense that its various strata are so intertwined that each stratum shares in the economic interests of the other strata, to a smaller or greater degree. Often, a bourgeois at one and the same time owns irrigation pumps and agricultural land and some urban real estate, undertakes transactions in one or more branches of commerce, and owns industrial stocks and shares if he is not the main founder of an industrial establishment. This mixed character of the Iraqi bourgeoisie may be illustrated by the development of the sources of finance of three prominent bourgeois families. The well-known family of Fattāḥ Pasha and Sons (Sulaymān and Nūrī) used to own some orchards and lands in Khālis, together with real estate in the form of shops, worked in the administration and army, and traded in textiles and grain. Despite the concentration of the wealth of this family in the woollen textile industry during the period 1926–64, it held substantial shares in the capital of a cotton trading and ginning company, the National Knitting Company, the Iraq Cement Company, the Vegetable Oil Extraction Company, etc. The wealth of this family might be estimated, prior to the Nationalization Laws of 1964, at between four and six million dinars. The family of Muḥammad Ṭāhir al-Baghdādī and his son ʿAbdu'l-ʿAzīz developed from commercial into industrial activity, especially in the cigarettes industry. M. T. al-Baghdādī engaged in trade before the First World War, and his wealth was then estimated at T£60,000. His son started his economic career in the tobacco trade with an annual income of 1,200–1,500 rupees. In 1934, this family established a joint company for the production of cigarettes which it completely controlled and owned within three years. It owns modern urban real estate which returns a relatively high proportion of its income, and participates especially in the tobacco and grain trade. Its wealth might be estimated at about two million dinars prior to 1964. Finally, the al-Jalabī family, especially ʿAbdu'l-Hādī and Sons, developed from agriculture and land speculation, foreign trade, and industrial ownership of stocks and shares. The wealth of this family might be estimated at between three and four million dinars prior to 1964. Thus, while two-thirds of the income of the Fattāḥ Pasha family accrued from industry, the remainder originated in trade, urban real estate and agriculture. Three-fifths of the income of the Baghdādī family came from urban real estate, the remainder from industry and trade. Finally, three-quarters of the income of the al-Jalabī family originated in land speculation, and the remainder in trade and industry.

The development of the export-propelled and the import-propelled sectors, the changes in the pattern of production and exports and the pattern of consumption and imports, and the transformations in the structure of employment and economic activity, throughout the past hundred years, have not been independent of one another, but have interacted with one another, and with other sectors of the economy. Thus the growth of Iraqi foreign trade was accompanied by the development of new and improved forms of transport. Up to the First World War, the development of river and sea transport provided relatively quicker, cheaper and safer means of communication than the traditional ones. This not only helped to link Iraq with the expanding world economy, but also various parts of the country with one another. Then came the construction of railways, the length of track growing from 121 kilometres completed at the outbreak of the Great War to about 1,500 kilometres during the later 1930's and then to 1,648 kilometres during the early 1950's. The interwar period saw the development of road transport. Thus, by 1931, the length of such roads was officially estimated at 7,217 kilometres, of which only 273 were paved. The number of commercial vehicles also more than doubled, rising from about 700 lorries in the 1920's to over 1,500 lorries in the 1930's.

Both the length of roads and the number of lorries increased during the war and postwar years. The length of roads rose to 8,000 kilometres, of which 2,500 kilometres were levelled and paved and 500 levelled only, during the early 1950's. The number of lorries also increased to about 7,000 during the same period.

However inadequate these means of communication were relative to the size and productive capacity of Iraq, they promoted not only the expansion of foreign and domestic trade, but also the unification of the country, the implementation of law and the establishment of order. They also undermined the basis of nomadic life and enhanced its decline, offered an alternative in the rise of pastoral production and settled agriculture, and hence followed the increase in rural population; they promoted the growth of industry from the 1930's and hence gave impetus to the growth of the urban population. Thus the external economies generated mainly by the growth of transport and the development of law and order, both of which were the results of the expansion of Iraqi trade with the advanced economies of Europe and America, contributed to the transformation of the structure of Iraqi society. These benefits or the external economies emanating from these developments extended beyond the foreign trade sector, to the economy of Iraq as a whole.

V. THE RISE OF A DEPENDENT ECONOMY

The ratio of foreign trade to national income (or population) is usually low in a primitive economy, but it rises rapidly with development. At the outset of the period of our study, Iraq was largely self-sufficient because so great a part of its production was made available by more or less self-sufficient producers of food or clothing, who handled a comparatively small amount of money, and traded only a very small part of their output. One consequence of the growth of trade and the decline of self-sufficiency was that, throughout the period of our study, foreign trade developed more rapidly than income or population. Thus, agricultural production increased at approximately 1·2 per cent per annum, and population at approximately 1·9 per cent per annum, while the growth of the export trade was as fast as 2·7 per cent, throughout the whole of the period, from the 1860's to the 1950's.

Moreover, the importance of foreign trade in the early stages of Iraqi development is also shown by the fact that in this stage leadership, in communication or trade, was in the hands of foreign entrepreneurs. It was the developing European countries, whose consumption was growing, that sought new sources of supply. European entrepreneurs were better informed about techniques, whether of production, or marketing transportation, which gave them an advantage over the nascent entrepreneurs of Iraq. In the course of a few decades, Iraqi entrepreneurs have both grown in number from a few hundreds before the First World War, to a few thousands during the interwar period, and then to many thousands during the postwar years, and acquired some of these techniques. With the advantage of operating more cheaply from one's home base, the Iraqi entrepreneurs have begun to compete with foreign entrepreneurs, during the interwar period, and to challenge them during the postwar years.

It is the deficiency of the home market which makes the role of foreign trade in economic development so important. These deficiencies arise, either in total demand in the response of key sectors of the economy, or in the attitude towards competitive struggle for markets. Accordingly, at low levels of economic activity, production for the foreign market is usually the turning point which sets a country on the road of economic growth. Merely to produce more for the home market is unprofitable, since extra receipts will not equal extra outgoings, unless some demand is captured from some other producers, and this requires innovation. Not only does the latter require new techniques, which at these levels usually come from abroad, but more important is the fact that the social atmosphere is not very conducive to innovation and competition for markets.

The general importance of international trade in the process of economic development is shown by the increasing ratio of foreign trade to the national income, the more rapid growth of foreign trade than income, and the entrepreneurial leadership of the mercantile community in the early stages of capitalist development.

In the absence of any national income calculations for Iraq up to the 1950's, it is only possible to calculate the value of exports and imports, reflecting production, consumption and investment, per head of the Iraqi population. It is probable that the changes in the ratio of foreign trade to national income move in the same direction as its ratio to population over long periods of time. During the 1860's, the value of foreign trade per head of the Iraqi population amounted to 650 *fils*; it rapidly rose to ID.1/400 during the 1890's, and then to ID.1/800 on the eve of the First World War. During the mid 1930's, the value of foreign trade per head of the Iraqi population rose to ID.3/100.

In 1939, the *per capita* income of Iraq was put at $48 or about ten dinars (at the current rate of exchange). As the population of Iraq was estimated then at about four millions, the national income would be about $192 millions or about ID.40 millions. Thus, the ratio of foreign trade, valued at ID.11·9 millions (excluding oil exports), to the national income was about 34 per cent. This would rise to 53 per cent, if the value of oil exports, which amounted to ID.9·4 millions, were included. This means that the development of foreign trade, during the 1864–1939 period, was at a rate higher than the rate of growth of national income, as its ratio rose from 6 per cent of the national income during the 1860's, to about 17 per cent on the eve of the First World War, and further up to 34 per cent in 1939. This also means that the foreign oil sector, especially its crude oil exports, began to play as important a part as foreign trade in the national income at the outbreak of the Second World War.

In addition, the ratio of the value of the export trade (excluding oil) to the national income amounted to 9 per cent in 1939; and if oil exports were included, it would rise to 32 per cent. This also reflects the importance that oil exports began to acquire in the national economy. As to the ratio of the value of the import trade to the national income, it amounted to 20 per cent at the outbreak of the Second World War.

The dependence of the Iraqi economy on foreign trade and oil increased gradually. In 1950, Iraq's national income amounted to ID.158 millions (at current prices), while the value of foreign trade (excluding oil) was about ID.57·6 millions, i.e. its ratio to national income rose to 37 per cent. If oil exports, amounting to ID.23·6 millions, were included, the ratio of the total value of foreign trade to national income would be 51 per cent.

But the ratio of the value of the export trade (excluding oil) to national income rose rather slightly to 12 per cent. This means that the rate of growth of domestic exports was about equal to that of the national income, and the rate of growth of oil exports was even lower than this. However, the ratio of the value of the import trade to national income continued to rise to about 24 per cent in 1950. This indicates that the rate of import growth was higher than that of the national income. This is consistent with the economic disequilibrium reflected in the increasing deficit on the balance of payments, the deterioration in the terms of trade, the decline of agricultural productivity, and ultimately the increasing economic dependence of the Iraqi economy on the foreign oil sector and the world market.

The dependence of the Iraqi economy on the foreign oil sector and its exports increased so much that the role of foreign trade (excluding oil exports) was reduced to a secondary place in the national economy. In 1957, Iraq's national income was estimated at ID.355·4 millions, while the ratio of her foreign trade (excluding oil exports), which amounted to ID.134·6 millions, to national income hardly increased, being only 38 per cent. If oil exports are included, the ratio of total foreign trade to national income rose remarkably to 70 per cent. The ratio of domestic exports to national income fell off significantly to 4 per cent, while the value of Iraqi exports, including oil which amounted to ID.114·1 millions, rose remarkably to 35 per cent of the national income. The ratio of imports to national income continued to rise significantly to 34 per cent on the eve of the 1958 Revolution.

This tendency towards the increasing dependence of the Iraqi economy on the foreign oil sector does not seem to have been counter-balanced by the effects of the policies of land reform and industrialization that came in the wake of the 1958 Revolution. Thus in 1962 Iraq's net national product at factor cost rose to ID.526·4 millions, while the ratio of her foreign trade (excluding oil exports), which amounted to ID.148 millions, to the national income declined to 28 per cent. If oil exports, which amounted to ID.223·7 millions, are included, the ratio of total foreign trade to national income improved very slightly, rising only to 70·5 per cent. The ratio of domestic exports to national income continued to decline to 3·5 per cent. But the ratio of total imports to national income declined to about 24 per cent, owing to the rise in the production of import substituting industries, under the favourable conditions of a relatively protectionist commercial policy.

The transformation of Iraq's subsistence economy into an 'export economy', or the tendency towards her increasing economic dependence, has been accompanied by a deterioration in her external economic relations, especially the unfavourable movement in her terms of trade, and the deterioration in her balance of trade and payments, principally during the period since the end of the First World War. The movement of Iraq's terms of trade tended to be in her favour as it moved from 84 during 1889–95 to 139 during 1896–1903 and further to 260 in 1904–11, as compared with 100 in the base years 1912–13. This was accompanied by a favourable balance on Iraq's trading account, as the value of the export surplus was about 10 per cent of the value of the export trade during 1880–1905. However, commercial policy played a secondary role, as the principal objective was the realization of maximum customs revenues, rather than the support of domestic development policy, this being Iraq's share of the Ottoman burden of foreign loans and investment through her contribution to the Ottoman Budget and Privy Purse by means of a gold outflow from Baghdad to Constantinople, up to the First World War. It was the favourable movement in the terms of trade and the very limited extent of foreign investment in Iraq that made for the rise of an export surplus which financed this outflow of gold to Turkey.

However, the interwar and postwar periods saw a general unfavourable movement in Iraq's terms of trade and a deterioration in her balance of trade. The index numbers of the terms of trade (excluding oil exports) were unfavourable, with the exception of the years of economic recovery of 1933–7, and of the Second World War. Thus, the terms of trade (excluding oil) moved from 36 in 1922–6 to 84 in 1946–51, and then fell off to 71 in 1952–8, as compared with 100 in the base years 1938–9. If oil exports are included, the terms of trade index tended to fall off more markedly to 52 during 1952–8. These unfavourable terms of trade were accompanied by a tendency towards trade deficit, which amounted to 228 per cent of the value of the domestic export trade in 1919–25, fell to 108 per cent during 1934–9, and rose again to 121 per cent during 1954–7.

Despite the changes that occurred in commercial policy with the emergence of some developmental elements during the 1927–58 period, as the imposition of low duties on productive imports such as to amount to virtual exemption on an increasing scale, and the imposition of relatively high duties on unnecessary consumption imports or on available import substitutes, it could not stem the unfavourable tendencies in the terms of trade and balance of payments. These two unfavourable tendencies have been accompanied by increasing foreign private investment, especially in the extractive oil industry. Thus the Turkish Petroleum Company started investing in Iraq in 1925, and by 1928 had raised its capital to £2 millions from £160,000 in 1914; by 1934, when Iraqi petroleum began to flow to world markets, total capital expenditure rose to $62 millions. In 1951, foreign oil investment in Iraq was estimated at £90 millions. This rose even more rapidly to over $600 millions in 1959.

The relationship between these three tendencies—the unfavourable movement in the terms of trade, the deterioration in the balance of trade and the increase in the inflow of foreign oil investment—may seem at first difficult to explain. But its economic analysis is simplified by assuming that the proportion of real national income (i.e. at constant prices) saved falls off with the fall in real national income itself. As the rise in import prices amounts to a fall in real national income, it would lead to an increase in the ratio of expenditure on consumption to the money national income and thence in its absolute total. As the value of domestic investment may also most probably rise, or at any rate, may not fall off with the rise in import prices, it is reasonable to conclude that the value of domestic expenditure varies with import prices, i.e., it rises with a rise in import prices and vice versa. On the assumption that the rising ratio falls off with the deterioration in the terms of trade, it follows that the value of foreign investment varies with import prices, i.e., it rises with a rise in import prices and vice versa.

The statistical analysis of Iraq's imports and exports in relation to her national income during the 1953–62 period has shown that, in the first place, there is a high correlation between imports and gross national income so that of each one million dinars increase in the latter, ID.237,000 or nearly one-quarter was spent on the former. Secondly, there was an even higher correlation between imports and oil revenues, so that of each one million increase in the latter, ID.858,000 or 86 per cent was spent on imports. Thirdly, the income elasticity of demand for imports, which is the ratio of the relative rate of change of imports to the relative rate of change of national income, was found to be as high as 1·054. Finally, the relation between exports and gross national income was, however, found to be so weak as to associate an increase in exports of one million dinars with only 1·9 million dinars of gross national product at factor cost prices. This implies a negative correlation coefficient between merchandise exports and gross national product (non-oil sector) at current factor cost prices, which means that merchandise exports have not been the most important determinant of the Iraqi national income during the 1953–62 period.[1]

This special relationship between imports and income on the one hand, and exports and income on the other, may also be illustrated in terms of the annual compound rates of growth of exports, imports and income during the last two decades and especially since 1952. While the rate of growth of total exports has been at about 19 per cent per annum during the 1949–64 period, the rate of growth of net national product at factor cost prices has been about 7·99 per cent per annum during the same period. This means that the rate of growth of exports has been higher than and in a sense inconsistent with the rate of growth of income, as the former has been mainly determined by the growth of world demand for oil exports which have, in turn, been determined by the increase in the production of the foreign oil sector, independently of the Iraqi domestic (non-oil) economy. It is the basic isolation of oil production and exports from the Iraqi domestic economy which explains the low or even negative correlation between Iraqi exports and national income, or the mutual inconsistency between their current rates of growth.

On the other hand, the rate of growth of imports has been about 10·4 per cent per annum during the 1949–64 period, while the rate of growth of net national product at factor cost prices has been about 7·99 per cent per annum during the 1953–62 period. This consistency between the rate of growth of imports and rate of growth of national income, or the high correlation between imports and national income, is tenable on the basis of the most important common factor as between imports and income, namely the rate of growth of oil revenues. It is the oil revenues which, at one and the same time, finance over 90 per cent of the total value of the import trade and provide between a quarter and a third of Iraq's national income.

The restriction of the role of the foreign oil sector mainly to the financial or monetary plane (as shown by the fact that the oil companies' expenditure on wages and local purchases never exceeded 5 per cent of the value of oil exports) means that the secondary stages consequent upon the process of expansion in oil production and trade occurred outside the

[1] M. A. Al-Atragchi, *Statistical Analysis of the Pattern of Merchandise Foreign Trade of Iraq, 1948–1962* (London University Ph.D. Thesis, 1965); and an unpublished paper on 'Iraq's Foreign Trade in Relation to Her National Income, 1953–1962', by the same author.

Iraqi economy. Through the consistency of the rate of growth of imports with oil revenues, there leaked out most of the multiplier effect (the ratio of income changes to investment changes) of the process of expansion, whereas, through the lack of consistency between rate of growth of oil exports and the rate of growth of domestic income, there leaked out most of the effects of the accelerator (the ratio of investment changes to income changes), with the consequent development of the oil refining and petrochemical industries outside the Iraqi economy.

It is this duality in the Iraqi economy, or its development into a mono-economy dependent almost entirely on oil production and exports, or the economically unbalanced relation between the foreign oil sector and the domestic economic sector, or finally the disequilibrium between Iraq's foreign trade and her home trade, which constitutes the end-result of the interaction between foreign trade and investment and the local backward economy of Iraq during the past hundred years. More recently, this lopsided development has been accentuated by structural inflation, as shown by the higher rate of increase in the supply of money (actual currency issues plus bank deposits) than in real output, as the former increased annually by 9·2 per cent, the latter by 5·3 per cent during the 1949–64 period. It has also been reflected in the low and decreasing rate of growth of gross domestic fixed capital formation, which increased at 2·5 per cent per annum during the 1957–62 period. At the same time, it is the removal of these basic manifestations of unbalanced economic growth, or the real organic integration of the oil industry and the domestic economy, which constitutes one of the most fundamental conditions for the future development of Iraq's national economy, as far ahead as we can foresee.

Growth Models for the Middle East

Z. Y. HERSHLAG

Some fundamental questions of the macro-model of growth

SEVERAL fundamental questions have been raised frequently in the context of the secular disparity of economic growth of the West and the East (including the Middle East):

(1) Why in the course of history has the West reached an exceedingly high level of economic development, while the rest of the world has lagged behind under conditions of growing disparity?

(2) Can underdeveloped economies make use of historical models of the developed countries, are they bound to follow similar stages of growth, or are jumps in the sequence of growth possible?

(3) What are the strategic factors of growth and of transition from backwardness to higher levels of economic performance?

(4) What is the degree of feasibility of normative growth models under economic, social, institutional and political conditions prevailing in the Middle East, or, in other words, what are the relative weights of the sharing, competitive and growth responses in Middle East societies?

If we were able to agree on *the* strategic factor or factors of growth and transition from stage to stage, we might give a satisfactory answer to the first question and, at the same time, render easier the answer to the second and the last one.

Not only were the presently still underdeveloped countries handicapped in comparison with the presently developed already hundreds of years ago, but according to empirical findings, even *today* they lag in GNP *per capita*, behind the pre-industrial *starting point* of the industrialized countries.[1] They lag behind in real income as well as in active economic attitudes owing to their prevailing social-institutional structure and a low degree of development mentality and entrepreneurship. Marx's dictum on freedom limited by the past heritage 'pressing like an Alp on the brains of the people'[2] should be amplified by the impact and pressure of tradition *on the institutional and economic set-up* in traditional societies.

On the other hand, the growing extent of an international flow of funds, knowledge and techniques and modern planning devices offer new

[1] Cf., in particular, M. G. Mulhall, *Industries and Wealth of Nations*, London 1896; C. Clark, *The Conditions of Economic Progress*, second ed., London 1951; S. Kuznets, in A. N. Agarwala and S. P. Singh, *The Economics of Underdevelopment*, pp. 135–53, and in U.N., *Proceedings of the World Population Conference*, 1954.

[2] Cf. K. Marx *Der Achtzehnte Brumaire des Louis Bonaparte*, second ed., p. 26.

opportunities of accelerated growth. Kuznets is right in stating that *modern* economic growth differs completely from *traditional* growth. Modern growth is characterized by simultaneous high and sustained increase of income *per capita* and high and sustained growth of population; by a shift in the industrial (sectoral) structure of product and of labour force; by urbanization; by changes in organizational units; by shifts in the structure of consumer expenditure; and by changes in the character and magnitudes of international flows.[3] But is all this equally applicable to less developed areas today? The hard dilemma of these areas is between structural requirements which involve gradual, evolutionary growth with regard for historical stages, on the one hand, and modern development which calls for rapid adjustments and non-conservative concepts, on the other.

Macro-economic models register three major turning points: Quesnay's *Tableau économique*, Marx's *Capital*, and Keynes's *General Theory*. These also reflect three stages of capitalist growth: ascendance, industrial dynamics and maturity. Interestingly enough, all three came into being on the heels of economic troughs and social distress. All were positive models with a normative inclination. For our present purpose we shall concentrate on macro-economic models of growth consisting of interdependent relations between magnitudes, expressed in a number of variables and constants consistent with each other, through the intermediary of coefficients reflecting the structure of the economy. The theory behind the model, but often also economic policy, decide which is the independent variable, or which are the independent variables, set as targets.[4]

Intermittently the issue has been reopened of the validity and applicability of one general model to all economies and to all periods. Not only economic historians, but also some 'pure' economists became convinced that 'various kinds of economies have different sets of rules', and that 'the General Theory was rooted in the situation of Great Britain in the 1930's; Keynes was rash in applying its conclusions equally to medieval England and ancient Egypt'.[5] With these qualifications, the employment of historical and normative models, representing a formalized and simplified analysis, may render easier the task of tracing the process of growth. Every formalization runs the risk of oversimplification, in particular in purely quantitative models. But economic variables *are* quantitative, even though under a strong impact of value variables. Without formalization and abstraction no theory is possible. If flexibility and common sense make the model more integrative by taking account of a sufficient number of factors, the model becomes more realistic and applicable.

[3] S. Kuznets, in W. W. Rostow, *The Economics of Take-off into Self-sustained Growth*, published by I.E.A., 1963.

[4] Cf. J. Tinbergen, *Central Planning*, 1964, p. 23. Cf. also J. Schumpeter, *The Theory of Economic Development*, *passim*.

[5] Joan Robinson, *Essays in the Theory of Economic Growth*, p. 34.

Historical and normative models

A *historical model* shows past relationships and the results of changes in strategic variables.

The inductive method of the historical, mainly German, school suggested a series of models of stages of economic growth as a sequence of socio-economic structures and events, but not necessarily true historical models based on causal and analytical relationship and interdependence. The theory of stages of the historical school, and *mutatis mutandis*, of W. W. Rostow, was an abstraction of the empirically found economic (and often social) relationships, through which a people *had* to pass in order to experience economic growth. The models differed in their respective stresses on economic organization, institutional framework, modes of production, etc., but in most of them the strategic factor of transition was absent or, at least, confused, thus rendering the explanation of transition impossible. Only Quesnay, List, Marx and Schumpeter, most of them hardly belonging to the historical school, pointed to the 'net product', 'industrialization', 'expanded reproduction', and the 'innovating entrepreneurship', respectively, as the responsible strategic factors. These factors of transition are of the utmost importance as the links of causality indispensable in a historical model. In its turn, causality can explain the static and dynamic models and assist in setting up a correct normative model. Theoretical, sometimes in defiance of historical, economists, often despise the usage of 'causality' and replace it by either positive or negative 'correlation'. This may be preferable in a static analysis but is hardly superior to causality in a historical or dynamic model. The exacting issue is to find the true causes and avoid the danger of the logical fallacy of '*post hoc ergo propter hoc*'. Certainly, causation, in particular in economic life, is circular, which means that all variables are interdependent; making a certain variable independent is rather a formal, mathematical procedure, although it is linked up with the theory and/or economic policies, which point to the *major* factor of economic performance.

Rather surprisingly, in face and even in defiance of the growing demand for replacing economic theory by 'social theory',[6] a sudden upsurge of the 'new economic history' drew attention to the possibility of applying econometric methods and models to the past and thus substituting the traditional historical model by econometric history, or the imaginatively termed cliometric model. It remains to be seen whether the model itself is truly imaginative too and whether it is helpful in economic-historical analysis. The 'new economic history' can be traced back to Schumpeter, not owing to the latter's concept of entrepreneurship and his new combinations of factors of production, but precisely owing to the weakest link

[6] Cf. Gunnar Myrdal, *Economic Theory and Underdeveloped Regions*, 1957, p. 100.

in Schumpeter's reasoning, namely, the rigidity of his interdependence of variables, when infinitesimal changes in the independent variables *must* effect certain definite changes in the dependent ones. To a certain degree, Schumpeter's criticism of the Historical School can be found in *his* interpretation of that School:[7] 'So far as the scientific part of his vocation is concerned the economist should first of all master historical technique.' Roughly it can be said that Schumpeter's own position was the opposite, namely that the economic historian must be first of all an economic analyst, a position also held by the 'new economic history'.

The 'new' school attempts a kind of laboratory exploration by isolating phenomena and neutralizing the '*cetera*', without necessarily employing the widely adopted economic reasoning of 'opening up' closed systems, but it tries also to employ hypotheses and figments to infer from 'conditions that were actually observed, a set of conditions that never occurred',[8] in order to compute, for example, hypothetical National Income in the *absence* of railroads. Historical study and analysis, based on an abstracted model, may lead to conclusions different from empirical findings and then either the analysis or the model prove wrong and require re-examination.

The 'new economic history' is clearly positivist in that it wants to investigate only phenomena compatible with direct or indirect quantitative measurement. It foregoes traditional institutionalism, historical circumstances and social environment, and instead draws heavily on economic theory. Its reliance on statistical evidence and inference is an underlying condition of the whole model-building, and not just an illustration, as in the more traditional methods. The new approach puts to the test propositions found in traditional history, but it substitutes the causal approach by a disguised teleological method, which can be attributed to all theories with a strong deductive element (designed to prove a theoretical 'image', such as the equilibrium of the Classical Theory, or the image of socialist ends of the Marxian theory). The representatives of this school would not admit, of course, the existence of a teleological flair in their method. Anyhow, they are not interested in the historical and circumstantial necessity or unavoidability of economic phenomena, such as, for instance, the development of the railways, but rather in their opportunity costs and in the 'actual' (though historically hypothetical) economic value of their alternatives, such as, for instance, canals and highways.[9] They try to measure the actual contribution of different sectors to economic growth, thus *possibly* changing the accepted explanation of factors of

[7] J. Schumpeter, *History of Economic Analysis*, 1954, p. 807.

[8] R. W. Fogel, 'The New Economic History, I. Its Findings and Methods', *The Economic History Review*, xix, 1966, p. 650.

[9] R. W. Fogel, *Railroads and American Economic Growth: Essays in Economic History*, 1964, in particular p. 237 ff.

growth and their relative importance.[10] Many accepted beliefs are challenged by the new school, though often a shift of emphasis on 'responsible' factors is not necessarily a 'new' revolutionary discovery, but a product of normal historical re-examination.[11] In general, much of the 'new' research concentrates on technology and productivity, throwing doubts, at least, on the interpretations by 'traditional' economic history, with much bearing also on normative models looking for leading sectors, forward and backward linkages, spread and backward effects, and *pôles de croissance*.

A *normative model*, the second one in which we are mainly interested in the present context alongside the historical model, represents the desired combination of factors of production, or the optimum combination, as effected by the political choice of instruments, mainly of the strategic variable which becomes the independent of the model. To discover this strategic factor (or factors) of growth, which can be employed normatively, due regard must be paid to the causal links of the secular growth curve.

Normative planning models are of relatively recent origin, first as a product of the First World War: partial planning, mainly of raw materials, by war-time Germany (partly adopted also by the Allies); overall communist Russian planning; and, rather extraordinarily for that period, partial industrial planning by Turkey in the 1930's. It can be safely said that empirical, trial-and-error planning models preceded theoretical normative models.

The normative model is a formalized dynamic forecast based on the extrapolation of trends and figures from the historical and static models, interrelated and bound by conditions of coherence and directed by realistic, i.e., real-factors-bound, policies. These policies, designed to bring about the maximization of the target chosen through optimal allocation of resources, normally select investment projects, both on the macro- and micro-level, based on one of the major criteria, such as the rate-of-growth, or the social marginal productivity criteria and, in particular, on the benefit/cost criterion ($r = b/c$).[12]

[10] For example, by the re-examination of slavery in America prior to the Civil War, they reach through sophisticated calculations the conclusion that although slavery might have interfered with new entrepreneurship, it nevertheless was an economically viable system. 'The case for the abolition of slavery thus appears to turn on issues of morality and equity rather than on the inability of a slave system to yield a high rate of economic growth,' R. W. Fogel, 'The New Economic History, I. Its Findings and Methods', *loc. cit.*, p. 647. Cf. also A. H. Conrad and J. R. Meyer, *The Economics of Slavery and other Studies in Econometric History*, 1964, *passim*.

[11] This is, for instance, the case in the reduction in ocean transportation costs by half between 1600 and the middle of the nineteenth century, *not* because of new equipment, but by elimination of piracy, resulting in less manning requirements and an increase in the size of markets, as explained by North. Cf. D. C. North, 'Determinants of Productivity in Ocean Shipping', in R. W. Fogel and S. L. Engerman (ed.), *The Reinterpretation of American Economic History*, 1967.

[12] Cf. J. Tinbergen, *Central Planning*, p. 28.

This benefit/cost ratio involves the issue of social *versus* private profit. In nationalized economies of the communist type, or in mixed economies with a strongly predominant public sector, of the recent Egyptian or Turkish type, this discrepancy has been allegedly minimized. However, in view of the growing importance of the profitability criterion for each individual plant even in socialist and centralized economies, the issue becomes more complicated. Aggregate or even infrastructure costs are self-evidently related to social or national benefits, but the situation is different with individual or sectoral projects. First, it is not easy to estimate fully their social (in the meaning of economic, but all-national) effects; second, it is a growing conviction of economists under different regimes that only economically sound and efficient firms are socially justified; but, third, imperfect competition, monopolistic devices, and overall national economic and non-economic considerations again strengthen the criterion of marginal social profit, rather than that of private (or, individual) profit. This benefit-cost ratio, which is equally applicable to historical, positive and normative models and has a long tradition since Quesnay's principle of rational economic activity,[13] fits well into modern approaches to economic history.

Prof. Tinbergen suggests[14] that 'planning should be carried on to the point where marginal revenue equals marginal cost', in similarity to all other economic activities. But this benefit/cost marginal concept is *not identical* with the benefit/cost ratio of the implemented programmes themselves. The former is a relative, hardly calculable ratio which invites an extremely difficult comparison of economic activities performed *with* and *without* planning, respectively. *Costs of planning* can possibly be calculated, but how can the *benefits of planning* be estimated? As a matter of fact, Prof. Tinbergen admits this point when saying that 'we must compare a situation in which planning has been applied with one in which it has not been applied leaving all other data unchanged'. This is a kind of figment reminding us of the 'new economic history'. In any case, costs of planning itself must be added to the marginal product cost. The original benefit/cost ratio should be substituted by a more detailed and specific equation in which the results of a planned economic action will be compared with those of an unplanned one. With

$b_{pr\ pl}$ — standing for marginal[15] benefit in planned product,

b_{pr} — marginal benefit in unplanned product,

[13] Cf. F. Quesnay's *Tableau économique*: 'Obtenir la plus grande augmentation possible de jouissance par la plus grande diminution possible de dépenses.'

[14] J. Tinbergen, *Central Planning*, pp. 49–50.

[15] Marginal—in the sense of response to additional investment, either in new or in existing activities.

c_{pr} — marginal cost of product, and
c_{pl} — marginal cost of planning

the equation will run:

$$\frac{b_{pr\ pl}}{c_{pr} + c_{pl}} = \frac{b_{pr}}{c_{pr}}.$$

The degree of feasibility of a solution of this equation will also lead to an answer of the frequently asked question, whether the very attempt to apply normative statistical models in particular to less developed economies does not involve a tremendous waste of time, energy and scarce human and economic resources, in view of the dubious planning results affected by non-calculable factors.

If, upon an analysis of the salient features of an economy, non-quantitative factors, such as cultural standards, quality of administration, technical levels, attitudes and mentality, appear to be particularly strong, an aggregate quantitative model may prove ineffective and futile since disregard for value variables can even be misleading. Then the analytical model steps in, or possibly, a partial model.

The application of a growth model to developing countries

A certain pattern and sequence of programming and planning underlies every planning process. First, a reasonable national accounting system must be drawn up to satisfy, as far as possible, the basic requirements of the theoretical model to be employed. Then trends are extrapolated from a positive, historic or static, model, and, on the basis of the initial data of the economy combined with the prevailing trends, a macro-economic forecast is made. This forecast, confronted with the aims of development set by the government, serves as the starting point for the first planning stage, namely the macro-economic stage, which can be followed by the sector-, project- and regional stages, concluded by the final stage in which changes, adjustments and final decisions on implementation are made. Eventually, a different procedure may be employed, namely, starting with the assembling of projects on a micro-level and proceeding to integrate them into a comprehensive macro-plan. The first procedure usually implies mandatory planning, while the second is more characteristic of an indicative planning. What must be done in any case, both for an econometric and an analytical model, is the extrapolation of the salient trends and features of the economy, mainly to reveal the major bottlenecks to be tackled by the plan, either in an integrated or a partial model.

The growth models, the endogenous-Schumpeterian[16] as well as the

[16] To Schumpeter, 'development' means 'only such changes in economic life as are not forced upon it from without but arise by its own initiative, from within', and 'that every process of development creates the prerequisites for the following'. J. Schumpeter, *Theory of Economic Growth*, pp. 63–4.

normative ones, involve a number of problems related to the time dimension of the model. These are, first of all, changes in propensities and in elasticities, in particular in income-elasticities. This leads to issues of entrepreneurship, resources for investment and the possibility of severe cuts in private consumption. Finally, equilibrium on a higher level of economic performance is rendered difficult by the emergence of new bottlenecks, such as: inflationary pressure resulting in misallocation of resources; balance-of-payments and monetary difficulties; controls affecting readiness to invest; demand pressure reflected in the clash between the social and economic aspects of income redistribution, between the requirements of the private and public sectors, as well as the clash between the requirements of firms and households; and discrepancies between the façade and hinterland, and/or between town and village.

Since Pigou's 'measuring rod of money' for comparative welfare, models of welfare and growth have developed in two, almost antithetic directions. On the one hand, econometric models gained ground, based on the quantitative nature of economic science, increasing statistical evidence and ever more refined analysis. On the other hand, the growing literature on newly developing economies revealed the inadequacy of quantitative concepts, in view of the scarcity of statistical evidence on the one hand, and the abundance of non-measurable qualitative factors interrelated with economic performance, on the other. Meanwhile, the re-emergence of the von Thünen-coloured space economics also brought into being a Robinsonian by-product. There 'is a sort of hubris in setting up a model in which all output is produced by human labour with the aid of man-made equipment, forgetting the kindly fruits of the earth. The foregoing model of [accumulation] cannot be applied, even in the broadest way, to actual problems until it has been supplemented by an analysis of the supplies of natural resources available to the economy. There is not much to be said about it, however, at the very high level of generality of the foregoing arguments, since, just because they are natural, natural resources cannot be aggregated.'[17]

Attempts to reconcile these two diametrically opposed approaches have not been successful so far. Also, an experiment to apply an essentially historical method of stages of growth to forecasts and planning aroused much criticism, even on historical grounds, particularly as the assumed strategic factor of change and transition, a kind of 'threshold rate' of investment, proved insufficient as a sole or even ever-important explanation of change; this in view of the undeniable impact of other economic and non-economic factors, which may even bring about a seemingly paradoxical negative capital-output ratio, if, for instance, a particularly

[17] Joan Robinson, *Essays in the Theory of Economic Growth*, p. 74.

bad agricultural season, or incompetence in the utilization of investment resources defeat growth expectations.

One of these factors, of a socio-institutional character, is reflected in the quality of response to the basic scarcity factor. D. Hall suggests three possible responses; the sharing response, the competitive response, and the growth response.[18] In every society and in every period there is certainly a mixture of all responses evident, but on the predominance of one of them depends the pattern of social and economic development. Growth response is evidently the desired reaction to scarcity at lower stages of welfare. But this growth response consists, in similarity to entrepreneurship, of growth mentality and spirit, on the one hand, and of growth material capacity, on the other, both in short supply under backward conditions.

The application of growth models to the Middle East

Growth response was more often than not absent in the Middle East in the past, since ruling strata were uninterested in growth, apart from sporadic instances, and the masses below them were too primitive and destitute to rise above the sharing and/or competitive responses. Today, most governments are growth-conscious, but the growth-responsive strata of the population are still too weak, both spiritually and materially, and the 'time horizon' of domestic entrepreneurship is too low.[19]

On the prevailing assumption that the major target of a growth model consists in the maximization of Gross National Product *per capita* and that capital investment is the strategic means to achieve this target, according to requirements derived from the capital-output ratio or the multiplier, the economic history of the Middle East becomes rather enigmatic. Although discontinuously, the Middle East did experience intermittently significant investment infusions, e.g., under Muḥammad ʿAlī, and later under Saʿīd and Ismāʿīl, and even under the British in Egypt, in schemes and sectors, such as the cotton plant and industry, the Suez Canal and other transport facilities, or the irrigation dams; from the 1850's on in Ottoman Turkey, in particular in the railways system; and in the interwar period in several countries, this time involving also the industrial sector.[20] The 1950's, and still more the 1960's, have registered an almost unprecedented upward trend in investments, largely within the framework of national development plans.

What were the actual results of all these development attempts? What is the lesson of the past? What kind of model is applicable to the economic

[18] Cf. Douglas Hall, *Ideas and Illustrations in Economic History*, 1964, p. 143.

[19] Cf. James Baster, *The Introduction of Western Economic Institutions into the Middle East*, Chatham House Memoranda (mimeographed), O.U.P., January 1960.

[20] Cf. B. Hansen and G. A. Marzouk, *Development and Economic Policy in the U.A.R.* (Egypt), 1965, pp. 4–5, and the present writer's *Introduction to the Modern Economic History of the Middle East*, 1964, *passim*.

history of the Middle East? What are the factors responsible for the trends of growth?

Insofar as statistical evidence for the Middle East in the nineteenth century can be relied upon, no serious rise in economic and social standards could be registered for that period. Even the developing heterogeneity of the society was precarious and the modern façade of foreign and domestic élite was extremely thin in comparison with the vast destitute, traditional and primitive hinterland. The persisting institutional structure, external non-progressive domination, incompetence and misallocation of resources proved stronger than material investments and defeated even such attempts at institutional change as the abolition of *iltizām* and *corvée*, and the extermination of such anti-progressive elements as the Mamluks and the Janissaries.

Almost no *historical* quantitative models exist for the Middle East as a whole or its individual countries. The economic history of the Middle East, in general rather neglected, has been told mainly in terms of chronology and pragmaticism. Facts and figures have been employed chiefly as illustrations of the story. Lack of adequate data, abundance of non-quantitative factors, but also indecision about methods have been behind this economic historiography.

It is not only the weakness of the historians but also of the theory and its applicability to the fragmented economic history of the Middle East, which rendered difficult the utilization of historical models for Middle Eastern studies. A reperiodization of regional economic history might certainly help in the abstracting of a historical model, but a rigid application of, for instance, a stages theory will presumably prove abortive. At the best, it would show that most of the Middle East has become stuck at the second Listian stage of 'improving agriculture, increasing commerce and rising manufacture', though in a somewhat modernized fashion.

The combined historical-typological approach, as applied to the Middle East, leads to the distinction of, at least, three different types of economies:

1. Countries still marking time in the first stage of economic development, namely a primitive, mainly agrarian, non-commercial, non-technical economy;
2. Countries in the transitional, pre-industrial stage, largely with a dualistic structure of a capitalist (or, eventually, socialist) façade and a preponderant traditional hinterland;
3. Countries, as in particular Israel, already economically and technically developed, but, first, too young for drawing final conclusions from their experience and, second, too singular and hardly representative as a historical model.

On the other hand, quite a number of *normative* models, either partial or aggregate, have sprung up intermittently for Egypt, Persia and Turkey. The main emphasis was put on industry and the quantitative element was reflected in the number of plants, volume of envisaged production and costs of investment, as already done more crudely by Muḥammad ʿAlī's administration. Only in the still partial, sectoral Turkish 5-year plans of the 1930's have strong elements of an input-output model been included, and this of a descriptive and detailed rather than analytical character.[21]

Quantitative aggregate macro-planning is of very recent origin, mainly in the 1960's, but it has spread quickly and widely over the area, in Egypt, Turkey, Jordan, Iran and Iraq and somewhat earlier in Israel.[22] These econometric models try, in Prof. Tinbergen's language, 'to find out how a certain optimum, seen as a goal, can be obtained by proper choices of the "action parameters" at the disposal of the agencies concerned'.[23]

The 'optimum seen as a goal' has been a straight-forward rate of growth of 7 per cent annually for almost all the economies concerned, although additional secondary, but nevertheless important, targets have been envisaged, such as equilibrium in the balance of payments, removal or, at least, reduction of open and disguised unemployment, monetary and price stability and greater regional and social equality. However, even in these plans, relationships established for major variables, such as output, consumption, investment, balance of payments, employment, etc., are rather flimsy, and the much desired high-level equilibrium is relegated to the aims of the long-term programming.

With regard to normative models, the Middle East has been widely influenced by a number of economic experts, intermittently invited to the area by governments and planning agencies. Also, official missions sent to the Middle East by the United Nations, IMF or IBRD, have often published their reports and recommendations. The official missions were usually inclined to emphasize the prevailing low propensity to save and the scarcity of investment funds, which, in combination with scarce technology and 'know-how', necessarily leads, in their view, to granting priorities to the utilization of agricultural potentials and small-scale, labour-intensive industries. This stress on priorities was, somewhat paradoxically, the result of a balanced-growth attitude, which attempted to avoid an over-emphasis on industrialization and economic and social imbalances. This

[21] Cf. T. C. İktisat Vekâleti, Sanayi Tetkik Heyeti, *2inci 5yıllık Sanayi Planı*, 1936.

[22] U.A.R., *Framework, Five-Year Plan, July 1960–June 1965, for Economic and Social Development*, 1960; State Planning Organization (Turkey), *First Five-Year Development Plan, 1963–1967*, 1963; The Jordan Development Board, *Five Year Program for Economic Development 1962–1967*, 1961; Plan Organization of Iran, *Third Plan Frame, 1341–1346 (September 1962–March 1968)*, 1961; Law No. 70 of 1961 (Iraq), *The Five-Year Detailed Economic Plan from 1961–1962 to 1965–1966*, 1961; for Israel, a number of plans, including the recent *Draft of a Development Plan for the National Economy for the Years 1965 till 1969*, 1964 (unpublished).

[23] J. Tinbergen, *Central Planning*, p. 4.

attitude favoured, as a matter of fact, a simultaneous maximization of several economic and social targets. But one of the fundamental conditions of every model is its coherence and the internal consistency of its interdependent relations. Therefore, apart from the von Neuman-Morgenstern objection to the pseudo-maximum utilitarian concept wishing to maximize two functions at once ('the greatest possible good for the greatest possible number'),[24] a series of elementary inconsistencies in targets may appear, contradicting the very theory behind the model. The underlying resources-balance-equation can be easily disturbed if a model aims simultaneously at increased consumption, increased investment, decreased foreign assistance and decreased working hours leading to a fall in production.[25]

A cautious approach, somewhat similar to that of international agencies, was that of Ragnar Nurkse (in particular for Egypt), with his strongly recommended 'balanced growth' theory,[26] and of Hollis B. Chenery (mainly for Turkey),[27] although both favoured greater stress on industrialization to break the vicious circle of poverty. This emphasis on industrialization as the chief instrument for attaining the goal of a high-income level of the economy through the 7 per cent growth target is also strongly brought out in the studies working on traditional lines of economic analysis such as Hansen's and Marzouk's book on Egypt.[28]

Most models, such as Rostow's with his 'threshold' rates of investment and growth for the 'take-off' period, or Harrod-Domar's with its strategic investment variable affecting the rate of growth through the capital coefficient, or Rostow-Hirschman's 'leading sectors', largely draw on historic experience adapted to the particular conditions of underdeveloped areas. More dynamic normative models have been implanted in the region by more demanding, radically planning-minded experts and advisers, such as Oskar Lange and Ragnar Frisch (for Egypt) and Jan Tinbergen (for both Egypt and Turkey). Their dynamic approach, stress on modern structural change and industrialization, reliance on international assistance as complementary to national savings and their rather ambitious target of 7 per cent growth of GNP *per annum*, very strongly appealed to local feelings enhanced by the spreading 'revolution of rising expectations'.

Although the recently prevailing tendency is to reject the 'balanced growth' theory as unfeasible[29] and to stress the inevitability of a scale of

[24] J. von Neuman and O. Morgenstern, *Theory of Games and Economic Behaviour*, 1944, p. 11.
[25] Cf. J. Tinbergen, *Central Planning*, p. 44.

[26] Cf. R. Nurkse, *Problems of Capital Formation in Underdeveloped Countries*, 1953, and his 'The Conflict Between "Balanced Growth" and International Specialization', in G. Haberler (ed.), *Equilibrium and Growth in World Economy*, 1961.

[27] In an unpublished report on Turkey's economy.

[28] B. Hansen and G. A. Marzouk, *op. cit.*, Preface, and p. 1.

[29] In M. Fleming's 'External Economies and the Doctrine of Balanced Growth', *Economic Journal*, 1955, p. 255, we read: 'The chances that diversified development in a

priorities in the process of investment decisions and their implementation, unbalanced growth, even though proved historically inevitable and analytically justified, has remained a major source of concern for developing economies, facing primary and secondary bottlenecks and inflationary pressure.

The dominant features of the growth models prevailing in the Middle East, much as in many developing countries elsewhere, are:

1. Five-year plan periods;
2. 7 per cent annual growth of GNP;
3. The assumption of a marginal capital-output ratio of 3, as a major instrument of the macro-stage planning;
4. Capital investment of 18–21 per cent of GNP as the strategic factor of growth;
5. The predominant position of the public sector in both financing and investment, either because of the large share of the infrastructure or owing to the spread of nationalization of industry and services,[30] in addition to the government's stake in land reforms;
6. Attempts at the setting up of econometric models, in which *desired*, rather than real and extrapolated, trends of savings, capital coefficients and rate of growth constitute the main variables.

The issue of refined models for less-developed economies with little available data is the bone of contention among economists. Some contend that refined models cannot be applied in the absence of reliable and sufficient data; others maintain that, on the contrary, precisely the peculiar and unsatisfactory state of national accounting in developing areas *requires* more refined methods of calculation and models.

As a matter of fact, in the Middle Eastern economies, a combination of a simple input-output matrix, regression analysis, stage-by-stage method and trial-and-error procedure is widespread. Turkey and, even more, Egypt have employed the Leontief-Frisch dynamic input-output matrix for some 20 (for Turkey) or 30 (for Egypt) lines of economic activity, thus combining the macro-economic with the sectoral stages, allowing in addition

---

variety of industries will play a mutually supporting, mutually validating role, as required by the balanced-growth doctrine, are greatest when the necessary additional capital is obtainable on easy terms, when unions can be prevented from pushing up real wages in industry, when reserves of underemployed agricultural labour are eagerly waiting to obtain industrial employment, when there are opportunities for economies of scale in the basic factor-producing industries and when, taken singly, the investments in question are only just not profitable.' Fleming's is not even a complete list of conditions underlying balanced growth and the latter can hardly be considered realistic.

[30] This applies to the past experience of Egypt under Muḥammad 'Alī and to Iran and Turkey between the two World Wars, as well as to present-day Turkey and, even more, Egypt, in which more than 40 per cent of GNP originates from public services and enterprises, and 90 per cent of total gross investment is made in the public sector.

for several hundreds of individual projects.[31] Under Middle Eastern conditions of poor national accounting and statistical evidence and the great impact of non-measurable value factors, more refined methods, such as simultaneous equations estimation or even multiple correlation analysis, are rarely employed and the use of econometric models seems to be out of proportion.

The individual projects and individual enterprises in general, are allowed in Egypt to respond to the market and its demand, thus leading to the preservation of a special kind of a planned market economy. In Turkey, where even in the new drafted second 5-year plan the rate-of-growth target prevails, not only investment but also production is directed and defined, in particular in the public sector, thus leaving less manœuvre for the market and price mechanism. A disturbing feature of the Turkish as well as the Egyptian plans is the, as empirically proved, unrealistic assumption of a protracted average annual growth of 4 and 5 per cent, respectively, in the agricultural sector. Under adequate conditions, these rates of growth *could* be achieved, thus stabilizing and securing the overall rate of growth, but this requires fundamental changes in planning, in the allocation of resources and also in the attitudes of both governments and farmers.

In a model suggested for Syria,[32] considered by its author, Dr. Khaled Abdo Shair, as applicable to any Middle Eastern economy, input-output analysis is employed, based on data mainly derived from national income statistics and from an industrial census. From the outset, however, one of the major difficulties appears in the application of the capital-output ratio. The latter should be extrapolated on a marginal basis, to satisfy the requirements of a realistic investment coefficient in the model. Shair suggests its extrapolation on an average basis as a ratio of capital stock to output.[33] This procedure, however, seems under Middle Eastern conditions to be even less feasible than the marginal investment basis, mainly because our knowledge of total capital stock is highly hypothetical. An additional error is made by the author's assumption that 'if a sector is to expand, we should logically start with the sub-sector which uses the least capital. Thus, the more the sector should expand, the greater is the capital-output ratio.'[34] As a matter of fact, rather the opposite can be assumed. Considerations other than capital-intensity are often more important in initial investment decisions, e.g., infrastructural requirements, construction, etc. In addition, increasing returns to scale, up to a certain point, through internal economies, as well as external economies effects, are liable to bring about at

[31] Despite the importance of regional planning for the Middle East, the existing development plans in the area tend to disregard the regional stage in their overall planning.

[32] Dr. Khaled Abdo Shair, *Planning for a Middle Eastern Economy, Model for Syria*, 1965.

[33] *Ibid.*, p. 27.

[34] *Ibid.*, p. 41.

least a temporary fall in capital-output ratio upon sectoral expansion. The model mentioned also suffers from dubious assumptions based on relatively high growth rates during the 1950's (5–6 per cent annually) despite relatively low investment (11 per cent of national income = 8 per cent savings *plus* 3 per cent capital inflow), i.e., a low capital-output ratio, erroneously attributed to utilization of idle land, a guess contradicted by figures given by the study itself.[35]

Consequently, Shair's model requires further elaboration and improvement, in particular if it has to fufil the conditions for a general growth model for the Middle East at large.

Although the Israeli case can hardly serve as an example of a historical model for the whole Middle East, it may be a good and applicable instance of a normative model.

Israel, or rather the Palestine Jewish community, historically reminds one broadly of the New World societies, mainly in three respects pertinent to economic development:

1. Intake of people and of entrepreneurial gift and activity;
2. Inflow of capital;
3. Creation of a hard-working community based on a modern, non-primitive, market-oriented agricultural sector.

The mainly Anglo-Saxon origins of the New World settlers, supported by active Italian, German, Dutch and Jewish elements, largely explain the rapid economic and industrial progress of North America, Australia and New Zealand, as opposed to the South American economies fed by the already declining Spanish and Portuguese empires. The Schumpeterian model with its stress on entrepreneurship as the strategic factor of growth quite nicely fits into these historical circumstances of both the big New World and the tiny Jewish Palestine community.

A resemblance also comes to the fore between the process of the industrialization of Israel telescoped into a short period of about 30 years (perhaps the 'classical' take-off) and the growth of the American and, perhaps, the whole Western economy in the recent 200 years. The intensification and the rapidly growing productivity of agriculture rendered it possible to dispense with a large proportion of the agricultural population and earners in favour of urbanization and the growing share of secondary and tertiary occupations, without impinging upon the population's food supply and standard of living. The Fisher-Clarkian model of the occupational and income structures serves well the Western and Israeli examples. On the other hand, lack of local entrepreneurship and/or its 'low time horizon', the peculiarity of foreign entrepreneurship and the lagging of agricultural productivity are behind the continued backwardness

[35] *Ibid.*, pp. 5–6.

of the Middle East as a whole and render both the Schumpeterian and Clarkian models inapplicable.

While the historical model of Israel corresponds more to Western experience, Israel's normative models are of importance to Middle Eastern normative growth models, mainly for three reaons:

1. The realistic approach, as reflected, for instance, in granting an important role to foreign financial resources in the lack of adequate local savings;
2. The relatively sufficient, non-conspicuous utilization of these resources;
3. The admission of the intricacies of planning and conscious development, in view of the great impact of exogenous and value factors on the growth model.

Consequently, Israeli planning, which is able to rely on rapid past development, on the strategic investment factor and on a quite adequate national accounting system, is very cautious with the application of econometric models. These elements of the Israeli growth model, namely, realism in the appraisal of physical and human resources[36] and of targets and the recognition of the intricacies of modern planning, can be a valuable contribution to overall Middle Eastern normative growth models.

Scope of research and projection of future trends

Even if the rate of investment is assumed as *the* strategic factor of growth and if an additional assumption is made of the availability of capital resources required by the 'threshold' rate of growth, *via* the capital-output ratio, i.e., about 20 per cent of GNP—the issue of *patterns* of investment stands out, apart from a number of other factors influencing investment efficiency. *Conspicuous consumption* and the 'demonstration effect' on consumption are frequently made responsible for secondary bottlenecks arising in backward countries in the period of transition to sustained growth. Also, in the Middle East these factors have been made responsible for an adverse impact on savings, for growing deficits in the balance of payments, and for misallocation of domestic resources. However, relatively little has been said on *conspicuous investment* apart from generalizations about waste of resources, mainly on exhibitionist construction. But, in particular in

[36] Israel has had so far a substantial supply of foreign exchange, following capital transfers of various kinds, but it aims at reducing its deficit on current account and its dependence on capital influx despite its success in building up significant reserves. Recently, Israel has reduced the trade gap from $570 million in 1964 to $450 million in 1966, by cutting the rate of increase in imports as well as by increasing exports to the amount of nearly $1 billion. Israel did not recoil from reducing its rate of growth from 11·5 per cent of GNP in 1963 to 1 per cent in 1966, thus even cutting *per capita* income. The still persisting 15 per cent of GNP deficit could be largely off-set by a change in the political and military situation and in defence expenditure.

the Middle East, ill-conceived patterns of investments and conspicuous investment, both in the past and in the present, deserve a much closer examination.

How often has the fundamental question been asked and examined, whether the profit expected, and later on realized, from investment exceeded the interest-cost by a margin large enough to cover the risk involved,[37] or, what has been the true benefit/cost ratio?

Let us take a typical example in Ismāʿīl's economic policies in Egypt during 1863–79. The national debt increased during that period by about 95 million pounds sterling. The real value of investments was estimated at about 40–45 millions, i.e., some 50 per cent. The balance was spent on public and royal consumption, or wasted in abortive or over-costly schemes. Thus, negative savings during the period mentioned amounted to some 40–45 millions. In other words, even the great boom, in particular of the 1860's, did not bring about lasting genuine savings. This, together with the patterns of investment themselves, falls in line with the concept of misallocation of resources following inflation. The interest-burden outstripped real profits on investments. The investments themselves, made mainly in construction—transport, communications, buildings and canals—seem to be highly over-estimated. Milner and Cromer were extremely critical of the real value of investments in that period and even more objective and favourable estimates have set it much below the historical costs.

This is a good case-study for both the analysis of investment-priorities decisions and the application of cliometrics to this chapter of economic history. In a more recent context, similar questions concerning the benefit/cost ratio can be raised with regard to the post Second World War development drive of individual Middle Eastern countries.

Although we should still think twice before applying the 'new economic history' method to research on the Middle East, with its particular and outstanding lack of reliable data for computation, hypotheses and re-assessment, this method can undoubtedly be useful to partial studies concerned with specific periods, sectors, economic institutions, individual projects, or, finally, applied theoretical concepts. For this purpose, the point of departure must be a disaggregation of the economic history of the Middle East in order to get a better and, possibly, quantified insight into the salient aspects of economic change, in resemblance to the analysis of a 'closed system' to be 'opened up' in the later stages of analysis. A re-aggregation following this method of research may result in a better and fuller understanding of economic processes experienced by the Middle East.

The list of such particular studies should include, for example, the re-examination of such chapters in the Middle East's economic history as:

[37] Cf. J. Robinson, *op. cit.*, p. 37.

the industrial drive of Muḥammad ʿAlī; infrastructure investments in the Ottoman Empire in the later nineteenth century; the particular case of the economic value of the *corvée*; the economic impact of oriental guilds and the true reasons for their disappearance; Ismāʿīl's financial and investment ventures; foreign investments in the area; the economic impact of the Suez Canal; the reassessment of the Baghdad railway; the full significance of the oil sector; re-examination of agriculture as the main source of capital formation;[38] the issue of disguised unemployment; economic implications of land reform; imputed values in national accounting; investment isoquants under Middle Eastern conditions; inflation as a secular companion of growth; capital- *versus* labour-intensive projects; or, confrontation of patterns of growth *with* and *without* planning. These would all be partial models only, but with far-reaching general implications and conclusions. From this disaggregated re-examination of outstanding issues of the economic past and present, an aggregated positive model may emerge, as a basis for a normative projection of the future, first in the form of a forecast and then of a normative growth model.

The difficulties and the intricacies of such a projection and of achieving the essential macro-target of growth, namely the sustained annual rate of growth of at least 7 per cent, can be shown in a very rough and general way.

The population of the Middle East (delimited by Egypt in the south-west and by Turkey and Iran in the north-east) will reach some 150 million in 1975, a rise of nearly 30 per cent above the 1965 level, according to extrapolated trends. To secure the present real income *per capita*, net product also must grow by 30 per cent, i.e., from less than $18 billion to at least $24 billion.[39] The incremental $6 billion requires investments of $18 billion in 10 years, at an incremental capital coefficient of 3, or average annual investments of $1·8 billion. This constitutes 10 per cent of the aggregate net product of the region.[40]

A target of doubling *per capita* income in 10 years (1965–75) up to an

[38] The old physiocratic model which makes growth dependent on capital formation and this, in its turn, on the rate of annual advances and reproduction, may be of interest to Middle Eastern growth models, insofar as domestic resources are concerned. Spengler rightly interprets the physiocratic argument when he says: 'In a sense then the agricultural surplus is the dynamic, growth-generating factor to which other branches of the economy accommodate themselves.' Cf. J. J. Spengler, 'Mercantilist and Physiocratic Growth Theory', in B. F. Hoselitz (ed.), *Theories of Economic Growth*, 1965, p. 59.

[39] An average real income of a flat $150 *per capita per annum* was assumed for the region as a whole, even though the real average might have been somewhat higher as a result of the much higher level of income in Israel, Lebanon and Kuwait, its somewhat higher level in Syria, Turkey, Jordan and Iran, the nearly average $150 in Egypt and Iraq, and the lower level of income in Yemen, Saudi Arabia and the Sheikhdoms.

[40] Incidentally, this percentage nearly equals the region's annual expenditure on defence, half of which, at least, for the Arab countries and Israel, has to be attributed to excessive spending caused by the Arab–Israeli conflict.

average of \$300 means an increment of \$150 *per capita* (by securing a total income of \$45 billion for the whole region), or an aggregate increment of \$27 billion in the final year.

The achievement of this target is conditional, *ceteris paribus*, on an aggregate investment of \$80 billion on a 10-year basis, and an average of \$8 billion annually, which amounts to 44 per cent of the national product in the first year and 20 per cent in the last.

This calculation is far from accurate, since, except for the rates of growth, the variables are arithmetic magnitudes and averages and not—as they should be—compound rates. Also not included are non-monetary, imputed investments, which might render possible an increase in income without accountable investment. However, its approximate exactness is corroborated by the fact that, for instance, Egypt, which since the mid-fifties has invested some 17 per cent of GNP annually (domestic and foreign resources), reached during that period, on an optimistic assumption, only 6 per cent total and 3 per cent *per capita* growth.[41] This confirms our estimated incremental capital-output ratio, as a floor ratio, as well as the required rate of investment, if real income is to be doubled every 10 years. As a matter of fact, a capital coefficient of 3 is quite optimistic, in view of the prevailing low efficiency and waste of resources.

Rates of domestic national savings in Middle Eastern *plans* fluctuate between 13 per cent and 25 per cent of GNP. Actual findings in recent years show a range of 10 per cent (and even less) to 14 per cent only. Non-availability of required funds results in cuts in investment projects and lower growth rates, either by decisions or by trial *and* in greater dependence on foreign resources.

Ex ante planned investment outlays from foreign sources, out of total investment, have ranged from 35 per cent to nil, e.g., in Egypt, on the assumption that towards the end of the 5-year plan period, no foreign funds, i.e., no net capital imports, will be needed; or, in Turkey, the same by the end of the second 5-year plan. All this with a growth target of doubling *total* and not *per capita* income in 10 years.

Unfortunately, the gap between the projections and the results of the mobilization of resources proved to be significant. *Actual* control figures show requirements of 35–50 per cent (of foreign in total capital resources) throughout the *whole* period, which is closer to the proportions reached at in our rough calculations above. Hansen and Marzouk found that one-third of current investment in Egypt has been financed during the first 5-year plan period by foreign sources.[42]

The large share of foreign financing is also evidenced by the growing deficit in Egypt's balance of payments, from 1·5 per cent of GNP in

[41] Cf. Hansen and Marzouk, *op. cit.*, p. 8.

[42] Hansen and Marzouk, *op. cit.*, pp. 14 and 21.

1946–51, to 7 per cent of GNP by 1966, or *more* than one-third of annual investments.[43] This, apart from the dwindling of foreign exchange and gold reserves from 65 per cent of GNP in the 1950's, to a negligible rate in the mid-sixties, and from economic losses incurred in the recent Arab-Israeli war.[44]

As for the future, on the overall Middle Eastern regional basis, one-third to one-half of required investment funds may come from oil royalties, assuming an increasing scale. This represents nearly all available local investment resources. It is true that other, non-oil countries, the 'have-nots', like, so far, Egypt or Turkey, accumulate certain savings, but these are levelled off by the utilization of a substantial part of royalties for current expenditures, including security.

If, at least, the *differential* spending on security of about 6 per cent of GNP resulting from the Arab-Israeli conflict could be diverted to investment, domestic savings for investment would come close to 20 per cent of GNP. As matters stand now, to double *per capita* income in 10 years, the region as a unit is in need of an additional $5 billion annually (equal to 20–25 per cent of aggregate GNP) from non-domestic sources. It does not seem to be easy to reach this target under the prevailing economic and political conditions in the area. During the period 1946–65, total U.S. *and* Communist Bloc aid to the Middle East did not exceed $10 billion, out of which at least $4 billion were for military purposes. That left $6 billion for economic aid, with, perhaps, $2 billion additional aid by other Western countries and direct private investment. The annual average of these $8 billion amounts to about $350–400 million for economic purposes, or (as an average of the total influx) about $600–700 million overall. Even though the average for the last decade was higher, largely due to the activity of the Soviet bloc, it does not exceed 15–20 per cent of actual requirements. In addition, this difficulty in achieving an adequate 'threshold rate' of investment and growth is only one, though a major restriction on the freedom of the growth model for the Middle East.

In this respect, greater emphasis on the rate of investment rather than on the rate of growth as the major target is more realistic, in view of the great number of endogenous and exogenous factors influencing the real rate of growth. This has not yet been admitted by most plans in operation in the Middle East. But even in those plans which, as in Egypt, did place the main stress on the investment target, too little attention was given to the elaboration of optimal investment criteria and investment patterns and too much was left to *ad hoc* decisions within the framework of annual

[43] Hansen and Marzouk, *op. cit.*, pp. 14 and 21.

[44] Before the war, Egypt's foreign exchange genuine earnings reached $78 million from tourism, $300 million from cotton and $260 million from the Suez Canal. Out of 7 million tons of crude oil, 5 million tons are presently in Israel's hands. Meanwhile Egypt's oil production has increased to about 10 million tons.

budgets (apart from the fact that the implementation of investment also lagged significantly behind the target).

The dissolution of the arbitrarily assumed regional unit into real national units will make some national economies happier, but others much more unhappy. Genuine co-operation between those national units through a regional planning entity may secure a more efficient and balanced use of resources. The limited domestic market, even of the total region, is a serious handicap, causing—*via* low demand—disincentives and inefficiency. This handicap becomes more outstanding if real, separate national economies are considered. Costs rise sharply in sub-optimal industries. For instance, the total steel consumption of Israel and the Arab countries was in 1964 1·9 million tons, while the optimum scale of one fully integrated steel mill is estimated at 4 million tons at which cost per unit stands at 100 (index-base), while for 2 million tons, it rises to 107, and at 100,000 tons to 191.[45] Exports are hardly an answer, for many sectors, in view of their low competitiveness. Under the prevailing patterns of trade and with the primary character of exports, the index of export quantum increased from 100 in 1952 to 117 in 1963, while the index of returns rose to 102 only, thus reducing the terms of trade (E/I) to 83.

The disquieting factor in Middle Eastern growth is not primarily its current average rate, which, until the June War, reached 6 per cent in Egypt and Turkey, 7–8 per cent in Jordan, or 10 per cent in Iran. Even if a discount is made for population growth, it still leaves an incremental *per capita* growth of 3–5 per cent; although in most countries *per capita* real income will, presumably, not be doubled in a decade, the prevailing trend is an important step forward in comparison with the past. The disturbing factors are, however, the incertitude of this growth trend, little progress towards *self-sustained* growth, the economic and social costs incurred by straining meagre domestic resources and spreading frustration among a population hardly participating in the incremental income and, so far, insufficient economic and social structural change in the direction of a modern, industrialized society.

The main deficiency of nearly all growth models, in particular of the quantitative ones, is the practical exclusion of the *quality* of the factors of production. Whether this is done for conceptual reasons or is due to the difficulties of quantification of value magnitudes, this disregard for, for instance, the quality of the human factors with all its cultural, behavioural, administrative or technological aspects, renders the model non-viable. Efficient utilization of human resources (U_h) depends not only on the relative shares of the economically active population (L) and of actual employment (E) (*deducting* open and disguised unemployment), but also,

[45] I am indebted to Mr. Michael Shefer for his helpful suggestions.

and perhaps mainly, on productivity per earner (P)[46] as expressed in a partial function, excluding physical capital: $U_h = f(L, E, P)$. This function can be, eventually, integrated in a general growth model of a combined Cobb–Douglas–Tinbergen type.

U_h is a measurable increasing function in which L and E can be compensated by P, as they are to a large degree in Israel. Under the particular Middle Eastern conditions, the explanation of success and failure of economic performance by the quality of the human factor and the degree of efficiency of the government machinery seems to be even more pertinent than capital investment. This holds true in spite of the immense difficulty of application to a quantitative growth model. But the realm of growth and planning offers no easy answers.

[46] Utilization of capacity, technology, sectoral structure of employment and product and the standards of labour itself, are reflected in productivity (P).

Middle East Economic Development, 1815–1914: The General and the Specific

CHARLES ISSAWI

In the century between the Napoleonic and First World Wars a world economy, based on western Europe, was built. Two aspects of this process may be distinguished. On the one hand, the various regions were successively integrated in a world-wide economic and financial system, through mechanical transport, mass migration, vast capital flows and a huge expansion in international trade. And on the other, the economy of the non-European countries was profoundly transformed. Thanks to the spread of security, the introduction of modern hygiene and the reduction of famine, death rates fell and population increased severalfold. In response to rising European demand for raw materials and helped by a sharp reduction in transport costs, agricultural output greatly expanded and export of cash crops multiplied; this in turn had deep repercussions on systems of land tenure, generally resulting in a shift from communal or tribal ownership to individual property rights. Handicrafts, exposed to the competition of European machine-made goods, were for the most part eliminated; and since, for a variety of economic, social and political reasons, modern factories did not rise to take their place, a process of de-industrialization occurred in many parts of the world. Social systems were also transformed and the already great inequality prevailing in these countries increased. For although the level of living of the masses probably rose in most places over the greater part of the period, the income and wealth of the upper strata grew much more rapidly. Lastly, the active agents of change were mostly foreign—either Europeans or Americans or immigrants from neighbouring countries, e.g., the Chinese and Indians in south-east Asia.

The above description fits the Middle East very closely for the period under review. The purpose of this paper is to examine whether and in what respects the region diverged from the prevailing patterns and trends. For this purpose four topics that lend themselves to quantitative analysis will be examined in some detail: population growth, foreign capital investment, mechanical transport and foreign trade. Five other topics will also be briefly discussed: agriculture, industry, levels of income, educational progress and agents of economic change. Wherever possible, comparison will be made with world totals and with figures for two other regions with sharply contrasting experiences, India and Japan; Japan was chosen as the most successful example of development in recent history while

India, on the contrary, represents a country that failed to develop rapidly in spite of a promising start in several fields. Lastly, an attempt will be made to determine whether the Middle East had its own distinctive pattern of development.

It goes without saying that this paper represents only a tentative first approach to a field that has received very little study. Essentially, it raises questions rather than providing answers. Its main purpose is to stimulate discussion and suggest topics for further research.

Population

In the nineteenth century population growth occurred in almost all parts of the world, but its extent varied considerably. The following table gives some crude estimates made by Carr-Saunders and Willcox, respectively.[1]

	Compound Annual Rate of Increase per 1,000					
	1800–1850		1850–1900		1900–1920	
Africa	1·1	0·0	4·7	6·9	7·7	—0·4
N. America	29·8	29·8	23·0	23·0	18·6	18·6
Latin America	11·1	7·2	13·0	13·0	18·6	18·6
Asia	4·3	2·0	5·4	2·8	2·8	6·1
Europe & U.S.S.R.	7·1	7·0	8·7	7·0	7·0	7·0
Total	5·1	3·4	7·3	5·9	5·9	7·1

For India, the population has been guessed at about 120 million in 1800. The 1872 census gave a total of 206 million, the 1911 census of 315, and the 1921 census of 319 million; about half the increase in 1872–1911 is attributable to improved methods of enumeration and additional areas covered[2] and the negligible growth in 1911–21 is due to the influenza epidemic. The 'real increase in population (allowing for the inclusion of new territory) in 50 years has been 88·6 million, i.e., 34·9 per cent',[3] giving a compound rate of growth of 6 per thousand. Accepting the 1800 guess of 120 million would imply a rate of growth of 7 for 1800–72, which may err on the side of exaggeration. Japan's population in 1800 was probably around 30 million. The 1872 census showed a figure of 33 million (which should probably be raised to 35 or 36 million) and that of 1920 of 56 million,[4] indicating rates of growth of 1 and 11 per thousand, respectively; however, the first figure should be slightly raised and the second reduced.

[1] *Cambridge Economic History of Europe*, vol. vi, Cambridge 1965, p. 58.
[2] *Ibid.*, p. 64.
[3] Vera Anstey, *The Economic Development of India*, London 1957, p. 605.
[4] *Cambridge Economic History*, p. 65.

For the Middle East estimates are of the very roughest. Egypt's population in 1800 is usually put at 2·5–3 million, but good reasons have been given for raising the figure to at least 3·5 million.[5] The first reliable census, that of 1897, put the total at 9·72 million and the 1917 census at 12·75 million, indicating rates of growth of 11 and 14 per thousand, respectively. For Iraq, where the first census was taken in 1947, Hasan's estimates show annual rates of growth of 13 between 1867 and 1890, 18 in 1890–1905 and 17 in 1905–19.[6] No reliable figures are available for Syria—which term is used throughout this paper to cover 'geographical' or 'greater' Syria. British consular estimates in the 1830's ranged from 1,000,000 to 1,864,000, but most of them fall between 1,250,000 and 1,450,000. Estimates for 1910–15 cluster around 3·5 million.[7] Assuming a figure of 1,350,000 for 1835 and 3·5 million for 1914 would suggest a rate of growth of 12 per thousand; putting the 1835 figure at 1,864,000 would reduce the growth rate to 8. If these figures are at all correct, they would indicate that the rate of growth of the population of the Arab countries was distinctly higher than those of Asia and Africa in general and India and Japan in particular. If this is so, it would mean that a large share of the increment in income achieved during the period under review was swallowed up by population growth. Available data on Algeria point in the same direction.[8] However, it should be remembered that not even an indication of the trend of population in Arabia is available, while that of the Sudan is usually believed to have fallen during the Mahdist period, following an earlier growth under Egyptian rule.[9]

Data for Turkey and Iran are even more fragmentary. The 1831 Ottoman 'census' put the number of males (*erkek*) in Anatolia at 2,384,000. If one assumes this to refer to adult males, a population of some 10 million is indicated—a figure of the same order of magnitude as other very rough estimates given by various European sources.[10] On the eve of the First World War, the population of the territory of what became the Republic of Turkey was put at 14,549,000.[11] Accepting these two figures at their face value would indicate the low growth rate of 5 per thousand in 1831–1914 (but see footnote 15, below). For Iran it is not even possible to say

[5] Gabriel Baer, 'Urbanization in Egypt, 1820–1907', in W. R. Polk and R. L. Chambers (eds.), *The Beginnings of Modernization in the Middle East*, Chicago 1968.

[6] M. S. Hasan, 'Growth and Structure of Iraq's Population, 1867–1947', *Bulletin of the Oxford University Institute of Statistics*, XX, 1958.

[7] For sources see Charles Issawi, *The Economic History of the Middle East*, Chicago 1966, p. 209.

[8] For a fuller discussion see Charles Issawi, 'Economic Growth in the Arab World since 1800', *Middle East Economic Papers* (Beirut), 1964.

[9] See Issawi, *Economic History*, pp. 332, and 469–70, respectively. [10] See *ibid.*, p. 17.

[11] Eliot G. Mears, *Modern Turkey*, New York 1924, p. 580, quoting *Statesman's Yearbook*. This figure is not necessarily incompatible with that of the census of 1927, viz., 13,648,000, in view of Turkey's huge war losses and the exodus of Greeks, Armenians and others.

whether the population in the latter half of the nineteenth century was larger or smaller than it had been at the beginning of that century. Thus Rawlinson put the total in 1850 at 10 million but in 1873 'after two desolating visitations of cholera and famine' at 6 million.[12] Other estimates for the 1880's range between 5 and 10 million, the two least unsatisfactory showing 7,654,000 for 1884 (by Houtum Schindler) and 6 million for 1888 (by a Russian scholar, Zolotarev). A later estimate by Houtum Schindler put the population in 1897 at 9 million, while Lorini gives a figure of 9,332,000 for 1899.[13]

As a very rough check on these figures, one can attempt some backward extrapolation. In 1956, when the first nation-wide Iranian census put the population at 18,955,000, that of Egypt was 23,532,000 and that of Turkey 24,771,000.[14] Assuming the same ratio to have prevailed in 1890 would indicate a figure of around 7 million for Iran, compared to about 9 million for Egypt. However, it seems highly unlikely that in 1890–1956 the Iranian rate of growth was as high as the Egyptian. This might indicate that the higher estimates given by Sir A. Houtum Schindler—a British-German general in the Iranian army, who knew the country well—are nearer the mark, a conclusion that tallies with Curzon's and Lorini's.[15]

As for Iran's rate of growth, for what it is worth, one can quote Curzon's guess, presumably based on the India Office records on which he drew so heavily, that at the time of his journey, a period 'free both from war and famine', the population was growing at $\frac{3}{4}$ per cent per annum.[16] And for what they are worth, most of the estimates of town populations quoted by him show some increase in the period 1800–90, often following sharp declines in the eighteenth century; however, there were some important exceptions, e.g., Isfahan and Meshed, whose populations seem to have declined.

Capital Investment

A United Nations study, *Capital Movements during the Interwar Period*, has put total long-term foreign investment outstanding in 1914 at $44,000 million. Of this over $2,000 million, or as much as one-twentieth, was in the Middle East.

[12] George Curzon, *Persia and the Persian Question*, London 1892, vol. ii, p. 492.

[13] *Ibid.* p. 493, *Encyclopaedia Britannica* (Eleventh Edition), s.v. Persia, and Eteocle Lorini, *La Persia economica*, Rome 1900, p. 378. L. A. Sobotsinskii, *Persia* (St. Petersburg, 1913), p. 12, quotes a 'contemporary' (1909) estimate by Medvedev of 10 million.

[14] United Nations, *Monthly Bulletin of Statistics.*

[15] The corresponding figure for Turkey would be about 10 million in 1890, which would imply a rate of growth of over 15 per thousand between 1890 and 1914; this figure seems too high, and it is therefore probable that the 1890 figure was well above 10 million. By the same token, the 1831 figure may have been somewhat below 10 million.

[16] *Op. cit.*, p. 493.

Total investment in Egypt on the eve of the First World War was over £E. 200 million, of which 94 million represented the outstanding public debt and the rest investment in the private sector.[17] For Turkey, the outstanding government debt at the time of the Lausanne conference was 161 million Turkish gold pounds, a figure not too significantly different from the one for 1914. Private foreign investment in 1914 was £66·4 million.[18] In Iran the only important private investment was that of the Anglo-Persian Oil Company, whose capital was raised to £4·2 million in 1914; the addition of the few Russian, British and other enterprises (banks, mines, transport, telegraphs, fisheries, etc.) would bring the total to well over £10 million.[19] As for the public debt, at the outbreak of war some £2 million was owed to Britain and the equivalent of about £4·8 million to Russia.[20]

The magnitude of foreign investment in Turkey and Egypt may be gauged by comparing it with the following figures, which represent total foreign investment in both the private and public sectors in 1913: India about £360 million, Japan about £200 million, China about £150 million, Brazil a little over £150 million, Mexico a little over £100 million. Relatively to their population the Ottoman Empire, and still more strikingly Egypt, had received an enormous amount of foreign capital. In Iran the scale of foreign investment was much smaller. It may be added that hardly any of the investment in the Ottoman Empire percolated to the Persian Gulf–Red Sea area; the exceptions were the Hijaz railway and some railway and irrigation construction in Iraq. Similarly the Sudan was only just beginning to attract foreign capital at the outbreak of war.

When, however, attention is turned to the *use* made of this foreign investment, the picture looks much less favourable. For whereas the bulk of the Indian and Japanese public debts helped to finance economic development, most of the Ottoman, Egyptian and Iranian public debts was either taken up in commissions and charges, or was used to repay earlier debts or to finance wars, or for indemnity payments, or was spent by the monarchs in various unproductive ways.[21] As a result these countries

[17] See A. E. Crouchley, *The Investment of Foreign Capital in Egyptian Companies and Public Debt*, Cairo 1936, and L. A. Fridman, *Kapitalističeskoye razvitiye Yegipta*, Moscow 1963, p. 13.

[18] For details see Issawi, *Economic History*, pp. 94–106.

[19] For details see Muḥammad ʿAlī Jamālzāde, *Ganj-i Shāygān*, Berlin 1335 A.H., pp. 98–117. The Russian Discount Bank's capital was 64 million gold roubles and the total value of the Russian property to which the Soviets renounced all claims in 1921 has been put as high as 600 million gold roubles. However, the latter figure includes various military installations and the basis of the valuation is not clear. See S. G. Gorelikov, *Iran*, Moscow 1961, p. 153, citing M. V. Popov, *Amerikanskiy imperializm v Irane*, Moscow 1956, p. 5.

[20] See Jamālzāde, *op. cit.*, p. 155, and Sir Percy Sykes, *A History of Persia*, London 1921, vol. ii, p. 523.

[21] Issawi, *Economic History*, pp. 94–106, 430–8.

found themselves saddled with debt charges that absorbed one-eighth of the Iranian budget, nearly a third of the Ottoman and almost half the Egyptian, and yet had very little to show in return.

Transport

Three factors shaped much of the development of transport in the Middle East: the region's location, the pattern of growth of steam navigation and the rivalries of the Great Powers. The high fuel consumption of steamships confined them to rivers and narrow waters for many decades; it was not until the 1870's that the greater part of international trade was carried by steamers rather than sailing ships. But within such waters steam navigation spread rapidly and by the 1830's the Mediterranean was criss-crossed by several lines. In the late 1830's British, French and Austrian lines provided regular services to Egypt, Syria and Turkey. After that progress was swift. Describing the situation around 1860, Farley reported: 'The mails leave London for Syria every Friday via Marseilles and every Monday via Trieste; while English steamers run regularly between Beirut and Liverpool'[22]—to which he could have added the Russian Black Sea line, which started operations in 1845 and served the Levant and Alexandria. And by 1870, there were three Egyptian, three British, five French, four Austrian, two Italian, one Russian and one Turkish steamship lines maintaining regular services to Egypt, and many others with ships calling at irregular intervals.[23] In the meantime, regular steamer services between India and Suez had been established in 1834, and between India and the Persian Gulf in 1861. It may be added that the opening of the Suez Canal not only attracted a vast volume of traffic to the Eastern Mediterranean but also strongly stimulated the development of steam navigation in general, by greatly facilitating fuelling on the Europe–Far Eastern route.[24]

Thus one may say that the Middle East was very adequately served by steamship lines connecting it with the outside world. It also had commercial steamboats on its navigable rivers at fairly early dates: the Nile in Egypt by 1841 and in the Sudan by the early 1860's,[25] the Tigris–Euphrates in 1862 and the Kārūn in 1888.

As regards railways, the other principal means of transport in the nineteenth century, the Middle East, with the definite exception of Egypt, was far less well equipped. In 1913 total railway track in the world was over 1,100,000 kilometres; of these 4,300 were in Egypt, 3,500 in the Ottoman Empire and 2,500 in the Sudan, i.e. less than 1 per cent of the world total,

[22] J. Farley, *The Resources of Turkey*, London 1862, p. 209.

[23] A. E. Crouchley, *The Economic Development of Modern Egypt*, London 1938, p. 142. See also Aḥmad al-Ḥitta, *Tārīkh Miṣr al-iqtiṣādī*, Cairo 1957, and N. Verney and G. Dambmann, *Les Puissances étrangères dans le Levant*, Paris 1900.

[24] See Max E. Fletcher, 'The Suez Canal and World Shipping', *Journal of Economic History*, 1958.

[25] See Richard Hill, *Sudan Transport*, London 1965.

a figure commensurate with neither the region's area nor its population. By that date India had 56,000 kilometres of railway and Japan 11,000. Two further facts stand out: the high development of railway transport in Egypt (which accounted for nearly half the regional total) and its absence in Iran.

By 1913 Egypt had a higher railway mileage per unit of *inhabited* area than almost any country in the world, and per unit of population than most countries.[26] It owed this position to an early start: Egypt had its first railway before Sweden or Japan, and it was not until the 1870's that the *total* railway mileage of Argentina and Brazil surpassed that of Egypt, while Japan did not catch up until the 1890's and China until after 1900. This in turn was largely due to the British desire for swift connections between Alexandria and Suez, the two steamship terminals on the route to India. A combination of factors made it possible for the British to push their railway scheme, against French opposition—just as the French were later to carry out the Suez Canal project, much more slowly and laboriously, against British obstruction. And after that the rulers of Egypt—first the viceroys and then the British—had enough freedom of action and sufficient resources to build a large network.

The completion of the trans-Egyptian railway greatly reduced the attraction of the rival route, through Mesopotamia, which also had its supporters in Britain. Other factors holding up railway development in Turkey, Syria and Iran were the weaker financial positions of these countries and the intensity of Great Power rivalries. One has only to read the diplomatic history of the Baghdad railway, or to follow the various projects and counter projects for railways in Iran drawn by the British and Russians, to realize what an important impediment this constituted. Here, too, except for Egypt and the Sudan, the contrast with India and Japan is striking.

Foreign Trade

International trade grew rapidly in the period under review. Rough estimates put the total (exports plus imports) in current prices at £320 million in 1800, £560 million in 1840, £1,450 million in 1860, £2,890 million in 1872–3 and £8,360 in 1913. Since prices were much higher in the period 1800–40 than in 1880–1913, the increase in real terms was greater than the twenty-five-fold rise registered in the above figures.[27]

Taking the Middle East as a whole, the expansion of foreign trade did not match the general advance. The Egyptian figure may indeed have been

[26] See Charles Issawi, 'Asymmetrical Development and Transport in Egypt, 1800–1914', in Polk and Chambers (eds.), *op. cit.*

[27] Albert H. Imlah, *Economic Elements in the Pax Britannica*, Cambridge, Mass., 1958, pp. 189, 94–8.

higher than the world average. The first reliable statistics put total trade in 1823 at £E.2·1 million; by 1860 the total stood at £E.5·1 million, by 1880 at £E.21·8 million and by 1913 at £E.60 million, a thirty-fold increase; moreover the 1823 level was probably higher than that of any of the previous fifty years or so.[28] But Ottoman trade almost certainly did not rise as fast, though comparison is vitiated by the fact that the area covered shrank steadily. In 1829 Ottoman trade with Britain and France amounted to £2·6 million, and total trade may be guessed to have been around £4 million. In 1876 the total was estimated at £54 million and in 1911 it stood at £63·5 million—perhaps a fifteen-fold increase[29]—and for the other parts of the region the growth in trade was surely much smaller.

The only available series for Iran, compiled by Entner, refers to that country's trade with Russia and shows a drop from an average of 10 million gold roubles in 1830–1 (a figure higher than that of previous years and reflecting the effects of the Treaty of Turkmanchai of 1828) to 6·9 million in 1860 and a recovery to 10·4 million in 1880; after that there was a rapid rise to a peak of 101·3 million in 1913.[30] In fact, however, Iran's total trade must have risen much less than ten-fold over the whole period. First, because the figures are in gold (1896) roubles, and therefore deflate the value of the 1830–1 totals, when prices were higher. (The figure for 1830–1 in account roubles was 25·2 million.) Secondly, because Russia's share of total trade probably rose appreciably over this period—it grew from 45 per cent of the total in 1901/2 to 63 per cent in 1912/13,[31] and in the late 1880's Curzon had estimated it at about £2 million (a figure that agrees fairly well with the Entner series) out of a total Iranian trade of some £7–8 million,[32] or say 30 per cent.

[28] For details see Issawi, *Economic History*, pp. 363–4.

[29] *Ibid.*, p. 30. For Syria the rise may have been of the same order, from say, £500,000 a year, in the 1820's to about £10 million in 1911—both figures referring to sea-borne trade, which rose far more rapidly than land-borne—see *ibid.*, pp. 208–9. For Iraq, Hasan puts average total trade at £438,000 in 1864–71, £1,760,000 in 1880–7, and £6,428,000 in 1912–13—see Muḥammad Salmān Ḥasan, *Al-taṭawwur al-iqtiṣādī fī al-'Irāq*, Beirut n.d., pp. 95 and 223.

[30] Marvin L. Entner, *Russo–Persian Commercial Relations, 1828–1914*, Gainesville, Fla., 1965, p. 8.

[31] *Ibid.*, p. 63.

[32] Curzon, *op. cit.*, vol. ii, pp. 562, 582. An earlier estimate had put the Russian share much lower. Even after doubling the figure for Persian imports from Russia, to take account of smuggling, total trade between the two countries in 1852–7 was put at 4·4 million thalers, out of a total Persian trade estimated at 42 million, or £6·3 million; however, the latter figure, which includes estimates for trade with Central Asia, may be somewhat too high. See Ernst Otto Blau, *Commerzielle Zustände Persiens*, Berlin 1858, pp. 164–5.

The League of Nations, *International Statistical Yearbook, 1928*, Geneva 1929, put Iran's imports in 1913 at $55 million and its exports at $38 million, or a total of $93 million (about £17 million). This would imply a three-fold increase in current prices in the sixty years preceding the First World War. Since price levels in the 1850's were close to those prevailing in 1913, the increase in real terms must also have been about three-fold.

Some increase must also have taken place in the first half of the nineteenth century. This is suggested by the fact that in 1831–56 trade through Trabzon, almost all of which

The few available data on Arabia and the Sudan also indicate that the rate of growth must have been rather low.[33]

Both India and Japan showed faster growth in their foreign trade than did the Middle East. Following the abrogation, in 1813, of the monopoly hitherto enjoyed by the East India Company 'the increase of trade with India [in 1814–32] has been enormous'.[34] By 1835–9 total trade averaged £18·7 million per annum (or about twice the 1814 level)[35] and in 1909–14 slightly over £250 million, a more than twenty-five-fold increase in one hundred years. In Japan total trade rose from an average of 36·0 million yen in 1868–70 to 1,511·4 million in 1913, a more than forty-fold increase.[36]

But although Middle Eastern foreign trade grew more slowly than did that of India and Japan, it played a relatively larger part in the economy of the region. Thus *per capita* trade in Egypt in 1913 amounted to $24·3, in the Ottoman Empire to $15·2, and in Iran to $10·3; the corresponding figures for India were $4·3 and for Japan $12·6. As a proportion of gross national product trade must have been far higher in the Middle East than in Japan and India.[37]

No less important is the difference in the composition of trade. By 1913 the Middle East's exports consisted almost entirely of agricultural produce, with some minerals from Turkey and a very small amount of oil from Iran. The same was true for India, except for some textiles. But Japanese exports already contained an appreciable proportion of cotton and silk textiles and other manufactured goods.

Agriculture

This large population growth and increase in exports presupposes an expansion of agricultural output, and all available evidence points to such a trend in most parts of the region. Generally speaking this was accomplished within the framework of peasant farming rather than plantation farming, and by extension of cultivated area rather than by intensification.[38] Hardly any attempts were made to improve methods of cultivation other than the foundation of the Ottoman Agricultural Bank in 1888 and one or

was in transit to or from Iran, multiplied twelve-fold (Blau, *op. cit.*, pp. 235–6). In the early 1850's Trabzon accounted for almost half of Iran's imports and a sixth of its exports.

Earlier figures are contradictory. In 1834 J. B. Fraser estimated Iran's total trade with Europe, including Russia, at £1 million (*ibid.*, p. 165). In 1836, W. Stuart put Britain's exports to Iran at just over £1 million and stated that Russia's were two-thirds higher (Curzon, *op. cit.*, vol. ii, p. 564).

[33] See Issawi, *Economic History*, Part V, Introduction, and Part VII, Introduction.

[34] Liverpool East India Committee, quoted in I. Durga Parshad, *Some Aspects of Indian Foreign Trade, 1757–1893*, London 1932, p. 132.

[35] *Ibid.*, p. 215.

[36] Bank of Japan, *Historical Statistics of the Japanese Economy* (1966).

[37] See Issawi, 'Asymmetrical Development'; the foreign trade and population figures were taken from the League of Nations *Statistical Yearbook*, 1928.

[38] For details see Issawi, 'Economic Growth', also Hla Myint, *The Economics of the Developing Countries*, London 1964, chapter 3.

two irrigation projects such as the Konya and Hindiyya dams, and there is no evidence of a rise in yields per acre.

The major exception to this statement was of course Egypt. Here extension of cultivation was impossible without irrigation works, which became steadily more elaborate and expensive in the course of the century. Conversion from basin to perennial irrigation naturally increased total annual yield per acre, since more than one crop could be grown on the same patch of land in a year and there was a shift to more valuable cash crops, especially cotton. But there is also evidence of a sharp rise in yields *per crop* per acre.[39] And at the turn of the century systematic efforts at intensification by means of selective breeding and application of chemical fertilizers were begun.[40]

India's experience recalls both that of Egypt and that of the rest of the Middle East. In most regions there was simply an extension of the cultivated area, with a switch to cash crops unaccompanied by a rise in yields. But there was also an enormous expansion of irrigation, and by 1913 government irrigation works watered an area of 25 million acres while private works accounted for a further 22 million. And starting around 1900 systematic research and experimentation was undertaken.[41]

Japan's development was completely different. Since most of the cultivable land was already under cultivation, growth could come only by raising yields, through intensification. This began as early as the 1870's and has been sustained to a remarkable degree ever since.[42]

Industry

'In India there was a much more definite hiatus than in the West between the decay of the handicrafts and the establishment of factories, during which certain types of demand were largely met by imports.'[43] In the Middle East the hiatus was even greater. For on the one hand the decline of some handicrafts, under the impact of European competition, began as early as the eighteenth century and was sharply accelerated from the 1830's on. And on the other the advent of modern industry was greatly delayed—

[39] See A. E. Crouchley, 'A Century of Economic Development', *L'Egypte Contemporaine*, (Cairo) 1939, and E. R. J. Owen, 'Cotton Production and the Development of the Egyptian Economy', D.Phil. Thesis, Oxford University, 1965.

[40] See Robert L. Tignor, *Modernization and British Colonial Rule in Egypt*, Princeton, N.J., 1966, chapter 7.

[41] See Anstey, *op. cit.*, chapter 7.

[42] See chart in U.S. Department of Agriculture, *Agriculture in 26 Developing Nations, 1948 to 1963*, Washington, D.C., p. 45. The most recent discussion of this question is in James I. Nakamura, *Agricultural Production and the Economic Development of Japan, 1873–1922*, Princeton, N.J., 1966.

[43] Anstey, *op. cit.*, p. 207. However the following judgement by a highly qualified scholar should be noted. 'The vast expansion of British cloth exports to India skimmed off the expanding demand. The handloom weavers were at least no fewer in number and no worse off economically at the end of the period than at the beginning. . . . The traditional sector, generally speaking, did not decline absolutely in economic significance,' Morris D. Morris, 'Towards a Reinterpretation of Nineteenth-Century Indian Economic History', *Journal of Economic History*, 1963.

indeed it was only just beginning to appear at the outbreak of the First World War, and did not really gain a foothold until the 1930's.[44]

India, on the other hand, continued to export handicraft textiles to Europe and elsewhere until early in the nineteenth century—it is worth recalling that Alexander Hamilton's report of 1791 demanded protection as much from Indian as from British goods; the decline of its handicrafts started around 1820 and modern industrialization began earlier than in the Middle East, in the 1860's, gathered strength in the last quarter of the nineteenth century and reached large proportions by 1914, in spite of a slackening after the 1890's.[45] As for Japan, there was practically no hiatus. For the handicrafts were immune to foreign competition until the opening of the country in the 1850's, and after that were greatly helped by the government to modernize and play an important part in the economy. And on the other hand, as early as the 1850's, and much more so after the Meiji restoration of 1868, modern industries were set up by the government or private enterprise, making of Japan a significant industrial power by 1914.[46]

Levels of Living

Only the most tentative statements are possible regarding trends in levels of living. In Egypt it is possible that there may have been a fall in levels of living (but surely not in *per capita* income) under Muḥammad ʿAlī, followed by a rise under his immediate successors. In the 1860's the cotton boom seems to have appreciably raised levels of living and during the British occupation there is also evidence of a distinct improvement.[47] For Syria, two scholars believe that there was a general impoverishment in the 1840's–50's,[48] but the decline in levels of living, if any, may well have been confined to the towns. It seems probable that from the 1860's until the First World War a steady, if slow, rise in *per capita* incomes and levels of living occurred. As for Iran, 'in periods of peace before the mid-nineteenth century the peasants were apparently better off than they are today'.[49] Clearly, one cannot draw conclusions for the region as a whole.

[44] See Issawi, *Economic History*, pp. 38–59, 452–60. For Muḥammad 'Ali's attempt at industrialization see *ibid.*, pp. 389–402.

[45] See Anstey, *op. cit.*, chapter 9, *Cambridge Economic History*, pp. 908–19, and Krishan Saini, 'Some measures of the economic growth of India, 1860–1913', unpublished paper, Columbia University.

[46] See *Cambridge Economic History*, pp. 875–99, and William W. Lockwood, *The Economic Development of Japan*, Princeton, N.J., 1954.

[47] See Owen, *op. cit.*, and Issawi, *Economic History*, p. 365.

[48] I. M. Smilianskaya, 'Razloženiye feodalnikh otnoshenii . . .', translated in *ibid.*, pp. 226–47, and Dominique Chevallier, 'Western Development and Eastern Crisis in the Mid-Nineteenth Century', in Polk and Chambers (eds.), *op. cit.*

[49] Nikki R. Keddie, *Historical Obstacles to Agrarian Change in Iran*, Claremont Asian Studies, Claremont, California, 1960, p. 4. See also A. K. S. Lambton, *Landlord and Peasant in Persia*, London 1953, pp. 143–5.

The course of events in India is at least as obscure. The most recent and authoritative survey of the state of knowledge in this field observes: 'It is dismaying to realize that even within very broad ranges of error we do not know whether during the past century-and-a-half the economy's performance improved, stagnated or actually declined,' and adds, 'This is true whether we attempt to measure performance in terms of *per capita* income or by any reasonable combination of qualitative-quantitative elements.'[50] As for Japan, 'some advance in living standards is evidenced in the decline of mortality rates, in increased *per capita* consumption of food and clothing supplies, and in the growth of public services of various kinds—especially in the cities', but most of the increase in national product was absorbed by population growth, capital investment and armaments.[51]

Educational Progress

Here one can be much more definite. Both in mass and in higher education the Middle East—which had started at a very low level in 1800—lagged behind other regions with distinctly lower *per capita* incomes. Thus Egypt's illiteracy rate in 1907 was 93 per cent, a figure equal to that of India but well above Burma's 71 per cent, Ceylon's 69 per cent and the Philippines' 51 per cent—not to mention Japan where already in the 1850's a male literacy rate of 40–50 per cent had been achieved and by 1914 'virtually the entire population had attained functional literacy, and compulsory school attendance was as close to 100 per cent as it could be'.[52] Illiteracy among the Turks (though not among the minority groups) must have been still higher, since the 1927 figure was 92 per cent (by which time Egypt's had fallen to 85 per cent) and in Iran higher still. As for higher education, by 1914 Egypt had only an embryonic university in Cairo, and Turkey a young and anaemic one in Istanbul,[53] in contrast to the small but far superior Indian universities (three of which were by then over sixty years old) and technical institutes, not to mention the excellent Japanese universities.

The one exception to the above statement is Lebanon, where illiteracy rates were almost certainly not above 50 per cent and which had two good foreign universities.

Agents of Economic and Social Change

Here too the main facts are clear, and very significant. In Japan the impetus for economic development came from the ruling circles, who kept a firm

[50] Morris, *op. cit.*; see also Anstey, *op. cit.*, chapter xvi. However, there is evidence of distinct progress in the forty or fifty years preceding the First World War—see Saini, *op. cit.*

[51] Lockwood, *op. cit.*, pp. 34, 138–50.

[52] Herbert Passin, *Society and Education in Japan*, New York 1965, p. 11—for details see Issawi, 'Asymmetrical Development'.

[53] At that time Robert College drew its students almost solely from minority groups—see Mears, *op. cit.*, chapter 5.

hold over the whole process. Foreign capital investment in the private sector was negligible and although foreign skills played an important part they did so under Japanese supervision and control.[54] In India, by contrast, the main impetus was British—not only through the government, which built the railways, ports and irrigation works, but also in the private sector: in foreign trade, plantations, finance and several industries. But much of the development was carried out by Indians, e.g. the cotton textile industry, which was almost entirely Indian, the steel industry and other branches. In this process Parsees played a leading part, but Hindus, notably the Marwaris, also had their share. The role of Muslims was negligible.[55]

In the Middle East the development that took place before 1914 was achieved almost entirely by foreigners or members of minority groups—Armenians, Greeks, Jews, Christian Lebanese and Syrians. The lack of interest of the Muslim majority—whether Egyptian, Turkish, Arabian or Iraqi—is striking, and has often been commented upon. Only in Syria, Iran and Hadramaut is there any evidence of commercial entrepreneurship among Muslims.[56] It may be added that the only country to receive any appreciable immigration was Egypt, which by 1914 had nearly a quarter of a million Europeans and somewhat fewer Armenians, Lebanese, Syrians and Jews, all of whom played a dominant part in the economy; mention should also be made of Jewish immigration to Palestine.

Conclusion

In drawing conclusions from the foregoing analysis, to see whether there was a specific pattern of economic development in the Middle East, an initial distinction should be made between the Mediterranean portion and the Persian Gulf–Red Sea portion of the region. The latter, which includes Iran, Iraq, Arabia and the Sudan, was relatively little affected by the changes taking place in the world until the exploitation of oil made of it, suddenly, the centre of the Middle East economy. Until the First World War, the impact of the world upon it had been mainly negative since European competition had severely hurt its shipping trade[57] and handicrafts without developing commensurately its other resources.

[54] Only one field was at first dominated by foreigners, the export trade. But even here 'by 1913 the bulk of overseas commerce was handled by Japanese firms, and half of it already moved in Japanese ships', Lockwood, *op. cit.*, p. 329.

[55] See Morris, *op. cit.*, Anstey, *op. cit.*, pp. 109–17, and D. H. Buchannan, *The Development of Capitalistic Enterprise in India*, New York 1934, chapters vii–xiii.

[56] See Issawi, *Economic History*, pp. 114–25, 505–13, Jamālzāde, *op. cit.*, pp. 93–117.

[57] Thus the total tonnage of vessels from the Persian Gulf entering Indian ports rose from nearly 100,000 tons per annum in the late 1850's to over 200,000 in the early 1900's and then fell well below its original level by the First World War—see *Statistical Abstract Relating to British India.* Since these figures cover not only Arab and Persian craft but British and other steamers plying between India and the Gulf, the fall in the former must have been very great. The same process occurred in the Red Sea region.

As for the Mediterranean region, here too there was much diversity, the trends observed being far more advanced in Egypt than in Syria or Turkey; the result of the foregoing discussion may be summarized as follows:

Population—growth probably started earlier than in other underdeveloped regions (including India and Japan) and therefore, even assuming that rates of increase were no higher than elsewhere, may have reached greater overall dimensions; this was certainly true of Egypt and possibly of Syria and Iraq.

Foreign Capital Borrowing—this was extremely high, and the proceeds were largely used unproductively, in contrast to India and Japan.

Transport—regular steamship connections with Europe were established very early; railways were highly developed in Egypt, much less so in Syria and Turkey.

Foreign Trade—growth was rapid, though slower than in Japan and, except for Egypt, slower than in India; however, both in *per capita* terms and as a percentage of gross national product, foreign trade was far greater than in India or Japan.

Agriculture—expansion of output was obtained by the extension of the cultivated area, not by intensification as in Japan. In Egypt even more than in India, irrigation played a leading part.

Industry—Middle Eastern crafts seem to have suffered more from foreign competition than did those of India and Japan; in addition, modern industry came much later.

Education—remarkably little progress was made in this field, probably less than in India, not to mention Japan.

Agents of Growth—these were drawn almost solely from foreign or minority groups, in sharp contrast with Japan and, to a far lesser extent, India.

Underlying the pattern formed by these trends are three basic, and partly interrelated, factors: the region's proximity to Europe and its strategic location, its social and political backwardness, and the nature of foreign economic and political control. To them should be added a fourth: the scarcity of those resources on which industry was based until the end of the nineteenth century, notably water-power, wood, coal and iron. Almost the only raw material available for industrialization was cotton.

Proximity accounts for the early date at which Europe began to impinge on the economy of the Middle East. It helps to explain the forging of transport links with Europe, the exposure of Middle Eastern handicrafts to devastating foreign competition, the expansion of Middle Eastern agricultural output in response to foreign demand, and the consequent rapid growth of foreign trade. Proximity may have impelled Europeans to help in establishing quarantines and other hygienic controls in the Middle East, to prevent the spread of epidemics, and in this way may have stimulated population growth.[58] It facilitated the migration to the Middle East of European entrepreneurs and technicians, who made an important contribution to the region's development and imposed on it a certain direction and pattern. And proximity certainly facilitated European economic and political control over the Middle East.[59]

The social and political backwardness of the region helps to account for the nature of its response to the impact of European economic expansion. Three aspects of this may be distinguished. First, the educational and cultural level of the Middle East was very low, even compared to other underdeveloped regions such as Japan and India, not to mention south-eastern Europe and Latin America.[60] Secondly its social structure was unfavourable for development. For various historical reasons, it had failed to produce a vigorous bourgeoisie and lacked autonomous bodies, such as city states, guilds and other corporations which could express, and defend, the interests of classes or groups interested in economic development; instead, control remained firmly in the hands of the military and civilian bureaucracy. Thirdly, and no doubt at least partly as a consequence, the economic ideas and policies of the government were singularly unenlightened. In Europe, the basic tenet of the Mercantilists was the need to promote exports in order to increase the output of local industry, and various measures were used to achieve this end. In the Ottoman Empire, however, exports were taxed at a higher rate than imports. Here prevailed a 'policy of provision', to use Hecksher's expressive term describing the medieval European attitude. The main objectives were not to promote local production but to meet the fiscal needs of the government and to ensure that the principal towns, and in particular Istanbul, would be adequately supplied. Some signs of a more enlightened policy appeared under Selim III but little came of it. And after that Middle Eastern statesmen, such as Reshid Pasha, swallowed the liberal prescription for economic growth and did little to help the economy until the latter part of the nineteenth century.[61]

The very low educational and cultural level of the Middle East, its

[58] For a detailed study see Robert Tignor, 'Public Health Administration under British Rule, 1882–1914', unpublished doctoral dissertation, Yale University, 1960. Rudimentary quarantines were established in several Ottoman ports in the first half of the nineteenth century.

[59] The following judgement deserves consideration: 'Had Japan been situated in closer proximity to the great industrialized nations of the West, her pattern of growth and structural change after 1868 would probably have been somewhat different. Both the pressure to industrialize, and the opportunity to do so, might have been somewhat diminished. She would have enjoyed more favorable access to large external markets for her coal, marine products, and high-value farm crops. Western consumer manufactures might also have competed more strongly in Japan than was the case, delaying the progress of industry.' Lockwood, *op. cit.*, p. 353.

[60] See Issawi, 'Asymmetrical Development'.

[61] *Idem*, *Economic History*, pp. 52–3.

social structure, and the form of its political institutions, meant that it had neither a half-way efficient government nor a native bourgeoisie that could take the country's economic development in hand and help to guide its course along the desired path. Hence when it was struck by the Industrial Revolution, with its demand for the exploitation of its raw materials, markets and transport possibilities, development had to be carried out by Europeans assisted by minority groups—if it was to be achieved at all. But development through such an implanted bourgeoisie had four fatal defects. First, a very large share of the fruits of progress went to foreigners or members of minorities; to take an extreme case, just before the First World War these two groups may have owned 15–20 per cent of Egypt's wealth and absorbed well over 10 per cent of its income. Secondly, the presence of educated foreigners or minority groups weakened the main pressure on the governments for the spread of education and the development of human resources in these countries. Thirdly, the existence and power of this bourgeoisie inhibited the growth of a native Muslim one. Lastly, because of this factor, the whole process of capitalist development in the region remained alien and was regarded as such by its inhabitants, a fact that helps to explain the measures taken against foreigners and minority groups in Turkey in the 1920's and in Egypt in the 1940's–50's. It should be added that in Syria and Lebanon foreigners played a different and far smaller part and development was much more indigenous.

Lastly, as regards foreign economic and political control, in a way the Middle East had the worst of both worlds. Japan, never having lost its full independence, was able to carry out the 1868 revolution and thereafter to guide the economy in the direction demanded by the national interest, as interpreted by the ruling group. India, by contrast, was subjected to outright British control. This had many drawbacks, which have been rightly stressed since the time of Adam Smith. But it had some advantages, which were strikingly foretold by Marx (see his brilliant 'The Future Results of British Rule in India', published in the *New York Daily Tribune*, July 1853) though carefully ignored by his followers. After the initial plunder and dislocation, British rule provided honest and efficient administration. It also ensured that the foreign debt was used productively, to build the largest irrigation system in the world and the third largest railway network, and to provide some education, and it transformed the land tenure system. And while not encouraging, and indeed often positively impeding, industrialization it 'laid down the material premises' for it.

In the Middle East, however, there was no complete foreign *political* control, except in Aden and in the Sudan after 1896. In the rest of the region there was much influence by rival powers, which jealously watched and checked each other. This led to the abortion of Muḥammad ʿAlī's attempt at development and of two promising revolutions, the Egyptian in

1882 and the Iranian in 1908–9 and to the stultification of much progress that might otherwise have taken place in Turkey, Iran and Syria. Even in Egypt the Capitulations and Caisse de la Dette thwarted many of Cromer's reforms.[62] Yet foreign *economic* control was overwhelming and led not only to the buttressing of the existing social order and to the creation of a deep feeling of discouragement but also to the sucking out of vast sums from the region in the form of payments of interest and dividends. This drain, together with the rapid population growth, wars, royal extravagance and possibly the rise in consumption levels, left little for investment in physical and human capital. The disastrous results of such a situation showed themselves most clearly in Egypt after the First World War, when the limits of cultivation had been reached and terms of trade deteriorated. Fortunately for the Middle East, it got a second chance, in the form of the discovery of its oil resources and a huge amount of foreign aid, and this is enabling it today to carry out a new programme of industrialization and modernization of its economy and society.

[62] Another important factor was the restrictions imposed on the Middle Eastern governments by international commercial conventions, which prevented them from giving tariff protection to their industries. But these restrictions had their counterpart in India and, until 1899, in Japan.

Structural Changes in the Egyptian Economy, 1937–1965

ROBERT MABRO and PATRICK O'BRIEN

Introduction

THE economic performance of Egypt during the nineteenth century and the early decades of the twentieth century has consistently been referred to as a typical illustration of 'lop-sided' development.[1] The economic activity of the country was centred on cotton: production, ginning and processing, financing of the crop, irrigation and public works, internal trade and exports. Cotton was the major source of rural and urban wealth as well as the cause of recurrent crisis. This almost exclusive reliance on a single export good implied a great deal of vulnerability to international forces over which Egypt could exercise little or no control.

TABLE 1. *Growth Rates of GDP 1913–1965*

Subperiods	Years	
1	1913–21	Almost zero on average, perhaps because of a decline during the war followed by a rise.
2	1922–28	2½% on average per annum.
3	1929–35	Decline at a rate of 1·5% on average per annum.
4	1936–39	Recovery at a rate of 3–4% per annum.
5	1940–45	Stagnation.
6	1946–51	High rates of growth, 7–8% per annum.
7	1952–54	Sharp decline.
8	1955–56	Slow recovery.
9	1957–60	Accelerated rate of growth (2·7%, 5·5%, 6·1% and 6·9% for the respective years).
10	1961–65	High rates of growth, 6% on average per annum.

Sources: B. Hansen and D. Mead, 'The National Income of the U.A.R. (Egypt) 1939–1962', Institute of National Planning, Memo No. 355.
National Planning Committee, Memo No. 121.
M. Anis, 'A Study of the National Income of Egypt', *L'Egypte Contemporaine*, Nos. 261 & 262 (1950).
B. Hansen, 'Planning and Economic Growth in the U.A.R. 1960–65', in P. J. Vatikiotis (ed.), *Egypt since the Revolution*, London 1968.

[1] C. Issawi, 'Egypt since 1880: A Study in Lop-sided Development', *Journal of Economic History*, xxi, 1961.

In Table 1 we have attempted to assess variations in the overall rate of growth from 1913 to 1965. A word of caution seems necessary at the outset. Income estimates are not very reliable for the prewar years, but since we are interested in relative changes rather than absolute levels, it should be possible to identify phases of stagnation, of accelerated growth or of decline by comparing the rate of growth in different periods.

It is possible to relate these different subperiods to international and domestic events. The effect of the world wars is clear in subperiods 1 and 5. The Great Depression explains the decline between 1928 and 1935, while the Korean Boom and its aftermath are readily identified in subperiods 6 and 7. Between 1945 and 1951, the economy benefited first from the resumption of foreign trade and from an investment boom following the wartime stagnation, partly financed by the accumulated Allied Debt in the form of sterling balances and later from the Korean Boom. Between 1913 and 1954, the Egyptian economy was strongly affected by fluctuations in cotton prices and the interruption of foreign trade in wartime. Egypt thus appears as a vulnerable open economy which depended heavily on cotton exports for overall growth. The impact of foreign trade on the rate of growth of National Income does not exclude the influence of other determinants. Surely changes in the rate and pattern of investment, fiscal and monetary policies, occasional crop failures and increases in agricultural productivity have all affected the rate of growth. But their contribution was probably much less significant between 1913 and 1954 than in subsequent periods.

Since 1954, the Government has assumed a more active role in the management of the economy. Government intervention, gentle during the first years of the Revolution, less timid during the First Industrial Plan (1957–60), became more decisively systematic and vigorous under the First Five Year Plan (1960–1, 1964–5).[2] A rapid glance at subperiods 8, 9 and 10 in Table 1 indicates the results. Sustained growth at an average annual rate of 6 per cent seems to follow an earlier phase when the rates of increase of GNP were rapidly lifted from 2 per cent to 7 per cent. A structural transformation of the economy initiated in the early 'thirties provided a favourable precondition to the success of recent policies. It became the significant feature of economic development in Egypt during the 1950's and the 1960's.

The purpose of this essay is to examine certain aspects of this structural transformation of the economy, brought about mainly through Government intervention which changed the pattern of investment and trade. How radical are the changes? Can we interpret them as indicating the emergence of a new economic set-up, structurally less vulnerable than the old system to external repercussions?

[2] P. K. O'Brien, *The Revolution in Egypt's Economic System*, Oxford 1966.

1. Changes in the Pattern of Investment

In traditional theory of the Harrod–Domar type investment is taken as the major determinant of growth. In Egypt comparatively high rates of growth achieved in the 1950's and early 1960's are indeed associated with an increase in the investment ratio. Changes in the sectoral pattern of investment seem, however, to have exerted a more significant influence.

We have attempted to relate the rate of growth of GNP to the investment ratio in the following model:

$$Y_t = a + bX_{t-2}$$

where Y = rate of growth of GDP, X = ratio of gross investment to GDP.

Due to lack of data, the analysis is restricted to the period 1952–3, 1964–5. The resulting equation is:

$$Y_t = -7{\cdot}682 + {\cdot}903X_{t-2} \quad R = {\cdot}7$$

The correlation coefficient is significant at the 5 per cent level. This mode with a two-year lag gave better results than alternative equations with different lags, which suggests that the average gestation period for investment amounted to two years. The estimate is not too unreasonable because capital expenditures on agriculture, heavy industry and major public works, a significant component of total investment during this period, are slow to mature.

The regression line further suggests that a minimum of 8 per cent of GDP needs to be invested before any growth occurs. Along the regression line any percentage increase in the investment ratio raises the rate of growth by 0·9 per cent. Thus the marginal gross investment/output ratio seems to be surprisingly low.

Our result may be due partly to the use of gross figures for both investment and domestic product. If it had been possible to use figures net of depreciation we would expect a regression line with no intercept and a higher incremental capital/output ratio. The model is also incomplete, since other important determinants of the rate of growth have not been identified. GDP figures should have been corrected for movements in the terms of trade and exogenous increases in productivity taken into account. If due allowance were made for all these sources of statistical bias, a much higher estimate of the capital coefficient should obtain.

There are, however, reasons to believe that the actual value of ICOR is comparatively small. The share of government, personal and other types of services—including trade and finance—in GDP, has been consistently high (around 32 per cent) for a long period stretching between 1937 and 1965. Services are a growing and labour-intensive sector of the economy that requires little investment. The contribution of the Suez Canal to the economy considerably increased after 1956 as a result first of nationalization and later of a remarkable growth in international shipping activity. The benefits that accrue during this period were unrelated to the amounts invested by the Canal Authority. It is also possible that the increased investment drew some excess capacity into fuller use (in the infrastructure and services only), created external economies and fostered the consumption of services. The stronger these forces, the lower the marginal capital/output ratio.

Finally, we must recall that an aggregate investment ratio may conceal changes in the sectoral pattern of investment. Higher rates of growth are consistent with a constant or slightly increased investment ratio if capital expenditures are reallocated from sectors with high ICOR to sectors with lower ICOR. Such a phenomenon seems to have taken place in Egypt between 1952 and 1956.

If we divide this period into three phases '52/53-'56/57; '57/58-'59/60; '60/61-'64/65 we notice that average rates of growth rose much faster than average investment ratios.

TABLE 2

Years	Average investment ratio	Average rate of growth
	%	%
1952/53-56/57	14	2·4
1957/58-59/60	14	6·1
1960/61-64/65	17	6·3

The small marginal change in the investment ratio was however accompanied by important shifts in allocation. The percentage of total investment allocated to each sector is as shown in Table 3.

The most remarkable trend in the pattern of investment is the decline of the share of housing from 32·8 per cent in subperiod 1 to 23 per cent in 2 and 10·8 per cent in 3. This is matched by increases in the shares of agriculture from 11·3 per cent to 13·8 per cent and 16·6 per cent respectively, of industry and of transport. The share of services declined slightly from 11·4 per cent in 1 to 10·2 per cent in 3. To assess the significance of these shifts, we need to evaluate the gross investment/gross output ratio of each sector. The larger the differences in the respective values of this coefficient, the greater the effects of reallocation on the rate of growth.

The large share of investment in housing (a sector with a very high capital/output ratio) helps to explain the relatively low rate of growth obtained in the '1952–1956' period. Higher rates of growth occurred under the First

TABLE 3. *Allocation of Total Investment to Selected Sectors*

Years	Agriculture*	Industry & Electricity	Transport & Suez Canal	Housing	Services†
	%	%	%	%	%
1. 1952–53	11·6	24·8	20·3	31·7	10·8
1953–54	11·2	29·1	18·3	34·7	10·5
1954–55	10·5	30·0	19·6	34·2	11·2
1955–56	10·5	33·5	17·1	30·2	10·7
1956–57	13·0	26·8	12·9	33·1	14·0
Average 1952–57	11·3	28·8	17·6	32·8	11·4
2. 1957–58	12·8	26·2	17·2	29·0	14·4
1958–59	13·7	30·0	18·2	22·1	15·4
1959–60	14·8	32·4	20·9	18·1	11·4
Average 1957–60	13·8	29·5	18·7	23·0	13·7
3. 1960–61	13·9	32·5	33·2	8·5	8·9
1961–62	14·9	22·5	28·3	15·1	11·4
1962–63	16·6	30·8	18·0	12·6	11·6
1963–64	18·1	37·8	12·1	10·0	9·6
1964–65	19·3	42·0	13·5	8·1	9·3
Average 1960–65	16·6	33·2	21·0	10·8	10·2

* Agriculture does not include the High Dam
† Services does not include Trade and Finance

Sources: U.A.R. Department of Statistics and Census, 'Ten Years of Revolution Statistical Atlas', Cairo, 1962
B. Hansen in P. J. Vatikiotis (ed.), *op. cit.*

TABLE 4. *Gross Investment/Gross Output Ratios*

Agriculture	2·4
Industry and Electricity	3·4
Transport and Communication	4·5
Housing	15·0
Services	1·8
Weighted average	3·4

Industrialization Plan (1957–60) not as a result of an increase in the gross investment ratio, but rather as a consequence of reallocation towards agriculture, transport and the services. This factor continued to operate, mainly in favour of industry, during the First Five Year Plan, helping to achieve the high rate of growth that obtained from 1960 to 1965.

Investment planning finds its justification here. The preference of the private investors for real estate, a common phenomenon in underdeveloped countries, was particularly strong in Egypt in the early years of the Revolution. Capitalists were reluctant to invest in industry and the land reform diverted funds from agriculture into housing. Whether houses are preferable to other commodities is a matter of judgement. If the aim, however, is to maximize the rate of growth, then neither the rate nor the pattern of investment are irrelevant. And this may imply some form of control.

2. *Structural Transformation and Sectoral Interrelationships*

The changing pattern of investment accelerated the structural transformation of the economy initiated in the early thirties.

TABLE 5. *Shares in GDP*

Years	Agriculture %	Industry & Electricity %	Construction %	Transport %	Housing %	Other* Services %
1937	49	8	2	3	7	31
1945	41	12	2·5	5	7	32·5
1952/53	33·5	15	3	6·5	7·3	34·7
1959/60	31	20	3·6	7	6	32·4
1964/65	27	22	5·3	9·5	4·5	31·7

* Includes Commerce, Finance, Government, etc.
Sources: See Table 1.

The most conspicuous features of this table are a steady decline in the contribution of agriculture to GDP, the emergence of an industrial sector giving rise to increased constructional and transport activities and the relative stability of the share of services in the national product. In other words, the average rates of increase of agricultural, 'services' and industrial income were respectively lower, equal to and higher than the average rate of growth of GDP. This pattern happens to conform to the ideas and expectations of most development theorists. A closer examination of sectoral interrelationships may however reveal some difficult problems.

(*a*) *Industry*

The rapid development of industry throughout the period 1937–65 reflects the strength of a political drive towards self-sufficiency. For many decades, since 1900, Egyptian economists have been bearing witness in their writings to the frustrating effects of British policies that emphasized specialization in cotton and the importance of free trade, both to the advantage of the Metropolis.[3] In this historical context, industrialization became an essential ingredient of the complex of aims and symbols associated with the idea of independence. But what about the real performance?

Statistical regression models may show that the growth of industry correlates with the rise in aggregate production even though the overall contribution of the industrial sector to GDP remains small (8 per cent in 1937, 22 per cent at the close of the First Five Year Plan). Egyptian industry however cannot be identified without qualifications as a 'leading sector'. Narrowly defined, leading sectors do not grow in response to other sectors but rather develop autonomously, often to exploit new demands, recently discovered resources or technical innovations. They transmit a strong impetus to the rest of the economy through a closely-knit network of linkages. To qualify for the adjective 'leading', a sector must make also a substantial contribution to the overall rate of growth.

The importance of linkages between the Egyptian industry and other sectors of the economy can be assessed from an examination of input–output tables constructed by the National Planning Committee.[4] Although inadequate for exact measurement and forecasting, these tables are still suitable for the purposes of qualitative analysis.

Forward linkages (deliveries of intermediate goods to other sectors) are particularly weak. In both the 1954 and 1959 tables less than 20 per cent of the intermediate goods produced by industry are supplied to other sectors, and this share does not appear to rise significantly in the 1962 table. The largest proportion of gross industrial output, 63 per cent in 1954 and 65 per cent in 1959, is for final demand. A most depressing feature is the share of investment goods in final use: less than 2 per cent in both years.

By contrast, backward linkages (supply of intermediate goods to the industrial sector) are relatively strong. Industry is the major receiver of intermediate goods delivered by the agricultural sector to the economy (80 per cent in both 1954 and 1959). Agricultural raw materials account for 50 per cent (1954) and 42 per cent (1959) of total domestic inputs supplied to the industrial sector. As in most underdeveloped countries, Egyptian manufacturing concentrates on processing the produce of the land. Greater diversification was however achieved under the First Five Year Plan.

Industry absorbed 50 per cent of the intermediate output of the 'services' sector (1959). The contribution of electricity (46 per cent of intermediate

[3] See for examples Congrès National Egyptien, 'Œuvres du Congrès National Egyptien tenu à Bruxelles le 22, 23, 24 Septembre 1910' (n.d.); El Sayed Hassan, *Essai sur une orientation nouvelle de l'économie égyptienne*, Toulouse–Alger 1927; Banque Misr, 'Creation des Industries Nationales et Organisation des Prêts industriels. Projet d'une banque industrielle égyptienne', Mimeo, Cairo 1929.

[4] Three tables were constructed, for 1954, 1959 and 1962 respectively.

output delivered to industry) and transport (23 per cent although smaller) is still very significant.

The figures derived from input–output tables may not be very accurate, but the pattern of interdependencies that emerge from the analysis is likely to bear a stronger relation to reality. It seems that Egyptian industry is essentially a producer of consumer goods. Its largest components can be viewed as the last stage of an integrated agricultural system. Absorbing most of its own intermediate output, the contribution of industry to the modernization of other sectors—measured by their demand for industrial goods—is rather limited. As Hazem El Beblaoui points out: 'Tandis que la demande agricole directe et indirecte constitue 30 pour cent de la production industrielle, la demande industrielle nécessaire pour la production agricole se réduit a 12 pour cent. Cette dernière observation confirme non seulement que l'industrie égyptienne est à base agricole, mais aussi que l'agriculture égyptienne n'est pas assez industrialisée. . . .'[5]

The significant link between industry and the rest of the economy comes basically through domestic—mostly urban—demand for finished manufactured goods. How far the level of expenditures on such products was itself determined by developments which raised incomes of households dependent on agriculture, construction, Government and other services is difficult to measure. But it seems reasonable to argue that changes in the level of this consumption were partly determined by the development of industry itself and partly by an expansion of Government employment, rather than by the growth of agricultural income.

Industry does not appear to contribute significantly to the *future* growth of the economy because its output of capital goods is almost negligible and its export capacity handicapped by high costs and inefficient initiative in trade promotion.

Nor can industrialization be simply equated with self-sufficiency. Production function studies have shown that the growth of industrial output is heavily dependent in Egypt on the rate of investment. The capital coefficient in the Cobb–Douglas function varies between ·65 and ·70 and the residual term of the equation—less than 0·5 per cent—is very small.[6] Egyptian industry has not benefited from the so-called 'exogenous' increases in total productivity that help to reduce the amount of investment —and therefore of imports—required to sustain a given rate of growth of output.

A policy of import substitution can be self-defeating when current production heavily relies on imports of intermediate goods. We shall show

[5] H. El Beblaoui, *L'Interdépendance agriculture-industrie et le développement économique (l'exemple de la RAU)*, Paris 1967, p. 26.

[6] E. Shamoon, 'Production functions and the Residual in Egyptian Manufacturing Industry', 1967, unpublished M.Sc. dissertation, School of Oriental and African Studies, University of London.

in a later section that the share of raw materials and semi-finished goods in total imports was much larger in 1965 than in 1952.

This analysis should not be construed as a case against industrialization but as a criticism of naive preconceptions about self-sufficiency and uncoordinated planning. Many a misguided decision is attributable to lack of communication between the numerous Government agencies that select independently their own projects, and to the inadequacy of their investment criteria.[7]

(*b*) *Agriculture*

The relative decline of the agricultural share in GDP, generally considered as an index of development, may have a less favourable interpretation against this background. The burden of supplying more food to a population increasing at an annual rate of 2·5 per cent, more raw materials to a growing domestic industry and more export goods to meet the rising import requirements of the country, falls squarely on agriculture.

Agricultural production failed to grow rapidly enough to meet these conflicting demands. The period is characterized by a slight decrease in the cotton area more than compensated by an increase in average yields. But the export capacity—allowing for changes in the terms of trade and occasional crop failures—remained fairly constant.[8] Progress was registered in the production and export of rice, a commodity that may acquire great importance in the new High Dam era. Food production rose by 48 per cent between 1937 and 1960 while total population almost doubled. Rapid urbanization and higher *per capita* income both added to the pressure on food supplies. Before 1937 Egypt was a net exporter of food, in 1965 foodstuffs accounted for 22·1 per cent of total imports. The balance of payments problem that arises in this context needs no further elaboration. The movement of resources from agriculture to industry characteristic of this period, can be theoretically justified if the balance of payments problem can be solved by the industrial sector. But Egyptian industry is neither equipped to produce capital goods—that compete with food for inputs—nor yet able to export large quantities of manufactured consumer goods—to meet the increasing requirements for both food and capital goods or to permit a reallocation of land as between cotton and food.

The priority given to the erection of the High Dam and the increased share of agricultural investment in total capital expenditures (see Table 2) indicate that Egyptian planners were conscious of the problem. They may have failed to realize that gestation lags are long when most projects are concerned with horizontal (land reclamation) rather than vertical expansion

[7] See O'Brien, *op. cit.*, and B. Hansen and G. Marzouk, *Development and Economic Policy in the U.A.R. (Egypt)*, Amsterdam 1965, ch. 11.

[8] D. Mead, *Growth and Structural Change in the Egyptian Economy*, Homewood, Ill., 1967, Statistical appendix table V.A. 6.

(drainage, high-yield seeds, etc.,) and that resources invested in the New Valley and to a lesser extent in the Tahrir Province would be largely wasted. Still, the performance of agricultural productivity—3 per cent increase of total productivity and 2 per cent of labour productivity per annum—since 1945 is no guide to the future.[9] The contribution of this sector may rise significantly on maturity of past investment and if the High Dam fulfils its promises.

The future of Egyptian development, granted the forthcoming improvements in agricultural productivity, also depends on the evolving pattern of sectoral relationships. Dualism is still the major characteristic of the economy. Industry failed to contribute to a modernization—which does not always imply mechanization—of agriculture that would lead to an increase in productivity and income, the necessary condition of an enlarged industrial market in the rural world. Stronger linkages result in higher rates of growth in both sectors. The technological improvements transmitted to agriculture may be translated through a larger market into economies of scale for industry.

(*c*) *Services*

The relationships between industry and the services are more difficult to assess. The sudden increase in employment and output of the construction sector between 1959 and 1965 was a reflection of both the level of investment activities under the Plan and the importance of their domestic component. The transport sector benefited somewhat from industrial expansion, but the most important cause of its remarkable growth is attributable to the Suez Canal, that is to international rather than domestic developments.

The sector labelled 'other services' has peculiar features. In National Income accounts this category is a mixed bag, including Government and Commerce and among many others bankers as well as pedlars, highly-trained professionals as well as domestic servants. It is striking that the share of this sector in GDP—the largest share in 1965—remained relatively stable throughout the period after 1937.[10] Development in the services cannot be properly understood without a reference to urbanization. Rural migration to towns, already significant in the early 'thirties, acquired momentum during and after the Second World War and ever since has not ceased to inflate the size of towns.[11] In the 'forties and early 'fifties when the industrial sector was relatively small, agricultural migrants were absorbed by the services and in the earlier years by the Allied Military Establishment.

[9] See Hansen and Marzouk, *op. cit.*, and B. Hansen, 'Planning and Economic Growth in the U.A.R. 1960–65', cited above.

[10] See Table 5.

[11] R. Mabro, 'Agricultural Underemployment, Industrial Expansion and the Lewis Model, 1939–65', *Journal of Development Studies*, July 1967.

It is possible to argue that the development of towns and the availability of a labour surplus in the urban services both favoured postwar industrialization by providing to the new sector cheap labour and a market. But in return, the impact of industrialization on employment, output and productivity in the services was uneven. D. Mead has shown that labour productivity increased significantly in 'Commerce and Finance', between 1945 and 1963, with very little expansion in employment, which suggests that a wide margin of excess capacity did exist in this sector at the end of the war.[12] The expansion of industry attracted new migrants and encouraged further urbanization. It created income which may have raised the demand for houses, lighting, domestic servants, transport, internal trade, entertainment and above all a wide range of public services. But the inflow of migrants—combined with the high natural rate of population growth—outstripped the absorption potential of industry and the burden of creating new employment fell again on the Government and the private 'services'. What proportion of new jobs in these sectors reflects their real needs and how much is 'parasitic' employment is difficult to assess. The growth of the services may partly reflect an adaptation of social and economic organization to population pressure. Jobs are often created less for the productive work they provide and more as a technique for the distribution of income.

The rise in the share of public consumption in GDP from roughly 14 per cent in 1959 to some 25 per cent in 1965 tends however to suggest that the Government was under pressure to expand employment for social reasons. Even if we allow for increased defence expenditure arising from the Yemen War (1963), and for the small increase in the share of expenditures on health and education from 4 per cent of GNP in 1959 to some 6 per cent in 1965, the residual increase in public consumption (costs of administration) would still be large. It seems unwarranted on economic grounds. A better allocation of expenditures from administration to social investment might have enhanced growth prospects for the long run.

The consequence of these employment and other policies is the emergence of a new class of military, civil servants and retired officers whose consumption patterns have larger components of services and manufactured goods than the rest of the population. The feed-back effects on the growth of services may have been significant. The design of an industrial output-mix heavily biased in favour of domestic consumer goods can perhaps be regarded as a political consequence of the emergence of this new class.

3. Trade

Changes in the volume and composition of trade are necessarily associated with changes in the levels and patterns of investment and output. The

[12] Mead, *op. cit.*, p. 145.

relationship operates indeed in two directions: the growth of income has an impact on trade, which is itself an 'engine of growth'. We shall concentrate on this latter aspect.

The mechanism through which commodities purchased outside Egypt affected its rate of growth can be revealed through a breakdown of imports. Table 6[13] shows that between 1952 and 1965 imports of food, capital goods and intermediate products have increased their shares at the expense of consumer goods. There are however important year to year fluctuations partly due to the instability of yields in agriculture to changes in domestic policies and to external repercussions. The Ministries of Mr. Aly Sabri and Mr. Zakaria Mohiedin had different attitudes towards economic policies and trade controls. In the aftermath of Suez—and the same phenomenon seemed to recur after the June war—controls on the import of consumer goods were relaxed. Fluctuations in the share of food imports are related to the availability of American aid. Despite these variations the trends are easily discernible.

Three influences have been at work: the expansion of industry (relatively more intermediate goods and less consumer goods), the high level of investment activities (a larger share of capital and intermediate goods) and the population explosion (more food).

Imports provided both an incentive and a strategy for industrialization. Foreign manufactured commodities pioneered the local market and often established channels of distribution which reduced both the risks and sales costs for local enterprises once established behind the tariff and quota wall. But import substitution often became 'the substitution of imports by imports'. The increasing share of intermediate goods in Table 6, unless explained by the rising requirements for capital formation, would lend some support to this view.

The direct relationship between imports and capital formation is more significant than variations in the share of intermediate goods for economic growth. Before 1960 imported machinery and other capital goods accounted for approximately a third of gross investment. Planners expected 42 per cent of total expenditure on gross fixed capital formation during the period 1960–1 to 1964–5 to be in foreign currency. The import content of investment turned out to be higher, nearer to 50 per cent under the First Five Year Plan. The bias in investment policy over the last decade towards industry in general and heavier industry in particular has resulted in increased demand for imports.

Imports of food increased from just under £E. 1 m. in 1939 to £E. 100 m. in 1965 with a peak of £E. 150 m. in 1962. Foreign food has performed the same function as imported capital goods in alleviating the effects of a likely and serious bottleneck in domestic supply. Classical growth theorists

[13] We are indebted to Mr. Samir Radwan for providing us with this breakdown.

Table 6. *Structure of Egyptian Imports 1945–65*

Year	Food		Consumer Goods		Raw Materials and Intermediate Goods		Capital Goods		Others		Total Imports	
	£E. 000	%	£E. 000	%	£E. 000	%	£E. 000	%	£E. 000	%	£E. 000	%
1945	9,742	16·3	21,649	36·2	20,232	34·0	7,974	13·4	72	·01	59,669	100
1946	9,149	11·0	35,870	43·2	26,209	31·6	11,269	13·6	386	·06	82,883	100
1947	10,365	10·2	42,583	41·7	30,341	29·7	18,599	18·2	163	·02	102,050	100
1948	37,953	23·4	54,254	33·5	40,432	25·0	29,340	18·0	191	·01	162,170	100
1949	34,054	20·5	51,966	31·3	42,709	25·7	35,764	21·5	1,790	·10	166,283	100
1950	46,712	21·8	73,302	34·2	48,375	22·6	42,755	20·0	3,119	·14	214,263	100
1951	61,021	23·0	108,186	40·7	64,424	24·2	29,559	11·1	2,778	·10	265,968	100
1952	66,794	29·6	55,394	24·5	58,356	25·8	44,787	20·0	460	·01	225,791	100
1953	47,384	27·1	37,333	21·4	50,552	29·0	38,460	22·0	984	·05	174,713	100
1954	20,899	11·2	67,834	35·3	57,359	30·7	41,913	22·4	644	·04	186,649	100
1955	20,034	11·0	46,879	25·8	64,430	35·4	50,048	27·5	525	·03	181,916	100
1956	41,854	17·2	83,955	34·5	69,579	28·6	47,644	19·6	198	·01	243,230	100
1957	44,688	16·7	120,997	45·2	61,844	23·1	39,906	15·0	133	·00	267,568	100
1958	45,259	19·6	43,405	18·8	79,137	34·2	63,184	27·3	165	·01	231,150	100
1959	48,172	22·4	43,573	20·2	68,844	32·0	54,475	25·3	112	·01	215,176	100
1960	77,862	30·0	40,570	15·5	80,408	31·0	61,461	23·5	91	·00	260,292	100
1961	92,060	32·7	32,516	11·5	88,112	31·3	68,628	24·4	185	·01	281,401	100
1962	150,372	40·6	47,687	13·0	106,653	38·8	65,078	17·6	68	·00	369,858	100
1963	117,761	28·6	76,709	18·7	124,707	30·3	91,150	22·2	804	·02	411,131	100
1964	97,629	25·8	78,103	18·0	129,352	34·2	83,556	22·0	15	·00	378,655	100
1965	100,282	22·1	87,512	19·3	146,869	32·4	118,973	26·2	33	·00	453,669	100

Source: The classification of imports in this table is based on a detailed breakdown of imports taken directly from U.A.R. Dept. of Statistics and Census, 'Statement of Foreign Trade', for the years 1954–61, and U.A.R. Central Agency of Mobilization and Statistics, 'Foreign Trade of the U.A.R.', for 1962–5.

first explained how limitations on food production would exercise an important restraint on economic growth. In their models, which do seem relevant to conditions in modern Egypt, the rate of growth accelerates when more labour is diverted from primary production to capital formation and sufficient food is made available for its maintenance. Thus the rate of investment depends on the size of the food surplus. In an open economy however other goods can be traded for food and the critical variable is the rate of growth of exports. If the expansion of exports is too slow the higher demand for food may either compete with the production of the agricultural export goods or with the imports of capital goods. On both counts it will act as a brake on growth, unless foreign aid is hurried in.

Clearly, Egypt's ability to sustain a 4 per cent annual rate of economic growth after 1945 and a 6 per cent rate since 1960 crucially depended on the rising level of and changes in the composition of its imports. Larger proportions of capital and intermediate goods favoured Egypt's development, but the higher share of food imports—not associated with a reallocation in favour of cotton in agriculture—may have acted as a constraint. This is, however, a complex issue. The expansion of services, partly a consequence of urbanization, explains 30 per cent of the rate of growth of output. Because of differences in the levels of rural and urban consumption, food can be considered as a necessary input of this expansion, the 'working capital' of the classical economists.

TABLE 7. *Imports and Exports as Percentage of GNP*

Years	£E. millions GNP	£E. millions Imports	Imports as a % of GNP	£E. millions Exports	Exports as a % of GNP
1952–53	905	201	22	146	16
1953–54	963	180	19	143	15
1954–55	1,014	184	18	145	14
1955–56	1,072	213	20	144	13
1956–57	1,125	255	22	157	14
1957–58	1,195	249	21	168	14
1958–59	1,256	223	18	163	13
1959–60	1,375	238	17·5	178	13
1960–61	1,467	271	18	183	12·5
1961–62	1,550	325	21	163	11
1962–63	1,679	390	23	193	11
1963–64	1,186	394	21	230	12·5
1964–65	2,032	416	20	240	12

Source: For GNP figures same sources as Table 1; for trade figures U.A.R. Dept. of Statistics and Census, 'Annual Statement for Foreign Trade', various issues.

The question now arises—how did the country finance a rising volume of imports? Certainly not through a corresponding rise in exports proceeds, despite occasional gains from an improvement in the terms of trade (e.g. the Korean Boom).[14] Thus throughout the postwar years the balance of trade and the balance of payments on current account steadily deteriorated.

Until 1958 finance for the growing deficit came from a fall in Egypt's foreign exchange and gold reserves. These reserves had been built up during the war from payments made by Allied armies and in 1945–6 from sales of accumulated cotton stocks. From 1958 a rising proportion of the deficit came to be financed by inflows of foreign loans, particularly from the U.S.A. (P.L. 480) and Russia. By the end of the Plan Egypt, already burdened by a large debt, relied almost entirely on foreign sources to finance the deficit.

Conclusion

Since 1945 and more impressively since 1960, the Egyptian economy has been able to grow at a much higher rate than at any period of this century. The Government deserves perhaps some credit for an intervention that affected the level and composition of investment. Industrialization was largely responsible for the structural transformation undergone by the economy. Industrialization provided also new incentives for rural migrants and accelerated the rate of urbanization, thus creating additional pressures on the 'services' sector in the towns. The patterns of consumption and trade changed.

Unfortunately, the structural transformation did not result in greater integration and stronger linkages. New relationships between the sectors of the economy failed to emerge. Industry is more dependent on agriculture than agriculture on industry and a large component of the 'services' sector is parasitically attached to the economy. Dualism is still the major feature of the country. The division runs through each economic sector as well as between rural and urban areas. Migration brought the dichotomy into the towns.

Since 1945 Egypt has been able to exercise greater control over its development policies and its rate of growth. Whether this implies less 'vulnerability' or greater 'self-sufficiency' depends on the various meanings given to these words and on the ideological connotations attached to them. Clearly, Egypt is an open economy, more dependent than ever for its economic development on a large and rising capacity to import. Theoretical discussion of developments has strongly emphasized that a rapid rate of industrialization depends on comparable rates of growth in agriculture and exports in order to obviate shortages of food and foreign exchange. Because of foreign aid and accumulated reserves, the Egyptian economy seems to

[14] See Table 7.

have grown at an impressive rate over the past two decades despite the virtually stagnant export volume and a relatively slow rise in agricultural output. In the future, with foreign exchange reserves exhausted and with diminished possibilities for foreign aid and loans, agriculture and exports are likely to emerge as far more serious bottlenecks to the rate of capital formation—unless of course the Egyptian Government can apply rigid measures to curb the growth of consumption or unless recent discoveries of oil solve the foreign exchange problem.

The Patterns and Problems of Economic Development in Rentier States: the Case of Iran

H. MAHDAVY

I

THE purpose of economic history is presumably analysis as well as collection of facts with a view to explaining certain uniformities that are believed to exist in the economic life of human societies. In other words, the art consists of formulating verifiable hypotheses and testing them against the facts of economic history. Few people have advanced hypotheses concerning the causes, prerequisites, patterns and problems of economic development that could have universal applicability, for all times and all places. The less ambitious approach consists in pinpointing and explaining certain uniformities within a more limited time span and for a more limited area. The area of our interest in this paper—that of the Rentier States—is not quite limited to the Middle East, though most countries of this region happen to belong to this category. As for the time span of our study, it is one of the objectives of this paper to suggest that the period roughly corresponding to 1950–6 represents a landmark in the economic history of the Middle East and that at least in the case of Iran the structure and sources of economic growth after this period are distinctly different from the decades preceding it.

But first let us consider what is meant by a Rentier State. Rentier States are defined here as those countries that receive on a regular basis substantial mounts of external rent. External rents are in turn defined as rentals paid by foreign individuals, concerns or governments to individuals, concerns or governments of a given country. Payments for passage of ships through the Suez Canal (after allowing for the operating and capital costs incurred) are external rents. The same holds for payments to the so-called transit countries in the Middle East that allow oil pipelines be passed through their territories. A moment's reflection will reveal that oil revenues received by the governments of the oil exporting countries can also be external rents. Some may prefer to look at oil royalties as compensation for the removal of certain exhaustible resources. This is the usual justification for the rent of mines. But apart from these so-called royalties, the governments of the oil exporting countries in the Middle East benefit from differential and monopolistic rents that arise from the higher productivity of the Middle Eastern oilfields and price fixing practices of the oil companies.[1] What is more important perhaps is to recognize that however one looks at them, the oil revenues received by the governments of the oil exporting countries have very little to do with the production processes of their domestic economies. The inputs from the local economies—other than the raw materials—are insignificant.[2] This lack of any meaningful relationship between the level of oil production and the local economies of the producing countries can be seen from Table 1. Whereas both for Iran

TABLE 1. *Production of crude petroleum and local expenditures of the oil industry, Iran and major oil producing countries of the Middle East, 1948 and 1958.* (*Production in thousands of barrels and expenditures in millions of dollars*)

	1948	1958
Iran:		
Production	190,334	301,526
Local expenditure*	125·0	105·3
Middle East†:		
Production	405,852	1,540,716
Local expenditure*	202·0	287·9

* Includes wages and salaries, payments to local contractors, purchase of local supplies etc.

† Includes Iran, Iraq, Kuwait, Qatar and Saudi Arabia.

Source: Charles Issawi and Mohammed Yeganeh, *The Economics of Middle Eastern oil*, London 1962, Appendix, Tables 1 and 5. (Figures rearranged.)

and a number of Middle Eastern countries, the production of crude petroleum has increased considerably (by 58 per cent and 280 per cent respectively between 1948 and 1958), the local expenditures of the oil companies have actually declined in the case of Iran and have increased by only $85·9 million for the group of countries considered. The input requirements of the oil industry from the local economies—at least for the inputs that have an opportunity cost—is so insignificant that for all practical purposes one can consider the oil revenues almost as a free gift of nature or as a grant from foreign sources. In fact, it may be worth taking note of the

[1] See Charles Issawi and Mohammed Yeganeh, *The Economics of Middle Eastern oil*, London 1962, pp. 105–6 and Table 30.

[2] The net value added attributed to labour in the Middle East oil industry during the period 1948–60 was calculated to be only 8 per cent of total net value added. The remaining 92 per cent was accounted for by capital and natural resources, capital being provided mostly by foreign concerns. See Issawi and Yeganeh, *op. cit.*, Table 31.

TABLE 2. *The relative significance of the oil industry and oil revenues in a number of Middle Eastern countries, selected years*

	Value added in oil industry as % of GNP	Oil Revenues as % of total Government Revenues	Shares of oil exports as % of total foreign exchange earnings
Bahrein			
1948	—		
1957	—	66	
1958	55	83	—
Iran			
1948	10	11	65
1958	15	—	57
1960	—	41	59
Iraq			
1948	10	7·5	34
1958	28	—	59
1960	—	61	78
Kuwait			
1948	70	—	—
1958	90	87	—
Qatar			
1948	90	—	
1950	—	90	
1958	90	—	
Saudi Arabia			
1948	20	65	64
1957	—	—	84
1958	50	—	87
1960	—	81	
Jordan			
1953	—	—	11
1954	3	—	18
1962	—	15	—
Lebanon			
1951	—	—	6
1952	2	—	6
1962	—	10	
Syria			
1949	—	1	
1957	—	—	8
1958	4	—	13
1961	—	25	—
U.A.R. (Egypt)			
1958	—	—	12
1959	3	—	12
1961	—	10	

Source: Tables 10 and 41 and Section C of Chapter viii of Issawi and Yeganeh, *op. cit.* Figures for certain years refer to fiscal years.

similarities that exist between external rents and foreign grants. In their economic effects, they are almost identical, so much so that countries like Jordan and Israel that receive substantial foreign grants may display a number of characteristics shared by Rentier States. However the temporary nature of foreign grants and the uncertainty attached to them introduce a different set of considerations which are usually absent in Rentier States.

Although most countries in the Middle East do receive some form of external rent, the amounts involved vary a great deal both in absolute amount and as percentages of total government revenues and foreign exchange earnings. Table 2 gives an indication of the relative importance of the oil sector in various Middle Eastern countries. If such extreme cases as Qatar and Kuwait are left aside, the value added in the oil industry as a percentage of Gross National Product varies from 10 to 55 per cent in oil producing countries and from 2 to 4 per cent in transit countries. The oil revenues as percentages of total government revenues and total foreign exchange earnings are much higher in both groups of countries. Although the stage at which a country can be called a Rentier State is determined arbitrarily, we are mainly interested in such cases as Iran, Iraq and Saudi Arabia in which the effects of the oil sector are significant and yet the rest of the economy is not of secondary importance. The 'size' of a country can clearly make a difference to the relative weight of a given amount of external rent. Typically, the Rentier States are 'small' in size; however with Algeria, Libya and Nigeria soon joining the group, the number of such countries may become quite significant.

It was stated earlier that the period 1950–6 constitutes a turning point in the economic history of the Middle East. Although the initial and terminal dates of this period are arbitrarily chosen, they are not devoid of all significance. Iran's oil nationalization movement began to gather momentum in 1950 and the Suez Canal was nationalized in 1956. The impressive changes that occurred during this period were not so much due to the normal growth of a large industry, but were rather imposed from outside as the result of *political* pressures in the Middle East. The oil industry had existed in Iran for nearly half a century and had not affected the Iranian economy in any appreciable way before. The political developments in Iran and Egypt—the two largest countries of the Middle East—enabled the governments of most Middle Eastern countries to appropriate a larger share of the rents that previously accrued to the oil companies as profits. A glance at table III will give an indication of the order of the magnitudes involved. Suffice it to say here that the current payments of the oil companies during the first five years after 1956 were over seven times as much as the payments during the entire thirty six years before 1950. Thus in spite of its relative size, the oil industry in the Middle Eastern countries cannot be considered as a 'leading sector'—whatever

TABLE 3. *Payments of the oil companies to the Governments of the Middle East, 1913–1949 and 1956–1960 (Million $)*

Period	Bahrein	Iran	Iraq	Kuwait	Qatar	Saudi Arabia	All Transit countries	Total
1913–49	18	483	135	26	1	146	12	821
1956–60	58	1,160	1,081	1,784	248	1,540	121	5,992

Source: Issawi and Yeganeh, *op. cit.*, Table 39. (Figures rearranged.)

that implies—in the usual way that certain other industries have been so labelled in the western economies. However, it can be argued that during the past decade or so the public sectors in countries that have been the recipients of external rents have affected the pace of growth and expansion of the rest of the region's economy to an extent seldom encountered in the history of this region or that of any other in the world.

The oil industry's major contribution is that it enables the governments of the oil producing countries to embark on large public expenditure programmes without resorting to taxation and without running into drastic balance of payments or inflation problems that usually plague other developing nations. And since the oil revenues typically increase at a faster rate than the GNP of the local economies, the public sector of the oil producing countries expands rapidly. This need not necessarily result in some kind of socialism, but may turn into what can be considered as a fortuitous *étatisme*. The government becomes an important—or even the dominant—factor in the economy. This is not to imply that the local economies are not dependent on oil or that any cyclical behaviour on the part of the oil industry (or even oil prices) will not affect the local economies. At least in Iran, this dependence can be observed very clearly. However, the dependence is indirect. It is through the *expenditure* side rather than through the inter-industry relationships of the oil industry with the rest of the economy that the mechanism works.

The closest problems to the case of Rentier States studied by economists and economic historians are the inflow of gold into sixteenth century Spain and the so called 'transfer problem' arising from the German reparation payments after the First World War. In modern studies of economic development, oil exporting countries are often treated as exceptional cases and are excluded from the sample of underdeveloped countries.[3] Perhaps one of the more crucial problems that needs to be studied is to explain why

[3] For an interesting exception see Nicolas Sarkis, *Le Pétrôle, Facteur d'Intégration et de Croissance Economique*, thesis (Paris 1961), Librairie Générale de Droit et de Jurisprudence, Paris 1962.

TABLE 4. *Iran's GNP and per capita GNP, 1959/60–1963/64 (Billion Rls.)*

	1959/60	1960/61	1961/62	1962/63	1963/64
1. GNP at current prices	292·5	331·3	342·6	348·9	369·6
Year to year % change	—	+13	+4	+2	+6
2. GNP at 1959/60 prices	292·5	314·0	324·6	327·7	345·9
Year to year % change	—	+7·4	+3·4	+1·0	+8·5
3. *Per capita* GNP at 1959/60 prices	Rls. 14,300 ($191)	Rls. 15,100 ($200)	Rls. 15,100 ($201)	Rls. 14,900 ($199)	Rls. 15,400 ($205)
Year to year % change	—	+4·7	+·8	−1·5	+2·9
4. GNP at 1959/60 prices excluding oil revenues	272·9	293·0	303·9	303·7	319·5
5. Year to year % change	—	+7	+4	—	+5

Source: Preliminary Estimate of Iran's National Income, the Central Bank of Iran.
Monthly Bulletins of the Central Bank of Iran.

the oil exporting countries, in spite of the extraordinary resources that are available to them, have not been among the fastest growing countries in the world. For most underdeveloped countries, lack of savings or shortage of foreign exchange constitute some of the major constraining factors in economic growth. No such limitations beset the Rentier States. And yet at least the rate of growth of the Iranian economy during the period 1955–65 has not been at all impressive (about 2 per cent on an annual *per capita* basis). Were we to exclude the oil revenues from the GNP calculations, the results would be still less impressive. Tables 4 and 5 provide partial evidence.

TABLE 5. *Average annual rates of change in Iran's GNP and per capita GNP, 1959/60–1963/64*

	GNP (current prices)	GNP (constant 1959/60 prices)	*Per capita* GNP (at 1959/60 prices)	GNP (at 1959/60 prices) excluding oil revenues
Average Annual Rates	6·25	4·3	1·47	4·0

Source: Table 4.

The explanations for this unexceptional performance may be sought in at least two different—though perhaps complementary—directions. One approach would be to focus attention on the kind of socio-political organizations that often prevail in this kind of (usually foreign-dominated) exporting country. It could be argued that the socio-political structure of these countries, saddled with legacies of open or disguised colonialism, is not conducive to rapid growth. This means that if organizational and political factors are accepted as important factors of production in an aggregative sense, then the degree of substitution between financial and organizational resources must be considered extremely low. The abundant financial resources cannot be properly utilized until the socio-political barriers to growth are removed independently. Iran's recent experience seems to lend support to this view: after the political upheavals of 1961–4 which forced the government to introduce a number of socio-economic reforms—notably land reform—the short-run performance of the economy has improved, even though additional factors such as weather conditions and availability of excess capacity in certain industries helped the process.

A somewhat different approach to the same problem would be to enquire whether additional causes may not be at work, so that even after the removal of socio-political barriers, a different set of problems may not hinder rapid growth. Spain was a major colonial power herself when the gold inflows were taking place; and yet, the Industrial Revolution took place not in Spain, but in England and in other European countries. Similarly, the apparent 'prosperity' of present oil producing countries should not be taken as an indicator of their performance as developing and industrializing nations. In fact this same prosperity may lull many people into believing that the problems of economic growth are much simpler than they really are.

The point to be stressed here is that extensive government expenditures *per se*, though stimulating to production by increasing demand, may not be sufficient for generating rapid economic growth. The nature and composition of this expenditure, as well as the general response from the rest of the economy on the supply side, can make a great deal of difference. Adam Smith spoke of productive and unproductive labour,[4] while Rostow insists that 'outlays for purposes other than consumption be distinguished with respect to their being productive or non-productive'.[5] Both are drawing attention to the fact that not all expenditures have equal growth effects. That an increase in demand may induce some increases in output is not being questioned here. What is being questioned is the extent and the nature of the growth that may occur. The experience of countries poorly endowed with natural resources may have interesting implications in this respect for those countries that are rich in resources. Consider the following explanation of Japan's industrialization:

> the main cause of the rise of industry has been Japan's need to overcome her limited endowment of natural resources. For this reason she has had to develop the trade pattern of an advanced country, exporting manufactured goods and importing raw materials. Although industrialization is usually attributed to changes in demand, more than 75 per cent of Japan's industrial growth is traceable to changes in supply conditions. These include substitution of domestic for imported manufactured goods, substitution of manufactured goods for primary products, and other technological changes. Although increased exports were of some importance up to 1935, increases in domestic and foreign demand together account for less than a quarter of the rise in the share of industry in GNP from 1914 to 1954.[6]

Industrialization need not of course be the only road to rapid growth. But apart from the fact that for most underdeveloped countries industrialization seems the main hope, increasing the overall productive capacity of an economy is greatly dependent on such factors as higher capital per

[4] A. Smith, *An Enquiry into the Nature and Causes of the Wealth of Nations*, Book II, Ch. III: Of the accumulation of capital or of productive or unproductive labour.

[5] W. W. Rostow, *British Economy of the Nineteenth Century*, Oxford 1948, p. 12.

[6] H. B. Chenery, S. Shishido and T. Watanabe, 'The Pattern of Japanese Growth 1914–1954', *Econometrica*, 30, 1962, p. 129.

worker, improvements in the technical skills of the labour force, greater specialization and realization of potential external economies in production. To allow technological and organizational improvements on the supply side to be effectuated and the benefits of external economies in production reaped, the input–output matrix of rentier economies has to change drastically so that the inter-industry demand part of the matrix does not remain 'underdeveloped' as compared with the final demand part. For if most of the external rent is used to import for consumption purposes, all the productive sectors of the economy will remain relatively untouched by these 'extraordinary' expenditures. The consuming sectors of the oil producing countries may consequently develop more meaningful relations with the productive sectors of the countries they import from than with their own local productive sectors. Government expenditures made possible by oil revenues thus need not induce a commensurate expansion in the rest of the economy.

This imbalance in the input–output matrix of rentier economies may not be so easy to rectify. The currencies of the Rentier States are typically overvalued and market wages do not generally reflect social costs which, in countries of ample supply of labour, are probably lower than the market costs. Imports thus become attractive and import substitution hazardous. Dudley Seers advances the theory that since the workers in the oil industry are paid higher wages than workers in other industries (which is certainly true in Iran), the level of wages is raised even further in all industries through a process of demonstration effect.[7] He further shows how unemployment and slow industrialization occur more frequently in oil producing countries than in other developing economies: 'Most non-petroleum economies have been feeling increasingly the tensions caused by a slow growth of exports and fast rise in imports: they have taken many measures which are in fact protective and employment-generating even if intended, in the first place, to protect reserves. A petroleum economy operates differently. Factors that elsewhere would express themselves in balance of payments crises, such as wage increases or inadequate initiative in developing local industry, will here cause growing unemployment.'[8] Devaluation as a remedy is not considered seriously in these countries because the governments of oil producing countries always try to maximize their foreign exchange receipts from the local expenditures of the oil companies.

In Iran, the government has recently tried to encourage industrial development by using policy instruments other than the exchange rate. Development plans are formulated—even though not fully implemented—on a comprehensive basis. In the private sector, a complicated system of imports quotas, customs duties and export subsidies has been introduced

[7] Dudley Seers, 'The Mechanism of an Open Petroleum Economy', *Social and Economic Studies*, 13, 1964. [8] *Ibid.*, p. 236.

while monopolistic concessions in certain fields have been granted to certain Iranian or joint (Iranian and foreign) groups. Cheap loans have also been made available. Most of the latter policies are inefficient from an economic point of view, iniquitious from a social point of view, and have proved cumbersome in practice. If devaluation is not feasible because the governments are usually in too much of a hurry to unload all their foreign exchange earnings on the market, a better alternative to the above-mentioned measures may be direct subsidization of industries having employment effects or widespread inter-industrial linkages. A yet quicker and more reliable way—from the point of view of realizing external economies—may be for the governments to invest directly in well-planned industrial complexes. The technological and labour force training programmes as well as any desired expansion in employment can be incorporated in such plans. This approach may also avoid some of the abuses of subsidization and the eventual inequality of incomes that typically prevails in such countries. In brief, what began as a fortuitous *étatisme* may have to move in the direction of a well-planned semi-socialist state if some of the short-run and long-run deficiencies of the Rentier States are to be avoided.

The danger that faces the Rentier States is that while some of the natural resources of these countries are being fully developed by foreign concerns and considerable government expenditures (usually in a few cities) are creating an impression of prosperity and growth, the mass of the population may remain in a backward state and the most important factors for long-run growth may receive little or no attention at all. To take an example, as far as public education is concerned, Iran is yet to reach in the 1970's the stage Japan had already passed in the 1850's! The organizational and technological shortcomings may turn out to be even more staggering. Furthermore, the gaps *vis-à-vis* developing countries may be widening over time, rather than narrowing. Whereas in most underdeveloped countries, this kind of relative regression will normally lead to public alarm and some kind of political explosion aimed at changing the *status quo*, in the Rentier States, the increasing welfare and prosperity (of at least part of the urban population) acquired through government expenditures and large imports pre-empts some of the urgency for change and rapid growth encountered in other countries. The blatant inequalities of income and wealth may create frictions, but not as much as in other countries since exploitation of a natural resource rather than the direct exploitation of the people is the main source generating the disparities. Consequently, the economic and technological backwardness of the Rentier States may easily coincide with a more serious kind of backwardness: socio-political stagnation and inertia. Under these circumstances one must be exceptionally wary of evaluating the developmental performance of a country on the basis of changes in such purely economic and average indicators as *per capita* income. Kuwait may have the highest *per capita* income in the world, but she will have to undergo drastic transformation in all facets of her economy and socio-political organization before she can be considered on her way to a genuine long-term growth.

II

To study the economic structure of Rentier States one may either use time series for a single country to show departures from past trends after the external rents have become significant in amount or utilize cross-sectional data to point out the deviations of Rentier States from more 'normal' patterns of growth. An attempt has been made here to apply both methods. But the low quality and inadequacy of the data—especially for the historical part—make either approach at best suggestive. The economic history of Iran, even for the more recent decades, has yet to be written.[9] Ideally, one would want to be able to trace the long-run changes in the sectoral distribution of output and labour force as well as changes in the patterns of private and public consumption and investment. But unfortunately the historical data are not available and the cross-section studies, in spite of their limitations, may prove of more help in this respect. However, a limited number of series, especially in the fields of foreign trade, government expenditure and investment, can be used to highlight certain contrasts between the two periods. Furthermore, during the period 1950–3, Iran came very close to a laboratory experiment with respect to the effects of sudden discontinuation of the oil revenues. Although the period was short and the oil revenues were not at that time as significant as they have become since, the experience is worth recalling for the light it may shed on the process of industrialization in the Rentier States. But first some of the contrasts between the pre- and post-nationalization trends have to be observed.

Table 6 shows oil production and government revenues from oil since 1910. Though the growth of production was considerable between 1915 and 1950 (from 376 thousand tons to 16·5 million tons), oil revenues did not increase rapidly. In 1950, oil revenues were still about £16 million. It is only after 1955—and in spite of the virtual denationalization of the oil industry in 1954—that the revenues shoot up to over £100 million in 1960 and £183 million in 1965. The effect of this sudden increase in oil revenues on Iran's foreign trade can partly be observed from Table 7. Iran's foreign trade before 1955 generally followed the trends of world

[9] See however *Tārīkh-i Sī-sāle-yi Bānk-i Millī-yi Īrān*, 1307–1337 (1928–1958), Bank Melli Press, Tehran 1959 (in Persian). N. Pakdaman, 'Economie Iranienne: Essai d'Analyse Structurale d'une Economie Sous-Developpée', thesis, Paris 1965; M. Agah, 'Some Aspects of Economic Development of Modern Iran', thesis, Oxford 1958.

TABLE 6. *Oil production and government revenues from the oil industry, Iran, selected years from 1910 to 1965*

Year	Oil production in metric tons	Oil Revenues of the Iranian government in £s
1910	—	—
1915	375,977	1,326,000
1920	1,385,301	469,000
1925	4,333,933	831,000
1930	5,939,302	1,288,000
1935	7,487,697	2,220,648
1940	8,626,639	4,000,000
1945	16,839,490	5,624,308
1950	31,750,147	16,031,000
1955	16,515,000*	32,323,764
1960	53,528,000*	101,877,471
1965	93,300,000	183,300,000†

* Converted from barrels into metric tons by assuming one metric ton = 7·3 barrels.
† Estimated.

Source: B. Shwadran, *The Middle East, Oil and the Great Powers*, New York, 1955.
Six Decades of Iranian oil Industry, Publication of National Iranian Oil Company, Tehran 1966.
Issawi and Yeganeh, *op. cit.*
Annual Report of the Central Bank of Iran, 1966 (in Persian).

TABLE 7. *Foreign trade of Iran, selected years from 1900 to 1960 (values in Million Rials; volumes in thousand tons)*

	Imports		Exports (excluding oil)	
	value	volume	value	volume
1900	255	—	147	—
1905	386	168	293	289
1910	485	249	375	273
1915	464	216	355	253
1920	482	131	137	49
1925	881	325	515	232
1930	610	370	459	183
1935	804	434	659	254
1940	865	317	940	215
1945	3,107	151	1,707	120
1950	6,242	504	3,563	194
1955	9,125	637	8,034	508
1960	52,657	1,914	8,360	446
1965	66,083	—	13,740	—

Source: Customs Administration Yearbooks, Tehran, Iran.

prosperity and depression.[10] It did not benefit very much from the prosperity of the decade or so before the First World War for internal political reasons (the Constitutional Revolution of 1906 and its aftermath) and it did not suffer too much during the depression periods of the interwar years because the government took over the control of foreign trade and embarked on extensive programmes of bilateral trade. Though the overall trend of exports and imports is upward during the first half of this century, it is only moderately so. The dramatic changes occur after 1955. Imports increase by over five times between 1955 and 1960 and the sharp upward trend seems to be continuing since 1965. The trend of Iran's imports leaves little doubt that we are basically concerned with two different regimes: the moderate rise of the first half of the century, and the sharp increases since 1955. As for exports, no such sharp increases can be observed. And the widening gap between imports and exports is the result of this disparity in growth rates which is of course filled out mainly by oil exports.

The government expenditures of Iran have been increasing rapidly since the 1930's. However the increases for the earlier periods given in Table 8 partly reflect the price inflation of the period just before and during the Second World War. In real terms, the expansion of public expenditure during recent years has probably been more pronounced. A further difference between the two periods which is not reflected in Table 8 is the

TABLE 8. *Government expenditures, Iran, selected years from 1930 to 1964 (in Million Rials)*

Year	Expenditure
1930	353
1935	750
1940	3,211
1945	7,762
1950	10,060
1955	23,500
1960	54,800
1964	74,700

Sources: H. Khajehnouri, *Survey of Education in Iran during the recent half century (in Persian)*, in *Survey of Manpower Problems*, Ministry of Labour and Social Affairs, Tehran 1966.
Public Finance Papers, Iran, U.N. publication, 1951.
Various reports and working papers of the Plan Organization and the Ministry of Finance.

[10] M. Djazaeri, *La Crise Economique Mondiale et ses Répercussions en Iran*, thesis, Paris, Librairie Technique et Economique, Paris 1937.

way in which government expenditures were financed. During the prewar period, expenditures were financed mainly through taxation—albeit a heavy and iniquitous indirect taxation—whereas after 1955, the oil revenues began to become the major source of revenue for government expenditures. This point will be touched on later, but the examination of Table 9 which shows the course of private fixed investment in Iran may

TABLE 9. *Private fixed investment in Iran, selected years from 1937 to 1959 (Million Rls.)*

Year	Agriculture	Industries	Construction	Transportation	Total
1937	10·0	74·9	279·3	44·9	409·1
1940	62·1	19·7	1,023·2	20·0	1,125·0
1943	134·7	10·6	491·7	9·6	646·6
1946	111·9	94·0	566·6	273·0	1,045·6
1949	246·1	369·7	1,195·3	563·7	2,374·7
1952	276·9	515·0	1,447·5	46·5	2,285·9
1955	336·6	1,267·0	4,095·9	841·2	6,540·7
1956	642·5	3,984·2	4,096·1	2,051·8	10,774·5
1957	877·9	4,999·7	4,974·8	2,448·1	13,300·5
1958	2,340·9	8,172·2	7,150·0	3,201·9	20,864·0
1959	2,711·0	14,069·6	10,175·0	3,840·3	30,795·9

Source: 'Private Fixed Investment in Iran 1316–1338 (1937/38 through 1959/60)', by Sharif Adib-Soltani, Plan organization of Iran, 1962, Table XII.

help to bring out two related points. Firstly, that the government expenditures of the prewar period, though mainly directed towards investment outlays—particularly in railways, roads and light industries—had little positive effect on private investment. Government investment in many industrial fields was competing with or even replacing private enterprise. Second, that after 1955, the rapid increase in private investment shows that not only is public sector investment not expanding at the expense of the private sector, but that its large outlays—as well as its loans and foreign exchange facilities—are to some extent inducing the private sector to follow the pace of economic activity set by the government. Between 1955 and 1959, there is a five-fold increase in private investment. In other words, the government outlays financed out of oil revenues not only did not replace private expenditures, they supplemented them. What is paradoxical however is that in spite of these heavy investments, the results over a ten or fifteen year period have not been more impressive than those obtained in less fortunate developing countries. The explanation lies only partly in corruption and waste of resources. A more serious shortcoming may be due to the lopsided composition of the investment outlays which emphasized residential, commercial and administrative construction and large-scale transportation and irrigation projects. The latter were often favoured by foreign consultants and contractors who pressed for the implementation of such projects without being sufficiently concerned with the question of economic feasibility.

The results of this period can be compared with the developments of the 1950–3 period. During the struggle for the nationalization of the oil industry, Iran virtually lost all her oil revenues, and in 1951 the Bank of England imposed restrictions on conversion of Iran's sterling holdings. This led to a *de facto* devaluation of the Rial: the U.S. dollar rose from 40 Rials in 1950 to 124 Rials in 1953. The effects of this devaluation and the more direct measures taken to restrict imports, contrary to the expectations of many Western observers, proved stimulating to the Iranian economy. The Korean War and the availability of some foreign exchange reserves and some foreign assistance were contributing factors, but the overall effect of import-substitution and export drive cannot be denied: '1950–3 was a period of industrial recovery. . . . Good crops and larger exports kept up the mass purchasing power, while restrictive measures gave the domestic industry welcome protection. With the return of profits to normal, many factories re-opened, new plants were installed and Iran actually became an exporter of manufactured articles such as mill textiles and matches. In textiles alone, in these three years eleven new factories with 110,080 spindles and 1,600 weaving looms, were installed.'[11]

The mechanism of this brief outburst of economic activity and some of its actual and potential problems are worth analysing. The stoppage of oil exports reduced the supply of foreign exchange and hence of imports. Because of the rise in the value of imported commodities, substitution of domestic products for marginal imports became profitable. This substitution occurred both in consumption and in production. Exports of non-oil commodities were also boosted. But the bulk of the exports consisted of raw materials which typically display supply elasticity only over longer periods of time. Even in the less traditional field of industry, the process of expansion could not have continued for long without running into labour and capital bottlenecks. If a fall in national income were to be averted, the decline in the use of a natural resource (oil) had to be compensated by employment of more capital and labour and/or better utilization of the existing capital and labour. The difficulty with countries like Iran is that because of their extremely low level of technology and national education—as well as their socio-economic rigidities—either their response to opportunities of this kind is slow or its dynamism is of short duration. If a country is to become more than a producer of raw materials—of any

[11] M. Agah, *op. cit.*, p. 212.

kind—and the growth of output is to be of a sustained kind, then the entire socio-economic framework of the country has to undergo a transformation. The level of education of the population and their technological sophistication have to be raised considerably. Also the necessary political and administrative mechanism for mobilizing national resources has to be devised. The government had begun to take important steps in this direction during the 1950–3 period.

The oil revenues offer unusual prospects for development precisely because they can make certain shortcuts in socio-economic transformation and long-range economic development possible. The effort and the sacrifice required to break through the educational, technological and organizational barriers are far less when relatively ample resources are available. However, the very existence of these resources and the expectation of ever increasing revenues in the future—for that is how most of the Rentier States think of their prospects—seem to affect the time preference of the governments in such countries: if in the future external rents are going to be more lucrative than in the past, then immediate increases in consumption and welfare assume an inordinately greater weight than increases in future consumption and welfare. This deprives the development effort of any urgency and worthwhileness. If the basic premise of ever increasing external rents were tenable, there would be little disturbing in this attitude. Countries like Kuwait could then be guaranteed a perpetual state of opulence, if not quite one of bliss. However, for any number of physical, technological and economic reasons, it is safer to assume that typically the revenues of any given single oil producing country should increase for a number of years, gradually flatten out and eventually decline. Viewed in a context of this sort—even though the duration of these phases cannot be estimated—the attitudes of the oil producing countries as reflected in their growth policies and plans are at best myopic. Instead of attending to the task of expediting the basic socio-economic transformations, they devote the greater part of their resources to jealously guarding the *status quo*.

III

In this section certain aspects of Iran's economic development over a ten to twelve-year period will be compared with those of a number of other developing countries. The indices used for showing patterns of growth in 'other countries' are a number of averages derived by Professor Kuznets and summarized in Table 8.1 of *Modern Economic Growth*.[12] Professor

[12] *Yale* 1966. It would have been better if these averages could have been purged of the data relating to countries which according to our criterion may be Rentier States themselves.

Kuznets' averages refer to groups of countries arranged by *per capita* Gross Domestic Product. In the case of Iran the use of *per capita* GDP may be misleading, since the difference between GDP and Gross National Product can be as much as 10 per cent of GDP owing to the operations of foreign oil companies.

The average *per capita* income of Iran was estimated to be $192 in 1963/4 by the Central Bank of Iran.[13] The relevant group of countries for purposes of comparison with Iran would appear to be the group whose *per capita* GDP ranges between $100 and $199 rather than the next group within the $200 to $349 range. However, both groups are usually given in the relevant tables to indicate possible trends of change.

Participation in Economic Activity

The aggregate population and labour force data of Table 10 refer to the 1956 census and to the 1966 population census results. That Iran's economically active population is only about 30 per cent of her total population (as compared with 39·2 per cent for the $100–$199 group of countries) can be explained partly by the high percentage of the population (46 per cent) under the age of 15 and partly by the low participation of women in economic activity. The latter point is confirmed by the Agricultural Sample Survey of 1960 and the Manpower statistics of 1964 (see Table 10).

The low participation of women in economic activity in Iran reflects more than religious prejudices or problems of defining 'economic activity'. It may reflect the accepted ethos of a typically patriarchal state. Countries like Iran or Saudi Arabia that pass quickly from being a traditional society to being a Rentier State may achieve fairly substantial average *per capita* incomes, without going through the organizational changes which are usually associated with the process of capitalistic (or socialistic) economic growth. The same economic (or even socio-political) organizations and mores associated with such organizations may prevail for a long time before the 'expenditure effects' of external rents begin to build up enough pressures to challenge them. If the results of the 1956 and 1966 censuses are to be considered accurate, then the decline in the percentage of the economically active population would seem disturbing. Only about 50 per cent of the decline can be accounted for by the increase in the number of students.

Sectoral Patterns of Output

As shown in Table 11, Iran's pattern of growth has this peculiarity that its A-sector[14] appears much closer to that of the group of countries in the range of $200–574 *per capita* GDP than to that of the group below $200.

[13] See *Estimate of Iran's National Income*, Tehran 1966.
[14] Comprising agriculture, forestry and fishing.

TABLE 10. *Participation in economic activity: Iran and other countries*

Iran			Kuznets' averages	
			$200–349 *per capita* GDP (17 countries)	$100–199 *per capita* GDP (24 countries)
Economically active as % of total population				
	1956 census	1966 census		
1. Total	31	27·3	38·7	39·2
2. Female	10	8·2	20·6	19·6
Economically active as % of rural population (1960 Agricultural sample survey)				
1. Total	32			
2. Male	52			
3. Female	11			
Number of workers in all establishments of Iran by sex (1st Quarter 1964). Dept. of Manpower, Ministry of Labour and Social Services				
	Number of employed	%		
Total	907,439	100		
Male	864,675	95		
Female	42,764	5		

Source: Documents cited above and S. Kuznets, *Modern Economic Growth*, Yale 1966, Table 8.1.

TABLE 11. *Share of major sectors in GDP, Iran 1959/60–1963/4 and other countries, early 1950's*

	Iran					Kuznets' averages	
% of GDP	1959–60	1960–61	1961–62	1962–63	1963–64	\$200–574 *per capita* GDP (5 countries)	Under \$200 *per capita* GDP (12 countries)
1. A – Sector	28·7	28·6	28·0	26·1	23·8	20·5	46·0
2. M+ Sector	19·1	19·5	19·7	20·5	21·5	34·0	21·5
3. Oil Sector	15·3	15·1	15·4	16·8	17·4	—	—
4. S – Sector	36·9	36·8	36·9	36·6	37·3	45·5	32·6
% of GDP (excluding oil sector)							
1. A – Sector	33·9	33·7	33·1	31·4	28·9		
2. M+ Sector	22·5	23·0	23·3	24·6	26·0		
3. S – Sector	43·6	43·3	43·6	44·0	45·1		

The M+Sector comprises mining, manufacturing, construction, water, energy, transport and communications. For definitions of the A – Sector and S – Sector, see p. 444 note 14 and p. 447 note 15.
Source: Kuznets, *loc. cit. Preliminary Estimate of Iran's National Income*, The Central Bank of Iran, Tehran 1966.

In 1963/4, the share of the A-sector in Iran's GDP was 23·8 per cent. By contrast, Iran's share of the S-sector[15] was somewhat higher than that of the countries with less than $200 *per capita* GDP. Once the oil sector is removed from GDP, the share of the S-sector in 1963/4 reaches 45·1 per cent which is very close to that of the group of countries with the higher per capita GDP. Although the number of years (five) for which GDP figures are available is not sufficient to show any trends, nevertheless, the increase in the shares of the oil sector and the S-sector may be considered as of some interest.

The relatively larger share of the S-sector can perhaps be explained by the following considerations:

(i) Since the external rents accrue to the government without substantially affecting the local economy, it is reasonable to expect the final demand part of the input–output matrix of rentier states to be more affected by the expenditure of the external rents than the inter-industry part.

(ii) Abundance of foreign exchange reduces the relative price of all importable goods as compared with non-importables—mainly services and rents. Whereas the prices of imported commodities are not affected by changes in internal demand, in the case of non-imported goods and services, it is in fact their prices that change in the first instance.

(iii) There may also exist a considerable monopoly element in the valuation of services in rentier countries over and above the monopoly elements usually found in most underdeveloped countries. Since the external rent is paid to the government, it is tempting for the government to reward its employees and supporters with regular salary increases, fringe benefits or lucrative contracts etc.

In the long-run this distortion in the valuation of product may have the effect of shifting manpower, talent and organizational ability from agriculture and industry into services.

Sectoral Distribution of the Labour Force. Table 12 shows that the distribution of the economically active population of Iran is closer to the average shares in the labour force of the various sectors in countries with less than $200 *per capita* GDP. Over 45 per cent of the economically active population was engaged in the A-sector and 28·3 per cent in the S-sector in 1964. This, in combination with the above-mentioned sectoral distribution of product, is sufficient to cause some disparity in sectoral product per worker. That the distribution of the labour force has not adjusted itself to sectoral productivity may be an indication both of the institutional rigidities and of the speed with which Iran has been economically affected by the oil revenues.

Sectoral Product per worker. Table 13 shows relative sectoral product per economically active population for Iran in 1963/4. The productivity

[15] Comprising trade, banking, insurance, government and other services.

TABLE 12. *Sectoral distribution of economically active population: Iran 1956 and 1964 and other countries, early 1950's*

	Economically active population of Iran (1956 census)		Estimated economically active population of Iran 1964		Kuznets' averages for share in labour force excluding unpaid family labour	
	Millions	% of economically active	Millions	%	\$200–574 *per capita* GDP	Under \$200 *per capita* GDP
A − Sector	3·326	56·4	2·733	45·5	37·9	57·6
M + Sector	1·396	23·6	1·570	26·2	29·8	19·5
S − Sector	1·186	20·0	1·691	28·3	32·3	22·9

Source: Iran's 1956 population Census and 1964 population sample survey. Kuznets, *loc. cit.*

of those engaged in agriculture and industry is respectively 0.53 and 0.82 of the average for the country. By contrast that of the S-sector is 1.31. Iran's sectoral product per worker would have been close to that of the more advanced countries (in the $200 to $574 *per capita* GDP range) were it not for her low product per worker in industry. The disparity between the A-sectoral and S-sectoral product per worker will probably widen, partly owing to a decline in product per worker in agriculture[16] and partly because the external rents are received and spent mainly in towns.

TABLE 13. *Relative sectoral product per economically active population for Iran 1963/64 and per worker for other countries, early 1950's*

	Iran	Kuznets' averages	
	Per economically active population	Between $200–574 *per capita* GDP (5 countries) per worker	Under $200 *per capita* GDP (12 countries) per worker
1. A—Sector to countrywide	·53	0·54	·80
2. M+ Sector to countrywide	·82	1·14	1·10
3. S—Sector to countrywide	1·31	1·41	1·42
4. S—Sector to countrywide (excluding oil)	1·60	—	—
5. M+ & S—Sector to countrywide	1·02	2·37	1·60
6. S—Sector to M+ Sector	1·61	1·24	1·29

Source: Tables 11 and 12, and Kuznets, *loc. cit.*

Manufacturing Sector. About 9 per cent of Iran's estimated labour force seems to have been engaged in manufacturing in 1963 as compared with 4·1 per cent and 13·9 per cent for the averages of groups with less than $200 and between $200 and $574 *per capita* GDP respectively (see Table 14). Iran's value added per worker engaged in manufacturing is however only slightly above that of the first group and considerably below that of the second group. The share of Iran's oil sector in value added is almost as large as that of all other industries in Iran (see Table 15). Once the share of the value added of the oil industry is excluded from the total, the share of other industries begins to approach that of the two groups of countries (Professor Kuznets' averages) given in Table 15. The higher share of textiles in Iran can partly be explained by historical reasons.

[16] The index of average productivity in agriculture dropped from 100 in 1959/60 to 94·6 in 1963/4. See *Estimate of Iran's National income,* cited above.

TABLE 14. *Number of workers engaged and value added per person in manufacturing, Iran, 1963, and other countries, 1953*

	Iran 1963	Kuznets' average (1953) $200–574 *per capita* GDP	Under $200 *per capita* GDP
Number of workers engaged	837,526	—	—
Workers engaged as % of total labour force (assumed to be 0·42 of population)	9%	13·9%	4·1%
Value added per person engaged in manufacturing	$595*	$1,389†	$567†

* Excluding the oil sector and in 1963 $. † In 1948 $.

Source: Iran's Industrial Census, 1963.
Kuznets, *loc. cit.*

Paper products, printing, publishing, chemicals, non-metallic minerals and basic metals in Iran have a smaller share in value added than in the two groups of countries—which may reflect Iran's lower degree of industrialization. However, the share of metal products in value added appears twice as much as that in the two groups of countries. Over 60 per cent of value added of 'metal products' reflects value added of transportation equipment which may be related to Iran's size and the volume of her foreign trade. The non-integration of the oil industry in the Iranian economy can be seen from the low share of chemicals.

Table 16 compares value added per worker in manufacturing in Iran with that of the two groups of countries. Again, more meaningful figures for Iran are those that exclude value added in oil industry from the total value added in manufacturing. Some 58 per cent of Iran's manufacturing labour force is engaged in textiles, clothing and footwear in which value added per worker is far less than the average value added per worker in all manufacturing (·57 and ·32 respectively). Relative value added per worker in these industries is also considerably below that of the two groups of countries given by Prof. Kuznets. By contrast value added per worker is relatively high in chemicals (4·40) and leather and rubber (2·23). However only 1·6 per cent of Iran's manufacturing labour force is engaged in these industries. Metal products show also a high relative value added per worker (2·19) and also comprise 9 per cent of the manufacturing labour force.

Distribution of GNP by Type of Use. Table 17 shows that private

TABLE 15. *Structure of manufacturing: shares in value added, Iran, 1963, and other countries, late 1950's*

	Iran			Kuznets' averages %	
	Value added in billion Rls.	Share in value added % (including oil)	Share in value added % (excluding oil)	$200–349 *per capita* GDP (7 countries)	$100–199 *per capita* GDP (16 countries)
Food, beverages and tobacco	13·2	19·1	35·8	34·3	38·2
Textiles	9·7	14·4	26·2	20·2	10·8
Clothing and footwear	1·4	2·0	3·8	4·3	5·4
Wood products	·9	1·3	2·4	4·0	7·2
Paper, printing and publishing	·4	·5	1·1	4·4	4·4
Leather and rubber	·8	1·2	2·1	3·3	2·2
Chemicals (excluding petroleum products)	1·4	2·0	3·8	9·4	10·1
Non-metallic minerals	·7	1·0	1·9	5·5	6·4
Basic metals	·1	·1	·2	4·4	1·9
Metal products	7·8*	11·3*	21·1*	9·2	10·6
All other (excluding oil industry)	·4	·5	1·1	1·2	2·6
Oil industry	32·1	46·6			
Total with oil industry	68·9	100			
Total without oil industry	36·8		100		

Source: Iran's Industrial Census 1963.
Kuznets, *loc. cit.*

* About 60 per cent transport equipment.

TABLE 16. *Value added per worker engaged in major industries as relative of value added per worker engaged in all manufacturing, Iran, 1963, and other countries, late 1950's*

	Iran					Kuznets' averages	
	Number of workers engaged	% of total employed	Value added per worker engaged Rls.	Value added per worker as relative of value added per worker engaged in all manufacturing sector		$200–349 *per capita* GDP (7 countries)	$100–199 *per capita* GDP (16 countries)
				Including oil Sector	Excluding oil Sector		
Food, beverage or tobacco	159,867	19	84,000	1·03	1·84	1·16	1·34
Textiles	383,744	46	25,300	0·31	0·57	0·91	0·72
Clothing and footwear	101,012	12	13,900	0·17	0·32	0·53	0·56
Wood products	32,733	4	27,500	0·34	0·61	0·69	0·67
Paper, printing and publishing	5,087	0·6	78,700	0·96	1·72	1·05	1·86
Leather and rubber	7,997	0·9	101,000	1·22	2·23	1·06	1·00
Chemicals (excluding petroleum products)	7,168	0·8	197,000	2·40	4·40	1·59	1·80
Non-metallic minerals	32,180	4	21,800	0·27	0·49	0·85	1·00
Basic metals	2,066	0·2	48,700	0·59	1·09	1·69	1·36
Metal products	79,772	9	98,000	1·19	2·19	0·87	0·81
All other (excluding oil)	11,307	1	35,500	0·43	0·79	0·80	1·33
Oil industry	14,583	2	2,200,000	26·7		—	—
Total with oil	837,526	100	82,100				
Total without oil	822,943		44,700				

Source: Iran's Industrial Census 1963, and Kuznets, *loc. cit.*

consumption expenditure in Iran is at a level nearer to the group of countries with \$200–349 *per capita* GDP than the group with \$100–199. Government consumption expenditure however seems below that of both groups, while Gross Domestic Capital Formation appears above that of the two groups for the years 1959/60 and 1960/1 and below it for the years 1962/3 and 1963/4.

Owing to the economic and political crisis of 1960–4, which was caused at least partly by a fall in oil prices and a decline in the rate of increase in oil revenues, the period 1959/60–1963/4 for which preliminary estimates of Iran's National Income are available may not prove particularly useful in determining long-run trends. Various economic indicators show that both government expenditures and investment have increased sharply since 1964—after a 70 per cent increase in oil revenues. Gross National Capital Formation shows greater degree of stability than GDCF. That the former in Iran is not very much above the averages given by Prof. Kuznets is an indication that oil revenues have not been used as 'additional' savings for capital formation. They have partly replaced ordinary savings.

The relatively lower share of government consumption in GNP may also be due to the fact that during these years the government had to adhere to a stabilization programme, more or less imposed on Iran by various international monetary and development authorities, as well as a group of lending countries. Total current government expenditures have of course been rising at a rate above the rate of growth of the economy.

Government Revenues and Expenditures. Table 18 gives an indication of the dependence of the Iranian government on oil revenues as its major source of finance. The share of oil revenues in total government revenues increases from 11 per cent in 1954 to about 50 per cent in 1965. Customs duties are another important item of government receipts. The foreign exchange earned from oil export makes large quantities of imports possible.

The low share of direct taxes in government revenues (about 7 per cent for Iran) reduces the redistributional power of fiscal policy in rentier countries. The government can only act through the expenditure side. Even for stabilization purposes, the fiscal policy cannot be as effective as in other countries, and consequently greater reliance must be placed on monetary policy. It is to be noted that the government of Iran receives about 70 per cent of its revenues from oil exports and customs duties alone. Although there is no reason why the governments of the oil producing countries should not be able to exercise greater fiscal control, at least over the expenditure side of their budgets, in fact they seldom do so: they spend whatever they receive.

Tables 19 and 20 give some indication of the trend of government

TABLE 17. *Distribution of GNP by type of use, Iran, 1959/60–1963/64, and other countries, 1950's (share in GNP%)*

	Iran					Kuznets' averages	
	1959/60	1960/61	1961/62	1962/63	1963/64	$200–349 *per capita* GDP	$100–199 *per capita* GDP
1. Private Consumption Expenditures	75·4	74·0	75·3	77·1	75·7	75·6	73·2
2. Government Consumption Expenditures	9·7	9·4	9·5	9·7	10·6	11·7	11·9
3. Gross Domestic Capital Formation	18·2	19·2	17·1	14·0	13·1	16·9	16·4
4. Net Change in Foreign Claims	−3·3	−2·6	−1·9	−0·8	+0·6	−1·5	−1·2
5. Gross National Capital Formation (= 3 + 4)	14·9	16·6	15·2	13·2	13·7	12·7	14·9

Source: Preliminary Estimate of Iran's National Income 1959/60–1963/64, The Central Bank of Iran, Tehran 1966.
Kuznets, *loc. cit.*

TABLE 18. *Iran's central government finance: major sources of revenue as percentages of total revenues, 1954–1965*

Revenues	1954	55	56	57	58	59	60	61	62	63	64	65
1. Oil Revenues (and concession bonuses)	11	37	39	47	51	40	42	42	46	46	61	50
2. Customs Duties	27	23	19	18	16	22	22	19	16	18	15	17
3. Direct Taxes	5	5	4	5	7	8	8	8	8	8	7	9
4. Other Taxes and Domestic Revenues	35	28	28	26	24	24	25	26	30	28	18	24
5. Foreign Grants	22	7	10	4	2	6	3	5	—	—	—	—
Total (%)	100	100	100	100	100	100	100	100	100	100	100	100

Source: Various estimates given at different intervals of time by the Ministry of Finance, Plan Organization, USOM/Iran etc. The figures used were not fully consistent in that some referred to actual receipts while others referred to budgeted revenues. The discrepancies however are not large.

TABLE 19. *Iran's central government finance: major expenditures as percentages of total expenditures 1954–9 and 1963–6*

	1954	55	56	57	58	59	1963	64	65	66
Defence	38	41	40	39	40	38	39	38	42	45
Education	16	14	20	22	18	18	23	21	22	23
Health and welfare	7	6	5	5	7	6	5	7	7	11
Government Investment	48	38	47	43	39	34	22	27	—	—

Source: Plan organization, Ministry of Finance, USOM/Iran and AID working papers at different intervals of time.

TABLE 20. *Government expenditure for health and education, Iran, 1959 and 1963, other countries, late 1950's* (% *of GNP*)

	Iran		Kuznets' average	
	1959	1963	$200–574 *per capita* GDP (7 countries)	Under $200 *per capita* GDP (15 countries)
1. Education	2·0	2·7	2·0	2·7
2. Health	0·7	0·5	1·2	1·0
3. Education and health	2·7	3·2	3·2	3·7
4. Share in private consumption expenditures (%)	3·5	4·5	4	5

Source: As for Table 19 and Kuznets, *loc. cit.*

expenditures. Defence expenditures account for about 40 per cent of total government expenditures, while education and health account for about 22 per cent and 7 per cent respectively. Iran's expenditure on health seems to be below that of the two groups of countries given in Table 21.

Table 19 shows Iran's government investment decline from 48 per cent of total government expenditures in 1954 to 27 per cent in 1964. Thus while oil revenues were assuming a larger proportion in total revenues, investment was becoming a smaller proportion of government expenditures.

The allocation of government investment funds is of some interest. Table 21 shows the revised version of Iran's Third Development Plan. The share of industries and mines is below 12 per cent while that of transportation and communications is about 24 per cent and that of urban

TABLE 21. *Iran's revised third plan programmes (1962–1968)*

	Rls. 140 Billion Programme		Rls. 200 Billion Programme*		Rls. 230 Billion Programme†	
	Billion Rls.	%	Billion Rls.	%	Billion Rls.	%
1. Agriculture and irrigation	30·3	21·6	45·0	22·5	49·0	21·3
2. Industries and mines	16·6	11·9	21·9	11·0	27·0	11·7
3. Fuel and power	26·1	18·6	27·0	13·5	41·5	18·0
4. Transportation and communications	30·0	21·5	50·0	25·0	56·0	24·3
5. Education	13·5	9·6	17·9	8·9	17·4	7·6
6. Health	10·0	7·2	13·9	6·9	13·5	5·9
7. Manpower	6·2	4·4	8·0	4·0	3·6	1·6
8. Urban development	4·5	3·2	8·0	4·0	7·0	3·1
9. Statistics	0·8	0·6	0·8	0·4	0·8	0·3
10. Planning and housing	2·0	1·4	7·5	3·8	14·2	6·2
Total	140·0	100·0	200·0	100·0	230·0	100·0

* Revised in 1963. † Revised in 1966.

Source: Plan Organization of Iran.

development and housing is about 9 per cent in the last revision of the plan. The allocations to agriculture and irrigation are mainly taken up by construction of large dams.

The 'constructional aspect' of economic development and the low priority accorded to industries and mines are only accentuated when *disbursement* figures rather than planned allocations are taken into account. Table 22 shows actual disbursements for the industries and mines sector of the plan. Only 9·4 per cent of funds allocated for investment in new industries were disbursed during the first half of the Third Plan period. The Second Development Plan taken at its mid-point also showed the same characteristics: low priority to industries (8 per cent of total allocations) and high priority to transportation (35 per cent) and other constructional activities (dams, city improvement plans etc.). See Table 23.

Structure of Foreign Trade. Table 24 shows total commodity trade of Iran to have increased from 11·4 per cent of GNP in 1954 to 29·7 per cent in 1965. Total commodity trade and services have increased during the same period from 14 per cent of GNP to 35 per cent. What is relevant here is not so much the absolute size of the proportion of foreign trade to GNP

TABLE 22. *Plan organization of Iran's disbursements for industrial and mining programmes, 1962–1965/6*

	Planned expenditures %	Actual expenditures as % of planned expenditures
1. Technical assistance to private investors in industries	2·2	21·2
2. Investment in existing public sector industrial units	9·6	52·1
3. Technical assistance to private investors in mining	1·1	52·7
4. Investment in new public sector mines	1·9	36·8
5. Investment in new industries	66·7	9·4
6. Long-term credit to investors and participation in their investment	18·5	48·1
	100·0	21·9

Source: Plan Organization of Iran.

TABLE 23. *Iran's revised second seven year development plan, 1955–62*

	Billion Rls.	%
1. Agriculture and Irrigation	18·9	22
2. Transportation and Communications	30·4	35
3. Industry and Mines	6·7	8
4. Social Affairs	11·7	13
5. Regional Development	12·2	14
6. Other Expenditures	7·0	8
Total	87·2	100

Source: Plan Organization of Iran.

(which may be related to the size of the country among other factors) but its rapid increase over a twelve year period.

The same Table also shows how the oil exports have increased from 20 per cent of total commodity exports to about 80 per cent during the 1962–5 period. Not only proceeds from exports of oil, but also the local expenditures of the oil companies and bonus payments to the government for new

TABLE 24. *Proportion of foreign trade to GNP, Iran, 1954–65 (% of GNP)**

	1954	55	56	57	58	59	60	61	62	63	64	65
1. Total commodity trade	11·4	15·1	19·4	21·7	24·6	24·6	23·2	21·1	21·7	22·1	27·0	29·7
2. Total commodity trade excluding oil exports	10·7	11·7	14·7	15·0	16·4	17·0	15·8	14·3	13·2	13·4	15·9	19·2
3. Total commodity and services traded	14·0	18·5	23·1	26·1	31·5	31·5	29·0	26·7	27·0	27·5	36·0	35·0
4. Value of oil exports as % of total commodity exports	20	57	61	68	71	73	73	77	81	80	84	79

* GNP figures for the years 1959–63 are from *Preliminary Estimate of Iran's National Income*, The Central Bank of Iran, Tehran 1966. The GNP figures for 1964 and 1965 were obtained by increasing the 1963 figure by 5 and 7 per cent respectively. Similarly, the figures for 1956–8 were obtained on a 5 per cent growth rate basis and 1955 and 1954 on a 4 and 3 per cent rate respectively. These rates are no more than 'informed guesses'.

Source: Monthly Bulletins, The Central Bank of Iran.

TABLE 25. *Foreign exchange receipts, Iran, 1954–65* (Million $)

	1954	55	56	57	58	59	60	61	62	63	64	65
Oil revenues	22	92	140	208	270*	261	285	291	342	388	665†	519‡
Year to year % change	—	+320	+51	+49	+30	−3	+9	+2	+16	+13	+72	−22
Purchase of foreign exchange from oil companies	12	47	40	48	74	77	74	100	95	83	89	93
Year to year % change	—	+290	−15	+20	+54	+4	−4	+35	−5	−13	+5	+4
Ordinary exports	95	70	90	98	86	95	106	88	82	97	89	132
Year to year % change	—	−26	+28	+9	−12	+10	+11	−12	−7	+18	−8	+48
Foreign loans and grants	81	92	141	116	62	114	124	152	54	19	34	116
Year to year % change	—	+14	+54	−18	−53	+82	+9	+23	−65	−65	+64	+240
Total	237	327	430	502	551	618	653	693	626	638	933	938
Year to year % change	—	+36	+32	+23	+10	+14	+5	+6	−10	+2	+52	+0·5

* Includes $25 million concession payment. † Includes $185 million concession payment. ‡ Includes $5 million concession payment.

Source: Monthly Bulletin, The Central Bank of Iran.

TABLE 26. *Proportion of imports to GNP and changes in oil revenues, Iran, 1954–65*

	1954	55	56	57	58	59	60	61	62	63	64	65
1. Proportion of imports to GNP	·08	·11	·13	·14	·17	·17	·15	·14	·13	·13	·16	·19
2. Ratio of changes in imports to changes in GNP	—	1·0	·62	·23	·70	·23	·02	−·27	−·33	·17	·74	·58
3. Year to year changes in imports (%)	—	+38	+30	+24	+25	+6	+7	−5	−4	+7	+27	+25
4. Year to year changes in oil revenues	—	+306	+52	+48	+34	−7*	+9	+2	+18	+13	+70	−17*

* The apparent decline in oil revenues is due to a lump sum bonus received by the Iranian government in the previous year for granting new oil concession. Thus the regular revenues from oil exports have not declined.

Source: Monthly Bulletins, The Central Bank of Iran. GNP figures for 1959–63 are from *Preliminary Estimate of Iran's National Income*, The Central Bank of Iran, Tehran 1966. Figures for other years are obtained according to the procedure described in Table 24.

concessions by various foreign concerns help in providing the foreign exchange needed for the expansion of imports. Total availability of foreign exchange and the rate of growth of its component parts is given in Table 25. The predominance of the oil revenues is evident.

The proportion of imports to GNP is shown in Table 26. It increases from ·08 in 1954 to ·19 in 1965. However, it is interesting to note that as in the case of government revenues and expenditures, the proportion of imports to GNP deviates from the trend during the 1960–4 period when the rate of increase of oil revenues slowed down owing to a decrease in oil prices. With the exception of these crisis years, the ratio of changes in imports to changes in GNP is extremely high, about ·50 to ·60.

Table 26 also brings out fairly close year to year changes in oil revenues and imports. It is interesting to observe that the year 1964, in which Iran's four year economic crisis ended, was the year in which the oil revenues increased by 70 per cent and Iran's total foreign exchange availability rose by 52 per cent.

TABLE 27. *Claims of the banking system on the private and public sectors, Iran, 1954–60 (Billion Rls.)*

	1954	55	56	57	58	59	60
Claims on private sector	8·06	9·72	10·82	13·98	22·61	32·24	—
Year to year % change	—	+20	+11	+28	+62	+42	
Claims on public sector	17·05	17·31	19·34	22·90	27·00	28·93	32·35
Year to year % change	—	—	+12	+20	+18	+6	+11
Total claims	25·11	27·03	30·16	36·88	49·61	61·17	—
Year to year % change	—	+8	+11	+22	+34	+23	

Source: International Financial Statistics, June 1962.

Behaviour of the Monetary System. Quite apart from the expansionary effects of the availability of foreign assets on the monetary system, it appears that credit creation by the banking system follows the inflow of oil revenues. No consistent set of figures is available for the entire period 1951–65 (the definitions of various indicators were changed by the Central Bank in 1960, the year it came into existence). Consequently, two different series have been used in Tables 27 and 28 to show how the monetary system's advances to the public and private sectors increased at annual rates ranging from 6 to 20 per cent for the public sector and 11 to 62 per cent for the private sector before the crisis of 1960–4. The same pattern seems to be developing after 1964.

The cyclical behaviour of the monetary system as far as the private

TABLE 28. *Net claims of the banking system on the private and public sectors, Iran, 1960–65 (in Billion Rls.)*

	1960	61	62	63	64	65
1. Net claim on private sector	29·4	33·8	36·0	39·6	48·8	56·1
2. Year to year % change		+15	+6·5	+10·0	+23·2	+15·0
3. Net claim on public sector	18·0	12·3	11·0	11·9	4·1	17·4
4. Year to year % change		−32	−10·6	+8·2	−65·5	+324·4
5. Total net claims	47·4	46·1	47·0	51·5	52·9	73·5
6. Year to year % change		−3	+2·0	+9·6	+2·7	+38·9

Source: The Central Bank of Iran, *Annual Report*, 1965.

sector is concerned can perhaps be explained by the fact that a considerable proportion of the private sector borrowing is used for financing imports. Once the oil revenues do not increase rapidly enough and measures are taken to reduce imports, this automatically affects the credit demand of the private sector. Government agencies reduce their investments both for lack of funds and in order to economize on foreign exchange—which also reduces their demand for credit from the banking system. Consequently, the monetary system finds itself subjected to pressures that follow the inflow of external rents. Given the ineffectiveness of fiscal policy as described above, monetary policy becomes a very weak instrument for implementing counter-cyclical measures.

Patterns of Income Distribution. Statistics for income distribution in Iran are very scanty. The wages and salaries of urban employed population are given in Table 29. It is worth noting that the annual wages and salaries of some 389,000 government employees are about 50 per cent more than the combined wages and salaries of some 785,000 operators and non-operators in the private sector. The wages and salaries of the government employees do not include allowances for travel, housing, medical expenses etc. The difference between the income levels of the governing groups and those of the governed is thus more than what the above figures indicate. The government employees may thus be turning into a privileged rentier class.

An attempt has been made in Table 30 to calculate the share of wages and salaries in GNP. But the figure of 45 per cent must be treated as only an approximation because of the arbitrary assumptions made in its derivation. That the share of income from the property may have increased during the Second Plan period is generally recognized and was stated explicitly in the Third Plan Frame. The reversal of this trend was considered

TABLE 29. *Urban employed population and their wages and salaries, Iran, 1964/65*

	Number of employed	Average weekly wages and salaries per employed (Rls.)	Total annual salaries and wages (Billion Rls.)
A. Operators:			
1. Agricultural workers	57,068	406·5	1·196
2. Unskilled workers	168,854	343·3	3·090
3. Skilled workers	264,976	632·6	8·700
4. Specialized workers	18,220	1,452·6	1·360
5. Highly specialized	3,356	6,785·9	1·183
Sub-total	512,474		15·529
B. Non-operators:			
1. Public sector employees	389,677	1,804·1	36·554
2. Private sector employees	263,698	690·5	9·467
Sub-total	653,375		46·021
Grand total	1,165,849		61·550

Source: 'A Study of Manpower Problems of Iran's Urban Sector', *Studies in Manpower Problems*, vol. 3, Ministry of Labour, Tehran 1966.

TABLE 30. *The share of wages and salaries in GNP, Iran, 1964/65*

	Billion Rls.
1. Wages and salaries of 1·166 million urban employed	61·550
2. Imputed* wages and salaries of 51,840 urban family workers	·919
3. Imputed† wages of 641,682 urban entrepreneurs and self-employed workers	36·000
4. Imputed* wages of 4·100 million rural employed	73·282
5. Total wages	171·751
6. Estimated 1964/65 GNP	405·600
7. % share of wages in GNP $\left(\frac{(5)}{(6)} \times 100\right)$	45

* Assumed to earn the wages of unskilled urban workers.

† Assumed to earn the wages of average workers from work alone. Any divergence from this average is treated as income from human capital.

Source: Tables 1, 4 and *The Manpower Sample Survey of Iran, 1964.*

to be one of the aims of the Third Plan. However, recent studies[17] by the Central Bank of Iran—though based on a limited sample—suggest that income distribution may have become more unequal during recent years. This was found to be more pronounced in larger towns, no doubt because property incomes tend to increase more rapidly in these towns. That land distribution has not checked the increasing disparities in income distribution is also of some interest. The government may have to use fiscal policy for redistributional purposes, even though from the revenue point of view, it may have little urge to do so.

IV

Since the mid-1950's, the Iranian economy has been subjected to the expenditure effects of rapidly increasing oil revenues and/or foreign loans obtained on the strength of future oil revenues. These expenditures have created a set of circumstances that hardly bear any resemblance to Iran's past experiences in economic growth. The repercussions of these expenditures have not been uniform in all sectors of the economy. Agriculture and industry have not thrived as has the services sector of the economy. Though at some points, linkages are being established between the traditional economy and the new superstructure of foreign trade and services that has emerged from the expenditure of external rents, the process is still haphazard and without a clear direction. Whatever direction there is seems still to be aimed at attracting more foreign 'participation' and developing and exporting more raw materials other than oil. This pattern is only too evident in such cases as natural gas, petrochemicals and aluminium. The basic problems of a raw material producing country are either not fully recognized or not seriously tackled. The result is that the mass of the Iranian people are hardly touched by the so-called development programmes that do absorb a considerable amount of the country's investment outlays. The people's participation in the economic activity—especially that of women—is extremely low. Industrialization is proceeding at a slow pace providing little opportunity for employment, and whatever of the investment funds is actually used in the industrial sector is not used to develop industries with the highest value-added per worker. There is considerable disparity of income and welfare between the rural and urban populations and in towns between those employed by the government and the workers in the private sector. Not only have government expenditures and programmes become increasingly dependent on oil revenues, the consumption patterns of the people are also thoroughly geared to the utilization of imported commodities. At the same time the level of the

[17] See *Preliminary Estimate of Iran's National Income*, Tehran 1966.

economy's technology, the nature of its socio-political organization and the standards of the people's general education and training are such that little optimism is warranted as far as the long-run growth prospects of the country are concerned. These prospects can of course be changed as the result of the adoption of appropriate policies, but for the time being the Iranian economy remains, as before, at the mercy of fluctuations in oil prices and weather conditions. On a more general level, the following points can perhaps be made:

(i) If the economic performance of most Rentier States is found to be as unimpressive as that of Iran during the period 1954–65, there would appear to be sufficient justification for doubting whether the availability of capital and foreign exchange are as crucial as they are sometimes assumed to be in the process of economic development.

(ii) Since organizational and technological factors can be collapsed together in the case of underdeveloped countries (for these countries are more concerned with utilizing what is already known and not so much with achieving new break-throughs in technology) the organizational aspects of economic growth, including the social and political structure of developing countries, assumes an importance seldom accorded to it. Political change may turn out to be the factor with the highest shadow price in Rentier States.

(iii) Even with the best of organizations, Rentier States will still have a number of special problems which they will have to solve if their economic growth is to continue smoothly and not be disrupted severely when the external rents begin to fluctuate or even decline. In constructing economic models for these countries, it would be advisable to introduce external rents as a major variable and establish the functional relationships that exist between it and other variables of the system. The shift from a raw material exporting country to an industrial economy would also have to be more deliberately planned.

(iv) For reasons that are partly technological and partly socio-political and economic, few of the Rentier States can remain Rentier States for very long periods of time. By concentrating on the issue of oil royalties, the oil producing countries may discover that they have ignored the most important aspect of having such a large industry on their soil: its potentialities for generating growth. Reversal of the oil company policy of input minimization from local economies and development of ancillary industries based on gas, power and petrochemicals may appear as the most logical way of passing through this transitional stage. Refining and marketing of petroleum by the producer countries will have the same effect.

(v) The socio-political aspects of Rentier States are also of some interest. A government that can expand its services without resorting to heavy taxation acquires an independence from the people seldom found in other countries. However, not having developed an effective administrative machinery for the purposes of taxation, the governments of Rentier States may suffer from inefficiency in any field of activity that requires extensive organizational inputs. In political terms, the power of the government to bribe pressure groups or to coerce dissidents may be greater than otherwise. By the same token, this power is highly vulnerable since the stoppage of external rents can seriously damage the government finances.

(vi) The problems of income distribution are not easy to solve in any underdeveloped country that tries to achieve rapid growth within the framework of a capitalistic method of production. The problems are more serious in Rentier States because of the concentration of vast external rents in few hands. The temptations for a government bureaucracy to turn into a rentier class with its own independent source of income are considerable.

The Profitability of Middle Eastern Oil Ventures: a Historical Approach

ZUHAYR MIKDASHI

THIS paper has the triple purpose of (1) outlining the problems attendant on the collection of information on the Middle East oil industry, (2) presenting a novel analytical approach for the study and evaluation of the economic performance of oil ventures, and (3) reviewing major findings of the author's recent historical analysis of the financial and related aspects of Middle Eastern oil concessions.[1]

I. Significance of a Historical Study of Profits in the Explanation of Sources of Conflict

The modern history of the Middle East has been dramatically influenced by the oil industry, and oil relations have been fraught with conflicts and crises between local governments on one hand, and oil concessionaires and their parent countries on the other hand. Yet historians writing on the Middle East have given too little attention to these developments. In general, they have neglected the inter-relation of economic and political factors in the problems that have confronted the Middle East.

The historian may ask himself what is the importance of a specialized historical study of income derived by oil companies and host countries in the Middle East.

A study of the size of income from oil production, and of how this has been divided between the host countries and the concessionaires, should serve to illuminate major sources of political conflict in the Middle East, and determine whether governments were well advised when they acted *vis-à-vis* oil companies with a view to increasing their revenue-take.

Although the basic differences have stemmed from economic factors, preconceptions and ignorance on the part of the oil producing countries have aggravated conflicts. So also have the policies and practices of the oil companies. Host countries have complained loudly that the distribution of oil income has been unfair. The author's study is designed to throw light on this issue.

Oil income, which is large in the Middle East, is essentially producers' rent representing an excess over the minimum return required to attract

[1] Zuhayr Mikdashi, *A Financial Analysis of Middle Eastern Oil Concessions, 1901–1965*, New York 1962.

capital to the area. This arises from the fact that Middle East oil deposits are extremely prolific and low cost compared with other sources of supply. The terms of the concessions and the oligopolistic structure of the international oil industry have helped to maintain a high level of economic rent for some oil producers.

II. The Search for Facts

A study of income derived by Middle Eastern oil ventures is a difficult undertaking. The researcher immediately faces problems both in the collection of objective facts and in the use of these facts. In examining these twin problems, the author finds it necessary to draw on his personal experience. He will later attempt to evaluate the significance of his research in this field.

Information on company income from the Middle East oil industry is relatively scanty, and this has invited speculation and surmises.

The author, like other writers, has been influenced by his environment. Having lived in the Middle East and the West, he has been subjected to various and conflicting preconceptions and prejudices current about the oil industry. Professor George Stocking, in his presidential address to the American Economic Association,[2] developed the idea that the problems an economist thinks about and the way he thinks about them are the product of his institutional milieu. This is especially true in an empirical study of a particular industry such as the petroleum industry.

To extricate oneself from environmental influence is not easy. Attitudes, whether consciously or unconsciously acquired, and whether they are held by oil companies or by host governments, are more often than not partisan and polemical. The parties which issued information were either pleading their cause or accusing others. Accordingly, a scholar should exercise continued vigilance in scrutinizing all information received and checking its validity and accuracy.

A wealth of information is available in U.S. Congressional hearings, various courts proceedings, and a number of governmental reports on the international oil industry. Although detailed financial statistics on the Middle East oil industry are not normally published in the annual reports of the major international oil companies, such information can be found at the Securities and Exchange Commission in Washington D.C. for American Companies, and at the Companies Registration Office in London for companies incorporated in England.

Some of the smaller, so-called 'Independent' oil companies frequently publish greater details about their Middle Eastern operations, and these can be used to make up for information not normally released by the

[2] George Stocking, 'Institutional Factors in Economic Thinking', *The American Economic Review*, 1959.

majors. This is particularly true of information on investments, costs and prices of Middle East oil.

The researcher can, given patience and perseverance, examine the mass of materials issued by oil companies or their spokesmen, and disentangle the objective and useful data on our subject matter. Such materials cover minutes of stock-holders meetings, addresses of executives, pamphlets, and company statements to the press. The author has found some company reports, not supposed to be published, in such institutions as the Hoover Library at Stanford University or the Bureau of Mines Library in Washington D.C.

Diplomatic correspondence is a source of valuable information. Unfortunately, however, correspondence of the diplomatic missions of the United States, Britain, France and other powers with oil interests in the Middle East has been published only partially. Moreover, free access to diplomatic correspondence in its entirety is restricted until the elapsing of a minimum period of 25 years in the U.S., and of 50 years in the U.K.

Disputes, whether arbitrated internationally or discussed openly in national or international forums, have led to the disclosure of information which would otherwise have remained secret. This is true, for example, of crises that have developed between the oil companies and the host governments of Iran, Iraq and Saudi Arabia. In the case of Kuwait, previously confidential information was released by the government to defend its oil policy *vis-à-vis* the country's political opposition and not with a view to accusing the oil companies.[3]

The Arab League, mostly through its petroleum congresses, offers a massive source of literature on the Middle East oil industry; some of the literature, however, is erroneous and prejudiced. The objective researcher must examine the congress papers and minutes of discussions with an alert and critical eye.

Local governments of the Middle East are learning more and more about their oil industry thanks to their successes in obtaining information from their own concessionaires. Governments' publications, especially those issued after 1950, can be reasonably trusted as to objective facts. The year 1950, it should be noted, witnessed the introduction of the so-called 50–50 split of profits between host governments and concessionaires. The enforcement of that formula necessitated the submission by oil companies of their revenue and expense figures. That was when the host countries began to develop a serious understanding of some financial and economic aspects of the oil industry.

The Middle East Research and Publishing Centre has proved a rich source of information on the area's oil industry. The Centre has a fine

[3] See, e.g., 'Statement of Ministry of Finance and Oil', printed in *al-Ṭalīʿa* (Kuwait, 4 May 1966).

library, a competent staff, and publishes a reliable summary of developments in its weekly entitled *Middle East Economic Survey*. But most of the sources of information on the Middle East oil industry, it should be acknowledged, remain outside the Middle East and chiefly in the countries of Western Europe and the U.S.A.

In trying to interview oil industry officials the author, like many other scholars, has been faced by reticence, occasionally verging on suspicion. Oil companies are commercial concerns which guard jealously information they consider vital to their protection from competitors or from the taxing authorities. Their caution increases when they are dealing with Middle Easterners for fear that the information offered could be used out of context and to their disadvantage.

To overcome the oil companies' suspicions, the author has found it worthwhile to offer some company officials concerned sections of preliminary drafts of his writings with a request that they check the facts. It is true that the officials of one company considered material submitted to contain a prejudicial description of their operations. It took some effort and time to convince them that the weight of evidence available to the author tilted the balance of the argument to what appeared to be an unfavourable evaluation of their operations. In fact, the writer had to begin his study with a mass of material—mostly supplied or issued by host governments at times of crisis—indicting the oil companies. The information published by oil companies was, in contrast, significantly less comprehensive.

Once oil company representatives were convinced of the scholarly goals of the writer, they suggested corrections, indicated sources of information previously not known to him, and gave generously of their time to discuss various aspects of the Middle East oil industry.

Neither was the cooperation of host governments always readily forthcoming. A few government officials also have fears about divulging so-called secret information—already publicly known, however, to Western groups interested in oil. Needless to say, an important reason for government officials' reluctance to cooperate is their ignorance of some of the complex aspects of the international oil industry.

The author is fortunate in having worked for, and having had intimate contacts with the Organization of the Petroleum Exporting Countries. There, he had access to primary but confidential information which—though not available for publication—offered him a unique opportunity for checking information collected from other sources.

III. Methodological Problems

The collection of relevant and objective data is, we have seen, a major hurdle in researching on the economic history of oil relations in the

Middle East. The other major task is to make proper use of the data collected.

The author's recent research has had a double purpose: to analyse and interpret (1) the determinants behind methods and rates of payments of major oil concessionaires to host governments in the Middle East, and (2) the financial performance of the parties concerned.

The author's objective in measuring and evaluating the financial results of the Middle East oil industry has led him to study (*a*) costs, (*b*) investments, (*c*) prices and (*d*) fiscal obligations. It is probably easier to ascertain and measure the fiscal obligations of oil companies than the other factors.

The author has managed to collect accounting data on costs, investments and prices. But accounting is an imperfect technique which aims at translating economic concepts and phenomena into figures. Needless to say, there are continuous improvements, and the practical application of economic concepts is nowadays less crude than it used to be.

Among the shortcomings of accounting techniques is the arbitrary allocation of depreciation charges per unit of time in a manner not usually consistent with the economic depreciation of assets. The proper valuation of the latter can be difficult at any time. Another shortcoming of accounting concerns the use of original costs in valuing assets. Inflation over the decades under study has been substantial, and the monetary units used do not have the same purchasing power.

Moreover, the accounting method of the average investment rate of return cannot be used for projects which have had a long time lag between the initial disbursements and the first year of earnings. This is true of the IPC Group of Iraq. There was an initial period of some ten years of investment during which period the accounting rate of return was nil. To average out periods of positive return with periods of no return would appear absurd. Some Middle East officials have been guilty of using recent or current accounting rates of return—which are high—to claim that the oil ventures in question have always been yielding such high rates.

Statistical studies on the profitability of Middle Eastern oil are few. Among the more important are those made by leading American banks (the Chase Manhattan Bank, and the First National City Bank of New York), by the U.S. Department of Commerce, by a few business consulting firms, and by host governments of the Middle East. These studies have something in common in that they use accounting figures. However, each study has adopted special assumptions, whether regarding elements to be included in assets representing the investment efforts or regarding the method of measurement of net profits derived from the use of these assets. Moreover, all these studies have confined their profitability estimates to a selected number of years. In general, the accounting method, while it purports to measure the profitability of a venture per period of time, namely a year, fails to show the true size of income and/or investment.[4]

On the other hand, the author has attempted to estimate the profitability of some Middle Eastern oil ventures from the date of their inception to the latest year available to him. His purpose has been to work out the average rate of return over the whole life of the enterprise. For the first time in a study of the historical profitability of the Middle East oil industry, he introduces the application of a method commonly used for evaluating the expected return from planned investment projects, and generally known as the discounted cash flow (DCF) method or the measure of the internal rate of return of capital. The DCF rate of return of a venture can be defined as that discount rate which equates cash disbursements of a capital nature and net cash earnings in the base year of the project.

The adoption of the DCF method has distinct advantages over the accounting average investment rate of return formula. It does away with the shortcomings of the latter deriving from the use of notional depreciation schedules in computing net assets and net income. Moreover, dealing with cash flows permits corrections for changes in the value of money more readily than dealing with book assets and profits. Also, the DCF technique weighs properly the time value of disbursements to, and revenues from, an oil venture while the commonly used accounting rates of return fail to reckon with this important factor.

The author has imputed cash flow tables for the Iraq Petroleum Company (IPC) Group of Iraq, the parent companies of Arabian American Oil Company (Aramco), and the parent companies of the Iranian Consortium. These tables are reproduced in the Appendix. Data available to the author on the Kuwait oil industry are not for publication. However, other researchers could also prepare cash flow tables from information accessible to the public on a few other oil ventures in the Middle East and elsewhere.

The author is not so bold as to assume that his calculations are completely foolproof. Indeed a number of his figures are rough approximations. He has had to adopt assumptions regarding the disbursement and receipt of funds by the oil ventures under study—assumptions which were considered reasonable by industry quarters. He assumed that annual disbursements of a capital nature were about equal to changes in total gross assets over consecutive years. The revaluation or retirement of assets introduces a calculable bias which is not considered significant enough to invalidate the principle and results of calculations.

In the computation of cash receipts, the author has had to impute for most of the years covered net cash earnings after tax. This requires

[4] See Ezra Solomon, 'Return on Investment: The Relation of Book Yield to True Yield', Society of Petroleum Engineers, Dallas, Texas, October 1963.

ascertaining the sales price of oil. Prior to 1950, no prices were published by Middle Eastern oil producers; thereafter so-called posted prices were published. The latter were first established at a level which the companies reckoned to represent the level of prices on sales to third parties. After 1957, posted prices have been maintained at a level much higher than sales prices to third parties. The latter benefited from 20 to 30 per cent discounts off the posted prices. The author, on the basis of price and expense information available from different sources, has estimated oil companies' earnings.

Some writers believe that it is impossible to estimate profits on oil exports from the Middle East. They argue that since most of the crude oil produced moves into integrated channels or is sold on long term contracts, no realistic price for crude oil exports can be determined. It is true that sales to third parties are relatively small. The economist, however, should not be deterred from attempting to measure the economic value of oil sold, no matter how imprecise his results may be.

In his DCF calculations, the author has been dealing with 'going concerns'. In order to calculate a rate of return for these concerns, the author has had to impute a market value of the venture in the terminal year. This is indeed a major limitation on the use of the DCF method for measuring the historical profitability of a going concern, and explains its current use only for bounded projects, i.e. projects which have been terminated or disposed of in one way or another.

The DCF rates of return computed by the author come out with one single average rate for each venture over its whole life. To the extent that an annual rate of return is also desirable for our analysis, the single average rate may prove inadequate if used alone. In principle, that drawback could be circumvented by deriving DCF rates on an incremental basis—a subject which merits thorough study. Moreover, cash flow tables can serve as a basis for computing an indicator of past profitability without necessarily computing a rate of return by the DCF method. The possible alternative approach would consist of relating the net cash earnings index to an index of disbursement streams with a view to assessing changes of yield relatively to changes of funds used.

To account for the fact that capital funds have a gestation period—probably averaging some three years—an appropriate escalation of these two indices would be required. A more complete picture can be offered if cash flows are prepared for upstream and downstream operations. This should include disbursements and receipts of funds in the production phase of an oil venture and in the various other phases of processing and trading the oil of that venture. The author has not carried out such calculations.[5]

[5] Mr. T. R. Stauffer is presently doing research of a nature akin to that done by the

IV. Results of Research and Analysis

Within the scope set in his work for analysing the profitability of Middle Eastern oil concessions, the author's research has thrown light on facts hitherto not known to the general public. It also has served to disprove some of the long held preconceptions on the Middle East oil industry and to clarify some of the widely circulating misapprehensions on the oil industry.

The study has brought to light the special relation which has existed between concessionaires and governments of their parent countries. Outsiders writing on the oil industry have generally assumed that the British Government, e.g., has continuously given full support to the actions and policies of the British concessionaire in Iran, viz., D'Arcy and his successor companies. Primary evidence available but not known by the general public interested in Middle Eastern oil shows that British Government officials have not always privately espoused the stand-point of the concessionaire. British diplomatic correspondence available at the Public Record Office shows spokesmen of the British Government acknowledging that the concessionaire's actions were occasionally unjustified. Yet the British Government condoned these actions, prompted primarily by expediency.

The study reveals another significant fact regarding the strategies and tactics used by concessionaires in their dealings with host governments. The historical records show that gratuities or 'douceurs' in various forms and sizes were offered occasionally by concessionaires and accepted by local rulers. This proved a 'quick' and effective way in the short run for doing business by concessionaires in societies where corruption prevailed. With the development of civic consciousness and public responsibilities, these practices have discredited both conniving rulers and concessionaires. The former have been for the most part replaced, and present oil managements are not likely to resort to such practices.

The study also reveals that host governments were not alone responsible for the infraction of concession agreements, and that concessionaires on occasion violated their contractual obligations. Governments could invoke as a reason for seeking changes in agreements the public interest and the exercise of their sovereign right to legislate. Concessionaires have had no equally valid excuse. In fact, oil companies have always made a point of the sanctity of contracts, and that they have never infringed the letter or spirit of agreements. But as a result of my research, I found the contrary. The refusal of the Anglo-Persian Oil Company (APOC) in the first two

author. Mr. Stauffer is writing his Harvard Ph.D. dissertation on the theory of capital with a case study regarding the measurement of return for the non-U.S. oil industry using a generalized cash flow basis.

decades of its operations to meet fully its contractual payments or the request of the Persian Government for arbitration of the matter is a glaring example of a concessionaire violating a concession agreement.[6]

The literature from Middle Eastern and other sources frequently refers to artificial manipulations of company accounts—at variance with the explicit provisions of agreements.[7] The Iranian Government, in particular, accused APOC in 1933 of following arbitrary accounting practices and of entering into fictitious transactions with a view to reducing the legitimate share of the Iranian Government in the concessionaire's profits. The author found no published evidence to support this charge. Nevertheless, the company was able in a few cases to interpret agreements in a partisan fashion to maximize its economic benefits.[8] Other official spokesmen of the Middle East have accused oil companies of having plundered their wealth; and to support their position some have produced studies of dubious objectivity and logic.[9]

The study of the financial aspects of leading oil ventures in the Middle East brings out the fact that all have been profitable. This is true regardless of the method of assessment or standard of comparison. The IPC Group of Iraq ranks lowest in terms of profitability amongst the companies studied (see Notes at end of Appendix). A figure of about 15 per cent is obtained on the DCF basis for the period 1925–63, after making adjustments for changes in the purchasing power of money.

The above mentioned DCF figure on the IPC group venture, and other DCF figures computed for other oil ventures, are very rough approximations. The author, in resorting to DCF calculations, has been interested primarily in the approach, not the figures. He expects other researchers, with better access to data, to obtain more accurate and reliable results (see Tables in Appendix). It is important to note that in the case of the Iranian Consortium, the accounting and DCF rates are both very high (close to 70 per cent), and do not show the same large disparity as in the case of the IPC group. A major reason for this is that the time-lag between the disbursements and receipts of funds was not as great. The Consortium's disbursements were followed immediately and in the same year by receipts, while in the case of the IPC Group it took some ten years after the initial disbursements were made before receipts started accruing.

What appears to be a not excessive DFC rate of return to the IPC Group venture in Iraq reflects a number of interesting facts: (1) that the host government has obtained relatively favourable financial terms and results if judged by the size of the economic rent derived from the venture, and

[6] Mikdashi, *op. cit.*, pp. 35–9. [7] *Ibid.*, pp. 39–40.

[8] Ref. the 'Interpretative' Agreement of 1920 between APOC and Iran; *ibid.*, pp. 16–19.

[9] As an illustration, one could refer to Abdallah Tariki's paper, *The Pricing of Crude Oil and Refined Products*, Second Arab Petroleum Congress, Beirut 1960.

(2) that the operations of the IPC group have not generated large economic rents to match those of other Middle Eastern oil companies. Indeed, the IPC venture in Iraq has been handicapped by the construction through transit countries of long and costly pipeline systems to the east Mediterranean. These pipelines were partly or completely put out of use for varying periods of time and for different reasons. Moreover, the rates of oil production and export were adversely affected by conflicts and crises between the IPC Group and host governments (the Iraq Government and the transit governments of Syria and Lebanon).

It is certain that access to new facts and the development of scientific techniques for measuring the economic performance of the Middle East oil industry offer new light and explanations in the history of the area. The author hopes to have contributed to opening up a new avenue for understanding the economic history of oil relations in the Middle East.

APPENDIX*

TABLE I. *Estimated cash flow of the IPC Group of Iraq, 1925–63 (£ million)*

Year	Disbursements	Receipts: Depreciation	Receipts: Net Income After Tax
	(1)	(2)	(3)
1925	·418		
1926	·397		
1927	·775		
1928	·560		
1929	·878		
1930	·756		
1931	1·633		
1932	2·966		
1933	5·297		
1934	3·072	·866	
1935	1·035	·866	1·719
1936	1·035	·866	1·219
1937	1·996	·866	2·268
1938	2·654	·866	3·034
1939	2·654	·866	2·367
1940	2·654	·866	3·039
1941	2·654	·866	2·204
1942	2·654	·866	3·661
1943	2·654	·866	5·361
1944	2·654	·866	6·284
1945	2·654	·866	6·936
1946	8·750	·866	7·041
1947	8·775	3·070	6·982
1948	20·054	3·006	4·889
1949	20·024	7·480	5·947
1950	20·216	9·133	13·100
1951	29·087	11·152	17·046
1952	33·205	7·557	44·448
1953	6·679	11·021	57·224
1954	9·352	7·932	74·496
1955	1·505	9·903	79·793
1956	4·203	8·838	74·239
1957	23·927	7·750	54·182
1958	11·056	10·797	61·809
1959	26·220	7·245	64·446
1960	7·744	13·495	71·640
1961	(−8·628)	3·286	72·164
1962	11·245	14·905	72·445
1963	2·452	7·024	82·862

* For sources, see Mikdashi, *op. cit.*

TABLE 2. *Estimates of accounting profitability of the IPC Group of Iraq, 1952–63*

	Average Net Assets £'000	Estimated Net Profits £'000	Accounting Rate of Return %
	(1)	(2)	(2) ÷ (1) × 100
1952	116,306	44,448	38·2
1953	123,610	57,224	46·3
1954	120,096	74,496	62·0
1955	116,123	79,793	68·7
1956	113,000	74,239	65·7
1957	117,425	54,182	46·1
1958	122,409	61,809	50·5
1959	125,756	64,446	51·2
1960	127,250	71,640	56·3
1961	120,238	72,164	60·0
1962	114,698	72,445	63·2
1963	113,477	82,862	73·0
1952–63	1,430,388	809,748	56·6

TABLE 3. *Estimated cash flow of Socal with respect to Aramco, 1934–64* ($'000)

Year	Disbursements to Aramco	Receipts: From Texaco, Down payment	Receipts: From Texaco, Pro rata payment	Receipts: From Jersey Socony, Pro rata payment	Receipts: From Aramco, Repayment of advances	Receipts: From Aramco, Dividends
	(1)	(2)	(3)	(4)	(5)	(6)
1934	250					
1935	1,375					
1936	1,375	3,000				
1937	1,500					
1938	1,500		110			
1939	3,134		980			
1940	3,134		1,255			
1941	2,745		657			
1942	2,745		628			
1943	2,745		684			
1944	2,745		1,941			
1945	10,700		5,308			
1946	10,700		9,437			
1947	10,700			18,617	39,883	
1948				7,500		3,000
1949				7,500		14,000
1950				9,550		17,106
1951				13,550		27,898
1952				14,750		28,249
1953				15,000		32,044
1954				17,000		85,059
1955				17,150		79,073
1956				17,600		79,675
1957				17,650		78,800
1958				18,250		106,500
1959				9,500		94,000
1960						100,000
1961						104,000
1962						121,000
1963						121,000*
1964						121,000*

* Estimates.

TABLE 4. *Estimated cash flow of Texaco with respect to Aramco, 1936–64* ($'000)

Year	Disbursements			Receipts		
		To Socal			From Aramco	
	To Aramco	Down payment	Pro rata payment	From Jersey Socony	Repayment of advances	Dividends
	(1)	(2)	(3)	(4)	(5)	(6)
1936		3,000				
1937	1,500					
1938	1,500		110			
1939	3,134		980			
1940	3,134		1,255			
1941	2,745		657			
1942	2,745		628			
1943	2,745		684			
1944	2,745		1,941			
1945	10,700		5,308			
1946	10,700		6,437			
1947				18,617	39,883	
1948				7,500		3,000
1949				7,500		14,000
1950				9,500		17,106
1951				13,550		27,898
1952				14,750		28,249
1953				15,000		32,044
1954				17,000		85,059
1955				17,150		79,073
1956				17,600		79,675
1957				17,650		78,800
1958				18,250		106,500
1959				9,500		94,000
1960						112,000
1961						117,000
1962						121,000*
1963						121,000*
1964						121,000*

* Estimates.

TABLE 5. *Estimated cash flow of Jersey-Socony with respect to Aramco, 1947–64* ($'000)

	Disbursements		Receipts
Year	Down payment to Aramco	Pro rata payment to Socal and Texaco	Dividends from Aramco
	(4)		(6)
1947	105,456	37,235	
1948		15,000	4,000
1949		15,000	18,667
1950		19,100	22,808
1951		27,100	37,197
1952		29,500	37,665
1953		30,000	42,939
1954		34,000	113,412
1955		34,300	105,431
1956		35,200	106,234
1957		35,300	81,800
1958		36,500	117,300
1959		19,000	113,000
1960			145,000
1961			154,000
1962			161,300*
1963			161,300*
1964			161,300*

* Estimates.

TABLE 6. *Estimates of Aramco's accounting rates of return on invested capital (in %)*

	Opec	Tariki
	(1)	(2)
1952		44·6
1953		39·8
1954		54·8
1955		54·9
1956	59	58·7
1957	58	55·2
1958	57	59·2
1959	62	60·6
1960	71	72·6
1961		81·5
Arithmetic Mean	61	57·6

TABLE 7. *Estimated cash flow of the Persian Consortium, 1954–64* (£'000)

Year	Disbursements*	Receipts	
		Depreciation	Net income after tax
	(1)	(2)	(3)
1954	48,321	3,612	3,106
1955	48,321	3,613	32,324
1956	14,288	7,595	54,792
1957	22,718	8,425	76,038
1958	19,533	9,089	58,893
1959	21,448	10,281	62,497
1960	9,051	10,949	67,918
1961	8,694	14,072	71,703
1962	2,011	14,790	79,460
1963	2,007	14,061	91,600
1964	26,998	15,215	114,333

* Disbursements = increases in assets (gross of depreciation).

TABLE 8. *Accounting profitability estimates of the Consortium, 1955–64*

	Average net Assets* £'000	Estimated net Profits £'000	Accounting rate of return %
	(1)	(2)	(2) ÷ (1) × 100
1955	82,537†	32,324	39·2
1956	85,820	54,792	63·8
1957	93,830	76,038	70·7
1958	105,038	58,893	56·7
1959	116,620	62,497	53·6
1960	120,181	67,918	56·5
1961	117,345	71,703	61·1
1962	109,402	79,460	72·6
1963	97,597	91,600	93·8
1964	95,007	114,333	120·3
1955–64	1,023,377	709,558	69·3

* Net assets = Total assets − Current liabilities.
† End of year.

Notes on DCF Rates

1. IPC group of Iraq: 13 to 15 per cent,
   assuming terminal values of about £560 to £1,800 million.
2. Aramco's owners:
   a—Socal: 28 per cent
   b—Texaco: 22 per cent
   c—Jersey–Socony: 20 per cent
   using an appraised value of Aramco of $2,667 million in the terminal year.
3. The Persian Consortium: about 70 per cent,
   using an appraised value of the Consortium of £700 million in the terminal year.

The Attitudes of British Officials to the Development of the Egyptian Economy, 1882–1922

E. R. J. OWEN

THE principal aim of this paper is to make a general survey of the attitudes of certain leading British officials in Egypt towards the development of the economy between 1882 and 1922. But in so doing an effort will also be made to describe the effects of some of the policies pursued, particularly in those areas where they exercised a deep and long-lasting influence on future economic progress. This may well seem too ambitious an undertaking. It could be argued, with justice, that the subject is too important and too complex to be dealt with in so brief a compass. Nevertheless it seems that some advantage might be gained from treating the period of British management of the Egyptian economy as a whole. In this way it becomes possible to draw attention not only to the ways in which policies developed over the years but also to a certain overall continuity of approach to Egypt's economic problems.

For the purpose of analysis, the years 1882 to 1922 have been divided chronologically into three parts, each of which has some basic characteristic in common. The first (1882–1906) was dominated by the figure of Lord Cromer, while the second (1907–13) and the third (1914–22) were greatly affected by two major events, the economic crisis of 1907–9 and the dislocations caused by the First World War respectively. However, such a division is, of course, no more than a convenient analytical tool. What is more important is to try and see the period in its entirety, for it is a basic thesis of the paper that British policy towards the Egyptian economy demonstrated a considerable degree of consistency throughout the forty years in question.

1882–1906

It is a commonplace of histories of British economic thought that one of the great changes which took place during the nineteenth century was the wane of interest in theories of development—that whereas men like Malthus and Ricardo were vitally concerned with the whole process of economic growth and devoted much of their energies to examining how it occurred, their successors took if all for granted and turned their interest elsewhere. This is largely true. From J. S. Mill's *Political Economy* onwards it is rare to find more than passing reference to what he called 'the advancement in material prosperity'. Once development could be seen to be inevitable it no longer had to be explained, it could be taken for granted.

Nevertheless, it would be wrong to suppose that British officials concerned with the management of Asian or African economies were totally without theoretical guidance. Even if contemporary textbooks were so empty of reference to economic growth, there was always something to be learned from what Professor Galbraith has called 'the conventional wisdom' of the age.[1] This is well illustrated in the case of Lord Cromer, the first British administrator to be called upon to deal with Egyptian economic problems in any concerted way. He, like many of his fellow Victorians, not only believed with Mill that most of the nations in the world 'gradually increase in production and population',[2] but also that the process would be more or less rapid according to whether certain kinds of conditions obtained. Central to his thinking was his conviction that growth was essentially a question of the development of a country's resources through the application of capital to productive works. Such capital could be raised domestically from the savers in the society or imported from abroad. But in either case it was his conviction that it would only be forthcoming in any quantity if there existed a framework in which enterprise could flourish. This was what he meant by the word 'security'—a shorthand for such things as law and order, an equable and efficient system of justice, and a legal code which preserved private property and in general allowed men to profit from the fruits of their labours.

Another prerequisite for progress was the creation of a certain infrastructure without which commercial interests could not be expected to come forward. On some occasions this might require action by the state. As Mill had put it:

> In the particular circumstances of a given age or nation there is scarcely anything really important to the general interest which it may not be desirable or even necessary that the Government should take upon itself, not because private individuals cannot effectively perform it, but because they will not. At some times and places there will be no docks, harbours, canals, works of irrigation, hospitals, schools, colleges, printing presses, unless the Government establishes them; the public being either too poor to command the necessary resources, or too little advanced in intelligence to appreciate the ends, or not sufficiently practised in conjoint action to be capable of the means.[3]

[1] The concept of 'conventional wisdom' is a useful one but difficult to use with precision. It is supposed to consist of ideas current among educated, thinking men. Thus, almost by definition, these ideas are of a very general kind and may not correspond closely with the kind of things academic economists are talking and writing about.

[2] *Political Economy*, vol. ii, London 1848, p. 244.

[3] *Ibid.*, p. 548. This passage was used by Sir John Strachey, a man who exercised a considerable influence over Cromer's thinking about development, as justification for a policy of using Government money and Government guaranteed loans to construct major public works in India, *India*, London 1888, pp. 120–1.

Otherwise, these aids apart, the Government should do nothing to interfere with the free exercise of enterprise. All restrictions on industry and trade should be removed, while the state confine itself only to those few things which it could do best. Any other course would lead to the stultification of that individual initiative upon which further progress so largely depended.[4]

One other tenet of Victorian 'conventional wisdom' must also be mentioned—the assumption that the development of a country's economy followed more or less the same pattern wherever it occurred. In Cromer's case this is well illustrated by the policies he pursued during his three years in India as Finance Member in the Viceroy's Council, 1880 to 1883.[5] India's first economic requirement, he asserted when introducing his first budget in March 1881, was that its resources should be developed without delay; and on this and subsequent occasions he went on to outline some of the ways by which such a requirement might be met. For one thing greater encouragement should be given to private individuals anxious to invest in the construction of new railways. Not only was it unlikely that the Government could perform this vital task entirely on its own, but he also hoped that such an initiative might lead Indian capitalists to come forward and take up some of the burden themselves. A second group of policies was designed to promote trade by freeing it from almost all the duties with which it was still encumbered, while a third went as far in the direction of assisting Indian industry as he felt able by introducing the principle that the administration purchase goods from local factories wherever they were as cheap and as well made as imports from Europe. It is also important to note that this last initiative was supported by arguments which suggested that he did not expect India to remain a purely agricultural country, and that he looked forward to a measure of industrialization, including the future establishment of plant to manufacture iron and steel.[6]

But of course Cromer was more of an Imperial administrator than an economist, and it would be wrong to look for the genesis of such policies solely within the confines of conventional economic wisdom. His whole approach to the question of development was also reinforced by what he took to be political necessity. If growth was the natural condition of a well ordered society, it was also absolutely essential in an Indian context, for only if the inhabitants came to believe that Britain was ready to attend to

[4] As an example of Cromer's view on this subject see his letter to the Editor of the *Spectator* in which he explained that he had turned down Campbell-Bannerman's invitation to become Foreign Secretary in 1905 because he did not want to become responsible for 'socialistic measures' which would run counter to all his most cherished convictions, Cromer to St. Loe Strachey, 3 April 1906, Cromer Correspondence, PRO FO 633/8.

[5] I have already tried to outline some of the impact of India on his approach to Imperial government in my 'The Influence of Lord Cromer's Indian Experience on British Policy in Egypt 1883–1907', *St. Antony's Papers No. 17*, Oxford 1965.

[6] For Cromer's Indian budget speeches see Parl. Papers 1881, vol. lxviii (especially pp. 303–9) and 1882, vol. xlviii (especially pp. 308–49).

their material interests would they be prepared to tolerate British rule. Strict economy in public expenditure was also important for two sets of reasons. It was not just that money would be more wisely spent if left to 'fructify' in the pockets of the peasant, but excessive taxation was a primary cause of rural discontent.

It was only after he had been in Egypt a number of years that Cromer had similar freedom of action to introduce schemes to develop the country's resources. For some time it was believed that the Occupation was to be of only a short duration, and expenditure had to be kept to a minimum in order to meet the many pressing financial obligations. Nevertheless, Cromer, following the lead given by Lord Dufferin, was sufficiently aware of the short-term political and economic advantage of a thorough-going reform of the system of irrigation to assign it a very high priority. To begin with his aim was largely to insure the land tax against the dangerous effects of a particularly low Nile, but later he took a more positive line and argued that a policy of increasing the value of Egyptian agricultural output was the easiest way of obtaining a continuous rise in Government revenue. Irrigation reform also had other virtues. It was a way of winning the allegiance of the peasants at a time when the alternative approach, a reduction in the level of taxation, was barred; and, as he wrote to the Foreign Secretary in 1886, it was a subject in which 'the good results of European administration can be readily brought home to the natives. Hence there is some chance that, in the event of withdrawal, our work would not wholly be undone'.[7] To this end Cromer gave those British officials in the Ministry of Public Works his full support. No other branch of the administration, with the exception of the army, was allowed as large a budget; only the Irrigation Department could count on money for long-term development projects.[8]

A more varied approach to questions of Egyptian development became possible in the early 1890's once the financial situation had eased and it had become apparent that the British Government were committed to an indefinite occupation. Primacy was given to schemes connected with the agricultural sector, progress taking place in three main directions.

Firstly, it was decided to increase the supply of summer water by building a dam at Aswān. This decision represented an important new departure. Hitherto efforts had been directed only at improving the system of irrigation which already existed; but now a more ambitious project was introduced, that of changing the type of agriculture practised throughout Middle Egypt so that crops could be grown all year round rather than only during the winter months. Again, although considerations of finance were

[7] Cromer (Baring) to Iddesleigh, 24 October 1886, C.C., PRO 633/6.

[8] R. L. Tignor, *Modernization and British colonial rule in Egypt 1882–1914*, Princeton 1966, pp. 113–14.

certainly relevant, the dam and its related works also represented the first step in the direction of a major long-term programme designed to maximize Egypt's agricultural potential by providing every piece of cultivable land with sufficient water to allow crops to be grown on it throughout the year.

A second area of activity involved efforts to improve the system of transport by the construction of agricultural roads and light railways. The former were financed and built by the provincial authorities, the latter by private capital. But in both cases it was the Government which took the initiative, either by passing the necessary legislation[9] or, where the railways were concerned, by advertising the fact that concessions were to be granted and by providing a guarantee of the profits up to a certain amount per kilometre.[10]

Thirdly, the method of collecting the land tax was reformed in such a way as to remove most of the existing inequalities by making the amount due more or less proportional to the rentable value of the land. At the same time the revision of the registers, following a cadastral survey, gave owners a more secure title to their property.

Cromer was quite content that such policies should lead to an improvement in agricultural incomes without the Government having to intervene directly in the production process itself, a policy of which he strongly disapproved. Nevertheless he was forced to modify this principle to some extent during the agricultural depression of 1894/5 when the price of all major crops fell so low that there was considerable hardship in a number of districts. In an effort to alleviate distress the Government agreed to supply a limited amount of cotton seed to the peasant cultivators at a low price. It also began to lend small sums of money in a few areas of the Delta. However, in neither case was the operation intended to be a permanent one. Cromer made it clear in his annual report for 1895 that he regarded the business of agricultural lending as something best left to the private banks. The Government did not have the resources to embark on such an activity. Nor was it wise that it should become the creditor of a large section of the rural population. On such occasions the Government might legitimately act as a pioneer, but he hoped that if the experiment were successful it might be possible to come to some arrangement with a private concern with a view to more extended operations.[11] This was in fact what happened three years later, in 1898, when the newly-created National Bank of Egypt agreed to take over the business of making small-scale loans in exchange for Government assistance in collecting the instalments when they fell due. Again, in the matter of supplying cheap seed, Cromer was only too happy to see this

[9] See, for instance, P. Gelat, *Répertoire de la législation et de l'administration Egyptiennes 1888–1892*, Alexandria 1893, pp. 403–4, 408.

[10] L. Wiener, *L'Egypte et ses chemins de fer*, Brussels 1932, pp. 493–4; A. Wright (ed.), *Twentieth Century impressions of Egypt*, London 1909, p. 183.

[11] Parl. Papers, 1896, vol. xcvii, pp. 997–9.

activity transferred to another private institution also founded in 1898, the Khedivial Agricultural Society. His anxiety to avoid further state intervention in the rural economy can also be seen in his attitude to the establishment of a Government Department of Agriculture. During the depression of 1894/5 he was subject to considerable pressure to create such an office which would take the lead in finding ways and means of safeguarding the future of the cotton crop. But here too Cromer was well content to leave activity of this kind to the Khedivial Agricultural Society, assisted by an annual Government subvention to its budget.

As it happened, the short-lived crisis of 1894/5 was a prelude to a period of unprecedented prosperity. To Lord Cromer, as well as to the other British officials who remembered the poverty and the frequent famines of India, this seemed a major triumph. As early as 1891 he had written to Goschen:

> So far as I know Egypt is the only agricultural country in the world whose wealth can, by human skill, be insured against all, or nearly all risks.

And he had concluded with the comment that: 'in the nature of things there is really nothing to prevent Egypt in our grandchildren's time from becoming one of the most prosperous countries in the world'.[12] Nine years later, at the turn of the century, there seemed no reason to doubt the accuracy of his prediction. The cotton harvest had doubled in size between 1890 and 1899; the value of the most fertile Delta fields had risen sharply; foreign investors were starting to pour money into any Egyptian enterprise connected with the sale or purchase or mortgage of agricultural land. But as time went on, some of Cromer's easy optimism began to give way to the realization that a seemingly effortless increase in prosperity was not the Egyptian norm. And in each of his four last annual reports he called attention to an aspect of the situation which he felt gave cause for concern. In 1903, for instance, it was the question of the pressure of population in certain districts forcing up rents;[13] while in 1905 he pointed to the evidence that cotton yields were beginning to decline. 'Probably the greatest danger which threatens Egypt', he added, 'lies in the fact . . . that the country depends too exclusively on one crop. . . .'[14]

However, the remedies he suggested hardly seemed to match the gravity of the situation he was attempting to diagnose: people should be encouraged to grow other crops like sugar and cereals in order to lessen the country's dependence on cotton; the decline in yields might be arrested by warnings against the dangers of over-cropping the land and the increased distribution of good seed by the Khedivial Agricultural Society; rural over-population could be lessened by providing men with the skills which would allow them to find employment outside agriculture. Meanwhile, the only hint that the

[12] Cromer (Baring), 28 December 1891, C.C., PRO FO 633/5.
[13] Parl. Papers, 1904, vol. cxi, pp. 220–1. [14] Parl. Papers, 1906, vol. cxxxvii, p. 505.

Government should play any role in these various processes came with his decision to establish a new department to supervise the expansion of facilities for technical and commercial education.

The reasons for this rather negative approach are not difficult to understand, for they follow directly from those basic principles which he felt should underlie official policy towards the whole question of development. His attitude to the question of Government assistance to agriculture is a case in point. Public works apart, there were a few operations which the administration might be forced to undertake in an emergency—among them the Delta-wide campaigns against locusts in 1904 and the cotton worm from 1905 onwards—but, as a rule, activities such as efforts to improve methods of cultivation or to introduce new crops were best left to private initiative. It was not just a case of lack of funds, there was also his profound belief that local enterprise could so easily be stultified by central direction.

But if Lord Cromer was unwilling to allow the Government more than a minimal role in the primary sector of the economy, he was even more sure that it would be quite wrong to do anything to diminish Egypt's dependence on agriculture by giving direct encouragement to industrial development. As a general rule, so he believed, the limits of state activity had been reached by two sorts of measures, the reduction (in November 1905) of the tariff on certain imported raw materials such as coal and wood from 8 to 4 per cent *ad valorem*, and efforts to improve the skills of the urban labour force by expanding the system of technical education. There were however, special cases. On at least one occasion he considered that it was of sufficient importance to the well-being of the Egyptian economy that he came to the assistance of an industry which had found itself in considerable difficulties. This was in 1906 when the Société Générale des Sucreries et de la Raffinerie d'Egypte was almost forced into liquidation and only saved by a reorganization of its finances which involved, among other things, the Government's purchase of the company's unprofitable network of light agricultural railways.[15] Further help was also provided by the Government's decision to waive the duty paid on sugar exports for one year.[16] But to offset this there was the notorious affair of the countervailing duty which, at Cromer's insistence, was placed on all Egyptian factory-produced cotton goods. I have dealt with this subject at some length in a recent article[17] and will say no more than that, for a variety of reasons—among them his belief in the principles of Free Trade, his fear of another political dispute similar to that which had marked the introduction of the Indian cotton duties in

[15] P. Arminjon, *La situation Economique et Financiere de l'Egypte*, Paris 1911, p. 242.

[16] J. Mazuel, *Le Sucre en Egypte*, Cairo 1937, p. 172.

[17] 'Lord Cromer and the development of Egyptian Industry', *Middle Eastern Studies*, 2, 1966, pp. 282–301.

1894 and, perhaps, his desire to propitiate the Lancashire cotton interests—he went to considerable lengths to prevent the two cotton factories established in Egypt at the turn of the century from obtaining any protection from the country's external tariff. Opinions as to the effect of this policy differ widely. But there can be no doubt that it did something, if not as much as is often supposed, to discourage other entrepreneurs from attempting to create new industrial enterprises.

Finally, we ought to take a brief glance at Cromer's educational policy. This is another controversial subject. But one thing at least is certain: neither he nor his advisers believed that there was any direct relation between education and development. Technical education was another matter, for here the link was clear. But there was no feeling that educational progress as such was of any particular value to the economy.

It was for these kinds of reasons that Cromer was inhibited from making more than token gestures in the direction of meeting the dangers which he believed might lie ahead. In conclusion it is also important to notice the way in which, in some measure, those very dangers were accentuated by another aspect of his approach to development, the extent to which he allowed Egypt's agricultural future to be determined by the point of view of the Irrigation Department—'Le vrai ministère de l'agriculture' as Scott Moncrieff called it[18]—the principal aim of which was simply to provide the fields with more and more water. Seen as a long term policy it would be difficult to quarrel with the department's avowed aim of bringing perennial irrigation to every part of the country's cultivated and cultivable land; but, in the short run, this had a number of harmful effects. Two were of particular importance. Firstly, the provision of extra summer water as a result of the repair of the Barrage and the construction of the dam at Aswān allowed the proprietors in perhaps a third of the Delta to substitute a biennial for a triennial cotton rotation between 1894 and 1907.[19] This in turn had a serious effect on the fertility of the soil. Secondly, for all the department's concern that the system of drainage be improved pari passu with that of irrigation, its efforts were on much too small a scale to prevent the marked rise in the level of underground water which was one of the primary causes of the decline in cotton yields that occurred in the years just before the outbreak of the First World War. It is not suggested that either of these harmful effects could have been entirely prevented by Government action. But had a Department of Agriculture existed it might at least have been able to point out the dangers of pursuing such a one-sided policy. As it was, the problem was left over for Cromer's successors, Gorst and Kitchener.

[18] Arminjon, *op. cit.*, p. 634.

[19] Based on calculations made by J. I. Craig to be found in his 'Notes on the Cotton Statistics of Egypt', *L'Egypte Contemporaine*, 6, 1911, pp. 176–9.

1907–1914

Lord Cromer's departure in May 1907 came at a time of considerable economic difficulties. The same spring recession in Europe had brought an end to a decade of mounting prosperity, causing Egyptian share prices to tumble, credit to dry up, and a number of firms to go into liquidation. This was followed, in 1908, by a sudden reduction in the value of agricultural output and, in 1909, by an alarming fall in cotton yields. The effects of these disasters were felt throughout the economy. Business confidence was rudely shaken; the price of land dropped sharply; many people found themselves unable to meet the instalments due to mortgages or bank overdrafts; local investment in Egyptian companies came almost to a halt. Recovery was long delayed and cannot be said to have been complete by the outbreak of war.

One important result of this prolonged depression was the stimulus it gave to a re-appraisal of Egypt's economic position. It raised, among other things, the whole question of the country's dependence on Europe and the wisdom of relying so exclusively on one crop of such uncertain returns. In official circles reflections of this kind naturally took second place to a discussion of the measures necessary to cope with the immediate effects of the crisis. But even there, the requirements of the situation led to a re-examination of many of the principal tenets which were central to Cromer's thinking about the process of development. Let us take the financial depression of 1907 first. One matter which was soon raised was the problem of the right relationship between the Government and the business community. During the Cromer period the activities of the latter had been subject to only the loosest controls. In part, this was a result of the Capitulations, which made the passage of any regulatory legislation affecting foreigners a matter for long and difficult negotiations with the Governments concerned. But Cromer himself was also averse to laws of this kind on grounds of principle. If business should not be encouraged by direct assistance from the Government it should not be discouraged either, for this would be to inhibit the investment of private capital in enterprises needed to develop the country's resources. Hence, little was done to restrain the speculative excesses which marked the height of the boom in company promotion in 1905 and 1906, the only measure of any importance being a regulation designed to prevent one of the worst abuses, the manipulation of founders shares, by restricting their issue to those cases where they were a return for some specific asset. However, as this rule applied only to Egyptian companies it was easily circumvented by concerns which had themselves registered abroad.[20] Gorst was ready to adopt a slightly more

[20] A. E. Crouchley, *The Investment of Foreign Capital in Egyptian Companies and the Egyptian Public Debt*, Cairo 1936, p. 63.

forceful approach and introduced a new law which allowed the Government to exercise some control over the operations of Egyptian stock exchanges.[21]

Secondly, the financial crisis re-activated the question of rural debt. Many proprietors who had bought land on credit were now in difficulties, others were affected by the fall in the value of their crops in 1908 and 1909. In these circumstances, arrears in payments owing to the Agricultural Bank rose from 3·1 per cent of the capital out on loan in 1907 to 17·7 per cent in 1909.[22] This led, in turn, to restrictions on further lending, as well as to a more thorough investigation of requests for advances. There was also some consideration of a suggestion put forward by Sir Paul Harvey, the Financial Adviser, that one way round the vexatious question of the lack of security for small loans might be to encourage the creation of agricultural co-operatives.[23] But in the event no new initiative was thought necessary, and it was left to Kitchener to try quite a different approach to the whole problem with his Five Feddan law designed to ensure that a peasant could not be deprived of his livelihood by the expropriation of all his land for non-payment of debt. His thinking on this subject was diametrically opposed to that of his predecessors. For Cromer and Gorst the main question was one of providing the small cultivator with sufficient credit to keep him out of the hands of the village usurer. Kitchener, on the other hand, was quite ready to make such advances very much more difficult to obtain by depriving the lender of any possible security. It was his belief that the peasants needed very much less working capital than had often been supposed and that it might be a very good thing if usurers would stop tempting them into debt.[24]

The disastrous cotton harvest of 1909 also produced a change in Cromerian policy. A Government commission was appointed to examine the causes of the fall in yield and, as a result of its recommendations, a Department of Agriculture was created in 1911 with special responsibility for measures designed to prevent any further decline. Two years later the department was upgraded to become a Ministry. A second group of recommendations concerned policies required to cope with the dangerous rise in the level of underground water. This led Kitchener to hasten the execution of a scheme for providing pump drainage for the low-lying areas along the Mediterranean coast. Plans had been drawn up before his arrival, but it was only after a clash with the Ministry of Finance (during which he secured the enforced resignation of Sir Paul Harvey) that he was able to obtain the large sums of money which were required.

[21] Tignor, *op. cit.*, p. 371.

[22] 'Memorandum Regarding the Agricultural Bank of Egypt', in Gorst, 20 March 1909, FO 368/284.

[23] *Ibid.*

[24] *Annual Report for 1912*, Parl. Papers 1913, vol. lxxxi, p. 214.

But if Gorst and Kitchener were willing to go to some lengths to modify a number of Lord Cromer's more important principles, they were in complete agreement with him as to the general lines along which Egyptian development should proceed. Like him, they placed most of their trust in large-scale public works and a policy of non-intervention in the country's commercial and financial life. By such means they hoped to increase agricultural output and to provide the sort of framework inside which private enterprise could flourish. As Sir Paul Harvey put it in a statement which Gorst repeated in his annual report for 1908:

> National prosperity can only be secured, in so far as it lies with the Government to secure it, by the steady development of the country's natural resources and the prudent and economical expenditure of its revenue.[25]

Again, like Cromer, Gorst and Kitchener were both willing to discuss the problems posed by monoculture and a rapidly rising population without appearing to suggest that they represented any very formidable difficulties. A good example of this occurs in the latter's report for 1912. Egypt was an agricultural country, he then wrote, and almost entirely dependent on cotton to pay for its imports and to service its debts. In the past, this dependence had exposed the economy to serious fluctuations, and it would undoubtedly do so again. However:

> so long as the cultivation of cotton remains as profitable as it is at present, that commodity will probably retain its place as the principal factor in Egypt's international exchanges, and its production will continue to absorb the preponderant share of the activities of the population. (Nevertheless) the Government is thoroughly alive to the expediency of developing the resources of the country in other directions, whether agricultural, mineral, or industrial. . . . The departments of Agriculture, of Survey, and of Technical Education, in their several spheres, are accomplishing useful work towards this end. . . .[26]

The programmes he referred to in this last sentence were as follows: the Department of Agriculture was experimenting with other crops which might be as profitable as cotton, the Survey Department was anxious to develop Egypt's mineral resources, oil in particular, with the assistance of private capital and the Department of Technical Education was doing its best (on a limited budget) to provide a well-trained labour force for the country's new factories. This was a programme with which Cromer would have been in whole-hearted agreement.

In these circumstances it was left to people outside Government, almost all of them Egyptians, to suggest a more radical approach to Egyptian development, involving the deliberate creation of an industrial sector of the economy. Not surprisingly such a policy was particularly popular among nationalists, for it seemed to offer the additional advantage of assisting the

[25] Parl. Papers, 1909, vol. cv, p. 349.

[26] Parl. Papers, 1913, vol. lxxxi, p. 213.

country to achieve that measure of economic independence without which, they felt, political independence would be virtually meaningless. Numerous examples of arguments of this sort can be found in, among other places, the speeches made at the meeting of the Egyptian Congress at Heliopolis in April/May 1911. Their relevance to the subject of this paper lies in the fact that they re-appear almost unchanged in the report of the Government Commission on Commerce and Industry, to which reference will be made in the following section.[27]

1914–1922

The outbreak of European war in August 1914 brought all such discussion about the development of the economy to a sudden halt. From then on, the primary concern of everyone in Government and business was with the problems produced by the dislocation of trade, the shortages of certain vital materials, and Egypt's direct involvement in the British war effort, problems which lasted well beyond the actual cessation of hostilities. The measures taken to cope with this situation inevitably led the administration to play a more active role in the management of the economy. No sooner had war been declared than Food Commissioners were appointed in each large town to fix the maximum permitted price for a number of basic necessities which it was felt might be in short supply. These were followed in 1915 by the creation of the Local Resources Board and the War Trade Department. But the main period of regulatory activity took place from the middle of 1917 onwards as shipping space became more and more difficult to obtain and Allenby's army began its final build-up for the Palestine campaign, culminating in the establishment of the Supplies Control Board in March 1918 with the executive powers necessary to carry out a comprehensive policy of economic management involving, among other things, the control of food supplies and the coordination of transport.

But if events made a consistent approach to Egyptian development impossible, the period is not without relevance to the subject of this paper. In a piecemeal way the war-time shortages acted as a great spur to the discovery and exploitation of new resources. Two groups of necessary commodities were particularly difficult to obtain from abroad, food and fuel. From about 1900 onwards Egypt had been unable to produce enough cereals for its growing population, and as soon as hostilities began there was a very justifiable fear that it would be difficult to obtain the necessary imports. It was therefore of particular importance to improve the yields of existing crops, a task which was taken up in earnest by the Botanical section of the Ministry of Agriculture after its formation in 1915. Experiments

[27] *Minutes of the Proceedings of the First Egyptian Congress,* Alexandria 1911, pp. 30–3, 161–6, 168–72, 174–8, etc.

were carried out to discover the best methods of cultivation, while new and more prolific strains were imported from abroad.[28] Later, as the war progressed and it became increasingly important to use every feddan of cultivable land to maximum advantage, much attention was also devoted to cotton and, in particular, to attempts to diminish the damage caused by a new and more recalcitrant pest, the pink boll worm. At the same time every effort was made to find alternative sources of fuel. A technical expert was invited from England to advise on the use of cotton sticks and other waste materials instead of coal. And the Government Analytical and Assay Office also carried out important experiments aimed at producing a better method of converting the oil newly discovered along the Red Sea into kerosene and benzene.

The exigencies of war also led the Government to seek means of developing Egypt's industrial capacity. It is true that it was still not considered possible to give any direct encouragement to private concerns. Thus in 1915 it was decided not to accede to a request for assistance from a British firm which was anxious to establish a factory in Egypt for making army uniforms, on the grounds that it could not be proved that its products would be cheaper than imports.[29] On the other hand, in 1916, the workshops attached to several of the Government's technical schools were utilized to make grenades and other military supplies;[30] while, in the same year, an official commission was appointed to enquire into the whole question of war-time shortages and to suggest ways of circumventing them by policies to promote Egypt's industrial and commercial development.[31] The Commission's report presented a persuasive summary of all the pre-war arguments in favour of some measure of industrialization—agriculture would not always be able to provide employment for an expanding population, the creation of new factories was a way of reducing the country's dependence on cotton, and so on. It also contained a detailed survey of the state of contemporary Egyptian industry and of the many problems which it faced, a list of new industries which might profitably be introduced, and suggestions as to how further development might be accelerated. In the event, the report had little or no practical effect while the war lasted. Its importance lies rather in the fact that it represents the first official assertion that industry had a vital role to play in Egypt's future development. Again, its often-stated assumption that the Government had a duty to assist the process of industrialization by taking certain positive steps, among them the imposition of a protective tariff, was clearly a radical departure from all of the policies pursued since 1882.[32]

[28] An account of this and other efforts to develop Egypt's resources during the war will be found in *Report for 1914–1919*, Parl. Papers 1920, vol. li, pp. 751-846.

[29] McMahon, 16 May 1915, FO 368/1253. [30] *Report for 1914–1919, op. cit.*, p. 807.

[31] *Rapport de la Commission du Commerce et de l'Industrie*, Cairo 1918, pp. 1–2.

[32] The Commission's willingness to abandon past precedent must certainly have been

The end of the war brought no immediate return to economic normalcy. Many commodities remained in short supply; the old regulatory bodies continued their work until well into 1919; new bodies like the Labour Disputes Conciliation Board were established as the need arose. In this atmosphere it was perhaps natural that the wartime approach to the question of exploiting Egypt's economic resources should also continue well after hostilities had come to an end. A good example of this was the creation of a Fisheries Department, with a view, as Allenby put it, to the better development 'of this important source of food supply'.[33] Its duties were to include the collection of much-needed information and the artificial stocking of inland water-ways. The Cotton Research Board was also set up at this time to coordinate all the efforts being made to prevent any further decline in yield and quality. Again, the high price of imported coal and the difficulty of obtaining a regular supply of oil caused the Government to extend its Petroleum Research Service with a view to meeting the fuel needs of its own departments and, eventually, of the State Railways as well. As a first step it was decided to undertake drilling operations and to purchase machinery for a small refinery.[34] Work on the latter began in 1920.

One other postwar initiative ought also to be mentioned, the creation in April 1920 of a Bureau of Commerce and Industry. Its two-fold purpose was to act as a link between the Government and the business community and to encourage the development of existing trades and manufacturing enterprises. Some idea of the way it proposed to approach the latter task can be learned from looking at a list of its activities during its first year of existence. These included a systematic inspection of existing industrial plant, the organization of a permanent exhibition of Egyptian products, and plans to introduce a system of voluntary registration of all companies, designed to help merchants in finding a wider market for their goods.[35] The establishment of such a bureau was the only one of the major recommendations of the Commission on Commerce and Industry to be implemented before 1922.

But if such measures represent movement in the direction of a little more public enterprise, a little more assistance to industry, this cannot be taken to imply that there had been any radical alteration in British thinking about the development of the economy. It is true that the period between the end of the war and the unilateral decision to grant Egypt independence in 1922 is too short to allow one to be categorical. Nevertheless, much of the evidence points to such a conclusion. For one thing, there was the rapidity

---

something to do with the fact that its President, Ismā'īl Ṣidqī, and two of its members were Egyptians with none of the attachment to Victorian Political Economy of a Cromer or a Gorst.

[33] *Report for 1914–1919, op. cit.*, p. 783.

[34] *Ibid.*, p. 785.

[35] *Annual Report for 1920*, Parl. Papers 1921, vol. xlii, p. 529.

with which war-time controls were dismantled once the postwar shortages were at an end. There was also the firm commitment to private rather than public development of resources illustrated by Allenby's assertion, apropos of the decision to build the state-owned oil refinery, that this in no way implied opposition to the development of a private petroleum industry.[36] Again, no effort was made to use Britain's powerful position in Egypt to re-negotiate the commercial conventions which pinned the external tariff at a uniform 8 per cent *ad valorem*. But perhaps the most important piece of evidence was the re-emergence after the war of the Ministry of Public Works as the arbiter of the economic future. Sir Murdoch MacDonald's *Nile Control Works*, published in 1920, is a concise account of the Ministry's approach. Egypt was 'a purely agricultural country'. The great expansion in its population in recent years meant that, for all the works of irrigation created in the past, facilities for crop production were now 'barely sufficient for its needs'. Thus, in future, it would be necessary for the rate at which new land was brought into cultivation to equal that at which the numbers of cultivators increased. MacDonald then went on to outline a plan which would allow water enough for the perennial irrigation of every piece of cultivable land which the country possessed within the next thirty-five years.[37] To anyone reading the report, the year when the scheme was to be completed, 1955, must have seemed impossibly far away. And they may have been pardoned for thinking that there was little need to try an alternative method of development.

Conclusion

One of the great dangers of attempting to cover so long a period in so short a space is that men's thinking is given a consistency that it did not possess. This is an inevitable distortion. The officials whose attitudes have been described were administrators, not economists or political philosophers; their approach to development was never so orderly as it has been made to seem. However, a study of their policies does reveal that each did hold certain key principles to which he looked for guidance. And as these principles stemmed in large measure either from the conventional wisdom of the age or from the nature of Egypt itself—the importance of the Nile, the central role of agriculture, and so on—it is not surprising that they imposed a certain uniformity of approach. Consistency was further assured by the fact that many of the leading British officials —Cromer, Kitchener, McMahon, and the first generation of irrigation engineers among them—had served in India and frequently drew upon their experience of that Empire. Thus it was that there was such general agreement about the role of public works, the need to encourage private enterprise, and the limits of Government

[36] *Annual Report for 1914–1919*, *op. cit.*, p. 786.
[37] *Nile Control Works*, Cairo 1920, Preface and pp. 1–5.

intervention in the economic life of the country. For someone like Cromer these general principles tended to reinforce each other so as to produce what almost amounted to a coherent system of beliefs. But even for a man like Kitchener, whose thinking was very much less doctrinaire, they still provided the only conceivable framework within which to view the question of development.

Policy cannot remain static, however. As time went on new problems were identified—the danger of rural overpopulation, the loss of commercial confidence in 1907, the threat to the economy posed by the decline in cotton yield, the Egyptian demand for a measure of industrialization, the war-time shortages. And these could only be met by a gradual increase in Government intervention and by giving limited encouragement to a greater diversification of economic activity. But policies of this kind meant no more than a slight change of emphasis. They did not alter the basic approach to Egyptian development established by Lord Cromer and adhered to so assiduously by his successors.

The India Office Records as a Source for the Economic History of the Middle East

M. E. YAPP

British involvement in the Middle East had two main points of origin.[1] The first was in Europe. Commercial relations in the area of the Eastern Mediterranean, which, from the sixteenth century, were grouped under the control of the Levant Company, led to the establishment of a number of agencies in that area.[2] The most important of these, of course, was at Istanbul, as the capital of the Ottoman Empire. Here the agent had a dual role as the representative of Company and Crown and his duties were commercial and diplomatic. After the extinction of the Levant Company, its remaining agents were taken over by the Crown. Together, the records of the Levant Company (SP 97, 105, 110) and of the Foreign Office (F.O. 78 and its continuations together with associated files), both of which are kept in the Public Records Office in Chancery Lane, London E.C.1. constitute the major source for British relations with the Ottoman Empire and themselves contain a vast amount of information about the economic history of the area.

The second point of origin, and that with which this paper is concerned, was India. The records of these operations are in the Commonwealth Office Records Department, access to which is through the separate India Office Library. These records, usually called the India Office Records, were moved at the end of 1967 to new premises at Orbit House, Blackfriars, together with the Library itself.[3]

The main interest of Englishmen in Eastern trade in the sixteenth century was the control of the trade in Eastern goods, especially spices. Itself virtually excluded from the Spice Islands by Dutch power, the English

[1] Leaving out the activities of the Muscovy Company, including the journey of Antony Jenkinson to Central Asia and the work of Elton and Hanway in Iran and Central Asia in the eighteenth century.

[2] The records of the Levant Company are described in A. C. Wood, *History of the Levant Company*, London 1935.

[3] For a useful outline description of the records relating to the period before 1858 see W. Foster, *Guide to the India Office Records, 1600–1858*, London 1919. A revised edition, to describe the records to 1947, is in preparation, but will not be available for some years. In the meantime, Miss Joan C. Lancaster, the Assistant Keeper, who has already achieved impressive results in making the records more accessible by organizing the preparation of duplicated lists of certain series, has produced a very useful short *Guide to Lists and catalogues of the India Office Records*, London 1966. It should be mentioned that duplicates of most of the series in the IOR, arranged rather differently, together with other information, exist in the National Archives of India, New Delhi.

East India Company was forced to concentrate its operations in India. From an early date the Company saw advantages in trade links with ports in the Persian Gulf and the Red Sea. The more northerly areas were seen as potential markets for English woollens, which were in little demand in India, and the silk products of northern Iran were desirable objects of trade. Also there was the desire, shared by other European powers, to acquire some control over those trade routes through the Middle East, which constituted the main alternatives to the sea route around the Cape of Good Hope. In the Red Sea area, Socotra was first visited in 1608 and Aden and Mocha in 1610. In the area of the Persian Gulf, the Company opened contacts with Iran in 1615; in 1617 a factory, or trading establishment, was opened at Shiraz, and trade begun through Jask. In 1622 a joint Anglo-Iranian force took Hormuz from the Portuguese. Thereafter, EIC trade in Iran was centred on Gombrun (Bandar ʿAbbās) on the mainland near Hormuz. In 1640 trade was extended to Basra and a factory established there.[4]

It is unnecessary to write a history of the trading operations of the EIC in the area of the Middle East. It is enough to say that those trading relations, which were established in the early seventeenth century, continued with occasional interruptions, and periodic movements, from one factory to another, until the end of the eighteenth century. From that time onwards, however, the problem changes its nature.

The EIC underwent a material alteration in its character in the course of the eighteenth century, when it acquired control over large territories in India. A process began which led, by 1833, to the loss of the last of its trading functions and its continuation as a governing institution for India. These governing functions too were taken over by the Crown in 1858. From 1858 to 1947 British India was governed by a Secretary of State, assisted by a Council, controlling the government in India.

At the same time that the Company lost its trading functions it became concerned by a new danger, a possible attack, or threat of an attack, by a European power on its possessions in India through the Middle East. It is unnecessary to discuss the extent to which this fear was justified or the degree to which it extended amongst influential politicians and officials at any particular date. It is sufficient to note that it became an important factor in decisions relating to the Middle East, at least from the French invasion of Egypt in 1798. In addition, the Middle East became important as a line of communication between India and Europe, first for mails, later, and particularly after the introduction of steam navigation, for passengers and, lastly, and especially with the opening of the Suez Canal, for goods.[5] Interest in the Middle East, therefore, shifted from an interest in

[4] See Sir W. Foster, *England's Quest of Eastern Trade*, London 1933.

[5] See H. L. Hoskins, *British Routes to India*, 1st ed. N.Y. 1928, 2nd ed. London 1966.

commercial possibilities to an interest in political developments and in bases for communications systems. For the economic historian this means that the records become much more plentiful and contain data affecting a much wider range of topics.

In order to know where to look for records and to know the type of information contained within the records, it is essential to know something of the history of British Indian involvement in the Middle East. A good example is that of Iran. Control over British relations with Iran changed hands five times before finally settling in the hands of the Foreign Office.[6] As a result the main source of information about Iran, in English records, before 1807, is in the records of the EIC. Between 1807 and 1810, when a contest took place for control of the Mission, it is necessary to look both at the Foreign Office Records in the PRO (FO/60) and in the EIC records. From 1811 until 1826 control was in the hands of the Foreign Office but it was vested in those of the EIC from 1826 to 1835 and in the hands of the Indian Government again for a short interlude in 1858–9. But throughout the whole period the EIC maintained a Resident at Bushire, who continued to correspond with the authorities in India, and who is the principal source of information for southern Iran and the Gulf. The same difficulty exists for other areas of the Middle East. The principal British agent in Iraq remained at least partly under the control of the Indian Government, although possessing consular status and carrying on correspondence with the Ambassador in Istanbul, until 1914. Information about the Red Sea area is also divided between the Foreign Office (FO 78 and 371) and British Indian Government archives.

A further need to understand something of the history of British relations with the area, before the records can be used with confidence, lies in the division of authority and, therefore, of record in British India. For many years the Government of the Bombay Presidency was responsible for control of relations with most of the British agencies in the Middle East, with the exception of Afghanistan and Iran. From the beginning, Afghanistan was regarded as the primary concern of the Supreme Government in Calcutta, because its rulers were held to represent a threat to northern India, and so to the British possessions in Bengal, although some information was collected at Bombay in the late eighteenth and early nineteenth centuries. Iran became the effective responsibility of the Supreme Government from Malcolm's first mission in 1799, although the Bombay Government retained direction of the activities of the Resident at Bushire. But in other areas the Bombay Government took the lead. Aden remained under the authority of the Bombay Government until 1932 when it became a Chief Commissionership under the Supreme Government, before

[6] M. E. Yapp, *Control of the Persian Mission*, University of Birmingham Historical Journal, vii, 1960, pp. 162–79.

becoming a Crown Colony in 1937. The Resident in the Persian Gulf, (originally the Resident at Bushire), remained under the Bombay Government until 1873 when he became responsible to the Supreme Government. For some time no-one knew who was responsible for the Resident in Baghdad, who was established in 1798, least of all the Resident himself, until in 1806 the Bombay Government was made responsible, an authority reluctantly shouldered until the Supreme Government eventually took control in 1843.[7]

It was, in general, the tendency for areas to move under the control of higher authorities—from Bombay to Calcutta, from Calcutta to London and from the Secretary of State for India to the Foreign Office. This was the inevitable result of the improvement in communications and in the machinery of Government in England and the development of closer links between events in Asia and Europe with the result that areas in the Middle East became of much greater political importance to England and involved relations with other European powers.

After first identifying the controlling authority for any given area at any given time it is necessary to discover in what series the relevant documents may be. But it should be said first that certain gaps do exist in the records. The EIC was by origin a trading company. Records were expensive to preserve and so only those which were useful for current work were preserved, with the exception of those which it was cheaper to preserve than to sort for destruction. And, although there was interest in history, it was not until 1771 that there was any attempt to create a Records Department and not until the nineteenth century that adequate preservation of records began. Even after this date there was frequent destruction. Wholesale disposals took place after the amalgamation of the records of the EIC with those of the Board of Control in 1858 and again in 1867. The criterion applied was whether the records appeared likely to be of office use. One of the most serious losses at about this time was the records of the Bombay Marine, which would have been an invaluable source of information for the history of the Persian Gulf in the early nineteenth century.[8]

For the period of commercial domination before 1800 the principal source is the *Factory Records*. Within this large general series is the *Original Correspondence* in 64 volumes, which is the main source for all areas in the seventeenth century. Parts of this correspondence have been published in the following. Sir George Birdwood and William Foster (eds.), *The First Letter Book of the East India Company 1600–19*, Quaritch 1893; W. Foster (ed.), *Letters Received by the East India Company from its Servants in the East 1613–1617*, 4 vols., London 1896–1902; W. Foster

[7] M. E. Yapp, 'Establishment of the East India Company Residency at Baghdad 1798–1806', *Bulletin of the School of Oriental and African Studies*, xxx, 1967, pp. 323–36.

[8] C. R. Low, *History of the Indian Navy 1613–1863*, 2 vols., London 1877, pp. i, ix.

(ed.), *The English Factories in India*, 13 vols., Oxford 1906–27; Sir Charles Fawcett (ed.), *The English Factories in India*, 4 vols., Oxford 1936–55.[9] The first letter book contains the surviving letters of the EIC's servants in this period. In fact relatively few survive. They were apparently handed to Richard Hakluyt for use in the compilation of *Purchas, His Pilgrimes*, 1625, which thus becomes the principal source for this early period, and seem to have been lost. The volumes edited by Foster which deal with the period 1613–55 are more or less a complete collection but after 1655 the volume of records preserved made it necessary to confine publication to a selection of the letters only, while the volumes which appeared under the editorship of the late Sir Charles Fawcett are only an account based on the records. It is therefore necessary to refer to the *Ms Original Correspondence* for any period after 1655.

Although the *Original Correspondence* is the principal collection for the seventeenth century it is not the only one within the *Factory Records Series*. Certain volumes in the *Miscellaneous Series* relate to the Middle East, e.g. Volume 12, Letter Book of Edward Knipe Supercargo of *Crispiana and Aleppo Merchant* to Surat and Persia 1642–4.[10] One problem in using the *Factory Series* is to identify the correspondence which refers to the Middle East. Many of the smaller factories corresponded, not directly with England, but with the principal factory in the area. In these cases it is necessary to look at the records of the principal factory. For the Middle East it was Surat for most of the sixteenth century and Bombay after 1687.

The *Factory Records Series* continues to be the principal English archival source for the history of the Middle East in the eighteenth century. The Series then becomes subdivided by areas. One such area was *Egypt and the Red Sea*, which series contains 40 volumes, covering the period from 1644 to 1869. Volumes 1–4 are letters from Mocha. After the unsuccessful attempt to open trade with Mocha in 1610 a factory was opened in 1618, which, because of the important coffee trade which developed, was maintained until 1752. Mocha remained the seat of the principal EIC agent in the area down to the annexation of Aden in 1828. Volumes 8–38 contain correspondence with various agents in Egypt. The EIC maintained agents at various times in Egypt, Aleppo and even in Istanbul, particularly to look after mails. Although the *Factory Records* do not compare with the Foreign Office Records as a source for the economic history of Egypt in the early nineteenth century, they do contain interesting information about the attempts to establish trade at the end of the eighteenth century and the problems of communications.

The other main area with which the EIC was concerned in this period

[9] See also *Calendar of State Papers, Colonial*, ed. W. M. Sainsbury.
[10] See *Extracts from Historical Ms Commission Reports*, p. 16.

was the Persian Gulf. *The Factory Records Series, Persia and the Persian Gulf*, has 135 volumes covering the period from 1620 to 1874. The seventeenth century has only part of one volume because this period, of course, is dealt with in the *Original Correspondence* but the eighteenth century is represented by some 22 volumes, originating chiefly from the factories at Gombrun and Basra. Volumes 2–13 are the *Gombroon Diaries*, volumes 14–20 are letters from Basra and Gombrun; volume 21 contains a particularly valuable report on British trade with Persia and Arabia.[11]

With the introduction of the political element in relations with the Gulf states, the material in the *Factory Records* becomes more general in character and contains a good deal of diplomatic correspondence. There is however still much information relating to trade and commercial negotiations. But the information is, from this point onwards, more or less duplicated in other sources, which are, in any case, more complete. Volumes from 53 onwards are largely duplicates of correspondence in the FO/60 series, although they still contain other letters, relating to Egypt, Syria, Iraq and Arabia.

Some other series also shed light on the economic history of the Middle East in the seventeenth and eighteenth centuries, although the *Factory Records Series* is pre-eminent within the EIC archives. The *Marine Records* also contains much information in the form of ship's logs, journals and logs, and the correspondence of the Marine Committee. The ships' journals are quite useful for the Middle East in the seventeenth century but the logs do not become particularly valuable until the series of important Indian Navy logs begin in the 1830's, when there are records of many voyages from Bombay to ports in the Gulf and the Red Sea. The *Miscellaneous Section* is particularly valuable for information relating to the introduction of steam navigation and the consequent growth of a new interest in the Gulf and Red Sea areas, especially the Euphrates Expedition of the 1830's (vols. 557 *et seq.*). There is also considerable information about trade, mostly by the EIC but also by other merchants in the area. The *Factory Records* are essentially the records of affairs which originated in the East and, consequently, contain most information about conditions in the area. But, according to the interests of the investigator, decisions made in England may also be of importance. The *List of General Records 1599–1879* (*1902*) describes the sources of information which relate to these.[12]

Records which relate to the nineteenth century are more difficult to describe because of their much greater number and their division among

[11] Used by L. Lockhart, *The Fall of the Safavi Dynasty and the Afghan Occupation of Persia*, Cambridge 1958, and M. Abu Hakima, *History of Eastern Arabia 1750–1800. The Rise and Development of Persia and Kuwait*, Beirut 1965. See also Abdul Amir Amin, *British Interests in the Persian Gulf*, Leiden 1967.

[12] See also *Guide to the Records of the Accountant General's Department, 1600–1955.*

more series of records. In general all records of the Indian Governments relating to the area of the Middle East in this period are contained in the *Secret and Political Records*. This follows from the nature of British interest in the areas and the need to preserve secrecy and to ensure that the relevant documents speedily reached the department of H.M. Government which was responsible (the Board of Control before 1858), because of the implications of relations with these areas for diplomatic relations with other European states.

The principal sources for the period before 1858 are the *Bengal Secret and Political Proceedings*, and its successors, the *India Secret Proceedings*, for those areas which came under the Supreme Government, and the *Bombay Political and Secret Proceedings* for areas subject to the Bombay Government. These however do not supply a complete record. Occasionally subjects were dealt with in the Political Department. A most important minute by the acting Governor General, Sir George Barlow, in 1806, dealing with the commercial Residency at Bushire, was deposited, not in the *Bengal Secret and Political Proceedings*, with other material on Iran but in the separate *Bengal Political Proceedings*. The repeated switching of departments can be confusing, as are the changes of nomenclature of departments and the series of records which they produce.

The *Proceedings*, or *Consultations* as they are sometimes called, were a record of work transacted in India of which copies were later sent to England. But it was also necessary for the Indian Governments to send to England despatches describing their actions and to accompany them with enclosures of all important material. These two series of *Secret Letters received from Bengal* (later *India*) and from *Bombay*, and their associated (and much larger series) *Enclosures to Secret Letters Received from Bengal* (from 1834 *India*) and from *Bombay*, really form duplicates of the correspondence contained in the *Proceedings*, although certain bulky reports, often containing valuable economic information, were not transmitted to England with the *Enclosures* but exist only in the *Consultations*.

From 1859 the system changes. The main series then becomes *India Foreign and Political Proceedings*. From 1875 three series emerge. The first is *Political and Secret Letters Received from Persia*. The second is *Secret Letters to and from Aden, Muscat, Persian Gulf and Zanzibar*. The third series is that of *Political and Secret Letters from India, Madras and Bombay*.

In the twentieth century there were further changes in the organization of correspondence. In 1911 the *Political and Secret Letters Received Series* come to an end and are succeeded by a series of *Political and Secret Files*. But already from 1902 onwards it had become the practice to abstract documents relating to certain important subjects, often extending over a period of years, and to group them in a separate series of

'*Subject*' files. Further reorganization took place in the 1930's but these records need not be described since they are not at present available for inspection.[13]

Before closing this brief list of the principal series of records relating to the Middle East it is worth while to describe two other collections in the India Office Records which are of some value, because they contain material which is in an easily usable form. The *Political and Secret Department Library* contains *inter alia* many confidential reports on routes, distances, communications, railways, etc. in Russian Central Asia, and a vast amount of information about Afghanistan. Included in this collection are a series of Gazetteers which represent digests of the information in the records and are of immense value, particularly the Gazetteer on Afghanistan, first compiled in 1871 under the editorship of C. M. Macgregor, which went through several later editions, each incorporating more information.[14] This Gazetteer is probably the most important single work on Afghanistan for the period before 1914, and in many ways comparable to the great *Description de l'Egypte* as a source. Another work of fundamental importance for the study of the area to which it refers is the excellent *Gazetteer of the Persian Gulf* by J. G. Lorimer, 2 vols., 1908–15. Other Gazetteers deal with other areas of the Middle East, including Iraq and Asia Minor.

A second, useful collection is that of *Political and Secret Memoranda 1840–1947* which also contains information in assimilable form including Henry Rawlinson's great *Report on the Dooranees*, the most important single account of land systems in Western Afghanistan in the first half of the nineteenth century.

Finally there is one series which, because of the heterogeneous nature of its contents, is difficult to describe. This is the *Home Miscellaneous Series*, containing over 800 volumes of official and private papers, some of which are useful for the economic history of the Middle East, and particularly trade in the seventeenth and early eighteenth centuries. There is an indispensable catalogue of this series by S. C. Hill (1927).

This is a brief, and by no means exhaustive account of the major sources available to the student of developments in the Middle East in the India Office Records. I have not considered the contents of the Library, although in the European Mss. collection there are some collections of very considerable value, e.g. the Masson Papers for Afghanistan. It now remains to say

[13] No description of the contents of the ordinary files is available, but there is a brief list of the contents of the Subject Files in *India Office Papers, Miscellaneous Lists*, which forms the principal guide to the Political and Secret Department Lists for the twentieth century. The recent adoption of the thirty year rule has made new material available.

[14] C. M. Macgregor, *Central Asian Gazetteer, Part II Afghanistan*, Calcutta 1871. Second Edition in three parts edited by W. S. A. Lockhart, 1882. Third Edition in five parts edited by W. R. Robertson, 1894–5. Fourth Edition edited by W. Malleson in six parts, 1907–10. Part II of Fifth Edition dated 1914 in IOL.

something of the type of information which is contained in these documents and its use to the economic historian of the Middle East.

Although one habitually uses the phrase as a convenient shorthand, there is really no such thing as economic information. Any information may bear upon economic decisions, which are, in essence, simply choices involving the allocation of scarce resources, which may be employed in production, distribution or exchange. Economic history is not the collection of information about subjects traditionally regarded as 'economic'. The failure to understand this led many older historians to turn away from sources, which a little theory, combined with induction, could have made of considerable use. It follows then that it could be argued, rather disarmingly, that all the sources described above are potentially useful to the economic historian. Although such a line of argument would at least have the merit of bringing this paper to an abrupt and probably welcome end, there are still some problems to be considered.

The India Office Records are primarily collections of information about British decisions and actions. They are not disinterested collections of information about the economies of Middle Eastern countries. The danger always exists that the inexperienced student will be led by his material into writing, not a study of economic development in the area but a study of British policy i.e. what Britain would have liked that development to be. In Collingwood's phrase we must put our sources to the question. That is, the student must have enough knowledge of theory to provide himself with a set of questions which will enable him to turn his material around so as to extract from it what it can tell him about the problems of the area itself.

In practice the problem is not so great as it is in dealing with chronicles. British officials were always interested in economic problems. In the sixteenth and seventeenth centuries the main interest was commercial. But the correspondence is not simply a catalogue of information about products exchanged. The EIC merchants believed that profitable trade depended on the existence of certain conditions, about which they diligently collected information. They did not confine themselves to the state of the market for the commodities in which they were particularly interested but recognized that profitable trade depended on the overall prosperity of the region concerned. So they supplied more general information about economic (and political) conditions in the areas which they visited. They described the trade, their competitors, Muslim and European, industrial development, currencies, rates of exchange on bills, port facilities, etc. Consequently, although their interests were basically commercial and confined to the periphery of the Middle East, they do supply information which can help to provide a picture of conditions in the interior.

From the beginning of the nineteenth century the quantity and variety of information increases considerably. Partly this is due to the better preservation of records. But it is a surprising fact that the change of interest from commerce to politics produced a much greater interest in the economies of the countries of the Middle East. The Middle East had always been a minor commercial interest of the EIC, but it now became a major political interest. And British diplomatic agents were all imbued with a conviction that a direct relationship existed between the economic prosperity of a country and the ability of its government to resist aggression from without and to suppress dissension within its frontiers, a notion now all too familiar to us all. British agents were particularly interested in the financial position of governments and went out of their way to collect budgets, and to send them to London with explanatory comments. John McNeil did this, as Minister in Tehran in the 1830's. Possibly because of their Indian experience they were all firmly convinced that agricultural prosperity was the key to the financial stability of the state and gave particular attention to this aspect. Thus we find in the exceptionally voluminous reports of John Malcolm during his missions to Persia much information of this sort, some of which he subsequently used in his history of Persia. Not all writers however were so fluent and indefatigable as Malcolm. Some, like Major Leech, the Political Agent in Qandahar, in 1839-40, were terse to the point of illiteracy, while some, like Samuel Manesty, the Resident at Basra, at the end of the eighteenth and beginning of the nineteenth centuries, were insane. Anyone using the reports of Commander Haines, the first British Resident at Aden, would do well to remember that he was eventually jailed for dishonesty, and it is necessary to guard against the ever present tendency of officials to blame their troubles on some convenient natural disaster. The result of this unevenness is that what we have is not the steady stream of comparable information which we should like, but the sort of irregular flashes of illumination which Lloyd George associated with lighthouses and Lord Kitchener.

In the case of Afghanistan this effect is enhanced by the intermittent nature of contacts with that country. Before 1808 knowledge about Afghanistan had advanced little beyond the 'Here be Tygers' stage.[15] In that year, however, the mission of Mountstuart Elphinstone provided a flood of information, only part of which found its way into his two invaluable volumes, *Account of the Kingdom of Caubul*, London 1815. In the volume *Home Miscellaneous 659* there are the reports of his companions, used only modestly by Elphinstone, which contain much additional information about the economy of Afghanistan. There followed another period of lack of interest before the first Anglo-Afghan War produced a

[15] In fact some information was available, e.g. George Forster, *Journey from Bengal to India*, 2 vols., London 1798, but government correspondence at the time shows extensive ignorance.

magnificent out-pouring of information. During the British occupation of Afghanistan from 1839–41 there was a steady movement towards greater and greater British control over the administration of the country. To control it effectively they needed information, and reports were produced which contained detailed information about systems of land tenure, revenue collection, currency, trade, budgets, and a host of other topics. One report for Jalalabad shows how each piece of land was held. In short the information produced in this period is of quite unparalleled value for the light which it throws on the Afghan economy.[16] Information becomes scarce again after 1843 until the Lumsden Mission of 1856, but the next major harvest came with the Second Anglo-Afghan War 1878–80. By using the information produced by these periods of considerable interest, and linking them with the regular reports of agents stationed in Afghanistan, it would be possible to produce a picture of economic change which, although it could not be expressed in quantitative terms for the period as a whole, could produce a surprisingly detailed collection of information for certain key areas such as that of Jalalabad.

The nature of British–Indian involvement with any area is an important factor in determining the amount of information which is available. Those areas which were directly administered produced the greatest quantity. Of considerable importance therefore is the history of Aden since 1839. The documents relating to this in the *Bombay Secret Proceedings* provide a continuous stream of information which can be used to describe, not only the development of the port of Aden, but also conditions in the interior of Arabia. After the negotiation of the Protectorate treaties in the 1870's this information covers a still wider area.

Another area for which the EIC records provide a major source of information is the Persian Gulf. From the seventeenth century factories had been established at various ports, but the extension of these agencies in the nineteenth century to the Arabian shore, including Muscat, of great importance in trade between India and the Gulf, and the steady increase in the powers of the Resident at Bushire and his involvement in the affairs of the Gulf, led to a large collection of information about piracy, the pearl trade, trade into the interior, and economic conditions generally in the Gulf area.[17] For the later nineteenth and early twentieth century there is considerable information with regard to Kuwait, including detailed trade reports. The dominant trading position of India with relation to the Gulf and the collection of information about it make it possible to construct a detailed picture of trading patterns in the area, which could

[16] Much of this information is footnoted by the author in three articles in the *Bulletin of the School of Oriental and African Studies:* 'Disturbances in Eastern Afghanistan 1839–42, xxv, 1962, pp. 499–523; 'Disturbances in Western Afghanistan 1839–41', xxvi, 1963, pp. 288–313; 'Revolution of 1841–2 in Afghanistan', xxvii, 1964, pp. 333–81.

[17] Used by J. B. Kelly, *Britain and the Persian Gulf 1795–1880*, Oxford 1968.

make it possible to shed some light on the movement of bullion in this period.

If we exclude Iran from consideration because of its early transfer to the Foreign Office the other area about which information was produced was Iraq, where the Residents at Basra and Baghdad (later the Resident in Turkish Arabia) produced information about this relatively little known area of the Ottoman lands. Of particular interest is the material relating to developments in communications, including the Baghdad Railway, and to irrigation. But it should not be supposed that Iran ceased entirely to be of interest to India. The contents of the Subject Files bear testimony to the continuing interest in oil, trade in southern Iran, famine relief, etc.

Finally, apart from information which relates to particular countries and areas there is a good deal of general information relating to the development of systems of communication, telegraphs, and navigation in the area, including the surveys of the Indian Ocean.[18] Scattered through all these records too is information relating to prices, wages, etc., which could be used by any future Thorold Rogers of the Middle East.

In conclusion it will be useful to attempt some general assessment of the value of these records in relation to other sources of evidence. The FO records which relate to the Ottoman Empire, with the exception of Egypt after 1882, valuable as they are, are not more valuable than the Foreign Ministry records of other European powers. They are of less value than the Austrian, comparable with the French. But with the important exception of the Russian Foreign Ministry records for Iran and the Uzbekistan State Archives for Soviet Central Asia, neither of which are normally available for inspection, the British Indian archives are quite unrivalled among European archival collections for the southern and eastern parts of the Middle East. The other European companies, with the exception of the Dutch EIC for the Gulf area in the eighteenth century, are of much less importance, and none compare for the nineteenth century.

The value of the British Indian records in relation to the records of Middle Eastern countries themselves depends on the existence and availability of the Middle Eastern records. For many areas they scarcely exist before the end of the nineteenth century, or the archives are in so confused a state that they cannot be used. It is also the case that they often appear in so enigmatic a form that, like the Khivan archives, it is difficult to wrest an intelligible meaning from them. In the twentieth century, of course, and especially since the First World War, as Middle Eastern states begin to collect and publish their own economic information, the British Indian records decline to relative unimportance as a source, except in so far as they deal with the more limited fields of those topics in which Britain

[18] W. A. Spray, *The Surveying and charting of the Indian Ocean: the British Contribution*, unpublished Ph.D. thesis, London University, 1966.

was directly concerned, e.g. oil production and trade. But for the nineteenth century, in particular, the British Indian records remain the major source of information about economic conditions in particular areas, especially Aden and parts of Arabia, the Gulf area and Afghanistan.

Index

ʿ*aṭā*ʾ, 37, 40–1.
Athens, 168, 170.
ʿAṭiyya b. Khalīfa, 123.
atmacacı, 181.
Australia, 387.
Austria, 80, 225–6.
ʿ*avarız*, 165.
Avignon, 100.
ʿAvrathisar, 181.
ʿAwjāʾ al-Ḥafīr, 83.
Ayalon, D., 118.
aʿyān, 342.
Ayās, 67.
Ayyūbids, 67–8, 124, 129.
al-Azdī, Muḥammad b. Aḥmad, 142.
Azov, 224.

Babinger, F., 16.
baç, 186.
Bachîr II Chihâb, 335, 337, 343–4.
Baer, G., 8–9, 279.
Bağdad, 171. *See also* Baghdad.
Baghdad, 48, 57, 64–5, 67, 196, 221–2, 240–2, 346, 351–2, 355, 361, 364, 369, 504, 512.
Baghdādī, family, 365.
Bahāʾ al-Dīn Qarāqūsh, 134.
Bahrein, 430, 432.
Baʿlabakk, 75.
al-Balādhurī, 42.
Balkans, 110, 160, 170, 174, 192, 209, 211–12, 221, 224.
Baltic, 64, 72–3, 85, 94.
Bāmyān, 84.
Bandar ʿAbbās, 214, 317, 502.
Banja Luka, 224.
Banyans, 316.
al-Barāwī, Rāshid, 278.
barcalo, 53.
Barcelona, 71.
Bardi, 34, 108.
Barfurūsh, 317.
Barkan, Ö. L., 159–60, 162, 233, 239.
Barlow, Sir George, 507.
barqalū, 53.
Barsbāy, sultan, 77, 119, 125.
Barthold, V., 139.
barut, 221.
Başbakanlık Arşivi, 164.
Baṣra, 64, 67, 171, 222, 231, 352, 361, 364, 502, 506, 510, 512.
Baybārs al-Manṣūrī, 136.
Bayezid I, 209, 214.
Bayezid II, 207, 238–9.
bayt, 338.
Beblaoui, H. El, 419.
Becker, 83, 139.
bedel, 190–1.
bedestan, 208.
Beğlerbeği, *see beylerbey*.
Beirut, 110, 227, 335, 400.
Bell, 83.
Bengal, 198, 503, 507.
Benjamin of Tudela, 71.
berāt, 164.
Berkovica, 181.
Bernheim, 45.
Berque, J., 274.
beylerbey, 186, 220–1.
bezzazistan, 208.
Bilecik, 224.
Biʾr al-Rubāhiyya, 73.
Birecik, 211.
Bitlis, 211.
Bitolia, 181.
Black Death, 33–4, 94, 97–9, 101, 103–4, 106, 109–10, 113–14.
Black Sea, 64, 67, 73, 110, 112, 126–7, 220, 223–4.
Bloch, Marc, 271.
Boccaccio, 99.
Bogrofča, 186.
Bologna, 110, 114, 168.
Bombay, 261, 503–7, 511.
Bor, 222.
Bosnia, 223, 225.
Bosphorus, 73.
Bottomore, T., 275.
Bozkır, 223.
Braudel, F., 274.
Brazil, 399, 401.
Brescia, 227.
Briggs, Asa, 270, 276.
Britain, 80, 322, 324, 354, 374, 399, 402–3, 470, 487, 512.
Bruges, 103, 106.
Brunschvig, R., 147.
Brusa, *see* Bursa.
Buçuk Tepe, 238.
al-Budayrī, 21.
Buḥayra, 222.
Bukhārā, 64–5.
Bulgaria, 174, 182–3, 208, 219–20, 224.
Burgundy, 102.
Burhān al-Dīn al-Maḥallī, 123.
Burma, 406.
Bursa, 168–70, 197, 207, 209–14, 217.
Bushire, 503–4, 507, 511.
buyūtāt, 320–1.
al-Būzajānī, 42.
Byzantine Empire, 108.
Byzantium, 31, 33, 35, 55, 63–6, 73, 238.

Caffa, 207, 210, 212. *See also* Kaffa.